The Blue Guides

City Guide
Paris
and Versailles

Delia Gray-Durant

A&C Black • London
WW Norton • New York

Tenth edition April 2001 © Delia Gray-Durant
Published by A & C Black (Publishers) Limited
37 Soho Square, London W1D 3QZ

1st (post-war) and 2nd editions L. Russell Muirhead © Ernest Benn Limited 1951, 1960
3rd edition by Stuart Rossiter © Ernest Benn Limited 1968
4th and 5th editions by Ian Robertson © Ernest Benn Limited 1977
6th, 7th and 8th editions by Ian Robertson © A&C Black (Publishers) Limited 1985, 1989, 1992
9th edition © Delia Gray-Durant and Ian Robertson

Historical introduction © Ian Robertson

Maps and plans drawn by RJS Associates, © A&C Black

Illustrations © Peter Spells

A CIP catalogue record of this book is available from the British Library.

ISBN 0–7136–0–7136–5294–2

Published in the United States of America by
WW Norton and Company Inc.
500 Fifth Avenue, New York, NY 10110

Published simultaneously in Canada by
Penguin Books Canada Limited
10 Alcorn Avenue, Toronto
Ontario M4V 3B2

ISBN 0–393–30073–0 USA

Delia Gray-Durant has lived and worked in Paris, and also had a home in the French Midi. As well as writing Blue Guides—she is also the author of *Blue Guide Southwest France*—she translates French art history publications and has contributed to British art publications. For several years she has devised and led art history and cultural tours.

Cover photograph of the doorway of the Petit Palais, Museum of Fine Arts, by Joe Cornish
Title page illustration Métro station entrance by Hector Guimard, 16e

Printed and bound in England by Butler & Tanner Ltd., Frome and London.

Contents

Paris ~ the guide

Maps and plans

Symbols used in this edition

☎   telephone
▤   fax
✉   e-mail address

🚇   Métro
🚊   RER

Introduction

It is exciting to have the opportunity to look closely at Paris at the turn of a century and its move into the second millennium has been fittingly spectacular. The city has continued in its unceasing impetus in the cultural sphere to build, rebuild, improve and expand. Projects that were begun before the millennium have now reached completion, while others begin. At the same time, Paris is promoting a new, greener image, with existing gardens receiving attention and the creation of new green spaces, despite the setback of the gales of Christmas 1999.

It has been a time to reflect on what was achieved in the preceding hundred years and certain centennial monuments are receiving deferential treatment corresponding to their age and will be rejuvenated to face the next century. Major projects embarked on for the 1900 Exposition Universelle included the Petit Palais and the Métro station entrances designed by Victor Guimard. A hundred years on the veil has been drawn temporarily over the **Musée du Petit Palais** (Ch. 27) while it undergoes a well deserved overhaul and we can look forward to seeing its extremely rich but fairly unknown collections to better advantage.

The **Métro** also celebrated its centenary in 2000 and between 1999 and 2001 Victor Guimard's iconic Art Nouveau style Métro stations are receiving attention. Although one of them resides in its entirety in MOMA, New York, these entrances were not listed as Historic Monuments in France until 1978. Paris has conserved two complete station entrances with the glass canopy intact (at Abbesses and Porte Dauphine, Chs 26 and 30) and, of the 180 originally built, 86 remain in part and these will be completely renewed.

Some landmarks that are considerably less than 100 years old have also been rejuvenated. Following much reorganising, the **Pompidou Centre** (Ch. 20), reopened on 1 January 2000, brighter and lighter than before. A victim of its own success, or more particularly the success of the panoramic views from the top, there are no more free rides up the escalator (so why not pay the fairly modest entrance fee and visit the newly arranged collections as well?). The spaces for the collections, divided between Historical (or Modern) for the period 1905 to 1960 and Contemporary for the period from 1960 onwards, have been extended and vastly improved, and architecture and design is now interspersed among the fine arts' galleries.

Other buildings that are well over 100 years old have also been given the 'treatment'. The west façade of **Notre-Dame** (Ch. 2) has finally reappeared from beneath its shrouds, presenting a strangely white and pristine face. More cleaning and restoration is scheduled for other parts of the exterior of the cathedral in due course.

One new project goes back way beyond the millennium, beyond previous millennia in fact, to the very beginnings of Paris. The **Archeo 2000** exhibition was launched by the **Musée Carnavalet** (the Museum of the History of Paris; Ch. 23) in autumn 2000 in the recently restored Orangery. Its objective is to increase public awareness of archaeological discoveries made towards the end of the 20C. Digs at Bercy from 1991 onwards brought to light a valuable group of objects, among them neolithic pirogues (dugout canoes) and these finds have revolutionised theories connected with settlements in the Paris basin 4000–6000 years ago. In addition, the results of vast amounts of research made over the last 30 years have been drawn together in a presentation of the origins of Paris up to the end of Antiquity. Discoveries that have rarely been seen by the public, such as Gallo-Roman wall paintings found in Rue Amyot, will be shown here. The Orangery at the Musée Carnavalet itself is an exceptional building being the only one of this type existing from the 17C.

The most important new museum to open since the last edition is the **Musée d'art et d'histoire du Judaïsme** (Museum of Jewish Art and History; Ch. 23). This is an extremely attractive museum with a variety of exhibits and has the added benefit of being housed in the completely refurbished 17C Hotel de Saint-Aignan in Rue du Temple in the 3rd arrondissement, an elegant building which had strong connections with the Jewish population in this district during the first part of the last century.

The final fine tuning at the **Louvre** (Ch. 15) was completed in 2000, with almost imperceptible changes. These include a handful of new rooms dedicated to Decorative Arts of the 19C, the final touches to Italian and Spanish and English paintings, and a permanent space for the Graphic Arts in each of the departments—where works will be seen in rotation.

The **Union des Arts Décoratifs** (Ch. 16) (which, it should be remembered, is integral with, but not part of, the Louvre) is gradually reopening and if any museum needed an overhaul this one did. The transformation is very impressive. The Union is made up of the Museum of Decorative Arts, the Museum of Fashion and Textile, and the Museum of Advertising. The last opened in 1999 as an exciting and innovative display using modern techniques and technology combined with temporary exhibitions; Fashion and Textile has rotating exhibitions and Decorative Arts has opened in part at the time of writing.

Other museums that have re-emerged are the **Musée de la Poste** (Ch. 7) at Montparnasse, with a comprehensive record of every aspect of the French postal service. The **Musée des Arts et Métiers** (Ch. 23) in the Temple district, after a long closure, now has an imaginative display of a wide range of objects from timepieces to aeroplanes, bringing together the innovatory and artistic aspects, as well as the history, of technology and science.

Several changes are taking place at the **Palais de Chaillot** (Ch. 29), built in 1937 and housing several museums. The former French Monuments Museum has closed and is scheduled to reopen in 2003, updated and restored. The **Musée du Cinema** is moving from the Palais de Chaillot to Bercy (Ch. 33) where work began in 2000 on the former American Centre designed by Frank Gehry, which is destined to be the new Maison du Cinéma. This will become the home of the Henri Langlois collections and house four projection rooms, space for one permanent and several temporary exhibitions, teaching units, the valuable collection of the Cinémathèque française and a documentation centre entirely devoted to the silver screen.

The transfer of the Museum of Cinéma to Bercy is an example of how the boundaries are pushing out from the centre so that once unfashionable areas have become in-places. Across the Seine from Bercy is the **Bibliothèque Nationale de France, François Mitterrand** (French National Library; Ch. 6) in the Tolbiac/Massena area of the 13th arrondissement which is also becoming an improved residential area. Certain areas of the library, a controversial building, are open to the public and exhibitions are held there.

This migration has been aided by the swish new Métro line, **Méteor** (Line 14), which opened in 1999 serving Madeleine, Pyramides, Palais Royal-Musée du

Louvre, Châtelet-Les Halles, Gare de Lyon, Bercy, Cour St-Emilion and Bibliothèque.

People are now talking about the Butte aux Cailles district in the 14th arrondissement, near Place d'Italie, and about the Belleville quartier (Ch. 31) in the 20th arrondissement. In recent years, artists and then Parisians in general have been drawn to Belleville, for its village-like atmosphere, its mixture of old and new, for the ethnic variety of its population and therefore its markets, music and cooking, and its steep and picturesque streets. The area also boasts a park high above Paris with great views.

La Villette, in the north-eastern corner of Paris, has very distinct attractions. The Cité des Sciences et de l'Industrie has been long established beside the Canal d'Ourcq, but there is also the Cité de la Musique. The **Musée de la Musique** (Ch. 31) is now fully open and the museology and musicality of this museum makes an expedition to this district even more rewarding.

The very latest major project, scheduled for 2004, is the **Musée Branly**, close to the Eiffel Tower. This brand new museum designed by Jean Nouvel, is the *grand projet* of Président Jacques Chirac. It will bring together the Arts of Africa, Asia, Oceania (Pacific and Australia) and the Americas, using exhibits gathered from the Musée de l'Homme, Musée National des Arts d'Afrique et d'Océanie, certain provincial museums and elsewhere. As a prelude, a small sample from these collections is being shown in galleries at the Louvre at the far end of Denon wing (enter by the Porte des Lions).

At the end of the old and the beginning of the new year, terrible gales hit Paris (and most of France), and vast numbers of trees were lost: 10,000 in Versailles, 17,500 in Parc de St-Cloud, and thousands in the parks of Paris. On the other hand, plans had already been made to celebrate the millennium by planting thousands of trees along the Paris meridian between Dunkerque and Barcelona, named the **Méridienne Verte**. An important new garden, somewhat anachronistically called the **Jardin Medieval**, has been created around the Musée du Moyen Age (Ch. 5) opened in 2000, a bonus for the Quartier Latin.

La Direction des Parcs, Jardins et Espaces Verts promotes Paris as the 'Capital with 400 gardens'. There are, in fact, 421 parks, gardens and cemeteries, divided into botanical, historical, contemporary and cemetery gardens; 175 have been created since 1979. The department has excelled itself with the production of quantities of printed information. These include a *Paris Plan Vert* (or Green Map); booklets on individual gardens; small guides, called *Sentiers-Nature*, with maps, which take you on a green walk around each arrondissement as well as the Bois de Boulogne, the Bois de Vincennes, and other parks; and a booklet called *La nature et les jardins*. Excellent guided tours are available at practically all the main gardens (mainly from April to October), some in English (see Gardens, in the practical information). During the summer there is music in many of the gardens and several concerts are free.

This edition of the *Blue Guide Paris and Versailles* has, therefore, attempted to take into account, as far as possible, all the changes to, or reopenings and closures of, museums and galleries and the detailed accounts of the contents of museums and galleries will help the reader to plan ahead. It is also a book to carry with you during your visit. Whether you have a couple of precious days or a drifting indeterminate time to linger, the overwhelming choice of attractions available makes a thoughtful organisation of your time essential and a deeper knowledge leads to a greater affection for this great city. This edition has a section devoted to architecture, designed as an at-a-glance chronological reference to Parisian buildings as an added planning aid.

Each visitor will approach a visit differently—you might prefer to dismiss the larger museums and go for something smaller, such as the Musée Maillol, the Musée Rodin, the Musée du Moyen Age, the Marmottan, or the new Jewish Museum. Others will be keen to discover the latest changes to the well-known sites such as Notre-Dame, the Pompidou Centre, the Louvre and the Musée des Arts Decoratifs. You may wish to spend more time on the outskirts, not only at Versailles, but also at St-Denis, St-Gemain-en-Laye, or Ecouen for example, which have great monuments or museums (or both), where you will gain a new insight into the Ile de France. There are also alternative means of transport for discovering Paris. The municipality has implemented a cycle programme, with the creation of cycle lanes and bikes can be hired. Batobus is a shuttle service that has six docking points along the Seine. You can jump on and off l'Open Bus or take a tram-train on a route between La Défense and St-Denis.

There are infinite possibilities for designing your visit and however good the preparations luckily it is impossible to eliminate totally the unexpected, the unknown, or the serendipitous moment and this is what makes every stay in Paris so special.

Delia Gray-Durant
April 2001

Acknowledgements

I am deeply grateful to all those people who have helped with the research involved in this book. My special thanks go to Brigitte Delattre at the Caisse National des Monuments Historiques et des Sites, and to Gabrielle Hufenbecher at the Comité Régional de Tourisme de Ile de France who provided introductions and documentation. I would also like to thank Marijke Naber at the Musée du Louvre for her continued support, and at other museums, individuals including Pascale de Sèze at the Union Centrale des Arts Décoratifs, Julia Fritsch at the Musée National de la Renaissance, Aggy Lerolle and Martine Sandjian at the Musée d'Orsay, Marie-Agnès Jallon at the Centre Pompidou, Odile Bordaz at the Château de Vincennes, Arielle Weintraub-Muntlak at the Musée d'art et d'histoire de Judaïsme, Jacqueline Robin at the Villa Savoye in Poissy, Sabrina Cook at the Cité de la Musique, Nicole Legrand at the Cité des Sciences et de l'Industrie, and to those whom I met at the Offices de Tourisme at Versailles, St-Denis and Rueil-Malmaison. The list of experts who have generously contributed time and advice is long and I hope that, even if I do not mention each one individually, they will understand that my gratitude remains undiminished and this book would not exist without them.

I am extremely grateful to friends in Paris such as Yvonne Laugier-Werth, Gregory Brown, Serena Poisson and her family, and Marie Eymard who have, as always, sustained and encouraged. On the home front, my thanks go to Gemma Davies at A&C Black who provided the opportunity again to work on *Blue Guide Paris and Versailles*, and of course to Will and Siân who are always there.

Paris surveyed

Paris lies on both banks of the Seine, near the centre of the Paris Basin, between 25 and 130m above sea-level and 150km (or over 320km by the windings of the river) from the sea. The Seine, the third in length of the four great rivers of France, enters this part of the Paris Basin some 500km from its source.

The great loop of the Seine divides the city into Left Bank (Rive Gauche) on the south and Right Bank (Rive Droite) on the north. It washes two islands, the Ile de la Cité, cradle of Paris, and the smaller Ile St-Louis. Spanned by numerous bridges, and lined by rapid thoroughfares, traffic roars alongside it and across it. But the Quais, lined with elegant façades, trees, bouquinistes, gardens, and historic monuments, remain the place for a leisurely walk and, between Pont de Sully and Pont d'Iéna, were declared a UNESCO World Heritage site in 1992. The river and its banks serve as a pleasant introduction to Paris while the sightseeing launches on the Seine offer unusual and attractive low-level views.

Paris in the 19C was bounded by a line of ramparts which, although they have long been demolished (tiny sections are still visible in places) and their sites built over, served to contain the population, denser than in any other European city (recently 20,164 inhabitants per square kilometre) in an area of 7800 hectares. The line of the 19C walls can be imagined by following the exterior Blvd Périphérique.

Pl. du Parvis-Notre-Dame on the Ile de la Cité, from which kilometric distances in France are measured, is a good starting point for exploring Paris. However, the carefully planned vistas from one bank of the river to the other are more obvious from Place de la Concorde. To the northwest is the most famous of avenues, the Champs Elysées, leading to the Arc de Triomphe and La Défense beyond, while in the opposite direction, through the trees of the gardens of the Tuileries, is the immense bulk of the Louvre. This is flanked, to the north, by Rue de Rivoli and its continuation, Rue St-Antoine, ending at Pl. de la Bastille; and further east, by the Rue du Faubourg St-Antoine, leading to Pl. de la Nation, and ultimately to Vincennes.

There are always many tourists, and the high season is not always when you might expect it. July and August are strange months in Paris, when Parisians desert their city in favour of the coast or countryside. Although it is possible to travel more easily by car during that period, some entertainments (such as theatres) and neighbourhood shops or restaurants are likely to be closed.

Ile-de-France

La Région d'Ile-de-France, which includes and surrounds Paris, consists of eight départements, as follows (with their postal prefix): the **Ville-de-Paris** (75) divided into *arrondissements* (see below) at the core. The three that lie immediately outside the periphery (*la proche banlieue*) are **Hauts-de-Seine** (92; préfecture Nanterre) to the west, **Seine-St-Denis** (93; préfecture Bobigny) to the northeast, and **Val-de-Marne** (94; préfecture Créteil) to the south-west. A second band around these (*la grande banlieue*) is made up of **Val-d'Oise** (95; préfecture Cergy-Pontoise) to the north, **Yvelines** (78; préfecture Versailles) to the west, **Essonne** (91; préfecture Ivry) to the south, and **Seine-et-Marne** (77; préfecture Melun) to the east. Some highlights (Versailles, Fontainebleau, Ecouen, St-Germain-en-Laye) of these départements are covered in the last section of the Guide.

The arrondissements

The municipal districts or arrondissements, of which there are 20 in central Paris, each with its Maire and Mairie (mayor and town hall), are important administrative and topographical entities. You can see on pp 2–3 of the Atlas that their numbering follows a spiral working out clockwise from the centre. The arrondissements are written 75001, 75002, etc., the prefix 75 indicating the département. The arrondissements touched on, in whole or in part, are indicated at the beginning of each Route. They used to be written 1er, 2e, etc. and this form is still sometimes used in text.

75001   Louvre: the western half of the Cité, the Louvre, Pl. Vendôme, Palais-Royal and St-Eustache.

75002   Bourse: also the Bibliothèque Nationale, Richelieu.

75003   Temple: comprising the north half of the Marais, Temple and Archives.

75004   Hôtel de Ville: includes the eastern half of the Cité, with Notre-Dame, Ile St-Louis and the Centre Pompidou, the southern part of the Marais with Pl. des Vosges, and bounded by Pl. de la Bastille to the east.

75005   Panthéon: the Quartier Latin, with the Sorbonne, Panthéon, Val-de Grâce and Jardin des Plantes.

75006   Luxembourg: with St-Germain-des-Prés, St-Sulpice and the Palais du Luxembourg.

75007   Palais-Bourbon: comprising the Faubourg St-Germain, Musée d'Orsay, Les Invalides, Ecole Militaire and bounded to the west by the Eiffel Tower.

75008   Elysée: with the Pl. de la Concorde, the Madeleine, the Champs-Elysées and Faubourg St-Honoré, and including Parc Monceau to the north, and Av. George-V to the west.

75009   Opéra: reaching up to Blvd de Clichy and Pl. Pigalle.

75010   Enclos St-Laurent: with Gares du Nord and de l'Est, and Hôpital St-Louis.

75011   Popincourt: the area north east of Pl. de la Bastille and reaching to Pl. de la Nation.

75012   Reuilly: the area south east of Pl. de la Bastille, including the Gare de Lyon and Bercy.

75013   Gobelins: the area south of Gare d'Austerlitz, including the Gobelins and Pl. d'Italie.

75014   Observatoire: including the Cimetière de Montparnasse, Parc de Montsouris and Cité Universitaire.

75015   Vaugirard: the area south west of the Tour Montparnasse and Av. de Suffren.

75016   Passy: between the Seine and Bois de Boulogne, its northern half crossed by Avenues Foch, Victor-Hugo and Kléber, radiating from the Etoile, and containing the districts of Chaillot, Passy and Auteuil.

75017   Batignolles Monceau: the area north west of the Etoile.

75018   Butte Montmartre: the area north east of Pl. de Clichy and reaching as far east as Rue d'Aubervilliers.

75019   Buttes-Chaumont: including La Villette.
75020   Ménilmontant: including Père Lachaise cemetery.

Métro stations. A list of convenient Métro stations is given at the beginning of most chapters: see also Atlas, pp 4–5.

Statistics

In 1999, the total municipal population of Paris was in round figures 2,125,000, with 11,000,000 in greater Paris. The total population of France in 1999 was 60,186,184. (A century or so earlier the figures were 2,269,000 for Paris and 39,238,000 for France.) Those interested in such figures and many other statistics should contact the INSEE Info Service, Tour Gamma A, 195 Rue de Bercy, 75582 Paris Cedex 12, ☎ 01 41 17 66 11, 🖷 01 53 17 88 09 (easily approached from the level of the Gare de Lyon).

PRACTICAL INFORMATION

Planning your trip

When to go

Parisian weather is changeable, particularly in the winter and spring, although long periods of fine weather occur each year. It can occasionally be oppressively hot in summer (30°C) for a few days, and bitterly cold in winter. The average number of days a year on which the temperature falls below freezing-point is about 35; the number of days of snowfall has averaged 15 in recent decades. Although spring in Paris is most people's ideal, the autumn can be glorious.

Tourist offices

In the UK General information, including how to get to Paris from the UK, with suggestions for accommodation and how to travel within France may be obtained from the **French Government Tourist Office**, Maison de la France, 178 Piccadilly, London W1V 0AL, ☎ 09068 244 123 (all calls charged at 60p per minute), 🖷 020 7493 6594. Maison de la France compiles a very useful *Reference Guide for the Traveller in France*. It also offers the following services: information office, travel agency, booking offices for *Air France*, *Brittany Ferries* and *SeaFrance*, and the *France Magasin* bookshop. Visit the French Travel Centre's web site at www.franceguide.com and to book holidays, www.holidaystore.co.uk.

Republic of Ireland French Government Tourist Office, 10 Suffolk Street, Dublin 2, ☎ 00353 1679 0813.

In the USA and Canada In the USA, **French Government Tourist Offices** are at 444 Madison Av., 16th floor, New York, NY 10022, ☎ 212 838 7800, 🖷 212 838 7855, with branches at 676 North Michigan Av., Chicago, Il. 60611-2819, ☎ 312 751 7800, 312 337 6339; 9454 Wilshire Blvd, Suite 715, Beverley Hills, Ca. 90212-2967, ☎ 310 271 6665, 🖷 310 276 2835.

The Canadian office is at 1981 Avenue McGill College, Suite 490, Montreal, Quebec H3A 2W9 ☎ 514 288 4264, 🖷 514 845 4868.

Travel agents and tour operators

Any accredited member of the Association of British Travel Agents will sell tickets and book accommodation. There are numerous excellent package deals offered by agents specialising in Paris. Look in the national press for special offers. A selection of UK-based tour operators specialising in holidays to Paris is:
Aeroscope, ☎ 01608 650 103, 🖷 01608 651 295, ✉ aerscope@aol.com
British Airways Holidays, ☎ 08702 424 243, 🖷 01293 722 704, www.baholidays.co.uk.
Euro Tours, ☎ 0870 333 0889, 🖷 01273 383 123, ✉ info@eurotours. co.uk; www.eurotours.co.uk.
Goodwood Travel, ☎ 01227 763 336, 🖷 01227 762 417, ✉ goodwood@ globalnet.co.uk; internet: www.concorde.co.uk.

Inghams (Just France), ☎ 020 8780 4480, ▤ 020 8780 7705, ✉ travel@ inghams.co.uk; internet: www.inghams.co.uk.
Paris Travel Service, ☎ 01992 456 611, ▤ 01992 456 609, ✉ paris@ bridge-travel.co.uk; internet: www.bridge-travel.co.uk.
Thomson Breakaway, ☎ 08706 061 470, ▤ 020 8210 4269.
Time Off, ☎ 0990 846 363, ▤ 020 8218 3636, www.timeoff.co.uk.

Passports

Passports are necessary for all British and American travellers entering France. British passports, valid for ten years, are issued at five regional Passport Offices in the UK and from Clive House, 70 Petty France, London SW1H 9HD. For all information, ☎ 0990 210 410. Passport forms are available from main post offices, branches of Lloyds Bank and some travel agents. Visas are not required for British or American visitors to France.

If you are from an EU country and intend to stay in France for more than three months, you should apply in advance for a *carte de séjour* from the nearest French Consulate or, if you are already in France, at the Préfecture de Police, Ile de la Cité (Salle Sud).

British subjects wanting to work in France should write to the Consular Section of the Embassy (see below) which will advise on the procedure to be followed, according to the status of the person concerned under EU regulations. It should be emphasised that it acts neither as an employment agency nor an accommodation agency.

Customs

Travellers by air pass through customs at the airport of arrival; EU travellers between EU countries may go through the blue exit and therefore do not need to go through Customs. However, selective checks are carried out. If travelling on international expresses, luggage may be examined on the train. If travelling by road, luggage may be checked at the frontier or at ports of departure and disembarkation.

In general, there are no limits on quantities of goods carried from one European Union country to another, provided tax has been paid on them in the country of origin and provided they are for personal use, but there are guidance levels: cigarettes 800, cigarillos 400, cigars 200, smoking tobacco 1 kg; spirits 10 litres; fortified wine (port, sherry) 20 litres, wine 90 litres (not more than 60 litres of sparkling), beer 110 litres. For passengers from outside the EU, the restrictions will vary and it is advisable to check with your local travel agent about allowances.

Embassies and consulates

In the UK French Embassy in London: 58 Knightsbridge, London SW1X 7JT, ☎ 020 7201 1000. French Consulate, 21 Cromwell Road, London SW7 2EN, ☎ 020 7838 2000; Visa Dept 6a Cromwell Place, London SW7 2EW, ☎ 0900 188 7733/020 7838 2050; French Chamber of Commerce, 21 Dartmouth Street, Westminster, London SW1H 9BP.

In the USA and Canada In the USA at 4101 Reservoir Road NW, Washington, DC 20007 (☎ 212 944 6000). In Canada at 42 Promenade Sussex, Ottawa, ON K2M 2C9 (☎ 613 789 1795).

Getting there

There are various ways of getting to Paris from Great Britain, by rail, air, sea and rail, or sea and coach. A car is not essential for getting around Paris and to its immediate surroundings as public transport is excellent (see below). In fact, a car can be a liability in central Paris except perhaps in August when the city is relatively empty. Car hire facilities are available at the airports and rail termini or in central Paris.

By air

From the UK Regular scheduled air services between England and France are operated by Air France working in conjunction with British Airways. Full information about flights from London and Gatwick and other cities in the UK to Paris Charles de Gaulle and Orly can be obtained from:

Air France, Colet Court, 100 Hammersmith Road, London W6 7JP, ☎ 08450 845 111, 📠 020 8782 8115, www.airfrance.co.uk.

British Airways, 156 Regent St, London W1R 5TA, ☎ 0990 444 000 (flight information), ☎ 0345 222 111, 📠 01612 475 707, www.britishairways.com.

British Midland, Donnington Hall, Castle Donnington, Derby DE74 2SB, ☎ 08706 070 555, www.britishmidland.com.

Buzz, Stansted Airport, Stansted, CM24 1RS, ☎ 0870 2407 070, www.buzz away.com.

Scotairways, Cambridge Airport, Cambridge CB5 8RT, ☎ 08706 060 707, 📠 01223 292 160, www.scotairways.co.uk.

Ryanair, Enterprise House, Stansted Airport, CM24 1QW, ☎ 0870 333 1231, www.ryanair.com.

For charter flights, check the national press.

From the USA For details of flights available from the USA contact the following airlines:

Air France, ☎ 800 AFPARIS, www.airfrance.com. Departures from Chicago, Houston, Los Angeles, Miami, JFK New York, San Francisco, Washington.

American Airlines, ☎ 800 433 7300, www.im.aa.com. Departures from Boston, Chicago, Dallas, Miami, JFK New York.

Continental Airlines, ☎ 800 525 0280, www.continental.com. Departures from Houston, Newark New York, Miami, San Francisco.

Delta Airlines, ☎ 800 241 4141, www.delta-air.com. Departures from Atlanta, Cincinnati, JFK New York.

Northwest Airlines, ☎ 800 225 2525, www.nwa.com. Departures from Detroit and many other cities.

TWA, ☎ 800 221 2000, www.twa.com. Departures from JFK New York, Saint-Louis.

United Airlines, ☎ 800 538 2929, www.ual.com. Departures from Chicago, Los Angeles, San Francisco, Washington.

In Paris *British Airways* has a Paris office at 13–15 Blvd de la Madeleine, 75009, ☎ 0825 825 400.

Air France has an office at 119 Av. des Champs-Elysées, ☎ 0802 802 802.

Airports

Paris is served by two international airports: **Roissy-Charles de Gaulle** (CDG), ☎ 01 48 62 22 80, 23km northeast of the capital, comprising two separate terminals; and **Orly** (south and west), ☎ 01 49 75 15 15, 14km south of the city.

Charles de Gaulle is linked by a shuttle and **RER B** train service with the Gare du Nord; Orly by shuttle and **RER C** with the Gare d'Austerlitz.

They are also connected by an *Air France* **bus service**, ☎ 01 41 56 89 00, leaving each terminal every 12 minutes.

CDG to Etoile/Porte Maillot, between 05.40 and 23.00.

Orly to Porte d'Orléans, Montparnasse Station and Les Invalides air terminal, between 05.00 and 23.00.

The Roissy Bus runs every 15 minutes between CDG and Rue Scribe (near Opéra Garnier), 05.45 to 23.00. The Orly Bus every 12 minutes between Orly and Denfert-Rochereau, 06.00 to 23.00. ☎ 08 36 68 77 14 for both.

Airport transfers between Orly and Roissy: Orly–CDG every 20 mins 06.00–15.00, every 30 mins from 15.00–23.30; CDG-Orly, every 20 mins 05.40–14.00, every 30 mins 14.00–23.00.

Taxis can be found at the airports and **car-hire firms** have offices there.

By train

The opening of the Channel Tunnel has transformed rail travel to Paris (and to Lille and Brussels) for those coming from Britain. For foot passengers from London, one of the pleasantest ways to travel is by *Eurostar* from Waterloo International Terminal, which brings you in just three hours to Paris Gare-du-Nord; or from the Ashford International Terminal, Kent, in two hours.

Information can be obtained and reservations made direct with Eurostar on ☎ 0990 186 186 (from outside UK +44 1233 617 575), and from most main line stations. Internet: www.eurostar.com.

For passengers and vehicles, the Eurotunnel, *Le Shuttle* drive-on, drive-off service terminal in England is at Cheriton, just west of Folkestone, M20 (Junction 11a); the French terminal is near Coquelles, some 5km southwest of Calais, A16 (Junction 13). There are up to four departures per hour during peak periods. The journey takes 35 minutes from platform to platform (25 minutes in the tunnel). For direct reservations, ☎ 08705 353 535, departure information: passenger information, including weather and road conditions ☎ 08000 969 992; www.eurotunnel.com. In France, information and reservations: ☎ 03 21 00 61 00.

Rail Europe, Rail Europe Travel Shop, 179 Piccadilly, London W1V 0BA (next to the French Government Tourist Office) or Call Centre ☎ 08705 848 848, www.raileurope.co.uk for information and bookings on all European rail services. The Paris office of *BritRail* is at Maison de la Grande Bretagne, 19 Rue des Mathurins, 75009, ☎ 01 44 51 06 00.

Railway terminals in Paris

The main stations are all on Métro lines and most have left-luggage offices (consignes) or lockers, trolleys, information bureaux, etc. Some, such as Gare d'Austerlitz and Gare du Nord, are also connected by regular bus services. *SNCF* information and reservations: main line, ☎ 08 36 35 35 35, in English: ☎ 08 36 35 35 39; Ile-de-France, ☎ 01 53 90 20 20 (French only).

The main stations of the *SNCF* are:

Gare d'Austerlitz (Map 15; 6–8), serving the Région Sud-Ouest (Tours, Bordeaux, Toulouse, Bayonne, the Pyrenees) and Spain and Portugal.

Gare de l'Est (Map 15; 6–8) for the Région Est (Reims, Metz, Strasbourg) and Luxembourg, Germany, Austria and Switzerland and Eastern European countries.

Gare de Lyon (Map 15; 6–8) for the Région Sud-Est (Lyon, Dijon, Provence, Côte d'Azur) and Italy, Switzerland, Greece. TGV Sud-Est.

Gare Montparnasse (Map 15; 6–8), terminus for the Région Ouest (Brittany, La Rochelle, etc.), and Aquitaine (the west-south-west of France). TGV Atlantique.

Gare du Nord (Map 15; 6–8) for the Région Nord (Lille, Brussels, Amsterdam, Cologne, Hamburg, etc., and also for boat-trains to Boulogne, Calais and Dunkerque). Eurostar terminus for London. TGV Thalys (Northern Europe).

Gare St-Lazare (Map 15; 6–8), another terminus of the Région Ouest (Normandy lines, Rouen, and boat-trains from Dieppe, Le Havre, Cherbourg, etc.).

There is also an Interprovincial service around Paris linking the TGV network.

Note: French Railways do not have ticket control at platform barriers. Passengers travelling in France must validate (*composter*) their ticket in an orange-red machine (which punches-and-date-stamps it) at the platform entrance before boarding the train or risk paying a fine.

By ferry

Brittany Ferries, ☎ 08705 360 360, www.brittany-ferries.com. Portsmouth–Caen/St Malo, Plymouth–Roscoff, Poole–Cherbourg.

Hoverspeed Fast Ferries, ☎ 08705 240 241, ⌨ 01304 865 203, www.hover-speed.co.uk. Dover–Calais 35 mins by Hovercraft, 50 mins by Seacat; Folkestone–Boulogne by Seacat, Newhaven–Dieppe.

P & O Portsmouth, ☎ 08702 424 999, ⌨ 01705 864 211, www.poportsmouth.com. Portsmouth–Le Havre and Portsmouth–Cherbourg.

P & O Stena Line, ☎ 08706 000 600, ⌨ 01304 863 464, www.posl.com. Dover–Calais.

SeaFrance, ☎ 08705 711 711, ⌨ 01304 240 033, www.seafrance.com. Dover–Calais.

By bus/coach

There are regular bus or coach services from the UK to Paris, and details may be obtained from ***Eurolines National Express***, 52 Grosvenor Gardens, London SW1W 0AU, ☎ 0990 143 219, www.eurolines.com.

By car

Motorists driving to Paris may obtain information from the automobile associations on necessary documents, routes, rules of the road, restrictions on caravans and trailers, availability of spare parts, insurance etc.

AA, Norfolk House, Priestley Way, Basingstoke, Hants RG24 9NY, ☎ 0990 500 600, www.theaa.co.uk

RAC, P.O. Box 1500 Bristol BS99 2LH, ☎ 08705 722 722 or www.rac.co.uk.

American Automobile Association, 1000 AAA Drive, Heathrow, Florida 32746-5063, ☎ 1407 444 7000.

Comprehensive motor insurance is advisable and you must keep your green international insurance card with you. Driving on a provisional licence is not allowed. At junctions, traffic from the right has priority unless otherwise indicated. Insurance facilities are available from *Europ Assistance*, Sussex House, Perrymount Road, Haywards Heath, West Sussex RH16 1DN, ☎ 01444 442 442, ✉ webmaster@europ-assistance.com, the AA and RAC or your motor insurance company.

Rules of the road

The use of safety belts is compulsory, crash helmets must be worn by motorcyclists; children under ten may not travel in the front seat (unless the car has no back seat); vehicles should have an international distinguishing sign and headlight beam converters, carry spare bulbs for headlights, left hand external mirror and warning lights or advance warning signal (triangle). The **Regional Road Travel Information Centre**, Ile-de-France ☎ 01 48 99 33 33, supplies information about traffic congestion and weather as well as itineraries.

The most rapid route from **Calais** or **Boulogne** to Paris is to take the A26 as far as Arras and then the A1. There are tolls (*péages*) to pay on these roads. From Dunkerque take the A25 to Lille and join the A1 at Lille. An alternative road is the A16 from Calais to Paris via Boulogne, Amiens and Beauvais.

If disembarking in **Le Havre** or **Caen**, the A13 brings you in to the west of Paris. This is a convenient route from southern England for those who might prefer to be based on the outskirts of Paris at, for example, St-Germain-en-Laye, Versailles or Fontainebleau.

If driving into central Paris, it is as well to check the number of the exit (*sortie*) from the motorway that you are aiming for prior to embarking on the Blvd Périphérique. Exits are usually well indicated, but be careful to get into the correct lane well in advance. The Blvd Périphérique is the efficient but often very crowded, inner ring road around Paris. Likewise it is important to make sure that you know which exit you need from the Périphérique (these are described as Portes, e.g. Porte Maillot, Porte de Vincennes).

Maps

For Paris and its immediate surroundings the following are recommended to supplement the Atlas section at the end of this Guide.

Michelin, *Plan de Paris* (no. 10, at 1:10,000), also available with street references as no. 12. (Their Paris Plan is perhaps more convenient when walking and it contains Métro and bus maps.) Nos 10 and 12 show the position of underground car-parks and 24-hour petrol stations and one way streets. Other maps published annually by Michelin are *Outskirts of Paris* (no. 101, at 1:50,000), *Environs of Paris* (no. 106, at 1:100,000), *Paris Region* (no. 237, at 1:200,000). The suburbs of Paris (with street indexes) are covered in nos 18, 20, 22 and 24. Map no. 9 concentrates entirely on forms of transport in Paris.

The *Institut Géographique National* (IGN) map of the *Environs de Paris* (no. 90, at 1:100,000) gives a good indication of contours and the general lie of the land. Paris is covered in detail in *Série Bleue* (no. 2314, est and ouest sheets, at 1:25,000); and the environs by *Série Verte* at 1:100,000, nos 8, 9, 20 and 21. *Série Rouge* no. 103 (*Carte de l'Environnement Culturel et Touristique*) at 1:250,000 helps to pinpoint tourist sites.

Travelling to or from Paris, Michelin's no. 236 is recommended and also *France-Grandes Routes* (no. 989), or the **IGN** *France-Routes: autoroutes* (no. 901), both at 1:1,000,000. Also available are the *Michelin Motoring Atlas France,* at 1:200,000, and their hardback *Road Atlas France*. Collins publish a *Road Atlas France* at 1:250,000, based on IGN maps.

The latest editions of maps can be found in London at **Stanfords**, 12–14 Long Acre, London WC2E 9LP: ☎ 020 7836 1321, 📠 020 7836 0189, www.stanfords.co.uk, and from most good booksellers in the UK, USA or France.

The London offices of the **Michelin Tyre plc** are at Edward Hyde Building, 38 Clarendon Road, Watford WD1 1SX; in Paris, **Pneu Michelin**, 46 Av. de Breteuil, south of Les Invalides, www.michelin-travel.com. **IGN Paris** is at 107 Rue La Boétie.

Getting around

Buses (*autobus*) and the underground railway (*Métro*) in Paris are controlled by the **RATP** (Régie Autonome des Transports Parisiens), offices 53 bis Quai des Grands-Augustins and Pl. de la Madeleine. For all information on Métro, bus and **RER**, call ☎ 08 36 68 41 14 (English), ☎ 08 36 68 77 14 (French). The RATP issues useful maps of the Métro, bus and **RER** networks, and a leaflet giving details of various summer excursions. The Michelin Map no. 9 (*Paris Transports*) is handy.

Smoking is forbidden on both buses and the Métro. The worst of the rush hour is between 08.00 and 09.00, and 17.30 and 19.30, and in some areas traffic is heavy between 12.00 and 14.00.

By Métro

The Métro (Métropolitan) provides a rapid means of transport throughout Paris from 05.30 to 00.30. The most convenient Métro stations are listed at the beginning of each route described in this Guide. Trains glide silently on rubber wheels through stations approximately 500m apart. Platforms at certain stations (e.g. Louvre, Hotel de Ville, Varenne) are decorated with reproductions of objects from nearby museums or sites. As in most large cities, avoid travelling alone late at night and beware of bag-snatchers and pickpockets.

The first line of the Métro was opened in 1900 and certain stations, notably the Bois de Boulogne entrance of Porte Dauphine, retain their Art Nouveau decoration, which have been the object of a campaign of restoration in 2000 to mark the centenary of the Métro. The latest line (no. 14) to open is called the Méteor and runs between Madeleine and Bibliothèque. The various lines are identified by number and by the names of the terminal stations: e.g. Ligne 1, Château de Vincennes–Pont de Neuilly. The direction in which the train is running is indicated by a sign naming the terminal station. At interchange stations, the passages leading to the line concerned are clearly indicated by an orange-lighted sign marked *Correspondance*, followed by the name of the terminal stations of the connecting line. Certain *correspondances* necessitate a long walk. There are tramways linking La Défense and Issy, and Bobigny and Saint-Denis.

By RER

RER (*Réseau Express Régional*) is a fast overground service with four lines, linked to the Métro and some *SNCF* train lines.

Line A runs west–east across Paris, between St-Germain-en-Laye (A1), Cergy-le-Haut (A3) and Poissy (A5) and Boissy St-Léger (A2) and Marne-la Vallée/ Chessy (Parc Disneyland) (A4) and is connected to the Métro at Etoile, Auber, Châtelet-Les Halles, Gare de Lyon and Nation.

Line B runs southwest–northeast through Châtelet-Les Halles and Denfert-Rochereau to Robinson (and Sceaux) (B2) and St-Rémy-lès-Chevreuse (B4) (link from Antony to Orly airport), and north from Châtelet-Les Halles via the Gare du Nord, to the airport of Roissy-Charles de Gaulle (B3), or Mitry-Claye (B5).

Line C, serves the west–north section, through Porte Maillot to Montigny-Beauchamp (C1) and Argenteuil (C3), west following the left bank of the Seine through St-Michel Notre-Dame, to Versailles-Rive Gauche (C5), St-Quentin-en-Yvelines (C7) and Versailles Chantiers (C8), and south to Pont de Rungis-Orly (C2), Dourdan-la-Forêt (C4) and St-Martin d'Etampes (C6).

Line D north–south through Châtelet-Les Halles to Orry-la-Ville-Coye (D1), Melun (D2) and Malesherbes (D4).

The Métro ticket is valid on these lines within central Paris but if you are travelling further afield a separate one must be bought at the interchange stations.

Travel passes and tickets

Tickets, valid on both Métro and buses, are sold individually or in tens (*carnet*) at all stations. The tickets operate a turnstile and should be retained until the end of the journey. The fare is the same for any distance on the main inner network, including all necessary changes.

Mobilis: a 1-day ticket valid for zones 1–2.

Paris-Visite: a ticket for 1, 2, 3 or 5 consecutive days of unlimited travel by Métro, *RER*, bus, suburban *SNCF* trains and the Montmartre Funicular in zones 1–3 (excluding airports), and zones 1–5 (including airports and Chessy-Marne-la-Vallée for Disneyland) and zones 1–8 if you want to go further.

Paris-Visite ticket also entitles you to reductions to numerous museums and monuments. It can be purchased at the *Paris Tourist Office* at 127 Av. des Champs-Elysées, in the main Métro, *RER* and *SNCF* stations, and at airports. In England it is on sale at the *French Travel Centre* (178 Piccadilly) and *French Railways* in London (179 Piccadilly) and *Eurostar* ticket desks at Waterloo and Ashford terminals and at the Paris airports.

Parissimo: an all-inclusive 3-day travel card for unlimited bus, Métro, tram and *RER* travel as far as La Défense and St-Denis-Stade de France. It also includes *L'Open Tour*, *Batobus* on the Seine (see below) and one prority entrance to the Louvre, enabling you to bypass the interminable queues. Available from tour operators and travel agents and prices vary according to the time of year.

Carte Orange: visitors staying more than a few days and planning to use public transport frequently are advised to buy (at any Métro station) a Carte Orange, for a week (*hebdomadaire*) or for a month (*mensuel*), for which you will need a passport-size photograph. You will be issued with an *SNCF* identification card, which you use to buy further weekly or monthly tickets. It is important to write the number of that card on your ticket.

SNCF/Paris: if you buy a train ticket from a railway station outside Paris, travel on the Paris Métro and bus is included.

By bus

This is the most pleasant way of travelling around Paris and is relatively easy as bus routes are displayed at bus stops and inside the buses. All bus stops are request stops (*arrêt facultatif*), and each is indicated by its name on the stop itself. All forms of travel pass and ticket listed below (Métro, Mobilis, Paris Visite, Parissimo, Carte Orange) will cover any journey on the Paris bus network. One Métro ticket from a carnet is valid for any one journey by bus (without changes) and should be punched (*composté*) in the small machine at the front of the bus. However, if you have one of the multi-voyage tickets, you can jump on and off buses with abandon (but do not punch your pass). Owing to the many one-way streets, buses do not necessarily return along the same route.

Daytime bus schedules run from around 07.00 to 20.30; some routes do not function on a Sunday; there is an evening service between 20.30 and 00.30; the *Balabus* takes you to the main tourist sites between Bastille and La Défense on Sundays and public holidays from April to September. The stops are marked Balabus (Bb). The *Monmatrobus* takes you on a round trip of Montmartre between the Mairie du 18C and Pigalle. *La Petite Ceinture* runs between the Portes de Paris, just inside the Blvd Périphérique. The 29 bus (from Gare St-Lazare to Porte de Montempoivre, via the Marais) is a new version of the old buses with an open platform at the back. For details of L'Open Tour, see below.

By car

Parking is severely restricted in central Paris and prohibited in many streets. Pay and display machines (*horodateurs*) dispense tickets usually lasting 2 hours either for coins or cards purchased in tabacs. There are underground car parks (e.g. Champs-Elysées, Place Vendôme, Louvre) but they are expensive. For information on residential parking, ☎ 01 44 67 28 28. Michelin maps indicate car parks.

Badly parked foreign cars are towed away as ruthlessly as native ones and may take hours to recover from one of the eight *fourrières* or pounds, and at a considerable charge; there will also be a heavy fine to pay. Alternatively, a clamp or *sabot* may be attached to a wheel. In either case, the owner should apply to the nearest police station (Commissariat).

By taxi

Taxis, which are not excessively expensive, can be hailed from the street or found at a taxi rank. (Each taxi rank has a phone number.) There are also phone cabs. Three tariffs (A, B, C) apply in Paris and are displayed inside the vehicle:

A = 07.00–19.00
B = 19.00–07.00, Sundays and public holidays;
immediate suburbs: B = 07.00–19.00
C = 19.00–07.00, Sundays and public holidays; outside suburban limits, tariff C.

Taxi drivers expect a tip of 10 per cent in addition to the charge on the meter. There is an additional charge for luggage, pick up from railway terminals, fourth adult passenger, large packages and pets.

Any complaints should be addressed to the *Service des Taxis*, Préfecture de Police, Service des Taxis, 36 Rue des Morillons, 75015 Paris, ☎ 01 55 76 20 00.

General information

Disabled travellers

Help for the disabled who wish to travel is expanding. Some of the carriers offer special concessions. *Eurostar* gives wheelchair passengers 1st class travel for 2nd class fares and *Le Shuttle* allows disabled travellers to remain in their cars for the journey. *Tripscope* offers a free travel and transport information service and advice on concessions, at Alexandra House, Albany Rd, Brentford, Mddx TW8 0NE, ☎ 08457 585 641, 📠 020 8580 7022, ✉ tripscope@cableinet.co.uk.

The Access Project, 39 Bradley Gardens, West Ealing, London W13 8HE, has a well researched document *Access in Paris* (also available to callers at the French Tourist Office, London) (a donation of £5 is suggested).

RADAR, 12 City Forum, 250 City Road, London EC1 V8AF, ☎ 020 7250 3222, gives specialist advice on all aspects of travel and publish *Getting There*, a guide to facilities at airports (£5).

The **Paris Tourist Office** has a pamphlet (in French) *Touristes Quand Même*, and other information.

In France, further information is available through the *Association pour la Mobilité des Handicapés*, 65 Rue de la Victoire, 75009, ☎ 01 42 80 40 20.

Embassies and consulates

British Embassy: 35 Rue du Faubourg St-Honoré, 75008, ☎ 01 44 51 31 00; British Consulate, 16 Rue d'Anjou (Visa Office), (near the Embassy) ☎ 01 44 51 31 00; visas: ☎ 01 44 51 33 01/01 44 51 33 03; passports: ☎ 01 40 39 80 64; resident permits: ☎ 01 40 39 80 65. The *Chamber of Commerce*, 31 Bossy d'Anglars, 75008; British Council, 9 Rue De Constantine, 75007.

US Embassy, 2 Av. Gabriel, 75008 (just north of the Pl. de la Concorde), ☎ 01 43 12 22 22.

Canadian Embassy, 35 Av. Montaigne, 75008, ☎ 01 44 43 29 00.

Australian Embassy, 4 Rue Jean Rey, 75015, ☎ 01 40 59 33 00.

New Zealand Embassy, 7ter Rue Léonard-de-Vinci, 75016, ☎ 01 45 00 24 11.

Irish Consultate, 4 Rue Rude, 75016, ☎ 01 45 00 20 87.

Emergencies

Police ☎ 17.	Fire brigade ☎ 18.
Medicalt ☎ 01 47 07 77 77.	SAMU (*Service Aide Médicale d'Urgence*) ☎ 15.
Dental ☎ 01 43 37 51 00.	Anti-poison centre ☎ 01 40 37 04 04.

Children's burns unit ☎ 01 44 73 62 54.

Adult burn centre ☎ 01 42 34 17 58.

For lost or stolen credit cards, see p 25.

Etiquette

The French, especially the older generation, may still be quite formal by Anglo-Saxon standards and will still generally shake hands at meeting and parting. It is safer to use the *vous* form of address with people you do not know although the

French *tu-toi* each other more readily than they used to. It is also polite to use Monsieur, Madame or Mademoiselle as a form of address (without the surname, which is fortunate when you have forgotten a name) even after knowing someone for a while. Overall, manners are becoming more relaxed whereas courtesy to foreign visitors, especially in museums, seems to have greatly improved.

Insurance

As members of the EU, British subjects are entitled to use the French health services but must have a form E111 (available from DSS offices and post offices) as this is necessary for any refund you will apply for in France. Note that it is essential to have the form signed by the doctor and keep prescriptions and all receipts for consultations, treatments and medicines. The average refund of medical expenses is about 70 per cent. You are also strongly advised to take out private insurance (available from travel agents and banks), which will not only cover the cost of any medical expenses and repatriation, but also loss of luggage, cash and other valuables.

Late-night chemists

Drugstore Champs-Elysées, 133 Av. des Champs-Elysées, to 02.00, Ὠ Charles-de-Gaulle Etoile.
Pharmacie des Arts, 106 Blvd du Montparnasse, to midnight, Ὠ Vavin.
Pharmacie Azoulay, 5 Pl. Pigalle, 75009, to 00.30, Ὠ Pigalle.
Pharmacie Dhéry, 84 Av. des Champs-Elysées, 24 hours, Ὠ George V.
Pharmacie Opéra, 6 Blvd des Capucines, to midnight, Ὠ Opéra.
Pharmacie St-Germain, 149 Blvd St-Germain, open until 01.00, Ὠ St-Germain-des-Prés.

Lost or stolen property

If identity papers are mislaid, in whatever circumstances, make a declaration at the nearest police station as a receipt will be needed for any further steps. Likewise for the loss of articles of value, a receipt will be needed for insurance claims. Lost or stolen credit cards should be reported to:
Carte bleue visa, ☎ 08 36 69 08 80   **Diner's Club**, ☎ 01 49 06 17 50
American Express, ☎ 01 47 77 72 00   **Mastercard Eurocard**, ☎ 01 45 67 53 53
American Express Travellers' Cheques, ☎ 05 90 86 00

Articles lost on the Métro or in buses are held for claiming for the first 48 hours at the terminus of the route concerned. Property lost on trains, at stations, on planes and at airports should be reclaimed at the lost property office of the terminus or airport in question.

When items have been lost in the street, theatres or cinemas, etc., enquire at the *Bureau des Objets Perdus*, Préfecture de Police, 36 Rue des Morillons, 75015 (open Mon, Wed 08.30–17.00, Tues, Thurs 08.30–20.00, Fri 08.30–17.30), Ὠ Convention ☎ 01 55 76 20 00.

Money and banks

Currency   The monetary unit is the franc, subdivided into 100 centimes. Bank notes of 20, 50, 100, 200 and 500 francs are in circulation, and there are also coins of 5, 10, 20 and 50 centimes, 1, 2, 5, 10 and 20 francs. Euro bank notes and coins will be introduced on 1 January 2002.

Banks   Branches of most French banks are open from 09.00 to 17.00 Monday to Friday; most branches close on Saturday morning. Not all banks have a foreign exchange service, but if they do, central branches of the principal banks may have a bureau de change open from 09.00 to 12.00. Most banks shut at noon on days preceding public holidays as well as on the holiday. **Bureaux de change** at the main train stations (Gares du Nord, de Lyon, de l'Est, de Montparnasse, St-Lazare, Austerlitz), are open daily from about 06.30 to 22.00 or 23.00. Those at the international airports operate a daily service from 06.00 to 23.00.

Changing money Larger hotels will also accept and exchange travellers' cheques, but usually at a lower rate of exchange than banks or bureaux de change. It is useful to have enough French currency for incidental expenses on arrival, particularly during a weekend. It is is worth shopping around for different rates of exchange and some bureaux de change do not charge commission. The majority of credit cards are accepted for most transactions, and cash may be obtained from cash dispensing machines bearing the Carte Bleue/Visa or Mastercard logo, the Eurocard symbol and from American Express machines. Some main post offices have change facilities.

Currency regulations There is no restriction on the amount of sterling you can take out of the United Kingdom. At present, you can take up to 50,000 francs out of France without declaring it. Visitors from outside the EU can claim back VAT (about 14 per cent) (TVA) on certain articles worth more than 1200 francs (enquire at the shop) but need to acquire a *Bordereau de vente* form which has to be stamped by Customs on the way out of France.

Medical services
Hospitals with English-speaking staff:
American Hospital in Neuilly, 63 Blvd Victor-Hugo, 92202-Neuilly ☎ 01 46 41 25 25.
British and American Pharmacy, 1 Rue Auber, open until 20.00 weekdays, until 20.00 Sat.
Franco-British Hospital, 3 Rue Barbès, 92300-Levallois-Perret, north-west of the Porte de Champerret ☎ 01 46 39 22 22 (🚇 Anatole France).

Personal security
As in any large city, do not leave objects of any value inside parked cars and beware of bag-snatchers and pickpockets in various guises, who are particularly common in the most touristy areas. Note that any parcels or luggage left about and apparently abandoned may be destroyed by the authorities. Most hotels have a safe-deposit system; sometimes there is a charge for this service, but it is worth the peace of mind.

You should carry official identification with you at all times (i.e. a passport or identity card). It hardly needs to be added that it is wise to leave a note of your passport details in a safe place. Identification is also necessary for changing travellers' cheques.

Post offices
Post Offices, indicated by the sign PTT, are open from 08.00 to 19.00 on weekdays, and until 12.00 on Saturdays. The main post office in Paris is at the Hôtel des Postes, 52 Rue du Louvre, 75001, which operates a 24-hour 7-day service.

The post office at 71 Av. des Champs-Elysées, 75008, is open from 08.00 until 22.00 Mon–Sat, and 10.00–12.00, 14.00–20.00 Sun.

Postage-stamps (*timbres*) are on sale at all post offices and tobacconists (*tabacs*). Letter-boxes are painted yellow.

Public holidays ~ jours feriés

1 January (*Jour de l'An*)	Easter Monday
Whit Monday (*Pentecôte*)	Ascension Day
1 May (Lily-of-the-Valley sold in streets)	Labour Day (*Fête de Travail*)
8 May (end of WWII in Europe)	14 July, Bastille Day (*Fête Nationale*)
15 August (*Assomption*)	1 November, All Saints' Day (*Toussaint*)
11 November (Armistice Day)	25 December, Christmas (*Noël*)

Sightseeing

By coach The following companies run tours with commentaries:

L'Open Tour, 2-day hop-on-hop-off ticket, every 25 mins, 09.45–19.00, over three sightseeing routes, ☎ 01 43 46 52 06.

Paris Vision, 214 Rue de Rivoli, ☎ 01 42 60 30 01.

Cityrama, 4 Pl. des Pyramides, ☎ 01 44 55 61 00.

Parisbus—les Cars Rouges, from the Eiffel Tower, tickets valid for two days, ☎ 01 42 30 55 50.

Touringscope, 11bis Blvd Haussman, ☎ 01 53 34 11 91; Paris Bus service (minibus exclusively), 22 Rue de la Prévoyance, 94300 Vincennes, ☎ 01 43 65 55 55.

By bike There are also tours of Paris by bike (*vélo*):

Escapade Nature, ☎ 01 53 17 03 18.

Paris à Vélo c'est Sympa, ☎ 01 48 87 60 01.

Paris Vélo Rent a Bike, ☎ 01 43 37 59 22.

Roue Libre (RATP), ☎ 01 53 46 43 77.

A map, *Paris Vélo*, giving cycle routes covering 130km through Paris and other information, is published by the Mairie de Paris.

By boat *Batobus* is a river shuttle service (no commentary), from the end of April to September, between the main sights stopping at the Eiffel Tower, Musée d'Orsay, Musée du Louvre, St-Germain-des-Près, Notre-Dame and Hôtel-de-Ville, ☎ 01 44 11 33 44.

Cruises with commentary, both during the day and after dark, April–September, are run by:

Les Bateaux-Mouches from Pont de l'Alma, ☎ 01 42 25 96 10.

Bateaux Parisiens, Quai Montebello (Notre-Dame) ☎ 01 43 26 92 55, or Eiffel Tower, (☎ 01 44 11 33 44.

Secrets of the Seine, lunchtime cruise on the *Crystal II* from the Eiffel Tower, with commentary, ☎ 01 44 11 33 55, www.bateauxparisiens.com.

Vedettes de Paris Ile-de-France, Port de Suffren (Bir Hakeim) ☎ 01 47 05 71 29.

Vedettes du Pont-Neuf, Sq. du Vert-Galant, Ile de la Cité, ☎ 01 46 33 98 38.

Canal trips are a less well-known means of discovering Paris, on the Canal St-Martin between the Arsenal Dock (Bastille) and Parc de la Villette:

Canauxrama (all year), Port de l'Arsenal, La Bastille, ☎ 01 42 39 15 00.

Paris Canal, between Musée d'Orsay and La Villette, ☎ 01 42 40 96 97.

Ourcq Loisirs, boat hire, 9 Quai de la Loire, ☎ 01 42 40 82 10.

Telephones

There are public call-boxes in most post offices, Métro stations, cafés, restaurants and at some bus stops (taxiphones). The majority of booths take only *Télécartes* (50 or 120 units), which you can buy at post offices, France Telecom agencies, tobacconists and railway stations. Reversed-charge calls (PVC) are accepted. Note that the charge for calls made from hotels may be as much as 40 per cent higher than for those made from public telephone boxes.

When calling abroad, dial 00 (international) followed by the country code. All French phone numbers are 9 digits, prefixed by 0 when calling inside France. Paris is prefixed by 01. Phone calls are less expensive in the evenings and at weekends.

UK 00 44   USA 00 1   Canada 00 1
Republic of Ireland 00 353   Australia 00 61

Telephone rates within France: at present the full tariff applies from 08.00–18.00 on week days, and until 14.00 on Saturday. Cheap rates apply between 19.00 and 08.00 and start at 14.00 on Saturdays.

Directories

For directory information in France, ☎ 12.
For international information ☎ 00 33 12 plus country code.
For the operator ☎ 13.
Telecom services (complaints etc.) ☎ 14.
Minitel, an information service linked to the phone, is available in most post offices: for telephone directory information, ☎ 36 11 (in English, ☎ 36 14) or consult *Le Bottin* in post offices, hotels, restaurants, shops, etc., or minitel in postoffices, or www.pagesblanches.fr.

Tourist information in Paris

The **Office de Tourisme et des Congrès de Paris**, has its Head Office at 127 Av. des Champs-Elysées, 75008, ☎ 01 49 52 53 54, 📠 01 49 52 53 00, www.paris-touristoffice.com It is open daily from 09.00–20.00 (Nov–March, Sun and public holidays, 11.00–18.00, closed 01/05). There are English-speaking staff who will answer queries concerning Paris and the environs, make hotel reservations for the same day, reservations for exhibitions, shows and concerts, tickets for sightseeing coaches or boats, brochures, currency exchange, etc. It sells for a small sum various useful booklets on museums and monuments, hotels, restaurants and annual events. You can also purchase a Paris Museum Pass here (see Museums, p 54).

Subsidiary branches of the tourist office are as follows:
Gare de Lyon, open Mon–Sat 08.00–20.00.
Mairie de Paris, 29 Rue de Rivoli, 70004, 09.00–18.00 Mon–Sat, closed public holidays.
Orly Airport, open 06.00–23.30, ☎ 49 75 00 90/01 49 75 01 39.
Regional Tourist Bureau for the Ile-de-France as a whole, Galerie du Carrousel du Louvre, 99 Rue de Rivoli, 754001.
Roissy Airport, open summer 06.30–23.00, winter 07.00–22.00, ☎ 01 48 62 27 29.
Syndicat d'Initiative de Montmartre, 21 Pl. du Tertre, 75018, ☎ 01 42 62 21 21.
Tour Eiffel, every day May–Sep 11.00–18.00.
Most towns in the environs of Paris have a Tourist Information Office.

Working hours

In France, small shops (e.g. *tabacs, boulangeries*) open earlier than in the UK (although most offices do not). Parisian cafés are open for a quick espresso on the way to work, and lunch is often at 12 noon (although less so in Paris than in the French provinces), whereas dinner is eaten late. Most food shops are open on Sunday mornings, and remain open until 18.00 or 19.00 on weekday evenings; but they are likely to be shut on Mondays.

Language

Increasingly many Parisians speak English and are often only too pleased to get some practice, but an effort to speak French is usually appreciated.

Hello/good day *bonjour*
Goodbye *au revoir*
See you later *à plus tard/à tout à l'heure*
Good morning/afternoon *Bonjour*
Good evening *Bon soir*
Good night (on retiring) *Bonne nuit*

Yes/no *oui/non*
OK/all right *OK/d'accord/ça va*

please *s'il vous plâit/s'il te plâit*
thank you (very much) *merci (beaucoup)*

today *aujourd'hui*
tomorrow *demain*
yesterday *hier*
now *maintenant*
later *plus tard*
in the morning *dans la matinée*
in the afternoon/evening *dans l'après midi/au soir*
at night *dans la nuit*

cold/hot *froid/chaud*
with/without *avec/sans*
open/closed *ouvert/fermé*
cheap/expensive *bon marché/cher*
left/right/straight on *à gauche/à droite/tout droit*
railway station *la gare*

bus station *la gare d'autobus/la gare routière*
airport *un aéroport*
ticket *le billet*
police station *le commissariat de police/la gendarmerie*
hospital *un hôpital*
doctor *le medecin*
dentist *le dentiste*
aspirin *une aspirine*

What is your name? *Quel est votre nom/quel est ton nom. Comment vous appellez-vous?/Comment t'appelles-tu?*
My name is ... *Mon nom est .../Je m'appelle...*

I would like ... *Je voudrais.../J'aimerais...*
Do you have ... *Avez vous..?/Est-ce que vous avez..?*

Do you speak English? *Parlez-vous anglais?/Parles-tu anglais?*
I don't understand *Je ne comprends pas*

Where are the toilets? *Où se trouvent les toilettes?*
Where is...? *Où est..?/Où se trouve...?*
What time is it? *Quelle heure est-il?*
At what time? *à quelle heure?*

How much is it? *ça coûte combien?/c'est combien?*	1 un
the bill *l'addition/la note*	2 deux
	3 trois
	4 quatre
Monday *lundi*	5 cinq
Tuesday *mardi*	6 seize
Wednesday *mercredi*	7 sept
Thursday *jeudi*	8 huit
Friday *vendredi*	9 neuf
Saturday *samedi*	10 dix
Sunday *dimanche*	11 onze
January *janvier*	12 douze
February *février*	13 treize
March *mars*	14 quatorze
April *avril*	15 quinze
May *mai*	16 seize
June *juin*	17 dix-sept
July *juillet*	18 dix-huit
August *août*	19 dix-neuf
September *septembre*	20 vingt
October *octobre*	30 trente
November *novembre*	40 quarante
December *décembre*	50 cinquante
	60 soixante
spring *le printemps*	70 soixante-dix
summer *l'été*	80 quatre-vingt
autumn *l'automne*	90 quatre-vingt-dix
winter *l'hiver*	100 cent

Where to stay

There is a vast choice of hotels and other accommodation in Paris. Nowhere within Paris is far from the centre by Métro and it can be agreeable to stay in districts that are less touristy and more residential. Listed below are hotels in Paris and in the areas around Paris that are covered by this guide.

Apart from direct booking, accommodation can be reserved through central reservation numbers (see below), through travel agencies or, in Paris, at the **Paris Tourist Office** (personal callers only) (see p 28), who will make advance bookings with a written confirmation and deposit, and on-the-spot reservations for the same night. These are automatically cancelled if not taken up within one and a half hours. They also sell a *Guide des Hôtels et Résidences de Tourisme* for Paris and region or you can look at their web site www.paris-touristoffice.com

It is wise to book rooms in advance, particularly during the high seasons, which are during the fashion salons in January and the start of July, the most popular tourist seasons of Easter, September and October and during the course of exhibitions and other trade fairs. Low season is mid-December, the rest of

January, the second half of July and August. In between these periods the season is described as 'normal' with patches of peak demand.

Useful publications are the Red Michelin guide to *Paris and environs: Hotels and Restaurants*, and Michelin, Kléber, and Gault-Millau guides, or the *Guide des Relais Routiers*. Local Tourist Information Offices provide lists of hotels in their area.

Hotels

All hotels are officially classified and are graded by stars awarded by the French Tourist Board, depending on their amenities and the type of hotel.

L☆☆☆☆	very high class, de luxe (1500–20,000F) (many in the 1er, 8e and 16e arrondissement)
☆☆☆☆	high class, comfortable (950–6000F)
☆☆☆	very comfortable (500–1050F)
☆☆	comfortable (250–750F)
☆	and without star (HT) simple with basic comforts (180–350F)

The classifications quoted above are approximate. Prices vary according to the position of the hotel, its grading and amenities, and also to the time of year. Prices given are the range for a twin/double in 2000 and the prices for singles, 4-bed rooms and suites will vary from these.

Only a proportion of hotels in the one and two-star categories have rooms with private bath and WC en suite, although many provide shower and bidet. Similarly, many hotels have no restaurant, although almost all provide a continental breakfast.

Prices include tax and service charges and must be displayed outside the hotel, at the reception and in the rooms. Breakfast is usually extra. Since 1994 a *Taxe de Séjour* (visitor's tax), has been levied on persons not liable for resident tax, which applies to all forms of paying accommodation from luxury hotels to camp sites, with rates varying from 1 to 7 francs per day per person.

Résidences de tourisme These are furnished apartments in collective units or separate housing, available for the day, week or month, but not as a permanent residence. They are a good alternative for visitors who want to cater for themselves. In some cases, the deal improves relative to the length of the stay. Prices must include tax and be displayed outside the building.

Booking Each reservation should be confirmed in writing, as should any cancellations. The hotel will normally ask for a deposit for each reservation. At certain times a total payment in advance may be required. In the event of a cancellation, the deposit will normally be kept. Hotels are not obliged to accept credit cards, but they usually do. It is the duty of the hotel management to issue an invoice for each payment. Do not leave valuables in the room, but place them in the hotel safe (if there is not a room safe).

The list of hotels below is organised by arrondissement (the postal districts in Paris) and by rating. It is not definitive, but is offered as a guideline to finding a place to stay in Paris. Large hotels outside the centre tend to be used by groups and those attending trade fairs.

Hotels in Paris

75001 ~ the Louvre

The western half of the Cité—the Louvre; Pl. Vendôme; Palais-Royal and St-Eustache:

Luxury 4-star

Hotels such as the *Castille*, 33 Rue Cabon, ☎ 01 44 58 44 58, fax 01 44 58 44 00; the recently revamped *Inter Continental Paris*, 3 Rue de Castiglione, ☎ 01 44 77 11 11, ▤ 01 44 77 14 60; *Le Meurice*, 228 Rue de Rivoli, ☎ 01 44 58 10 10 ▤ 01 44 58 10 15; and the *Ritz*, 15 Pl. Vendôme, ☎ 01 43 16 30 30, ▤ 01 43 16 36 68, are priced anywhere between 2160–4300F for a double.

4-star

Clarion Saint-James & Albany, 202 Rue de Rivoli, ☎ 01 44 58 43 21, ▤ 01 44 58 43 11. An elegant building with a garden and courtyards, and more affordable prices than others in the category and area. 1100–1800F.

Costes, 239 Rue Saint-Honoré, ☎ 01 42 44 50 00, ▤ 01 42 44 50 01. One of the 'in' places to stay; entirely renovated, elegant and opulent, with courtyard and spa. 2250–3500F.

3-star

Brighton, 218 Rue de Rivoli, ☎ 01 47 03 61 61, ▤ 01 52 60 41 78. Very competitive prices in an old established hotel opposite the Tuileries and a couple of steps away from the Louvre. 580–950F.

Comfort Hotel Louvre Montana, 12 Rue Saint-Roch, ☎ 01 42 60 35 10, ▤ 01 42 61 12 28. Well placed comfortable small hotel. 580–1090F

Le Loiret, 5 Rue des Bons Enfants, ☎ 01 42 61 47 31, ▤ 01 42 61 36 85. Well priced, well placed and practical. 530–590F.

Relais du Louvre, 19 Rue des Prêtres St-Germain-l'Auxerrois, ☎ 01 40 41 96 42, ▤ 01 40 41 96 44. Great position opposite the Tuileries, beautifully renovated. 862–992F.

Novotel Paris Les Halles, 8 Pl. Marguerite-de-Navarre, ☎ 01 42 21 31 31, ▤ 01 40 26 05 79. For lively modernism, this is the place. 980–1220F.

De la Place du Louvre, 21 Rue des Prêtres St-Germain-l'Auxerrois, ☎ 01 42 33 78 68, ▤ 01 42 33 09 95. Plenty of atmosphere, plenty of art work and comfortable for the price. 720–855F.

75002 ~ Bourse

Luxury 4-star

Westminster, 13 Rue de la Paix, ☎ 01 42 61 57 46, 01 42 60 30 66, another old-established hotel which has been beautifully restored, with top-class restaurant. 1650–2600F.

Edouard VII, 39 Av. de l'Opéra, ☎ 01 42 61 56 90, ▤ 01 42 61 47 73. Luxury and style with Art Deco reception. 950–1500 F.

3-star

Ascot-Opéra, 2 Rue Monsigny, ☎ 01 42 96 87 66, ▤ 01 49 27 06 06. A good central location near Opera Garnier and the *grands magasins*, in the mansion where Offenbach once resided. 690–930F.

Hotel Malte Opéra, 63 Rue de Richelieu, ☎ 01 44 58 94 94, ▤ 01 42 86 88 19. Conveniently situated, comfortable hotel with air conditioning and patio. 790–1290F.

2-star
Grand Hotel de Besançon, 56 Rue Montorgueil, ☎ 01 42 36 41 08, 📠 01 45 08 08 79. Reasonably priced, situated just north of Les Halles. 650–750F.

75003 ~ Temple
The northern part of the Marais:
3-star
Pavillon de la Reine, 28 Pl. des Vosges, ☎ 01 40 29 19 19, 📠 01 40 29 19 20, www.pavilion-de-la-reine.com. Well-known hotel with pretty courtyard in a 17C house on the charming Place des Vosges in the Marais. 1850–2300F.

75004 ~ Hôtel de Ville: the eastern half of the Cité, the Ile St-Louis, and the southern part of the Marais
4-star
Jeu de Paume, 54 Rue St-Louis-en-l'Ile, ☎ 01 43 26 14 18, 📠 01 40 46 02 76, www.HotelJeudePaume.com. Classily converted 17C real tennis court with 30 light and calm rooms. 905–1550F.

3-star
Bastille Speria, 1 Rue de la Bastille, ☎ 01 42 72 04 01, 📠 01 42 72 56 38, globe-market.com/h75004-speria.htm. Practical and well situated in this increasingly popular area. 580–670F.
Bretonnerie, 22 Rue Ste-Croix-de-la-Bretonnerie, ☎ 01 48 87 77 63, 📠 01 42 77 26 78. Delightful, intimate hotel with a friendly atmosphere tucked away in the Marais. 640–790F.
Caron de Beaumarchais, 12 Rue Vielle du Temple, ☎ 01 42 72 34 12, 📠 01 42 72 34 63. Wonderful small hotel deep in the Marais, with 18C décor and all modern comforts. 730–810F.
St-Merry, 78 Rue de la Verrerie, ☎ 01 42 78 14 15, 📠 01 40 29 06 82. Close to Les Halles and the Pompidou Centre, 17C former presbytery has 11 rooms furnished with period furniture. 400–1800F.
Deux Iles, 59 Rue St-Louis en l'Ile, ☎ 01 43 26 13 35, 📠 01 43 29 60 25 and *Lutèce*, 65 Rue St-Louis-en-l'Ile, ☎ 43 26 23 52, 📠 01 43 29 60 25. Adjacent small and classy hotels with picturesque features; under the same management. 870F.
Saint-Louis, 75 Rue St-Louise-en-l'Ile, ☎ 01 46 34 04 80, 📠 01 46 45 33 95. A small gem on the island, tastefully maintained and with every comfort. 795–895F.

2-star
Grand Hotel Jeanne d'Arc, 3 Rue Jarente, ☎ 01 48 87 62 11, 📠 01 48 87 37 31. An old house tucked away in the Marais. 400–490F.
Grand Hotel Malher, 5 Rue Malher, ☎ 01 42 72 60 92, 📠 01 42 72 25 37. Small independent hotel between Rue de Rivoli and Rue des Rosiers in the Marais, with attractive accommodation. 580–730F.
St-Louis Marais, 1 Rue Charles V, ☎ 01 48 87 87 04, 📠 01 48 87 33 26. Fine old building of the Marais. 650–750F.

75005 ~ the 'Latin Quarter'
3-star
Elysa Luxembourg, 6 Rue Gay Lussac, ☎ 01 43 25 31 74, 📠 01 46 34 56 27. Very pleasant hotel well situated near to the Jardins de Luxembourg. 560–760F.

Notre Dame (de), 19 Rue Maître-Albert, ☎ 01 43 26 79 00, ▯ 01 46 33 50 11. Charming and well-kept little hotel in a corner of the Latin Quarter. 702–762F.
Parc Saint-Severin, 22 Rue de la Parcheminerie, ☎ 01 43 54 32 17, ▯ 01 43 54 70 71. 26 rooms impeccably kept and attractively furnished, some with a view of the adjacent church. 600–1000F.
Select Hotel, 1 Pl. de la Sorbonne, ☎ 01 46 34 14 80, ▯ 01 46 34 51 79. On the doorstep of the Eglise de la Sorbonne, with plant-filled atrium. 670–805F.

2-star

Grands Hommes, 17 Pl. du Panthéon, ☎ 01 46 34 19 60, ▯ 01 43 26 67 32. Situated next to the mausoleum of the great men (and women) of France with largish rooms. 780–800F.
Jardins de Luxembourg, 5 Impasse Royer Collard, ☎ 01 40 46 08 88, ▯ 01 40 46 02 28. Pretty place to stay which was frequented by Sigmund Freud in the 19C. 740–840F.
des Carmes, 5 Rue des Carmes, ☎ 01 43 29 78 40, ▯ 01 43 29 57 17. Refreshed and modernised after complete refurbishment, an inexpensive base in the Quartier Latin. 510–610F.
TimHotel Jardin des Plantes, 5 Rue Linné, ☎ 01 47 07 06 20, ▯ 01 47 07 62 74. With roof terrrace and sauna, a practical small hotel. 680–750F.

1-star

Esmeralda, 4 Rue St-Julien-le-Pauvre, 75005, ☎ 01 43 54 19 20, ▯ 01 40 51 00 68. A very small hotel on the Left Bank and near the Seine, which has one or two rooms with great views. 420–450F.

75006 ~ Luxembourg
4-star

d'Aubusson, 33 Rue Dauphine, ☎ 01 43 29 43 43, ▯ 01 43 29 12 62. Old building, new hotel with featuring exposed beams and antiques. 1300–2000F.
Lutétia, 45 Blvd Raspail, ☎ 01 49 54 46 46, ▯ 01 49 54 46 00. A large early 1930s establishment that is comfortable and dependable. 990–1990F (suites up to 12,000 F).
Relais Christine, 3 Rue Christine, ☎ 01 40 51 60, ▯ 01 40 51 60 81, ✉ relaisch@club-internet.fr. Perfect combination of old and new at the heart of the Left Bank yet calm; vaulted breakfast room. 1800–2250F.
Relais Saint-Germain, 9 Carrefour de l'Odéon, ☎ 01 43 29 12 05, ▯ 01 46 33 45 30. Charming small hotel where everything is thoughtfully arranged for total comfort and luxury. 1290–1800F.
Saint-Grégoire, 43 Rue de l'Abbé-Grégoire, ☎ 01 45 48 23 23, ▯ 01 45 48 33 95. Attractive rooms and small garden; reasonable prices for the category of hotel. 790–990F.
Victoria Palace, 6 Rue Blaise Desgoffe, ☎ 01 45 49 70 00, ▯ 01 45 49 23 75, www.ila-chateau.com/victoria. Wallow in the plush Louix XVI décor with soft upholstery in warm colours and every comfort. 1700–2000F.

3 star

L'Abbaye, 10 Rue Cassette, ☎ 01 45 44 38 11, ▯ 01 45 48 07 86, www.hotel-abbaye4in.com. In an 18C building described as between courtyard and garden, and quiet. 960–1580F.
Angleterre St-Germain-des-Prés, 44 Rue Jacob, ☎ 01 42 60 34 72, ▯ 01 42 60

16 93. Long-time favourite, former British Embassy and residence of Hemingway, with olde-worlde rooms and lots of flowers. 712–1212F.

Buci Latin, 34 Rue de Buci, ☎ 01 43 29 07 20, 🖷 01 43 29 67 44, www.bucilatin.com. Charming hotel of character in the heart of the Latin quarter next to the famous market. 970–1250F.

L'Hotel, 13 Rue des Beaux-Art, ☎ 01 44 41 99 00, 🖷 01 43 25 64 81. Oscar Wilde once stayed here; eclectic décor, loads of charm, and well appointed. 800–2800F.

De l'Odéon, 13 Rue St-Sulpice, ☎ 01 43 25 70 11, 🖷 01 43 29 97 34, www.hotelodeon.com. Small hotel in picturesque 16C building with grandiose beds. 820–1412F.

Madison, 143 Blvd St-Germain, ☎ 01 40 51 60 00, 🖷 01 40 51 60 01. Hotel of great charm prettily decorated, with classical revival lounge. 910–1460F.

Libertel Prince de Conti, 8 Rue Guenegaud, ☎ 01 44 07 30 40, 🖷 01 44 07 36 334. Elegant yet intimate hotel in an 18C building with a patio. 920–1250F.

Relais Medicis, 23 Rue Racine, ☎ 01 43 26 00 60, 🖷 01 40 46 83 39. The 16 light and quiet rooms are decorated in primary colours; patio with fountain. 1100–1595F.

Saints-Pères, 65 Rue des Saints-Pères, ☎ 01 45 44 50 00, 🖷 01 45 48 67 52. Surprisingly quiet for this busy area, with rooms on the garden front. 750–1050F.

La Villa Saint-Germain, 29 Rue Jacob, ☎ 01 43 26 60 00, 🖷 01 46 34 63 63. Modern and zany for the smart set. 800–1800F.

Louis II St-Germain, 2 Rue St-Sulpice, ☎ 01 46 33 13 80, 🖷 01 46 33 17 29. 22 rooms in an 18C building at the heart of St-Germain, with pretty bedrooms and exposed beams. 555–820F.

2-star

Atlantis Germain-des-Près, 4 Rue du Vieux Colombier, ☎ 01 45 48 31 81, 🖷 01 45 48 35 16, www.paris.com. Simple hotel in convenient location. 585–690F.

Michelet-Odéon, 6 Place de l'Odéon, ☎ 01 46 34 27 80, 🖷 01 46 34 55 35. Good basic hotel in the centre of St-Germain. 500–850F.

Recamier, 3 bis Pl. St-Sulpice, ☎ 01 43 26 04 89, 🖷 01 46 33 27 73. Next to St-Sulpice church in a pleasant square, modest hotel with budget prices. 460–640F.

Hotel de Saint-Germain, 50 Rue du Four, ☎ 01 45 48 91 64, 🖷 01 45 48 46 22. Small hotel with tiny rooms but good value. 520–695F.

1-star

Saint-André-des-Arts, 66 Rue St-André-des-Arts, ☎ 01 43 26 96 16, 🖷 01 43 29 73 34. Rooms with bath or shower, budget prices. 480F.

75007 ~ Palais-Bourbon

Faubourg St-Germain; the Musée d'Orsay; Eiffel Tower:

4-star

Montalembert, 3 Rue de Montalembert, ☎ 01 45 49 68 68, 🖷 01 45 49 69 49, www.montalembert.com. Comfort and luxury is the name of this 1920s hotel. 1750–2300 F

Le Tourville, 16 Av. de Tourville, ☎ 01 47 05 62 62, 🖷 01 47 05 43 90, www.hoteltourville.com Modernised accommodation with carefully chosen lighting and colours. 650–1100F.

3-star

Bourgogne et Montana, 3 Rue de Bourgogne, ☎ 01 45 51 20 22, 🖷 01 45 56 11 98. Elegant themed suites, simple rooms. 900–1500F.

Duc de Saint-Simon, 14 Rue de St-Simon, ☎ 01 44 39 20 20, 🖷 01 45 48 68 25. Charming hotel with romantic bedrooms, garden and vaulted bar. 1075–1475F.

Lenox, 9 Rue de l'Université, ☎ 01 42 96 10 95, 🖷 01 42 61 52 83. Small and elegant in a great area. 650–1100F.

2-star

Quai Voltaire, 19 Quai Voltaire, ☎ 01 42 61 50 91, 🖷 01 42 61 62 26. Views of the Seine and handy for the Orsay and Louvre. Favoured in the 19C by artists and writers. Might be noisy. 550–920 F.

75008 ~ Elysée

Place de la Concorde, the Madeleine, the Champs-Elysées and Faubourg St-Honoré:

Luxury 4 star

Le Bristol, 112 Rue du Faubourg-St-Honoré, ☎ 01 53 43 43 00, 🖷 01 53 43 43 01, exceedingly comfortable and lavish and large, 2500–4600F.

Hôtel de Crillon, 10 Pl. de la Concorde, ☎ 01 44 71 15 00, 🖷 01 44 71 15 02, 2550–4100 F.

George V, 31 Av. George-V, ☎ 01 53 53 28 00/0800 526 648, its Art Deco glory totally restored following a mega-overhaul costing 300 million francs, 3300F upwards.

Plaza Athénée, 25 Av. Montaigne, ☎ 01 53 67 66 65, 🖷 01 53 67 66 66, 2600–4000F.

Prince de Galles, 33 Av. George V, ☎ 01 53 23 77 77, 🖷 01 47 20 61 05, boasts an open patio on the roof, 1910–3485F.

4-star

Balzac, 6 Rue Balzac, ☎ 01 44 35 18 00, 🖷 01 42 25 24 82. Discreet, luxurious and appreciated by those in the know, with new bar and excellent restaurant. Prices 1700–2200F

Beau Manoir Best Western, 6 Rue de l'Arcade, ☎ 01 42 66 03 07, 🖷 01 42 68 03 00. 17C-style bedrooms and plenty of charm, near the Madeleine. 1200–1155F.

California Paris Champs-Elysées, 16 Rue de Berri, ☎ 01 43 59 93 00, 🖷 01 45 61 03 62, www.hroy.com/california. Endowed with art works a pretty patio. 1950–2500F

Château Frontenac, 54 Rue Pierre-Charron, ☎ 01 53 23 13 13, 🖷 01 53 23 13 01. Very comfortable, good service, and excellent position; prices reasonable. 980–1800 F.

Claridge Bellman, 37 Rue François-Ier, ☎ 01 47 23 54 42, 🖷 01 47 23 08 84. Select, modern luxurious hotel with 40 rooms. 800–1500F.

Résidence Maxim's de Paris, 42 Av. Gabriel, ☎ 01 45 61 96 33, 🖷 01 42 89 06 07. Hotel designed by Pierre Cardin resembles a superbly furnished and appointed private castle. 2000–2250F.

Royal Monceau, 37 Av. Hoche, ☎ 01 42 99 88 00, 🖷 01 42 99 89 90, the sort of hotel that the rich and famous return to, magnificently appointed and every need catered for. 2200–3500F.

3-star

Arcade, 9 Rue de l'Arcade, ☎ 01 53 30 60 00, ▤ 01 40 07 03 07. Centrally placed near the *grands magasins*, yet roomy, attractive and quiet. 790–980F.

Lavoisier (Le), 21 Rue Lavoisier, ☎ 01 53 30 06 06, ▤ 01 53 30 23 00. A pleasant and refined hotel following a complete refurbishment. 790–1190F.

Résidence Monceau, 85 Rue du Rocher, ☎ 01 45 22 75 11, ▤ 01 45 22 30 88. Not glamorous, but good basic hotel. 700F.

2-star

d'Albion, 15 Rue de Penthièvre, ☎ 01 42 65 84 15, ▤ 01 49 24 03 47. A modest hotel with 26 rooms, most with bath. 430–480F.

75009 ~ Opéra
As far as Blvd de Clichy and Pl. Pigalle
Luxury 4-star

Scribe, 1 Rue Scribe, ☎ 01 44 71 24 24, ▤ 01 42 65 39 97. This is one of the great old establishments, on the doorstep of the opera, and richly decorated and furnished. 2275–2700F.

3-star

Bergère Opéra Best Western, 34 Rue Bergère, ☎ 01 47 70 34 34, ▤ 01 47 70 36 36. Delightful hotel, near the shops and the opera, but quiet. 690–1090F.

Châteaudun, 30 Rue de Châteaudun, ☎ 01 49 70 09 99, ▤ 01 49 70 06 99. Quiet, convenient, and reasonably priced. 760F.

Leman, 20 Rue de Trévise, ☎ 01 42 46 50 66, ▤ 01 48 24 27 59. Attractively redecorated in tasteful modern style, with vaulted breakfast room. 390–730F.

Opéra Cadet, 24 Rue Cadet, ☎ 01 48 24 05 26, ▤ 01 42 46 68 09. Practical and well situated modern hotel. Garage. 1040F.

Du Pré, 10 Rue Pierre Semard, ☎ 01 42 81 37 11, ▤ 01 40 23 98 28. No frills, but good value accommodation and handy for Gare du Nord. 545–580F.

Tour d'Auvergne, 10 Rue de la Tour d'Auvergne, ☎ 01 48 78 61 60, ▤ 01 49 95 99 00. Not exactly tasteful, but adequate accommodation. 562–712F.

2-star

Arts (Des), 7 Cité Bergère, ☎ 01 42 46 73 30, ▤ 01 48 00 94 42. Inexpensive, friendly, family run hotel—excellent value. 360–400F.

Chopin, 49 Passage Jouffroy (10 Blvd Montmartre), ☎ 01 47 70 58 10, ▤ 01 42 47 00 70. This freshly redecorated 19C hotel is quite a bargain. 450–490F.

75010 ~ Gare du Nord and Gare de l'Est
3-star

Grand Hotel du Danemark, 27 Rue des Récollets, ☎ 01 46 07 03 74, ▤ 01 46 07 14 00. Close to Gare du Nord and the Canal St-Martin, this is a practical and well kept hotel with competitive prices. 440–500F.

2-star

Apollo, 11 Rue de Dunkerque, ☎ 01 48 78 04 98, ▤ 01 42 85 08 78. A good bargain hotel closed to the Gare du Nord. 445–500F.

Hôtel Français, 13 Rue du 8-Mai-1945, ☎ 01 40 35 94 14, ▤ 01 40 35 55 40. Pleasant and comfortable budget hotel. 385–470F.

75011 ~ northeast of the Pl. de la Bastille to Pl. de la Nation
2-star

Beaumarchais, 3 Rue Oberkampf, ☎ 01 53 36 86 86, ▤ 01 43 38 32 86. Recently revamped, this is quite a bright and zany place. 450–500F.

Hotel de Nevers, 53 Rue de Malte, ☎ 01 47 00 56 18, ▤ 01 43 57 77 39. Basic clean facilities. 180–275F.

75012 ~ southeast of the Pl. de Bastille
Including the Gare de Lyon and Bercy:

3-star

Belle Epoque, 66 Rue de Charenton, ☎ 01 43 44 06 66, ▤ 01 43 44 10 25. Old and modern combined. 850–1040F.

Pavillon Bastille, 65 Rue de Lyon, ☎ 01 43 43 65 65, ▤ 01 43 43 96 52. www.france.paris.com. Bastille is a trendy and lively *quartier* and this pleasant hotel is a stone's throw from the opera Bastille. 550–955F.

Claret, 44 Blvd de Bercy, ☎ 01 46 28 41 31, ▤ 01 49 28 09 29. An ancient establishment with standard accommodation. 600–650F.

Le Zephyr, 31bis Blvd Diderot, ☎ 01 43 46 12 72, ▤ 01 43 41 68 01, www.teaser.fr/paris hotel. Comfortable, modern and reliable. 550–690F.

2-star

Nouvel Hôtel, 24 Av. du Bel Air, ☎ 01 43 43 01 81, ▤ 01 43 44 64 13. Tidy and friendly with attractive prices. 400–570F.

75013 ~ Gobelins
South of the Gare d'Austerlitz, including the Gobelins and Pl. de l'Italie:

3-star

Grand Hôtel des Gobelins, 57 Blvd St-Marcel, ☎ 01 43 31 79 89. Near the Jardin des Plantes, excellent value for money. 520–670F.

Vert Galant, 41 Rue Croulebarbe, ☎ 01 44 08 83 50, ▤ 01 44 08 83 69. 15 attractive rooms near the Gobelins (tapestry) Manufacture. 400–500F.

2-star

Résidence les Gobelins, 9 Rue des Gobelins, ☎ 01 47 07 26 90, ▤ 43 31 44 05. Young and colourful. 425–465F.

75014 ~ Observatoire
3-star

Delambre, 35 Rue Delambre, ☎ 01 43 20 66 31, ▤ 01 45 38 91 76. Famous for the fact that the Surrealist group leader, André Breton, once lived here. Pleasantly presented. 460–550F.

l'Orchidée, 65 Rue de l'Ouest, ☎ 43 22 70 50, ▤ 01 42 79 97 46. Built around a courtyard, this is a well-kept residence. 456–850F.

Le Parnasse, 79 Av. du Maine, ☎ 01 43 20 13 93, ▤ 01 43 20 95 60. Attractive and inexpensive. 545–580F.

2-star

Istria, 29 Rue Campagne-Première, ☎ 01 43 20 91 82, ▤ 01 43 22 48 45. Former famous visitors include Man Ray, Marcel Duchamp and Louis Aragon; simple but comfortable. 580–600F.

75015 ~ Vaugirard
Southwest of the Tour Montparnasse and Av. de Suffren:
3-star
Frantour-Paris-Suffren, 20 Rue Jean-Rey, ☎ 01 45 78 50 00, ▤ 01 45 78 91 42, www.hotelworld.com. Large and reliable, with well-equipped standard rooms. 750–1600F.
Nikko de Paris, 61 Quai de Grenelle, ☎ 01 40 58 20 00, ▤ 01 40 58 24 24. Huge and business-like, with bar, brasserie and restaurants. 1690–1980F.

75016 ~ Passy
Between the Seine and the Bois de Bologne, including the districts of Passy, Chaillot and Auteuil:
Luxury
Le Raphaël, 17 Av. Kléber, ☎ 01 44 28 00 28, ▤ 01 45 01 21 50. Relatively small, top-notch establishment dating from the 1920s favoured by a rich and famous clientele for its refined luxury; rooftop restaurant. Around 2820F.

4-star
Pergolèse, 3 Rue Pergolèse, ☎ 01 40 67 96 77, ▤ 01 45 00 12 11 www.hotel.pergolese.com. Interesting modern décor where the welcome is warm and clients are cosseted. 1100–1800F.
Square, 3 Rue de Boulainvilliers, ☎ 01 44 14 91 90, ▤ 01 40 71 95 07, www.hotelsquare.com. On the opposite side of the Seine from the Eiffel Tower and Parc Citroën, but state-of-the-art design and super cool colour-coded décor. Only 22 rooms. Prices 1400–2100 F.

3 star
Bouquet de Longchamp, 6 Rue du Bouquet Longchamp, ☎ 01 47 04 41 71, ▤ 01 47 27 29 09. Intimate hotel around a courtyard. 532–912F.

2-star
Keppler, 12 Rue Keppler, ☎ 01 47 20 65 05, ▤ 01 47 23 02 29. Not far from the Champs-Elysées, pleasant hotel and good value. 470–480F.

75017 ~ Batignolles Monceau
Northwest of the Etoile:
3-star
de Banville, 166 Blvd Berthier, ☎ 01 42 67 70 16, ▤ 01 44 40 42 77, www.hotelbanville.fr A little outside the tourist area, with only 39 rooms, this 1930s hotel is well appointed and reasonable. 890F.
Eber Monceau, 18 Rue Léon-Jost, ☎ 01 46 22 60 70, ▤ 01 47 63 01 01. Great little hotel with 15 reasonably-priced rooms and 3 suites, Renaissance décor and patio. 610–690F.
Etoile Pereire, 146 Blvd Pereire, ☎ 01 42 67 60 00, ▤ 01 42 67 02 90. Quiet and pretty with garden. 702–802F.
Regent's Garden Best Western, 6 Rue Pierre-Demours, ☎ 01 45 74 07 30, ▤ 01 40 55 01 42, www.france-hotel-guide-com/h75017reggarden.htm. Classic hotel with Second Empire décor and garden. 740–980F.

2-star
Batignolles (Des), 26-28 Rue des Batignolles, ☎ 01 43 87 70 40, ▤ 01 44 70 01 04. Basic amenities and courtyard, near Montmartre. 320–360F.

75018 ~ Butte Montmartre
Northeast of the Pl. de Clichy as far east as Rue d'Aubervilliers:
4-star
Terrass, 12 Rue Joseph-de-Maistre, ☎ 01 46 06 72 85, 📠 01 42 52 29 11. Old-established family-run hotel with wonderful views. 1320–1470F.

2-star
Eden, 90 Rue Ordener, ☎ 01 42 64 61 63, 📠 01 42 64 11 43. Behind the Butte de Montmartre. Adequate and clean. 420F.
Ermitage, 24 Rue Lamarck, ☎ 01 42 64 79 22, 📠 01 42 64 10 33. Delightful *petit hôtel* right next to Sacré-Coeur. 500F.
Prima Lepic, 29 Rue Lepic, ☎ 01 46 06 44 64, 📠 01 46 06 66 11. The aura of Montmartre is condensed in this hotel, although a trifle idiosyncratic. 500F.
Regyn's Montmartre, 18 Pl. des Abbesses, ☎ 01 42 54 45 21, 📠 01 42 23 76 69. Deep in Montmartre, some rooms recently done up. 435–475F.

75019 ~ Buttes-Chaumont, La Villette
4-star
Holiday Inn Paris Pantin La Villette, 216 Av. Jean-Jaurès, ☎ 01 44 84 18 18, 📠 01 44 84 18 20. Convenient for the Cité de Musique and the Cité des Sciences. 1050F.

3-star
Forest Hill Paris La Villette, 28 ter Av. Corentin-Cariou, ☎ 01 44 72 15 30, 📠 01 44 72 15 80.

2-star
Le Laumière, 4 Rue Petit, ☎ 01 42 06 10 77, 📠 01 42 06 72 50. Impeccably kept and bargain prices. 290–380F.

Global booking services
Hotel groups with central reservation facilities (bookings usually taken until 3 pm for the same night.)

Abotel, France: 01 47 27 15 15.
Best Western, UK: 0800 39 31 30; Spain: 900 993 900; USA: 800 528 1234.
Concorde, UK: 0800 181 591; France: 0800 05 00 11; Spain: 900 200 136; USA: 800 888 4747, www.concorde.hotels.com.
Hilton Intl., UK: 0345 581 595; France: 0800 90 75 46; Spain: 900 993 246; USA: 1800 445 8667, www.hilton.com.
Holiday Inn/Crown Plaza, UK: 0800 897 121; France: 0800 905 999; Spain: 900 99 3119; USA: 1800 327 0200.
Ibis, UK: 0208 237 74 74; France: 03 20 60 86 42.
Libertel/Utell, UK: 0990 300 200; France 01 44 74 17 47; USA: 1 800 44.
Mercure, UK: 0208 283 4500; France: 01 60 77 22 33; USA: 800 MERCURE.
Meridien, UK: 0800 402 215, 0800 335 522, 0800 404 404; France: 01 40 55 67 85 www.forte-hotels.com.
Parisotel, France: 01 44 51 19 52.
Sofitel, UK: 0208 283 4500; 0208 283 4560; France: 01 60 87 90 90; USA: 1 800 SOFITEL.
TimHotel, UK: 0990 300 200; France: 01 44 15 81 47.
Westin, UK: 0800 325 95 95 95, Spain: 900 971 910, USA: 1(800)WESTIN-1.

Résidences de Tourisme/Apartments

75002 ~ Bourse
4-star
Metropole Opéra, 2 Rue de Gramont, ☎ 01 42 96 91 03, 🖷 01 42 96 22 46. 9 studios, day 650–790F, week 4550–5530F; and 24 apartments, day 950–2400F, week 6650–9800F.

75008 ~ Elysées
The Pl. de la Concorde, the Madeleine, the Champs-Elysées and Faubourg St-Honoré:
4 star
Beverley Hills, 35 Rue de Berri, ☎ 01 53 77 56 00, 🖷 01 42 56 52 75. Apartments up to 5 rooms. 2 room: day 1500–2500F, week 8400–15400F.
Claridge Champs-Elysées, 74 Av. des Champs-Elysées, ☎ 01 44 13 33 33, 🖷 01 42 25 04 88. 45 studios, and apartments. Studio, day: 1200–1450F, week 8400–10150F; 2-room apartment day: 1435–1960, week: 9044–33852F.
Suites Saint-Honoré, 13 Rue d'Aguesseau, ☎ 01 44 51 16 35, 🖷 01 42 66 35 70. 3 and 4 room apartments, and 4 duplex. 3-room apartment: day, 2700–6400F.

75009 ~ Opéra
Alba Opéra, 34 ter Rue de la Tour-d'Auvergne, ☎ 01 48 78 80 22, 🖷 01 42 85 23 13. Pretty studios and apartments. Studio, day 620–700F, week 2800–3430F; apartment: day 1200–1400F, week 6650–7700F.
Résidence Hôtel des Trois Poussins, 15 Rue Clauzel, ☎ 01 53 32 81 81, 🖷 01 44 21 80 21. Offers rooms as well as studios, and nicely turned out. Studios with kitchens 640–910F per day, 3500–6000F per week.

75011 ~ northeast of the Place de la Bastille
2 star
Résidence Trousseau, 13 Rue Trousseau, ☎ 01 48 05 55 55, 🖷 01 48 05 83 97. Modern and renovated, with a garden. Studios 450–850F per day, 3000–3500F per week; apartments 900–1500 per day.

75013 ~ Gobelins
2 star
Amhotel-Inn City Choisy, 96 Av. de Choisy, ☎ 01 44 23 22 02, 🖷 01 45 82 71 05. Modern residential hotel, with 22 studios. Day 360–410F, week 2380–2520F.

75014 ~ Observatoire
Cité Ripoche, 35 Rue M. Ripoche, ☎ 01 44 12 55 00, 🖷 01 44 12 55 01. 14 studios. Day 350–450F, week 3300–3800F.

75016 ~ districts of Passy, Chaillot, Auteuil
2 star
Espace Greuze, 30 Rue Greuze, ☎ 01 40 56 99 50, 🖷 01 40 56 99 69. Apartments, 2 rooms: week 4655–4893F, 3 rooms: week 5243–6986F.

75017 ~ Batignolles Monceau
Résidence Hotel Malesherbes, 129 Rue Cardinet, ☎ 01 44 15 85 00, 🖷 01 44 15 85 29. 21 studios: day 400–550F, week 2450–3350F.

75019 ~ Butte-Chaumont, La Villette
3 star
Maeva La Villette, 28 bis Av. Corentin-Cariou, ☎ 01 44 72 42 00, 📠 01 44 72 42 42. 27 studios: day 345–620F, week 2370–3900F, and 45 apartments: day 440–770F, week 2950–4850F.

Résidences de Tourisme/Apartments, central booking
Citadines/Orion, France: 01 41 05 79 05, 📠 01 41 05 78 83.
France Appartements, France: 01 56 89 31 00, 📠 01 56 89 31 01.
Home Plazza Bastille, France: 01 40 21 22 230, 📠 01 47 00 82 40.
Libertel/Utell, UK: 0990 300 200; France 01 44 74 17 47; USA: 1 800 44.
Paris Appart. Services, France: 01 40 28 01 28, 📠 01 40 28 92 01.
Paris Lodging, France: 01 43 36 71 69, www.ifrance.com/parislodging.
PSR (Paris Séjour Reservation), France: 01 53 89 10 50; USA: 312 587 77 07; www.PSRyourhomeinParis.com.
Pierre et Vacances, France: 01 45 58 87 00.

Hotels in Ile de France

Paris La Défense ~ 92060, Hauts de Seine
4 star
Sofitel Paris La Défense Centre, 34 Cours Michelet, ☎ 01 47 76 44 43, 📠 01 47 76 72 10. Classy modern hotel at the centre of this commercial district. 1500–1750F.

Rueil Malmaison ~ 92500, Hauts-de-Seine
3 star
Le Cardinal, 1 Pl. Richelieu, ☎ 01 47 08 20 20, 📠 01 47 08 35 84. Situated at the centre of this pleasant town. 730F (special weekend tariffs).

Fontainebleau ~ 77300, Seine-et-Marne
4 star
Grand Hôtel de l'Aigle Noir, 27 Pl. Nap.-Bonaparte, Fontainebleau, ☎ 01 60 74 60 00, 📠 01 60 74 60 01. Rooms come in a variety of historic styles in this up-market hotel close to the park of the chateau. 790–1050F.
Grand Hôtel Mercure Royal Fontainebleau, 41 Rue Royale, ☎ 01 64 69 34 34, 📠 01 64 69 34 39. Bright and comfortable hotel in a prime situation.

3 star
Napoléon, 9 Rue Grande, ☎ 01 60 39 50 50, 📠 01 64 22 20 87. Very attractive centrally placed hotel around a courtyard. 490–800
Hôtel Legris et Parc, 36 Rue du Parc, ☎ 01 64 22 24 24, 📠 01 64 22 22 05.

2 star
Hôtel Victoria, 112 Rue de France, ☎ 01 60 74 90 00, 📠 01 60 74 90 10. Friendly and intimate hotel. 250–365F.

Barbizon ~ 77630, Seine-et-Marne

Le Bas Bréau, 22 Rue Grande, ☎ 01 60 66 40 05, 📠 01 60 69 22 89. Formerly a hunting lodge, this is an elegant place to stay and to eat in lovely surroundings. 900–1500F.

Hostellerie Les Pléiades, 21 Rue Grande, ☎ 01 60 66 40 25, 📠 01 60 66 41 68. Smallish but comfortable rooms, with a pretty décor. 270–550F.

St-Germain-en-Laye ~ 8100, Yvelines
4 star

Cazaudehore et La Forestière, 1 Av. du Président-Kennedy, ☎ 01 30 61 64 64, 📠 01 39 73 73 88. Utterly charming hotel on the edge of the forest with a renowned restaurant. 990F.

Le Pavillon Henri IV, 21 Rue Thiers, ☎ 01 39 10 15 15, 📠 01 39 73 93 73. The birthplace of Louis XIV, and frequented by Alexandre Dumas and Offenbach. Situated near the château in a park. 980–1280F.

Versailles ~ 78000, Yvelines
Luxury 4 star

Trianon Palace, 1 Blvd de la Reine, ☎ 01 30 84 38 00, 📠 01 39 49 00 77, www.westin.com Sumptuous and historic hotel overlooking the park. Luxury spa and top-class restaurant.

4 star

Sofitel Versailles, 2 bis Av. de Paris, ☎ 01 39 53 30 31, 📠 01 39 53 87 20. Placed very conveniently for the château at the centre of the town. 1290F.

3 star

Hotel Résidence du Berry, 14 Rue d'Anjou, ☎ 01 39 49 07 07, 📠 01 39 50 59 40, www.hotel-le-versailles.f. Smallish and beautifully turned out hotel. 520–1350F. (Special weekend tarifs.)

2 star

Angleterre, 2 bis Rue de Fontenay, ☎ 01 39 51 43 50, 📠 01 39 02 45 63, www.hotel-angleterre-versailles.fr. 18 rooms at budget rates. 300–350F.

Home Saint-Louis, 28 Rue St-Louis, ☎ 01 39 50 23 55, fax 01 30 21 62 45. Smallish hotel a little way from the centre with simple accommodation and quiet surroundings. 220–350F.

 # Eating and drinking

Restaurants

Paris has a staggering 8000 or so eating establishments of every kind and category and the restaurant scene is constantly adapting to new trends. A selection of restaurants is included at the beginning of each chapter, with brief descriptions and price ratings. Prices, of course, vary wildly and at the top end of the market the sky's the limit. Most visitors will probably not be eating *haute cuisine* all the time, and it is still possible to eat inexpensively in Paris although all the inexpensive restaurants will not necessarily be good value for money. A brasserie will not quibble (unless you misguidedly try to eat only a salad chez Lipp) if you order just one dish. The lowest price for a good set lunch menu might be around 60–80F, and lunch (between 12.30 and 14.00) is often better value than dinner. It is worth adapting the rhythm of your day to accommodate this if food is important.

Restauration rapide/menu rapide is fast food, e.g. the French equivalent of MacDonalds is *Quick*.

Dinner is not normally served before 20.00; extras such as quality wine and coffee can bump up the bill although bread is always included. By law, all restaurants have to display menus and prices outside and a service charge of 15 per cent will be included—but no-one will complain if you leave a little extra for good service. Always check your bill (*l'addition*).

As a very basic indication, the restaurants listed in the *Blue Guide* are categorised: £ (inexpensive, up to 200F), ££ (moderate, anywhere between 200F and 400F), £££ (400F upwards).

There are, of course, plenty of specialised French gastronomic guides listing or recommending a great range of eating-places in and around Paris, detailing the quality, price, type of food and setting. Many restaurants are closed on Sunday evenings, and during August. It is advisable to book well in advance (weeks rather than days) at the famous or fashionable restaurants.

The chains

There are several restaurant chains that offer a reliable, standardised meal, such as *Léon de Bruxelles*, which specialises in mussels and chips; the *Bistros Romain* with reasonably priced two-course menus, often including *carpaccio à volonté* (as much as you can eat) and copious desserts; *Bar à Huitres* (Montparnasse, St-Germain and Bastille) specialises in shellfish; *Batifol*, bistrot-type food; *La Dame Tartine* (Beaubourg, Bastille, Tuileries Gardens, and St-Cloud Park), open sandwiches and snacks; *Hippopotamus*, grills, open until 5 am, etc. Like everywhere else in Europe, pizzerias abound and the French make very good pizzas.

More up-market groups include *Brasseries Flo*, which has some lovely Art Nouveau and Art Deco properties; restaurants *Detourbe* which offer a fixed-price dinner menu (Rues N. Charlet, 15e, Duret 16e, Rue Pierre Demours, 17e); *l'Amanguier* (Blvds Montmartre and Montparnasse, Avs des Ternes and de Madrid, and Rue du Théâtre). The typical simple French bistrot is becoming a rare species but worth the search, and several fashionable chefs (Rostrand, Savoy and Cagna) also have a bistrot (or bistrots) as well as their gastronomic restaurants. Terence Conran opened the *Alcazar* in Paris in 1998.

Museum eateries

The Parisians have woken up to the fact that it's great to take a break for refreshments during the marathons that are many galleries and museums: the Louvre has quite a choice; the Musée d'Orsay has a couple; and there are various restaurants belonging to the Costes Group in or near museums (*Café Marly* at the Louvre, the Pompidou Centre's trendy new rooftop restaurant, *Restaurant Georges*, and *Café de la Musique* next to the Cité de la Musique at La Villette). There is a cafeteria in the garden of the Musée Rodin, a *Salon de Thé* in the Musée Jacquemart André, and in the Musée Maillol.

Restaurants with views

Restaurants with views are found in the Eiffel Tower, the Institut Arabe, in the department store La Samaritaine (*Le Toupary*), and the Tower Montparnasse. In several of the public gardens of Paris there are restaurants, cafés or snack bars: for instance, in the Bois de Boulogne, the Bagatelle gardens, the Tuileries, the Parc des Buttes Chaumont.

Cafés

The cafés of Paris are legion and always popular, especially when it is fine enough to sit outside on the pavement (or *terrasse*). Take heed, prices are usually higher on the terrace than sitting down inside, and it is cheaper still to stand at the bar for your coffee or drink. A glass of ordinary wine (*un petit blanc/un petit rouge*) or a beer in a standard café may be cheaper than a coffee, a sparkling water or a coca cola. A small draught beer is a *un demi pression*.

Coffee is an espresso if you simply order *un café*. A *café crème/café au lait* is with hot milk and usually in a large cup, served at breakfast. Some cafés (but not all) serve *un petit crème*. If you would prefer coffee with cold milk, ask for *une noisette*. If you want a longer, less strong coffee, ask for a *café allongé* or *à l'américain*. **Tea** usually comes as a tea bag with separate hot water, and with milk (*thé au lait*), lemon (*thé citron*) or plain (*thé nature*). **Hot chocolate** (*chocolat chaud*) is a popular drink, especially in the morning.

A **Continental breakfast** (*petit déjeuner*) is served in the mornings at many cafés and will consist of fresh baguette or rolls and/or croissants, brioches etc., with a choice of coffee, tea or hot chocolate. The breakfasts in hotels have improved over recent years, and some hotels serve a buffet breakfast.

Cyber cafés are among the 'in places' to be seen—such as *Web Bar*, 32 Rue de Picardie, 75003.

Wines

Rouge, blanc or *rosé* wine can vary from excellent to pretty rough. The mark-up on wine is very high, but in the more modest restaurants, house wine is still served in a *pichet* or *carafe* (litre, *demi* or *quart*) for a very reasonable price.

A list of dishes

Many French culinary terms and processes are universally known, but the following may be helpful:

Les potages ~ soups
bouillon, broth
consommé, clear soup
crème, thick soup
potage, thick (vegetable) soup

Hors-d'oeuvre and salads
croque monsieur/croque madame, toasted cheese and ham sandwich/topped with an egg
crudités, raw vegetables, usually sliced, chopped, or grated
tapénade, a purée of olives, sometimes with capers, anchovies
salade Niçoise, with tomato, anchovy, onions and olives

salade panachée, mixed salad
salade verte, green salad; also *Salade simple*, or *de saison*
pissaladière, provençal onion and anchovy pie
aïoli, a mayonnaise of vinegar, oil and crushed garlic, often eaten with fish

Les oeufs ~ eggs
à la coque, soft-boiled
mollets, medium-boiled
durs, hard-boiled
sur le plat or *au plat*, fried
pochés, poached
en cocotte, baked in a ramekin
brouillés, scrambled

omelette aux fines herbes, savoury
omelette; *au jambon*, ham omelette,
etc., and an infinite variety of others

Les poissons, les coquillages et crustacés (or fruits de mer) ~ fish and shellfish

escargots, snails
anchois, anchovies
anguille, eel
bar, sea bass
barbue, brill
bellon, a type of oyster
brandade de morue, salt cod and potatoes (sort of fish pie)
brochet, pike, often the base of quenelles
cabillaud, cod
calmar, squid
carpe, carp
colin, hake
coquilles St-Jaques, scallops
crevettes, prawns or shrimps
cuisses de grenouilles, frogs' legs
daurade, sea bream
écrevisse, fresh-water crayfish
églefin, haddock
friture, deep fried whitebait
fruits de mer, seafood/shellfish
harengs, herrings
homard, lobster
huitres, oysters
langouste, crayfish or lobster
langoustine, Dublin Bay prawns
lotte, monkfish, *lotte de rivière*, burbot
loup, sea bass
maquereau, mackerel
merlan, whiting
mérou, brill
morue, salt cod
moules, mussels
mulet, grey mullet
palourdes, clams
poulpe, octopus
praires, clams
quenelles, fish (often pike) or meat
made into a light dumpling roll,
served in a sauce
raie, skate (often served '*au beurre*
noir', with black butter)

rouget, (red) mullet
St-Pierre, John Dory
sandre, pikeperch
saumon, salmon
saumon fumé, smoked salmon
thon, tuna
truite, trout

Les viandes ~ meat

Meat may be ordered *bleu*, very rare;
saignant, rare; *à point*, medium; or
bien cuit, well done
agneau, lamb
bavette/onglet, beef flank steak
boeuf, beef
(*bifteck* is a franglais word which has
been in use since 1786)
carré d'agneau, cutlets
cassoulet, a stew of white haricot
beans, goose fat, Toulouse
sausage, pork and probably goose
or duck, originating in the southwest
chateaubriand, fillet steak
cochon de lait, sucking-pig
daube, a stew; other forms are *pot-au-*
feu and *marmite*
gigot d'agneau, leg of lamb
mouton, mutton
porc, pork; see below
queue de boeuf, ox-tail
ris de veau, sweetbreads
rosbif, roast beef
veau, veal
viandes froides, cold meats

La charcuterie ~ pork products, cured or cooked meats

abbats, offal
andouille, smoked chitterling
sausage
boudin blanc, veal, chicken or pork
sausage
boudin noir, blood sausage
cervelles, brains
foie, liver
foie gras, goose liver
jambon, ham
jambon cuit, York ham

jambon fumé, smoked ham
jambon cru, *jambon de Bayonne*, cured ham
pieds de porc, pigs' trotters
rillettes, potted shredded pork
rognons, kidneys
saucisses, sausages; *saucisson*, salami sausage
terrines, potted meats

Les volailles et le gibier ~ poultry and game

caille, quail
canard, duck
caneton, duckling
cerf or *chevreuil*, venison
dinde or *dindon*, female and male turkey
faisan, pheasant
lapin, rabbit
lièvre, hare
marcassin, young wild boar
oie, goose
confit d'oie/de canard, goose/duck conserved in its own fat
palombe, wood pigeon
pintade, guinea-fowl
poulet, chicken
poularde, capon
sanglier, wild boar

General terms

basquaise, with tomato and pimento
bercy, with wine and shallots
biologique, organic (becoming more popular)
bourguignonne, cooked in red wine, with bacon, mushrooms and small onions
chasseur or *forestière*, with mushrooms Lyonnaise, with onions
meunière, cooked slowly in butter
parmentier, with potatoes
périgourdine, with truffles and/or foie gras
provençale, with oil, tomatoes and garlic
tartare, raw minced steak (occasionally tuna or salmon)

Les légumes et aromates ~ vegetables and herbs

ail, garlic
aïoli, a mayonnaise of crushed garlic
aneth, dill
artichaut, globe/leaf artichoke; *fonds*, hearts
asperges, asparagus
basilic, basil
bettrave, beetroot
cannelle, cinnamon
céleris, celery
céleri-rave, celeriac; *céleri-rave remoulade*, in mustard sauce
cèpe, wild mushroom (boletus edulis)
cerfeuil, chervil
champignons, mushrooms
chicorée, Belgian endive
chicorée frisée or *scarole*, curly chicory
chou, cabbage
choucroute, sauerkraut
choufleur, cauliflower
choux de Bruxelles, Brussel sprouts
ciboulettes, chives
concombre, cucumber
cornichon, gherkin
cresson, watercress
échalote, shallot
épinards, spinach
estragon, tarragon
fenouil, fennel
fève, broad bean
flageolet, flageolet bean
genièvre, juniper berry
girolle, wild mushroom (chanterelle)
gratin dauphinois, sliced potatoes cooked in cream
gratin savoyard, similar, but with the addition of eggs and cheese
haricot blanc, white haricot bean
haricot vert, French green bean
huile de noix, walnut oil
huile d'olive, olive oil
laitue, lettuce
lentilles, lentils
mâche, lamb's lettuce
mesclun, mixed young salad leaves
morille, wild mushroom (morel)
navet, turnip

oignon, onion
oseille, sorrel
persil, parsley
petits pois, green peas
pissenlit, dandelion leaves
poireau, leek
pois chic, chick pea
poivre, pepper
poivron, sweet pepper
pomme de terre, potato
potiron, pumpkin
radis, radish
riz, rice
romarin, rosemary
topinambour, Jerusalem artichoke

Les fromages ~ cheeses

Note that cheese is always served before the dessert in France.
There are numerous regional varieties. Most are made from cow's milk, otherwise marked **e** for ewe (*brebis*) or **g** for goat (*chèvre*). Only some of the more usual types are listed.
Normandy: Bondon, Camembert, Livarot, Pont-l'Evêque, Boursin
Northern France and Ile-de-France: Mimolette, St-Paulin, Brie, Coulommiers
Brittany: Port-Salut
Touraine, Poitou and Périgord: St-Paulin, Chabicou (g), Ste-Maure (g)
Berry and Burgundy: Valençay (g), St-Florentin and Epoisse
The Pyrenean region produces several, mostly cow, but also ewe-cheeses
The Causses in the southwest produce the renowned blue, Roquefort (e) and Pelardon des Cévennes (g)
The Auvergne is noted for the Bleu-d'Auvergne, Cantal, St-Nectaire and Fourme-d'Ambert
Alsace and Lorraine: Carré-de-l'Est, Munster and Rocollet
The Franche-Comté produces Comté, and further south, Bleu-de-Bresse
Savoy is noted for Beaufort, Emmental, Reblochon and Tomme
Lyonnais and Dauphiny, the Rigotte-

de-Condrieu; the Picodon and St-Marcellin (both g) are reputed
There are also many varieties of cream cheeses; *fromage blanc* is a fresh white cheese often eaten with sugar
Fondue Savoyarde is melted cheese (often Vacherin), wine and kirsch

Les desserts et fruits

abricot, apricot
ananas, pineapple
banane, banana
bavarois, cream dessert
beignet, fritter/doughnut
cannelle, cinnamon
cassis, blackcurrant
cerise, cherry
citron, lemon
coing, quince
compote de fruits, stewed fruit
crème caramel, *crème caramalisé*, caramel custard
figue, fig
flan, solid custard pie
fraises, strawberries
fraises des bois, wild strawberries
framboise, raspberry
glace, ice cream
groseille, red or white currant
île flottante, floating island (poached meringue floating on egg custard)
liégeois, coffee or chocolate sundae
marron, chestnut, *marron glacé*, candied chestnut
mendiant, mixed almonds, raisins, etc.
miel, honey
mûres sauvage, blackberry
myrtille, bilberry
noisette, hazel-nut
noix, walnut
pamplemousse, grapefruit
pâte d'amande, almond paste/marzipan
pâte de coings, quince jelly
pêche, peach
poire, pear
pomme, apple
pruneau, prune
prune, plum

mirabelle, small yellow plum
reine-claude, greengage
raisins, grapes; *raisin sec*, raisin
sucre, sugar
tarte Tatin, caramelised upside-down apple tart

Patisseries et confiseries ~ pastries, cakes and confectionery
confiture, jam; *confiture d'orange*, marmalade
crêpes dentelles, pancakes

dragées, sugared almonds
en brioche, baked in dough
gâteaux secs, biscuits
gaufres, waffles
macarons, almond paste macaroons
millefeuille, multiple layers of puff-pastry, often with jam and cream
nougatines, caramelised ground almonds
pain d'épices, spiced honey-cake or gingerbread
petits fours, fancy biscuits
viennoiseries, type of bread and pastries

Pain ~ bread

Pain is usually bought at boulangeries; the most popular is *une baguette*, a long thin roll, especially good from reputable Parisian bakers. There are smaller versions of the baguette, *une ficelle* and others of varying shapes made from the same dough. This bread does not keep—it is best eaten straight away. *Pain de campagne* is a larger, rustic, loaf and there has been an increase in recent years of other types of bread such as *pain complet*, wholegrain, *pain aux noix*, walnut bread, and *pain de seigle*, rye bread (traditionally served with oysters). A *tartine* is buttered bread.

Entertainment

For up-to-date information on theatres, cinemas, cabarets, night clubs, cultural events, sporting events, fairs, exhibitions and shows, consult the Tourist Office telephone information ☎ 01 49 52 53 53, or their web site (see below). Weekly information can be found in *Pariscope* or *l'Officiel des Spectacles* on sales at newsstands.

Tickets

Tickets for most events can be purchased at the **Paris Tourist Office** (in person). They are also available from the following:
FNAC Billetterie, ☎ 01 49 87 50 50, or in person at other **FNAC** outlets.
Virgin Megastore in the Carrousel du Louvre.
Kiosque, 15 Place de la Madeleine and Esplanade de la Tour Montparnasse, sells half-price tickets on the day of the performance.
In London:
Globaltickets (**Edwards & Edwards**), 1 Regent Street, SW1Y 4XT, ☎ 020 7734 4555.
Michael Cooks' Ticket Finder, 74 Mortimer St, W1N 8HL, ☎ 020 7631 0671.
Voyages Vacances Intl., The Linen Hall, 162/168 Regent St, W1R 5TB, ☎ 020 7287 3171, www.helloparis.co.uk.

Theatre, opera and ballet

Theatres

The national, or state-subsidised, theatres are:

Comédie-Française, Pl. André-Malraux, 75001 (☎ 01 44 81 15 15).

Théâtre de l'Odéon), Pl. Paul-Claudel, 75006 (☎ 01 44 41 36 36).

Théâtre National Populaire (TNP), Palais de Chaillot, 75016 (☎ 01 53 65 30 00).

Théâtre National de la Colline, 17 Rue Malte-Brun, 75020 (☎ 01 44 62 52 52).

Théâtre de la Ville, Pl. du Châtelet, 75004 (☎ 01 42 74 22 77), theatre, dance, variety.

Théâtre du Châtelet, Pl. du Châtelet, 75004 (☎ 01 40 28 28 40) concerts, opera, variety.

Opéra National de Paris, Palais Garnier, 75009, and **Opéra National de Paris Bastille**, 75012 dance, opera, cinema, ☎ 08 36 69 78 68, and www.operat-de-paris.fr.

Opéra-Comique, Salle Favart, Pl. Boïeldieu, 75002 (☎ 01 42 44 45 46).

Some theatres close for some weeks in the summer and on one evening a week, usually Monday or Tuesday. Smoking is forbidden. Note that tickets bought through an agency will cost as much as 25 per cent more than at the box-office of the theatre concerned, usually open between 11.00 and 18.30 or 19.00.

Concerts

Salle Pleyel, 252 Rue du Fb. St-Honoré, 75008 (☎ 01 45 61 53 00).

Théâtre des Champs-Elysées, 15 Av. Montaigne 75008 (☎ 01 49 52 50 50); Théâtre du Châtelet (see above).

Salle Gaveau, 45 Rue La Boétie, 75008 (☎ 01 49 53 05 07).

Maison de l'ORTF (or **de la Radio**), 116 Av. du Président-Kennedy, 75016 (☎ 01 56 40 15 16).

Cité de la Musique, 221 Av. Jean Jaurès, 75019 (☎ 01 44 84 44 84), and www.cite-musique.fr.

For information on free concerts in the city's gardens (May–September), contact the *Paris Tourist Office*, the *Information Office* at the Mairie de Paris or any district Town Hall.

Church music and organ recitals are frequently held at such churches as Notre-Dame, St-Eustache, St-Germain-des-Prés, St-Louis-des-Invalides, St-Séverin, St-Sulpice, St-Roch, St-Clotilde, St-Etienne-du-Mont, Saint-Merri, Saint-Germain l'Auxerrois and La Madeleine, and special concerts are usually well advertised. *Musique et Patrimoine*, ☎ 01 47 76 67 00, for information on organ recitals preceded by a short lecture.

Cafés-théâtres and chansonniers

Informal revues or pithy political satires, for which a fairly thorough knowledge of the language and latest *argot* is needed, still exist, one of the most famous being *Au Lapin Agile* in Montmartre.

Cabarets and dinner shows

Paris is famous for these shows, which vary from 'artistically exotic or erotic' to grossly vulgar. Among the more up-market establishments of long-standing are: *Crazy Horse Saloon*, 12 Av. George V, 75008 (☎ 01 47 23 32 32).

Lido, 116bis Av. des Champs-Elysées, 75008 (☎ 01 40 76 56 10).
Folies Bergère, 32 Rue Richer, 75009 (☎ 01 44 79 98 98).
Moulin Rouge, 82 Blvd de Clichy, 75018 (☎ 01 53 09 82 82).

Cinemas

Cinemas abound (the French are great cinema goers), and Paris claims nearly 350 screens, showing films of all kinds. Programmes normally change on Wednesdays. Prices charged in the better-known cinemas can be high but the seats are very comfortable. Many cinemas show films in VO (*vérsion originale*), i.e. foreign-language films that are not dubbed (but have sub-titles).

Art exhibitions

Although smaller shows devoted to individual artists can be seen at any number of galleries and art-dealers' shops, many of them in the 6e arrondissement, the more important temporary exhibitions are held in the Grand Palais, Petit-Palais, Musée d'Orsay, Palais de Tokyo, Musée des Arts Décoratifs, Centre National d'Art et de Culture Georges Pompidou and other leading art galleries.

Sports

General information about a variety of sporting events, sporting facilities, addresses of tennis-clubs, squash-courts, golf-courses, swimming-pools, etc. in Paris and environs, may be obtained from the Paris Tourist Office (or consult their web site), see above, the Direction de la Jeunesse et des Sports, 17 Blvd Morland, 75004. The most popular new sports venue is the Stade de France at St-Denis (see Ch. 39).

Gardens

There are guided visits to the Gardens of Paris, either thematic (e.g. historic gardens, modern gardens, cemeteries, etc.), and a half-day coach tour of the gardens. Information and 'Green Map' available from the Paris Tourist Office, the Hôtel de Ville, or ring the Service des Visites des jardins de la Mairie de Paris, 3 Av. de la Porte d'Auteuil, 75016, visits ☎ 01 40 71 75 60, general information ☎ 01 40 71 76 07. There are visits conducted in English during the summer at Père Lachaise Cemetery, Parc Citroën, and Parc de Bercy.

Children's Paris

Zoos
Ménagerie du Jardin des Plantes.
Parc zoologique du Château de Thoiry.
Parc Zoologique de Paris, Bois de Vincennes.

Parks and gardens
Aquatic Centre, Aquaboulevard, 4–6 Rue Louis Armand, 75015, with giant waterslides, heated pool and wave machine.
Jardin d'Acclimatation (🚇 Sablons).
Jardin d'enfants des Halles.
Jardin du Luxembourg.
Parc Floral de Paris, Vincennes.
Parc de la Villette (🚇 Porte de Pantin).

Theme parks
Disneyland Paris, 77777 Marne-la-Vallée (32 km from Paris 🚇 *RER* A).
Parc Astérix, 60128 Plailly (30km from Paris (🚇 *RER* B3).
France Miniature (78990 Elancourt).

Science areas
Centre d'Information et de Documentation Jeunesse, 101 Quai Branly, 75015, offers general information on activities in museums, etc.
La Cité des Sciences et de l'Industrie, Parc de la Villette.
Grande Galerie de l'Evolution.
Palais de la Découverte.
Musée de la Poupée (Doll Museum).

Paris from above
There are several monuments or buildings that offer spectacular views over Paris (some free, some to be paid for). These include:
Arc de Triomphe.
Butte Montmartre and the Basilica of Sacré Coeur.
Eiffel Tower.
Grande Arche de la Défense.
Institut du Monde Arabe.
Panthéon.
Parc de Belleville (20e arrondissement).
Pompidou Centre.
La Samaritaine (department store).
Tour Montparnasse.
Towers of the Cathedral of Notre Dame.

 # Shopping and markets

The really smart shops and designer boutiques are in the 1er, 6e, 8e and 16e arrondissements, particularly around Rue du Faubourg-St-Honoré. But in fact every district of central Paris has good and less pricey shops.
The best known **department stores** are:
Carrousel du Louvre, 99 Rue de Rivoli (closed Tues), is a fashionable covered shopping centre (🚇 Palais Royal/Musée du Louvre).
Les Galeries Lafayette and *Au Printemps*, at 40 and 69 Blvd Haussmann respectively (🚇 Havre Caumartin, Chaussée d'Antin).
Marks & Spencer stores (Rue de Rivoli, 🚇 Châtelet), and Blvd Haussmann (🚇 Havre Caumartin).
La Samaritaine (🚇 Louvre, Châtelet, Les Halles).
For **antiques**:
Le Louvre des Antiquaires, Pl. du Palais Royal, 75001 is the main, and expensive centre (🚇 Palais Royal/Musée du Louvre).
   Many antique shops and *brocanteurs* (second-hand dealers) are in the 6e, including:

Village Suisse (closed Tuesday–Wednesday), west of the Ecole Militaire (🚇 La Motte Piquet).

Village Saint-Paul (🚇 St-Paul).

Carré Rive Gauche (🚇 Rue du Bac).

Marché aux Puces (open Saturday–Monday), a few minutes' walk north of the Porte de Clignancourt Métro, is the most extensive and best known flea market and sometimes produces bargains among the bric-à-brac.

Auctions are held regularly at the rebuilt *Salle Drouot*, 6 Rue Rossini, 75009. Nearby, in the Rue Drouot and further south in the arcades of the Palais-Royal, are the haunts of philatelists and an open-air stamp market is held Thursday–Sunday, at Av. Matignon, Rond-Point des Champs-Elysées.

Art and craft work is found at the Viaduc des Arts, 9–129 Av. Daumesnil, not far from the Bastille.

Markets

Colourful markets devoted to **flowers** are held in the Pl. Louis-Lépine (not far east of the Conciergerie), on the east side of the Madeleine, at the Pl. des Ternes, and Pl. de la République. On Sundays, the flowers of the Pl. Louis-Lépine give way to a bird market, while opposite, on the Quai de la Mégisserie, is a pet market.

Outdoor markets not too far from the centre are at:

Rue de Buci (just north of the Odéon Métro), 75006.

Rue Cler, 75007.

Rue Daguerre (Denfert-Rochereau).

Rue Lepic, 750018 (Abbesses).

Rue de Lévis (north-east of the Parc de Monceau), 750017.

Rue des Martyrs, 75009.

Rue de Montorgueil (leading north from Les Halles Métro), 75002.

Rue Mouffetard, 75005.

Place Monge, 75005.

Av. Président Wilson, 75016.

There are often lively neighbourhood food markets on a Sunday morning.

Covered arcades, built at the end of the 18C or in the 19C, have come back into fashion, among them:

Galerie Véro-Dodat (1826), 75001 (🚇 Palais-Royal).

Passage du Caire (1798), 75002 (🚇 Sentier).

Passage des Pavillons, 6 Rue du Beaujolais, 75001 (🚇 Pyramides).

If you are determined to shop 'til you drop, try a *Paris shopping tour*, with fashion brands at low prices (☎ 01 42 94 13 87, or *Shopping Plus*, by shopping theme (☎ 01 47 53 91 17).

Bookshops

Bookshops continue to proliferate throughout central Paris, but differ widely in the range of books stocked and in the quality of their service. English newspapers and magazines can be found at a price at many kiosks near the centre. A selection of books in English is provided by *Brentano* (37 Av. de l'Opéra), *Galignani* (224 Rue de Rivoli: near the Tuileries Métro) and *W.H. Smith* (248 Rue de Rivoli), among others.

Museums, collections and monuments

A table giving hours of admission is printed below, but it is wise to check opening times by telephone or in the press as during strikes or public holidays there will probably be unscheduled closures. As a general rule, the national museums are closed on Tuesdays, and the municipal museums are closed on Mondays; but see below. Some museums have late openings, close early, or may be shut between 12.00 and 14.00, although the large museums tend to stay open. The same guidelines may also apply to other monuments, and churches, except for the major ones, are frequently closed. In some museums the admission fee is reduced or entrance is free on some or all Sundays.

Museum Pass (La Carte Musées et Monuments) This card gives direct entry to some 70 museums and monuments in Paris and the surrounding region. It can be bought at participating museums and monuments, the Paris Tourist Office and the Ile-de-France Tourist Information Centre (Carrousel du Louvre), major métro stations, FNAC ticket counters and Batobus stops. It is available for 1, 3 or 5 consecutive days. It avoids having to queue in the busier museums and is a great advantage for the Louvre, as it enables you to bypass the long queues and enter faster by Passage Richelieu or Porte des Lions. Note that it cannot be used for temporary exhibitions or guided tours. In the section on the Louvre (Ch. 15) there is advice on alternative means of acquiring tickets in advance for that museum. www.intermusees.com

Lecture tours are organised by several bodies. Walking tours are promoted by the Caisse Nationale des Monuments Historiques et Sites, are listed in a bi-monthly brochure, *Visites Conférences* obtainable from the Hôtel de Sully, 62 Rue St-Antoine, 75004, directly or by mail, ☎ 01 44 61 21 69/44 61 21 70. Information on guided walks can also be found at Mairies of each arrondissement, from the Paris Tourist Office, and in certain newspapers and publications such as *l'Officiel des Spectacles* and *Pariscope*. No advance booking is normally necessary: just turn up at the right place at the time stated, and pay the fee. The tour is taken by a competent, trained French-speaking guide-lecturer.

Entrance fees All museums charge an entry fee. The quality of general catalogues of permanent collections is constantly improving, especially in the larger museums, and English versions are quite frequent. Many are published by the *Editions de la Réunion des musées nationaux* (a list of catalogues in print by this organisation is available from the bookstalls of any of the national museums) or by the Musées et Monuments de France.

Hours of admission Some museums will not allow entry some 45 minutes before closing time. Sections of some museums may be closed at times other than those indicated (note especially at the Louvre, Ch. 15). Many are closed on Bank holidays (*jours fériés*) and most of these are listed below, but it is always wise to double-check.

Tourist Offices have information on museums in Paris and the Ile de France with up-to-date admission times and charges.

NB. **GT** indicates guided tour only.

Arabe, Institut du Monde
Quai St.-Bernard, 5e.

Tues–Sun 10.00–18.00.
Closed Mon.
Page107
www.imarabe.org

Arc de Triomphe de l'Etoile
Place Charles-de-Gaulle, 8e

1 Apr–30 Sept 09.30–23.00,
1 Oct–31 March 10.00–22.30.
Closed a.m. 8/5 and 11/11;
all day 1/1, 1/5, 14/7, 25/12
Page 293
www.monuments-france.fr

Archives Nationales
60 Rue des Francs-Bourgeois, 3e,

Mon–Fri 12.00–17.45,
Sat–Sun 13.45–17.45.
Closed Tues.
Page 262

Armée, Musée de l'
see Invalides

Art Moderne de la Ville de Paris
11 Av. du Prés.-Wilson, 16e

Tues–Fri 10.00–17.30,
Sat–Sun 10.00–18.45.
Closed Mon and some public
holdiays
Page 303
www.paris-france.org/musees

Art Naif, Musée
2 Rue Ronsard, 5e

Open daily 10.00–18.00
Closed 1/1, 1/5, 25/12
Page 289

**Arts Décoratifs,
l'Union Centrale des**
107 Rue de Rivoli. 1er
(see also **Musée de la Publicité**)

Tues–Fri 11.00–18.00, 21.00 Wed,
Sat, Sun 10.00–18.00.
Closed Mon & 1/1, 1/5, 25/12.
Page 219
www.ucad.fr

Arts et Métiers
60 Rue Réamur, 3e

Tues–Sun 10.00–18.00, 21.30 Thur.
Closed Mon and public holidays.
Page272
www.cnam.fr/museum/

Arts et Traditions Populaires
6 Av. du Mahatma-Gandhi 16e
(Bois de Boulogne)

Wed–Mon 09.45–17.15.
Closed Tues.
Page 315
www.culture.fr/culture/atp/mnatp

Assemblée Nationale Palais Bourbon GT when not in session

Palais Bourbon, Blvd St-Germain, 7e | Sat 10.00, 14.00, 15.00.
Page 144

Assistance Publique
47 Quai de la Tournelle, 5e

Tues–Sat 10.00–17.00.
Closed Sun, Mon, public holidays, Aug.
Page 289

Balzac, Maison Honoré de
47 Rue Raynouard, 16e

Tues–Sun 10.00–17.40.
Closed Mon and public holidays.
Page 310

**Bibliothèque Nationale,
Cardinal Richelieu,
Cabinet des Médailles**
58 Rue de Richelieu, 4e

Mon–Fri 113.00–17.45,
Sat 13.00–16.45, Sun 12.00–18.00.
Page 229
www.bnf.fr

**Bibliothèque Nationale,
François Mitterand**

GT Tues–Sat 14.00, Sun 15.00.
Page 111

Bourdelle
16 Rue Antoine-Bourdelle, 15e

10.00–17.40; closed Mon & public
holidays.
Page 120

Camondo, Nissim de Camondo
63 Rue de Monceau, 8e

Wed–Sun 10.00–17.00.
Closed Mon & Tues
Page 299
www.ucad.fr

Carnavalet
23 Rue de Sévigné, 3e

Tues–Sun 10.00–17.40.
Closed Mon & public holidays.
Page 265

Catacombes
1 Pl. Denfert-Rochereau 14e

GT Tues–Fri between 14.00 & 16.00,
Sat 09.00–11.00, 14.00–16.00.
Page 118

Cernuschi
7 Av. Velasquez, 8e

Tues–Sun 10.00–17.40.
Closed Mon and public holidays.
Page 300

Chapelle Expiatoire
Sq. Louis XVI, 8e

Thur, Fri, Sat 13.00–17.00.
Closed 1/1, 1/5, 25/12.
Page 285

Chasse (hunting)
60 Rue des Archives, 3e

Wed–Mon 10.00–12.30, 13.30–17.30.
Closed Tues.
Page 263

Cinema/Henri Langlois
Bercy Park, 12e

Opening 2002
Page 332
www.maison-du-cinema.com

Cluny; see Moyen Age-Thermes

Cognacq-Jay
8 Rue Elzévir, 3e

Tues–Sun 10.00–17.40.
Closed Mon & public holidays.
Page 270

Conciergerie
1 Quai de l'Horloge, 4e

Summer 09.30–18.30,
winter 10.00–17.00.
Closed 1/1, 1/5, 1/11, 11/11. 25/12.
Page 82

Découverte, Palais de la
Grand Palais
Av. Franklin-Roosevelt, 8e

Tues–Sat 09.30–18.00,
Sun & public holidays 10.00–19.00.
Closed Mon, 1/1, 1/5, 14/7, 15/8, 25/12.
Page 293
www.palais-decouverte.fr

Delacroix, Musée
6 Rue de Furstenberg, 6e

Wed–Mon 09.30–17.00.
Closed Tues & 1/1, 1/5, 25/12.
Page 131

Dolls (Musée de la Poupée)
Impasse Berthaud
22 Rue Beaubourg, 3e

Tues–Sun 10.00–18.00.
Closed Mon.
Page 248

Eiffel Tower
Champs de Mars, 7e

Lift 10 June–31 Aug 09.00– 24.00,
1 Sept–9 June 09.30–23.00,
10 June–31Aug 09.00–24.00,
1 Sept–9 June 09.00–18.30.
Page 157
www.eiffel.tower.com

Egouts de Paris
South end of Pont de l'Alma, 7e

1 May–30 Sept 11.00–17.00,
1 Oct–30 Apr to 16.00.
Closed Thurs, Fri & last 3 weeks Jan.
Page 150
www.paris-france.org

d'Ennery (oriental art)
59 Av. Foch, 16e

Thur–Sun 14.00–18.00.
Page 314
www.muséeguimet.fr

Evolution, Grande Galerie d'
(Jardins des Plantes)
36 Rue Geoffrey-St-Hilaire, 5e

Wed–Mon 10.00–18.00,
Thur 10.00–22.00.
Closed Tues.
Page 110

Gobelins (tapestries)
42 Av. de Gobelins, 13e

GT Tues–Thurs 14.00 & 14.15.
Page 112

Grande Arche
La Défense, 92400

Mon–Fri 11.00–17.00,
Sat, Sun 10.00–17.00.
Closed Tues.
Page 318

Guimet
6 Pl. d'Iéna, 16e
and
Galerie du Panthéon Buddique
annexe

Wed–Mon 10.00–18.00.
Closed Tues.

Wed–Mon 09.45–18.00
Closed Tues.

19 Av. d'Iéna	Page 305
	www.guimet.fr
Musée Hébert	Mon, Wed, Thur, Fri 12.30–18.00.
85 Rue de Cherche-Midi, 6e	Sat, Sun 14.00–18.00.
	Page 148
Henner	Tues–Sun 10.00–12.00, 14.00–17.00.
43 Av. de Villiers, 17e	Closed Mon.
	Page 301
History of France, Museum of the	Mon–Fri 12.00–17.45,
Hôtel de Soubise, 3e	Sat–Sun 13.45–17.45.
	Closed Tues.
	Page 262
Homme, Musée de l'	Wed–Mon 09.45–17.15.
Palais de Chaillot, 16e	Closed Tues & public holidays.
	Page 308
Hugo, Maison de Victor	Tues–Sun 10.00–17.40.
6 Pl. Des Vosges, 4e	Closed Mon & public holidays.
	Page 260
Invalides, Les (army museum)	1 Apr–30 Sept 10.00–18.00,
also Plans-Reliefs	1 Oct–31 March 10.00–17.00.
Esplanade des Invalides, 7e	Tickets for 3 museums and
	Napoléon's tomb.
	Closed 1/1, 1/5, 1/11, 25/12.
	Page 150
	www.invalides.org
Jacquemart-André	Daily 10.00–18.00.
158 Blvd Haussmann, 8e	Page 297
	www.musee-jacquemart-andre.com
Jardin des Plantes (Histoire	07.30–20.00 (or sunset).
Naturelle)	Page 109
57 Rue Cuvier, 5e	www.mnhr.fr
Japon, Maison de la Culture	Tues–Sat 12.00–19.00,
101bis Quai Branly, 15e	Thurs to 20.00.
	Closed 25/12–02/01.
	Page 158
	www.mcjp.asso.fr
Jeu-de-Paume	Tues 12.00–21.30,
Pl. de la Concorde, 1er	Wed–Fri 12.00–19.00,
	Sat, Sun 10.00–19.00.
	Closed Mon.
	Page 162
	www.jeudepaume.org
Judaïque, Arts et Histoire	Mon–Fri 11.00–18.00,
Hôtel de St-Aignan	Sun 10.00–18.00.

71 Rue du Temple, 3e

Page 275

Légion d'Honneur, Musée
2 Rue Bellechasse, 7e

Tues–Sun 14.00–17.00.
Closed Mon.
Page 144

Libération, Mémorial du
P. Leclerck & J. Moulin
23 Allée de la 2e DB,
Jardin Atlantique,
Gare de Montparnasse, 14e

Tues–Sun 10.00–17.40.
Closed Mon and public holidays
Page 120

Louvre, Musée du
Pyramid (Cour Napoléon)
Palais du Louvre, 1er

Wed–Mon 09.00–18.00, 21.45 Mon.
Closed Tues.
Page 170
www.louvre.fr

Maillol Musée
59-61 Rue de Grenelle, 7e

Wed–Mon 11.00–18.00.
Closed Tues & public holidays.
Page 148

Marine
Palais de Chaillot, 16e

Wed–Mon 10.00–17.50.
Closed Tues and 25/12, 1/01, 1/05.
Page 308

Marmottan
2 Rue Louis-Boilly, 16e

Tues–Sun 10.00–17.30.
Closed Mon.
Page 310
www.marmottan.com

Médecine, Musée d'Histoire
12 Rue de l'Ecole de Médecine, 6e

14.00–17.50.
Closed summer Sat, Sun;
winter Thur & Sun & some public
holidays.
Page 126
www.unif.paris.fr

Mickiewicz, Musée
6 Quai d'Orléans,
Ile St-Louis, 4e

Thur 15.00–18.00.
Page 92

Mineralogy, Museum of
Ecole des Mines
Blvd St-Michel, 6e

Tues–Fri 13.30–18.00,
Sat 10.00–12.30, 14.00–17.00.
Closed Sun, Mon, public holidays.
Page 126

de la Mode et du Costume
Rue de Rivoli, 1er

Tues–Sun 10.00–17.40.
Closed Mon & public holidays.
Page 303
www.paris.france.ors

Monnaie (Mint)
11 Quai de Conti, 6e

Tues–Fri 12.00–17.30,
Sat–Sun 12.00–17.30.
Closed Mon & some public holidays.
Page 124

Montmartre, Musée du Vieux
12 Rue Cortot, 18e

www.monnaiedeparis.fr
Tues–Sun 11.00–18.00.
Closed Mon, 1/1 1/5 25/12.
Page 289

Monuments Français
Palais de Chaillot, 16e

Closed for restoration until 2002.
Page 308

Moreau, Gustave
14 Rue de la Rochefoucauld, 9e

Mon & Wed 11.00–17.15,
other days 10.00–12.45, 14.00–17.15.
Closed Tues & 1/1, 1/5, 25/12.
Page 284

Moyen Age-Thermes
6 Pl. Paul-Painlevé, 5e

Wed–Mon 09.15–17.45.
Closed Tues & some public holidays.
Page 101

Musique, Cité de la
221 Av. Jean-Jaurès, 19e
(La Villette)

Tues–Sat 12.00–18.00, 19.30 Fri,
Sun 10.00–18.00.
Closed Mon.
Page 321
www.cite-musique.fr

Notre-Dame, Cathedral
Crypte Archéologique
Pl. du Parvis Notre-Dame, 4e

Summer 09.30–18.30,
winter 10.00–17.00.
Closed 1/1, 1/5, 1/11,
11/11, 25/12.
Page 86

Notre-Dame de Paris, Musée
10 Rue du Cloitre Notre-Dame, 4e

Wed, Sat, Sun 14.30–18.00.
Page 90

Océanographique Institut
195 Rue St-Jacques, 5e

Tues–Fri 10.00–12.30, 13.15– 17.30,
Sat, Sun 10.00–17.30.
Closed Mon.
Page 115
www.oceano.org

Observatoire
61 Av de l'Observatoire, 14e

GT first Sat of month 14.30.
Page 117

Opéra Garnier
Pl. de l'Opéra, 9e

Daily 10.00–17.00.
Closed 1/1, 1/5.
Page 278 & 279
www.opera-paris.fr

Orangerie
Pl. de la Concorde

Wed–Mon 09.45–17.15.
Closed Tues and public holidays.
Page 162

Orsay, Musée d'
1 Rue de la Légion d'Honneur

Summer Tues–Sun 09.00–18.00;
winter Tues–Sat 10.00–18.00,
Sun 09.00–18.00.
Thurs until 21.45.
Closed Mon & 1/1, 1/5, 25/12.

Page 133
www.musee-orsay.fr

Palais de Justice
2 Blvd du Palais, 1er

Page 83

Panthéon
Pl. Ste-Geneviève, 5e

Summer 10.00–19.30,
winter 10.00–18.15.
Closed 1/1, 1/5, 1/11, 11/11, 25/12.
Page 98

Pasteur, Musée
Institut Pasteur
25 Rue de Dr-Roux, 15e

Daily 14.00–17.30.
Closed public holidays & Aug.
Page 120

Petit Palais
Av. Winston Churchill, 8e

Tues–Sun 10.00–17.40.
Closed Mon & some public holidays.
Page 292
(Closed for renovations)

**Photography, Maison Européene
de la Photographie**
5–7 Rue de Fourcy, 4e

Wed–Sun 11.00–20.00.
Closed Mon–Tues & public holidays.
www.mep-fr.org
Page 254

Picasso
5 Rue de Torigny, 3e

Summer Wed–Mon 09.30–18.00,
winter Wed–Mon 09.30–17.30.
Closed Tues & 1/1, 25/12.
Page 271
www.oda.fr/aa/musee-picasso

Police, Musée de la Préfecture de
1bis Rue des Carmes, 5e

Mon–Fri 09.00–17.00,
Sat 10.00–17.00.
Closed Sun and public holidays.
Page 100

Pompidou, Centre (Musée
National d'art moderne)
4e

Wed–Mon 11.00–21.00,
closed Tues & 1/5.
Page 238
www.centrepompidou.fr

Postal Museum
34 Blvd Vaugirard, 15e

Wed–Mon 10.00–18.00.
Closed Tues & public holidays.
Page 120

**Publicité, Musée de la Union
Central des Arts Décoratifs**
107 Rue de Rivoli, 1er

Tues–Fri 11.00–18.00, Wed 21.00.
Sat, Sun 10.00–18.00.
Closed Mon, 1/1, 1/5, 25/12.
Page 219
www.museedelapub.org

Rodin, Musée
77 Rue de Varenne, 7e

Summer Tues–Sun 09.30–17.45,
winter Tues–Sun09.30–16.45
Closed Mon & 1/1, 25/12.
Page 146

Romantique, de la Vie

Tues–Sun 10.00–17.40.

16 Rue Chaptal, 9e

Closed Mon & public holidays.
Page 284

Sainte-Chapelle
Blvd du Palais, 4e

Summer 09.30–18.30,
winter 10.00–17.00.
Closed 1/1, 1/5, 1/11, 11/11, 25/12.
Page 84

**Service de Santé des Armée,
Musée de**
1 Pl. A.-Laeran, 5e

Tues, Wed 12.00–17.00,
Sat, Sun 13.30–17.00.
Closed Mon, Thur.
Page 116

**Serrure, Musée de la
(Musée Bricard)**
1 Rue de la Perle, 3e

Mon 14.00–17.00,
Tues–Fri 10.00–12.00, 14.00–17.00.
Closed Sat & Sun.
Page 263

Sciences et de l'Industrie
30 Av. Corentin-Cariou, 19e
(La Villette)

Tues–Sun 10.00–18.00.
Closed Mon & 1/5, 25/12.
Page 323
www.cite-sciences.fr.

UNESCO
7 Pl. Fontenoy, 7e

Mon–Fri 10.00–18.00.
Closed public holidays.
Page 156
www.unesco.org

Villette, La;
see Science et de l'Industries and
Instrumental

Villas la Roche and Jeanneret
8–10 Sq. Dr-Blanche, 16e

Mon–Thur 10.00–12.30, 13.30–18.00,
17.00 Fri.
Closed Sat, Sun & public holidays.
Page 311

Vincennes, Château de
Vincennes, 94300

Daily 10.00–12.00 and 13.15–18.00.
1 Oct–31 Mar to 17.00.
Closed 1/1, 1/5, 1/11, 11/11, 25/12.
Page 333

Zadkine, Musée
100bis Rue d'Assas, 6e

Tues–Sun 10.00–17.40.
Closed Mon; and public holidays.
Page 132

Environs of Paris

**Ecouen
Château de
Musée de la Renaissance**

Wed–Mon 09.45–12.30,
14.00–17.15.
Closed Tues, 1/1, 1/5, 25/12.
Park summer 08.00–19.00,
18.00 in winter.
Page 373

Fontainebleau
Château de
June–Oct 09.30–17.00,
July & Aug 09.30–18.00,
Nov–May 09.30–12.30, 14.00–17.00.
Closed Tues, 1/1, 1/5.
Page 379

Musée de l'Auberge
Ganne, Barbizon
1 April–12 Nov 10.00–12.30,
14.00–18.00, 13 Nov–30 March
to 17.00,
open all day Sat, Sun and most
public holidays.
Closed Tues.
Page 387

Maisons-Laffitte
Château de
1 Apr–15 Oct 10.00–12.00, 13.30–18.00,
16 Oct–31 Mar until 17.00.
Closed Tues, 1/1, 1/5, 1/11, 11/11,
25/12.
Page 365

Malmaison
Château de
Mon, Wed, Thur, Fri 10.00–12.00,
13.30–16.30,
Sat, Sun 10.00–17.00.
Closed Tues & 1/1, 25/12.
Page 357

Bois-Préau, Château de
Currently closed. (Thur–Sun
12.30–18.30 winter until 18.00.)
Page 360

Poissy
Villa Savoye
82 Rue de Villiers
1 Apr–31 Oct Wed–Mon 09.30–12.30,
13.30–18.00, 2 Nov–31 Mar to 16.30.
Closed Tues and public holidays.
Page 364

St-Denis
Basilique de
1 Apr–30 Sept Mon–Sat 10.00–19.00,
Sun 12.00–19.00,
1 Oct–31 Mar to 17.00, Sun to
17.00.
Closed 1/1, 1/5, 1/11, 11/11, 25/12.
Page 367

Musée d'Art et d'Histoire
22 Rue G. Péri, St-Denis
Wed–Sat 10.00–17.30,
Sun 14.00–18.30.
Closed Tuesday & public holidays,
Page 372

Christofle, Musée
Check with Tourist Office.

112 Rue Ambroise Croizat   Page 372

St-Germain-en-Laye
Antiquitiés Nationales   Wed–Mon 09.00–17.15.
Pl. du Château   Closed Tues & some public holidays.
                                                  Page 362

Debussy, Musée Claude   Tues–Sat 14.00–18.00.
38 Rue d Pain   Page 363

Prieuré (Nabis)   Wed–Fri 10.00–17.30,
2bis Rue Maurice-Denis   Sat & Sun 10.00–18.30.
                                                  Page 363

Sceaux
Château de   April–Sept Wed–Mon 10.00– 18.00,
(Musée de l'Ile de France)   Oct–March Wed–Mon 10.00– 17.00.
                                                  Closed Tues & 1/1, Easter, 1/5,
                                                  1/11, 11/11, 25/12.
                                                  Page 376

Sèvres
Musée Nationale de Céramique   Tues–Sun 10.00–17.00.
                                                  Closed Mon.
                                                  Page 337

Versailles
Château de Versailles   2 May–30 Sept Tues–Sun 09.00–18.30,
                                                  1 Oct–30 Apr Tues–Sun 09.00–17.30.
                                                  Closed Mon & some public holidays.
                                                  Page 341
                                                  www.chateauversailles.fr

Grand Trianon &   1 Apr–30 Oct Tues–Sun 12.00–18.30,
Petit Trianon   1 Nov–30 March Tues–Sun 12.00–17.30.
                                                  Closed Mon.
                                                  Page 355

Grandes Heures du Parlement   2 May–30 Sept Tues–Sun 09.00–18.30,
                                                  1 Oct–31 Apr Tues–Sun 09.00–17.00.
                                                  Page 348
                                                  www.assemmblee-nat.fr

Gardens/Parks   Summer daily 07.00–dusk,
                                                  winter daily 08.00–dusk.
                                                  Page 353

The cemeteries of Père Lachaise (p 325), Montmartre (p 286), and Montparnasse (p 119) are normally open from 07.30–18.00 in summer, and from 08.00–17.00 in winter; that of Picpus is open during the afternoon only.

Glossary

Acajou, mahogany
Arc-boutant, flying buttress
Archivolt, the series of mouldings which form the ensemble of an arch
Ardoises, slates
Autel, altar
Boiseries, decorative woodwork
Caissons, en, coffered
Carrefour, crossroads
Carrelages, floor tiles
Caserne, barracks
Chevet, exterior of an apse; also **abside**
Colonnette, little column for a vaulting shaft
Contreforts, buttresses
Corbels, wooden or stone projections supporting a beam or parapet, and often elaborately carved
Dessus de porte, a painting above a door
Donjon, keep
Douves, moat; wet or dry
Ebeniste, cabinet-maker
Eglise, church
Email, enamel
Escalier, staircase, à vis, spiral
Flèche, spire
Hôtel, mansion
Hôtel de Ville, town hall, also **Mairie**

Hôtel-Dieu, principal hospital in many towns
Jeu de Paume, a real tennis court
Jubé, rood-screen
Mansarde, the roof of which each face has two slopes, the lower steeper than the upper, named after the architect François Mansart (1598–1666)
Nacre, mother of pearl
Narthex, an ante-nave, porch or vestibule to a church or basilica
Nef, nave
Oeil-de-Boeuf, small circular, sometimes oval, window (bull's eye)
Piece d'eau, an expanse of water, usually ornamental
Porte-cochère, carriage gateway
Poutres, beams or joists
Rez de Chaussée, ground floor
Tierceron, curved rib in Gothic vaults springing from the same point as the intersecting diagonal rib, and rising to the end of the ridge-rib
Tympanum, space, often decorated, between door lintel and arch
Vermeil, silver-gilt
Vitrail, stained-glass window
Voussoires, wedge-shaped stones used in constructing arches or vaults

BACKGROUND INFORMATION

Historical introduction

The Romans

The foundations of modern France may be said to date from the crossing of the Alps by the Romans in 121 BC and the establishment of the province (Latin provincia; modern Provence) of Gallia Narbonensis. Important remains such as the Pont du Gard and the theatres and amphitheatres at Nîmes, Arles and Orange are still extant. But the whole of France as we now know it did not become subject to Rome until after Julius Caesar's decisive defeat of Vercingetorix at Alésia in 52 BC. In the previous year Caesar had first mentioned—under the name of Lutetia—the fortified capital of the Parisii, an insignificant Gallic tribe, confined on islands in the Seine, which he nominated as the rendezvous of deputies from conquered Gaul. Lyon, however, was the Roman capital of Gaul throughout.

In spite of occasional local revolts, Rome gradually imposed her government, roads, speech and culture on Gaul. By c AD 300 the country had become partially Christianised, St Dionysius (Denis) being its first bishop, but by then a series of Barbarian invasions began. In 292 Paris became a base of the Emperor Constantius Chlorus, and then more importantly for the Emperor Julian the Apostate (356–60), although it was not until 360 that the name was applied to the river-port. Barbarian mercenaries (among them Visigoths and Burgundians) were employed to defend the frontiers of the Empire in its decline, but they wearied of their alliance with the degenerate Gallo-Romans, and after the repulse of Attila and his Huns at the Chalon (451) became virtually masters of the land, the most powerful tribe being the Salian Franks under their legendary leader Merovius.

The Merovingians

Merovius's grandson Clovis I (481–511) defeated Syagrius (the Roman governor of Soissons) in 486, and the Alemanni at Tolbiac in 496, after which he adopted the Christian religion. In the following year Paris opened her gates to him (traditionally on the advice of Ste. Geneviève), although he did not make it his official capital until 508. According to Frankish custom, the kingdom was divided on his death between his three sons into Austrasia (between the Meuse and the Rhine), Neustria (the territory to the northwest, from the Meuse to the Loire) and Burgundy (to the south), and although the Merovingians remained in control, the dynasty was weakened by internecine warfare during the next two centuries.

Eminent among the Merovingians was Chilperic I (king of Neustria from 561–84) and Dagobert (king of Austrasia from 622 and of all France from 628 until his death in 638). Paris remained the political centre of conflicting Frankish interests, its growing population overflowing to form suburbs around monasteries situated on both banks of the river; but after the death of Dagobert, who refounded the abbey of St-Denis, most of the power passed into the hands of the 'maires du Palais', one of whom, Charles Martel (714–41), an Austrasian, was to defeat the invading Moors at Poitiers in 732. In 751 Pepin, Martel's son, deposed Childéric III, the last of the Merovingians, and founded a new dynasty.

The Carolingians

Although Pepin resided occasionally at Paris, his son Charlemagne, in alliance with the Pope, extended his dominion over Germany and Italy, and was crowned 'Emperor of the West', or 'Holy Roman Emperor'. He moved the seat of government from France to Aix-la-Chapelle (present-day Aachen). Not only a great ruler, Charlemagne also presided over a remarkable revival of learning and education. However, the system of dividing territories on the death of kings was to cause the eventual disintegration of the empire, and in 843, by the Treaty of Verdun, those areas which were to form modern France were transferred to his grandson Charles 'le Chauve'. Further division ensued, and France became little more than a collection of independent feudal states controlled by dukes and counts.

The situation was further disturbed by the invasion of Scandinavian or Norse pirates. By 912 the Vikings had settled in Rouen and had carved out the duchy of Normandy for themselves, in 885 having besieged and pillaged Paris itself from their encampment (possibly on the present site of the Louvre). The Cité had been defended by Eudes, Duc de France and comte de Paris, who in 888 deposed Charles 'le Gros', but the Carolingian dynasty staggered on for another hundred years. It was a century of disunity for France, distinguished politically by the growth of Norman power, and religiously by the foundation in 910 of a Benedictine abbey at Cluny, soon to gain fame and influence.

The Capetians

Hugh Capet was elected by the nobles at Senlis in preference to any more incapable Carolingians, and he and his successors proceeded to make Paris the centre of their tiny 'royal domain'—at first only the Ile de France. But this policy frequently brought them into conflict with independent spirits, one of whom, William, duke of Normandy, in 1066 invaded and conquered England. Paris grew steadily in size and importance, particularly on the North Bank, and during the reign of Louis VI, if not earlier, a second town wall was thrown up. The 'Hanse Parisienne', a league of merchants, was established, marking the foundation of the municipality.

The marriage in 1152 of the future Henry II of England to Eleanor of Aquitaine (the divorced wife of Louis VII), whose dowry brought Henry about one-third of France, was to cause a power struggle between the two countries which lasted three centuries. In 1095 Urban II preached the First Crusade at Clermont; in 1198 the Abbey of Cîteaux was founded; in c 1115 Clairvaux was founded by St. Bernard, who in 1146 was to preach the Second Crusade at Vézelay. In 1163 the foundation-stone of **Notre-Dame** was laid and some years later Philippe Auguste built the fortress of the Louvre. This religious enthusiasm was in part the reason for the expulsion of the Jews. The cathedral schools of Paris (at which Guillaume de Champeaux and Abélard had taught) were united to form one **University**, which was granted its first statutes by Pope Innocent III in 1208. This was established on the **Left Bank** of the Seine, where the growing student population settled; the **Right Bank** became the centre of commerce, industry and administration. Some streets were paved; the two ancient wooden bridges were replaced by ones of stone; and the city was enclosed by an extensive line of fortifications.

In the political field **Philippe Auguste** won back a large part of the lost provinces (Normandy and Anjou), inflicting a heavy defeat on the allies of John of England at Bouvines in 1214. The bloody Albigensian Crusade of 1209–13 eventually delivered Languedoc to French rule. During the long reign of **Louis IX**, the **Hospice des Quinze-Vingts** and the theological college of the **Sorbonne** were founded, the latter to become a dominant influence in the University. The **Palais de la Cité** was rebuilt (parts of which, notably the Sainte-Chapelle, still exist), and the office of Provost was reformed; statutes were drawn up for the many guilds, which were to remain in force until the Revolution. Louis, canonised in 1297, was a great crusader, and eventually lost his life at Tunis. With the death of Charles IV in 1328 the direct branch of the Capetian dynasty became extinct.

House of Valois

The claim of Philippe de Valois to the throne was disputed by Edward III of England, who invaded France, precipitating the **Hundred Years War** (1337–1453). He routed the French army at Crécy (1346) and inflicted a further defeat on Jean II at Poitiers in 1356. The ravages and depredations of both French and English soldiery roused the peasants (the Jacquerie) and the burgesses to revolt. In Paris, **Etienne Marcel** (Maire du Palais and provost of the merchants) took advantage of the situation to increase the influence of the municipality, but he offended public opinion by attempting to hand over the city to Charles of Navarre, and was assassinated in 1358. Two years later, by the Treaty of Brétigny, England reduced her claims only to Aquitaine and Calais, but before long desultory warfare between the two countries broke out again and continued until the French had won back a large part of their lost territory, largely due to the tactics of Du Guesclin.

Charles V was able to bring back some order to the kingdom. He built the fortress of the **Bastille**, but anarchy returned during the following reign, when his weak-minded son **Charles VI** provoked the citizens of Paris—at that time numbering some 280,000—by excessive taxation. Although the resulting revolt of the 'Maillotins' was bloodily suppressed, the king became the pawn of rival regents and for the next 40 years France suffered from dissensions between the aristocratic party, the Armagnacs, and the Burgundians, the popular party (Jean II had made his fourth son, Jean sans Peur, Duke of Burgundy).

Seizing the opportunity, **Henry V of England** invaded France, and supported by the Burgundians, defeated a French force at Agincourt (1415). By the Treaty of Troyes (1420) he received the hand of Catherine, Charles VI's daughter, together with the right of succession to the throne. But in 1422 Henry died at Vincennes, only seven weeks before the death of Charles VI. **Charles VII**, by himself no match for the English and Burgundians, found a champion in **Jeanne d'Arc** (Joan of Arc; 1412–31). But the English continued to control Paris until 1436. In 1429 John, Duke of Bedford repelled an assault led by Joan, who, after a brilliant campaign, defeated the English at Orléans in May of that year.

Captured at Compiègne by the Burgundians in 1430, she was handed over to the English, condemned as a heretic by a court of ecclesiastics, and burned at the stake in Rouen. But the successful revolt she had inspired continued, and by 1453 only Calais remained of the once extensive English possessions in France. A vivid account of conditions prevailing in Paris during the years 1405–49 is given in the anonymously compiled 'Journal d'un Bourgeois de Paris'. The poet Villon was born here in 1431.

With the reign of **Louis XI** the change from a medieval social system to the modern state was accelerated. A brilliant and unscrupulous politician (and relieved of the menace of England, then occupied with the domestic 'War of the Roses'), he proceeded to crush the great feudal lordships which encroached on his territory, the most threatening being that of **Charles the Bold** ('le Téméraire') of Burgundy. The Peace of Péronne (1468) gave the Burgundians a momentary advantage, but Louis managed to win over Charles' English allies by the Treaty of Picquigny (1475). After Charles' death before the walls of Nancy in 1477, Louis soon overwhelmed his lesser adversaries, and brought Arras, the Franche-Comté, Anjou, and Maine into direct allegiance to the crown. In 1469/70 the first printing-press in France was set up in the Sorbonne; and in 1484 the first meeting of the Estates-General was convened at Tours, near which, in the Loire valley, several châteaux were being rebuilt as royal residences.

The following half century was principally occupied with indecisive campaigns in Italy, the only tangible result of which—particularly during the reign of François I—was the establishment in France of the cultural concepts of the Italian Renaissance. Among the more important literary figures of the period were Marot, Rabelais, Du Bellay, and Ronsard, the last two being members of the poetic circle known as La Pléïade.

Charles VIII and **Louis XII** were successive husbands of **Anne de Bretagne**, whose dowry, the important duchy of Brittany, was formally united to France in 1532 on the death of her daughter, wife of François I. The reign of **Henri II** saw the acquisition by France of the Three Bishoprics (Metz, Toul, and Verdun), while Calais fell to the Duc de Guise in 1558. In 1559 Henri II concluded the treaty of Cateau-Cambrésis with Felipe II of Spain, thus ending the Italian wars. In 1564 an edict fixed the beginning of the year as 1 January, inaugurating the 'new style' of dating.

The short reign of **François II**, who while still dauphin (aged ten) had married Mary Stuart, Queen of Scots, was followed by that of his brother **Charles IX**. At the instigation of **Catherine de Médicis** (1519–89), his bigoted and domineering mother, Charles signed the order for the massacre of protestant Huguenots on the Eve of St Bartholomew (23 August 1572). (Catherine was mother also of Henri III, and of Marguerite de Valois, the first wife of Henri of Navarre.) From 1560 until the promulgation of the Edict of Nantes in 1598, the country was ravaged, sporadically, by the Religious Wars of the League (La Ligue). In 1588 the ultra-Catholic Henri, Duc de Guise, was murdered at Blois by **Henri III**, against whom he had been an overt rebel. The king himself was assassinated at St-Cloud the following year.

House of Bourbon

The parents of **Henri IV** (of Navarre) were Jeanne d'Albret (daughter of Marguerite of Navarre) and Antoine de Bourbon, of the Bourbon branch of the Capetian dynasty, descending from Robert of Clermont, sixth son of Louis IX. A Protestant, Henri eventually defeated the Catholics at Ivry (1590), but was unable to enter the besieged capital until 1594, after he had ostensibly abjured his faith with (it is said) the cynical remark that '*Paris vaut bien une messe*'. Despite his conversion, he granted Protestants freedom of worship by the Edict of Nantes. Among the many who joined in the general recognition of Henri as the legitimate heir to the throne was Montaigne, whose '*Essays*' were published in part in 1580.

Peace established, Henri set about enlarging the **palaces of the Louvre** and the **Tuileries**, planned several squares including the Place Royale, and completed the Pont Neuf. However, with his assassination by Ravaillac in 1610, religious restlessness returned, and the admirable reforms and economies instituted by the **Duc de Sully** (1560–1641), his able minister, were brought to nothing by the extravagant favourites of young **Louis XIII** (whose mother, Marie de Médicis, Henri had married in 1600 after his divorce from Marguerite de Valois). On Henri's death, Marie became Regent, but in 1624 **Cardinal Richelieu** (1585–1642) took over the reins of government. His main aim was the establishment of absolute royal power in France, and of French supremacy in Europe. He suppressed all Protestant influence in politics, capturing their stronghold, La Rochelle, in 1628. Anyone defying Richelieu suffered severe penalties, and numerous fortresses throughout the country were dismantled in the process of repression. The cardinal then turned his attention to the Habsburg power, which since the reign of Emperor Charles V had surrounded the frontiers of France, and, in alliance with Gustavus Adolphus of Sweden, Richelieu involved France in the Thirty Years War. The campaigns of the Grand Condé (1621–86; a member of a collateral branch of the Bourbons) resulted in the temporary acquisition of Picardy, Alsace and Roussillon.

In 1635 and 1640 respectively, the **Académie Française** and the Imprimerie Royal were founded; a fifth wall was erected around Paris, where several new quarters arose, such as the **Pré-aux-Clercs** (Faubourg St-Germain), the **Ile-St-Louis** and the **Marais**, which became a favourite residence of the nobility. Marie de Médicis built the **Palais du Luxembourg**; Anne of Austria, consort of the king since 1614, founded the church of **Vâl-de-Grace** in thanksgiving for the birth of a son (later Louis XIV) in 1638; and Richelieu built for himself the Palais-Cardinal, later the **Palais-Royal**.

Richelieu had been succeeded meanwhile by **Cardinal Mazarin** (1602–61), who carried on his predecessor's policies. Although France was assured of the possession of Alsace and the Three Bishoprics by the Treaty of Westphalia in 1648, the expenses of campaigning were crippling. Civil war broke out, known as 'La Fronde', from which no one—the insurgents, Mazarin, Condé or Marshal Turenne (1611–75)—emerged with much credit. During the Fronde, Condé (who had defeated the Spaniards at Recroi in 1643), allied himself with Spain (who had not subscribed to the Treaty of Westphalia), but Turenne's victory at the Battle of the Dunes (1658) forced Spain to accept the Treaty of the Pyrenees the following year.

On Mazarin's death in 1661 **Louis XIV**, who had succeeded as a minor in 1643, decided to govern alone, duped by the conviction that '*L'État c'est moi*'. The nobility were reduced to being ineffectual courtiers, and the king selected his ministers from the *haute bourgeoisie*, some, such as **Colbert** (1619–83), being very able. He then launched a series of costly wars of self-aggrandisement, which although they eventually increased the territory of France—its frontiers fortified by Vauban (1633–1707)—were to bring his long reign to a disastrous close. At the same time his indulgence in such extravagant projects as the building of a palace fit for the 'Roi Soleil' at **Versailles** (extended by Hardouin-Mansart, with gardens laid out by Le Nôtre and its lavish decoration supervised by Le Brun), where Louis had chosen to transfer his court in 1672, further beggared the country. At Versailles most of the great artists of this and succeeding reigns were gathered, while among composers Lully (from 1652 until his death in 1687), Couperin and (in the following reign) Rameau provided music to entertain the court.

In Paris, which had now grown to a metropolis containing some 500,000 inhabitants and 25,000 houses, boulevards were laid out on the lines of Etienne Marcel's wall. The **Hôtel des Invalides** was founded in 1671. The University quarters were incorporated within the city, which had become one of the cultural centres of Europe—Corneille, Molière, La Fontaine, Boileau and Pascal (the latter associated with the activities of the reforming Jansenists of Port-Royal) making their home there—while the salons of Mme de Rambouillet and Mme de Sablé, among others, had become the influential intellectual rendezvous of such figures as La Rochefoucauld, the Scudérys, and Bossuet. Meanwhile, in 1685, Louis had revoked the Edict of Nantes, which again imposed Catholicism on the whole country.

The king's preoccupation with '*La Gloire*' involved him first in the rapid campaign of 1667–68, which secured the possession of several towns in Flanders; while the Dutch War of 1672–78 ended in the Peace of Nijmegen and the absorption of the Franche-Comté. Less successful were the campaigns against the League of Augsburg (or the Grand Alliance; 1686–97), and of the war of the Spanish Succession (1701–13), in which French forces suffered repeatedly at the hands of Marlborough and Prince Eugène (at Blenheim in 1704; Ramillies in 1706; Oudenaarde in 1708; and Malplaquet in 1709), although Marshal Villars won a victory at Denain (1712) after the withdrawal of the English from the war.

'If greatness of soul consists in a love of pageantry, an ostentation of fastidious pomp, a prodigality of expense, an affectation of munificence, an insolence of ambition, and a haughty reserve of deportment; Lewis certainly deserved the appellation of Great. Qualities which are really heroic, we shall not find in the composition of his character.' Such was Smollett's condemnation. Life at court during the latter part of the reign and subsequent regency (under Philippe, duc d'Orléans; 1715–23) is brilliantly recorded in the '*Mémoires*' of the Duc de Saint-Simon. Several bad harvests (particularly in 1726, 1739 and 1740) decimated the peasantry—who formed four-fifths of the population of 20,000,000 in 1700—but colonial trade improved, and merchants thrived in such provincial centres as Bordeaux, Nantes, and Marseille.

The marriage in 1725 of **Louis XV** to Marie, daughter of Stanislas Leszczynski (the deposed king of Poland) drew France into the War of the Polish Succession (1733) and further ruinous wars followed, including that of the Austrian Succession (1740-48) (in which Louis was allied with Frederick the Great of

Prussia in opposition to England and Holland, who supported the cause of Maria Theresa, Empress of Austria). In spite of Saxe's brilliant victory at Fontenoy (1745) the French gained little, while the English improved their position as a maritime power, and Prussia likewise gained in strength. The Seven Years War (1756–63), in which France was allied to Austria, was disastrous for France, and saw the loss of flourishing colonies in India, North America and the West Indies. By 1788 the cost of these wars had created a situation whereby three-quarters of the State expenditure was being spent on reducing the national debt and on defence.

Nevertheless, grandiose buildings continued to be erected in Paris, such as the **Panthéon** and the **Palais-Bourbon**; but a sixth wall, raised as a customs-barrier by the powerful and rapacious farmers-general of taxes, only fostered further discontent (*'Le mur murant Paris rend Paris murmurant'*). In contrast to the general degradation of his court and the corruption and negligence rife among his administrators, the reign of Louis XV was made illustrious by some of the great names in French literature: Voltaire, Rousseau, Montesquieu, Marivaux, the Encyclopédistes (Diderot, Condillac, Helvetius, d'Alembert, et al), who frequented the fashionable salons of the Marquise de Lambert, Mme de Tencin, Mme du Deffand, Mlle Lespinasse, Mme Geoffrin, or Baron d'Holbach, and others of lesser influence. But many of the philosophers vehemently attacked both the establishment and the clergy, and their ideas undoubtedly helped to sow the seeds of revolution. At the same time the expulsion of the Jesuits in 1764, after years of struggle with the Jansenists, removed one of the pillars of the Ancien Régime.

On his succession **Louis XVI** found the populace critical of his predecessor's extravagance and lack of military success, but was too weak to cope with the interminable financial crises (in spite of the reforms initiated by Turgot from 1774 and of Necker from 1777). 'This man is rather weak but not imbecile, but there is something apathetic about both his body and his mind he has no taste for instruction and no curiosity', wrote the Austrian Emperor Joseph I, after visiting his brother-in-law, while he urged Marie-Antointette to abandon 'the vortex of dissipation around her' and seek 'rational company', prophetically remarking that otherwise 'the revolution will be cruel'. Economic problems were precipitated by bad harvests, particularly in 1787–88, when there were grain riots in many French towns, including Paris and Grenoble. These crises inspired reforms, which, if accepted, would have adversely affected the privileged estates ('Les Privilégiés')—the upper ranks of the clergy (the First Estate), and the majority of the nobility (the Second Estate)—who therefore rejected them. Louis' foreign policy, which supported the American colonies in their struggle for independence from England, was not only financially disastrous, but indirectly did much to disseminate democratic ideals.

In an attempt to reform methods of taxation—for Les Privilégiés held innumerable hereditary rights by which they avoided paying taxes, yet levied them to their own advantage—the king convoked an assembly of the Etats généraux. The 1165 deputies elected met at Versailles on 5 May 1789, for the first time since 1614. The first political act of the Third Estate, the Non-Privilégiés (which numbered almost 600) was the creation of a **National Assembly** (17 June), which, meeting separately in the Jeu de Paume on the 20th, swore not to disband until a constitution had been given to the country which would limit royal autocracy and guarantee liberty, equality and fraternity. Three days later Mirabeau defied the king: '*Nous sommes ici par la volonté du peuple etêon ne nous arrachera que par la force des baïonnettes*'; and on 9 July, reinforced by many of the clergy and a minority of the nobility, the renamed Assemblée constituante set to work to frame such a constitution. But two days later Necker, who had promised further financial reforms, was dismissed by the king, and it was feared that this gratuitous act would be followed by the dissolution of the Assembly.

The Revolution

The citizens of Paris—and also in the provinces at Dijon, Rennes, Lyon, Nantes, and Le Havre—were provoked into a more open rebellion, culminating in the storming of the Bastille on 14 July; but while the next few months saw numerous reforms, there was little political or economic stability, and tensions heightened. In an attempt to avoid bankruptcy, church lands were nationalised, which produced some opposition. Many of the nobility—a class shortly, but temporarily, to be abolished—sought asylum abroad. The king and his unpopular consort, **Marie-Antoinette,** were virtually prisoners in the Tuileries; they attempted to flee the country but were arrested (at Varennes in June 1791) and brought back to Paris. On 1 October 1791 a new Legislative Assembly was formed, which in the following April declared war on Austria to forestall foreign intervention. The Assembly was at first led by the moderate Girondins, but the following year the extreme Jacobins under Danton, Robespierre and Marat, seized power and, as the National Convention, meeting on 20 September (the day on which the victory of Valmy turned the tide of war in France's favour), established the Republic.

On 21 January 1793 Louis XVI was executed in the Place de la Révolution, an act followed by the setting-up in March of the dictatorial Committee of Public Safety, which, suspicious of the moderate party, ruthlessly suppressed all those suspected of royalist sympathies. The guillotine was in constant action. In July Marat was assassinated, and even the Dantonists found themselves to be a moderating force, opposed to the even more bloodthirsty Hébertists. But **Robespierre** (1758–94), chief architect of the Reign of Terror, brooked no rivals, and early in 1794 both Hébert and Danton were guillotined. However, after further weeks of ferocious intimidation, the reaction came and on 27 July (9 Thermidor; see below), Robespierre's own head fell.

By 1795 the Girondins were again in control, although the Royalists continued to make determined efforts to change the course of events, particularly in the Vendée, where they were eventually suppressed by Hoche. On 28 October 1795 a Directory of five members assumed power. One of the five was Barras, to whom the young Corsican general, **Napoléon Bonaparte** (1769–1821), owed his promotion as general of the Interior. During the next four years French republican armies under Bonaparte won notable successes abroad, especially in campaigns against the Austrians (whom he was to crush at Marengo on 14 June, 1800). Returning to Paris after his failure to destroy the British fleet at the Battle of the Nile, Bonaparte found the tyrannical Directory generally detested, and with the help of the army and of Siéyès, established the Consulate by a coup d'état on 9–10 November 1799. Bonaparte became First Consul, assisted by Siéyès and Roger Ducos. A new constitution awarded him the consulate for life but such was his personal ambition that he declared himself 'Emperor of the French', and was crowned Napoléon I (1804–15) in Notre-Dame by Pope Pius VII (18 May 1804). A Civil Code, largely retaining the liberal laws of the Revolution, was laid down. Paris was embellished with monuments and bridges, as befitted the capital of an expanding empire, and was further enriched by the spoils of conquest.

First Empire

Faced by a new coalition of Britain, Austria, and Russia, Napoléon shattered the last two at Austerlitz in 1805, and imposed on them the humiliating Peace of Pressburg, but his fleet had been virtually destroyed at Trafalgar only six weeks earlier. In the following year Prussian armies were cowed at Jena and Auerstadt, and a further campaign against Russia was ended by the Treaty of Tilsit, which brought temporary peace to the Czar. Austria attempted to renew the struggle, but suffered disastrous defeats at Essling and Wagram. The subsequent Peace of Vienna (1809) marked perhaps the apogee of the emperor's power.

Meanwhile, his brother Joseph had been imposed on the Spaniards, whose guerrilla methods of carrying on the war in the Peninsula caused a continual drain on Napoléon's reserves of power. Britain sent out two expeditionary forces to assist the incapable Spaniards, and under Wellington they inflicted a series of defeats on the French, among them Salamanca, and culminating in the battles of Vitoria (1813) and—on French territory—Toulouse.

Napoléon himself had just returned from the disastrous invasion of Russia, where the 'Grande Armée' although successful at Borodino, was virtually anni-hilated by the winter. The Prussians, recovered from their previous defeats, were able to retaliate at Leipzig (October 1813), and with the Russians and Austrians entered France. Paris itself surrendered to the Allies (31 March 1814) after skir-mishing on the heights of Montmartre. The emperor abdicated at Fontainebleau, and retired to the island of Elba.

The Monarchy restored

The **Bourbons** were restored, but the Treaty of Paris (30 May 1814) restored the frontiers of 1789. During 'the Hundred Days' (26 March–24 June 1815), Napoléon made a desperate attempt to regain absolute power, having claimed at Grenoble (en route to Paris from Elba) that he had come to deliver France from 'the insolence of the nobility, the pretensions of the priests and the yoke of for-eign powers'. His defeat at Waterloo (18 June) and subsequent banishment to St Helena, where he died in 1821, enabled the king—**Louis XVIII**—to resume his precarious throne, which he was only able to retain by repressive measures: the University was supervised by the clergy. The reign of his successor, **Charles X** (1824–30), under whom were passed the reactionary Ordinances of St-Cloud, suppressing the liberty of the press and reducing the electorate to the landed classes, only proved that the Bourbons could 'learn nothing and forget nothing'. The '**July Revolution**' of 1830 lost him his throne.

House of Orléans. Louis-Philippe (1830–48; son of Philippe-Egalité d'Orléans of the Revolution) was chosen as head of the 'July Monarchy', and the upper-middle class, who had striven for power since 1789, now achieved it. Most of the urban populace, however, still lived in pestilential conditions: some 19,000 Parisians of a total of about 900,000 died in an outbreak of cholera in 1832. The total population of France was then about 32,500,000. The only other towns of any size were Lyon and Marseille, with about 115,000 each, and Bordeaux and Rouen with about 90,000 each. France was still essentially a country dominated by agriculture and by a rural population.

The king devoted himself, with perhaps more energy than taste, to the further embellishment of the capital, and many pretentious buildings date from this period. Gas lighting had first been installed there in 1814. In 1840 the body of

Napoléon was transferred with much pomp to its last resting-place under the Dôme des Invalides. The city was surrounded by a ring of fortifications in 1841–45, but these could not defend the 'citizen-king' against his people. Socialist ideas were spreading, but the conservative policy of Guizot opposed any reforms, and in the '**February Revolution**' of 1848 Louis-Philippe was overthrown. In June 1848, during the brief military dictatorship of Général Cavaignac, some 4000 workmen were killed, another 1500 shot, and 11,000 imprisoned or deported to Algeria. In the elections which followed, which introduced universal male suffrage, the electorate leapt from 250,000 to 9,000,000. Among famous literary figures during the first half of the century were Balzac, Chateaubriand, Hugo, George Sand, Stendhal, Flaubert, Gautier, and Sainte-Beuve.

The Second Republic

A Second Republic was set up by the provisional government, and **Louis Napoléon** (Bonaparte's shrewd and cynical nephew, who as pretender had already made two abortive attempts to regain the throne), was elected Prince-President by almost 75 per cent of those who voted; but such was the sentimental prevalence of the idea of Empire, that in December 1851 a coup d'état (involving the temporary imprisonment of some 30,000 in opposition) led to his election as the Emperor Napoléon III (1852–70) some months later, thus inaugurating the Second Empire.

Having adopted the clever but misleading motto of '*L'Empire c'est la paix*', he proceeded to embroil the country in a succession of wars, firstly in the Crimea (1854–56), and then in Italy, which he undertook to deliver from Austrian oppression, afterwards receiving Savoy and Nice in recompense. But he stopped Garibaldi and his followers capturing Rome. Meanwhile he continued the expedient policy of his predecessor, by clearing the mass of congested, evil-smelling, and tortuous lanes of old Paris, which had so favoured the erection of barricades in 1830 and 1848 and the spread of cholera. In their place Baron Haussmann laid out a number of broad boulevards which are still characteristic of much of the centre, while from 1861 Garnier's Opera-house, representative of the expansive taste of the time, was being built, and the Bois de Boulogne and the Bois de Vincennes were transformed into public parks.

But these peaceful projects were halted abruptly in 1870 when Napoléon III declared war on Prussia. The inglorious campaign ended with the capitulation of Sedan, where the emperor was taken prisoner and deposed. He died in exile at Chislehurst (England) in 1873.

Third Republic

Léon Gambetta and **Adolphe Thiers** were largely instrumental in forming the Third Republic, which had been proclaimed (4 September 1870) while German troops advanced on Paris, which was laid siege to on 19 September, its defenders commanded by Trochu. After a four-month siege and much suffering and famine, Paris capitulated on 28 January 1871. At this time the fortified enceinte of Paris almost 34km long, and had 67 entrances or gates. A circle of 17 detached fortresses were built at strategic points beyond this boundary wall. The Louvre had been turned into an armament workshop, the Gare d'Orléans (now Austerlitz) into a balloon factory, and the Gare de Lyon into a cannon-foundry;

but the army was ill-prepared. Order was not re-established until the Communard Insurrection (18 March–29 May) had been crushed at the cost of pitched battles in the streets, in which 3000–4000 Communards were killed, and the destruction of parts of the Tuileries and other public buildings such as the Hôtel de Ville. Retaliatory measures included the summary execution of 20,000–25,000 Parisians, including women, mostly of the working classes; and the deportation of a further 4000–5000. Thiers, who was ultimately responsible for these mass killings, was then declared Président. An amnesty bill, introduced by Gambetta, was not adopted until 1880.

By September 1873 the last occupying troops had gone, but France was left to pay a heavy war indemnity and lost the provinces of Alsace and Lorraine. Various political crises, embittered by the reprehensible 'Dreyfus affair' (1894–1906), in which Alfred Dreyfus was falsely accused of betraying France to a foreign government, coloured much of the period up to the outbreak of the First World War. An 'Entente Cordiale' between Britain and France was established in 1904, putting an end to colonial rivalry and paving the way to future co-operation. In 1903 the '*Loi sur les Associations*' was passed, and in 1905 the Church was separated from the State, both essential measures to counteract the powerful influence the ecclesiastics and religious orders still had on education. During these decades building continued apace and the economy continued to grow. The '**Grand Palais**' and '**Petit Palais**', a new **Hôtel de Ville**, the **Gare d'Orsay**, the **Eiffel Tower** and the basilica of **Sacré-Coeur** exemplify the taste of an age, differing facets of which were well described by Zola and later by Proust. In 1910 extensive areas of Paris were inundated by the flooding of the Seine.

Two World Wars

War with Germany broke out on 3 August 1914. French troops were dramatically reinforced at the Marne by some 11,000 men rushed to the front in Parisian taxis: citizens had the satisfaction of hearing the din of battle gradually recede and little damage was done to the capital by air raids or long-range bombardment. But although Paris was saved from another occupation, ten departments were overrun, and the attrition of four long years of trench warfare followed with the Battle of the Somme, culminating in the terrible bloodbath of Verdun in 1916. On 11 November 1918 an armistice was signed. The provinces lost to France through the Treaty of Versailles in 1871 were restored, although **Clemenceau**, the 'Tiger', France's Prime Minister, wanted more. Nothing, however, could compensate for the staggering loss of life during the war years. For every ten Frenchmen aged between 20 and 45, two had been killed—a total of over 1,300,000. Slowly, and only partially, the country recovered her strength, even if politically she showed little initiative. In Paris, Thiers' fortifications were demolished in 1919–24, affording an opportunity to lay out a new ring of boulevards. A number of new buildings were erected for the Exhibition of 1937, including the **Musées d'Art Moderne** and the **Palais de Chaillot**. Meanwhile France's passive defensive policies were concretely expressed in the construction of a costly and supposedly impregnable barrier along the German frontier—the Maginot Line (named after a minister of war)—which, after the outbreak of the Second World War (September 1939), was side-stepped by invading armoured divisions in May 1940.

Demoralised French forces, in no state to resist and not capable of mounting a successful counter-attack, capitulated to the triumphant Reich, while a high proportion of the British army was able to re-cross the Channel from Dunkerque (27 May–4 June 1940) in a fleet of open boats sent to their rescue. The Germans proceeded to occupy the northern half of the country and the Atlantic coast, over-running the rest of France after 11 November 1942. For the rest of the war, the slowly growing underground Resistance Movement did what it could to thwart the collaborating policies of the 'Vichy Government' (1940–44) presided over by the octogenarian Marshal Pétain, hero of Verdun, and Pierre Laval, among others.

Meanwhile, a provisional government had been set up in London by **Géneral Charles de Gaulle** (1890–1970), and Free French forces co-operated in the liberation of France. Allied troops disembarking in Normandy and in the south of France (6 June and 15 August 1944 respectively) converged on Paris, which was free by late August. France was able to participate in the victory celebrations of May 1945 and even occupy a small 'zone' of Germany as one of the victorious Four Powers.

Fourth Republic

In October 1946 the Fourth Republic was proclaimed, of which Vincent Auriol (1947–54) and René Coty (1954–58) were presidents. Women now had the vote and proportional representation was adopted. Slowly, despite many changes in government and despite defeat in Indo-China and revolt in Algeria, the country was restored to economic prosperity after the physical and moral devastation of war. In 1957 a Common Market (EEC) was established, in which France, West Germany, Italy and the Benelux countries were founder members.

Fifth Republic

In 1958 de Gaulle prepared a new constitution, which was approved by a referendum, and the general was elected the first president of the new republic by universal direct suffrage, for a period of seven years. The powers of the head of state were considerably—some would say inordinately—increased: he nominates the prime minister, who in turn recommends the members of the government; he can make laws and refer decisions of major importance to popular vote by referendum; in extreme cases he has the power to dismiss the National Assembly.

In 1962 Algerian independence was proclaimed; reversing earlier immigrations, a remarkable number of Algerians can now be seen in the towns of France. In 1965 de Gaulle was returned to power with enthusiasm but with a reduced majority. In May 1968 a serious 'Student Revolution' took place in Paris, which precipitated overdue educational reforms. The following year de Gaulle resigned and was succeeded by Pompidou, who died in office in 1974. His successor was Giscard d'Estaing whose somewhat cavalier attitude to the mass of his country-men produced a reaction, and a swing to the Left, with Mitterrand moving into the Elysée. But, Mitterrand immediately alienated many of his supporters by the inclusion of Communist ministers in the government, a devious manoeuvre which in turn provoked reaction, and launched an ill-timed programme of nationalisation. In spite of instituting changes in the electoral system in an attempt to retain Socialist control, they lost the election of March 1986, when Jacques Chirac, who had been the right-wing *maire* of Paris since 1977 (when the title was changed from that of Préfet de la Seine) became Prime Minister, inaugurating what was called a period of 'cohabitation' with the Socialist President. Mitterand in 1988 was re-elected, and the Socialist party returned to power in the National Assemby.

In 1989, the bicentenary of the Revolution was celebrated by the inauguration of a prestigious opera house at the Place de la Bastille. In 1995 Jacques Chirac won the presidential election, beating the Socialist Lionel Jospin (Mitterand, dying of cancer, stood down) but his new right-wing government found itself faced by acute economic and social problems. Partly because of the attempt to meet the financial guidelines for the projected European Monetary Union, unemployment rose to levels not seen since before the Second World War. This, coupled with increasing racial tensions, gave the National Front, the ne-fascist party led by Jean-Marie Le Pen, an opportunity to increase its vote. The Fifth Republic approaches its 40th birthday amid seemingly unsolvable crises.

THE GUIDE

Ile de la Cité and Ile St-Louis

1 • The Ile de la Cité

> ■ Arrondissements: 75001, 75004
> ⊜ Cité, Pont-Neuf-La Monnaie
> ⬢ St-Michel-Notre-Dame, Châtelet-Les Halles

There are several restaurants and bars in the western part of the island including:

Le Bar du Caveau, 17 Place Dauphine, ☎ 01 43 54 45 95, ££

Chez Paul, 15 Place Dauphine, ☎ 01 43 54 21 48. A long-established, traditional favourite with sympathetic surroundings, £

Taverne Henri IV, 13 Place du Pont Neuf, ☎ 01 43 54 27 90, which specialises in cheeses, £

Nearer to Notre-Dame are:

La Colombe, 4 Rue de la Colombe, ☎ 01 46 33 37 08. Touristy but attractive, with terrace, £

Le Vieux Bistrot, 14 Rue Cloître Notre-Dame, ☎ 01 43 54 18 95. Good quality cooking despite the touristy address and faded décor, £–££

The Ile de la Cité (**Map 8; 3–4 and p 80**), the earliest inhabited part, lies in the river like a ship—the *pointe* its prow and Notre-Dame its poop—moored to both banks by numerous bridges. The freighted vessel on a sea argent has figured in the arms of Paris since the '*sceau des marchands de l'eau*' (the seal of the water merchants) became the seal of the first municipal administration at the time of St Louis in the 13C, with its device '*fluctuat nec mergitur*' (tossed but not engulfed). In its stylised form as the logo of the Mairie de Paris it is found all over the city.

Some of the most important monuments of Paris are concentrated in this small area at the heart of Paris: the Cathedral of Notre-Dame, sparkling after a recent restoration; the Conciergerie, a former royal palace that became a prison for royalty during the Revolution where hundreds were imprisoned and died; and the Sainte-Chapelle, best known for its wonderful 13C stained glass. Traces of the Roman past of Paris are found beneath the forecourt of Notre-Dame and there are also the delights of the flower market (see p 85) on the north, the quiet charm of Place Dauphine to the west and the gardens of Square Jean XXIII behind the cathedral, beyond which is the touching memorial to martyrs of the deportation.

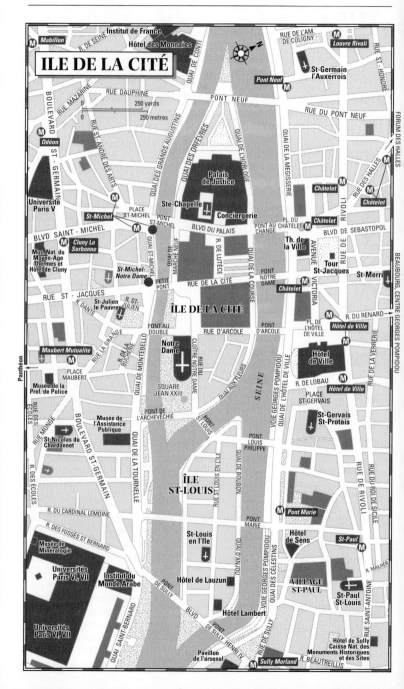

ILE DE LA CITÉ

*Cathédrale Notre-Dame,
Ile de la Cité*

The Conciergerie and the Sainte-Chapelle are described in Chapter 1 while the Cathedral of Notre-Dame is covered in Chapter 2.

History of the Ile de la Cité

The Cité was the site of the original Gallic settlement of *Lutèce* or *Lutetia Parisiorum*, the capital of the Parisii settled c 52 BC by the Romans. After the destruction of the later Roman city on the Left Bank, the island became the site of Frankish Paris and remained the royal, legal and ecclesiastical centre, with fourteen parishes in the Middle Ages, long after the town had extended onto both river-banks. Despite the incursions of the 19C, its historic importance is still evident as an ecclesiastical, judicial and legal headquarters.

The Cité derives its importance from its situation at the crossroads of two natural routes across northern France. The Capetian kings were the great builders of the Cité, and it remained little changed from 1300 to the Second Empire (mid 1850s), when Baron Haussmann, after massive demolition of the medieval quarters, left it more or less with its present appearance.

From the Quai du Louvre the picturesque **Pont Neuf** crosses the western extremity of the island. Despite its name, it is the oldest existing bridge in Paris, begun by Baptiste du Cerceau, completed in 1607, and repaired several times since. It was also the first to be built with pavements, but without houses lining each side. The Pointe de la Cité is occupied by the Sq. du Vert-Galant, whose name alludes to the amorous adventures of Henri IV. Steps lead down behind the statue of the gallant King (Lemot, 1818), to a small shaded garden from where you have fine panoramas of the mainland buildings. The *Vedettes du Pont Neuf* (sightseeing boats) depart from here.

East of the Pont-Neuf, entered by Rue Henri-Robert, is **Pl. Dauphine**, retaining two rows of houses, some dating from the reign of Louis XIII, but many altered since then. This little square contains one or two restaurants.

Other bridges connecting the Cité to the Right Bank of the Seine are **Pont au Change** (1860), which acquired its name in the 12C when goldsmiths and moneylenders set up shop on the medieval bridge, the present one replacing a 17C stone bridge lined with buildings; **Pont Notre-Dame**, rebuilt in 1913 on the site of the main Roman bridge; and beyond, **Pont d'Arcole** (1855), named after a youth killed in 1830 leading insurgents against the Hôtel de Ville.

To the south, the island is connected to the Left Bank by **Pont St-Michel**, rebuilt several times since the late 14C (most recently in 1857), giving a fine view of the façade of Notre-Dame. Beyond is the **Petit Pont** (1853), on the site of another Roman bridge. Until 1782 it was defended at the southern end by the Petit Châtelet, the successor of the Tour de Bois that in 886 held Viking or Norman marauders at bay. From the west front of Notre-Dame, the **Pont au Double** (1882) replaced a mid-17C bridge where the toll of a diminutive coin known as a *double* was charged; while from the eastern extremity of the Cité, **Pont de l'Archevêché** (1828) (named after the archbishop's palace pulled down in 1831), allows a good view of the apse of Notre-Dame, with its profusion of flying buttresses.

Conciergerie

Follow the Quai de l'Horloge on the north bank of the island, to just beyond the twin towers, to the entrance of the Conciergerie, which occupies part of the lower floor of the Palais de la Cité. This was a royal palace before the building became known as one of the world's most infamous prisons.

• Open 1 Apr–30 Sept 09.30–18.30, 1 Oct–31 March 10.00–17.00, closed 1/1, 1/5, 1/11, 11/11, 25/12, ☎ 01 53 73 78 50.

History of the Conciergerie

At the centre of Lutèce and then Paris, Roman governors and the first French kings had their palaces on this site until the second half of the 14C. The three distinctive round towers facing the river are vestiges of the royal palace built by Philippe le Bel (1285–1314). After the old palace was abandoned in favour of the Louvre and Vincennes it became the seat of power for the Parlement, a judicial body, and residence of the Concièrge, a high-ranking officer of the Crown with powers of justice. Over time the name became associated with the place of imprisonment of those judged and its former role of royal palace was forgotten. Its infamy grew during the Revolution when a succession of the celebrities of the day, some 2780 people, both Royalist and Jacobin, passed their last hours in the Conciergerie. Included among them were Marie-Antoinette, Mme du Barry, Camille Desmoulins, Charlotte Corday, Danton, André Chénier, the poet, and Robespierre. From 1793, the Revolutionary Tribunal was installed in the Great Chamber marking the reign of the Terror.

The visit starts with part of the medieval palace (restored recently). The **Salle des Gardes** is a handsome vaulted room, c 1310, divided down the middle by three pillars. The impressive four-aisled Gothic **Salle des Gens-d'Armes**, constructed 1302–13 by Enguerrand de Marigny, served as a refectory for some 2000 members of the royal household and contains a portion of the black marble table once used here. Near the far end, to the left, is the lower part of the vaulted kitchens with four huge fireplaces built in the 14C during the reign of Jean le Bon (1350–64). The four western bays of the hall are known as the Rue de Paris, an area reserved for the *pailleux* (prisoners who slept on straw, being too poor to pay for their term in jail). This leads to the first part of the **Revolutionary Prison**, dating from 1780 (restored 1989) and the **Galerie des Prisonniers**, off which are small spaces reserved for the Clerk, who took the prisoners' names, the Concierge's office, and the room where prisoners were prepared for execution. The chapel where the Girondins were incarcerated was a small royal chapel that had been restored in 1776, and Marie-Antoinette's Chapel was the Queen's cell, turned back into a chapel at the Restoration. The **Cour des Femmes**, where the female prisoners took exercise, has a fountain and stone tables. A poignant reminder of the tragic past of the Conciergerie is the re-creation of **Marie Antoinette's cell**, the last room on this level. Upstairs, there are rooms with memorabilia from the prison and the blade of a guillotine, as well as reconstructions of cells. Here you can watch a short video film with English subtitles.

On leaving the Conciergerie, turn right into Blvd du Palais passing beneath the Tour de l'Horloge (see below). Unlikely as it may now seem, the Cour du Mai, on the right, was named after the maypole set up here annually by the society of law clerks.

The **Palais de Justice**, a huge block occupying the whole width of the island, is a great but inglorious result of 19C rebuilding, the main architects of which were Louis Duc and P.-J.-H. Daumet. The Conciergerie and the Sainte-Chapelle (see below) are the oldest surviving parts and are both embraced within its precincts.

History of the Palais de Justice

The site was occupied as early as the Roman period by a palace in which Julian the Apostate was proclaimed emperor in 360; the Merovingian kings, when in town, divided their time between the Thermes (see p 101) and this Palais de la Cité within the city walls. Louis VI died in the palace in 1137 and Louis VII in 1180. St Louis (Louis IX) altered the palace and built the Sainte-Chapelle. From 1431 it was occupied entirely by the Parlement, which had previously only shared it with the king, but it was at the Revolution that it acquired its present function.

Here, in the 16th Chambre Correctionelle, the trials of Flaubert's *Madame Bovary* and Baudelaire's *Les Fleurs du Mal* (29 January and 20 August 1857 respectively) took place.

The 18C buildings were greatly enlarged in 1857–68 and again in 1911–14. In the mid-19C, the 14C tower at the northeastern corner, with a clock copied from the original dial designed c 1585 by Germain Pilon, was virtually rebuilt. Splendid to look at, this replaced the first public clock in Paris. Likewise, the upper part of the north façade was rebuilt in the 19C in an attempt to reproduce the original 14C work by Enguerrand de Marigny. The domed Galerie Marchande, dominating the Cour du Mai, is embellished with sculptures by Pajou.

The most interesting part of these law courts may be entered directly from the boulevard just north of the Cour du Mai, by stairs up to the **Salle de Pas-Perdus**. This magnificent hall, which replaced the great hall of the medieval palace (where in 1431 the coronation banquet of Henry VI of England was celebrated), was rebuilt in 1622 by Salomon de Brosse and restored in 1878 after being burned by the Communards. At the far end of the room, divided in two by a row of arches, and to the right, is the entrance to the Première Chambre Civile, formerly the Grand Chambre or Chambre Dorée (restored in the style of Louis XII), a vestige of the old palace and perhaps originally the bedroom of Louis IX. Later it was used by the Parlement, in contempt of which Louis XIV here coined his famous epigram '*L'Etat, c'est moi*'.

Sainte-Chapelle

The Sainte-Chapelle, entered from Blvd du Palais, was built by the saintly Louis IX and dedicated in 1248. A remarkable building, it is best known for its stained glass and its exceptional lightness and delicacy.

• Open 1 Apr–30 Sept 09.30–18.30, 1 Oct–31 March 10.00–17.00, closed 1/1, 1/5, 1/11, 11/11, 25/12, ☎ 01 53 73 78 50.

History of Sainte-Chapelle

The Sainte-Chapelle was planned both as a royal chapel and as a resting place for precious and costly relics acquired from Baudouin II, the Emperor of Constantinople, among them the Crown of Thorns and fragments of the True Cross. The importance attributed to these relics is reflected in the sumptuousness of the original building, whose design has been ascribed to Pierre de Montreuil, who also worked at St-Denis and St-Germain-en-Laye. The west window was replaced in 1485 by a Flamboyant rose. Damaged by fire in 1630, the chapel was slowly rebuilt only to be put under risk of demolition at the end of the 18C as the Revolution left it in a perilous state. Thankfully, enthusiasm for all things medieval, engendered by the Romantic movement in the 19C, resulted in the saving by Lenoir of most of the statues and a full-scale restoration between 1837 and 1857 by Duban, Lassus (who reconstructed a leaden flèche in the 15C style, the fifth on this site), Viollet-le-Duc (chief architect of the Monuments Historiques created in 1830 to safeguard the national heritage) and his successor Boeswillwald.

From the outside, the impression of great height, actually 42.50m, in proportion to its length (36m) and breadth (17m) is accentuated by the buildings that crowd in around it. The chapel in fact consists of two superimposed levels: the smaller lower one, dedicated to the Virgin Mary, was for the use of servants and retainers; the upper chapel, originally linked directly to the palace, with its lofty windows and rich stained glass, was reserved for the royal family and court. The portal consists of two porches, one above the other; the statues are 19C restorations. The balustrade is decorated with a motif of *fleurs de lys* and carved on the pinnacle above the south tower is a Crown of Thorns.

The interior of the **Chapelle Basse**, with carved oak bosses and 40 columns supporting the upper chapel is darkened by the decoration of Emile

Boeswillwald, who attempted to reproduce its medieval décor painted with the *fleurs de lys* of France and the towers of Castille. The glass is 19C and three-lobed arcades and medallions enhance the walls. There are several 14C–15C tombstones in the pavement.

A narrow spiral staircase leads to the **Chapelle Haute** (20.50m high); royalty had an entrance direct from the palace. In contrast to the gloominess of the lower chapel, the upper chapel is a revelation, appropriate as the shrine of the precious holy relics. A virtuoso achievement of the Middle Ages, the structure is reduced to clumps of tracery and supports, between walls of richly coloured glass. Linking the blind traceried arcades of the lower part and the soaring windows are statues of Apostles under baldaquins—the 4th and 5th on the left and the 4th and 5th to the right are 13C. The upper chapel, originally inlaid with gilt and glass to give the effect of enamels emphasised the relationship to a shrine or reliquary. Ideally, to take full advantage of the stained glass, the Sainte-Chapelle needs to be seen in bright daylight. The two deep recesses under the windows of the 3rd bay were the seats reserved for the royal family. On the south side is a small chapel built at the time of Louis XI to enable the monarch to participate in mass without being seen.

In the centre of the restored arcade across the apse is a wooden canopy beneath which the relics used to be exhibited on Good Friday; those few surviving the Revolution are in the treasury of Notre-Dame.

The **stained glass** was skilfully restored in 1845 and, although some glass has been lost, a large proportion dates from the 13C. The glass reads from left to right and from bottom to top, and binoculars are a great help. Of the three east windows, on the left are scenes from the life of *St John the Evangelist* and the *Childhood of Christ*; the central one, considered the most outstanding, dwells on *Christ's Passion*; and on the right are the stories of *St John the Baptist* and of *Daniel*. All the other windows, except one, deal with the Old Testament, reading from northwest: *Genesis*, *Exodus*, *Numbers*, *Deuteronomy* and *Joshua*, *Judges*, *Isaiah* and the *Rod of Jesse*. Then the three apse windows are followed by *Ezekiel* —92 of the 121 scenes are original—*Jeremiah* and *Tobit*, *Judith* and *Job*, *Esther*, and the *Book of Kings*. The southwest window depicts the *Legend of the True Cross* with illustrations of the translation of the relics to Paris by St Louis. However, this is one of the least well preserved and contains only 26 of the original 67 scenes. The 86 panels from the *Apocalypse* in the large rose-window, which are the easiest to read, were a gift of Charles VIII.

You leave the Chapelle Haute by the second spiral stair.

Opposite the Cour du Mai, Rue de Lutèce leads between (right) the Préfecture de Police and (left) the domed Tribunal de Commerce (by Bailly; 1860–65), behind which the **Marché aux Fleurs** offers a colourful and sweetly scented contrast. A bird market is held here on Sundays.

The Quai des Orfèvres on the south side of the island owes its name to the goldsmiths who were established here between 1580 and 1643. Much later, as the site of the headquarters of the detective branch of the French police, the quartier became famous through Maigret, Georges Simenon's detective hero.

2 • Notre-Dame

> Cité

On the eastern side of Rue de la Cité is **Pl. du Parvis Notre-Dame**, a space which Baron Haussmann increased sixfold by his demolitions. Here you are face-to-face with the oldest of Paris's emblems, the Cathedral of Notre-Dame, the ribcage of the Cité and of Paris, with all its associations from pre-Christian times, royal marriages, Quasimodo, and presidential funerals. The Parvis or forecourt is at the very heart of Paris and road distances are calculated from a symbolic centre marked by a bronze flagstone engraved with the arms of the town and the four points of the compass. Traced on its paving is the outline of part of the earlier cathedral of St-Etienne (Stephen).

On the left is the Hôtel Dieu, the hospital for central Paris, rebuilt in 1868–78 to the north of the site where the first hospital was founded by St Landry, Bishop of Paris, c 660. The old Hôtel Dieu, built at the same time as Notre-Dame (12C), was razed by Haussmann. In the past, ecclesiastical authorities brought condemned heretics to trial on the Parvis where they knelt to acknowledge their sin and beg absolution before execution.

Near the west end of the Parvis is the entrance to the **Crypte Archéologique**. Superimposed layers of architectural remains of all periods of the Cité's past were uncovered here in 1965 during excavation work for the adjacent underground car-park. The site is well presented with dioramas and models explaining the growth of the district prior to the ravaging fire of 1772. Sections are illuminated by press-button lighting and explanatory notes are printed both in French and English.

• Open 1 Apr–30 Sept 10.00–18.00, 1 Oct–31 March 10.00–17.00, closed 1/1, 1/5, 1/11, 11/11, 25/12, ☎ 01 43 29 83 51.

The path runs above the foundations of the late-3C Gallo-Roman rampart, more of which is seen later. Further to the east, beyond the excavated area, lie the foundations of the west end of the Merovingian cathedral of St-Etienne (6C). After passing display cases of artefacts from the dig, you follow the foundations of the demolished Hospice des Enfants-Trouvés and other medieval buildings which flanked Rue Neuve Notre-Dame—some on the right as you approach the exit date from as early as the 2C. On the left are vestiges of hypocausts, etc.

Cathédrale de Notre-Dame

To the east of the Parvis or forecourt rises Notre-Dame **(Map 8; 4)**, an immensely important building in the history of the development of Gothic architecture. Begun in 1163, it developed the new style initiated at St-Denis, which became known as Gothic. The west front, with its magnificent rose window, was completed in the 13C. Notre-Dame was in its turn a major influence on church architecture in the Ile-de-France and all over Europe. Despite successive alterations, this building represents a text-book example of the evolution of the Gothic style from the 12C to the 14C.

• Open 08.00–18.45, closed Sat 12.30–14.00, ☎ 01 42 34 56 10.

History of Notre-Dame

Bishop Maurice de Sully, who died in 1196, was the inspiration behind the move to replace two earlier churches, St-Etienne and Notre-Dame, by a single building on a much larger scale. St-Etienne, founded by Childebert in 528 (see above), replaced a Roman temple of Jupiter more or less on the site of the present cathedral. Tradition holds that the foundation stone of the new cathedral was laid by Pope Alexander III in 1163. Between that date and the consecration of the main altar on 19 May 1182 the choir and double ambulatory were finished except for the high vault. The second phase of work, which completed the transepts and most of the nave, extended from c 1178–1200. From 1190–1220 the west front was built up to the rose window and during this period the second nave aisle was being erected. The rose itself dates from 1220–25 and the towers from 1225–50.

However, modifications were already being made c 1225 to the earlier sections, notably the enlargement of the clerestory windows all around the church. In 1235–50 a series of chapels was built between the nave buttresses. Around 1250 the north transept was extended and the porch built by Jean de Chelles who also began c 1258 the extension of the south transept which was completed by Pierre de Montreuil. Pierre de Chelles built the *jubé* (rood screen) at the beginning of the 14C and he, followed by Jean Ravy, was responsible for the chapels around the apse (1296–1330). The latter *maître d'oeuvre* began the flying buttresses, which took the strain of the high vaults and whose dramatic proportions provoke comparisons with the rigging of a ship. Jean Ravy's successors, Jean le Bouteiller and Raymond du Temple, completed work on the great vessel by the second half of the 14C.

For some three centuries the fabric of the cathedral remained relatively untouched and provided the setting for many important events. The School of Music at Notre-Dame was influential during the late 12C and 13C. In 1186 Geoffrey Plantagenet (the son of Henry II) was buried here after his sudden death in Paris. Henry VI of England at the age of 10 was crowned king of France here in 1431. Many royal marriages were celebrated within its walls, including those of James V of Scotland to Madeleine of France in 1537, François II to Mary Stuart (1558), Henri of Navarre, the future Henri IV, to Marguerite de Valois (1572) and Charles I of England (by proxy) to Henrietta Maria (1625).

Changes in taste and emphasis during the reigns of Louis XIV and Louis XV brought about major alterations. Tombs and stained-glass were destroyed, the *jubé* and the stalls were condemned, and in 1771 Soufflot desecrated the trumeau and part of the tympanum of the central portal to allow a processional dais to pass through. Much of what survived this destruction was lost during the Revolution. But the cathedral was still used for great ceremonies: in 1804, Napoléon I was crowned Emperor by Pius VII and in 1853 Napoléon III and Eugénie de Montijo were married here.

By 1844, due in great part to Victor Hugo's Romantic novel *Notre-Dame de Paris* (1831), or *The Hunchback of Notre-Dame*, which helped to engender an interest in Gothic architecture, Notre-Dame was thought worth a thorough restoration. This was begun under the direction of Lassus and Viollet-le-Duc.

A century later, on 26 August 1944, the thanksgiving service following

Général de Gaulle's entry into liberated Paris took place at Notre-Dame. The cathedral continues to be the scene of occasional ceremonial functions, state funerals, etc, the latest of which was the state's adieu to François Mitterand, in January 1996. The first stage of a long renovation of the building was completed to coincide with the start of the 21C when the wraps covering the west façade were taken down to reveal the startlingly bright, clean elevation.

Exterior

The **west front**, composed of three distinct storeys, is a model of clarity and harmony. A masterful design of verticals and horizontals divides the elevation into regular and complementary sections, its construction continued through the entire first half of the 13C. The central **Porte du Jugement**, c 1220, is medieval only in essence. The figure of Christ on the trumeau dates from 1885, the *Last Judgement* was restored by Viollet-le-Duc, and most of the other sculptures are also 19C.

The **Porte de la Vierge** on the left, slightly earlier, is a fine composition. The Virgin on the central pier is a restoration, and the statues of saints were remade by Viollet-le-Duc. However, the scenes relating to the *Life of the Virgin* in the tympanum are 13C: in the lower register, the *Ancestors of the Virgin*, in the middle, the *Resurrection of the Virgin*, and in the upper register, her *Coronation*.

The sculptures of the **Porte de St Anne** (right) are mostly of 1165–75, designed for a narrower portal, with additions of c 1240. On the pier is *St Marcellus* (19C); above are scenes from the life of *St Anne and the Virgin*, and the *Virgin in Majesty*, with Louis VII (right) and Maurice de Sully (left). The two side doors retain their medieval wrought-iron hinges.

In the buttress niches flanking the doors are modern statues of St Stephen, the Church, the Synagogue and St Denis. Above, across the full width of the façade, is the *Gallery of the Kings of Judah*, reconstructed by Viollet-le-Duc. Its 28 statues were destroyed in 1793 because the Parisians assumed that they represented the kings of France but fragments discovered in 1977 are now in the Musée du Moyen Age. The magnificent **rose-window**, 9.6m in diameter, is flanked by double windows within arches. Higher still is an open arcade on slender columns.

The massive **towers** never received the spires that were originally intended. It is possible to climb the 387 steps inside and it is worth the effort for the view

Central portal, Notre-Dame

of Viollet-le-Duc's flèche and the rooftops. You enter by the north tower then pass an exhibition about the building; have a close-up from the gallery between the towers of the suitably chimerical creatures redesigned by Viollet-le-Duc; and see the great bell, Emmanuel, recast in 1686 and weighing 13 tonnes, in the south tower, recalling Quasimodo, Victor Hugo's bell-ringer. It is possible to climb even higher up the south tower. Open 1 Apr–30 Sept 09.30–19.30, 1 Oct–31 March 10.00–17.00, closed 1/1, 1/5, 1/11, 11/11, 25/12, ☎ 01 44 32 16 70.

Like the west front, the **side façades** and **apse** also consist of three distinct and receding storeys; the bold and elegant flying buttresses of the latter were an innovation by Jean Ravy. The **south porch**, according to a Latin inscription at the base, was begun in 1257 under the direction of Jean de Chelles. The story of *St Stephen* (a reference to the earlier church dedicated to him) in the tympanum and the medallions depicting student life, are original. The **north porch**, slightly earlier, has an original statue of the *Virgin* and, in the tympanum, the *Story of Theophilus*. Just to the east of this porch is the graceful **Porte Rouge**, probably by Pierre de Montreuil. To the left, below the windows of the choir chapels, are seven 14C bas-reliefs. The flèche (90m above the ground), a lead-covered oak structure, was rebuilt by Viollet-le-Duc in 1860, after the original was destroyed in the 18C.

Interior

The interior is fairly regular in its layout with only slight discrepancies. The shift in axis between the nave and choir and the increased width of the latter (48m) over the former are hardly discernible. Despite the large clerestory windows with modern glass (1964), the interior tends to be rather sombre, and is usually very busy. On the left when entering is a bookstall, and visitors are encouraged not to enter the ambulatory except for devotional purposes.

The height of the ten-bay **nave**, 33m—very daring for the time—confirmed the prestige of the principal ecclesiastical building in Paris. The sheer elevations of the nave and shallow mouldings of the upper storey emphasise the wafer thin-ness of the walls relative to their height. In contrast, short cylindrical piers, a throw-back to St-Denis, surround the nave and the apse. Triple shafts of equal size rise uninterrupted from the capitals to the springing of the sexpartite vaults. The nave is flanked by double aisles and a double ambulatory surrounds the choir (five bays) and 37 chapels surround the whole. The total length of the cathedral is 130m. A vaulted triforium overlooks the nave whereas the gallery around the choir has double openings.

The change in master of works c 1178 resulted in the contrast between the piers with shafts on the east and the piers with pilasters to the west. The upper part of the transept bays and west bay of the choir were remodelled in the 19C to approximately their original 12C disposition.

The shallow transepts contain two of the three **rose-windows** that have retained some original 13C glass. The north is the finest and best preserved and represents kings, judges, priests and prophets around the Virgin. The south was much restored in 1737 and, with Christ at the centre, it figures saints, apostles and angels, with the wise and foolish virgins. The rose in the west contains scenes of the labours of the months, the signs of the zodiac, vices, virtues and prophets with the Virgin, but was almost entirely remade in the 19C.

In the **side-chapels** of the nave hang seven 17C paintings from an original 76 (by Charles le Brun, Sébastian Bourdon and others), presented by the Goldsmiths' Guild of Paris between 1630 and 1707. Against the south-east pillar at the crossing stands a 14C image of the Virgin, known as Notre-Dame de Paris, and against the north-east pillar is St Denis by Nicolas Coustou (18C).

The **choir**, completely altered in 1708–25 by Louis XIV in fulfilment of his father's vow of 1638 (to place France under the protection of the Virgin should he father a son; this vow was realised after 23 years of marriage when the Louis XIV was born), under the direction of Robert de Cotte, was not spared by Viollet-le-Duc. Behind Viollet-le-Duc's altar is a *Pietà* (1723) by Nicolas Coustou, the base by Girardon, part of the *Voeu de Louis XIII*. The statue of Louis XIII (south) is also by Coustou; that of Louis XIV (north) by Coysevox (both 1715). Of the original 114 stalls, 78 remain, adorned with bas-reliefs from the designs of Jules Degoulon, with canopied archiepiscopal stalls at either end. The bronze angels (1713) against the apse-pillars escaped the Revolutionary melting-pot.

In the first four bays of the choir are the remains of the mid-14C choir screen which, until the 18C, extended round the whole apse; the expressive reliefs on the exterior were unhappily restored and repainted by Viollet-le-Duc. In the blind arches below are listed some of the eminent people buried in the church.

The **ambulatory** contains the tombs of 18C–19C prelates. Behind the high altar is the tomb-statue of Bishop Matiffas de Bucy (d. 1304). In the 2nd chapel south of the central chapel is the theatrical tomb, by Jean-Baptiste Pigalle, of the Comte d'Harcourt (d. 1769); here also are the restored tomb-statues of Jean Jouvenel des Ursins and his wife (d. 1431, 1451).

On the south side of the ambulatory is the entrance to the sacristy, now containing the **treasury**, a somewhat indifferent collection of ecclesiastical plate, reliquaries and cult objects. Open Mon–Sat 09.30–11.30, 13.00–17.00, closed Sun and Christian feast days. In the west is the main organ, 1733, by Cliquot rebuilt in 1868 by the Cavaillé-Coll workshops.

At No. 10 Rue du Cloître Notre-Dame is the **Musée Notre-Dame de Paris** with collections relating to the history of the cathedral. Open Wed, Sat and Sun, 14.30–18.00.

Sq. Jean XXIII, to the east of the cathedral, is a pleasant little garden with a fountain and benches on the site of the 17C archbishop's palace. Further east, another garden, **Sq. de l'Ile-de-France**, was the Canons' Walk. At the far end near the water and down a flight of steps, is a stark but deeply moving **Mémorial des Martyrs et de la Déportation** of 1962 by Henri Pingusson. The names of some 200,000 French men, women and children deported to German concentration camps during the 1939–45 war are recorded here. There is also a simple tomb to an unnamed deportee.

3 • Ile St-Louis

■ Arrondissement: 75004

Ⓜ Cité, Pont-Marie, Sully-Morland

The small island is perfect for an afternoon stroll and to stop off at:
Auberge de la Reine Blanche, 30 Rue St-Louis en l'Ile, ☎ 01 46 33 07 87. Reasonable traditional cooking, £
Bertillon, 31 Rue St-Louis en l'Ile, ☎ 01 43 54 31 61. The ice-cream parlour famous for over 100 flavours, £
Brasserie de l'Ile St-Louis, 55 Quai de Bourbon, ☎ 01 43 54 02 59. For decades a popular haunt of the British—beer and unpretentious Alsatian cooking, £
La Charlotte en l'Ile, 24 Rue St-Louis en l'Ile, ☎ 01 43 54 25 83. Tea-shop, £
La Flore en l'Ile (near the Pont St-Louis), Quai de Bourbon, ☎ 01 43 29 88 27. Café and tea-shop, £
Le Monde des Chimères, 69 Rue St-Louis en l'Ile, ☎ 01 43 54 45 27. Offers good quality classic cooking in an old house with modern décor, £–££

Just a footbridge away from the Ile de la Cité is its smaller sister, the enchanting Ile St-Louis (**Map 8; 4–6/9; 3–5 and p 80**). This tranquil and elegant backwater, with no Métro station, is a sought-after residential area reached on foot from the Ile de la Cité via Pont St-Louis (dating from 1614, but replaced in 1969). The Ile St-Louis boasts no major monuments just a harmonious architectural setting and river views for quiet contemplation. There are one or two pleasant hotels tucked away in this secluded spot.

History of Ile St-Louis

The Ile St-Louis was formerly two islets which were not linked until the 17C when, as an annexe of the Marais to the north, it became the site of a number of imposing mansions, several designed by Louis Le Vau, the leading French Baroque architect. These jostle for place in the few narrow streets or present a dignified and subtly-hued cordon facing out to the river.

The island is connected to the north bank by **Pont Louis-Philippe** (rebuilt 1862); beyond stands **Pont Marie** (1635), named after the original developer of the island, Christophe Marie, crossing to Quai des Celestins. Further east, the island and river are intersected obliquely by **Pont de Sully** (1876), at the northern end of which, beyond Sq. H.-Galli, stands the striking Hôtel de Fieubet. On the south side of the island, **Pont de la Tournelle** of 1928 (the last of a succession since 1369), crosses from Rue des Deux-Ponts to the Quai de la Tournelle.

The main street, **Rue St-Louis en l'Ile**, does not have the views of the river and its banks but has retained an aura of times past. It is endowed with one or two good buildings, including at no. 51 the **Hôtel Chenizot**, with a fine decorated doorway and balcony of 1726 by Pierre de Vigny.

The church of **St-Louis en l'Ile** could be passed by unnoticed if it were not for the curious openwork spire and the clock of 1741. Begun in 1664 to replace the by then outgrown original chapel, St-Louis en l'Ile was based on designs by the great architect Louis Le Vau. It was finished in 1726 by Jacques Doucet. The bright Baroque interior has ornamental stone-carving executed under the direction of the painter Philippe de Champaigne's nephew Jean-Baptiste de Champaigne, who is buried here (d. 1681). As well as several 18C paintings and furnishings of some interest, the church contains a 16C Flemish polychromed wood relief of the *Dormition of the Virgin*, and six Nottingham alabaster reliefs.

Typical of the grander *hôtels particuliers* built on the eastern part of the island is the **Hôtel Lambert** at no. 2, begun in 1641 by Le Vau, the interior decorated by Eustache Le Sueur and Charles Le Brun, among others. It is now privately owned but the terraced garden and oval gallery designed by Le Vau can be glimpsed from the Quai d'Anjou.

The extreme easterly tip of the island is a tiny triangular square, Sq. Antoine-Louis Barye, named after the sculptor Antoine-Louis Barye.

Across the Seine is a view of the Left Bank with the Institut du Monde Arabe to the south east (see Ch. 6), and the adjacent Science Faculty Building, with its tower, built on the site of the old Halles aux Vins.

No. 3 Quai d'Anjou, on the north eastern side of the island, belonged to Le Vau; no. 9 was the home of the artist Honoré Daumier from 1846. No. 17, the **Hôtel de Lauzun**, 1657, attributed to Le Vau, was the residence 1682–84 of the Duc de Lauzun, commander of the French forces at the Battle of the Boyne in 1690, when he was defeated by King William III of Britain. From 1842 it became a popular meeting place for artists and writers, and both Baudelaire and Théophile Gautier rented rooms here. The artists responsible for its splendid decoration were Le Brun, Le Sueur, Patel and Sébastien Bourdon. (Visits to the interior are extremely limited and it is necessary to reserve months ahead: ☎ 01 42 76 57 99.) Ford Madox Ford's literary periodical *Transatlantic Review* was published from No. 29.

Further west, 13 and 15 Quai de Bourbon, the Hôtel Le Charron (17C), has a mansard window with the old pulley used for hoisting goods. No. 1 was the cabaret or inn Franc-Pinot.

Turning south, you pass at no. 6 Quai d'Orleans the **Musée Adam Mickiewicz**, with a Polish library and souvenirs of the poet (1798–1855), and also of Chopin.

The South or Left Bank: La Rive Gauche

4 • Quartier Latin

■ Arrondissement: 75005
◉ St-Michel, Cluny-La Sorbonne, Maubert-Mutualité, Card. Lemoine, Luxembourg
◭ Saint-Michel-Notre Dame

Le Balzar, 49 Rue des Ecoles, ☎ 01 43 54 13 67. 1930s brasserie of the Flo group, good traditional fare, ££
Le Bar à Huîtres, 33 Rue St-Jacques, ☎ 01 44 07 27 37. Oyster bar for those who love a seafood platter (see also Montparnasse and Bastille), £
A selection of restaurants includes:
Bistrot d'à Côté St-Germain, Michel Rostaing, 16 Blvd St-Germain, ☎ 01 43 54 59 10, £
Les Bouchons de F. Clerc, 12 Rue de l'Hôtel-Colbert, ☎ 01 43 54 15 34. Newish bistrot, excellent wine at reasonable prices. £–££
Café de la Nouvelle Mairie, 19–21 Rue des Fossés St-Jacques, ☎ 01 44 07 04 41. Chic snacks and scruffy students, £

Bistrots come in all guises:
Campagne et Provence, 25 Quai de la Tournelle, ☎ 01 43 54 05 17. Mediterranean influence and good value limited choice menus, £
Les Fontaines, 9 Rue Soufflot. ☎ 01 43 26 42 80. Trendy café-restaurant that comes highly recommended, £

Forgón St Julien, 10 Rue St-Julien-le-Pauvre, ☎ 01 43 54 31 33. Small restaurant serving Spanish dishes, good tapas and paella, £–££
Perraudin, 157 Rue St-Jacques, ☎ 01 46 33 15 75. A homespun, down-to-earth bistrot, £

Among the brasseries:
Le Reminet, 3 Rue des Grands-Degrés, ☎ 0144 07 04 24. Small, popular, reasonable, a few veggie dishes as well as meaty ones, £
La Rôtisserie du Beaujolais, 19 Quai de la Tournelle, ☎ 01 43 54 17 47. Same ownership as *Tour d'Argent*, but more affordable traditional fare, ££
La Timonerie, 35 Quai de Tournelle, ☎ 01 43 25 44 42. The touch of an alchemist transforms simple ingredients into tours de force, £–££
La Tour d'Argent, 15 Quai de la Tournelle, ☎ 01 43 54 23 31. It is among the upmarket establishments still going strong. Legendary institution overlooking the Seine, with sky-high prices and up-dated haute-cuisine, ££

Although associated with the young, the Quartier Latin, is one of the oldest parts of Paris and contains the majority of the educational and scientific institutions of the University of Paris. There are still many signs of student life (but probably little Latin spoken). The district holds a vague yet irresistible attraction to many visitors, and cafés and bookshops abound, but the crass commercialism, fast-food restaurants and constant frenetic hustle and bustle of the main artery, the Boul Mich (Blvd St Michel) can be a disincentive to linger. The *quartier's* more picturesque character is found in the side streets where there are many reminders of the past, despite being dissected by Blvd St-Germain in the mid-19C. The two major Gallo-Roman remains of Paris—the Arènes de Lutèce and the Thermes de Cluny—are here (see Ch. 5 for the latter) as well as three of the most interesting lesser-known medieval churches, St-Séverin, St-Etienne-du-Mont, and St-Julien-le-Pauvre, and the great necropolis on the hill, the Panthéon. During the student revolution of 1968, the old *pavés* (cobblestones) were used as missiles and have been replaced by dull slabs.

History of the Quartier Latin

The name Quartier Latin goes back to the language spoken by scholars who congregated around the brilliant and outspoken theological scholar, Pierre Abélard (d. 1142), on the Montagne Ste-Geneviève. He came here following his removal, c 1100, from the school attached to Notre-Dame where he had confounded his master, Guillaume of Campeaux, in disputation. Abélard continued to challenge the established canons of the Church and later proved to be a writer of genius, but his place in history was established by the scandal of his seduction and marriage to Heloïse, his pupil and niece of Canon Fulbert of Notre-Dame. After the couple failed to keep their vow of celibacy, Fulbert's fury knew no bounds and he ordered Abélard's castration. (There is a monument to the couple in Père Lachaise cemetery, see Ch. 32.)

In its earlier history, the Quartier Latin was the site of Roman *Lutetia*, on the south bank of the Seine opposite Ile de la Cité (see Ch. 1). In 1968, rising student unrest at the University of Nanterre on the outskirts of Paris, provoked by poor academic standards and overcrowding, spread to the Left Bank which became the theatre of many student riots during the *évenements* of May. The Revolution escalated to a nationwide general strike lasting until 30 May when President de Gaulle's appeal finally restored calm, and in subsequent years many universities were hastily expanded and new faculties built (see p 100).

Place St-Michel (Map 8; 3) is linked to the Cité by Pont St-Michel, with the Fontaine St-Michel at its south end (1860), incorporating a memorial to the Resistance of 1944. From the Place, Blvd St-Michel leads south to Carrefour de l'Observatoire, in part following the Roman Via Inferior. Part of Haussman's scheme for Paris (see Ch. 25), it links the right and left banks of the Seine, and Blvd St-Germain. Immediately to the east of Pl. St-Michel is a still decrepit corner of Old Paris penetrated by ancient streets or alleys such as Rue de la Huchette, Rue Xavier-Privas and Rue du Chat-qui-Pêche (named after an old shop-sign).

St-Séverin

From Place St-Michel, take Rue de la Harpe and then take the first turning left, to arrive at St-Séverin, an interesting church, built from the 13C–16C combining early and late Gothic styles overlaid with various modifications of later periods.

History of St-Séverin

The first simple church was built here in the 13C on the site of an oratory of the time of Childebert I in which Foulque of Neuilly-sur-Marne had preached the Fourth Crusade (c 1199). The church was enlarged at the end of the 13C and the beginning of the 14C, but only the first three bays of the nave escaped a fire in 1448. Rebuilding work began in 1452 and went on until 1498. In the 17C the church was drastically altered like many churches at the time. The *jubé* was demolished and the choir partially classicised at the request of Mlle de Montpensier, niece of Louis XIII, 'La Grande Mademoiselle'.

The early 13C **west door**, with foliate carvings between the colonettes, was brought piecemeal from St-Pierre-aux-Boeufs in the Cité in 1837 (Virgin and Child, 19C). The upper two storeys date from the 15C. On the left is a tower of the 13C, completed in 1487, with a door that was once the main entrance; the tympanum dates from 1853, but in the frame is a 15C inscription *Bonnes gens qui par cy passés, Priez Dieu pour les trespassés* ('Good people who pass through here, pray to God for your sins'). To the left of the tower, a niche holds a statue of St Séverin (1847). On the south are the galleries of the 15C charnel house, the only one left in Paris.

The **interior** is impressively broad compared to its length, with a double ambulatory but no transept. The difference in style between the first three bays, built in the 13C, and the remainder, which are 15C, is quite obvious. The earlier bays contain late 14C glass from St-Germain-des-Prés, but much restored; from the fourth bay on, the glass is mid-15C. One of the subjects on the south side of the nave is the *Murder of Thomas Becket*. The west rose-window contains a *Tree of Jesse* (c 1500) masked by the organ of 1745, once played by the composers Fauré (1845–1924) and Saint-Saëns (1835–1921).

The double **ambulatory** is a tour de force of Flamboyant architecture with a dynamic central column around which shafts spiral to burst into leaf in the vaults like a palm tree. The stained glass of the apse chapels is by Jean Bazaine (1966). Off the southeast chapel is the Holy Communion Chapel designed by Jules Hardouin-Mansart in 1673. The liturgical furnishings are by Georges Schneider (1985–89) and the chapel contains a series of engavings, *Miserere*, 1922–27, by Georges Rouault, displayed here since 1993.

To the east of Rue St-Jacques is **Rue Galande**, one of the oldest streets in Paris (14C). It has retained traces of earlier times, and on no. 42 is a carved relief of the life of St Julian.

The church of **St-Julien-le-Pauvre** (Map 8; 6), rebuilt c 1170–1230 by monks of Longpont, a Cluniac abbey, stands on the site of a succession of chapels dedicated to St Julien the Hospitaller or the Poor Man. Despite degradation and many restorations it retains the air of a solid late-Romanesque country church and there are two original carved capitals in the chancel. It was used in the 13C–16C as a university church and in 1655–1877 by the former Hôtel-Dieu for various secular purposes. Since 1889 it has been occupied by Melchites (Greek Catholics) and an iconostasis obscures the east end. The present west front was built in 1651.

The small garden adjacent to the church, **Sq. René Viviani**, is adorned not only with some architectural elements, possibly from Notre-Dame, but the oldest tree in Paris, a *Robinia* (false acacia) planted in 1601. From here is a classic view of Notre-Dame.

From the northeast side of this square runs Rue de la Bûcherie. The bookshop, **Shakespeare & Co.** at no. 37 established its reputation as the rendezvous of interwar American writers and by publishing James Joyce's *Ulysses* in 1922, at its first home in Rue de l'Odéon. No. 13 was occupied by the Ecole de Médecine from 1483 to 1775, with a rotunda built in 1745.

South of Sq. René Viviani is Rue du Fouarre (named after the straw on which the students sat), the centre of four 14C schools of the University, and referred to by Dante who is said to have attended lectures here.

A short distance along **Rue Monge**, leading southeast, is (left) **St-Nicolas-du-Chardonnet**, its name a reminder that an earlier church was built in a field of thistles. The major part of the present church was built 1656–1709; only the tower (1625) remains of the previous building. Le Brun designed the finely carved door on Rue des Bernardins. In the 19C, Blvd St Germain shaved the east of the church necessitating a rearrangement of the apsidal chapel, and the main façade on Rue Monge was not completed until the last century.

The interior contains some interesting furnishings while the ornamental glass chandeliers add a decadent touch. In the first bay is Le Brun's painting of the *Martyrdom of St John the Evangelist*, and in the first chapel on the right is Corot's study for the *Baptism of Christ*; in the transept are two paintings by Nicolas Coypel. Outstanding are a monument by Girardon of Bignon, the jurist, d. 1656 (second chapel on the right of the choir), and the splendidly theatrical tomb of Le Brun's mother, designed by Le Brun (8th chapel round the apse); in the same chapel is a monument to Le Brun (d. 1690) and his widow, by the sculptor Antoine Coysevox.

To the west of Rue Monge, under the wall of the former Ecole Polytechnique, is a triangle of greenery, **Sq. Paul Langevin**. The fountain is 18C and the two headless statues are from the old Hôtel de Ville. The statue is of the poet François Villon. Steps lead up to the Jardin Carré, a modern public garden in the former college's courtyard (see below), with a bronze, *La Spirale*, by Meret Oppenheim (1986).

Turn east down the Rue des Ecoles (crossing Rue Monge) to reach (left) Rue de Poissy. At no. 24 are the remains of the 14C refectory of the ancient Collège des Bernardines.

At the north end of this street, where it meets Quai de la Tournelle, stands the restored 17C **Hôtel de Nesmond** (at nos 55–57), containing the offices of La Demeure Historique. This association of owners of historic residences, founded in 1924, is devoted to promoting public interest in privately owned châteaux and publishes information about them.

At no. 47 is the former convent of the Miramiones or Filles Ste-Geneviève, founded by Mme de Miramion (died 1696). It has a small museum devoted to the history of the hospitals of Paris, the **Musée de l'Assistance Publique** (open 10.00–17.00, closed Sun, Mon, public hols and Aug, ☎ 01 40 27 50 05). No. 15 is *La Tour d'Argent*, one of the oldest top-class eating places in Paris built on the site of a tavern dating from 1582. The restaurant is on the top floor looking across to Notre-Dame, and below is the small Musée de la Table.

At 32 **Rue du Cardinal Lemoine**, the next main street to the east running south from the *quai*, stood the Collège des Bons-Enfants, where Vincent de Paul founded his congregation of mission-priests. Further south, no. 49 is the **Hôtel le Brun**, built by Germain Boffrand, and later occupied by Watteau and by Buffon (for Buffon, see Ch. 6).

Climbing southwest at the junction with Rue Monge, you reach Rue Clovis, where a section of Philippe Auguste's 13C perimeter wall is visible. No. 65 Rue du Cardinal Lemoine, the Institution Ste-Geneviève, was the **Collège des Ecossais** (Scots College), re-founded here in 1662 by Robert Barclay. (It was originally founded at another location in 1326 by David, Bishop of Murray. Occasional visits with Monuments Historiques.) This street meets Rue des Ecoles and the quarter of the old schools.

At 5 Rue Descartes (running across Rue Clovis) is the entrance to the former **Ecole Polytechnique**, founded in 1794 for the training of artillery and engineer officers. This most prestigious of the *Grandes Ecoles* (colleges created by the Convention to provide technical experts needed by the Empire), transferred here in 1805 to the old buildings of the Collège de Navarre and the Collège de Boncourt, and moved to the outskirts of Paris in 1977. The gardens are open to the public (see above).

At 34 Rue Montagne-Ste-Geneviève, further down the hill, are remains of the Collège des Trente-Trois, named after its 33 scholarships, one for each year of Christ's life.

At 23 Rue Clovis is the entrance to the **Lycée Henri-IV**, one of Paris's great schools, which took over the site of the old Abbaye Ste-Geneviève in 1796. Little remains of the original abbey demolished in 1802 except the courtyard tower, with Romanesque base and two Gothic upper storeys (14C–15C). The former refectory (now the chapel) is an over-restored 13C building. The kitchens are also medieval.

St-Etienne-du-Mont

On the right is St-Etienne-du-Mont (**Map 8; 6**), an unusually pretty church with some original features. Essentially a late-Gothic structure with Renaissance decoration, it was almost continuously in construction from 1492 to 1586. It has sheltered the shrine of Ste-Geneviève, patron saint of Paris, since the destruction of the old church. But its most unusual asset is a *jubé* or rood screen, rarely found still intact in French churches.

History of St-Etienne-du-Mont

Originally St-Etienne adjoined the abbey church possibly accounting for the choir, nave and façade being on slightly different axes. In 1610, Marguerite de Valois laid the foundation stone of the façade, which has three pedimented tiers with a small rose window in each of the upper ones in a curious combination characteristic of the transitional style of architecture from late Gothic to Renaissance. The statues are 19C. The tower, begun in 1492, was completed in 1628 and on the north flank is a picturesque porch of 1632.

The luminous **interior** gives an impression of height because of the tall aisles. Its originality lies in the elegant gallery that links the supporting pillars of the nave and choir. Several of the large windows contain Renaissance stained glass. The ambulatory is wide with ribbed vaulting and heavy pendant bosses, the longest above the crossing. The celebrated fretted stone *jubé*, built in 1525–35, is a virtuoso piece of stone carving with magnificent sweeping spirals at either side of the central pierced balustrade. The design is attributed to Philibert de l'Orme, and the work was probably carried out by Antoine Beaucorps. The date 1605 on the side refers only to the door to the spiral.

The **organ**, over the west door, has a richly carved case by Jean Buron dating from 1631–32, with Christ of the Resurrection at the summit. The works are 17C, renovated in the 19C. The pulpit is the work of the great sculptor Germain Pilon, with later sculptures designed by Laurent de la Hyre.

The **stained glass** ranges in date from c 1550 to c 1600; the high nave windows by N. Pinaigrier, date from 1587–88, and include scenes of the *Resurrection, Ascension* and the *Coronation of the Virgin*. The transept glass (1585–87), also by Pinaigrier with J. Bernard, includes various saints and the *Crucifixion*. The high windows in the choir contain glass of the 1540s onwards, and in the ambulatory are fragments of 16C glass mixed with 19C work.

The church has many **furnishings** of note. Above the first chapel in the choir is an ex-voto to Ste Geneviève, with the provost and merchants of Paris, by François de Troy (1726), while higher, to the right, is a similar subject painted by Largillière of 1696. On either side of the chapel are the epitaphs of Pascal and Racine (by Boileau), whose graves are at the entrance to the Lady Chapel. Also buried in the church are Charles Rollin (1661–1741), the historian, and the artist Eustache Le Sueur (1616–55). In the next chapel south of the choir is the copper-gilt shrine of Ste Geneviève (1853), containing a fragment of her tomb; her remains were burned by the mob in the Pl. de Grève (Pl. de l'Hôtel de Ville) in 1801.

From the next bay runs a corridor, at the end of which (right) is the presbytery, built in 1742 for Louis d'Orléans (son of the Regent), who died here in 1752. On the left is the **charnier**, or gallery of the graveyard, with 12 superb windows of 1605–09; the joy of these is that the glass panels are at eye level and the most notable are no. 1, *The Miracle of Rue des Billettes*, no. 2, *Noah's Ark*, no. 9, *Manna from Heaven*, and no. 10, *The Mystic Wine-press*.

The Panthéon

Across Pl. Ste-Geneviève **(Map 8; 6)**, south west of St-Etienne-du-Mont is the unmistakable and grandiose bulk of the Panthéon. The building was inspired by the Pantheon in Rome with its dome and peristyled portico. Situated on the Mont de Paris, the highest point on the Left Bank (60m), this was the legendary burial-place of Geneviève (5C; see also Ch. 30), later regarded as the patron saint of Paris. At the Revolution it became the necropolis of the great and famous. Open summer 09.30–18.30, winter 10.00–18.15 (last admission 45 mins before closing), closed 1/1,1/5, 11/11, 25/12, ☎ 01 44 32 18 00.

History of the Panthéon

In 1744, lying ill at Metz, Louis XV vowed that if he recovered he would replace the abbey church of Ste-Geneviève, then in a ruinous state. The present building was begun 20 years later, although not completed until 1790. Its architect, Jacques-Germain Soufflot, died of anxiety, it is said, because the construction showed signs of subsidence as its foundations were laid above Roman clay pits.

In 1791, the Constituent Assembly decided that the building should be used as a Panthéon or burial-place for distinguished citizens, and the pediment was inscribed with the words *Aux Grands Hommes la Patrie reconnaissante*. From the Restoration to 1831 and from 1851 to 1885 it was reconsecrated, but on the occasion of Victor Hugo's interment in 1885 it was definitively secularised.

The Panthéon, built in the shape of a Greek cross, is 110m long, 82m wide and 83m high to the top of its majestic dome. The pediment above the portico of Corinthian columns contains a masterful relief by David d'Angers, representing *France between Liberty and History*, distributing laurels to famous men.

The **interior** is coldly Classical, using the giant Corinthian order. Saint Geneviève's tomb was originally intended to lie below the cupola. The vast space is enlivened with a series of huge (everything is colossal here) murals, made possible when 42 windows were walled up during the Revolution. The most notable of these is the series of the *Life of Ste Geneviève* by the Symbolist painter Puvis de Chavannes, recognisable by their calm dignity and quiet colours. The only true exponent of the technique of fresco painting to work in the Panthéon and an admirer of the art of the Quattrocento, Puvis began the series in 1874 in this ideal working environment and it brought him general acclaim. Note in particular the panel showing the saint watching over Paris and bringing supplies to the city after the siege by the Huns.

In the east end is a work representing the Convention, by Sicard and against the central pillars are monuments to Jean-Jacques Rousseau by Bartholomé, right: left, to Diderot and the Encyclopédistes by Terroir.

The **dome**, supported by four piers united by arches, contains three distinct shells, of which the first is open in the centre to reveal the second, with a fresco by Antoine Gros. Within the dome, in 1852, the physicist Léon Foucault gave the first public demonstration of his pendulum experiment proving the rotation of the Earth, dramatically reconstructed (commentated by audio-visual displays in the aisles).

The **crypt** (enter by the northeast) contains the tombs of Jean-Jacques Rousseau (1712–78), Voltaire (1684–1778), and Soufflot, the architect. Of the famous men whose remains have been re-interred in the vaults, the most eminent are Victor Hugo (1802–85) and Emile Zola (1840–1902); Marcelin Berthelot (1827–1907), the chemist; Jean Jaurès the socialist politician (1859, assassinated 1914); Louis Braille (1809–52), benefactor of the blind; the explorer Bougainville (1729–1811); and Jean Moulin (1899–1944), the Resistance hero. The heart of Léon Gambetta (1838–82), one of the proclaimers of the Republic in 1870, is enshrined here. Jean Monnet (1888–1979), the 'Father of Europe', was buried in the Panthéon on the centenary of his birth, and most recently the remains of Pierre and Marie Curie (in 1995) and André Malraux (in 1996) were translated here.

It is now possible to climb up into the **Colonnade** encircling the dome for an unusual and interesting view over historic Paris.

At no. 11 Rue Pierre and Marie Curie is the **Musée Marie Curie** in the laboratories (decontaminated in 1981) where Marie Curie worked.

In the northwest corner of the Pl. du Panthéon, on Rue Soufflot, is the Law

Faculty building, begun by Soufflot in 1771, and subsequently enlarged. The **Bibliothèque Ste-Geneviève**, on the northern side of the Place (10 Place du Panthéon), began as the library of the Abbaye Ste-Geneviève. The Collège de Montaigu, founded in 1314, and where Loyola, Erasmus and Calvin were students, stood on this site until the 19C. The present building (1844–50), by the great architect Henri Labrouste, is an important structure because it is an early example of a metal frame building, using both wrought and cast iron. Students work under the splendid iron and glass roof of the reading room. It also has a highly original exterior, a cross between a 16C Florentine palace and a 19C railway station. (Visits on request in writing or apply for a one-day reader's pass.)

The library contains a large collection of manuscripts, incunabula, and some 120,000 volumes from the 16C to 19C MSS of Rimbaud, Verlaine, Baudelaire, Gide and Valéry. It also houses the Scandinavian Library with some 160,000 volumes.

On the other side of the library in Rue Cujas, is the Collège Ste-Barbe, founded in 1460, the oldest existing public educational establishment in France. In Rue Valette, to the east of the library, was the Collège Fortet (no. 21) where Calvin studied in 1531. At 1bis Rue des Carmes is the **Musée de la Préfecture de Police** (Museum of the History of the Prefecture of Police), with a section devoted to the Resistance and the Liberation of Paris (open 09.00–17.00, Sat 10.00–17.00, closed Sun and public holidays) with records of important conspiracies, arrests, famous characters, archives, unique weapons and uniforms, and evidence from famous criminal cases.

From Rue Cujas or Rue Soufflot turn right into **Rue St-Jacques**, an ancient and important thoroughfare which follows the course of the Roman road, the Via Superior, from Lutetia to Orléans, and formed part of the pilgrimage route to Santiago de Compostela in the Middle Ages. (Its southern section is described in Ch. 7.) On the right is the **Lycée Louis-le-Grand**, formerly the Jesuit Collège de Clermont, founded in 1560 and rebuilt in 1887–96. Molière, Voltaire, Robespierre, Desmoulins, Delacroix and Hugo studied here.

The next building is the **Collège de France**, its entrance in the Pl. Marcelin-Berthelot (**Map 8; 6**). In the courtyard, with its graceful portico, is a statue of the scholar Guillaume Budé (Budaeus; 1468–1540), under whose influence it was founded by François I in 1530 with the intention of spreading Renaissance humanism and counteracting the narrow scholasticism of the Sorbonne. Independent of the University, its teaching was free and public. The present building was begun in 1610, completed by Jean-François Chalgrin c 1778 and has since been enlarged.

Sq. A.-Mariette-Pacha, next to the Collège de France, contains statues of Dante (1882), Ronsard (1928) and C. Bernard, Prof of Medicine 1947–78 (1946), and in Impasse Chartière nearby is a monument to the Pléiade, a group of Renaissance poets that originated in the vanished Collège Coqueret, founded on this site in 1418–1643.

La Sorbonne

To the west of the Collège de France is the Sorbonne (**Map 8; 5**), founded as a theological college in 1253 by Robert de Sorbon (1201–74), chaplain to Louis IX. It was rebuilt at Richelieu's expense by Jacques Lemercier in 1629 but, with the exception of the church, the present buildings date from 1885–1901.

History of La Sorbonne

The University of Paris, which disputes with Bologna the title of the oldest university in Europe, arose in the first decade of the 12C out of the schools of dialectic attached to Notre-Dame. Transferred by Abélard to the Montagne Ste-Geneviève, the university obtained its first statutes in 1208, and these served as the model for Oxford and Cambridge and other universities of northern Europe. By the 16C it comprised no fewer than 40 separate colleges.

Before the end of the 13C the Sorbonne had become synonymous with the faculty of theology, overshadowing the rest of the university and possessing the power of conferring degrees. It was noted for its religious rancour, supporting the condemnation of Joan of Arc, justifying the St-Bartholomew's Day massacre and refusing its recognition of Henri IV, a former Protestant. Nevertheless in 1469 it was responsible for the introduction of printing into France, by allowing Ulrich Gering and his companions to set up their presses within its precincts.

In the 18C it attacked the *philosophes* and in 1792 was itself suppressed, was refounded by Napoléon and became in 1821 the seat of the University of Paris. The student revolution of May 1968 eventually brought about overdue reforms in the university system, and in 1970 the University of Paris was replaced by the formation of 13 autonomous universities in the region. Paris IV and Paris III (Letters, French Civilisation and Human Sciences faculties) are based here.

The courtyard and galleries can be visited; the great staircase and amphitheatre, can be seen on application at the main entrance at 17 Rue des Ecoles (☎ 01 40 46 20 15).

The ponderous buildings, which still house the university library of 700,000 volumes, the Académie de Paris and minor learned institutions, include the Grand Amphithéâtre or main lecture hall, containing the best work in the building, the mural *Le Bois sacré* by Puvis de Chavannes.

The **Chapelle de la Sorbonne**, facing Pl. de la Sorbonne was founded in the 13C and rebuilt by Jacques Lemercier in 1635–42 at the expense of Richelieu. The dramatic tomb of the great cardinal (1585–1642) was designed by Le Brun and sculptured by Girardon (1694). The chapel is open only for temporary exhibitions or concerts.

5 • The Musée du Moyen Age

■ Arrondissement: 75005
▣ Cluny-La Sorbonne, Maubert-Mutualité, Odéon, St-Michel
▣ St-Michel-Notre Dame

The 15C **Hôtel de Cluny** (Map 8; 5), north-west of the entrance to the Sorbonne and adjacent to the Gallo-Roman thermae, is one of the finest extant examples of medieval French domestic architecture in Paris. It houses the **Musée du Moyen Age-Thermes et Hôtel de Cluny**, an intimate museum of special charm. As well as the Roman remains, a remarkably well-conserved vestige of antique Paris, there is a superb collection of the arts and crafts of the Middle Ages, from gold artefacts of the

Visigoth and Merovingian periods, through remnants of stonecarving from Notre-Dame de Paris, to the celebrated series of 15C tapestries, *The Lady with the Unicorn*. Since autumn 2000 it has been endowed with a Medieval Garden. The entrance is in the right-hand corner of the courtyard, beyond an archway.

- The museum is open 09.15–17.45, closed Tues and public holidays, ☎ 01 53 73 78 00. There are frequent guided visits and cultural activities. There is also sound and touch equipment for the non- or partially sighted.

History of the Hôtel de Cluny

The property was bought in 1340 by Pierre de Chalus, Abbot of Cluny in Burgundy, to establish a residence in the area of the university. The mansion that replaced the earlier building was built c 1490 by Abbot Jacques d'Amboise, as the town house of the abbots, who rarely occupied it. The building is important architecturally as an early example of a house standing between a courtyard and a garden. Louis XII's widow, Mary Tudor, (1496–1533) lived here for a time.

At the Revolution, the mansion became national property but in 1833 it was taken over by Alexandre du Sommerard and filled with the treasures that he spent his life collecting. These were bought by the State and supplemented by many new acquisitions during the long curatorship of his son, Edmond du Sommerard (d. 1889), and since. Subsequently the thermae became the repository of original stonework removed from major Parisian monuments during renovation.

Ground floor

Among the outstanding tapestries in the first rooms is *The Resurrection* (c 1420) the oldest tapestry in the museum, *The Grape Harvest* (early 15C) and *The Deliverance of St Peter*, 1460. The set of six scenes illustrating the activities of a noble household of c 1500, entitled *La Vie Seigneuriale* c 1500–25, hangs in **room 4** with other furnishings of the same period. Also displayed are the 15C *Altarpiece of the Passion*, in wood with painted panels, and a small statue of St Denis, holding his head in his hand according to the legend of his martyrdom.

The textiles and embroidery in **room 3** range from 6C–14C. Some are Coptic or Byzantine; others, of French, Italian and Spanish origin, include examples of Hispano-Moresque fabrics. An example of the highly regarded English production of the early 14C is the *Embroidery with Leopards*, the stylised creatures surrounded by foliage and young girls, embroidered in gold on velvet. In the small **room 5** are alabasters, mainly from Nottingham.

Room 6 displays precious panels of stained glass including the section of a circular medallion from St-Denis (before 1144); part of a window depicting *St Timothy* (c 1160) from Alsace; a scene of the *Charity of St Nicholas* from Troyes (c 1170–85), and various pieces from the Sainte-Chapelle, Paris (early to mid-13C).

In the corridor, **room 7**, where the medieval and antique buildings join, are various tombstones including that of Jean de Sathanay (1360) from the Cluny college chapel and Pierre de Montreuil's portal of the Chapel of the Virgin from the interior of St-Germain-des-Prés.

Turn right through the portal into **room 8**, Salle Notre-Dame-de-Paris, a spacious area arranged to exhibit sculptural fragments removed from Notre-Dame de Paris during the Revolution. These include the original 13C heads from the gallery of the Kings of Judah, discovered in 1977 during excavation work in Rue de la Chaussée d'Antin; a magnificent Adam, c 1260; a heavily restored yet vigorous nude figure, originally painted, from the south transept; also fragments of statue columns from St-Anne's gate.

Rooms 9, 10 and 11, across the corridor, contain many carved ivories (4C–12C) among which is the sensual Ariadne (Constantinople, 6C), and an 8C English diptych remarkable in being carved on both sides. Having been re-used in the 9C, the later decoration is typical of the Carolingian Renaissance. There are also many fine examples of medieval statuary in wood and stone. Among important examples of Romanesque carving from Paris is a group of 12 capitals from the abbey church of St-Germain-des-Prés (mid-11C) and large, richly carved capitals from Ste-Geneviève-de-Paris (c 1100). Three early Gothic heads come from the abbey church of St-Denis. There are also two very moving 12C French Crucifixions in polychrome wood from provincial France.

Statues of the Apostles (1241–48) removed from the Sainte-Chapelle during restoration in the 19C remained in the museum and are on display along with a group of 12C Catalonian historiated capitals. Note the Gothic 'sway' of the ivory Virgin and Child. Several fine carved stone retables from the Paris area include one of 1250–60 from St-Denis showing the Baptism of Christ and of 1259–67 from St-Germer-de-Fly and a 14C altarpiece with Scenes of the Passion. Also to see are fragments of 12C mural paintings.

Under **room 12** is the frigidarium of the Gallo-Roman baths, remarkable in that it still retains its 2C vault, unique in France. The room (20m by 11.5m and 14m in height) with the piscina on the northern side, is all that remains in its entirety of the baths, assumed to have been built during the 1C and modified later (212–17): only partial ruins remain of its tepidarium and caldarium and the palestras (gymnasiums) facing Blvd St-Germain, but the rest was demolished in the 16C and 19C. Underground chambers on the north side still exist. The museum's collection of Gallo-Roman sculpture is displayed here as well as some early medieval pieces of masonry and stone-carving. The area is regularly used for concerts.

First floor

On the first floor, in the circular **room 13**, are displayed the series of six exquisite millefleurs tapestries known as *La Dame à la Licorne* (or Unicorn). This gallery is equipped with fibre optic lighting deliberately kept dim for conservation reasons. There is also sound and touch equipment for the non-sighted (in French).

History of La Dame à la Licorne tapestries

These tapestries, probably designed by a Parisian artist but woven, in silk and wool, in Northern Europe between 1484 and 1500, were commissioned by Jean le Viste, a Lyonnais lawyer whose family arms—gules, a band azure with three crescents argent—are frequently repeated in the designs. The tapestries hung for a long time in the Château of Boussac in the Creuse until brought to public notice by both Prosper Mérimée, Inspector of Historic Monuments, and the writer George Sand. They were acquired by the museum in 1882 and have undergone a number of restorations.

Visually stunning, with rich red backgrounds, blue islands of colour, and different types of trees, the panels are scattered with thousands of delicate flower, animal and bird motifs. In each the lady appears differently attired, sometimes accompanied by her maid, and always flanked by the mythical, elusive Unicorn, symbol of purity, and a Lion. In several of the panels a monkey and a pet dog are also included.

Five of the tapestries present the theme of the senses. Taste: the lady feeds the monkey and a parakeet from a bowl of sweetmeats. Hearing: in which the lady plays a portable organ. Sight: in which the Unicorn gazes into the mirror held before him by the lady. Smell, where the monkey sniffs a flower while the lady weaves a garland, and touch: in which the lady gently grasps the horn of the unicorn. Opposite and in isolation, is the sixth tapestry in the series, known by the enigmatic motto *A mon seul désir* embroidered above the pavilion before which the lady stands while returning jewels to a casket held by her maid. The iconography remains a mystery.

Among the late medieval religious works from all parts of Europe in the large gallery, **room 14**, are several altarpieces. The most noteworthy is the *Altarpiece of the Blessed Sacrament* from Averbode in Brabant (1513) the work of Jan de Molder, carved with the Mass of St Gregory in the centre and the Last Supper on the right. The numerous representations of Virgins and female saints include an early 16C *Virgin reading to the Child* from the Lower Rhine and a late-15C *St Mary Magdalen* from Brussels carved in wood. Also of note are a painted *Pietà* from Tarascon (mid 15C), the elegantly carved head of the funeral effigy of Jeanne of Toulouse (c 1280), and a disturbing wooden *Head of Christ*, c 1470, from Franconia. There is a rare example of an English painting of *Scenes of the Life of the Virgin*, c 1325, and this room also contains the elegantly animated Prodigal Son tapestries, c 1520.

In the corridor (**room 15**) are various medieval domestic objects and examples of the locksmith's craft.

Room 16 is devoted to the arts of **goldsmiths and enamellers**. The centre-pieces, part of the magnificent Treasure of Gurrazar, include three Visigothic votive crowns with their pendant crosses, dating from the late 7C; and the Golden Rose (1330), given by the Avignon Pope John XXII to a count of Neuchâtel. There is also Gallo-Roman and Merovingian jewellery, including gold torques, bracelets, buckles, ornamented belts and fibulas; late Roman and Byzantine cloisonné enamelwork; two rock crystal lionheads (4C–5C), from the Roman Empire; enamels from the Rhineland and Meuse.

Among the fine examples of late 12C–14C **Limoges** enamelwork are reliquaries, chalices, pyxes, shrines, plaques, croziers and crucifixes; two reliquaries of St Thomas Becket (1190–1200) with the scene of the Archbishop's assassination; the 13C *Reliquary of the Sainte-Chapelle* commissioned by Louis IX, like a miniature chapel and engraved with three decapitated saints; the *Picture-reliquary of Ste-Geneviève*, c 1380, acquired in 1989, showing the patron saint of Paris and the legend of the candle; and a finely worked gilded silver Virgin with the Child standing on her knee which is the *Reliquary of the Umbilicus of Christ* (1407). The so-called Colmar Treasure consists of early 14C coins and jewellery found in a wall of the Rue des Juifs, Colmar, in 1853. There are also processional crosses from Barcelona (mid-14C) and from Siena (mid-15C); a collection of cameos, intaglios and glyptics; and the *Reliquary of St Anne* (1472) by Hans Greiff of Ingolstadt. The finely engraved portable triptych showing the *Dormition of the Virgin* (Nuremberg, 15C) whose central plaque was found in London in 1994.

Room 17 has 14C and 15C stained glass and ivories; also ceramics and a fine collection of Hispano-Moresque ware and other lustreware from Manises (Valencia).

In **room 18** are the reassembled choir-stalls, with irreverently carved misericords, from the abbey of St-Lucien at Beauvais (1492–1500). Illuminated manuscripts with Book of Hours, signs of the zodiac, a page of antiphons (end 11C) and the text of law written for Louis IX, which can be leafed through.

Room 19 contains some choice pieces: the early-11C gold antipendium (altar front) possibly intended as a donation for Monte Cassino from Emperor Henry II and Empress Cunegonde, who are portrayed as minuscule figures at the feet of Christ, but which in fact ended up in Basle Cathedral; the 12C Stavelot (Meuse) retable, with a Pentecostal scene of Christ and the Apostles; and a gospel binding of the 12C in nielloed and gilded silver.

Adjacent is the **chapel** (**room 20**), a masterpiece of Flamboyant vaulting from a central pillar, with a filigree of delicate moulding between the main ribs. There are two 14C fonts and a 15C carved wooden door from Provins.

Starting by the staircase and continuing in the adjoining room, is a series of tapestries depicting the *Life of St Stephen*, based on 23 scenes taken from *The Golden Legend*, woven c 1500 for Jean Baillet, Bishop of Auxerre for the cathedral. The tapestries, brought to the museum in 1880, are in remarkable condition. Although they have never been restored, the colours are still strong and every painstaking detail clearly revealed. Like a strip cartoon with captions, the scenes are arranged in alternate interior and exterior settings, the first part dealing with the life and martyrdom of St Stephen and the second with the legend of the relics.

In **room 21** you will find mainly **Italian works** such as three 14C polychrome wooden sculptures: a Tuscan *Angel of the Annunciation* (end 14C), the bust-reliquaries of *St Ursula* (c 1340) and one of her 11,000 maiden companions, St Mabilla (c 1370–80). Also a 14C Sienese *St John the Baptist*. There is a collection of gilded and engraved glass (*églomisé*). Other small artefacts include a collection of late medieval wooden combs with intricate decoration, embroidered alms purses, bakery moulds, etc. The tapestry has *Scenes of the Life of the Virgin, with a Donor* (late 15C). Hanging in **room 22** is a mid-15C painting of the Jouvenel des Ursins family standing in line, commissioned for their chapel in Notre-Dame de Paris. Two small examples of domestic stained glass include one of chess players (15C) and a small monogrammed roundel in grisalle, c 1450–60. Also here are two carvings from the late Middle Ages, from the school of Hans Geiler of Fribourg. In **room 23** are arms and armour in different materials and games pieces in ivory and bone, dating from 11C/12C to 1500. On the walls are three small tapestries depicting courtly culture (15C).

There is a helpful bookshop and boutique (☎ 01 53 73 78 22) with a large selection of information on the society, arts and music of the Middle Ages. Later objects, from the era of the Renaissance but part of the collections of this museum, are to be seen at Ecouen: see Ch. 40.

Jardin Médiéval

The Musée du Moyen Age has blossomed in 2000 with the creation of a garden. Although described as a medieval garden, it is a contemporary interpretation of themes and symbolism found in the museum and does not claim to reproduce an actual 15C garden. It is entered from Blvds St-Michel and St-Germain and divided into distinct enclosed areas around the building with areas for repose.

The **Forêt de la Licorne** evokes medieval woodland with restful glades and wattle fences and the animals found in the famous tapestries populate the children's area. The domesticated traits of a medieval garden are presented in the three-tiered enclosed terrace behind the museum, with medicinal and culinary plants essential to the composition. The **hortus conclusus**, where the rose reigns, is doubly symbolic: the **Jardin céleste** is dedicated to the Virgin, the **Jardin d'amour** to courtly love. The flower meadow on the site of the former abbots' garden is adorned with the mille fleurs represented in the tapestries and a fountain, allegory of the rivers of Paradise.

The shady **Chemoin creux** recalls the old paths of the Montagne Sainte-Geneviève while the courtyard on the museum is planted with old fashioned flowers. The tiny **Square Paul Painlevé**, opposite the entrance to the museum, carpeted with annuals, contains a statue of Montaigne by Landowski and of Puvis de Chavannes by Desbois; also a replica of the *Roman She Wolf*, given by Rome to Paris in 1962.

6 • Southeast of the Quartier Latin

■ Arrondissements: 75005, 75013
🚇 Jussieu, Cardinal Lemoine, Maubert-Mutualité, Pl. Monge, St-Marcel, Gare d'Austerlitz, Les Gobelins, Censier-Daubenton, Quai de la Gare, Bibliothèque
🚉 Gare d'Austerlitz

L'Anacréon, 53 Blvd St-Marcel, ☎ 01 43 31 71 18. Down-to-earth setting, friendly ambience and generally good cooking, £–££
L'Atlas, 12 Blvd St-Germain, ☎ 01 44 07 23 66. Modern Moroccan cooking with wide choice, £
L'Auberge Etchegorry, 42 Rue Croulebarbe, ☎ 01 44 08 83 51, near Gobelins, atmospheric restaurant with hearty cooking from the Basque region, £–££
Bibliothèque Nationale Mitterand has a small cafeteria, £
Bistrot d'à Cité,16 Blvd St-Germain, ☎ 01 43 54 59 10. A Rostang offshoot, loved by the in-crowd, but chose carefully, £–££
Café de la Mosquée de Paris,

☎ 01 43 31 18 14. Tea shop for sticky pastries, attached to the mosque, £
Café de la Poste, 7 Rue de l'Epée-de-Bois, ☎ 01 43 37 05 58. Pleasant and inexpensive café, £
Chez Henri au Moulin à Vent, 20 Rue des Fossés St-Bernard, ☎ 01 43 54 99 37. Legendary French dishes such as frogs legs, £–££
Restaurant E. Marty, 20 Av. des Gobelins, ☎ 01 43 31 39 51. An institution, authentic 30s brasserie and quality brasserie food, £–££
Institut du Monde Arabe, 1 rue des Fossés-St-Bernard, has three eating places: on the 9th floor, *Le Ziryab* restaurant with panoramic views, ££, ☎ 01 40 51 39 27/01 53 10 10 20,

and a cafeteria, *Le Moucharabieth* £, and on the ground floor the *Café Littéraire* £, a place to relax with a mint tea.
Moissonnier, Rue des Fossés-St-Bernard, ☎ 01 43 29 87 65. Reliable Lyonnais cooking in a well-established bistrot, £–££
Le Mouffetard, 116 Rue Mouffetard, ☎ 01 43 31 42 50.

Battling to keep its character; good coffee and croissant, £
Le Petit Navire, 14 Rue des Fossés-St-Bernard, ☎ 01 43 54 22 52. Provençal style cooking which is ever popular, £
Toutoune, 5 Rue de Pontoise, ☎ 01 43 26 56 81. Provençal gaiety and careful attention to the cooking, £

This area, on the Left Bank, is slightly less on the tourist track than the area around St Michel, yet has enough places of interest for a day or two of thorough exploration. The sites described in this chapter range from the botanical gardens of Paris, the Jardin des Plantes with the Grand Galerie de l'Evolution which re-opened in 1994 to the historic Gobelins Tapestry Factory. The Paris Mosque and the Institut du Monde Arabe (IMA), with spectacular views from the top floor down on the Seine and Notre-Dame are near the Jardin des Plantes. There is also the new and controversial Bibliothèque Nationale de France which makes for an interesting comparison with London's new British Library.

The 1960s block and tower at the east end of Rue des Ecoles houses Paris VI and Paris VII, the Faculty of Science of the University of Paris. On the northwest side, Rue des Fossés St-Bernard descends towards the Seine and the Pont Sully. The very beautiful **Collection of Minerals** of the Université Curie are exceptionally well presented at 34 Rue Jussieu, open Wed–Mon 13.00–18.00, closed Tues, ☎ 01 44 27 52 88.

Here, until their transfer to Bercy, stood the huge bonded warehouses of the Halles aux Vins, itself on the site of the Abbaye de St-Victor. Dispersed in 1790, Thomas Becket and Abélard had resided in the abbey and Rabelais had studied in its library.

Rue Linné ascends from Rue Jussieu to Rue des Arènes bringing you up to the remains of the 1C amphitheatre, the **Arènes de Lutèce**. This is the second most important Gallo-Roman site in Paris (the baths are the first, see Ch. 5), which fell into ruin in the 3C and was used as a necropolis in the 4C. Only discovered in 1869 and fully excavated since 1883, a large chunk was lost during the construction of Rue Monge and the site has suffered from over-enthusiastic restoration. The arena is surrounded by the gardens of Sq. Capitan named after Dr Capitan, who restored the ruins in 1917–18, and is a popular place for playing boules or eating sandwiches.

Institut du Monde Arabe (IMA)

The Institut du Monde Arabe (IMA: **Map 9; 5**), beside the Seine at 1 Rue des Fossés-Saint-Bernard, is well-known to Parisians but perhaps often overlooked by overseas visitors. Inaugurated in 1987, it was founded to further cultural and scientific relations between France and some 21 Arab countries. The sleek and complex building, designed by Jean Nouvel, has 9 levels above ground and two below. The design echoes, in a totally 20C manner, certain aspects of Arabic

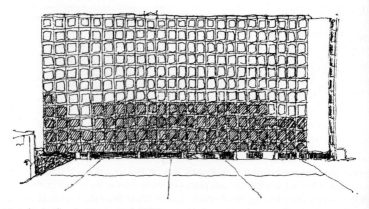

Monde Arabe, inaugurated 1987

architecture such as the unique window shutters, or *moucharabiehs*, of the south façade which function like a camera lens, expanding and contracting in reaction to the sun's intensity through the medium of photo-electric cells; they can also be operated mechanically. The building is arranged around an interior court or *ryad* (with glass lifts), and a book tower or *ziggourat*.

Areas of the Institute that are open to the public include a museum, temporary exhibition spaces, a cinema, book and gift shop, library and documentation centre plus **La Médiathèque Jeunesse** (for children). On **level 0** is the *Café Littéraire* and glass lifts in the centre of the building take you to the *Restaurant Ziryab* and *Cafeteria Le Moucharabieth* on level 9 where there also is a terrace with bird's eye views down on the Seine and Notre-Dame. Open Tues–Sun 10.00–18.00, closed Mon, library closed Sun (☎ 01 40 51 38 38; www.imarabe.org).

The **permanent collection**, exhibited in the museum on three levels (starting on level 7 and working down), is dedicated to the art and civilisation of the Arab world from pre-Islamic time to the present day, presented chronologically. This small but elegantly laid-out museum is concerned with the development of the religion of Islam and of the part played by the Arab world in the history of science. The **arts and crafts of Islam**, from the 9C to the 19C, include ceramics, manuscripts, metalwork, ivories, fabrics and glass objects; also textiles, rugs, costumes and jewellery from throughout the Arab world. The Institute's excellent **temporary exhibitions** are an important part of the Parisian cultural scene. These are mounted almost once a year and present different aspects of the Arab world, its heritage and culture such as Morocco in 1999–2000, including its influence on Matisse; Coptic Egypt and Andalucia in 2000 and 2001.

Between the Quai St-Bernard and the Seine, in the Tino-Rossi gardens on the riverside, extends the **Musée de Sculpture en Plein Air** (Map 9; 5), created in 1980 with examples of mostly contemporary sculpture. There are works by some 29 artists, including César, Stahly, Ipousteguy, Nicolas and Olivier Debré as well as Brancusi and Zadkine. The most eyecatching is Schöffer's gyrating metallic tower, with its struts and discs.

Jardin des Plantes

There are three entrances to the Jardin des Plantes, officially the **Muséum National d'Histoire Naturelle** (**Map 9; 7**)—from the semicircular Pl. Valhubert on the river side, opposite Gare d'Austerlitz; at the junction of Rue Linné with its continuation, Rue Geoffroy-St-Hilaire, near the Fontaine Cuvier (1840), to the north-west; and in Rue Geoffroy-St-Hilaire. The whole museum is due for a lengthy overhaul.

This oasis of 28 hectares encompasses botanic gardens, a group of museums, and other attractions, several of which will entertain and inform younger visitors, notably the menagerie (zoo), the maze, and the Grande Galerie de l'Evolution. As well as unrivalled collections of wild and herbaceous plants, there are alpine, rose, and ecological gardens, tropical greenhouses, and in May and June magnificent displays of peonies and iris.

• The Jardin des Plantes is open from 07.30–20.00 (depending on sunset); the Menagerie Mon–Sat 09.00–17.00 or 18.00 (or sunset), April–Sept Sun 09.00–18.30; the greenhouses Mon–Fri 13.00–17.00, Sat, Sun 10.00–18.00, winter 17.00 (☎ 01 40 79 30 00). There are facilities for the handicapped and refreshments in the gardens and the Grand Galerie.

History of the Jardin des Plantes

Founded in 1626 under Louis XIII for the cultivation of medicinal herbs by the royal physician Guy de la Brosse, the garden was first opened to the public in 1640. Its present importance is mainly due to the great naturalist, the Comte de Buffon (1707–88), who was superintendent from 1739 and greatly enlarged the grounds. Known until 1793 as the Jardin du Roi, it was then reorganised by the Convention under its present official title and provided at that time with 12 professorships. The National Museum of Natural History is a public institute with the triple role of research, conservation and dissemination of knowledge. The library owns a remarkable collection of botanical manuscripts, including the *Vélins du Roi*, illustrated by Nicolas Robert and others; also works by Redouté.

Several of the distinguished French naturalists who taught and studied here are commemorated by monuments in or near the garden. A statue of the naturalist J.-B. Lamarck (1744–1829), by Léon Fagel of the early 20C, faces the Place Valhubert entrance and another by the same artist of the chemist Eugène Chevreul (1786–1889) stands in the northern part of the gardens. Chevreul's research on the principles of harmony and colour contrasts had an important influence on the Impressionist painters' colour theories and he was, for a time, director of the dyeing department at the Gobelins tapestry factory. Buffon's likeness faces the Grande Galerie.

Among other scientists associated with the Jardin des Plantes are the zoologist Geoffroy Saint-Hilaire (1772–1844), Louis Daubenton (1706–99), and the botanists Joseph de Tournefort (1656–1708) and Bernard de Jussieu (1690–1777).

The Maison de Cuvier, home of Georges Cuvier (1769–1832), zoologist and paleontologist, was later occupied by Henri Becquerel (1852–1908) who discovered radioactivity here in 1896. The Administrative Department is housed in the Hôtel de Magny, built in 1650.

From the Esplanade Milne Edwards in front of the Grande Galerie, formal gardens bordered by plane trees create an orderly floral vista with a backdrop of modern Paris, while behind the northern avenue is a host of less regimented gardens.

On the right of the rue Linné entrance is the Butte, a charming hillock with a maze and the first cedar of Lebanon (from Kew Gardens) to be planted in France, in 1734. At the summit is the famous Gloriette, a metal structure of 1786 and sundial bearing the inscription *Horas non numero nisi serenas*: I only count the bright hours.

Animals from the royal collection at Versailles and of street showmen formed the nucleus of a Menagerie in 1792. It now occupies most of the northern side of the gardens and contains more than 1000 animals. The Greenhouses, built in 1830–33—one known as 'Australian' and the other 'Mexican'—are in the western section.

Grande Galerie de l'Evolution

Part of the Museum of Natural History (nearest entrance 36 Rue Geoffroy-St-Hilaire), the Grande Galerie de l'Evolution re-opened in 1994 after a closure of nearly 30 years. It was one of President Mitterand's '*grands projets*' and offers an exciting visual experience besides the natural history content. Open Wed–Mon 10.00–18.00, Thur to 22.00, closed Tues; café on level 1 and facilities for the handicapped (☎ 01 40 79 30 00).

Originally this opened in 1889 as the Zoological Gallery but the building and the specimens deteriorated and the museum was closed in 1965. The present exhibition space uses the central nave, balconies and side galleries of the old building. The theme of the museum revolves around the History of Evolution, whose drama unfolds through the different levels of the museum and the concepts of modern museology to convey a powerful scientific message in a magical way. The permanent exhibition combines carefully selected and restored specimens—the smaller ones suspended in transparent display cases to great effect—with audio visual presentations, models and etched glass.

The **ground floor**, excavated to reveal stone arcades, evokes the watery underworld and takes you across various marine zones, from the deep to the shallows and on to the coast and dry land. Arctic regions have to be crossed on the way to **level one** and a change in climate. Here, among other displays, is a cavalcade of animals across the African savannah and the tropical forests of South America. Lifts fly you past exotic birds to **level three** to be greeted by the oldest specimen in the museum, the rhinoceros that belonged to Louis XV. The balconies, devoted to the evolution of living organisms, provide a spectacular view down onto the nave of level one. The exhibition continues on **level two** with the science of selectivity and man's role in evolution, including some most disturbing effects on the environment. Behind the balcony on the east side is a gallery devoted to extinct and endangered species. This chapel-like room, with its original wooden display cabinets, is classified as an historic monument and contains a clock made for Marie-Antoinette.

Other public galleries, arranged along the southern side of the gardens, are open Wed–Mon 10.00–17.00, Sun 10.00–18.00; 10.00–17.00 winter; closed on public holidays. **Mineralogy** has an interesting collection including a group of giant crystals from Brazil, originally destined for industrial use, which amount to three-quarters of the world's known stock. The **Palaeontology and Compared Anatomy Gallery**, next to the Austerlitz entrance, is frequently mistaken for the Grande Galerie de l'Evolution. The spirit of the period has been preserved in this gallery where skeletons and fossils are presented in the manner of the 17C. The staircase which sweeps you to the upper floor has splendid metal bannisters with a chrysanthemum and fern motif.

To the west of Rue Geoffroy-St-Hilaire is a green-tiled mosque, the **Mosquée de Paris**, complete with minaret, inaugurated in 1926, which is open to the public 09.00–12.00 and 14.00–18.00, guided visits (entrance on Rue des Quatrefages). Inspired by the mosques of Fez, it commemorates the 100,000 Moslems who died for France in 1914–18. The religious buildings are grouped around a courtyard and in the prayer room are some magnificent carpets. The decorative materials were made in North Africa and much of the décor has a Hispano-Mauresque feel. Part of the mosque, but entered from the corner of Rue Daubenton and Rue G. St-Hilaire, is a tea-room and shop.

The sad example of 1960s' utilitarian architecture west of Rue G. St-Hilaire, on Rue Censier, is the Faculty of letters, languages and sociology, Paris III, Sorbonne nouvelle. Not far to the south is Blvd St-Marcel which leads northeast to meet Blvd de l'Hôpital.

To the right of this junction stands the huge **Hôpital de la Salpêtrière** (Map 9; 7), founded in 1656 as a home for aged or abandoned women. The criminal wing, built in 1684, is associated with Manon Lescaut, in the novel by Abbé Prévost.

The main building, by Le Vau and Pierre Le Muet, dates from 1657–63; the domed chapel of St-Louis, built in 1670–77 by Libéral Bruant, can hold 4000 people. Statues by Antoine Etex were added after 1832. As a whole, it is a notable example of the austere magnificence of the architecture of the period and may be compared to Les Invalides. In contrast, is the post-modernist Pavilion of the Child and Adolescent, 1985. Dr Jean-Martin Charcot (1825–93), the hypnotist, is commemorated by a monument to the left of the gateway; his consulting-room, laboratory and library have been preserved intact.

Adjacent to the south is the Hôpital de la Pitié, transferred in 1911 from Rue Lacépède, where it had been founded by Marie de Médicis in 1612.

To the north east is **Gare d'Austerlitz**, the main railway terminus for Tours, Bordeaux, Bayonne and Toulouse (**Map 9; 7**). Between 1870 and 1871 (during the Siege of Paris), the station, then known as the Gare d'Orléans, was turned into a balloon factory.

The *quartier* southeast of the station, on both sides of the Seine, has been undergoing a major transformation over the last few years. New apartments, office blocks and roads, the Charles de Gaulle bridge and a footbridge connecting this bank with the new Parc de Bercy (see p 332) have been constructed, as well as the new Métro line 14, Méteor. Quai d'Austerlitz, faces the new buildings of the Ministère des Finances on the far bank of the Seine, and Quai de la Gare, opposite the Palais Omnisport, is the site of the new Bibliothèque Nationale de France, François Mitterand.

Bibliothèque Nationale de France, François Mitterand

Opposite the footbridge, beside the Seine half way between the Pont de Bercy and the Pont de Tolbiac, is the new Bibliothèque de France, a veritable fortress for books to which the major part of the national collection was transferred 1996–98 from the Bibliothèque Nationale, Cardinal de Richelieu (see p 230).

The last of Mitterand's *grands projets*, this mammoth construction is the design of Dominique Perrault and was begun in 1990. It consists of four L-shaped 80m-high towers, each of 20 storeys, simulating books opened at right angles, standing at the corners of a hollow rectangular podium. The whole Tolbiac site covers 7.5 hectares. The stark and open esplanade (60,000sq m) is approached by wide steps of silvery-grey hard-wood, and decorated with evergreen bushes trapped in metal cases. Only on reaching the top of the steps do the sunken gardens (12,000sq m), planted with tall pines and silver birches, come into view. The 11 upper floors of each glazed tower-block, designed to contain offices and the book stacks, had to be lined with wooden shutters for protection. Altogether, there is a storage capacity for over 15,000,000 volumes. The reading rooms themselves, arranged around the gardens, evoking a vast, glassed-in cloister, cover a total area of 58,000sq m. The library is equipped with all the latest technological services and facilities.

The vast interior spaces are panelled in woven metal, wood and concrete and softened with hectares of rust colour carpet. The funishings are also Perrault's designs.

The area immediately surrounding the library, as well as parts of the interior, are open to the public. Take the escalators (east and west) from the esplanade down to the two main entrances and entrance halls at each end of the **haut-de-jardin** (upper garden level). Anyone can come into this area and there are limited guided visits (in French) of the building Monday to Saturday at 14.00, Sunday 15.00 (advisable to book in advance, ☎ 01 53 79 59 59). Here are also exhibition spaces for temporary exhibitions based on the collections, a bookstall and a cafeteria. The 1650-seat library on this level is open to anyone over 16 (with a daily or annual reader's ticket on sale in the entrance halls) and provides open access to 300,000 specifically acquired volumes, not part of the patrimonial collection.

The **rez-de-jardin** (garden level), is open only to readers and has 2000 places for researchers who have access to the closed stack collections as well as a collection on open access of some 400,000 volumes. The reading rooms and collections on both levels are organised into five departments, four of them thematic and one devoted to audio-visual material.

The present Bibliothèque Nationale at the Richelieu site will retain manuscripts, maps and plans, engravings, photographic material, coins and medals, and the performing arts and music collections; see Ch. 18.

Blvd St-Marcel runs southwest of Blvd de l'Hôpital to meet Av. des Gobelins, beyond which it divides to be continued by Blvd Arago to the west and Blvd de Port-Royal. A short distance south of this junction on the right and northwest of Pl. de l'Italie is **La Manufacture Nationale des Gobelins**, the famous tapestry factory that has been a state institution for over 300 years. The Manufacture brings together three great weaving workshops, Gobelins and Beauvais for tapestries and Savonnerie for carpets. This is a fascinating guided visit (in French), which can be taken on Tues–Thur at 14.00 and 14.45 (☎ 01 44 08 52 00, groups ☎ 01 44 61 21 69).

History of Les Gobelins

The renown of Les Gobelins began in 1662, when Colbert brought together Louis XIV's weaving workshops at this site, and its importance in the manufacture of tapestries has survived for over 300 years. The buildings were originally named after Jean Gobelin (d. 1476), head of a family who had set up their dye-works here on the banks of the Bièvre in 1443. The court painter, Le Brun, supervised the manufacture which, by 1667, included the royal furniture factory with silversmiths and cabinet makers, as well as the best Flemish weavers. The production was destined exclusively for the embellishment of royal palaces and as diplomatic gifts. The royal carpet factory, established at the Louvre by Henri IV in 1604, subsequently moved to a *savonnerie* (soap-factory) at Chaillot. The Savonnerie factory was placed under the artistic direction of Le Brun in 1663, and finally in 1826 transferred its workshops to Les Gobelins. The Beauvais tapestry workshops were a private enterprise founded in 1664, which reached its peak in the 18C. All three workshops came under the administration of the Mobilier National (or National Furniture Store) in 1937. However, the Beauvais works moved to Les Gobelins only in 1940 after the destruction of their workshop (although in 1989 part of the production returned to Beauvais).

The tapestry is still woven by hand on both high-warp (Gobelins), and low-warp looms (Beauvais). The highly skilled weaver works on the reverse side of the tapestry; the painting that he is copying is placed behind him and reflected in a mirror. The average amount of tapestry produced per person per day is 15sq cm. Both traditional designs, which feature a border, and modern designs, since 1945 without a border, are used.

In the former chapel, designed by Jacques V. Gabriel in 1723, hang two tapestries after cartoons by Raphael for the Vatican and copied at Gobelins in the early 18C. The visit takes you across Rue Berbier-du-Mets, behind the factory, which now covers the non-calcareous waters of the Bièvre, which used to flow between the dye-works and workshops. Little remains of the 15C but there are 17C/18C buildings; there are plans to renovate part of the site and create a museum. The Mobilier National, designed by Perret in 1938, and the gardens of Sq. René-le-Gall, are where the kitchen gardens of the weavers used to be.

Av. des Gobelins ends to the south at **Pl. d'Italie**, the hub of seven important thoroughfares. Going north on Av. des Gobelins, you will come to **St-Médard** (**Map 8; 8**), dedicated to the St Swithin of France. The nave and west front are of the late 15C; the choir, in construction from 1550 to 1632, was classicised in 1784, when the Lady Chapel was added. The church was sacked by the Huguenots in 1561, and not much 16C glass survives.

To the west of the church, the narrow, shabby but busy **Rue Mouffetard**, an ancient thoroughfare (the lower end is closed to traffic), climbs north through a tatty but picturesque district with a good street market and a village-like atmosphere. Several of the houses, although frequently altered, stand on medieval foundations. In Rue de l'Arbalète, at no. 3, Auguste Rodin was born in 1840. Eventually you pass (right) Pl. de la Contrescarpe, where no. 1 has a tablet commemorating the Cabaret de la Pomme-de-Pin, immortalised by Rabelais and the Pléiade.

Also in this district, but slightly to the west, in Rue Pierre-Brossolette, at the

Ecole de Physique et de Chimie industrielles, Pierre and Marie Curie did their experimental work in 1883–1905. Further west, and best approached by Rue d'Ulm (leading south from the Panthéon), is the Maronite church of N.-D. du Liban, facing Rue Lhomond. The Collège des Irlandais, founded in 1578 by John Lee and re-founded in 1687 by English Catholics as a seminary, stands at the corner of the adjacent Rue des Irlandais.

At 45 Rue d'Ulm is the **Ecole Normale Supérieure**, established in 1794 for the training of teachers and sited here since 1843. Pasteur worked in laboratories here between 1864 and 1888.

7 • Val-de-Grâce and Montparnasse

■ Arrondissements: 75005, 75014, 75015
Ⓜ Luxembourg, Port-Royal, Denfert-Rochereau, Vavin, Montparnasse-Bienvenue
🚆 Cité-Universitaire, Denfert-Rochereau

L'Amanguier, 46 Blvd. du Montparnasse, ☎ 01 45 48 49 16. Traditional food of reliable quality and prices, £

La Bélièr, 74 Rue Daguerre, ☎ 01 43 20 25 84. Bar, bistrot, budget menu, and great ambiance. Music after 10 pm, £

La Cagouille, 10–12 place Brancusi, ☎ 01 43 22 09 01. With terrace, for fish lovers only, produce straight from the market, ££

The brasseries where the Existentialists gathered in the 20s on Blvd du Montparnasse are still popular:

Closerie des Lilas, 171 Blvd du Montparnasse, ☎ 01 43 26 70 50/43 54 21 68. 1930s style bar and restaurant, slip in for a *coup de champagne*, ££

La Coupole, ☎ 01 43 20 14 20. Seats 600 but still gets crowded, ££;

Le Dôme, ☎ 01 43 35 25 81. Professional, specialises in oysters, pricey, ££

Le Dôme Bistrot, 1 Rue Delambre, ☎ 01 43 35 32 00. Charming but simple setting, where fish reigns, £–££

Giovanna, 22 Rue Edouard-Jacques, ☎ 01 43 22 32 09. Minuscule place, for home-made pasta and Italian and Moroccan dishes, £

Le Select, 99 Blvd du Montparnasse, ☎ 45 48 38 24. Popular bar, £

Near the park are:

Au Rendez-Vous des Camionneurs, 34 Rue des Plantes, ☎ 01 45 42 20 94. Friendly, comfortable, inexpensive, good quality, £

Au Vin des Rues, 21 Rue Boulard, ☎ 01 43 22 19 78. Robust Lyonnais cooking and wine at affordable prices, £

Bistrot Montsouris, 27 Av. Reille, ☎ 01 45 89 17 05. Unpretentious, mainly seafood, £–££.

Noura, 121 Blvd du Montparnasse, ☎ 01 43 20 19 19. Lebanese food with plenty of choice but variable quality, £

Pavillon Montsouris, 20 Rue Gazan, ☎ 01 45 88 38 52. Belle époque pavilion with regular clients and good cooking, £–££
Philippe Detourbe, 8 Rue Nicolas-Charlet, ☎ 01 42 19 08 59. The crowds rush here for the set five-course dinner menu, £–££

Picrocole, 9 Rue Vandamme, ☎ 01 43 21 57 58. Relaxed neigh-bourhood bistrot with 30s bar and courtyard; reasonable prices, £–££
Villa Toscane, 36–38 Rue des Volontaires, ☎ 01 43 06 82 92. Tiny idiosyncratic place, serving reasonable Italian menus, £

Montparnasse with its former literary and bohemian associations, now a busy shopping and residential area, has a slightly seedy charm and is watched over by the dark silhouette of the Montparnasse Tower. The monuments of the *quartier* are not among the most famous but include the marvellous Baroque church of Val-de-Grâce as well as the Paris Observatory, the Cité Universitaire in its gardens, the Tour Montparnasse, the Postal Museum, and the former studio of the sculptor Bourdelle. There is the curiosity of the Jardin Atlantique, planted on top of the mainline station of Montparnasse, and its famous cemetery is the resting place of Jean-Paul Sartre.

Rue St-Jacques (Map 8; 7; see Ch. 4 and below), is the connecting link between the Quartier Latin and Montparnasse via the Val-de-Grâce. This major artery of the Left Bank since Gallo-Roman times was followed in the 19C by Blvd St-Michel which runs a similar parallel route.

At no. 195 is the **Centre de la Mer et des Eaux: Institut Océanographique**, which has aquariums and frequent exhibitions; open Tues–Fri 10.00–12.30, 13.15–17.30, Sat, Sun 10.00–17.30. A little further along on the right is **St-Jacques-du-Haut-Pas**. This unadorned Classical building (1630–88) was originally the site of a hospice for pilgrims on the road to Santiago de Compostela and its 17C severity reflects its Jansenist connections. It was completed in 1712 with the help of the Duchesse de Longueville (1619–79) who is buried here, together with Jean Duvergier de Hauranne (1581–1643), prominent Jansenist, and Jean-Dominique Cassini (1625–1712), the astronomer. It has a fine organ, with a case dating mainly from 1609, transferred here from the church of St-Benoît-le-Bétourné and entirely rebuilt in 1971.

No. 254, at the corner of Rue de l'Abbé-de-l'Epée, is the **Institut National des Sourds-Muets**, a hospital for the deaf and dumb, founded by the Abbé de l'Epée (1712–89) about 1760. It was taken over by the State in 1790 and reconstructed in 1823. In the courtyard is a statue of the Abbé by Félix Martin, a deaf and dumb sculptor (1789).

Further on, at no. 269 (left) is the **Schola Cantorum**, a free conservatoire of music, established in 1896 by three pupils of César Franck, including Vincent d'Indy. The buildings (1674), by Charles d'Avilère, are those of the English Benedictine monastery of St Edmund, founded in France in 1615, which occupied this site from 1640 until the Revolution and is still an English property. The salon and staircase are good examples of 17C decor, and the chapel, where the exiled James II's body lay in state in 1701, is now a concert hall.

Rue St-Jacques widens opposite the magnificent Baroque façade of **Val-de-Grâce** (**Map 8; 7**), one of the best preserved examples of 17C architecture in Paris.

History of Val-de-Grâce

Anne of Austria commissioned François Mansart to build Val-de-Grâce in fulfilment of a vow for the birth of Louis XIV in 1638 after 23 years of childless marriage. The first stone of the new works was laid by the young king in 1645 and under Mansart's direction the church was built up to the entablatures of the nave and lower storey of the façade. But a year later Mansart was dismissed and the project was completed by Jacques Lemercier, Le Muet and Le Duc, and completed by 1667. The remains of royalty interred here, including Anne of Austria (wife of Louis XIII) and Marie-Thérèse (wife of Louis XIV), were dispersed at the Revolution.

In 1624 a Benedictine convent under the patronage of N.-D. du Val-de-Grâce was founded, which became a military hospital in 1790 and the Army Medical School was added in 1850. A new hospital was built at the end of the 20C. In the courtyard is a bronze statue of Napoléon's surgeon, Baron Larrey (1766–1842), by David d'Angers.

The porticoed and pedimented façade of the church is a splendid example of the Counter-Reformation style introduced by the Jesuits, and the lead and gilt **dome** (by Le Duc), one of the finest in France, shows the influence of Roman Baroque.

The highly Classical interior was decorated (1662–67) by François and Michel Anguier, Pierre Sarazin and others and the dome painting, *La Gloire des Bienheureux* (1663), is by Pierre Mignard. The high-altar, with its six huge twisted marble columns, is inspired by Bernini's baldacchino or canopy over the saint's tomb in St Peter's, Rome; the sculptured Nativity on it is a copy of Michel Anguier's original (now at St-Roch, see p 225). In the chapel on the right of the choir is a portrait of *Anne of Austria borne by an angel*; and in the Chapel of the Sacrament is the *Communion of the Angels*, by J.-B. de Champaigne. The St-Anne Chapel once contained the hearts of royalty.

Musée du Service de Santé des Armées, 1 Pl. A.-Laveran, ☎ 01 40 51 51 94, Tues, Wed 12.00–17.00, Sat–Sun 13.30–17.00.

Val-de-Grâce was only one of the many religious houses which, until the Revolution, were established in this district and some of the neighbouring street names recall vanished convents: Rue des Ursulines and Rue des Feuillantines.

Across Blvd de Port-Royal are two hospitals. The maternity hospital on the right has, since 1818, occupied the buildings of Port-Royal de Paris, a branch of the Jansenist abbey of Port-Royal-des-Champs (southwest of Versailles), destroyed at the instigation of the Jesuits in 1709. However, the chapel completed by Le Pautre in 1647 still stands, basically unaltered, and has kept some of the furnishings including, in the chapter house, the woodwork.

The extensive buildings of the Hôpital Cochin on the left of Rue Faubourg-St-Jacques lists George Orwell and Samuel Becket among its more famous patients. On the right, at no. 38, is the Hôtel de Massa (1784), transferred here from the Champs-Elysées in 1927, re-erected, and now occupied by the Société des Gens de Lettres.

Next turn right into the pleasant Rue Cassini, lined with early 20C buildings in variations of the Modern style although nos 2–6 contain fragments of old masonry. Many of these houses were built as artists' studios and the English engraver, S.W. Hayter, lived at no. 12.

Observatoire

The Observatoire, the oldest working observatory in the world, was founded by Louis XIV. On 21 June 1667 the meridian of Paris was established and determined the orientation of the building. It is indicated by a copper line embedded in the paving of the second floor (2° 20' 14" east of Greenwich). The Paris meridian was replaced by Greenwich in 1884. The four sides of the building face the cardinal points of the compass, and the latitude of the southern side is the recognised latitude of Paris (48° 50' 11" north) which, until 1912, was the basis for the calculation of longitude on French maps. The Observatoire is also the headquarters of the Bureau International de l'Heure, and a speaking clock is installed in its cellars.

The Observatoire was designed by Claude Perrault and completed in 1672. One of its directors was Jean-Dominique Cassini (1625–1712), the first of the family of astronomers and cartographers. The famous Danish astronomer Olaf Römer (1644–1710), worked here from 1672.

Application to attend a guided tour (first Saturday of each month) should be made in writing to the Secrétariat at 61 Av. de l'Observatoire, 75014 Paris (☎ 01 40 51 22 21).

In the entrance is the original speaking clock (1933). On the first floor of the main building is a **Museum of Astronomical Instruments**, and the contents of the Rotunda in the west tower illustrate the history of astronomy. From the second storey is a staircase to the terrace and in the east cupola is an equatorial telescope of 38cm aperture.

For the leafy gardens behind the Observatory, take Rue du Fb. St-Jacques to the entrance on Blvd Arago, open to the public from 1 April to 15 October, at 13.00. At no. 65 is a gate opening onto a hidden garden, known as the Cité Fleurie, which a group of artists' studios constructed from scraps salvaged from the Universal Exposition of 1878.

In the angle between Rue Cassini, Av. de l'Observatoire and Av. Denfert-Rochereau is the former Couvent du Bon Pasteur, now a centre for handicapped children. It encompasses the Pavillon Fontainier (water tower) built in 1624 as part of the rebuilding of the Roman aqueduct carrying water from Rungis to supply the Left Bank and the fountains of the Luxembourg Gardens, brought back to life by Marie de Médicis. On Av. Denfert-Rochereau is the Hôpital St-Vincent-de-Paul, with a chapel of 1650–55.

Slightly further north on Blvd Raspail (no. 261) is the **Cartier Foundation for Contemporary Art**, in a building by Jean Nouvel opened in 1994, which organises exhibitions of contemporary art by international artists. It has a garden landscaped by Lothar Baumgarten. Open 12.00–20.00, closed Mon (☎ 01 42 18 56 67).

Where Blvd Arago and Av. Denfert-Rochereau meet is a large junction, **Place Denfert-Rochereau**, known as the Place d'Enfer until 1879, when it received its present name in honour of the defender of Belfort during the Franco-Prussian War. The earlier name originated as Via Inferior, the Roman road (now Blvd St-Michel) leading south to the Ile de la Cité, parallel to and west of the Via Superior (now Rue St-Jacques). In the centre of the Place is a reduced version of Bartholdi's sculpture of the *Lion of Belfort* and the area is cheered up by four small squares planted with trees. In Square Ledoux on the south-west side are the remnants of twin pavilions of the old Barrière d'Enfer where levies were collected. These heavily rusticated remains of the wall of the *fermiers généraux* (1784) were designed by the great Neo-classical architect Claude Nicolas Ledoux.

The entrance to **Les Catacombes** is in the eastern pavilion of the Barrière. Guided visits lasting about 45 minutes take place Tues–Fri between 14.00 and 16.00, and Sat–Sun 09.00–11.00; 14.00–16.00 (☎ 01 43 22 47 63). (Take a torch and wrap up warm.) The tour starts with the historic background, then a macabre series of galleries lined with bones and skulls leading to a huge ossuary containing the debris of over six million skeletons.

This labyrinthine series of underground quarries, covering about 850 hectares and 20m down, first provided stone in Roman times. The 160km of tunnels extend from the Jardin des Plantes to the Porte de Versailles and as far as Montrouge and Montsouris. In the 1780s they became a charnel-house for bones removed from four overfull graveyards in the city, particularly the Cimetière des Innocents (see Ch. 19), and most of the victims of the Terror were transferred here. It took 15 months to transport these remains. In 1944 the Catacombs served as a headquarters of the Resistance Movement.

Leading south from Pl. Denfert-Rochereau, Av. René-Coty approaches the **Parc de Montsouris**, covering 16 hectares and laid out in 1875–78 as part of Haussmann's scheme to provide green spaces around the capital. The gardens imitate the informal English style with lawns and some 1400 trees in groups; near its north-east corner is a lake. As well as sculptures in stone and bronze, such as Etex's *Les Naufrages* (1882) and *Drame au désert* (1891) by Georges Gardet, there is also a bandstand, a café, and a marionnette theatre. The area west of the park is worth exploring for examples of 20C architecture.

Facing the south side of the park spread over about a kilometre along Blvd Jourdan, is the **Cité Universitaire**, founded in 1922 on the site of the 19C fortifications, to provide accommodation for about 7000 students in a park-like setting. The architecture of the 37 national halls of residence, designed to evoke national characteristics, includes wide spectrum of styles from 1922 to 1960. The Maison Internationale (1936), was financed by John D. Rockefeller but the most innovative building of the time was Le Corbusier's sleek Swiss Hall (1930–32) introducing revolutionary new elements, including *pilotis* (i.e., built on piles). A later example of Le Corbusier's work, in conjunction with Lúcio Costa, is the partly painted exposed concrete brutalism of the Brazilian Hall (1952). Other important buildings are the Japanese pavilion, designed by P. Sardou, the Dutch Hall, by M. Dudok, 1927, and the Fondation Avicenne, which is the most recent (1966–68) and exemplifies French architecture of the period.

Montparnasse

Returning to the Observatoire and continuing north, Av. Denfert-Rochereau brings you to the Carrefour de l'Observatoire. Straight ahead is the extravagant **Fontaine de l'Observatoire** (1875) by Germain Davioud, with Carpeaux's group of figures representing the four quarters of the globe, and bronze horses and turtles by Frémiet. To the northwest is François Rude's statue of Marshal Ney (1769–1815), who was shot nearby (and buried in Père Lachaise cemetery) for supporting Napoléon on his return from Elba. The *Closerie des Lilas*, behind it, built in 1903, altered in 1925, was one of the famous literary watering holes of the 1920s.

From the Carrefour de l'Observatoire the seemingly endless Blvd du Montparnasse runs northwest across Blvd Raspail, where to the north stands Rodin's statue of Balzac. This junction is the centre of a quarter which partly supplanted Montmartre as the principal artistic and bohemian rendezvous early in the 20C. Both Henry Miller and Ernest Hemingway have described the café life, disreputable and otherwise, of the district in its heyday.

To the southwest and parallel to Blvd du Montparnasse, is the Blvd Edgar-Quinet, with the main entrance of **Cimetière Montparnasse** (Map 7; 8), an 18-hectare site laid out in 1824. The list of the late and great buried here is impressive: Maupassant, Baudelaire, J.-K. Huysmans, Leconte de Lisle, Sainte-Beuve, Jean-Paul Sartre, Ionesco and Beckett among writers; César Franck, Saint-Saëns and Gainsbourg among composers and musicians; Fantin-Latour, Gérard, Houdon, Rude, Soutine, Zadkine, Bourdelle, Bartholdi and Brancusi, among artists and sculptors; Pierre-Joseph Proudhon, the social reformer; Arago, the scientist and politician; Alfred Dreyfus; Charles Garnier, the architect; André Citroën, the car manufacturer. A plan is available at the office just inside the gate.

History of the area

The district has inevitably changed since the 1920s, retaining only fading associations with late 19C and early 20C artists and intellectuals who inhabited the area. As well as the writers and critics who lived here (Sainte-Beuve, Rilke, Romain Rolland), Rodin, Carolus-Duran, Gauguin, Modigliani and Whistler at some point in their careers had studios in and around Montparnasse, and Trotsky frequented the Rotonde before 1917. It is still home to some artists, and the boîtes in Rue de la Gaîté and elsewhere continue to attract visitors. The large brasseries, such as *Le Dôme*, *La Coupole* and *La Rotonde*, while altered in character, are still popular.

The area is now dominated by the insolent **Tour Montparnasse** (200m high), a high-rise office block built in 1973, the first of its kind, and still an intrusion. Perhaps the only way to beat it is to go up it and there are impressive panoramic views from the open-air terrace on the 56th floor (1 Apr–30 Sept, weekdays 09.30–22.00, weekends 09.30–23.00; 1 Oct–31 March 09.30– 22.00; charge).

Adjacent to the Tour, and forming part of the glass and concrete complex, is the **Gare Montparnasse** (Map 7; 7), 18 storeys high, surrounding the station platforms on three sides.

The station, which serves Brittany and the Atlantic coast, has been the subject of a long series of improvements not least of which is **Le Jardin Atlantique**, built above the station. Enter the garden from Place des Cinq-Martyrs-du-Lycée-Buffon or from the mainline station. This urban breathing space uses metal, wood, marble and granite structures, with a central lawn featuring an intermittent fountain, the Ile des Hespérides, evoking the sound of waves on a seashore, and a meteorological centre. There is a sandy area for children and coastal plants are used to harmonise with the theme. On the west is a sports area; on the east a raised walkway and a group of small thematic gardens organised around the pavilions of the Blue Waves and of the Pink Rocks, intended to evoke ocean and sky.

Entering from the Jardin Atlantique (the Tower end) are the resolutely modern **Museums of Philippe Leclerc de Hauteclocque (Marshal Leclerc) and Jean Moulin**, which present aspects of these men's roles in the Second World War, Free French and Resistance. One room is dedicated to the Liberation of Paris. Open 10.00–17.40, closed Mon and public holidays (☎ 01 40 64 39 44).

At 34 Blvd de Vaugirard, north west of Montparnasse station, is the recently reopened **Musée de la Poste**. The updated museum presents some 500 years of the history of the French postal system in 15 rooms. The main sections, displayed chronologically and thematically, cover history, philately, art and society and the postal service today, illustrated using a range of exhibits. There are scale models, unusual objects and old letter-boxes, the earliest stamps and their printing, methods of communication and transport, through to postmen evoked by old costumes and prints. There is also a room devoted to the development of the air-mail service, telecommunication and the mechanisation. Open 10.00–18.00, closed Sun and public holidays (☎ 01 42 79 23 45).

Further to the west is Blvd Pasteur, off which to the southwest runs Rue du Docteur-Roux, with (left) the **Institut Pasteur**, founded by Louis Pasteur (1822–95) in 1887 and built by private subscription. Pasteur's apartment has become the **Musée Pasteur**, containing family memorabilia and the mausoleum with the chemist's tomb. (Open every day, 14.00–17.30. ☎ 01 45 68 82 82.)

At 16 Rue Antoine-Bourdelle, north of and parallel to Blvd de Vaugirard, is the discreet **Musée Bourdelle**, devoted to the sculptor Antoine Bourdelle, who lived and worked here from 1885 until his death. Open 10.00–17.40, closed Mon and public holidays (☎ 01 49 54 73 73).

Bourdelle's entire collection was donated to the Ville de Paris by his widow in 1949. This charming time-warp encompasses a small courtyard open to the street and the studios and furnished living apartments. A gallery for plaster models was added in 1961 and in 1990–92 a two-level extension was built for permanent and temporary exhibitions as well as a gallery for graphic arts (by appointment only) and a library. On display are studies, plaster casts and bronzes of his best known works. Bourdelle tended to work on a monumental scale and among powerful models and casts for larger works are the *Monument to General Alvear*, for Buenos Aires (1913–23); *Hercules the Archer*; and studies for the Hartmannweilerkopf crypt in Alsace; *Monument to Mickiewicz*; and *La France*. A pupil of Rodin, Bourdelle's earlier works, such as *Beethoven aux Grands Cheveux* (1891) show Rodin's influence while his later, more Classical style, appears in the reliefs for the Théâtre des Champs-Elysées (1912–13), strongly influenced by the dances of Isadora Duncan. Among his pupils were Giacometti and Germaine Richier.

8 • Faubourg St-Germain, eastern sector ~ Luxembourg and St-Germain-des-Prés

■ Arrondissement: 75006

🚇 Pont-Neuf, Odéon, Luxembourg, St-Sulpice, St-Germain-des-Prés, Mabillon

 The cafés which were once hangouts for impoverished intellectuals are now rather expensive but still something to experience:

Café des Deux Magots, 6 Pl. St-Germain-des-Près, ☎ 01 45 48 55 25. Named after the wooden Chinese statues inside, ££

Café de Flore, 172 Blvd St-Germain, ☎ 01 45 48 55 26. Art Deco décor, ££

Others include:

Alcazar, 62 Rue Mazarine, ☎ 01 53 10 19 99. Large, modern Conran restaurant, has become the rage, £–££

Allard, 41 Rue St-André-des-Arts, ☎ 01 43 26 48 23. A winning institution run by husband and wife team, £–££

L'Arbuci, 25 Rue de Buci, ☎ 01 44 32 16 00. Unusually intimate brasserie, serves sea-food and spit-roasts, £–££

La Bastide de l'Odeon, 7 Rue Corneille, ☎ 01 43 26 03 65. Bright Provençal cuisine, moderately priced, £

Le Bistrot d'Henri (Chez Henri), 16 Rue Princesse, ☎ 01 46 33 51 12. Classic friendly bistrot, £

Les Bookinistes, 53 Quai des Grands-Augustins, ☎ 01 43 25 45 94. One of chef Guy Savoy's other places. Trendy, £–££

Le Bouillon Racine, 3 Rue Racine, ☎ 01 44 32 15 60. Belgian cuisine in splendid Art Nouveau setting, music Mon & Thur, £

Brasserie Lipp, 151 Blvd St-Germain, ☎ 01 45 48 53 91. Beautiful brasserie which still attracts beautiful people, ££

La Cafetière, 21 Rue Mazarine, ☎ 46 33 76 90. French/Italian dishes, a happy unison, £–££

Casa del Habano, 169 Blvd St-Germain, ☎ 01 45 49 24 30. For cigar afficiandos, smoke along with classic Spanish food, ££

La Catalogne, 4-6-8 Cour du Commerce-St-André, ☎ 01 55 42 16 19. A modern bistrot, in the Catalonian tourist office, £–££

Aux Charpentiers, 10 Rue Mabillon, ☎ 01 43 26 30 05. Authentic Parisian bistrot where the carpenters guild once met, £–££

Lapérouse, 51 Quai des Grands-Augustins, ☎ 01 43 26 68 04. Favoured for its charming 19C décor on 4 floors, expensive, £££

Le Muniche, 7 Rue St-Benoît, ☎ 01 42 61 12 70. 1930s' brasserie with classic dishes, £–££

Le Palanquin, 12 Rue Princesse, ☎ 01 43 29 77 66. Vietnamese restaurant with some surprises and wonderful beamed interior, £–££

Le Petit Zinc, 11 Rue St-Benoît, ☎ 01 42 61 20 60. Fashionable Art-Deco with good affordable food, £–££

Polidor, 41 Rue Monsieur le Prince, ☎ 01 43 26 95 34. Lively and popular Bistrot with good, inexpensive fare, £

Le Procope, 13 Rue de l'Ancienne Comédie, ☎ 01 40 46 79 00. Established 1686, Paris's oldest café, attractive but touristy, £–££

Restaurant des Beaux Arts, 11 Rue Bonaparte, ☎ 01 43 26 92 64. Bit more up-market than when a student dive, but good value, £

La Rotisserie d'en Face, 2 Rue Christine, ☎ 01 43 26 40 98. Cagna's Left Bank Bistrot; reasonable set-price menus, ££

As emblematic of Paris as the Quartier Latin or Montparnasse, but timelessly elegant and fashionable, Faubourg St-Germain fascinates every visitor. This chapter covers the area between Blvd St-Michel, Rue des Saints-Pères and Blvd Raspail with its network of old streets. The oldest of the major churches of Paris, St-Germain-des-Prés, is close to the famous literary cafés *Les Deux Magots*, *Le Flore* and *Brasserie Lipp*. Smart but discreet hotels and restaurants, antiquarians selling books and bibelots, and modern galleries stand cheek-by-jowl with the best in fashion boutiques and one of the most colourful street markets in central Paris, Rue de Buci. The district's main buildings are the Institut de France, the Hôtel de la Monnaie, with a museum of coins and medals, and the Palais du Luxembourg standing in its famous gardens. There is a small museum dedicated to the sculptor Zadkine and another to Eugène Delacroix; the Neo-classical St-Sulpice contains work by the painter. Ch. 10 describes the part of the Faubourg which lies in the 7th arrondissement.

History of Faubourg St-Germain

Faubourg St-Germain stretches south from the Seine opposite the Louvre, between the Institut de France to the east to Pont de la Concorde to the west. In the Middle Ages much of this area, the property of the Abbaye St-Germain-des-Prés, was open country with a *bourg* which developed outside Philippe-Auguste's walls bounded in the 13C by Rues du Vieux-Colombier and des Saints-Pères. Early in the 14C more houses were built, and in the 17C the abbey enclosure was gradually dismantled. With the 16C–17C religious revival, several convents were built here and, in 1670, the Hôtel des Invalides was constructed on the west outskirts. By 1685 the new Pont Royal provided easy access to the Palais des Tuileries, the home of the court during the Regency (1715–23). This, together with the creation of the Ecole Militaire, was the main reason for building this new aristocratic quarter, which gradually supplanted the Marais. About half the houses were built between 1690 and 1725, a quarter between 1725 and 1750, and most of the rest between 1750 and 1790. In style they are very similar; often the more handsome façades face the interior garden, and the gateway or *porte-cochère* from the street leads to the *cour d'honneur*.

Haussmann in the mid-19C created the main thoroughfares, Blvd St-Germain, Rue de Rennes, and Blvd Raspail, obliterating small streets, houses and *hôtels particuliers*. The most characteristic streets of the once noble *faubourg* (suburb) are Rue de Lille, Rue de l'Université, Rue St-Dominique and Rue de Grenelle. About 100 old mansions remain, many of them converted to house embassies or government offices. The 6e and eastern half of the 7e arrondissements are still two of the most pleasant districts of Paris.

Blvd St-Michel to Rue Bonaparte and Rue de Rennes

Institut de France

Pl. de l'Institut, on the south bank of the Seine, facing the Louvre, is flanked by the curved wings of the Institut de France (**Map 8; 3**). These prestigious premises, with their gilded dome, are among the most attractive on this reach of the quais. The building may be visited Sat and Sun, by prior arrangement with the Secrétariat, 23 Quai de Conti, ☎ 01 44 41 43 35 (weekdays).

History of the Institut de France

This is an outstanding edifice, without parallel in 17C France, the oval cupola and semi-circular façade embodying characteristics typical of Roman Baroque. Louis Le Vau was responsible for the initial design, on the axis of the Cour Carrée of the Louvre, and it was built between 1662–91, the architects Lambert and d'Orbay carrying on where Le Vau left off. The Institut, founded in 1795, acquired the building in 1806 and moved from the Louvre.

The building was erected in accordance with the bequest of Cardinal Mazarin. A powerful statesman, Mazarin was first Minister of France while Anne of Austria acted as regent (1643–61) during the minority of Louis XIV. He gave 2 million livres in silver and 45,000 livres a year for the establishment of a college for 60 gentlemen of the four provinces acquired by the Treaty of the Pyrenees: Artois, Alsace, Roussillon and Piedmont (Pinerolo), known from then as the Collège des Quatre-Nations rather than by its official title, Collège Mazarin.

The east wing of the Institut and the adjacent Hôtel de la Monnaie (see below) cover the site of the Hôtel de Nesle (13C), in which was incorporated the 13C Tour Nesle or Hamelin, the river bastion of Philippe Auguste's wall (which ran south east parallel to Rue Mazarine). The western part, known as the Petit-Nesle and the workshop of the goldsmith Benvenuto Cellini in 1540–45, was demolished in 1663. The eastern part, or Grand-Nesle, rebuilt in 1648 by François Mansart, became the Hôtel de Conti, and in 1770, the Hôtel de la Monnaie (Mint).

The Institut de France comprises five academies: the exclusive Académie Française, founded by Cardinal Richelieu in 1635 and restricted to 40 members, whose particular task was the editing of the dictionary of the French language; the Académie des Beaux-Arts (1816), founded by Mazarin in 1648 as the Académie Royale de Peinture et de Sculpture; the Académie des Inscriptions et Belles-Lettres, founded by Colbert in 1663; the Académie des Sciences, also founded by Colbert, in 1666; and the Académie des Sciences Morales et Politiques, founded in 1795 and reconstituted in 1832. The Institut is also responsible for several collections, among them the Musée Marmottan. An annual general meeting of all five academies is held on 25 October.

The Académie Française holds special receptions for newly elected members who are known as *Les Immortels* (because their ranks are always refilled). Only in 1980 was the first woman member, the writer Marguerite Yourcenar, elected.

Institut de France, Quai de Conti

From the first octagonal courtyard, beyond which are two others, one of them the Kitchen Courtyard of the old college, an elegant staircase (1824) by Vaudoyer leads to the **Bibliothèque Mazarine**. Little changed since the 17C, it contains c 450,000 vols, 4600 manuscripts and 2100 incunabula. Originally the Cardinal's personal library, it opened to scholars in 1643, became the first public library in France and was considerably augmented by other collections during the Revolutionary period. The Institut library is also in this wing, together with several rooms decorated with academic statues and busts of eminent academicians.

In the former chapel in the west wing is the Salle des Séances Solennelles. Restoration has undone the damage caused by Vaudoyer, and Mazarin's tomb, by Coysevox, has been returned from the Louvre. The room contains some 400 seats (green for members of the Académie Française; red for the others), and is used for receptions and general meetings.

The riverside embankment here, as elsewhere in this reach of the Seine, is lined with the bookstalls of the *bouquinistes* or second-hand booksellers. At 13 Quai de Conti is the Hôtel Guénégaud or de Sillery-Genlis, by François Mansart (1659), often visited by Napoléon as a young officer; Napoléon's surgeon, Baron Larrey, lived here from 1805 to 1832.

No. 11, the **Hôtel de la Monnaie**, the former Mint, is a dignified building by J.-D. Antoine, who made it his home. The handsome doorway is ornamented with Louis XV's monogram and elegant bronze knockers; above is the *fleur-de-lys* escutcheon supported by Mercury and Ceres. From the handsome 18C vestibule, a double staircase on the right ascends to the the Salle Guillaume Dupré, in the centre of the building, which is (apart from the modern ceiling) representative of the best Louis XVI style. This and the adjacent rooms are used for temporary exhibitions.

On the opposite side of the courtyard in the former ateliers or workshops of the mint is the **Musée de la Monnaie**, open 11.00–17.30, Sat–Sun 12.00–17.30; closed Mon and some public holidays (☎ 01 40 46 55 33). The visit starts on the ground floor to the right. This gallery is divided into nine sections and takes you through the evolution of French currency from the time of Roman Gaul to the Revolution with the aid of coins and medals displayed in transparent vertical mounts and presentations explaining clearly the different periods. The visit continues on an upper floor with three sections devoted to the period from the Revolution to the present day. On a lower level, the last section is the Machine Room. There is an audio-visual presentation on the ground floor. Although in 1973 the minting of French coins was transferred to a new establishment at Pessac, near Bordeaux, some pieces are still minted here such as medals, prototypes and *coins d'essais* as well as collectables and jewellery. The ateliers can be visited by prior appointment on Wed and Fri afternoons; telephone two days in advance.

In the adjacent boutique (entrance also on Rue Guénégaud), there are medals and a tempting array of other replicas, as well as jewellery for sale.

At no. 5, on the corner of Rue Guénégaud, Col de Marguerittes, of the Resistance, set up his headquarters while conducting operations for the liberation of Paris 19–28 August 1944. A segment of Philippe Auguste's wall is visible at the end of the adjacent Rue de Nevers (entered below an arch).

Continuing from the southern end of the Pont Neuf, Rue Dauphine, cut in 1607, runs through picturesque streets, passing on the left at 9 Rue Mazet the site of Chez Magny, a literary rendezvous in the 1860s. The Carrefour de Buci with its enticing **street market** is a veritable assault on the senses.

Quai des Grands-Augustins, between Pont St-Michel and the Pont-Neuf, built in 1313, is the oldest quai in Paris. It took its name from a convent situated here from 1293 until its demolition in 1797 and is bordered by fine mansions, from the 14C to 16C. There are several good restaurants on the quay (see above). Rue Séguier, lined with old houses, leads south to meet Rue St-André-des-Arts, also containing several notable 17C–18C buildings (nos 27, 28 and 52).

From Pl. St-André-des-Arts, to the east, Rue Hautefeuille leads south; no. 5, the Hôtel des Abbés de Fécamp, has a pretty turret. Also running south Rue de l'Eperon shortly meets (right) Rue du Jardinet. At the end of this the alley is the entrance to the Cour de Rohan (16C–17C), originally part of the palace of the Archbishop of Rouen, with an old mounting block still in place. Pass through an archway and turn left to see, through the window of the boutique at no. 4 in the Cour de Commerce-St-André, the base of one of Philippe Auguste's towers.

At no. 9, opposite, popular myth has it that Dr Joseph-Ignace Guillotin, professor of anatomy, perfected his 'philanthropic beheading machine', although in fact he merely proposed to the *Assemblée constituante* that beheading should be the only method of capital punishment, preferably by machine. A mechanic built one model to the specifications of the secretary of the College of Surgeons, Dr Louis, which was put into operation on 25 April 1792, and was first known as the Louisette.

Rue de l'Ancienne Comédie (the next street to the west) takes its name from the Comédie Française of 1689–1770, which occupied no. 14, while opposite is *Le Procope*, created in 1686, which claims to be the oldest café in Paris and was the favourite haunt of many generations of writers—Voltaire, Balzac, George Sand and Oscar Wilde among others (see above).

At no. 42 Rue Mazarine, back towards the Institut, was the site of the jeu de paume de la Bouteille, where the Abbé Perrin established the Opéra in 1669–72; it was then occupied by Molière's company in 1673–80, and by the Comédie-

Française in 1680–89. No. 12 is the site of another *jeu de paume*, where the Illustre Théâtre was opened in December 1643 by Molière's company. No. 30, known as the Hôtel des Pompes, was until 1760 the headquarters of the *pompiers* or fire brigade of Paris, founded in 1722.

In the mid-19C, Blvd St-Germain was cut through the meandering urban lanes leading south from the river. Opposite Rue de l'Ancienne Comédie, beyond the Pl. Henri-Mondor, is the Carrefour de l'Odéon, both busy crossroads. At the Café Voltaire, which stood there, a banquet was held in honour of Gauguin before he left for Tahiti in 1891.

To the east, at 12 Rue de l'Ecole de Médecine, is the old **Faculty of Medicine** on the site of the Collège de Bourgogne and Collège des Prémontrés. Gondouin was responsible in 1769–76 for the courtyard and pedimented entrance, a grandiose Classical structure, enlarged by Ginain between 1878–1900.

In the courtyard is a statue of the anatomist Xavier Bichat (1771–1802) by David d'Angers (1788–1856). The library contains c 600,000 volumes and commentaries of the heads of the faculty from 1395 onwards. Also of interest are the lecture hall, the **Musée d'Histoire de la Médecine** (open 14.00–17.30, closed summer: Sat, Sun, winter: Thur, Sun and some public hols, ☎ 01 40 46 16 93), and the Salle du Conseil, hung with four Gobelins tapestries of the Louis XIV period, after Le Brun. Opposite is the entrance to the former refectory of the Couvent des Cordeliers, a 15C Franciscan house.

At no. 5, the Institut des Langues Modernes occupies the old domed Amphithéâtre du Jardin du Luxembourg St-Côme (1691–94), with an attractive portal. This was originally the lecture-hall of the College of Surgery. A plaque commemorates the birth of the actress Sarah Bernhardt (1844–1923).

Further east (left) at the corner of the southern section of Rue de Hautefeuille (no. 32), Gustave Courbet had his studio in the former chapel of the Collège des Prémontrés.

Rue de l'Ecole-de-Médecine narrows at the eastern end before meeting Blvd St-Michel. From its western end, a flight of steps ascends to Rue Monsieur-le-Prince (de Condé). To the left, on meeting Rue de Vaugirard, is the Lycée St-Louis, built by Bailly on the site of the Collége d'Harcourt (1280), where the writers Racine and Boileau studied. Its entrance faces Pl. de la Sorbonne.

Adjacent to the south end of Rue Monsieur-le-Prince is Pl. Edmond-Rostand, looking across to the Panthéon (see Ch. 4). To the south, on the right of Blvd St-Michel, the Ecole Supérieure des Mines occupies the Hôtel de Vendôme, an 18C building enlarged after 1840, its principal façade facing towards the Luxembourg Gardens. It contains a **Museum of Mineralogy**, open Tues–Fri 13.30–18.00, Sat 10.00–12.30, 14.00–17.00, closed Mon, Sun, public holidays (☎ 01 40 51 91 39).

The Jardin and the Palais du Luxembourg

One of many entrances to the Jardin du Luxembourg (**Map 8; 5**) is a few paces south of Pl. Edmond-Rostand. This extensive garden (23 hectares), embellished by more than 80 statues, two fountains and a pond, forms a pleasantly refreshing area in a *quartier* with few green spaces and on sunny weekends it is packed with people of all ages taking the air. Planned in the 17C, it was radically altered in 1782 and 1867, although the basic layout follows to some extent the one that was first created for Marie de Médicis. You will find cafés, a bandstand, carousel, marionnette theatre and children's play area and you might also see chess-players locked in combat.

Steps descend from the east terrace to lawns surrounding an octagonal pond with a fountain. Beyond the formal west terrace is the Jardin Anglais enclosing a replica of the *Statue of Liberty* by Bartholdi, given to the United States in 1885. To the southwest is a fruit garden. Due south, beyond Pl. André-Honnorat, the impressive perspective between the two branches of Av. de l'Observatoire was achieved at the cost of the Carthusian monastery demolished at the Revolution. Landscaped during the First Empire (1804–15), these gardens are named Jardin Robert-Cavelier-de-la-Salle and Jardin Marco-Polo.

North of the central octagonal pond, on the right, at the end of an oblong pool, is the **Fontaine Médicis**, attributed to Salomon de Brosse (c 1627), in the style of an Italianate grotto. It was moved here in 1861. In the central niche is *Polyphemus about to crush Acis and Galatea*; on either side are *Pan* and *Diana*, the work of Augustin Ottin (1866). At the back is a low-relief, the *Fontaine de Léda*, brought from the Rue du Regard in 1855.

A small selection of the many scattered sculptures, some of distinctly dubious quality, includes Stendhal by Rodin, George Sand by François Sicard, Leconte de Lisle by Denys Puech (1898), the Seller of Masks by Zacharie Astruc (1883), a monument to Watteau by Henri Gauquié, a bust of Beethoven by Bourdelle, and the monument to Eugène Delacroix by Dalou.

The Palais du Luxembourg

The Palais du Luxembourg (**Map 8; 5**) was once a royal residence. Heavily rusticated, it is more attractive outside than in. The northern façade, where the main entrance is surmounted by an eight-sided dome, is original; the south façade, facing the gardens, is a 19C copy by Gisors. The two wings, terminating in steep-roofed pavilions, with three orders of columns superimposed, are connected by a single-storeyed gallery.

History of the Palais du Luxembourg

The Luxembourg was built by Salomon de Brosse in 1615–27 for Marie de Médicis, widow of Henri IV, who, it is said, sought a refuge from the noisy Louvre to a more rural setting reminiscent of Tuscany and a palace recalling the Pitti Palace, her birthplace in Florence. She acquired the mansion of the Duc de Tingry-Luxembourg (the Petit-Luxembourg; 1570–1612), hence its name. The building was altered in 1808 and enlarged in 1831–44.

After Louis XIII's death, the palace passed to her second son Gaston, Duc d'Orléans, and the Palais Médicis became known as the Palais d'Orléans. Subsequently, it belonged in succession to Mlle de Montpensier, the Duchesse de Guise (1672), Louis XIV (1694) and the Orléans family.

It was used as a prison during the Revolution and in 1794 the Directory transferred the seat of government from the Tuileries to the Luxembourg. In 1800 it became the Palais du Consulat, under the Empire it was the Palais du Sénat and later the Chambre des Pairs (House of Lords). Several important people were tried here, including Louis-Napoléon Bonaparte after his attempted coup in 1840. From 1852 to 1940, except for a short time, the Palais was the meeting-place of the Senate, the upper chamber of the French Republic. In 1940–44 it was occupied as the Luftwaffe's headquarters and reverted in 1958 to the Senate.

The **interior**, drastically remodelled by Jean Chalgrin under Napoléon I, is decorated in the sumptuous 19C manner, replete with an indifferent group of statues and paintings, historical and allegorical. The celebrated series of paintings devoted to the *Life of Marie de Médicis*, by Rubens, which once hung in the palace, is now in the Louvre.

Notable is the luxuriously gilt Cabinet Doré, Marie de Médicis's audience chamber. Other rooms (on the first floor) occasionally open to the public are the Salles des Conférences, the hemicycle of the Salle de Séances and the library, overlooking the gardens, with magnificent paintings by Delacroix. Those above the window show *Alexander Placing the Poems of Homer in Darius's Golden Coffer* and, in the cupola, the *Limbo of Dante's Inferno*.

The adjoining **Petit-Luxembourg** (now the residence of the President of the Senate) was presented to Richelieu by Marie de Médicis in 1626. It includes the cloisters and chapel of the Filles du Calvaire, for whom the queen built a convent; the chapel is a charming example of the Renaissance style; the cloister forms a winter-garden. To the west is the Orangery, once occupied by a museum, some of the former contents of which now embellish the Musée d'Orsay.

A few paces to the north east of the Palais, in isolation and surrounded by arcades, stands the **Odéon**, **Théâtre de l'Europe**, a focus of attention during the student *Manifestations* in 1968. It was built 1779–82 as the Théâtre-Français in the form of a Classical temple, by Wailly and Peyre in the garden of the demolished Hôtel de Condé. The name was changed to Théâtre de l'Odéon in 1797 and it had to be rebuilt by Chalgrin after a fire in 1799, re-opening in 1808. The ceiling of the auditorium was decorated by André Masson in 1965 and the theatre has hosted many controversial and memorable plays.

From its north entrance, Rue de l'Odéon, bordered by 18C houses, slopes downhill towards the Carrefour de l'Odéon. At no. 12 once stood the Librairie Shakespeare (Shakespeare and Co, see Ch. 4), founded by Sylvia Beach, where in 1922 the first edition of James Joyce's *Ulysses* was published, in an edition of 1000 numbered copies.

The main entrance of the Palais du Luxembourg, is in **Rue de Vaugirard**, the longest street in Paris, stretching from Blvd St-Michel to the Porte de Versailles. The wide and stately Rue de Tournon, with its fine 18C façades and elegant shops, runs gently down to the Blvd St-Germain, and continues on to the river and the Institute as Rue de Seine, flanked by attractive houses.

The next street, turning right off Rue de Vaugirard, Rue Bonaparte, becomes narrower and more interesting the other side of Blvd St-Germain as it approaches the Seine. A commercial street, it is a great place to linger and admire the numerous antique shops and art galleries. Between Rue de Vaugirard and Pl. St-Sulpice is a small garden, l'Allée du Seminaire where, under shady chestnuts is the Fontaine de la Paix, originally in Place St-Sulpice. Rue Bonaparte skirts **Place St-Sulpice**, since 1844 embellished with the Fontaine des Quatre-Evêques by Visconti with statues of four famous preaching bishops: Bossuet, Fénelon, Massillon and Fléchier. A charming and elegant part of the Left Bank, in June the square hosts an antiques fair.

At no. 6 is a dignified mansion by Servandoni (1754), the first of a range which never materialised. Although the merchandise in the shops in the neighbourhood is changing, traditionally this has always been the place to buy ecclesiastical artefacts.

St-Sulpice

The wealthiest church on the Left Bank, St-Sulpice (**Map 8; 5**) is a fine Italianate building, imposing mainly for its size. The sober west front, like a Roman theatre, features a two-storey colonnade of superimposed Doric and Ionic orders. The north tower, topped by a balustrade, is 73m high; the unfinished south tower is 5m lower. The scale of the project and the change in style of the elevations, notably the Jesuit or Baroque characteristics of the transept arm, are evident from Rue Palatine on the south flank.

History of St-Sulpice

A succession of masons and a succession of designs mark the character of this church. Begun in 1646 by Gamard, to replace an older church, it was continued on a larger scale by Gittard in 1670. After an interval from 1678 to 1719 work was resumed by Oppenordt, still on the designs of Gittard, but the tower added above the crossing had to be demolished after 1731. The building of the west front was entrusted to Giovanni Servandoni, a Florentine, who was replaced in 1766 by Maclaurin. His successor, Chalgrin, built the north tower in 1778–80, but the south tower was left incomplete.

In the form of a Latin cross, the **interior** is spacious and regular in Counter-Reformation style, measuring 115m long, 57m wide, and 33m high, with high arcades to the aisles. The **organ**, one of the largest in existence (6588 pipes), was built in 1781 and remodelled in 1860–62; the case was designed by Chalgrin, with statues by Clodion and decoration by Duret. The church is noted for its music and organ recitals.

Among the furnishings are two huge *Tridacna gigas* shells serving as holy-water stoups, presented to François I by the Venetian Republic; supported by 'rocks' carved from marble by Pigalle. The late-18C pulpit, designed by Wailly, bears gilded figures of Faith and Hope by Guesdon, and Charity by Dumont.

The lateral **chapels** are decorated with frescoes. The most important are the late works (1855–61) by Delacroix in the first chapel on the right. These vigorous images of spiritual conflict represent, in the vault, *St-Michael Vanquishing the Devil*, on the left, *Jacob Wrestling with the Angel*, and on the right *Heliodorus Chased from the Temple*. In the 5th chapel is the tomb, by Slodtz, of the curé Languet de Gergy (1674–1750), founder of the Enfants Malades, and responsible for the completion of the church.

In the paving of the south transept is a bronze table connected by a **meridian line** with a marble obelisk in the north transept. At noon the sun's rays, passing through an aperture in a blind window in the south transept, strike the meridian at specific points according to the time of year: during the winter solstice the sun strikes the obelisk, and during the spring and autumn solstice, the ray strikes the bronze table.

The **sacristy** on the south has some good 18C woodwork. The statues against the pillars of the choir are by Bouchardon and his workshop (1740), and the stalls are 18C. The high windows are 17C except the Sacré Coeur, which is of 1885. The sizeable, domed **Lady Chapel** was designed by Servandoni but, damaged by fire in 1762, its trappings were restored by Wailly in 1774. The original painting by F. Lemoyne (1731–32) in the cupola has undergone several alterations. The four easel paintings are by Carle van Loo (1746–51) and the subtly lit marble Virgin (placed here in 1774), in the niche behind the altar, is by

Pigalle, with angels by Mouchy. The bronze altar relief is by M.A. Slodtz (1730). Remains of the 16C church may be seen in the crypt.

Continue north to cross Rue du Four. Beyond is the busy intersection of the recently renamed **Place Jean-Paul Sartre et Simone de Beauvoir** (formerly Place St-Germain-des-Prés). Diagonally opposite are the best-known and still popular cafés of Paris made famous by the elite of the artistic and literary world—Romantics, Surrealists and Existentialists—who patronised them up to the 1950s, *Café des Deux Magots* and *Café de Flore* (see above).

St-Germain-des-Prés

Dominating the north of the square is the revered and reassuring tower of St-Germain-des-Prés. Although heavily rebuilt and restored, this is the oldest church in Paris and the only one retaining any considerable remains of Romanesque work.

History of St-Germain-des-Prés

A part of the great Benedictine abbey founded in 558 by Childebert I, who was buried there, as was St Germanus, Bishop of Paris (d. 576), this site was also the burial place of the Merovingians. The church was rebuilt at the beginning of the 11C, and the nave completed up to the vaults by 1050. The base of the west tower dates from this time. Pope Alexander III consecrated the enlargement of the chancel in 1163 and in the 13C the master mason, possibly Pierre de Montreuil, came up with a solution to the long-standing problem of how to vault the curved section of an ambulatory. The ensemble was embellished at this time with a Gothic Lady Chapel and cloisters. A small section of the cloisters stands in the gardens.

In the 17C, when it was the chief house of the reformed Congregation de St-Maur, the wooden roof of the nave was replaced by a neo-Gothic vault, the transepts were remodelled (c 1644), and the bell-chamber of the tower was added. Badly desecrated at the Revolution, drastic alterations in the 19C included the rebuilding of the Lady Chapel in 1819, the truncation in 1822 of the two towers flanking the choir and the restoration of the upper part of the west belfry.

The massive flying buttresses of the choir are among the earliest in France. The west porch dates from 1607, but retains the jambs of a 12C door and a battered lintel depicting the Last Supper. A fragment of the 11C tympanum was found during excavations in 1971–73. The beautiful **chapel of St-Symphorian**, begun in the 6C and once the Merovingian necropolis, with 11C–12C frescoes, which is on the right (south) of the entrance, is open on Tues and Thur 13.30–17.30 (free guided tour in French).

The **interior** (65m by 21m, and 19m high), an important architectural document of the transition from Romanesque in the nave to the earliest Gothic in the choir, was painted all over with murals from 1842–64, by Hippolyte Flandrin and friends. The neo-Gothic vaults of the nave and the aisles date from 1644–46. The sculpted capitals are copies (1848–53) of the originals now in Musée du Moyen Age, with the exception of one remaining in the northwest corner.

To the right in the **south aisle** is a marble image of N.-D. de Consolation, presented to the Abbey of St-Denis by Queen Jeanne d'Evreux in 1340. In the south transept is the tomb, by Girardon, of Olivier and Louis de Castellan, killed in the king's service in 1644 and 1669.

The small marble columns in the triforium of the **choir** are re-used material from the 6C antecedent of this church, the abbey of St-Vincent and their bases and capitals are 12C. When cleaning work was done on the ambulatory in the 1950s, the 12C structure and capitals of some of the **eastern chapels** came to light. In the first ambulatory-chapel is the tomb of Lord James Douglas (1617–45; son of the first Marquess of Douglas), commander of Louis XIII's Scots regiment, killed near Arras. In the second chapel are tombstones of Descartes (1596–1650) moved from Ste-Geneviève in 1819 and of Mabillon. The fourth chapel has fragments of mid-13C stained glass. The Lady Chapel was rebuilt and decorated in the 19C.

In the **north aisle** is the tombstone of Nicolas Boileau (1636–1711) trans-fered from the Sainte-Chapelle, and the tomb of William Douglas, 10th Earl of Angus (1554–1611), who died in the service of Henri IV. In the north transept are a statue of St Francisco Xavier, by G. Coustou, and the theatrical tomb, by G. and B. Marsy, of John Casimir V, King of Poland, Abbot of St-Germain in 1669, who died in 1672.

In the little gardens of Square L.-Prache to the north are fragments of sculptures from the Lady Chapel (1212–55) and Picasso's *Head of a Woman* given in 1959 in homage to Guillaume Apollinaire. In Square F.-Desruelles on the Blvd St-Germain side of the church is a statue of the potter, Bernard Palissy and a mon-umental portico in ceramic and stone made at the Sèvres works by Risler for the Great Exhibition of 1900.

In 1857, six years before he died at 6 Rue de Furstenberg (or Fürstemberg) Delacroix built a studio in the adjoining Pl. de Fürstemberg, which with its four Paulownias, is now less of a back-water than it once was. This was later shared by Monet and Bazille, and now contains the **Musée Delacroix**, open 09.30–17.00, closed Tues and 1/1, 1/5, 25/12 (☎ 01 44 41 86 50). This is where Delacroix pre-pared the works for St-Sulpice and it now contains memorabilia and small paint-ings. The little garden has been returned to the form it had during Delacroix's time.

West of Rue Bonaparte and Rue de Rennes

Rue Bonaparte continues north, intersecting Rue Jacob. The Hôtel du Marquis de Persan (nos 7–9) was the birthplace of the painter Edouard Manet in 1832.

The main entrance of the **Ecole National Supérieur des Beaux-Arts** (School of Fine-Arts) (**Map 8; 3**), is at 14 Rue Bonaparte. Begun in 1820 by Debret and fin-ished in 1862 by Duban, it replaced the convent of the Petits-Augustins, founded in 1608, of which certain relics remain. It was here that Alexandre Lenoir (1762–1839) collected together numerous pieces of sculpture, saving them from destruction during the Revolutionary period (including the tombs of the kings from St-Denis). At the Restoration many, but not all, were returned to their place of ori-gin or dispersed among museums. The building was further enlarged in 1885 by the acquisition of the Hôtel de Chimay (see below). This was the first great archi-tectural school and of course many celebrated 19C and 20C artists studied here.

The courtyard of the school can be seen from the street and is open on the third Monday of each month (not during academic holidays, ☎ 01 47 03 52 15). For temporary exhibitions enter by Quai Malaquais.

Façade by Philibert Delorme in the courtyard of the Ecole des Beaux-Arts

If you do get inside the courtyard, you see the former convent church (c 1600) (occasionally used for temporary exhibitions) with, re-erected against the south wall, the central part of the façade of the Château d'Anet (c 1540), by Philibert Delorme. This façade is cited as the earliest example in France of the correct use of the three orders of architecture according to Vitruvius. In the vestibule are more souvenirs of Anet and the small hexagonal Chapel des Louanges, on the Rue Bonaparte side, was built by Marguerite de Valois. Its dome is the earliest built in Paris (1608). An arcade from the Hôtel de Torpane (c 1570) and the façade from the Hôtel de Chimay are also preserved. Scattered around the courtyards and inside the buildings are many pieces of sculpture, while the Salle de Melpomène is used to display the work of students when competing for the Grands Prix de Rome.

Leading south west from the Pl. St-Germain-des-Prés is Rue de Rennes, with the tall finger of Tour Montparnasse (see Ch. 7) in the distance. A little way on the left is Rue de Cassette, one of the oldest in this district with 18C houses. Turning right at the end of this street into **Rue de Vaugirard**, you pass the domed St-Joseph-des-Carmes, once the chapel of a Carmelite convent, dating from 1613–20, and containing several 17C canvases. In the crypt are the bones of some 120 priests massacred in the convent garden in September 1792. Joséphine de Beauharnais, later Madame Bonaparte, was one of many imprisoned here during the Terror.

Adjacent are the buildings of the Institut Catholique, founded in 1875, the most prestigious Catholic teaching establishments in France. Here, in 1890, radio waves were discovered by Edouard Branly (1844–1940).

Past the Institut Catholique is the crossroads with Rue d'Assas. Tucked away on the south (left) side of Rue d'Assas, at 100 bis, across a mini sculpture garden, is the **Musée Zadkine** (Map 8; 7) (10.00–17.40, closed Mon, ☎ 01 43 26 91 90). The home and studio from 1928 of the Russian-born sculptor Ossip Zadkine, on exhibition are about 100 of the 300 works bequeathed by his widow including a model for *La Ville détruite* for Rotterdam, and several tributes to Van Gogh. This interesting little museum demonstrates the range of Zadkine's sculptures, from his early Cubist-inspired work through Expressionism and Abstract style.

Turning right into Rue d'Assas, and recrossing Rue de Rennes, you reach the eastern part of Rue du Cherche-Midi which derives its name from an 18C sign on no. 19 representing an astronomer tracing a sundial and contains several attractive 17C–18C houses.

From the busy Carrefour de la Croix-Rouge, sporting a centaur sculpted by César as a *Hommage to Picasso* (1988), Rue de Sèvres leads south west. (For the west section of Rue de Sèvres and Rue de Grenelle, see Ch. 10.)

Across this junction is Rue du Dragon, the possible site of the pottery workshop of Bernard Palissy. Victor Hugo as a young man lived at no. 30. The next street along, Rue de Grenelle, parallel with Rue du Dragon, is Rue des Saints-Pères which runs north and crosses Blvd St-Germain.

On the east side of Rue des Saints-Pères, after crossing St-Germain, is a minuscule garden, named after a Ukranian poet, Taras-Chevtchenko (1814–61). The church of the Ukranian Catholic community in Paris (St-Vladimir-le-Grand) now occupies the Chapelle St-Pierre, rebuilt in 1611, the sole relic of the Hôpital de la Charité, here from 1605 to 1937.

Further north, at the corner of Rue de Lille, is the Ecole des Langues Orientales, founded by the Convention in 1795. The artist Edouard Manet died at 5 Rue des Saints-Pères and at no. 45 is the **Museum of Anatomy–Delmas-Orfila-Rouvière** (to visit, ☎ 01 42 86 20 47).

Rue des Saints-Pères brings you back to Quai Malaquais and a number of 17C–18C mansions. Henrietta Maria (the widow of Charles I) lived at no. 17, part of the Hôtel de Chimay (Ecole des Beaux Arts), built by François Mansart c 1640, and altered in the 18C. No. 9, at the corner of Rue Bonaparte, the Hôtel de Transylvanie, is a good example of Louis XIII architecture (1622–28).

9 • Musée d'Orsay

> ■ Arrondissement: 75007
> 🚇 Musée d'Orsay, Solférino
> 🚋 Musée d'Orsay
>
> *Café des Hauteurs*. This café on the upper level serves light meals, £. There is also fast food on the level above *Café des Hauteurs*, £
>
> *Restaurant du Musée*, ☎ 01 45 49 47 03. This popular belle époque style restaurant was part of the former hotel, £–££

• Open Tues–Sun, summer 09.00–18.00, winter 10.00–18.00, Sun 10.00–18.00 all year, Thur until 21.45. Closed Mon, 1/1, 1/5, 25/12. ☎ 01 40 49 48 14, recorded information ☎ 01 45 49 11 11. Main entrance, 1 Rue de la Légion d'Honneur.

The Quai d'Orsay is dominated by the huge and ornate bulk of the former Gare d'Orsay, still bearing the names of destinations it once served—Orléans, Bordeaux, Toulouse, etc. It has two great clocks above the massive glazed arcades, and large allegorical figures look out from its façade across the river to the Tuileries Gardens. The new footbridge, the **Pont de Solférino**, opening in 2001, will link the Quai and the Tuileries.

The Musée d'Orsay was inaugurated in December 1986 (**Map 7; 2**). This remarkable metamorphosis of railway station into museum is extremely popular with art-loving Parisians. The aim of the museum is to continue, chronologically, where the Louvre leaves off, bringing together national collections of the second half of the 19C and the early 20C. It is an important record of the different themes of mid-19C art and follows the evolution of art through Impressionism and beyond. The works exhibited include all aspects of the visual arts: painting and drawing (including pastels), sculpture, decorative arts and photography, but the museum is probably best known for the collection of Impressionist paintings. The works assembled came from the Louvre, the Jeu de Paume, the Palais de Tokyo, the Musée de Luxembourg and provincial museums, and through donation and acquisition.

History of the Musée d'Orsay

The building was originally the Gare and Hôtel d'Orsay, erected in 1898–1900 by Victor Laloux on the site of the ancient Cour des Comptes, set ablaze in 1871 during the Commune. With a metal frame, intended to be both functional and decorative, the elevation towards the Seine was faced with stone to complement the Louvre on the opposite bank. The hotel façade faced west on Rue de la Légion d'Honneur. Edouard Detaille, the artist, remarked ironically at the time that the railway station looked exactly like a Palais des Beaux-Arts, but 86 years were to elapse before the transformation took place.

By 1939 the station had virtually outlived its usefulness because of its comparatively short platforms and then was put to a succession of uses. The belated revival of interest in the conservation of 19C industrial architecture saved the condemned building and the decision was taken to convert it into a museum.

The architects chosen for the museum were Renaud Bardon, Pierre Colboc and Jean-Paul Philippon of ACT and the architect/designer responsible for the interior was Gae Aulenti. Certain rooms retain their original decoration of the 1900s.

The museum is also the site of frequent temporary exhibitions as well as concerts, films and lectures. There is a bookshop, library, postcard shop and boutique (with access from the exterior) and a mailbox; facilities for the disabled are available (ask at reception).

The collections

The main permanent collection—approximately 4700 paintings, 500 pastels, 2260 sculptures, 1300 objets d'art and 45,000 photographs (exhibited in rotation)—is shown on three floors. Separate sections are devoted to individual collections, including the collections of Chauchard, Gachet, Kaganovitch, Mollard, Personnaz, and Moreau-Nélaton. The 16,000 square metres for permanent exhibitions is divided into some 80 separate sections or galleries and a well planned visit will save both time and frustration. On the **forecourt** of the museum are bronzes commissioned for the first Trocadero Palace built for the Paris Universal Exposition of 1878, and on Rue de Lille are works of 1925 by Bourdelle.

The first impression of the **interior** is of space and light. The building is in total 220m by 75m and the coffered vault—with its 1600 rosettes—of the central hall alone, which once spanned the platforms, is 138m in length, 40m wide and 32m high. The architects wanted to create a museum on a human scale without losing the original perspectives. The installations use a great deal of pale, polished Buxy stone and are designed neither to emulate nor to vie with the original building. The museum aims to present all aspects of the art of the period (mid-19C to early 20C). A representative selection of sculpture produced in the 19C is shown to advantage in the central aisle. A large section is dedicated to the stiff and formal Salon paintings produced in quantity by followers of David, Ingres and Canova. Work of the Romantic era is well represented, as is Symbolism and the early *plein air* painters, such as the Barbizon School. And there are examples of Art Nouveau artefacts. In fact, all the art against which the Impressionists reacted, or from which Impressionism developed. The remarkable collection of Impressionist works is in a series of rooms on an upper level followed by the art of the early 20C which developed out of Impressionism.

Work is on-going to rooms around the Seine gallery on the ground floor, and these will reopen at the end of 2001. Further reorganisations to the museum may involve changes to the layout of the works compared to the plan and the description below.

Ground floor

On the ground floor, with its entrance below the great clock of the terraced central aisle, are displayed some of the more important sculptures by Rude, David l'Angers, Pradier, Préault and Barye. The 19C works come into their own in this large, lucid area which throws up the contrast between the marble and bronze and the severely geometric partitions that flank the aisle.

On the left as you enter is one of the most extreme examples of Romanticism, albeit in a Classical guise: ***Napoléon Awakening to Immortality*** (1846), by François Rude, a plaster of the monument made for Fixin, Burgundy.  The creative energies of Jean-Baptiste Carpeaux are given full recognition, and outstanding are the ***Ugolin group*** (1862), the ***Four Quarters of the World*** bearing the celestial sphere (1867–72) for the fountain on Avenue de l'Observatoire, and ***La Danse*** (1869), commissioned for the façade of the Opéra. Facing the main aisle is a huge canvas by Thomas Couture, ***Roman Decadence*** (1847), much praised in its time. Works by Rodin, Camille Claudel, Bourdelle, Maillol and Joseph Bernard are on the terraces around the central aisle and other sculptures are scattered through the galleries (see below).

Central Hall, Musée d'Orsay

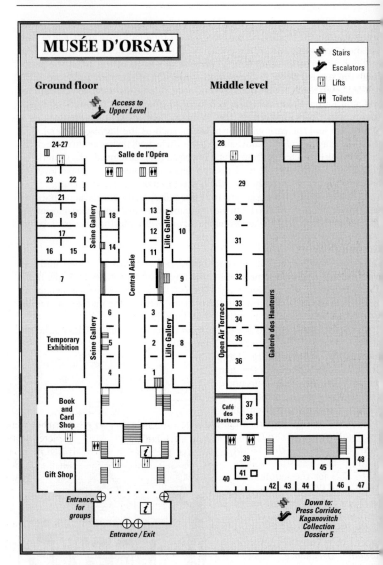

MUSÉE D'ORSAY

	Stairs
	Escalators
	Lifts
	Toilets

Ground floor

Access to Upper Level

24-27

23 22

21

20 19

17

16 15

7

18

14

Salle de l'Opéra

13

12 10

11

Central Aisle

9

Seine Gallery

Lille Gallery

Temporary Exhibition

6

3

5

2 8

4

1

Book and Card Shop

Gift Shop

Entrance for groups

Entrance / Exit

Middle level

28

29

30

31

32

33

34

35

36

Open Air Terrace

Galerie des Hauteurs

Café des Hauteurs

37

38

39

40 41

42 43 44

45

46 47

48

Down to: Press Corridor, Kaganovitch Collection Dossier 5

Rooms 1–3 On the right as you enter the central aisle, are works from the period up to 1880, including two dominant yet contrasting painters and their followers, the Neo-classical **Jean-Auguste-Dominique Ingres** and the Romantic **Eugène Delacroix**. Representative of their works are Ingres' *La Source* (completed 1856) and Delacroix's *The Lion Hunt*. *The Tepidarium* (1853) by Théodore Chassériau—student of Ingres, admirer of Delacroix and later the teacher of Moreau—was inspired by one of the thermae discovered at Pompeii. The technically competent but vacuous works of Salon painters such as Alexandre Cabanel and Winterhalter (c 1805–73) are in this section.

Rooms 9–10 In the Lille Gallery are history paintings and portraits (1850–80) and an eclectic group of works, and rooms 9–10 are devoted to the decorative arts of the period 1850–80.

Rooms 11–13 The museum owns several important works by **Puvis de Chavannes** (1824–98), a profound influence on many later painters including the Symbolists and Seurat. The *Poor Fisherman* (1881), *Young Girls by the Sea* (1879), and *The Pigeon* and *The Balloon*, both painted during the Siege of Paris (1870–71). Close by are works by **Gustave Moreau**. Early (i.e. before 1870) works by **Edgar Degas**, include the finely tuned family group, *The Bellelli Family* (1858/60), portraits of *Hilaire de Gas*, the artist's grandfather (painted on a visit to Italy in 1857) and of *Thérèse de Gas* (1863), *Before the Race* (1862/80), *The Orchestra of the Opéra* (1868/69) and the unfinished *Semiramis Watching the Construction of Babylon* (1861).

Rooms 4–6 and Seine Gallery Crossing the central aisle diagonally you find work of the mid-19C. Not only are there paintings by **Honoré Daumier**, such as *The Laundrywoman* (c 1863) but also his remarkable series of 36 painted clay caricature busts of *Parliamentarians*, modelled from 1831.

The paintings of the 1860s include Ernest Meissonier, *Campagne de France*, and pleasant but undemanding rural scenes by Jules Breton, Rosa Bonheur, Constant Troyon, Félix Diem, Eugène Isabey, early Delacroix, and small animal bronzes by Bayre. From this period are the gentle silvery landscapes of **Jean-Baptiste Corot**; works by the **Barbizon painters**: Théodore Rousseau (1812–67), Charles Daubigny (1817–78), and Diaz de la Peña, who paved the way for open-air painting; and the atmospheric and dignified canvases of **Jean-François Millet**, including *The Gleaners* (1857), *The Angelus* (1858/9) and several portraits and landscapes.

Room 7 The large, and sometimes sombre, works of **Gustave Courbet** were both controversial and influential. The *Burial at Ornans* was considered scandalous at the Salon of 1850, because of its blatant realism. Its counterpart, equally huge and impressive, is *The Artist's Studio* (1855) with Baudelaire depicted on the right, reading. A more recent acquisition is Courbet's beautiful nude entitled *The Origin of the World* (1866). During renovations in 2001, not all the works usually in rooms 14 and 18 will be on display.

Room 14 On the right of the Seine Gallery, are works by **Edouard Manet** before 1870. This stunning group of paintings includes *Portraits of his Parents* (1860), *Lola de Valence* (1862), *Bullfight* (1865–66), *The Balcony* (c 1868–69), with Berthe Morisot in the foreground, the audaciously defiant *Olympia* (1863), and *Portrait of Zola* (1868), with the previous painting in the background. The *Fife-Player* (1866) contrasts the rigorous play of black and white with the red trousers of the musician. There are some delicious still lifes.

Room 18 Early works by **Claude Monet** (in and around room 18) are shown with pre-1870 works of his friends and colleagues, **Auguste Renoir** and Frédéric Bazille, and reveal the early experiments that led to Impressionism. Paintings by Monet include *Portrait of Mme Gaudibert*, two sections from *Le*

Déjeuner sur l'herbe (1865/6), *Women in a Garden*, painted in the open air, and *The Magpie*, the black and white bird against the subtle whites of a snow-covered landscape. Here also are works executed before 1870 by Renoir, *Bazille Painting* (1867); and by Bazille, *Portrait of Renoir*.

Rooms 15–17 and 19–23 At the time of writing these rooms were being renovated. The following works will be returned to these galleries, but may alternate at times with temporary exhibitions.

Many of these painters were close to the Impressionists or were their forerunners. Henri Fantin-Latour, recorded the artistic milieu of the day in *The Studio in the Batignolles* (1870), showing Manet at the easel and grouped around him Monet, Bazille, Zola, Renoir and others; and in *A Corner of the Table* are the poets Verlaine and Rimbaud. There are also charming small marine paintings by Boudin, Lépine (1836–92) and Jongkind (1819–91).

In the Antonin Personnaz collection are 14 landscapes by **Camille Pissarro** from 1870 to 1902: *Winter at Louveciennes* (c 1870) and green scenes such as *Landscape at Chaponval* (1880) and *Woman in an Enclosure* (1887) show the evolution of his later style; *Bridge at Argenteuil* (1874) by Monet; *The Place Valhubert* and *Paris, Quai de Bercy in the Snow* (somewhat different from its present aspect, see Ch. 33) by Guillaumin and *Woman Sewing* (c 1880/82) by the American, Mary Cassatt her only painting in the Orsay. The Eduardo Mollard collection includes Jongkind, *The Seine at Notre-Dame*; Boudin, the well-known *Beach at Trouville* (1864), and Sisley's, *The Bridge at Moret-sur-Loing* (1893).

Part of the museum's fine collection of pastels are usually shown on this floor. Canvases by Adolphe Monticelli among others are representative of the harsh light of Realism. Orientalism refers to paintings inspired mainly by North Africa and Egypt. In the footsteps of Ingres and Gérôme are Guillaumet *Evening Prayer in the Sahara* (1863) and *The Desert* (1867); Fromentin, *The Land of Thirst*.

Below the main vault of the building is the **Opéra room**, devoted to architect Charles Garnier and the construction of the Paris Opéra, started in 1862 (see also p 278). This contains a maquette of the entire Opéra quarter at 1:100 as it was in 1914 (beneath a transparent floor); a model of the Opéra shown as a cross-section; and a maquette of the stage built for the Universal Exhibition of 1900.

On the Seine side of the eastern extremity of the museum (**rooms 24 to 27bis**) is Richard Peduzzi's Architectural Tower. Successive elevations of the tower demonstrate architectural features of public and private constructions of the period 1850–1900. Stairs from this level take you up through the Architectural Plans and Design section with maquettes and examples of furniture by such as Augustus Pugin, Philip Webb, Charles Rennie Mackintosh, Frank Lloyd Wright, Otto Wagner and Adolf Loos.

Upper level
Escalators, discreetly tucked away behind the Opéra display, ascend to the upper level and the Impressionist galleries (rooms 29–34). The majority of these works were moved here from the Jeu de Paume and are displayed in roughly chronological order. This very popular part of the museum is often crowded.

Rooms 29–34 The first gallery contains the Etienne Moreau-Nélaton collection (other parts of this collection are dispersed in the Orsay, and in the Louvre). One of the most notorious picnics of all time is here, *Le Déjeuner sur l'Herbe*

(1863) by Manet. The contrasting flesh and fabric, the juxtaposed still life and abandoned blue dress are still provocative.

This extraordinarily rich collection also includes an all-time favourite by Monet, *The Poppies*, a halcyon moment, while intrusive 19C engineering features in *The Railway Bridge at Argenteuil* (c 1875). Also Fantin-Latour's *Hommage to Delacroix*, Sisley, *The Footbridge at Argenteuil*, and further works by Pissarro.

In the following galleries you will find: James Whistler, *Arrangement in Grey and Black*, *Whistler's Mother* (1871), composed with austere harmony. Two tender interpretations by Berthe Morisot, *The Cradle* (1872) and *Young Woman in a Ballgown* (1879), contrast with the vigorous *Floor Planers* (1875) by Gustave Caillebotte.

Among works by **Degas** is the moving portrayal of dejection *The Absinthe Drinkers* (1876) compared with the oblique glimpse of *The Dancing Class* (1873–76); also *The Stock Exchange* (c 1878–79), the fatigue of *Women Ironing* (c 1884–86), and several horse-racing scenes. Bronzes by Degas include the 14-year-old *Dancer wearing her tutu*. Manet is represented by *On the Beach at Berck-sur-Mer* (1873), the marvellous *Lady with the Fans* (1873–74),

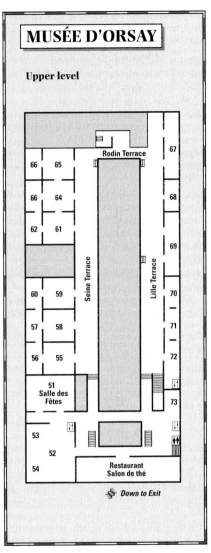

and at his most impressionistic in the portraits of *Mallarmé* and of *Clemenceau*.

Works before 1880, a turning point in Impressionism, include Monet's *Regatta at Argenteuil* (c 1872), the *Fête in the Rue Montorgueil* (1878), and *St-Lazare Station* (1877). Landscapes by Pissarro include *Red Roofs*. The effects of dappled light are used by **Renoir** in paintings of 1876 such as *Dancing at the Moulin de la Galette* and *The Swing*; also, among his sculptures, is a bust of Mme Renoir.

Later Impressionist works by Monet include *Woman with the Sunshade* (1886), five of the series of views of the *Cathedral at Rouen*, showing the effects of light at different times of day (1892–93), one example of the *Haystacks* series. By Renoir are the joyful *Dance in the Country*, and the more restrained *Dance in the Town* of 1883, and *Girls playing the Piano*.

Rooms 35, 36–38 In these rooms are a large number of the best-loved paintings by **Vincent van Gogh**. From the dark and brooding early paintings, Van Gogh's work erupts into the vigorous impasto and intense colour of *The Portrait of Dr Paul Gachet* (1890), one of three portraits of the doctor who befriended the Impressionists and whose collection was donated to the museum by his children. The collection includes van Gogh's *The Bedroom at Arles* (1889); two *Self-portraits*, of 1887 and 1889, electrifying in the use of colour and the tense energy of the brushstrokes; and the intense *Church at Auvers-sur-Oise* (1890); *The Siesta*, after Millet, 1889–90, could be called rhapsody in blue and gold.

The museum possesses a significant cross-section of the works of **Paul Cézanne**. From Cézanne's earlier period are the *Portrait of Achille Emperaire* (1869/70), and the *Still Life with Soup Tureen* (c 1877). Examples of his monumental mature works include *The Card-players* and *Woman with a Coffee-pot*. Landscapes are represented by the *Bay at Estaque* (c 1878–79), the *Bridge of Maincy* (1879), *Poplars* (1879–82) and *Mont Ste-Victoire* (c 1890). *Still Life with Onions* (1896/98), and *Apples and Oranges* (c 1899) combine the textures of voluptuous fruit and heavy fabrics. *Bathers* (c 1890), was his last and largest canvas of male nudes.

Also in this area are Toulouse-Lautrec's panels for La Goulue's booth at the Foire du Trône and the later pastels by Degas.

The adjacent *Rooftop Café* provides a curious version of Paris through the hands of the huge clock, and panoramic views from the terrace.

Rooms 39–44 Late works by **Monet** and **Renoir** include by the former, *The Houses of Parliament, London, Sunlight in the Fog* (1904), *Lily Pond*, 1899 and 1900, and *Blue Waterlilies* (c 1916–18), and blue iris in *The Garden at Giverny* (1900). Renoir's *Large Bathers* (c 1918–19) is considered the culmination of his art.

Examples of **Odilon Redon**'s mysterious and luminous work include *The Buddha* (1906/07), pastel, and *Portrait of Gauguin* (1903/05). There are pastels by Ker-Xavier Roussel (1867–1944), Maurice Denis, Georges Rouault (1891–1959) and a watercolour by Piet Mondrian (1872–1944). Rooms at the western end of the museum include the Gachet collection, work by **Henri (le Douanier) Rousseau** such as *Portrait of a Woman* (c1897) and the *Snake Charmer* (1907). Next are the Pont Aven painters Emile Bernard and Paul Sérusier, and **Paul Gauguin**, covering periods in Brittany and in the South Seas (from 1875 to 1903), evolving through an impressionistic style to an emphasis on flat patterning and symbolic use of colour: *Washerwomen in Pont-Aven* (1886), *La belle Angèle* (1889); *Tahitian Women on the Beach* (1891), *And the Gold of their Bodies* (1901) and *Self Portraits* of 1893/94 and 1896.

Rooms 45–48 Works from the 1890s are in the last rooms on this level. Neo-Impressionism or Pointillism, represented by **Georges Seurat** in his preparatory sketches for *La Grande Jatte*, *Poseuses*, and *The Circus* of 1890/91; *Port-en-Bessin, avant-port, marée haute* (1888). Pointillism or Divisionism becomes coarser and richer in the hands of Paul Signac, Henri Cross (1856–1910) and Maximilien Luce (1858–1941); **Henri Matisse** adapts the technique in *Luxe,*

Calme et Volupté (1904) to shimmering horizontal dashes captured within an outline.

Works by **Toulouse-Lautrec** include *Jane Avril Dancing* (c 1891), *La toilette* (1896), and *Cha-U-Kao* (the female clown) (1895); room 48 is devoted to small format paintings by the Nabis, including Pierre Bonnard, Maurice Denis; Félix Vallotton and Edouard Vuillard. (The larger works by these artists are on the floor below, the Middle Level.)

Escalators or stairs take you down to the Press Corridor, which traces the development of images in the press over the period, and to the Gallery of Dates. This brings you also to the Kaganovitch collection (**room 50**), including Gauguin's *Breton Peasant Women*, and works by Monet, Sisley, Renoir, Van Gogh and others.

Middle level

Cross the press corridor to reach escalators descending to the middle level of the museum. On this level is the restaurant (see above), which is not too expensive but the queues build up at midday.

Rooms 51–54 present the **Decorative Arts of the Third Republic**. The former ballroom (Salle des Fêtes) of the station hotel has been restored to its original glitzy glory, with gilded mirrors and chandeliers. Large portraits of society beauties and frivolous paintings by William Bouguereau, mingle with sleek statues by Denys Puech (1854–1942) and Ernest Barrias. The stuccoed rooms in the northwest angle deal with the creation of public monuments, many of which still embellish Paris, through preparatory paintings, maquettes and models.

A footbridge brings you to the next section, the **Seine Terrace** overlooking the central aisle, with Monumental Sculpture 1870–1914 by Barrias, Coutain, Frémiet and Gérôme, mainly addressing themes of conflict, power or heroism, for example Frémiet's *Saint Michael*.

Rooms 55, 57–58 Leading off the terrace are a number of rooms devoted to **Naturalism** and **Realism**. Among them are paintings by Bastien-Lépage (1848–84), Léon Bonnat (1833–1922), Jacques-Emile Blanche (1861–1942), Philip Wilson Steer and Jean-Léon Gérôme's bust of *Sarah Bernhardt* (c 1895). There are also works by Sir Lawrence Alma-Tadema (1836–1912) and small bronzes by Dalou.

Rooms 59 and 60 Among the Symbolist works here are Burne-Jones' (1833–98) *The Wheel of Fortune*; and paintings by Gustav Klimt (1862–1918), Edvard Munch (1863–1944) and James Ensor (1860–1949).

Rooms 61–66 Adjacent is a fascinating section containing **Art Nouveau** production from several European countries. There are samples of jewellery by René Lalique; glass, ceramics and enamel work by Emile Gallé and the School of Nancy as well as Albert Dammouse; also stained glass by Louis Comfort Tiffany and Jacques Gruba. There is also an interior design by Redon (1899).

There are examples, perfectly crafted and sometimes exquisitely over-the-top, of **furniture and woodwork**. The craftsmen include Hector Guimard, Alexandre Charpentier with a dining room of 1901, Jean Dampt, Louis Majorelle, with the bedroom suite, Nénuphars (c 1905), Eugène Vallin, F.-R. Carabin, Henry Van de Velde, and Peter Behrens with chairs (c 1902).

Outside these rooms and on the east landing is an important collection of sculpture by **Auguste Rodin** (1840–1917). Among numerous busts is the marble, entitled *La Pensée*, of the head of Camille Claudel, whose impressive bronze group entitled *L'Age mûr* (Maturity) is also in this section.

Rooms 67–69 are used for temporary thematic exhibitions. **Sculpture** continues on the **Lille Terrace** with Emile Antoine Bourdelle (1861–1929) and Aristide Maillol.

Rooms 70-72 Passing a section devoted to temporary exhibitions, you reach to the left, the last series of rooms containing paintings, largely post-1900, of work by the Nabis: Denis, Bonnard, Vuillard, Vallotton and Ker-Xavier Roussel. There are large decorative panels by Edouard Vuillard, as well as canvases: *In bed* (1891) and *Portrait of Thadée Natanson*. Among Pierre Bonnard's contributions are *The Croquet Party*, and others showing a heavy debt to Japanese art.

Among collections of early **photographs** (shown in rotation) are representative examples of the art of Eugène Atget, Edouard Baldus, L.-A. Humbert de Molard, Félix Nadar, Charles Nègre, Piere Petit, Georges Charles Beresford, Julia Margaret Cameron, Lewis Carroll, Roger Fenton and George Shaw.

10 • Faubourg St-Germain: western sector: Musée Rodin, Musée Maillol

■ Arrondissement: 75007
🚇 Solférino, Musée d'Orsay, Assemblée Nationale, Invalides, Varenne, Sèvres-Babylone, Rue du Bac
🚉 Musée d'Orsay, Invalides

Arpège, 84 Rue de Varenne, ☎ 01 45 51 47 33. This is seriously grand, innovative cooking, with an emphasis on vegetables; the *menus surprises* live up to their name, £££

Au Babylone, 13 Rue de Babylone, ☎ 01 45 48 72 13. Lunch only, for unassuming well cooked bistrot food, £

Aux Fins Gourmets, 213 Blvd St-Germain, ☎ 01 42 22 06 57. Basic and down-to-earth southwestern cooking, a favourite, £

Le Bamboche, 15 Rue de Babylone, ☎ 01 45 49 14 40. Small and stylish, but new owner not yet tested and tried, ££

Le Bistrot de Paris, 33 Rue de Lille, ☎ 01 42 61 16 83. Careful cooking and presentation draw the locals, £–££

Bistrot de l'Université, 40 Rue de l'Université, ☎ 01 42 61 26 64. Tiny 30s bistrot, with old trappings and honest food and prices, £

Le Divellec, 107 Rue de l'Université, ☎ 01 45 51 91 96. A sophisticated, up-market, fish restaurant. Lunch menu affordable, £££

L'Epi Dupin, rue Dupin, ☎ 01 42 22 64 56. Very popular bistrot, book weeks ahead, good value good food, £–££

Gaya Rive Gauche, 44 Rue du Bac, ☎ 01 45 44 73 73. Sought-out Goumard-Prunier seafood annex,

refined, excellent quality, ££
Joséphine 'Chez Dumonet', 117
Rue du Cherche-Midi, ☎ 01 45
48 52 40. Somewhat up-market
bistrot—good but watch the bill,
££
A La Petite Chaise, 36 rue de
Grenelle, ☎ 01 42 22 13 35.
Established in 1680, but still
serving a good value meal, £
Au Pied de Fouet, 45 Rue de
Babylone, ☎ 01 47 05 12 27.
Very small, extremely popular,
wildly good value; come early, £
Le Recamier, 4 Rue Recamier,
☎ 01 45 48 86 58. Elegant, old-
fashioned, with terrace, serving
Bugundian food and wine, ££
Le Roupeyrac, 62 Rue de
Bellechasse, ☎ 01 45 52 33 42.
Near the Orsay, simple, limited
choice, crowded weekday
lunchtime, £
Le Télégraph, 41 Rue de Lille,
☎ 01 42 92 03 04. Revamped
in Art Nouveau style, spacious,
trendy, and fairly easy on the
pocket, £–££
The two museums, *Maillol*,
☎ 01 42 22 59 58, and *Rodin*,
☎ 01 45 50 42 34, both have
pleasant cafeterias, £

Rather grander than the eastern sector, this part of Faubourg St-Germain
accommodates several embassies and ambassadorial residences in its elegant
17C and 18C *hôtels particuliers* while the Palais Bourbon is home of the
Assemblée Nationale. There are also are two exceptionally fine smaller museums
established in beautiful houses, each dedicated to a sculptor, Auguste Rodin and
Aristide Maillol.

Quai Voltaire (Map 7; 2), the continuation of Quai Malaquais (see Ch. 8) separates this sector of Faubourg St-Germain from the Seine and is linked to the
Right Bank and the Louvre by Pont du Carrousel. To the west extend Quai
Anatole France and the Quai d'Orsay. The former is dominated by the Musée
d'Orsay (see Ch. 9).

Quai Voltaire was popular with writers and artists in the 18C and 19C. Not
surprisingly, one of these was Voltaire (1694–1778), who died at no. 27; also
Ingres died at no. 11 in 1867; Delacroix lived at no. 13 in 1829–36, and Corot
later. Baudelaire lived at no. 19 in 1856–58 while writing *Les Fleurs du Mal*, and
Wagner completed the libretto of *Die Meistersinger* at the same address in
1861–62; later tenants included Sibelius and Oscar Wilde.

Opposite the west end of the Musée d'Orsay is the grandly colonnaded **Palais de
la Légion d'Honneur**, the former Hôtel de Salm. One of the last *hôtels particuliers* to be built in the district, with its triumphal arch, vast courtyard and motto
Honneur et Patrie, there is a touch of pomposity about it. However, the rotunda
with Corinthian columns facing the *quai* is elegant.

History of the Palais de la Légion d'Honneur

Built in 1782–86 for a German count who was put to death in 1794, the
house became the Swedish Embassy in 1797 and Mme de Staël, the ambassador's wife, gave her famous receptions here. In 1804 it was bought by the
government for the grand chancellory of the Legion of Honour and was
restored to its original form in 1878, following a severe fire during the
Commune.

The entrance to the **Musée National de la Légion d'Honneur et des Ordres de Chevalerie** is at 2 Rue de Bellechasse. Open 14.00–17.00, closed Mon, ☎ 01 40 62 84 25. The contents of the museum are related to the history of the French Orders of Chivalry since Louis XI, together with foreign heraldic trappings. One room deals with the Royal Orders: the Ordres de Saint-Michel, du Saint-Esprit, de Saint-Louis, etc. Another with the history of the Legion of Honour which replaced all the other honours after the Revolution. A military and civil order, it was instituted in May 1802 by Napoléon and comprises five classes in ascending order: Chevalier, Officier, Commandeur, Grand-Officier and Grand-Croix. Those awarded it have the right to wear a discreet little red rosette in their buttonhole.

At 80 Rue de Lille (to the south) is the Hôtel de Seignelay built by Gabriel Boffrand in 1714. Boffrand, France's finest Rococo architect, also built the adjacent **Hôtel de Beauharnais** (1713), one of the best in this area. Sold first to Jean-Baptiste Colbert, nephew of the Great Statesman Colbert, it was then acquired by Eugène de Beauharnais in 1803 and was the occasional the home of his sister Queen Hortense. In 1814 it became the Prussian legation, in 1871 the German Embassy, and is now the German ambassador's residence. The curious neo-Egyptian peristyle characterises a fashion that was introduced after Napoléon's Egyptian expedition of 1798.

A few minutes' walk west to the end of Blvd St-Germain brings you to the **Palais Bourbon**, seat of the Assemblée Nationale (**Map 7; 1**), facing Pont de la Concorde. Open Sat 10.00, 14.00, 15.00, at 33 Quai d'Orsay, ID required, ☎ 01 40 63 60 00.

History of the Palais Bourbon

In 1722–28 a mansion was erected on this site for the Dowager Duchess of Bourbon, daughter of Louis XIV, of which only the inner courtyard and main entrance (at 128 Rue de l'Université) have survived. The Prince de Condé enlarged the palace between 1764 and 1789, incorporating the Hôtel de Lassay. The Palais became national property at the Revolution, was transformed into the meeting-place of the Council of Five Hundred, and was later occupied by the Archives (1799–1808). Since 1815 it has been used by the Chambre des Députés, the French equivalent to the British House of Commons. Its name was changed to the Assemblée Nationale in 1946.

In 1940–44 the Palais Bourbon was the headquarters of the German military administration of the Paris region. At the time of the Liberation considerable fighting took place in the neighbourhood, causing some damage to the building and the destruction of over 30,000 volumes in the library.

The north façade (1804–07), a neo-Hellenistic piece of imperial bombast designed principally to balance the Madeleine when seen from Pl. de la Concorde, is entirely decorative and consists of a portico of twelve Corinthian columns. The low reliefs on the wings are by Rude and Pradier. Inside, the semicircular *salle de séances* (1828–32) has bas-reliefs by Lemot (1798), statues by Pradier, Desprez and others, and a Gobelins tapestry after the School of Athens (Raphael). Other rooms contain historical paintings by Horace Vernet (1789–1863) and by Delacroix (in the Salon du Roi and library). The Galerie des Fêtes (1848) connects the building to the Hôtel de Lassay (1724), the official residence of the President of the Assembly.

Further along Quai d'Orsay stands the Ministère des Affaires Etrangères (Foreign Office), built in 1845. Adjacent, on the Esplanade des Invalides, is Gare des Invalides (1900) adapted in 1945 as the Air France Aérogare (Air Terminus). For the Hôtel des Invalides and Musée de l'Armée, see Ch. 11.

Turning east along Rue de l'Université, you shortly reach Pl. du Palais Bourbon, an elegant ensemble of Louis XVI houses built to the same pattern after 1776.

At 108 Rue de l'Université (entrance at 121 Rue de Lille, parallel to the north) in the former Hôtel Turgot (18C), is the **Institut Néerlandais**, with a good collection of Dutch and German drawings. Open to the public during exhibitions and conferences.

Further east (on the far side of Blvd St-Germain), at 51 Rue de l'Université, is the magnificent **Hôtel de Soyécourt** (1707, by Lassurance), also known as the Hôtel Pozzi di Borgo; no. 24, the Hôtel de Sennecterre, has a notable courtyard façade. Rue de Bellechasse leads south back to Blvd St-Germain, flanked to the west, at this point, by the extensive buildings of the Ministère de la Défense (by Bouchot; 1867–77), with a clock-tower at the corner of Rue de Solférino.

Nos 1, 3 and 5 Rue St-Dominique, running west from Blvd St-Germain, date from c 1710; nos 10–12 (since 1804 part of the Ministère de la Défense) occupy the former Couvent des Filles de St-Joseph (1641). Nos 14–16, in the same block of buildings, the Hôtel de Brienne (1714 and 1730), was acquired by Lucien Bonaparte in 1802. No. 28 was the Hôtel Rochefoucauld-d'Estissac (1710), while further west, the Hôtel de Sagan (no. 57), built by Brongniart in 1784 for the Princess of Monaco, is now the Polish Embassy, and was the British Embassy prior to the purchase of the Hôtel de Charost (see Ch. 28).

South of Rue St-Dominique rises the uninspired Gothic-revival church of **Ste-Clotilde**, built in 1846–56, where César Franck was organist from 1858 until his death in 1890. In the little patch of greenery, Square Samuel-Rousseau, is a commemorative monument to Franck (1891) by Lenoir.

Follow Rue de Bellechasse south to **Rue de Grenelle**, a street of numerous embassies and ministries. At no. 41, the Conseil de la Résistance and the Comité Parisien de la Libération organised operations for the rising of 19 August 1944.

To the east of the junction, at no. 106 Rue de Grenelle, is the Temple de Pentémont of the Reformed Church (1747–56) by Constant d'Ivry, originally the chapel of a Bernardine convent. No. 102, the very fine **Hôtel de Maillebois**, was remodelled by the architect Jacques-Denis Antoine in 1783. No. 87 is the Hôtel de Bauffremont (1721–36), with a curved façade. No. 85, the Hotel d'Avaray was built by Leroux 1718–23, and was tastefully renovated in 1920 when it became the Netherlands Embassy. No. 79, the pale yellow and white Hôtel d'Estrées, the Russian Embassy, was built by Robert de Cotte in 1713.

Retracing your steps towards the west, you pass no. 110, the Hôtel de Courteilles (1778); no. 116, the old Hôtel de Brissac, was rebuilt in 1709 for Marshal de Villars by Boffrand. No. 101, opposite, the former Hôtel Rothelin (or de Charolais), built by Lassurance in 1700; nos 138 and 140 were built by Jean Courtonne in 1722 and decorated by Lassurance in 1735 for Mlle de Sens. Marshal Foch (1851–1929) died in the former; the latter is occupied by the Institut Géographique National. No. 127, the Hôtel du Châtelet, and one of the finest examples of the Louis-XV style, and was used as the Archbishop's Palace in 1849–1906. The Hôtel de Chanac, at no. 142, opposite (by Delamair; 1750), is now the Swiss Embassy.

Musée Rodin

Off the Blvd des Invalides, opposite the Hôtel des Invalides (see Ch. 11), at the end of Rue de Varenne (no. 77), is the Hôtel Biron (**Map 7; 3**), host to the Musée Rodin.

- The museum is open summer: 09.30–17.45, garden to 18.45; winter 09.30–16.45, garden to 17.00; closed Mon and 1/1, 25/12, ☎ 01 44 18 61 10. Bookshop and a garden café, open March–Sept.

This stately mansion and its gardens provide an ideal setting for the important and comprehensive collection of works by Auguste Rodin, which he donated to the State in 1916. Together with many original marbles and bronzes, there are plaster casts, maquettes, drawings and watercolours. There is also his personal collection of art, antiquities and furniture, together with some 8000 old photographs associated with the sculptor. Perhaps the most popular museum in Paris dedicated to a single artist, it owes much of the charm to the 18C building.

History of the Musée Rodin

The mansion, built in 1728–30 by Aubert and Gabriel, was occupied by the Duc de Biron in 1753, and in 1820 by a religious community, expelled in 1904. Much of the painted and gilt panelling, which had been removed, has been recovered and replaced. From 1908 Rodin rented a studio, along with other artists and writers including the poet Rainer Maria Rilke, his secretary at that time. He gradually took over more rooms and lived here until his death in 1917.

Nearly 500 of Rodin's sculptures are on show in the museum, from early seminal works to his best known masterpieces, grouped chronologically and thematically. The presentation demonstrates the revolutionary nature of his art, in comparison with academic sculpture at the time, and his debt to Michelangelo. He opened new vistas in sculpture in much the same way as the Impressionists did in painting, although he was not as vigorously criticised.

In the **front courtyard** are several of his major commissions. Near the entrance, and seen from the street, is the large group, the *Burghers of Calais*; on the right, among the conical yews, is the *Thinker*, while nearby is his *Balzac*. To the left are the *Gates of Hell*, based on Ghiberti's Baptistry Gates in Florence, the iconography inspired by Dante's Inferno. Intended for the Musée des Arts Decoratifs but never installed they were, in fact, cast only in 1926.

The **entrance hall** has portrait busts of *Rodin* by Bourdelle and Desbois and bronzes of *St John the Baptist* and the vigorous *L'Homme qui marche*. A visit begins to the left on the ground floor, past the shop, with rooms that have small and often pretty or ornamental works of the period (1860–80), including the terracotta, *Young Woman with a Flowered Hat*. The oval Salon with its original woodwork, contains *The Age of Bronze* (1875–76), his first freestanding figure of precise anatomical proportions, which caused controversy at the time as it was erroneously reputed to have been cast from a live figure.

The next two galleries overlooking the garden concentrate on sculptures of couples and the human body—*Adam and Eve*, *Paolo and Francesca*, a version of his best known work, *The Kiss*, and examples of fragments of figures, such as

The Hand of God; also examples of the technique based on Michelangelo's unfinished works, which Rodin brought to a state of perfection, where a highly polished figure emerges from rough hewn marble or stone.

In the room devoted to Camille Claudel, Rodin's pupil and lover, are compositions modelled on her such as *La France* and *l'Aurore*. Her exceptional and sensitive talent as a sculptress is demonstrated in the bronze *L'Age Mûr* (1898), *Gossips*, and *The Wave* (1897–1902) in onyx and bronze (acquired in 1995). The next two rooms concentrate on women, in the symbolic sense, such as *Eve*, and portraits of women such as Eve Fairfax, the suffragette, Lady Sackville-West, and Mrs Potter-Palmer, some of them souvenirs of amorous adventures. The last room on the ground floor, room 9, has rotating exhibitions of his drawings.

The *Gates of Hell* provided Rodin with a source of motifs such as the *Three Shades* on the staircase, and the first rooms of the upper galleries contain studies for and variations on the *Gates of Hell*. There is a room devoted to studies for the *Burghers of Calais*. The upper rooms overlooking the garden have preparatory works for public monuments, including clothed and unclothed versions of Balzac. The group of male busts—*Clemenceau*, *George Bernard Shaw*, *Gustav Mahler* and *Puvis de Chavannes*—reflects the sculptor's intellectual and political connections. In his later years he was inspired by dancers, including Isadora Duncan who at one time occupied studios in this building. Among later works (1890–1905) is the gravity-defying *Iris, Messenger of the Gods*, headless and leaping.

Paintings collected by Rodin include three glorious works by Van Gogh: the celebrated *Portrait of Père Tanguy*, *Les Moissoneurs* and *La Vue du Viaduc à Arles*; there is also a female nude by Renoir, and Monet's *Paysage de Belle-Isle*.

The **gardens**, which can be visited independently, were remodelled in 1993. The formal layout, flanked by mature trees, frames to advantage the elegant south façade of the Hôtel. Scattered in the garden are more Rodin works, including *Whistler's Muse*, *Cybele*, *Bastien Lepage*, *Claude Lorrain* and, in the pool, *Ugolino and his Children*. On the west side is the pleasant cafeteria. The small building by the entrance is the 19C chapel of the former convent, used for temporary exhibitions.

There is an annexe to the museum at Meudon, Rodin's home, see Ch. 35.

No. 72 in Rue de Varenne is the Hôtel de Castries (1700), and no. 69 is the Hôtel de Clermont by Leblond (1711). Just beyond is the **Hôtel de Matignon** (no. 57), built by Courtonne in 1721 and altered in the 19C. The Austro-Hungarian Embassy 1888–1914, since 1935 it has been the residence of the Président du Conseil (or Prime Minister). One of the most beautiful hôtels in the faubourg, it has an unusually large garden. The statesman Talleyrand (1754–1838) lived here in 1808–11.

At no. 53 Edith Wharton 'spent ... rich years, crowded and happy ...' 1910–20. No. 50, the handsome Hôtel de Gallifet, with an Ionic peristyle built by Legrand in 1775–96, is now the Italian Institute; their embassy is at no. 47. (See below for the continuation of the route north from Rue du Bac.)

Turning south, nos 118–120 Rue du Bac, the Hôtel de Clermont-Tonnerre, are two matching mansions of the early 18C with doors designed by Toro. No. 128 the Séminaire des Missions Etrangères, founded in 1663, protects relics of martyred missionaries and has a leafy garden open to the public. Nos 136–140 are the Hôtel de la Vallière, with handsome portals, occupied by the Soeurs de Charité. The chapel of the Médaille Miraculeuse (which can be visited) is an important shrine.

To the left is the Grands Magasins du Bon Marché, built on the site of an asylum, the Petites Maisons. To the east is Sq. Boucicaut, named after the founder of Bon Marché with an imposing monument by Moreau-Vauthier, of 1914. To the west is the Jardin de Babylone, which opened to the public in 1978, in part of the park of the former Hôtel de la Vallière.

A short distance to the southwest, at 42 Rue de Sèvres, is the Hôpital Laënnec, formerly a women's hospice, founded c 1635, with its original courtyard and chapel. At no. 95 is the Eglise des Lazaristes, with a silver shrine containing the body of Vincent de Paul (1576–1660), canonised in 1737.

Running parallel to Rue de Sèvres, is Rue du Cherche-Midi (eastern section, see Ch. 8). At no. 38 (no. 56 Blvd Raspail) is the Maison des Sciences de l'Homme, built in 1968 on the site of the Prison Militaire du Cherche-Midi, where many French patriots were imprisoned between 1940 and 1944. At no. 87, the Hôtel de Montmorency (1743), is the **Musée Hébert**, open Wed–Mon 12.30–18.00, Sat–Sun 14.00–18.00; closed Tues, certain public holidays (☎ 01 42 22 23 82). Ernest Hébert, painter of Italian landscapes and society portraits and cousin of the writer Stendhal, lived in this aristocratic mansion typical of the second half of the 19C.

Musée Maillol

From Rue de Varenne, Rue du Bac leads north, crossing Rue de Grenelle, where to the right (no. 57–59) is the **Fontaine des Quatre-Saisons**, built by Bouchardon in 1739 to feed the water supply of the quartier. To maximise the limited space in this narrow street, the fountain is designed in a semi-circle. The sculptures represent the City of Paris with the Seine and Marne at her feet, with bas-reliefs of the Seasons. The *hôtel particulier* was built on land that once belonged to the Couvent des Récolets. The poet and dramatist Alfred de Musset (1810–57) lived here from 1824 to 1840 and in the 20C century, jazz enthusiasts frequented the Cabaret de la Fontaine des Quatre Saisons.

The Fondation Dina Vierny has endowed this building with the Musée Maillol (**Map 7; 4**) which opened in 1995. This charming and well-presented museum also has a delightful small restaurant in the basement. The buildings still reveal traces of the past including the cellars of the old convent. Open 11.00–18.00, closed Tues and public holidays, ☎ 01 42 22 59 58.

History of the Musée Maillol

Dina Vierny met Aristide Maillol (1861–1944) in 1934, when she was 15 and he 73, and in her he recognised the ideal figure he had been modelling all his life. Their association lasted for ten years, during which Vierny began collecting. She opened a gallery in St-Germain-des-Prés after the war and, as she was a native of Russia, launched avant-garde Russian artists such as Poliakoff. Vierny created the Foundation after donating a number of Maillol's sculptures to the Tuileries Gardens in 1964.

The concept of a museum developed over 15 years and the skilful adaptation of the old buildings is due to Pierre Devinoy. The visit starts on the site of an old poissonnerie (fish market). The gallery with exposed original timbers is dedicated to Maillol's monumental works, including *La Rivière*, 1938–43, and versions of those exhibited in the Tuileries.

A spiral staircase takes you to the upper floor, to rooms mainly devoted to different aspects of Maillol's work. The first room contains the bronze sculpture, *La Méditerranée*, 1902–05, pensive and serene, which early established him among the great Modern sculptors. A painter initially, his works in crayon, pastel, chalk and charcoal and paintings in oils are exhibited in the upper rooms, and include *Portrait of Dina*, 1940, and *Dina with a Scarf*, 1941. Examples of Maillol's diverse talents—ceramics, wood and stone carvings—are often on show.

In galleries on the second floor are earlier works such as the Impressionistic painting, *Seated Woman with Sunshade*, 1895, and tapestry designs. And in a bright white space are nine bronzes of between 1900 and 1931 including *Pomone*, 1910.

Dina Vierny's private collection comprises **modern and contemporary art**, including work by Odilon Redon, Renoir, Maurice Denis and Gauguin. There is a gallery of Matisse drawings, drawings and watercolours by Dufy, as well as carvings and watercolours by Gauguin. Vierny was an early supporter of naïve artists, here represented by Douanier Rousseau, Louis Vivin and Camille Bombois among others. The collection also includes works by each of the Duchamp brothers: Marcel Duchamp, one of the original Dadaists, Raymond Duchamp-Villon, and Jacques Villon.

Russian non-figurative art includes works by Poliakoff, Kandinsky, Charchoune, Boulatov, Yankilevski and Oscar Rabin, and the Constructivist Jean Pougny. Ilya Kabakov, one of the first proponents of Installations, built for the museum *The Communal Kitchen* which is located below the ground floor. There are also sculptures by Gilioli, Couturier and Zitman, and a vast collection of drawings by Degas, Picasso, Bonnard, Ingres, Cézanne, Suzanne Valadon, Foujita, and others. The museum mounts temporary exhibitions and some of the works in the permanent collection are exhibited in rotation.

Half-left across Blvd St-Germain, government offices occupy two early-18C houses: no. 246, the Hôtel de Roquelaure (1722), by Lassurance and Leroux, has a fine courtyard. Guillaume Apollinaire lived and died at no. 202. To the right (east) of the junction, Rue St-Guillaume crosses the boulevard. At no. 27 is the 16C Hôtel de Mesmes, enlarged in 1933, now the Institut National d'Etudes politiques; no. 16, the Hôtel de Créqui, built in 1660–64, and extended in 1772, was for a time the home of poet, statesman and historian Alphonse Lamartine (1790–1866).

Across the Boulevard, the continuation of Rue du Bac leads north to the Seine. It took its name from the ferry operating there before the construction of the Pont Royal. No. 46 Rue du Bac, is the stylish Hôtel de Boulogne, c 1740.

To the east is the former Dominican church of **St-Thomas-d'Aquin**, begun in 1682 by Pierre Bullet in the Jesuit style, and completed, with the construction of the monks' choir in the east, behind the altar, in 1722 and façade, in 1765–69. The light interior with pale stained glass is very effective. The *Transfiguration* on the vaults of the choir was painted by Lemoyne, and the organ of 1771 was restored in the 19C and again in the 20C.

11 • Les Invalides

■   Arrondissements: 75007, 75015
🚇   Invalides, Varenne, La Tour-Maubourg, St-François-Xavier
🚏   Invalides

L'Affriolé, 17 Rue Malar, ☎ 01 44 18 31 33. Welcoming and assured, the a la carte-style menu is good value, £

Le Bellecour, 22 Rue Surcouf, ☎ 01 45 51 46 93. Reassuringly traditional and unfashionable, £–££

Bistrot de Breteuil, 3 Pl de Breteuil, ☎ 01 45 67 07 27. Popular place for basic French fare, and terrace, £

Chez l'Ami Jean, 27 Rue Malar, ☎ 01 47 05 86 89. Authentic Basque cuisine in intimate and congenial surroundings, £

D'Chez Eux, 2 Av Lowendal, ☎ 01 47 05 52 55. Generous servings of south-western dishes—for the really hungry, ££

La Fontaine de Mars, 149 Rue St-Dominique, ☎ 01 47 05 46 44. Inexpensive and friendly home-style cooking, £–££

La Gauloise, 59 Av de la Motte-Picquet, ☎ 01 47 34 11 64. Basic traditional cooking, £

Paul Minchelli, 54 Blvd Latour Maubourg, ☎ 01 47 05 89 86. Minimalist seafood cooking—back to the basic fish. Art Deco style, ££

Le Violin d'Ingres, 135 Rue St-Dominique, ☎ 01 45 55 15 05. Rustic yet refined cooking, good price/quality ratio, £–££

The wider, more spacious avenues to the west of Faubourg St-Germain are dominated by the magnificent building of Les Invalides, unmistakable from its gilded dome announcing the burial place of Napoléon I. Within the ensemble are also the St-Louis church and the Musée de l'Armée. The grandest approach to the sweeping panorama of Les Invalides at the end of its esplanade is from the Right Bank across the ornate Pont Alexandre-III (see Ch. 27). In stark contrast to Les Invalides, further to the west rises the skeletal silhouette of the Eiffel Tower, and to the east the modern mass of the Tour Montparnasse.

Esplanade des Invalides, 487m by 250m, was laid out in 1704–20 by Robert de Cotte and planted with rows of elms but a gradual deterioration led in 1978 to the replanting of the whole area with lawns and scented lime trees. In the north-east corner is the Aérogare and to the west, Quai d'Orsay extends as far as Pont de l'Alma.

At no. 63 on the *quai* is the American Church, built in a Gothic style in 1927–31. The public entry to the **Egouts de Paris** (sewers), a dubious but popular visit, where you can learn about the history of the Paris water system and Haussmann's sewers, is next to the Pont de l'Alma (opposite 93 Quai d'Orsay). Open 1 May–30 Sept 11.00–17.00, 1 Oct–30 Apr to 16.00, closed Thur, Fri and last 3 weeks of Jan (☎ 01 53 68 27 81). James Joyce lived, from 1935 to 1939, at 7 Rue Edmond-Valentin, a short distance south west off Av. Bosquet.

Pl. des Invalides, at the end of the Esplanade, is the junction of several major avenues. Av. de la Motte-Picquet leads southwest to the Ecole Militaire and the Parc du Champ de Mars (see Ch. 12). Along the east flank of the Hôtel des Invalides is Blvd des Invalides into which run Rue de Grenelle and Rue de Varenne; in the angle with the latter is the Musée Rodin (see Ch. 10).

On the south side of Les Invalides, approaching from Pl. Vauban, is the **Jardin de l'Intendant**, a fine formal garden based on plans by Robert de Cotte but carried out only in 1980. It is organised around a large pool and the borders are punctuated by cone-shaped yews; the architect Jules Hardouin-Mansart (1646–1708) is remembered in a 19C statue by Ernest Dubois.

The Hôtel des Invalides

The Hôtel des Invalides (**Map 7; 3**), the headquarters of the military governor of Paris, was founded by Louis XIV in 1671 as a home for disabled soldiers, the first enduring institution of its kind. At one time it housed between 4000 and 6000 pensioners or *invalides* and now some 80 war veterans are accommodated here in one of the most modern hospitals in Paris. There are entrances on both the north and south sides.

History of the Hôtel des Invalides

The buildings, which form a majestic ensemble, are based on designs by Libéral Bruant and, after his death (1697) the work was carried on by J. Hardouin-Mansart. During the Revolution it was known both as the Temple de l'Humanité and Temple de Mars. It was restored under Napoléon I, who was later buried beneath its Dôme. The buildings encompass several museums: the Musée de l'Armée, the Musée des Plans Reliefs, the Musée de l'Ordre de la Libération, also the Eglise St-Louis and the Eglise du Dome, and Napoléon's Tomb (see below).

• Tickets cover three museums and entry to Napoléon's Tomb (the main entrance to which is in the Pl. Vauban). **Musée de l'Armée**, daily 1 Apr–30 Sept 10.00–18.00, 1 Oct–31 March to 17.00, closed 1/1, 1/5, 1/11, 25/12 (☎ 01 44 42 37 72); **Napoléon's Tomb** until 19.00, 15 June–15 Sept. **Musée des Plans-Reliefs**, as above (☎ 01 45 51 95 05); **Musée de l'Ordre de la Libération**, open Mon–Fri 1 Apr–30 Sept 10.00–18.00, 1 Oct–31 March 10.00–17.00, Sat and Sun pm only via Musée de l'Armée (☎ 01 47 05 04 10). To the right of the gateway of the main façade is the main ticket office; there is another ticket office, a cafeteria and shop on the southern side (near the entrance to the Dôme Church.

Between the Esplanade and the Invalides are fortifications in the style of Vauban, with a ditch and bossed walls. Facing out are two artillery batteries: the unmounted Batterie Trophée, and the Batterie Triomphale, whose salvoes announcing victory were last heard at the end of the First World War. The Batterie Triomphale was removed by the Germans in 1940. Made for Frederick the Great in 1708, these pieces were captured by Napoléon in 1805.

The dignified **north façade** is 200m long and four storeys high, with a pavilion at each end surmounted by stone trophies and flags. The remaining decoration is concentrated in the attic storey around the dormer windows. Flanking the main entrance are copies of the original statues of Mars and Minerva by

Guillaume Coustou (1735). Above the central door, the equestrian bas-reliefs of Louis XIV accompanied by Justice and Prudence, by Pierre Cartellier, replaced in 1815 the original designed by Coustou that was destroyed during the Revolution.

The entrance brings you to the vast Cour d'Honneur (102m by 64m) with 60 sculpted dormer windows and sundials. Either side of the courtyard are entrances to the Musée de l'Armée and opposite is the door of the church of St-Louis, above which are Seurre's original bronze statue of Napoléon, which formerly topped the Vendôme Column (see p 225), and an astronomical clock (1781).

The **Eglise St-Louis** (the chapel of Les Invalides or the Soldiers' Church) was built (c 1679–1708) by Bruant and Hardouin-Mansart. The rather bare interior, with a gallery built at the same level as the dormitories of the disabled, is hung with captured regimental colours. In 1837 it resounded to the first performance of Berlioz's *Grande Messe des Morts*. The organ (1679–87) is by Alexandre Thierry, with a case possibly designed by Hardouin-Mansart. A sheet of plain glass behind the high altar separates the chapel from the Dôme des Invalides. There are memorials to those who fell on the field of battle and the coffin and pall used in the translation of Napoléon's remains in 1840. The graves of numerous French marshals and generals lie are in vaults below (no admission).

On leaving the chapel, turn left along the Corridor de Metz to reach the entrance of the Dôme. At the foot of the staircase to the right of the entrance to the church, is one of the Renault cars (the 'Marne taxis'), which, commandeered by Général Gallieni, carried troops to the Front in September 1914, so saving Paris from the advancing Germans.

The **Dôme des Invalides**, begun by J. Hardouin-Mansart in 1677 and finished in 1706, was added to the church of St-Louis as a chapel royal. In the niches on either side of the entrance are statues of Charlemagne and St Louis by Coysevox and Nicolas Coustou. The **ribbed dome**, the most splendid in France, is roofed with

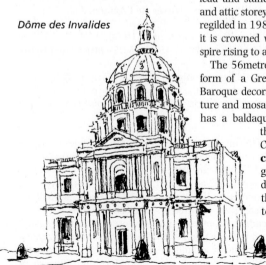

Dôme des Invalides

lead and stands on a balustraded base and attic storey. In each bay are trophies, regilded in 1989 with 12kg of gold, and it is crowned with a lantern and short spire rising to a height of 107m.

The 56metre-square interior is in the form of a Greek cross with an ornate Baroque decoration of paintings, sculpture and mosaic paving. The main altar has a baldaquin of the mid-19C and there are paintings by N. Coypel in the vault. The **chapels** on the upper level, going in an anti-clockwise direction from the right of the entrance, contain the tombs (some enshrining only hearts) of Joseph Bonaparte (d. 1844), Vauban (d. 1707), tomb of 1847 by Antoine Etex; Ferdinand Foch, Marshal of France (d. 1929), tomb by Landowski; Lyautey, soldier and colonial administrator (d. 1934), tomb by Albert Laprade; La Tour d'Auvergne (d. 1800), the first grenadier of the Republic; and Turenne, soldier (d. 1675), first buried at St-Denis, his remains were saved from destruction, and his tomb is by Le Brun, Tuby and Marsy. The last chapel, St-Jérome, stands empty. Relics of the Roi de Rome (1811–32), Bonaparte's only son, who died prematurely of phthisis and was originally buried in Vienna, were brought here by the Germans in 1940, but since 1969 have lain in the vaults of the crypt.

As you approach the circular gallery under the dome you look down on the seriously imposing **Tomb of Napoléon**, designed by Visconti, in which the Emperor's remains were placed in April 1861, 40 years after his death on St Helena (see p 360). They were brought to Les Invalides in December 1840 and lay in the Chapel St-Jérome while the sarcophagus was being prepared.

Descend the steps to the crypt to appreciate fully the proportions (4m by 2m and 4.5m high) and colours (dark red Finnish porphyry and green Vosges granite) of the tomb. The inscription at the entrance is taken from Napoléon's will, '*Je désire que mes cendres reposent sur les bords de la Seine, au milieu de ce peuple français que j'ai tant aimé*': ('I desire that my mortal remains rest on the banks of the Seine, in the midst of the French people whom I have loved so dearly'). It is surrounded by a gallery with ten bas-reliefs after Simart representing the benefits conferred on France by the Emperor. Facing the sarcophagus are 12 figures by Pradier symbolising his greater victories, between which are six trophies of colours taken at Austerlitz. The statue of *Napoléon in his Coronation Robes* is also by Simart.

Musée de l'Armée

The Musée de l'Armée comprises a vast collection of arms and armour, weapons, uniforms and military souvenirs. The building also houses the Musée des Plans-Reliefs (see below), a library and a small cinema.

On the west side of the Cour d'Honneur are the extraordinarily rich **Collections of Arms and Armour**, with weapons of all periods, many of artistic interest and masterpieces of damascening and chasing. Begin on the right with Salle François I (recently renovated).

To the left of the entrance to this wing is the Salle Henri IV, concentrating on jousting armour. Note the diminutive 'sample' suits. On the right of the corridor leading from the vestibule is a small room with arms dating from before the 9C. Further on is the important **Pauilhac Collection** which contains the only remaining example of a 16C French painted harness. The Louis XIII room contains an outstanding collection of firearms and suits of armour which belonged to Henri III, Louis XIII, Henri IV and Louis XIV.

La Galerie de l'Arsenal recaptures the atmosphere of arsenals of the past. And there are also collections of Oriental arms and armour from Turkey, Persia, India and China. Among individual helmets of interest is that of the Ottoman sultan Bajazet II (1447–1512). On the exterior walls of the Cour d'Angoulème (north) is the Danube Chain, which the Turks used to hold their vessels in position during the Siege of Vienna in 1683.

On the **second floor** are galleries devoted to the 1914–18 and the 1939–45 Wars, illustrated by documents, scale models, and films, describing the movements of troops during the principal campaigns. Occupied France, France during the Liberation, and the sad history of deportations are also covered, as are the Normandy Landings. There is an exhibition dedicated to General de Gaulle.

A room on the third floor is devoted to artillery and a collection of scale models, dating back to the end of the 16C, is presented in the Gribeauval Room.

The museum continues in the east wing ground floor with a historical circuit introduced by the **Vauban Room**. The **Turenne Room** (Emblems) contains a collection of 17C to 20C colours and frescoes, and a relief floor plan of the Hôtel des Invalides (before 1757). On the **upper floors** is a series of rooms devoted to the military exploits of the Ancienne Monarchie (1618–1792), set out in chronological order. Among the numerous plans, engravings, prints and portraits, are macabre curiosities such as the cannon-ball that killed Turenne in 1675 and the perforated back-plate of his cuirass. Note also the colours of the Irish Clancarthy regiment (1642).

Some 20 rooms devoted to **Revolution and Empire** have sections concentrating on the Revolutionary, Directory and Consulate periods, with numerous Napoleonic souvenirs, including one of Bonaparte's grey coats; his tent and furniture and the stuffed skin of his white horse, Vizir, which outlived the Emperor by eight years. Other displays show Napoléon at St Helena, and the period 1830–52. (See also Ch. 37.) There are also sections devoted to the **Second Empire**, **Crimean War** and **Franco-Prussian War** of 1870, with early photographs, and paintings by Alphonse de Neuville and Edouard Detaille.

The autonomous **Musée des Plans-Reliefs** on the attic floor is a fascinating collection of some 100 recently-renovated relief models in a revamped display. These models of fortified sites, built to the scale 1:600, served a practical military purpose. They were begun from 1668 onwards, at the time of Vauban, and the practice of ended after the Franco-Prussian War (1870–71).

The original idea is attributed to Louvois (1641–91), Louis XIV's minister of war. Secreted until 1776 in the Louvre, they were then moved to Les Invalides, where they have for the most part remained. The display is divided between fortifications along the Channel, the Atlantic and Mediterranean coasts and the Pyrenees.

The **Musée de l'Ordre de la Libération** is a repository of memorabilia connected with the fighters for France Libre and the Resistance, and the 1036 companions who received the Cross of the Liberation created by de Gaulle in 1940. (Entrance also 15bis Blvd Latour-Maubourg.)

12 • The Ecole Militaire and Tour Eiffel

■	Arrondissements: 75007, 75015
🚇	Ecole Militaire, Cambronne, Bir-Hakeim, Champ-de-Mars, La Motte Picquet-Grenelle, Javel, Lourmel, Balard, Convention, Porte de Vanves
🚌	Champs-de-Mars/Tour Eiffel, Blvd Victor

7e arrondissement
L'Auberge du Champ de Mars, 38 Rue de l'Exposition,
☎ 01 45 51 78 08. Inexpensive

eating that packs no surprises, £
Au Bon Acceuil, 14 Rue de Monttessuy, ☎ 01 47 05 46 11. Very popular, must book, excellent cooking, ££

Le 6 Bosquet, 6 Av. Bosquet, ☎ 01 45 56 97 26. Newish bistrot with cheerful atmosphere and Burgundian dishes, £
Le Bourdonnais, 113 Av.de la Bourdonnais, ☎ 01 47 05 16 54. Flawless cooking with excellent set menus, but pricey, £££
Les Olivades, 41 av de Ségur, ☎ 01 47 83 70 09. A new slant on Provençal cooking, but easy on the pocket, £
Le Petit Troquet, 28 Rue de l'Exposition, ☎ 01 47 05 80 39. Near the Eiffel Tower, pleasant bistro and freshly cooked food, £
Thoumieux, 79 Rue St-Dominique, ☎ 01 47 05 49 75. Rugged rural cooking from the centre of France, £

Eiffel Tower
Jules Verne, 2nd Floor, ☎ 01 45 55 61 44. Reach giddy heights by combining spectacular views and top quality cuisine, £££
Altitude 95, 1st Floor, ☎ 01 45 55 20 04. Brasserie food priced within reason, Zeppelin décor and great views, ££
There are more down to earth snack bars on ground, 1st and 2nd floor.

15e arrondissement
L'Amanguier at 46 Rue du Théâtre (M. Dupleix), ☎ 01 45 77 04 01. Belongs to a small group of a reliable, pleasant restaurants with traditional cooking, £
Café du Commerce, 51 Rue du Commerce, ☎ 01 45 75 03 27. Down-to-earth bistrot choices on three floors around an atrium, £
Les Celebrités, Hôtel Nikko, 61 Quai de Grenelle, ☎ 01 40 58 21 29. Refined yet confident. cooking with a view of the Seine, ££–£££
Les Coteaux, 26 Blvd Garibaldi, ☎ 01 47 34 83 48. Wine bar and wide choice of eaux de vie, £
La Dinée, 85 Rue Leblanc, ☎ 01 45 54 20 49. Outstanding and inventive fish dishes in a calm contemporary setting, ££
Morot-Gaudry, 8 Rue de la Cavalerie, ☎ 01 45 67 06 85. In view of Eiffel Tower, reliable but slightly unadventurous fare, ££
L'Os à Moëlle, 3 Rue Vasco-de-Gama, ☎ 01 45 57 27 27. Terrific value for money using fresh market produce, £
Le Suffren, 84 Av. de Suffren, ☎ 01 45 66 97 86. Always popular, always open, lively brasserie, £

This walk brings into close focus the Eiffel Tower, its familiar profile and great height looming over the district, set in one of the great vistas of Paris stretching from the Ecole Militaire across the Champ des Mars gardens and the Seine, to the Palais de Chaillot. It is worthwhile visiting the buildings of UNESCO for the architecture and the works of art assembled there. On Quai Branly, in the 15e, is the Japanese Cultural Centre, and some distance along the Seine's south-westerly curve, is Parc Citroën.

Radiating from the semi-circular **Pl. Vauban** (Map 7; 3), south of the Les Invalides, are four major avenues: Av. de Villars, wide tree-lined Av. de Breteuil, Avenue de Ségur, and Avenue de Tourville. Av. de Villars runs southeast and, by the neo-Renaissance façade of the church of St-François-Xavier (1875), becomes Blvd des Invalides.

Av. de Tourville, west from Pl. Vauban, leads directly to UNESCO, the Ecole

Militaire and the Tour Eiffel. But on foot it is more fun to take the varied and interesting route to the Champ de Mars along Rue de Grenelle which passes, to the south Rue Cler, a pedestrianised street with a lively market on certain days.

UNESCO

Between Avenues Ségur, Lowendal and Suffren, on Pl. de Fontenoy, are the buildings of UNESCO, headquarters of the UN's Organisation for Education, Science and Culture which is open to visitors Mon–Fri 09.00–18.00 (☎ 01 45 68 16 42, recorded information ☎ 01 45 58 10 60). The main **UNESCO Building**, designed by an international team of French and American architects Bernard Zehrfuss and Marcel Breuer and the Italian engineer, Pier Luigi Nervi, was begun in 1954 and inaugurated in 1958. The number of member states of UNESCO has increased from the original 37 to 186, and its multi-national character is reflected in all aspects of its design.

This large complex consists, in fact, of three major buildings. The main building is the Y-shaped Secretariat of seven floors in concrete and glass, the Ségur façade enlivened by an extraordinary spiral fire escape. Supported by 72 pylons (*pilotis*), the huge ground-floor hall is tiled with Norwegian quartzite and decorated with works by Afro (Italy) Apper (Netherlands) and Matta (Chile), and the French photographer Brassaï.

The square building to the west has, on an exterior wall, a mosaic by Bazaine, next to which is a delightful **Garden of Peace** designed by Noguchi (1904–88) in which everything comes from Japan, such as the *Nagasaki Angel* and the cylindrical Meditation Space with a pond of granite exposed to the bombing of Hiroshima, since cleaned. Near it are the five sculptures, *Signaux Eoliens*, by Vassilakis Takis. The Conference Building has fluted concrete walls and an accordion-pleated concrete roof covered in copper. It contains a huge murals by Picasso and Rufino Tamayo. On the vast Piazza, between Avenues Lowendal and Suffren, are works by Alexander Calder, Henry Moore, Giacometti, *Symbolic Globe* (1995) by Erik Reitzel, and *Birth of a New Man*, Zurab Tsereteli, marking the 500th anniversary of the discovery of America. Other works include two ceramic walls by Miró and Llorens Artigas, a bronze relief by Hans Arp, a painting by Victor Vasarely, a tapestry by Le Corbusier and in the Miollis building, an installation by Soto.

To the north is the **Ecole Militaire** (Map 6; 4–6), a handsome structure covering part of the former farm and château of Grenelle, built by J.-A. Gabriel, and enlarged in 1856. 18C railings separate the Pl. de Fontenoy from the elegant Cour d'Honneur, profusely embellished with Corinthian columns and pilasters. The figure of Victory on the entablature is in fact modelled on Louis XV, but this seemingly went unnoticed by Revolutionary iconoclasts.

History of the Ecole Militaire

The school was founded in 1751 by Louis XV for the training of noblemen as army officers. It was opened in 1756 and completed in 1773. In 1777 its rigid rules for entry were modified to accept the élite of provincial military academies and thus in 1784 Bonaparte was chosen from the Collège de Brienne. It is now a staff college training the upper echelons of the armed services.

On written application to the Chef des Moyens Généraux, BP 132, 0472 Armées, or ☎ 01 44 42 41 96, giving details of dates and participants, a visit to certain areas is possible Mon–Fri, 09.30–17.00. Bonaparte was confirmed in the chapel (1768–73), which is decorated with nine paintings of the *Life of St Louis*, during his training.

Off Pl. Cambronne to the south west is Rue Frémicourt and its extension, Av. Emile-Zola, leading due west to Pont Mirabeau: see below.

Between the Ecole Militaire and the Seine lies the **Champ-de-Mars**, almost 1km long, laid out in 1765–67 as a parade ground on the market-gardens of the old Plaine de Grenelle.

History of the Champ-de-Mars

The ground was the scene of several early aeronautical experiments by J.-P. Blanchard in 1783–84 and others. It was the theatre of the celebration to mark the first anniversary of the storming of the Bastille, the Fête de la Fédération (14 July 1790), and of Napoléon's Champ de Mai on his return from Elba. Used as a racecourse after the Restoration, the parade ground was transformed and reduced in 1860 and became the site of five universal exhibitions. In 1908 work, lasting 20 years, was begun to create the park that we see now with central lawns, avenues of trees and less formal areas either side. There is a bandstand, marionette theatre, and other amusements. Among the sculptures is the *Monument of the Rights of Man*, near the Rue de Belgrade (southeast) commissioned for the bicentenary of the Revolution from Yvan Theimer. Captain Alfred Dreyfus was publicly degraded here in December 1894, the start of *l'affaire Dreyfus* in which he was falsely accused of delivering documents concerned with the national defence to a foreign government (see Ch. 23).

The Eiffel Tower

The Tour Eiffel (**Map 6; 3**), at the river end of the Champ-de-Mars, is a masterpiece of 19C engineering. Yet, at the beginning of the 21C, its audacious proportions (318m high including the television installation) still take your breath away. An inseparable part of the Paris landscape, it remains the most emblematic monument of the city and continues to inspire painters, poets and film makers.

History of the Eiffel Tower

Opened in 1889 for the Universal Exhibition marking the 100th anniversary of the Revolution, the Tour Eiffel aroused as much controversy then as the Pompidou Centre or the Louvre Pyramid do today. Originally granted only 20 years of life, its new use in radio-telegraphy in 1909 saved it from demolition. Erected by the contracting company owned by the engineer Gustave Eiffel (1832–1923), the tapering lattice-work tower is composed of 18,000 pieces of metal weighing over 7000 tonnes (total weight 10,100 tonnes), the design was mainly due to the engineers Maurice Koechlin and Emile Nouguier and the architect Stephen Sauvestre, while its four feet are supported by masonry piers sunk 9–14m into the ground. It is repainted every seven years, and the 17th application of paint was in 1995. The Eiffel Tower bronze, exclusive to the monument is, in fact, gradated from a lighter tone at the summit to a darker one at the base to enhance the impression of perspective.

The first and second levels are reached by lift and stairs, and the third, 276m from the ground, by lift only. On a clear day, particularly about one hour before sunset, this is the ultimate place to view Paris. Ascent by lift, 10 June–31 Aug 09.00–24.00, 1 Sept–9 June 09.30–23.00; ascent on foot, 10 June–31Aug 09.00–24.00, 1 Sept–9 June 09.00–18.30. An all-time favourite, there can be a long wait for the lift at peak times.

On the vast Level 1 there are two lighthearted, interactive presentations providing information on the history and technology of the structure called Feroscope and Cineiffel and a laser system that measures the oscillations of the summit. You can also see are the old hydraulic pump and a section of the original spiral staircase. There are bars, shops, a post office and a brasserie, *Altitude 95*. On Level 2 is the Visitors Galaxy, a virtual construction of the Tower, information on the working of the original hydraulic elevator, and the restaurant *Jules Verne*. At the top level, apart from spectacular views, is a reconstruction of Gustave Eiffel's office.

Pont d'Iéna spans the Seine to the Palais de Chaillot (see Ch. 29).

A new museum is planned for 2004 on Quai Branly, between the Eiffel Tower and Pont d'Alma, which will be known as the **Musée du Quai Branly**. The architect is Jean Nouvel and it will contain Primitive Arts from Africa, Asia, Oceania and the Americas (see the Louvre, Ch. 15).

At 101bis Quai Branly, between the Eiffel Tower and Pont de Bir-Hakeim, is the **Maison de la Culture du Japon à Paris**, designed by Masayuki Yamanaka and inaugurated in 1997. This provides a permanent centre where Japanese culture can be presented in all its aspects through exhibitions, concerts, etc. Open 12.00–19.00 Tues–Sat (☎ 01 44 37 95 00).

Southwest of Av. de Suffren is the 15e arrondissement, a densely populated residential area that remains mainly unknown to the visitor but has two important 20C gardens. The next bridge, Bir-Hakeim, is crossed by the Métro, and from it Blvd de Grenelle leads southeast. At no. 8 a plaque records the round-up of thousands of Parisian Jews in the *vélodrome* (cycle-track) here in July 1942 before their deportation.

Quai de Grenelle continues southwest past Sq. Bela Bartok, a little verdant valley created in 1981 among the high-rise buildings flanking the Seine. On the opposite bank is the Maison de la Radio (see p 303). Stretching between Pont de Bir-Hakeim and Pont de Grenelle is an artificial island, the **Allée des Cygnes**, with a pleasant, tree-lined walk. At the western extremity is a scale replica in bronze of Bartholdi's *Statue of Liberty*, a gift from the Parisian community in the United States in 1885 in return for the original presented by France to New York.

Further still is Pont Mirabeau (1895–97), leading to Auteuil, and to the southeast, at 25–35 Rue de la Convention, is the Imprimerie Nationale (founded 1640), moved here in 1925 from the Hôtel de Rohan (visits in French by written application one month ahead, Mon–Thur 13.00).

On the riverside beyond Pont Mirabeau the site of the former car factory was transformed in 1992–99 into the **Parc André-Citroën**, open 07.30–dusk, Sat, Sun and public holidays, 09.00–dusk. Rigorous, architectonic, it is the creation of Alain Provost and Gilles Clément working in association with three architects, Patrick Berger, Jean-Paul Viguier and François Jodry. There are three principal sections: the White Garden to the east, the Black Garden to the south, and the main park dominated by two huge rectangular greenhouses. The principal perspective descending towards the Seine is flanked by banks of evergreen magnolias and beech hedges, with box and yew, trimmed into disciplined shapes. Water is a determining element of the park—a large fountain, canals, lily-ponds, water courses and *jets d'eau* account for about a hectare of the total. On the northeast side is a series of parallel rectangular gardens each planted to a different colour scheme. Opposite each is a small high greenhouse.

The plants in the Jardin des Métamorphoses, on the other side, evoke alchemical transmutations. In contrast to the formal gardens, closer to the river there are stretches of wild gardens described as Jardin des Roches and Jardin en mouvement.

At the opposite end of the arrondissement, to the southeast, close to Blvd Lefebvre and between Rues des Morillons, des Périchaux and Brancion, the **Parc Georges-Brassens**, laid out 1977–85 and one of the most successful new gardens, takes the name of the poet-singer who lived in the *quartier*. This was the former hamlet of Vaugirard and was until the end of the 18C an important vineyard. The vineyards became market gardens in the 19C and abattoirs until 1974. Some vestiges of the old buildings have been integrated into the gardens. Among its attractions are a pond and fountain, an aromatic and medicinal garden, and vines.

Beyond Blvd Victor and Pont du Garigliano, is the Blvd Périphérique (Quai d'Issy; with the Porte de Sèvres further east), on the far side of which is the Héliport de Paris, while adjacent to the east are various buildings of the Armée de l'Air and other Service departments, exhibition areas and Palais des Sports.

The Right Bank

13 • Place de la Concorde to Place du Carrousel

■ Arrondissements: 75001/75008
Concorde, Tuileries, Palais-Royal

Les Ambassadeurs,
Hôtel de Crillon, 10 Pl.
de la Concorde, ☎ 01 44 71 16
16. Beautiful dining room, views
over Place de la Concorde, cuisine
and service to match; top of the
range, £££

In the Jardin des Tuileries are:
Café Very, ☎ 01 47 03 94 84.
Stylish and attractive, ££
La Dame Tartine, ☎ 01 47 03 94
84. Open sandwiches, snacks, £
See also listings for Chapters. 17
and 24.

Place de la Concorde

Place de la Concorde (**Map 2; 7–8**) is one of the world's most impressive squares, next to the Seine and midway between the Etoile and the Ile de la Cité. Even the traffic constantly swirling around it does not detract from the great perspectives and the skilful landscaping of this huge open space, devoid of buildings on three sides. Its design dates from the First Empire, but its present appearance dates from 1852, when Jacques-Ignace Hittorff (1792–1867) redesigned the Place. In 1995 the 18 green-bronze and gilded *colonnes rostrales* (rostral columns), made for the July festivities of 1838, were renovated and reinstalled. the ornamental columns are decorated to resemble the prow of a ship, and symbolise, like the city's coat of arms, the importance of the river to the history of Paris.

History of the Place de la Concorde

In 1757, the then empty site to the west of Paris was chosen to receive a bronze statue of Louis XV commissioned by the *echevins* (magistrates, see Hôtel de Ville, Ch. 21). The statue, by Bouchardon and Pigalle (model in the Louvre) was unveiled in 1763 and the surrounding square, the creation of Jacques-Ange Gabriel, named Place Louis XV. The celebrations with fireworks to mark the marriage of the Dauphin Louis and Marie-Antoinette in 1770 resulted in 133 onlookers being crushed to death in a ditch. In 1792 the statue was replaced by a huge figure of Liberty, designed by Lemot and the square was renamed Pl. de la Révolution. In the same year the perpetrators of the theft of the crown jewels (see below) were executed here by guillotine. On 21 January, 1793 the same fate befell Louis XVI on the site now occupied by the fountain nearest the river, and between May 1793 and May 1795 the blade claimed 1119 victims. The square received its present name in 1795 at the end of the Terror, but it was subsequently renamed Place Louis XV at the Restoration (1815) before it finally reverted to Concorde under Louis-Philippe (1830).

On the north side of the square are two handsome colonnaded mansions designed by Gabriel in 1763–72, originally intended as official residences, with pediment sculptures by M.-A. Slodtz and G. Coustou the younger. The one on the

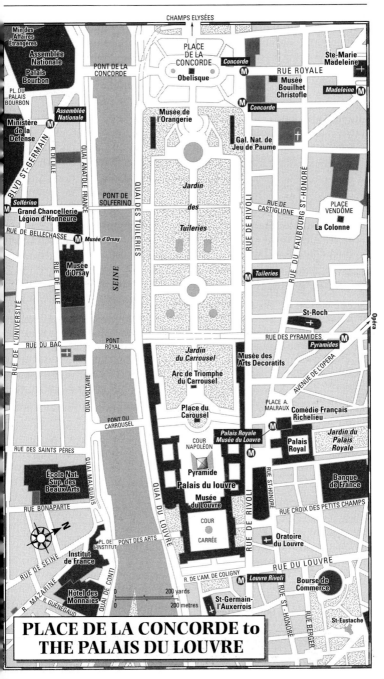

CHAMPS ELYSÉES

Min des Affaires Etrangères
Assemblée Nationale
Palais Bourbon
PL. DU PALAIS BOURBON

PONT DE LA CONCORDE

PLACE DE LA CONCORDE
Concorde Ⓜ
Obelisque

Ste-Marie Madeleine
RUE ROYALE
Musée Bouilhet Christofle
Madeleine Ⓜ

Ministère de la Défense
Assemblée Nationale
Ⓜ

BLVD ST-GERMAIN
R. DE LILLE
QUAI ANATOLE FRANCE

Musée de l'Orangerie

Concorde Ⓜ

Gal. Nat. de Jeu de Paume

Solferino Ⓜ
Grand Chancellerie Légion d'Honneure
RUE DE BELLECHASSE
Ⓜ *Musée d'Orsay*

PONT DE SOLFERINO

Jardin

des

RUE DE RIVOLI
RUE DE CASTIGLIONE
RUE DU FAUBOURG ST-HONORÉ

PLACE VENDÔME
La Colonne

RUE DE LILLE
Musée d'Orsay

QUAI DES TUILERIES

SEINE

Tuileries

Tuileries Ⓜ

RUE DE L'UNIVERSITÉ
RUE DU BAC

PONT ROYAL

St-Roch
RUE DES PYRAMIDES
Pyramides Ⓜ

Opéra →

QUAI VOLTAIRE

Jardin du Carrousel
Arc de Triomphe du Carrousel
Place du Carrousel

Musée des Arts Decoratifs

AVENUE DE L'OPERA

RUE DES SAINTS PÈRES

PONT DU CARROUSEL

PLACE A. MALRAUX
Comédie Français Richelieu

Palais Royale Musée du Louvre Ⓜ

Palais Royal

Jardin du Palais Royale

École Nat. Sup. des Beaux Arts
RUE BONAPARTE

QUAI MALAQUAIS

COUR NAPOLÉON
Pyramide
Palais du louvre
Musée du Louvre

RUE ST-HONORÉ
RUE DE RIVOLI

Banque de France

RUE CROIX DES PETITS CHAMPS

Ⓜ

N

Institut de France

PL. DE L'INSTITUT PONT DES ARTS

COUR CARRÉE

Oratoire du Louvre

RUE BONAPARTE
RUE DE SEINE
R. MAZARINE
R. GUENEGAUD

Hôtel des Monnaies

QUAI DE CONTI

QUAI DU LOUVRE

R. DE L'AM. DE COLIGNY
St-Germain-l'Auxerrois

Louvre Rivoli Ⓜ

RUE DU LOUVRE

Bourse de Commerce

RUE ST-HONORÉ
RUE BERGER

St-Eustache

0   200 yards
0   200 metres

PLACE DE LA CONCORDE to THE PALAIS DU LOUVRE

right, from which the crown jewels were stolen, is now the Naval Ministry. The left-hand building has long been shared between the Automobile Club and the prestigious *Hôtel Crillon*. Between these buildings Rue Royale leads to the church of the Madeleine (see Ch. 24) and the Palais-Bourbon (National Assembly) (see p 144) can be seen to the south across the Seine.

On the west of Pl. de la Concorde, the dramatic sweep of the Av. des Champs-Elysées (see Ch. 27) towards the Arc de Triomphe is framed by replicas of the *Marly Horses* (originals in the Louvre), two groups by G. Coustou, which were brought from the Château de Marly in 1794. The winged horses are balanced at the west entrance of the Tuileries Gardens, opposite, by replicas of Coysevox's equestrian groups (originals in the Louvre). Across the gardens the view extends as far as the Louvre.

Pont de la Concorde, on the south side of the Place, with magnificent views up and down river, was built by Perronet in 1788–90 and widened in 1932. Stone from the Bastille was used in the construction of the upper part (so that Parisians could feel they were treading upon the relics of tyranny!).

In the centre of the Place, on the site of Louis XV's statue and then Liberty, rises the **Obelisk of Luxor**, a monolith of pink syenite, almost 23m high and of 230 tonnes in weight. It originally stood before a temple at Thebes in Upper Egypt and commemorates in its hieroglyphics the deeds of Rameses II (13C BC). It was presented to Louis-Philippe in 1831 by Mohammed Ali (the donor of Cleopatra's Needle in London). The pedestal, of Breton granite, bears representations of the apparatus used in its erection in 1836 (see also Musée de Marine, Ch. 29). The two fountains, by Hittorf, copies of those in the piazza of St. Peter's at Rome, are embellished with figures symbolising inland and marine navigation.

Eight 18C stone pavilions around the Square, by Gabriel, support statues (restored in 1989) by Caillonette, Cortot and Pradier personifying the eight provincial capitals. Strasbourg (as capital of Alsace, lost to France in 1871) was hung with crêpe and wreaths until 1918.

The pillars of the gateway opening from the Pl. de la Concorde are crowned by replicas of equestrian statues of Fame and Mercury, by Coysevox (brought from Marly in 1719). Inside the gates, north and south of the western end of the Jardin des Tuileries are two public galleries, the Jeu de Paume and the Orangerie.

The Galerie National du Jeu-de-Paume and the Musée de l'Orangerie

The Galerie du Jeu-de-Paume is so named because it was originally a real (royal) tennis-court built in 1851. The building once contained the Impressionist collections that were transferred to the Musée d'Orsay in 1986 and it has been revamped by Antoine Stinco to hold temporary exhibitions of contemporary works. Open Tues 12.00–21.30, Wed–Fri 12.00–19.00, Sat, Sun 10.00–19.00, closed Mon (☎ 01 47 03 12 50). There is a small café.

To the south across the Tuileries Gardens is the **Musée de l' Orangerie** (Map 2; 8) which is undergoing reorganisation and will reopen at the end of 2001. Open 09.45–17.15, closed Tues, and all public holidays including the Mondays following Easter and Whitsun (☎ 01 42 97 48 16).

Monet's sensational series of mural paintings, *Les Nymphéas* (see also Ch. 29), was installed here in 1927. Since 1984 it has been the permanent home of the Jean Walter and Paul Guillaume collection of some 144 outstanding Impressionist and early 20C works.

Impressionist paintings include Monet's *Argenteuil* (1875), contrasts of red boats against bright green waterweed; and Sisley's *The Montbuisson Road at Louveciennes* (1875).

Among the 14 works by **Cézanne** in the collection are *Apples and Biscuits* (c 1880), the portraits of *Paul Cézanne*, the artist's son, and *Madame Cézanne* (1885); also *In the Park of the Château Noir* (c 1900) and *The Red Rock*, c 1895, constructed from small planes of colour. There are several studies of young girls by Renoir, such as a version of *Young Girls at the Piano* (1892) and *Yvonne and Christine Lerolle at the Piano* (c 1897–98), studies of his children, *Gabrielle and Jean* (c 1895), *Claude Playing* (c 1809), and *Claude Dressed as a Clown* (1909), as well as some lush nudes.

The 28 examples of works by **André Derain** are mainly dark and monumental nudes from his post-Fauves period including *The Artist's Niece* (1931) and *Portrait of Mme Guillaume* (c 1929). In the museum are portrait tributes to the art dealer collector, Paul Guillaume, by Modigliani and van Dongen as well as Derain.

Several of the paintings by Matisse are typical decorative interiors with odalisques painted during the 1920s in Nice. By Henri Rousseau (le Douanier) are *The Wedding* (c 1908), and *Père Junier's Cart* (1910) which the Surrealists raved about. Picasso's blue tendency is represented by *The Embrace* (1903), and his rose period by *Les Adolescents* (1906), while his later monumental nudes are exemplified in *Bathers* of 1921 and 1923. There are also works by Utrillo and by Marie Laurencin and the collection includes examples of the impasto Expressionist paintings of Chaïm Soutine, the Lithuanian member of the School of Paris, such as *Le Petit Pâtissier* (c1922) and *La Table* (c 1925).

Stairs descend from the central gallery to the two oval rooms designed with the approval of **Monet** for the famous waterlily murals, *Les Nymphéas* of c 1914. Drenched in colour and reflected light, the panels submerge the onlooker in vibrating lilacs and blues, intense greens and acid yellows.

Jardin des Tuileries

The Jardin des Tuileries (**Map 2; 8**), the best known and oldest of all the gardens of Paris, covering over 28 hectares, still retains the basic formal layout that Le Nôtre designed in 1664. Re-landscaping work has been undertaken with the aim of returning the garden to something like its original character and glory. With about 100 statues beneath some 2800 trees (mainly chestnuts and limes, but also maples, planes and elms), although some were lost in the gales of Christmas 1999, the garden extends eastwards to the Pl. du Carrousel, uninterrupted now that Av. du Gén.-Lemonnier has gone underground. As in practically all Parisian public gardens, the grass is for looking at, not walking on.

Beneath the Jeu-de-Paume is a **Librarie du Patrimoine**, a bookshop stocking publications produced by Editions du patrimoine.

History of the Jardin des Tuileries

At the beginning there were vineyards and fields and then in the 12C, the site, beyond the city walls, was occupied by tile-kilns (*tuileries*). The area was requisitioned by François I in the 16C for his mother, but it was not until Catherine de Médicis assumed power in 1564 that the palais and the gardens took shape. Enclosed in walls, this garden, in the Italian style, was the work of a team probably including Philibert Delorme, architect of the Tuileries Palace (see below), Pierre Le Nôtre (grandfather of André), Bernard Palissy the ceramicist. Later, during the reign of Louis XIV, important alterations were undertaken by André Le Nôtre, notably the enlargement of the main alley and the creation of the two large pools and terraces. At this time it became Paris's first public garden.

From the 17C dances, concerts and firework displays took place in the garden, it was a fashionable promenade until the Palais-Royal took over this privilege, and from the Revolution it was even more popular when cafés and restaurants opened. The major changes in the 19C were the construction of the Orangerie (1853), Jeu de Paume (1861), and the creation of the Carrousel Garden (1871). The gardens were always intended to be viewed from the palace terrace to the east. Louis XV introduced sculptures in the 18C and these have been added to in the 20C.

Terraces extend along both sides of the gardens. On the south, overlooking the Quai des Tuileries is the Terrasse du Bord-de-l'Eau. A footbridge, Pont de Solférino, crosses to the Quai Anatole-France. On the north side, the Terrasse des Feuillants, skirting the Rue de Rivoli, is named after a Benedictine monastery. To the east, nearly opposite the Rue de Castiglione, was the site of the *manège*, the riding-school of the palace, where the National Assembly met from 1789 to 1793, and where Louis XVI was condemned to death.

The Tuileries Garden has three distinct parts: the Octagon to the west, the Grand Couvert, a wooded central area and, to the east, the formal gardens and Round Pond of the Grand Carré.

The **Octagon** is an open area determined by the large Octagonal pond. Around it are replicas of 17C–18C statuary, some of the oldest in the garden (originals in the Louvre), by N. and G. Coustou and Van Cleve. On the steps to the south is *Hommage à Cézanne* by Maillol and to the north, a copy of Coysevox's bust of *Le Nôtre* (original in St-Roch). There are also works by Rodin, Henry Moore and Henri Laurens.

The wide central avenue of the **Grand Couvert** is flanked by chestnut and limes in echelon, which shade works by Jean Dubuffet, Etienne Martin, Giacometti, Max Ernst, David Smith and Germaine Richier. The marble exedra and ponds have been renewed in the eastern part. There are cafés and children's play areas.

The third section, the **Grand Carré**, from the Round Pond to Av. du Gén.-Lemonnier, was the original palace garden and certain essential elements of Le Nôtre's original designs were respected during the renovation between 1991–96. These had been the *jardins réservés* or private gardens of Louis-Philippe, and and were then turned into informal English-style gardens by Napoléon III. The flower beds are densely populated by statues notably by G. and N., Coysevox and Le Pautre.

A terrace designed by Ming Pei in 1993, marked by two huge late 17C vases by Robert and Legros, has been built over Av. du Gén.-Lemonnier linking the Tuileries and the Carrousel Gardens and reinstating the perspectives of the historic site. This is now the setting for Dina Vierny's donation in 1964–65 of 18 bronzes by Aristide Maillol. Yew hedges have been shaped to provide an all-year-round structure to this area.

The **Arc de Triomphe du Carrousel**, a copy on a reduced scale of the Arch of Septimus Severus at Rome (14.60m high instead of 23m), is enhanced by pink and white Corinthian columns. It was begun in 1806 from designs by Fontaine and Percier to commemorate the victories of Napoléon I in 1805, depicted in the marble bas-reliefs on the four sides. It is surmounted by figures of soldiers of the Empire and a bronze chariot-group by Bosio (1828) representing the Restoration of the Bourbons.

Arc de Triomphe du Carrousel

The original group incorporated the antique horses, looted by Napoléon from St Mark's, Venice, in 1797 but returned in 1815.

The main west wing of the former Palais des Tuileries no longer exists, except for the **Pavillon de Flore** and the Pavillon de Marsan (to the south and north respectively), both of which have been restored or rebuilt. They now form the western extremities of the wings of the Palais du Louvre; see below. The Pavillon de Marsan accommodates the museums of the Union Centrale des Arts Décoratifs (see Ch. 16).

History of the Palais des Tuileries

The Palais des Tuileries was begun in 1564 by Philibert Delorme for Catherine de Médicis. Delorme was succeeded by Jean Bullant and then, in 1595, by Jacques II Androuet du Cerceau and Louis Métezeau, who were responsible for the Pavillon de Flore. The Pavillon de Marsan was built in 1660–65 by Louis Le Vau and his son-in-law François d'Orbay. Both pavilions were partly rebuilt and restored in 1875–78 by Lefuel.

Louis XVI was confined here after being brought from Versailles until 10 August 1792. It was the headquarters of the Convention. The Tuileries became subsequently the main residence of Napoléon I, Louis XVIII (who died here), Charles X, Louis-Philippe and Napoléon III. In May 1871 the Communards set fire to the building which, like the Hôtel de Ville, was completely gutted. Its charred remains stood until 1884, when the main wing was razed, and the site was converted into a garden in 1889.

The Arc du Carrousel was the main entrance to the courtyard of the Tuileries from the Cour du Carrousel. The Pl. du Carrousel, which derives its name from an equestrian fête given here in 1662 by Louis XIV, lies to the east of the arch. Until the middle of the 19C this was a small square surrounded by a labyrinth of narrow alleys, almost encircled by the royal palaces (see history of the Louvre, Ch. 14).

The archways to the north lead to the Rue de Rivoli and those on the south give onto the Quai des Tuileries opposite the Pont du Carrousel. To the east lies the

Cour Napoléon, and the main entrance to the Musée du Louvre, below its distinctive glass pyramid (see Chs 14 and 15). To the west is a distant view towards the Arc de Triomphe and the towers of La Défense beyond. Underground is the shopping mall, the Carrousel du Louvre (see Ch. 14).

14 • Palais du Louvre

> ■ Arrondissements: 75001
> 🚇 Palais-Royal-Musée du Louvre, Louvre-Rivoli, Tuileries, Pont-Neuf

This chapter describes the history and architecture of the Louvre Palace. The Palais du Louvre (**Map 8; 1**) which occupies an extensive site between the Rue de Rivoli and the Seine. This was one of the most magnificent of the world's palaces, and the Grand Louvre project, initiated by President Mitterand in 1981, which reaches its conclusion in 2002, has revitalised and re-enhanced the most majestic public building in Paris.

The Musée du Louvre is described in Ch. 15, and the Musée des Arts Décoratifs in Ch. 16.

Despite its apparent homogeneity, the Louvre as we see it now is the result of many phases of building, modifications and restoration. It can be divided into two main parts: the Old Louvre, comprising the buildings surrounding the Cour Carrée to the east and the long gallery along the bank of the Seine, and the New Louvre, the 19C buildings north and south of the Cour Napoléon, together with their extensions to the west which were originally part of the Tuileries Palace.

History of the Palais du Louvre

The derivation of the name is unclear, but it was already in use when it first appears in history as one of Philippe Auguste's fortresses (1190–1202), which stood at the south-west corner of the Cour Carrée. A fascinating outcome of the Louvre project is the incorporation of the remains of the old fortress into the museum (see Ch. 15). Charles V (1364–80) made the castle one of the official royal residences, endowed it with his famous library and carried out improvements, including new buildings and a handsome staircase.

Subsequent monarchs preferred other palaces until François I (1515–47) planned the total demolition and reconstruction of all the west and south sides of the fortress. The west side of the Cour Carrée, to the south of the Pavillon Sully, part of the early 16C palace, is the oldest visible elevation. The work was begun by Pierre Lescot shortly before the king's death, and was continued under Henri II. Jean Goujon was responsible for the sculptural decorations. Their elegant Classical style set the tone for all later additions.

Under Charles IX, Henri II's son, the Petite Galerie was begun and a long gallery planned to connect the Louvre with the Tuileries, his mother Catherine de Médicis' new palace outside the Paris wall. At the time of Henri IV, Luis Métezeau and Jacques II Androuet du Cerceau built the Grande Galerie from 1594–1606, the first part of the royal design (Grand Dessein) to enlarge the Louvre and the Tuileries. The Pavillon de l'Horloge (later called

Pavillon de Sully) and the north half of the west façade were the work of Lemercier, 1639–42, but the pavillon was the only part decorated, with large caryatids from the workshop of Jacques Sarazin (17C).

From 1654, during the minority of Louis XIV, work proceeded mainly in the court apartment of the queen mother, decorated by Romanelli and Angier, under the supervision of Lemercier. In 1661 the destruction of the second floor of the Petite Galerie and the royal decision to renew the Grand Dessein of Henri VI resulted in the Apollo Gallery, the main floor of the Petite Galerie, and new buildings on the west. The quadrangle was extended and from then on could be described as the Cour Carrée. Several architects, including Bernini and Le Vau, submitted projects for the main façade to the east. However, the great colonnade of 52 Corinthian columns and pilasters that now forms the exterior east façade (facing St-Germain-l'Auxerrois; see

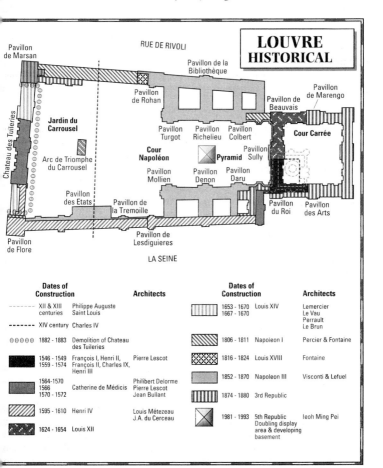

LOUVRE HISTORICAL

Dates of Construction		Architects	Dates of Construction		Architects
XII & XIII centuries	Philippe Auguste Saint Louis		1653 - 1670 1667 - 1670	Louis XIV	Lemercier Le Vau Perrault Le Brun
XIV century	Charles IV		1806 - 1811	Napoleon I	Percier & Fontaine
1882 - 1883	Demolition of Chateau des Tuileries		1816 - 1824	Louis XVIII	Fontaine
1546 - 1549 1559 - 1574	François I, Henri II, François II, Charles IX, Henri III	Pierre Lescot	1852 - 1870	Napoleon III	Visconti & Lefuel
1564-1570 1566 1570 - 1572	Catherine de Médicis	Philibert Delorme Pierre Lescot Jean Bullant	1874 - 1880	3rd Republic	
1595 - 1610	Henri IV	Louis Métezeau J.A. du Cerceau	1981 - 1993	5th Republic Doubling display area & developing basement	Ieoh Ming Pei
1624 - 1654	Louis XII				

Ch. 21) was the work of Claude Perrault, and Le Vau. (The decorations of th Cour Carrée were not completed until the 19C.) But Louis XIV, preoccupie with his new palace at Versailles, soon lost interest in these buildings, whic were left in a state of disrepair and occupied by the academies. It was not unt 1754 that Louis XV commissioned Gabriel to renovate and restore the palac

Under Napoléon I part of the North Gallery along Rue de Rivoli was begu and in 1810 the wedding feast of Napoléon and Marie-Louise of Austria wa celebrated in the Salon Carré. The building was attacked during the revolu tions of 1830 and 1848 and the building of the New Louvre was undertake at the time of Napoléon III by Visconti in 1852. The Galerie du Bord de l'Ea was largely rebuilt in 1861–68. After Visconti's death the work was continue by Lefuel, who made several radical modifications to its decoration and com pleted it in 1871. In that year it was set on fire by the Communards, thoug serious damage was limited to the library (see Palais des Tuileries, Ch. 13). Th Pavillon de Marsan, part of the Tuileries Palace, was rebuilt by Lefuel.

In 1793 the Musée de la République was opened in the Louvre, which, wit a change of name, has remained the national art gallery and museum eve since. By 1981 it was decided that the museum lacked sufficient space for bot visitors and workshops, so the north wing, occupied by the Ministry of Financ since 1871, was handed back in 1989 and the Ministry transferred to a ne building at Bercy. The ambitious **Grand Projet du Louvre** began in 198 when President Mitterand approved the plan proposed by Ieoh Ming Pei (Chinese-born American architect) to construct a glazed pyramid as the ne entrance to the museum. The alterations to the buildings included the excava tion of the Cour Carrée to expose the foundations of the medieval fortress an the palace of Charles V, now called the Medieval Louvre. The north side, know as the Richelieu Wing was, until 1989, occupied by the Ministère des Financ which has been transferred to a new building at Bercy. This wing has bee extensively rebuilt and adapted to accommodate the enlarged Musée du Louvr

La Pyramide

The Pyramid, elegant and innovative yet controversial, this tip of the iceber symbolising the metamorphosis and spread of the Musée du Louvre, has becom a famliar and favourite sight during the last decade. 30m square and 20m hig it has transparent walls supported by a trussed steel frame. Designed to overcom problems of light and space, aggravated by the proximity of the Seine whic makes deep excavation impossible, the glass reflects and refracts light as well permitting uninterrupted views of the mellow façades of the palace. It takes u less space than conventional building shapes and now shines like a crystal in stone showcase.

Centrally placed in the Cour Napoléon between the Pavillon Richelieu and th Pavillon Denon, it is flanked by three subsidiary pyramids and seven fountain with triangular basins of Brittany granite. Between it and the Carrousel Arch an equestrian statue of Louis XIV, a lead copy of 1988 after Bernini's original Versailles. The statue, but not the Pyramid, is on the same axis as the Tuileri and the Champs-Elysées and the Arc de Triomphe.

The Pyramid (west side) is the main entrance to the museum with steps and a escalator descending into a spacious well or vestibule, the Hall Napoléon (fr entry; see Ch. 15) clad in pale stone and flooded with light from the glazed el

Pyramid, Cour Napoléon, Palais du Louvre

vations of the Pyramid. From here, passages lead to the basements, to the Cour Carrée, and to the South and North Wings. On the central column is a plaque commemorating the fact that on 18 November 1993, President Mitterand dedicated the whole Palace du Louvre to the museum. In this area are the information desk, the auditorium group reception desk, the museum bookshop, restaurants and cafés.

The **Carrousel du Louvre**, is the smart and popular underground shopping precinct reached from the Métro Palais Royal-Musée du Louvre, or from escalators descending from 99 Rue de Rivoli and from Hall Napoléon under the Pyramid. It can also be entered from the underground parking, below the Jardins du Carrousel, access Rue du Général Lemonnier. Another glass pyramid, this time inverted, provides daylight for this area. There is a large food hall with a wide variety of cafés and specialist boutiques. From here, passages lead directly to extensive underground car and coach parks. A section of the fortifications planned by Charles V and rebuilt at the beginning of the 16C, which came to light during excavations here, has been preserved.

Below the Pl. du Carrousel and Cour Napoléon is a complex providing space for the reserves of the Louvre, studios for the restoration of works of art, service areas and other facilities.

Three bridges cross the Seine from the Louvre to the Quai Voltaire. To the west is the Pont Royal, a five-arched bridge by Père F. Romain (1685–89); the last pillar on either bank has a hydrographic scale indicating the low-water mark (zero; only 24m above sea-level), besides various flood-marks. The Pont du Carrousel (1834; rebuilt in 1939) retains four seated figures by Petitot and Pradier from the original structure.

The pedestrian Pont des Arts, built of cast iron by Cessart and Dillon in 1801–03, derived its name from the Palais des Arts as the Louvre was then called. It was dismantled for several years then rebuilt in a similar style to the original in 1983–85. The new footbridge, Passerelle Solférino, crosses the Seine between the Musée d'Orsay and the Tuileries gardens. Designed by Marc Mimram, it opened in 2000 after a few difficulties.

The Louvre's medieval history is well illustrated and explained in several rooms devoted to the subject, which lie east of the Hall Napoléon (see Ch. 15).

15 • The Musée du Louvre

> ■ Arrondissement: 75001
> 🚇 Palais-Royal-Musée du Louvre
>
> *Le Café Marly*, entrance on the north side of Cour Napoléon, ☎ 01 49 26 06 60, is a fashionable watering hole that overlooks Cour Marly inside and Cour Napoléon from the terrace. £ *Carrousel du Louvre* has a large food hall with a number of self-service cafés serving a variety of foods.
>
> In the Hall Napoléon there are self-service cafés/bars: *Café du Louvre*, *Café Napoléon Les Cafés de la Pyramide*, which can be reached without buying a ticket for the museum
>
> *Le Grand Louvre Restaurant* (☎ 01 40 20 53 20), the most elegant and expensive restaurant in the building, ££
>
> Inside the museum are three café/restaurants serving snacks and light meals: *Café Denon*, the most recent to open, also on the first floor Denon (via Egyptian funerary objects) *Café Mollien*, Denon, first floor, near room 77 *Café Richelieu*, first floor, Richelieu, has a terrace which is open in the summer

The background to the Louvre Museum and practical information for visiting is given below, while the exterior of the Palais du Louvre, and its architectural history, is described in Ch. 14.

The **Grand Projet du Louvre**, which began in 1983, will be completed by the end of 2002. On 18 November, 1993, 21,500m^2 of new exhibition space were inaugurated in the Richelieu Pavilion, and since then modernisation has continued in the Denon and Sully Pavilions. As a result of the Grand Projet there are better facilities for receiving some 5 million visitors a year. The increased exhibition space allows for a vastly improved presentation of works and for better conditions of conservation, as well as the reorganisation of collections into more coherent themes or schools and logical chronological order. The areas of technical and scientific support have also been extended. The final gesture, at the initiative of President Chirac, was the installation in 2000 of a selection of pieces from the collection of arts of Africa, Asia, Oceania (Pacific and Australia) and the Americas, the flagship for the new museum to be opened on Quai Branly in 2004. The new entrance, the Porte de Lions, at the west end of Denon Pavilion is the direct route to this collection as well as to Spanish and Italian paintings. With the work nearing completion, the Musée du Louvre, extended and rejuvenated, is one of the largest museums and art galleries in the world. To give some indication of the staggering size and scope of what has been undertaken, the museum will has doubled its exhibition surfaces, from 31,000 to 60,000m^2, and increased the number of works exhibited from 20,600 to 34,000. The former role of the building as a palace can be discovered through information in certain rooms, giving political, architectural and decorative history and there is a free brochure-guide of the history (in French, see below).

History of the collection

The nucleus of the royal art collection was formed by François I at whose request Leonardo da Vinci spent the last few years of his life in France (d. 1519, Amboise). Henri II and Catherine de Médicis carried on the tradition and Henri IV (1589–1610) created a room for antiquities in the Palace; Louis XIV added to the Cabinet des tableaux du roi and the Cabinet des desseins which became the basis of the present collection; Louis XVI acquired some important paintings of the Spanish and Dutch Schools and planned the opening of a museum in the Louvre. During the 18C the Académie de Peinture et de Sculpture (founded 1648) had a permanent exhibition and also held biennial exhibitions of the works of its members here which, during the years 1759–81, were the subject of Diderot's Salons.

In 1793 the Musée de la République was opened to the public, and during the next few years a large number of the most famous paintings of Europe—spoils of conquest by the victorious Republican and Napoleonic armies—were exhibited here; after 1815 the French government was obliged to restore some works of art to their former owners. Under Louis XVIII, the *Vénus de Milo* and over a hundred pictures were acquired. Champollion, the Egyptologist, persuaded Charles X to acquire prestigious Egyptian collections.

Advice for visitors

The Louvre Museum is stunning and exciting, but its immensity and diversity are daunting. There are several ways of tackling a visit and it is probably advisable to start with a preconceived plan tailored to individual preferences or time available. All the old favourites are on view, albeit frequently rearranged—80 per cent of the objects have been moved from their previous positions. Many pieces not previously on view have come out of storage, and there has been a considerable programme of restoration.

The **main entrance** of the Musée du Louvre is situated in the west side of the glass Pyramid which is in the centre of the **Cour Napoléon**. Cour Napoléon can be reached at street level from the west, from the east via the Cour Carrée and from the north via the Passage Richelieu. An alternative route of entry is from the underground shopping precinct, the Carrousel du Louvre (see Ch. 14) via 99 Rue de Rivoli or from the Métro. In **Passage Richelieu** (between the Cour Marly and Cour Puget) there is an entrance for ticket-holders and for groups. There is a second, smaller entrance, **Port des Lions**, in Denon accessed from the Quai or the Esplanade des Tuileries, which leads directly to certain collections, notably the section on arts from Africa, Asia, Oceanie and the Americas.

Cour Napoléon is flanked by three blocks of buildings or wings which are named on the orientation panels inside the museum: Sully (the four sides of the Cour Carrée) to the east; Denon (to the south); and Richelieu (to the north); see plan.

- The galleries of the Musée du Louvre are open Wed–Mon 09.00–18.00; until 21.45 on Mon (short tour) and Wed; closed on Tues and certain public holidays. Due to lack of staffing, certain galleries are closed on certain days each week (including Wed eve). It is therefore important to check this when planning a visit to avoid disappointment. (Recorded message in English, ☎ 01 40 20 51 51, information desk ☎ 01 40 20 53 17, or www.louvre.fr).

- Reduced entrance fee after 15.00 and Sundays; free to persons under 18, and to everyone on the first Sunday of each month. At peak times there can be a long wait to enter the Pyramid and to buy tickets in the Hall Napoléon. This can be avoided by using a Carte Musées et Monuments (see p 54) or by buying your ticket in advance via the Internet (see above); in France, at 400 sales outlet: Fnac, Carrefour, Continet (☎ 0803 808 803) or Virgin Megastore, Galeries Lafayette, Le Printemps, ☎ 0803 346 346, or through Minitel 36–15 Louvre. All groups have to book in advance, ☎ 01 40 20 53 63, 📠 01 42 86 04 63.

Once inside the Pyramid, a spiral stair, an escalator and a lift (for the handicapped) descend from the entrance to the spacious **Hall Napoléon**. It is a help to remember, when orientating yourself, that the main reception area, Hall Napoléon, is below ground. From here escalators (and lifts) ascend to the lower ground floor, which provides access to the three main wings, Richelieu, Sully and Denon. In the Hall Napoléon is an information desk giving details of times of lectures, guided tours (in English), etc.

Free orientation leaflets, in English and eight other languages, are available at the information desk. Also free are the pamphlet *Les nocturnes de lundi* (French only) for a visit of the highlights of the collections on Monday evenings, and *Histoire du Palais du Louvre: itinéraire pour une visite* of the history of the building (French only). (All the English information is signalled in red.)

The collections are colour-coded according to category: brown for History of the Louvre, red for paintings, pink for prints and drawings, blue for Greek, Etruscan and Roman antiquities, green for Egyptian antiquities, gold for Oriental antiquities, purple for objets d'art, buff for sculptures. Behind the desk are two large display boards with 14 video screens giving information on the permanent collections and daily activities. There are cloakrooms and toilets on this level.

- Tickets (for the permanent and temporary exhibitions combined) may be purchased at three ticket desks (not always all open). Audio-guides (English commentary covers 350 works, French 900 works) can be hired at the entresol level of the three museum wings. The museum mounts about 10 temporary exhibitions a year, and holds lectures, films and concerts in the auditorium (☎ 01 40 20 67 89 recorded information). There is an audio-visual room open from 10.00.

  Virtually the whole museum is accessible by the disabled and wheel chairs can be borrowed free (☎ 01 40 20 59 90); there is an area for blind and partially sighted visitors in the foreign sculpture section of Denon.

- Many galleries have broadsheets in several languages, with information on exhibits. Also wall panels giving the history of certain rooms. For those who have limited time the Louvre publishes in English a small First Visit guide; in addition, also guides for certain departments (*Petit guide* and *Guide du visiteur*) for sale in the bookshops.

- Hand cameras are admitted without charge. The use of flash and tripods is prohibited.

- On the southwest corner of the reception area is the museum bookshop with information on the Louvre and art history in general (☎ 01 40 20 52 06).

There are also bookstalls in the museum itself. In the passageway linking Hall Napoléon with the Carrousel du Louvre is a boutique selling postcards and slides of objects in the Musées Nationaux and another selling *moulages* or casts in bronze, resin or plaster together with replicas of jewellery (good quality but pricey), and copies of other objects from the national collections. The Chalcographie du Musée sells an extensive range of prints, many made from the original plates.

CyberLouvre (☎ 01 40 20 67 30), with CD-Roms, websites, data banks, is open 10.00–18.30 (to 19.45 Mon and Wed) every day except Mon and some public holidays, and is free. In the same area are a post office and exchange facilities.

Visits The (seven) departments of the Louvre plus the section from Musée Branly are distributed throughout the three wings. Each level is subdivided into ten sections and each section consists of several galleries. In outline, the collections are arranged as follows:

Paintings French School, 14C–17C, Richelieu second floor, and 17C–19C, Sully second floor (Richelieu escalator); large French 19C paintings, Denon first floor. Northern Schools–Dutch/Netherlandish, Flemish, German, Richelieu second floor. Italian, Spanish and English Schools and Icons, Denon first floor.

Prints and Drawings Denon west, Flore Pavilion, apply in writing or fax (01 40 20 53 51) to use the Consultation Rooms. Works from this department are not on permanent display but works on paper, pastels, cartoons and miniatures are exhibited in rotation in galleries of the individual schools of painting, i.e. drawings and prints from the Northern Schools in Richelieu, from the French School in Sully, from the Italian Schools in Denon. There are also temporary exhibitions.

Greek, Etruscan and Roman Antiquities Denon lower ground floor and ground floor and Sully ground floor and first floor. Pre-classical Greek objects are on Denon lower ground floor; Roman marbles and sculpture are on Denon ground floor. Smaller objects such as glass, bronze and silver and ceramics, Sully first floor.

Egyptian Antiquities Sully, east and south sides: ground floor Pharaonic Egypt, Thematic Circuit; first floor, Pharaonic Egypt, Chronological Circuit. Roman and Coptic Egypt are on Denon lower ground floor.

Oriental Antiquities Richelieu, ground floor and around Cour Khorsabad: Assyrian and Mesopotamian sections. Sully ground floor, the north and west sides, Near Eastern section including Iran, Levant, pre-Islamic Arabia, and Cyprus. Islamic Art is at the east end of Richelieu lower ground floor.

Objets d'Art Richelieu first floor, including the Apartments of Napoléon III, and Sully first floor. The Crown Jewels are in the Apollo Gallery, Denon first floor.

Sculptures Richelieu lower ground floor and ground floor, including Cours Marly and Puget, French sculptures from the Middle Ages to the 19C. Denon lower ground floor, north and west sides, 11C–15C Italian and Spanish and 12C–16C Northern; Denon ground floor, 16C–19C Italian and 17C–19C Northern sculptures.

Arts from Africa, Asia, Oceanie and the Americas Opened in April 2000 in the Flore pavilion, at extreme west of Denon. Entry is included in the general ticket and the recommended entrance is Porte des Lions.

Medieval Louvre Sully lower ground floor.

Medieval Louvre

This section adds a fascinating dimension to understanding the Louvre Palace's history with the aid of paintings, sculptures, models and the foundations of Philippe Auguste's fortress. It was made possible following the excavation in 1983–84 of the moats constructed by Philippe Auguste in 1190. From the Hall Napoléon below the Pyramid, take the escalator opposite the information desk up to Sully lower ground floor. Follow the passage leading east to a central point with massive reliefs of 1559–65, attributed to Jean Goujon, taken from the façade of the Louvre. Adjacent rooms (start on the right) are devoted to the History of the Louvre Palace. Maquettes explaining the development of the fortress and palace are supplemented by drawings, fragments of masonry, engravings and paintings as well as a reproduction of the *Très Riches Heures of the Duc de Berry* (1413–16) showing the castle at the time of Charles V. Continue eastwards along the passage to the Medieval Louvre.

Passing through a massive rusticated wall by Le Vau (17C) (re-sited), you reach sombre vaulted galleries below the west part of Sully where the site of the Tour de la Fauconnerie, built by Philippe Auguste, is traced on the floor in black. In 1367, Charles V transferred his library to three floors of the tower, and its name changed to the Tour de la Librairie. Various displays explain the excavations of 1983–84, when 16,000m^3 of earth was moved, and include archaeological finds from the debris.

The next section brings you to the moat surrounding the massive foundations of the two surviving walls of the medieval fortress, forming its north and east sides excavated below the southwest corner of the Cour Carrée. This outer moat was filled in by Lemercier in 1624 and by Le Vau in 1660. The Tour du Milieu (12C), like the Tour de la Taillerie beyond, shows signs of considerable battering. Between this and the next tower is the base of the drawbridge support and a well of 1660. The basements of the twin towers formed the eastern entrance of the Château du Louvre, and the support for its drawbridge.

The circular donjon (keep) of the earlier fort, established at the turn of the 13C by Philippe Auguste to form a quadrilateral 70m by 77m, was razed and in 1528 the surrounding moat was filled in. On the left is a well, probably 14C. Skirting the foundations of this keep (15m in diameter and 7m high, formerly 30m high), are some of the additions made at the time of Charles V. The area was excavated and the walls strengthened in 1984–87, and the moats given ceilings to sustain this south-west corner of the Cour Carrée.

Shuttered concrete passages lead to a vaulted basement room below the present Salle des Cariatides, called the Salle St-Louis. Archaeological finds extracted from this site and from the Cour Napoléon reveal life in the old castle. Some 900 objects or fragments were discovered in the well of the keep and 169 of them have been painstakingly reassembled to reveal items of Royal ornamental apparel.

At the far end of the moat is the entrance to the Crypte du Sphinx, and to Egyptian Antiquities.

Paintings

French School

The rooms devoted to the French School of painting, displayed in historical order, are arranged as follows: 14C–17C, **Richelieu** second floor, 17C–19C **Sully** second floor. The large scale 19C French paintings are in **Denon** first floor, rooms 75 and 77. To reach the start of the French School paintings, take the Richelieu escalator (or lift) from Hall Napoléon up to the second floor. French prints, drawings, cartoons and pastels are in Rooms 20–23, 41, 42, 44 and 45.

The first three rooms, opposite the escalator, are common to both Northern European and French Schools of the end of the 14C and beginning of the 15C, when Franco-Flemish artists, working at Paris, Dijon and Bourges, developed the International Gothic style.

Rooms 1–3 Anon. (c 1350), *Portrait of Jean Le Bon* (1319–64) is a rare 14C easel painting on wood and the only existing French portrait of this period; grisaille on silk of the *Liturgical Cloth of Narbonne* (c 1375), probably for use during Lent, with Charles V depicted in the border; the *Calvaire* by Beaumetz, the *Large Round Pietà*, attributed to Malouel, and Henri Bellechose *Retable of St-Denis* (1415–16) were commissioned by Philippe le Hardi for Champmol, Burgundy. French, Flemish and Italian influences combine in Jacquemart de Hesdin, *Carrying of the Cross*.

After room 3, paintings from the Northern Schools continue in the galleries to the left and French painting to the right.

Rooms 4 and 5 School of Avignon, seat of the papal court in the 14C, which produced such brilliant works as the *Thouzon Retable* (two sections) (c 1410). Barthélémy d'Eyck, *Crucifixion*, and Enguerrand Quarton, *Pietà* of Villeneuve-les-Avignon, a masterpiece of drama and pathos. New currents were introduced from the north by Nicolas Froment, *Matheron Diptych*, and Josse Lieferinxe *Crucifixion and Visitation*.

Room 6 Jean Fouquet (c 1420–80) was significant for his bold and simplified forms in both miniatures and full-scale portraits, such as *Charles VII* and *Guillaume Juvenel des Ursins*. His influence is seen in the (anon.) *Retable of the Parlement of Paris* (c 1455)—note the view of the Louvre in the background. From the centre of France, Jean Hey (the Maître de Moulins), fragments of a *Retable of the Bourbons*.

Rooms 7 and 8 16C portraiture is dominated by **Jean Clouet** (c 1485–c 1541). The attribution of his celebrated *Portrait of François I* (c 1530) was the subject of long debate; François Clouet, *Portrait of Pierre Quthe, Apothecary* (1562); *Elisabeth of Austria* (wife of Charles IX, painted in 1571); attributed to François Quesnel (c 1543–1616), *Portrait of Henri III*; and several works by followers of F. Clouet. Among small portraits, largely anon. are portraits of *Jean Babou de la Bourdasière*, *Michel de l'Hospital*, *Catherine de Médicis*, and also *The Ball at the Wedding of Anne, Duc de Joyeuse*; several by Corneille de Lyon (1505–74) or his school, including Pierre Aymeric.

Rooms 10 and 11 The **First and Second Schools of Fontainebleau**. Italian artists brought to Fontainebleau by François I in the 16C introduced the Mannerist

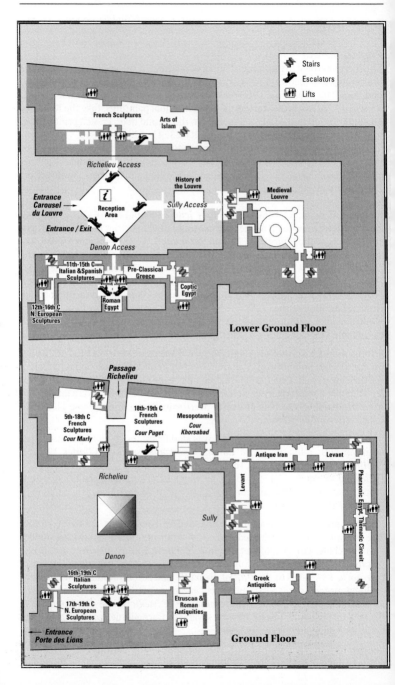

Lower Ground Floor

Ground Floor

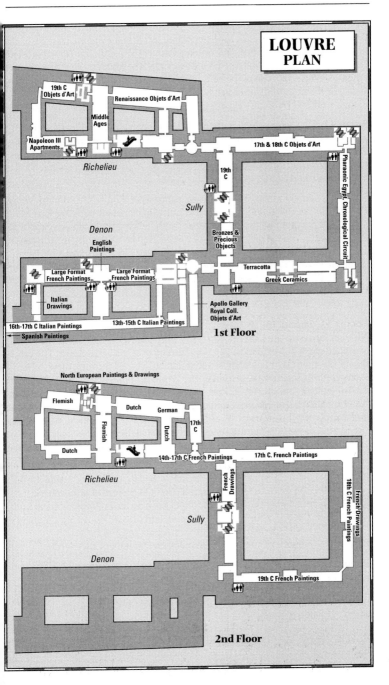

LOUVRE PLAN

1st Floor

- 19th C Objets d'Art
- Renaissance Objets d'Art
- Middle Ages
- Napoleon III Apartments
- 17th & 18th C Objets d'Art
- *Richelieu*
- Pharaonic Egypt. Chronological Circuit
- 19th C
- *Sully*
- *Denon*
- English Paintings
- Bronzes & Precious Objects
- Large Format French Paintings
- Large Format French Paintings
- Terracotta
- Greek Ceramics
- Italian Drawings
- 16th-17th C Italian Paintings
- 13th-15th C Italian Paintings
- Apollo Gallery Royal Coll. Objets d'Art
- Spanish Paintings

2nd Floor

- North European Paintings & Drawings
- Flemish
- Dutch
- German
- Flemish
- Dutch
- 17th C
- Dutch
- 14th-17th C French Paintings
- 17th C. French Paintings
- *Richelieu*
- French Drawings
- 18th C French Paintings
- *Sully*
- French Drawings
- *Denon*
- 19th C French Paintings

style and profoundly affected the art of the period. Among the main exponents in the First School were Jean Cousin the Elder whose *Eva Prima Pandora*, was one of the first nudes painted in France; and Antoine Caron (1521–99) *The Tiburtine Sibyl*. The elegant, *Diana the Huntress* (c 1550) (anon.), is possibly an idealised portrait of Diane de Poitiers, mistress of the king. Of the Second School (late 16C), a *Portrait of Gabrielle d'Estrées* and one of her sisters; others introduced a decorative character to their work, see Dubreuil's *Hyante et Climène offrant un Sacrifice à Vénus*.

Room 11 The **Caravaggist painters**: Valentin de Boulogne, *The Concert with Antique bas-relief, Tavern scene, The Innocence of Suzanne, The Judgement of Solomon*; Nicolas Régnier, *The fortune-teller*; Claude Vignon *The Young Singer* and *The Death of St Anthony*; Simon Vouet, *St William of Aquitaine*; Nicolas Tournier, *Crucifixion*.

Room 12 Large works by the Court painters of Louis XIII: Simon Vouet, *Presentation at the Temple* (1641), a strong and confident painting, one of his many altarpieces, this one commissioned by Richelieu for the Jesuit church of St-Paul-St-Louis. Vouet's delight in golden yellows is revealed fully in *Allegory of Wealth, Celestial Charity* and *Virtue* (previously known as Victory); Jacques Blanchard *Charity*; Eustache le Sueur, *Reunion of Friends*; one of several portraits by Philippe de Champaigne (1602–74), of *Richelieu*, and *Louis XIII crowned by Victory*, commemorating the siege of La Rochelle (1628); also some early works by Poussin (see below).

Rooms 13, 14 and 16–19 There follows a series of rooms filled with the work of **Nicolas Poussin**; the Louvre owns 38 of his paintings, a quarter of the total in existence. Born in Normandy, Poussin spent most of his life in Rome. The evolution of his rigorous, intellectualised style can be followed through these galleries. From the large scale of *Apparition of the Virgin to St James Major* (1629) (room 12), he turned to a smaller format and recreated antiquity for the cognoscenti. Among paintings of his first Roman period (1624–40) are: *Bacchanals, Echo and Narcissus, Inspiration of the Poet*; and the philosophical themes and Arcadian scenes of his mature years: the celebrated *Arcadian Shepherds* and the grave *Self-portrait*. Rooms 16–18 with noble landscapes: *The Seasons* series (1660–64), and finally his last work, *Apollo and Daphne*.

Room 15 Less well represented is Poussin's artistic opposite **Claude Gellée**, called Le Lorrain or Claude in English (c 1600–82), painter of atmospheric landscapes and ports who also spent most of his working life in Rome: *Seaport in the Setting Sun, View of a Port with the Capitol*, and *Ulysses returning Chryseis to her Father* (1644), *Arrival of Cleopatra at Tarsa* (1642–43).

Room 17 presents a changing exhibition of the Painting of the Month.

Room 19 has large scale **altar paintings** (17C) by the founders of the Académie Royale in 1648, the major contributors being Eustache le Sueur (1616–55), *St Paul at Ephesus*; Poussin, *The Miracles of St Francis Xavier*; Laurent de La Hyre, *The Apparition of Christ to the Three Marys*; Philippe de Champaigne, St Philip; and Sébastien Bourdon (1616–71).

Rooms 20–23 to the south, are reserved for examples from the collection of French Graphic Arts (drawings, cartoons, engravings, etc) exhibited in rotation, changing every three to six months.

Rooms A, B, C leading out of room 19 contain three collections: Beistegui, Lyon and Cröy (see below).

Room 24 The series of 22 paintings of the life of St Bruno, founder of the Carthusian order, by Eustache le Sueur, was completed in 1648.

Room 25 evokes the decoration of 17C Parisian houses.

Rooms 26 and 27 Small scale (*du cabinet*) religious paintings, by a variety of painters, including the greatest, along with still lifes, are found in the side galleries.

Room 28 Georges de la Tour deliciously anecdotal *The Card-sharper*, and the sensitive image of *St Thomas* are both lit with natural light in contrast to *St Irene nursing St Sebastian*, *The Adoration of the Shepherds* and *Mary Magdalen watching a Candle* where the effect of candlelight throwing dramatic shadows plays a key role.

Room 29 The genre scenes of the Le Nain brothers, Louis (c 1600–48), Antoine (c 1588–1648), and Mathieu (c 1607–77) range from subdued colours and quiet dignity, thought to be the work of Louis, to more Baroque works by Mathieu. Among their works are *The Travellers' Rest*, *The Peasant Family*, *The Forge*, *The Hay-wain*, *The Corps de Garde*.

Room 31 Portraits and religious works of the 17C. These include Philippe de Champaigne, *The Prévôt des Marchands*, *Portrait of a Man*, *Portrait of Jean-Antoine de Mesme*, and *The Last Supper*. His masterpiece of 1662, *The Artist's daughter with Mère Catherine-Agnès Arnauld*, was painted in thanksgiving for the miraculous cure of his daughter. Compare with the sumptuous *Equestrian portrait of Chancellor Séguier*, by Le Brun, c 1661.

Room 32 holds Le Brun's *Battles of Alexander*.

Room 33 has religious paintings by Jean Jouvenet.

Rooms 34–35 are dedicated to the **painters of the court of Louis XIV**: Le Brun, Mignard, Rigaud. The celebrated full-length likeness of *Louis XIV* in 1701, by **Hyacinthe Rigaud**, is the Baroque portrait of absolute monarchy. Nicolas de Largillière, a popular portraitist among the upper bourgeoisie, e.g. *The Artist with his Wife and Daughter*, also painted religious subjects such as *The Finding of Moses*. Other painters in this group include Pierre Mignard, *Self-Portrait*; and Antoine Coypel.

Rooms 36 and 37 Antoine Watteau painted the monumental but enigmatic *Pierrot* (also known as Gilles), also *Portrait of a Gentleman*, *The Two Cousins* and *L'Indifférent*. The term *fête galante* was coined for his vision of a lazy, melancholic day of late summer, *Pilgrimage to Cythera* (1717). Gems of 18C elegance from the La Caze Collection of 1869 by Watteau, Boucher, Chardin, Lancret (1690–1743), and Jean-Baptiste Pater (1695–1736).

Rooms 38–40 18C paintings created for the domestic market. Typical of **Jean-Baptiste-Siméon Chardin**'s marvellous still lifes are *The Ray* and *Le Buffet*, where perilously perched dishes and fruit form a pyramid of reds and greys. Studies of children include *Le Souffleur*, *Young Man with a Violin*; and genre scenes, *Le Bénédicité*. Paintings of pure pleasure by **François Boucher**

are pertly pink half-dressed ladies: *Renaud and Armide* (1734), *Diana getting out of her Bath* (1742); also *Venus asking Vulcan for arms for Aeneas* (1732).

Room 41–42 and 44–45 The Couloir des Poules, overlooking the Seine has 18C Graphic Arts (shown in rotation), including pastels and miniatures.

Room 43 overlooking the Cour Carrée, has large mid-18C paintings by Restout (1692–1768) and Pierre Subleyras (1699–1749), and a portrait by Chardin.

Room 46, the **Boucher Gallery**, includes Jean-Baptiste Oudry (1686–1755), *Bittern and Partridge Watched by a White Dog*; Louis Tocqué (1696–1772), *Marie Leszczynska* (1740); Claude-Joseph Vernet (1714–89), *View of Naples*; Jean-Baptiste Perronneau (1715–83), *Mme de Sorquainville*; Boucher landscapes: *Le Moulin* and *Le Pont* (1751).

Room 47 *Portrait of Denis Diderot* (1767) by Louis-Michel Van Loo (1707–71); Chardin Still lifes, Vernet and Jean-Baptiste Greuze, such as *The Agreement of the Village* and *The Dead Bird*.

Rooms 48 and 49 Jean-Honoré **Fragonard**, made his name in Paris with *The High Priest Coroesus sacrificing Himself to save Callirhoe*, 1765, in a grand style from which he soon turned to lighter themes dashed off with rapid, vibrant brushstrokes: fantasy figures, of which the Louvre owns eight, include *Music* and *Portrait of Marie-Madeleine Guimard*; other paintings are *Women Bathing* (c 1770), *Adoration of the Shepherds* (c 1775) and *Le Verrou* (c 1777) oppose sacred and profane love. Hubert Robert painted large picturesque ruins in France: *Le Pont du Gard* (1787), *The Triumphal Arch at Orange*, *The Maison Carrée*, and *Temple of Diana* (Nîmes). Among works by **Joseph Vernet**, *The Entrance to the Port of Marseilles* (1754), *The Ponte Rotto*; Elisabeth Vigée-Lebrun, *Portrait of Hubert Robert*.

Room 51 Examples of portraits as well as the moralistic and sentimental work of Jean-Baptiste Greuze.

Room 52 **Vigée-Lebrun** was encouraged to paint by Vernet, whom she painted in 1778 (see above); also portraits of women and children. The work of two other women, Anne Vallayer-Coster, 1744–1818, and Adélaïde Labille-Guiard (1749–1803) is exhibited here.

Room 53 the **Salle Vien**, has Classical and religious themes, large format, including *Three Graces*, 1794, by Baron Jean-Baptiste Régnault and Baron François Gérard, *Psyche and Cupid*, 1798. The butterfly above Psyche's head symbolises inconstancy.

Room 54 Here are examples of **Jacques-Louis David**'s work are shown together with paintings by his followers. David's rigorous, Neoclassical style influenced all French painting via his pupils Gros, Gerard and Ingres. Jacques-Louis David (1748–1825), *Madame Trudaine* (unfinished); in the same vein, Baron Antoine-Jean Gros, *Portrait of Madeleine Pasteur*; Baron François Gérard (1770–1837), *Portraits of his wife*, of *Comtesse Regnauld de Saint-Jean d'Angély*; Marie-Guillemine Benoist, *A Black Woman*, also Louis Girodet (1767–1824) and Pierre Guérin (1774–1833).

Room 56 has works by Pierre-Paul Prud'hon, *Young Zephyr balancing above the Water*; *Bath of Venus*.

Rooms 55, 57, 58, 59, landscapes and genre paintings of around 1800. The 125 studies of Italy by Pierre de Valenciennes are exhibited in rotation; Eugène Isabey, *The Wooden Bridge*. Genre paintings include works by Louis Boilly.

Room 60 Jean-Auguste-Dominique Ingres, pupil of David, consummate draughtsman and one of the great portraitists, *Portraits of L.-F. Bertin, senior*, and of *C.-J.-L. Cordier*; also *The Turkish Bath*, *La Baigneuse de Valpinçon*, and the composer *Cherubini*.

Rooms 61 and 62 are devoted to the great Romantic painters, Géricault and Delacroix. **Théodore Géricault**, *The Mad Woman*. **Eugène Delacroix**, *Self-portrait*, *Hamlet and Horatio*, *Portrait of Chopin*; *Algerian Women in their Apartments*.

Room 63 Brought together here are the followers of Ingres, and Orientalists, such as Théodore Chassériau, *Toilette d'Esther*; Léon Bénouville, Hippolyte Flandrin and Paul Flandrin.

Rooms 64–72 Two major collections: **Moreau-Nélaton**, donated in 1906, and **Thomy-Thiery** donation of 1902. Among them are many works by **Jean-Baptiste Camille Corot** especially in rooms 68 and 73, such as the *Pont de Mantes* (c 1868), *View of the Colosseum*, and the gentle *Souvenir of Castelgandolfo* (c 1865), *La Femme à la Perle* and the *Mother Superior Mère Marie-Héloïse des Dix Vertus* (1852). Also works by Delacroix including *Rebecca carried off by the Templar* (1858); Jean-François Millet, *Les Botteleurs de Foin* (1850); Eugène Isabey and Thomas Couture. Landscapes by the Barbizon artists Théodore Rousseau, Nino Diaz de la Peña, Daubigny (1817–78), Decamps, Huet, Troyon, and Eugène Fromentin. (The Impressionist works from the Moreau-Nélaton collection are at the Musée d'Orsay.)

Room A The **Beistegui collection** (between the staircases Henri II and Henri IV), donated in 1953 on the condition that the works are always exhibited together, has a range of works mainly of the 18C–19C, including a 14C *Virgin and Child* (Flemish) and a late 15C *Portrait of the Dauphin Charles Orlando* (son of Charles VIII and Anne of Brittany) by the Maître de Moulins. There are numerous portraits by Fragonard, *Portrait of a young artist* and others, also by Largillière, Jean-Marc Nattier (1685–1766), van Dyck, Thomas Lawrence (1769–1830), Zuloaga (1870–1945), Carlos de Beistegui, Meissonier (1815–91) and David; Ingres' likeness of his friend *Bartolini*, the sculptor; and work by Gérard. Also Rubens' *The Death of Dido*, and Goya's magnificent portrait of the *Marquesa de la Solana*.

Rooms B and C Two more collections, **Cröy** and **Lyon**, donated in 1930–32 and 1971 respectively. The large donation of 3800 drawings and paintings, by the Princess Louis de Cröy, consists mainly of paintings of the Northern schools with landscapes by Valenciennes. The Hélène and Victor Lyon donation, of 17C–18C Northern and Venetian paintings includes landscapes by Jan van Goyen (1596–1656), Bernardo Strozzi (1581–1644), Canaletto (1686–1768); Giandomenico Tiepolo, and a cross section of late-19C French works by Cézanne, Degas, Jongkind, Monet, Pissarro, Renoir and Toulouse-Lautrec.

For later paintings of the French School, see Musée d'Orsay, Ch. 9.

Rooms 75 and 77 Denon first floor, **large 19C French paintings**. Take the escalator from Hall Napoléon and then the staircase towards *Winged Victory*; turn right halfway up these stairs, to start in Salle Daru (room 75). The theatrical works of **J.-L. David**, inspired by antiquity, include *Andromache Mourning Hector* (1783), *The Sabine Women* (1799), and *The Oath of the Horatii* (1784), widely seen as extolling Republican virtues although commissioned for the Crown; the brilliant historical record of *The Coronation of Napoléon I by Pope Pius VII in Notre-Dame, 2 December 1804* (1805–07). David's genius as a portrait painter is demonstrated in *M. Sériziat, His wife and son*; *Madame Récamier*; *The Marquise d'Orvillers*; *Pope Pius VII*; and in his *Self Portrait*. Baron Gros, *Christine Boyer*, first wife of Lucien Bonaparte, Prud'hon a rather wistful *Empress Joséphine at Malmaison* (1805).

Jean-Auguste-Dominique Ingres (1780–1867): *Romulus Conqueror of Acron* (1812), *La grande Odalisque* (1814), *Portraits of the Rivière Family* (1805), *The Apotheosis of Homer*, *Oedipus and the Sphinx*, and *Roger and Angelique*. On a lighter note are works by Pierre-Narcisse Guérin (1774–1833) *L'Aurore et Cephale* (1810) and Vigée-Lebrun's *Self Portrait with Daughter*.

Great Romantic paintings, in Salle Mollien, room 77, include Baron Gros *Bonaparte visiting the Plague-striken at Jaffa* (1804); **Delacroix**, *Death of Sardanapolos*, *Dante Crossing the Styx*, *Massacre at Chios* (1824), *Liberty leading the People* (1831), *Women of Algiers* (1834). **Géricault** offers high drama in *Raft of the Medusa*; and portraits by Chassériau. Also work by Paul Delaroche, Alexandre Descamps, Ary Scheffer *Paolo and Francesca*, and Victor Schnetz (1787–1870).

English School
Room 76 The modest collection of English paintings is in **Salle Denon**, on Denon first floor surrounded by large format French paintings. The Louvre owns paintings by Thomas Lawrence (1769–1830), *Charles William Bell, John Julius Angerstein and his wife* and a portrait of their children; by the great landscapists, **John Constable** (1776–1837), *Weymouth Bay, Helmington Dell* (Suffolk) and **J.M.W. Turner** (1775–1851), *Landscape with a River and a Bay* (c 1845). Works by the great 18C English portraitists include Joshua Reynolds (1723–92), *Master Hare*; **Thomas Gainsborough** (1727–88), *Conversation in the Park, Lady Gertrude Alston*; George Romney (1734–1802), *Sir John Stanley*. Also Joseph Wright of Derby (1734–97), *The Lake of Nemi*; *Portrait of a Man*. Johan-Heinrich Fuseli (1741–1825) *Lady Macbeth Sleepwalking*; John Linnell (1792–1882), *Hampstead Heath*. Also two Scottish painters, Allan Ramsay (1713–84), *Lord Elcho*, and Henry Raeburn (1756–1823), *Innocence—Portrait of Nancy Graham, Capt. Robert Hay of Spott*. Richard Parkes Bonington (1801/2–28), who spent much of his short life in France, *View of Venice*. There are also examples of the work of John Hamilton Mortimer, and Angelica Kauffmann (1741–1807) who was born in Switzerland but spent some years in England.

Northern Schools
The 36 rooms, designed by I.M. Pei and devoted to the Northern Schools of painting—Dutch/Netherlandish, Flemish, and German, with some 840 works—are in **Richelieu** second floor. To reach the Northern School galleries, take the same route as for French Paintings (Richelieu second floor). The first three rooms are

common to Northern and French Paintings (see above). Prints and drawings are in Room 12.

Room 3 The style known as **International Gothic**, developed throughout Europe between about 1370 and 1450, especially in paintings from Bohemia, Lombardy, Burgundy and France, characterised by elegance, decorative refinement and a celebration of courtly life. *Retable from the Chapelle Cardon* (c 1400), the 15C *Virgin Writing*, and a *Virgin and Child* from Bohemia. Turn left.

Rooms 4 and 5 15C Dutch and Flemish paintings. A deliberate breakaway from the brilliant but superficial qualities of International Gothic, by Robert Campin and Jan van Eyck, occurred in the southern Netherlands c 1420–25. By a pupil of Campin, Rogier van der Weyden (1399/1400–64), the *Braque Family Triptych* (c 1450), a work of intense colour and feeling, and the *Annunciation* with sparkling details; **Jan van Eyck**, *Virgin with Chancellor Nicolas Rolin*; Rolin, donor of this exceptional painting, was the rich and powerful Chancellor of Burgundy. Petrus Christus, *Pietà*.

Many artists followed Van Eyck's innovations in Bruges including **Hans Memling**, of German origin, *The Mystic Marriage of St Catherine* (Virgin and Child surrounded by Saints), *Portrait of an Old Woman*, triptych of the *Resurrection with the Martyrdom of St Sebastian*, the *Virgin of Jacques Floreins*, triptych of the *Flight into Egypt*; Gérard David, *Triptych of Mary of the Sedano Family*, *Marriage at Cana*; Cornelis van Dalem, *Farmyard in Winter*; Brueghel the Elder *Beggars*, *Sacrifice of Abraham*; Lucas van Leyden, *The Card-dealer*, *Lot and his Daughters*; the last and strangest painter represented is **Hieronymus Bosch**, with his famous *The Ship of Fools*.

Room 6 is described as the **Studiolo d'Urbino**. With work by Juste de Gand Justus of Ghent, active 1460) and Pedro Berruguete is a series of 28 portraits of illustrious or wise men: saints and sages, of poets and scholars, including Dante, commissioned by Federico da Montefeltro for the Ducal Palace at Urbino.

Room 7 15C German works from Cologne and other artistic centres are presented here: the dramatic and sensual oeuvre of the Master of the St Bartholomew Altarpiece (active c 1500), *Descent from the Cross*, painted for an Antonite community; narrative cycles by the Master of the Legend of St Bruno and by the Master of the Legend of St Ursula (dressed in sumptuous costume, Ursula is shown departing on a pilgrimage to Rome, spurning the pagan king who demands her hand in marriage); Master of St Germain-des-Prés, active in Paris c 1500, *Pietà*, with a view of the Louvre and St-Germain-des-Prés.

Room 8 Important **German paintings of the Renaissance** period, between 1495 and 1550, characterised by a remarkable original fusion of German, Netherlandish and Italian art. **Albrecht Dürer**, *Self-Portrait* (1523), *The Grieving Christ*; **Lucas Cranach the Elder**, *Venus in a Landscape, St Peter and St Paul*, part of a retable, portraits presumed to be of *Magdalena Luther* and of *Frederick the Wise*, and *The Effects of Jealousy*; five portraits by **Hans Holbein the Younger**, purchased by Louis XIV: *Sir Henry Wyatt, Anne of Cleves, Erasmus* (painted for Sir Thomas More), *Nicolas Kratzer* (Henry VIII's astronomer), and *William Warham, Archbishop of Canterbury*; representative of the Danube School, Wolf Huber and Hans Sebald Beham.

Room 9 and room 10, the small gallery, have works by Netherlandish painters of the first half of the 16C, from Bruges and Antwerp. Quentin Metsys (1465–1530), *Moneylender and his Wife* (note the reflection in the round mirror), a small *Pietà*, and *Virgin and Child*, with a bunch of grapes before an open window; Jan Gossaert (Mabuse), the beautiful *Diptych of Jean Carondelet (Chancellor of Flanders) and the Virgin*; Joos van Cleve, *Virgin with Dominican Offering his Heart* (c 1510–15), and *The Last Supper*; Joachim Patinier, *St Jerome in the Desert*; Barent van Orley, *Holy Family*. Small works by Lucas van Leyden (1494–1533); Pieter Brueghel the Elder; Jan van Scorel.

Room 11 16C Netherlandish painters, known as the Romanists, who were influenced by studying antiquity, often during a stay in Italy. Jan Massys, *David and Bathsheba*; Jan van Hemmessen, *The Young Tobias Restoring his Father's Sight* (1555); Pieter Brueghel the Younger, *Parable of the Blind Men*, a 17C copy of the work of 1568 by Bruegel the Elder.

Room 12 Rotating exhibition of Graphic Arts of the Northern Schools.

Rooms 14 and 16 are small-scale landscapes and still lifes of end 16C–beginning 17C: Jan (Velvet) Brueghel, *The Battle of Arbela*; Jacob Fopsen van Es, *Still Life*.

Rooms 13 and 15 The **Dutch and Flemish works of the late 16C and early 17C** are grouped under the heading Mannerist, and exhibit the exaggerated tendencies of this style which spread throughout Europe from Italy. The main exponents of landscape are Paul Bril and Jan Brueghel, *Virgin and Child with a garland of flowers*, and *Air and Earth* (part of a series of the four Elements); there is also an early Rubens' *Landscape*. A virtuoso *Still Life* by Georg Flegel, sports a fly on the loaf of bread.

Rooms 17–26 17C Flemish painting, dominated by **Peter-Paul Rubens** (1577–1640). Early paintings (room 17) by Rubens include *Ixion deceived by Juno, Hercules and Omphale* (c 1602–05), and *Adoration of the Magi*; in the same room, Anthony van Dyck, *Martyrdom of St Sebastian*; and other contemporaries of Rubens.

Room 18, the **Medici Gallery** presents, against light-green walls, **Rubens'** resplendent series of 24 huge allegorical works depicting the *Life of Marie de Médicis*. Designed in 1622–25 to decorate the Luxembourg Palace, this was the painter's greatest single achievement and this gallery is a major success of the Louvre Project. These paintings glorify the life and achievements of the Queen in an appropriately exuberant and eulogistic manner, in chronological sequence. Running from left to right, each canvas represents a major event of Marie's life starting with her birth in April 1575. Other scenes include her arrival at Marseilles on 3 November 1600, the birth of her son Louis, her coronation at St-Denis and the series ends with the reconciliation with her son, Louis XIII, in 1619. Above the door, between portraits of her parents, is Marie de Médicis as *Reine Triomphante*. This great series influenced later French artists as different as Watteau and David.

Room 19 at the other end of the Medici gallery, overlooking Cour Napoléon, has huge, mainly religious, paintings: Jacob Jordaens; Jacob van Oost; Gaspart de Crayer; Van Dyck, *Crucifixion*; Philippe de Champaigne, *Assumption of the Virgin*.

Rooms 21–22 Return through the Medici gallery and across Escalier Lefuel (room 20), for further works by **Rubens**, including a tenderly executed portrait of his wife *Hélène Fourment with two of her Children*, *Baron Henri de Vicq* (c 1625), a portrait of the ambassador who obtained for the artist the commission to paint the Medici canvases; among landscapes by Rubens is the unforgettable *Kermesse*—the village wedding. Room 22 contains Rubens' sketches. Also a study for the *Head of an Old Man* by Van Dyck.

Rooms 23 and 25 Mainly **David Teniers**; also small 17C Flemish genre paintings by his contemporaries such as Brouwer, Sorgh, and Craesbeeck, and Pieter Meulener (1602–54).

Rooms 24–26 Works by **Van Dyck** (1599–1641), and Jacob Jordaens (1593–1678), *Jesus Banishing the Merchants from the Temple*. Works by Van Dyck include two religious works, *Virgin with Donors* (1630–32), and the moving *St Sebastian supported by the Angels*. An example of his mythological paintings is *Venus and Vulcan* (1626–32) painted just before his departure for England; portraits executed during his Antwerp and Italian periods (before 1632) of *Marchesa Spinola-Doria*, *A Lady of Quality and her Child* and its counterpart *A Gentleman and his Child*; and from his years in England is *Charles I of England* (c 1637). Also in this gallery is Jan Davidsz de Heem (1606–1683/84), *The Dessert*, and Sir Peter Lely 1618–80), *Portrait of a Man* (c 1658).

The last 12 rooms are devoted to Dutch paintings arranged by genre, rather than around a single artists, with the exception of Rembrandt. The paintings follow more or less chronologically, emphasising the variety and wealth of the Dutch School.

Rooms 27–29 Works from the first half of the 17C, a transition between two schools: **Frans Hals**, of Flemish origins, represented by majestic portraits of *Paulus van Berestyn*, and of his third wife, *Catherine Both van der Eem*; his growing preference for restrained colours is found in *Old Woman* and *Buffoon with a Lute*. Other portraitists include Verspronck, *Portrait of Anna van Schoonhoven*; Willem van der Vliet, *Portrait of a Man Seated*; Miereveld, *Portrait of Jan van Oldenbarneveld*.

Landscape is dominated by Van Goyen, *Two large Sailing Boats and Animals* and *View of Dordrecht*, and Solomon van Ruysdael, *The Landing-stage*, whose compositions often consist mainly of sky, brilliantly painted. Other landscapists are Pieter de Nyn (1597–1639), Abraham de Verweer (1617–50); and the painter of Brazil, Frans Post (1608–69).

Among painters specialising in **architecture** are Saenredam, *Interior of a Church Haarlem*; and Steenwyck *Jesus at the House of Martha and Mary*. Cornelis van Poelenburgh and others were evidently influenced by Italy, and Dutch genre scenes are typified by Adam van Breen, *Skaters*. Still Life has a privileged place in Dutch painting, and its Flemish origins are recalled in *Flowers* by Bosschaert and Van der Ast.

Fine examples of **large history or genre painting** typical of Caravaggist artists are Gerard van Honthorst, *The Concert* and *The Lute Player*. More sober is Ter Brugghen from Utrecht; also Frans Hals, *The Bohemian* and Judith Leyster *Joyful Company*, Jan Woutersz (Stap), the *Old Man*, and Pieter de Grebber, *Tattooing Lesson*.

Room 30 Further examples of landscapes.

Room 31 is devoted to **Rembrandt van Rijn** (1606–69), and includes two introspective *Self-Portraits* of 1633, one *Bareheaded*, the other, *Wearing a Toque and Chain* uses a rich palette and play of light; the decor of *Self-Portrait with an Architectural Background* (1647) has been reworked by another hand; a fourth self-portrait is of the *Artist in his Old Age at his Easel* (1660). From the 'Baroque' years, 1630–40, *The Philosopher in Meditation*, the *Archangel Raphael taking leave of the Family of Tobias*, and *Holy Family*. From his more mature and mystical period come *Christ at Emmaus* (1648), the stunning *Bathsheba* (1654) and *St Matthew and the Angel* (1661). Perhaps the best known of all Rembrandt's work in the Louvre is the monumental *Bathsheba Bathing*, with copper tones, soft and tangible flesh, and deep velvety shadows. A more violent note is struck by *The Slaughtered Ox* (1655), whereas the imaginary *Landscape with Castle* (c 1640) is an enchanted vision.

Room 32 Works by the pupils, imitators and followers of Rembrandt.

Rooms 33–39 Dutch paintings from the middle to the end of the 17C. **Room 33**. *The Fish Market* by Adriaen Van Ostade; Isaac Van Ostade, *Frozen Canal;* and the Van der Helst's *Reepmaker Family* as well as works by Ferdinand Bol and Jacob Van Ruisdael. **Room 34** contains Cuyp's *The Walk*, Berchem's *Landscape and Animals*; the *Oudekerk at Delft* by Van Vliet, and *View of Amsterdam* by Backhuiysen. **Room 35** revolves around the work of Gerard Dou, including *The Bible Reading* and the *Trumpet*. Also in this room are *The Ford* by Berchem, *Flowers in a Crystal Jug* by Mignon and more landscapes. **Room 36** has *Still Lifes* by Metsu (1629–67) and work by Steen. There is more landscape, genre and still life in room 37. In **room 38** are two works by **Jan Vermeer**, the *Lacemaker* (c 1679), with perfect colour and light used to convey intense concentration, and another intimate interior scene of a small group using cool blue tones, called *The Astronomer*. Nearby are Pieter de Hooch's *The Drinker*, and the favourite *Courtyard of a Dutch House*; Jacob Ruisdael, *The Ray of Sunshine*. Room 39, the last room, is dedicated mainly to the 15 works by Wouwerman, along with Jan Weenix, and Hobbema.

Italian Schools

The richly endowed Department of Paintings of the Italian Schools 14C–18C, **Denon** first floor, reopened after renovations in 1999. From Hall Napoléon take the Denon escalator to the lower ground floor, then the lift to Denon ground floor, cross Pre-Classical Greece on your left and up the staircase past the *Winged Victory*. Starting in the east of Denon and ending in the former Rubens gallery (room 14), at the west of the Grande Galerie, the revised circuit displays the works in a coherent chronological order. The Salle des Etats (room 6) contains the *Mona Lisa*. Rooms 9–10 are assigned to cartoons, prints and drawings.

Rooms 1 and 2 Salle Percier et Fontaine and Salle Duchâtel (near the *Winged Victory*), have 15C and early 16C frescoes: two elegant works by Botticelli (1445–1510), were created for Villa Lemmi, near Florence (1480/83); a large *Crucifixion with Saint Dominic* by Fra Angelico of striking simplicity; also three frescoes by Bernardino Luini (1485–1532).

Room 3, Salon Carré, contains works by **Florentine masters of the 13C–15C**. The large altar painting *Madonna and Child in Majesty with Six*

Angels by Cimabue (c 1240–1302), is an early attempt to bring a certain naturalism and depth to a fundamentally Byzantine composition. Note in the painted frame the 26 medallions of Christ, angels, prophets and saints. The freer, more lifelike interpretation of figures by Giotto (c 1266–1337) is found in *St Francis Receiving the Stigmata*.

The great 15C Florentine painter, **Fra Angelico** (c 1387–1455), in his triumphant *Coronation of the Virgin*, handles a traditional religious subject with a novel use of perspective. The large 14C *Crucifixion*, from the workshop of Giotto was originally suspended above an altar. At the extreme of each arm are St John the Evangelist and the Virgin, the Pelican at the top symbolising the Resurrection. Paolo Uccello, *Battle of San Romano*, 1432, is one of three panels on the same theme (others in Florence and London). Combined with brilliant colours, the result is a charmingly decorative if oddly wooden battle scene. School of Fra Filippo Lippi, a large and sophisticated *Nativity*.

Sandro Botticelli was the most important Florentine artists of the second half of the Quattrocento (15C), admired for his refined and delicate approach. The intense and compact composition, set off in a fine carved frame, is a moving painting of a youthful *Madonna and Child*, surrounded by Angels who resemble fresh-faced adolescents; also *Portrait of a Young Man, The Madonna of the Guidi of Faenza, Madonna and Child with St John the Baptist*. Small works include Fra Angelico, *Angel in Adoration*; School of Fra Angelico, *Herod's Feast*.

Room 4 covers **Siena and Northern Italy, 13–15C**: Pisanello c 1395–1454), *A Princess of the House of Este*; Gentile da Fabriano (c 1370–1427), *Presentation at the Temple*—note the detailed attention to the architectural setting and materials. By the Sienese painter Sano di Pietro (c 1405–81), *Five Episodes from the Life of St Jerome*, where the central scene depicts the saint extracting a thorn from the lion's paw; Perugino (1445–1523) *Apollo and Marsyas*, a musical contest; also Master of the Observance, *St Anthony*, part of a polyptych; by Sassetta (1400–50) are scenes from the polyptych painted (1437–44) for the church of San Francesco, Sansepolcro, the majority of which are in London: *Madonna and Child with Angels, St Anthony of Padua* and *John the Evangelist*; Pesellino (c 1422–57), *St Francis of Assisi Receiving the Stigmata*, and *St Cosmas and St Damien nursing the sick; Luca* Signorelli (c 1441/50–1523), *Birth of St John the Baptist*; Piero della Francesca (c 1416–92) *Portrait of Sigismondo Malatesta* revealing his intellectually rigorous style and predilection for sharp profiles. Jacopo Bellini, from Venice, father of Gentile and Giovanni and father-in-law of Mantegna, *Madonna and Child with Donor*.

Small works include: Simone Martini, from Siena who worked for a time in Avignon, *Christ bearing the Cross* (c 1342), a small vivid section of a polyptych of the *Passion*; Guido da Siena (active 1260–70), *Nativity*, and *Presentation at the Temple*.

Rooms 5, 8 and 12 The paintings along the great length of the Grande Galerie are arranged so that dialogues are set up between the works on opposite walls. The first section has 15C–16C paintings from Tuscany and northern Italy. The precise draughtsmanship of **Andrea Mantegna** (Padua and Mantua) produced the *Crucifixion* and *St Sebastian*. The exaggerated perspective of the *Virgin of Victory* (1496) suggests it was intended to be viewed from below. 15C Florentine painters include: Ghirlandaio (1449–94), *The Bottlenosed old Man and his Grandson*, Bartolommeo di Giovanni (active end 15C), *Marriage of Thetis and Peleus*, and *Wedding Procession*; Piero di Cosimo (1462–1521), *Madonna and Dove*.

Among painters of the 15C from the **Venetian School** are Antonello da Messina (1430–79), a Sicilian who spent several vital years in Venice: *Christ à la Colonne*, *The Condottiere*; **Giovanni Bellini**, the greatest artist of his family, he raised Venetian art to level of that of Florence. His personal vision is represented in several works including *Crucifixion* and *Virgin and Child with Saints*. Carpaccio (1437–1525), *St Stephen Preaching in Jerusalem*, note the use of colour and architecture; Jacopo de Barbari (1440–1516), *Madonna at the Fountain*; Cima da Conegliano (c 1459–c 1518), *Madonna and Child with St John the Baptist* and *The Magdalen*; Marco Palmezzano, *Christ supported by angels*; Catena (c 1495–1531), *Portrait of Giangiorgio Trissino*.

From Perugia, Pietro di Cristoforo Vannucci, called Perugino (1445–1523), who strongly influenced his pupil, Raphael: *Tondo depicting The Madonna and Child with St Catherine and St John the Baptist and St Sebastian*.

The end of the Quattrocento and first quarter of the Cinquecento (16C), called the **Italian High Renaissance**, when perfect harmony and proportion were sought, produced some of the greatest Italian painters.

The Louvre is rich in works by **Leonardo da Vinci** (1452–1519). An air of mystery and sensuality envelopes *The Virgin of the Rocks* (1482), probably earlier than the London version; the *Madonna and Child with St Anne* is an extraordinarily vital yet closely knit group of three generations expressing tenderness and compassion. Also by Leonardo are an *Annunciation* and *St John the Baptist* and *La Belle Ferronnière* (because of the metal chain around her forehead).

Room 6, Salle des Etats. Leonardo's most celebrated portrait, is traditionally assumed to be of *Mona Lisa Gherardini* (correctly Monna, the Italian for lady), third wife of Francesco di Zanobi del Giocondo. She is also known as La Gioconda and in French La Joconde. Now in a specially protected niche and brightly lit, this innovative yet enigmatic portrait using soft tonal modelling, positively glows. Leonardo worked on it intermittently between 1503 and 1506 and brought it to France when he came at the invitation of François I in 1516. Purchased by the king, it became the most valued piece in the royal collection. In August 1911 it was stolen but was recovered in Florence in December 1913.

In the same gallery, there are glorious works demonstrating the Venetian tradition for dynamic use of colour which was brought to its zenith by **Titian** (c 1485–1576) in such works as *Lady at her Toilet*, *Allegory representing the Wife of Alfonso d'Avalos being entrusted to Chastity and Cupid*, *Venus of the Pardo*. The gentle *Concert Champêtre*, the first in the tradition of *fêtes champêtres*, was for long attributed to Giorgione, who heavily influenced Titian, but is now considered to be an early Titian. Religious works include *Supper at Emmaus*, *The Entombment*; and portraits: *Man with a Glove*, from Louis XIV's collection, and *François I* (taken from an image on a medal).

Tintoretto (1518–94) combined the 'colour of Titian and the drawing of Michelangelo' to produce a highly personal style; works include *Paradise*, a preparatory work for the Doge's Palace. Dominating this gallery is the huge painting by **Paolo Veronese**, *Marriage at Cana* was painted for San Giorgio Maggiore, Venice and the intensity of its colours were rediscovered when it was restored in 1989–92. Others by Veronese are the so-called *La Belle Nani*, *Supper at Emmaus*, and *Jupiter striking down the Vices* with its tumbling giants.

Room 8, Grande Galerie, has a section devoted to the **Roman School**, including Raffaello Sanzio, called **Raphael** (1483–1520) Raphael (1483–1520)and his followers. By the master, *La Belle Jardinière* (1507) is heavy with religious symbolism, and one of several such groups of the Holy Family, each a version of the pyramidal composition pioneered by Leonardo. The *Portrait of Baldassare Castiglione* (poet and diplomat) was purchased by Louis XIV from the heirs of Cardinal Mazarin in 1661. Works commissioned by Pope Leo X for François I: *The Large St Michael*, the monumental *Holy Family of François I*, and *St Margaret*. Other works by Raphael include *Self-Portrait with a Friend*, where the artist stands behind another figure who turns towards him. Giulio Romano (c 1499–1546) who trained with Raphael and also practised architecture, is described as a pioneer of the Mannerist style. He produced the sumptuous *Portrait of the Vice-Queen of Naples* (formerly known as Joanna of Aragon); Andrea del Sarto (1486–1530), *Charity*; Sebastiano del Piombo (c 1485–1547).

Correggio (1489?–1534), associated with an extreme use of sfumato and a tenderly voluptuous quality, as in *The Mystic Marriage of St Catherine of Alexandria*, *Jupiter and Antiope* and *Allegory of the Vices and Virtues*. Lorenzo Lotto (c 1480–c 1556), *The Woman taken in Adultery*, *Christ bearing the Cross*.

Among the **Mannerists**, work by Jacopo Pontormo, *Virgin and Child with St Anne and Four Saints*; Bronzino (1503–72); Georgio Vasari (1512–74). Lorenzo Lotto (c 1480–c 1556) and Arcimboldo (1527–93), famous for his curious compositions made up of fruit and vegetables.

Rooms 9–10 have been reserved for 16C and 17C Italian cartoons and drawings which will be exhibited in rotation.

Room 12 The greatest Italian painter of the 17C was **Caravaggio** (c 1499–1546), who threw himself passionately into both his life and work and whose artistic influence spread throughout Europe. The message in *The Fortune-Teller* is clearly legible. *Death of the Virgin* (1605–06) was considered scandalous at the time because of the earthy realism of the figures and the dramatic contrasts of light and shade. There is also *Portrait of Alof de Wignacourt*.

The most talented of the Carracci family, from Bologna, was Annibale: *The Virgin appearing to St Luke and St Catherine*, *Hunting and Fishing*. Guido Reni, who was influenced by the Carracci, fell out of fashion in the 19C but is now admired as a great colourist: *St Sebastian*, *Ecco Homo*. Domenichino (1581û1641), pupil of Annibale Carracci: *Herminia among the Shepherds*, *St Cecilia*; Guercino (1591–1666), *The Raising of Lazarus*.

Room 13 is named after Salvator Rosa (1615–73), from Naples, the prototype Romantic artist: *Landscape with Hunters*; Pietro da Cortona (1596–1669), one of the founders of the Roman High Baroque: *Venus as a Huntress Appearing to Aeneas*. Bernardo Strozzi, the leading Genoese painter of the 17C, was influenced by Rubens and Van Dyck: *Holy Family*. Luca Giordano (1634–1705), Bernado Strozzi (1581–1644) *Madonna of Justice*.

Room 14, Gallery Piazzetta, previously contained the Médicis cycle, now has large format 18C Italian paintings: Giambattista Piazzetta (1682–1754), huge

Assumption of the Virgin; Giovanni Paolo Panini, *Concert in Rome* (26 November 1729).

Rooms 15–18, the small side galleries, contain 17C paintings from Genoa, Naples, Bologna and Rome and Still Lifes; works by Sassoferrato (1609–85) *Annunciation* and *Child Jesus found sleeping.*

Rooms 19–22, 18C paintings: Giuseppe-Maria Crespi was the most individua Bolognese artist of the time, best known for his genre scenes, such as *Woman with Flea.* Room 21, Giovanni Battista Lampi, *Count Stanislas Felix Potocki and his sons.*

Rooms 23–25, Venetian scenes by Canaletto (1697–1768), *The Molo* (c 1730) of which there are about 10 versions, and by Michele Marieschi, *View of Santa Maria della Salute.* Francesco Guardi painted views of Venice in a freer and more expressive mood than Canaletto such as the eight scenes depicting festivities for *The Coronation of the Doge Alvise IV Mocenigo.*

Room 24, 18C Venetian scenes: Pietro Longhi, *Presentation.*

Room 25, perhaps the greatest painter of the 18C, Giambattista (Giovanni Battista) **Tiepolo**, was the last in a line of fresco artists and produced exuberan yet delicate work: *The Last Supper.* His son and assistant, Giandomenico Tiepolc painted *Carnival Scene* and *The Charlatan* (or The Tooth Puller).

Spanish School

The Spanish School, is in the former Pavillon des Sessions at the far west of **Denon** first floor, and the adjacent Petits Cabinets (rooms 26–30 and 32). Access these rooms through the Porte des Lyons directly, or go right through to the end of Italian Paintings. It is not a vast collection, but is notable for a fine series of masterpieces acquired relatively recently. Louis-Philippe amassed a magnificient collection exhibited in the Louvre 1838–48, but these works followed the King in exile to London and were dispersed in 1853.

Room 26, Murillo Room, the former Médici Gallery, is dedicated to the Golden Age of Spanish painting (17–18C). Brought together here are seven large works of **Bartolomé Estabán Murillo**, *The Angels' Kitchen*, is one of a series of 12 painted for the Franciscan convent at Seville. *Birth of the Virgin* is typical for its soft tints. Murillo is famous for sweet Madonnas, but also for a number of paintings on the theme of picturesque urchins, of which *Young Beggar* (1650) is a good exmple. Juan Carreño de Miranda, *Foundation of the Trinitarian Order*; Francisco de Zurbarán, *St Bonaventura at the Council of Lyon, St Bonaventura's Corpse Exposed*; and a delightful *St Apollinaire*. **El Greco** (1541–1614), a characteristic work of heavy pathos, *Crucifixion with two Donors* (signed in Greek characters) c 1579; and *St Louis, King of France with a Pageboy.* José de Ribera, the fine *Adoration of the Shepherds, St Paul the Hermit, Deposition* and *Clubfooted Boy* (1642); Valdès Leal (1622–90), *Virgin of the Immaculate Conception between St Philip and St James Minor* (1654); Luis de Morales, *Deposition from the Cross*; several works by Herrera (1585–1654).

Room 27, Martorell Room, 15C–16C masterpieces from Valencia and Catalonia. Master of Burgo de Osma (early 15C), retable with the *Virgin and*

Child, and two panels *St John the Baptist* and *St Ambrose*; Bernardo Martorell, *Four episodes from the Life of St George* (c 1430–35).

Room 28, Huguet Room, 15C–16C works from Catalonia and Castille: Jaime Huguet, *Flagellation* and *Lamentation*; Juan de Borgoña (active 1495–1536), *The Virgin, Saint John* and *Two female Saints with St Dominic*; Master of St Ildefonse, active in Toledo and Valladolid.

Room 29, Francisco Collantes (1599–1656), *The Burning Bush*; Vincente Carducho (1570–1638), six episodes from the *Life of St Bruno*; five small portraits attributed to Sanchez Coello and a portrait by El Greco.

Room 30, 17C Spanish painting: **Diego Velázquez,** *Queen Mariana of Austria*; *Portrait of the Infanta Margarita, aged three years*; and attributed to Velázquez, *Infanta María Teresa*; smaller works by Murillo, El Greco and Alonso Cano in the cabinets.

Room 32, Goya Room, 18C Spanish Painting. **Francisco Goya** absorbed varied influences (Tiepolo, English portraitists, Velázquez) to become the most original artist of his period and, according to André Malraux, the father of modern painting. Gathered here are the striking portrait of *Ferdinand Guillemardet* (c 1798), *Woman with a Fan* (c 1810), and portraits of *Mariana Waldstein, Marquesa de Santa Cruz* and *Evaristo Pérez de Castro* and two small paintings *The Unequal Wedding* and *Christ in the Garden of Olives*. (For Goya see also the Beistegui bequest, Sully.) Luis Meléndez, *Self-Portrait* and *Still-life*. Also work by Bernardo German y Llorente and one by the Portuguese Domingo Sequeira.

Room 31 contains **Greek and Russian Icons.** These are mainly 16C to 17C (other icons can be found in Objets d'Arts, Richelieu). Cretan School, end 15C–beginning 16C, *St John the Baptist*, and Russian, 16C, *The Virgin of Georgia* from Novgorod.

Prints and Drawings

The **Department of Prints and Drawings** (Arts Graphiques) owns some 130,000 works on paper (drawings, pastels, miniatures, etc.); the Edmond de Rothschild collection comprises 3000 drawings and 40,000 engravings; and there are 16,000 engraved plates. Because these works are fragile and susceptible to light, they are not on permanent public exhibit but are displayed on a rotational basis every three to six months. They are divided between the appropriate schools of painting: French School in **Sully** second floor (rooms 20–23, 41, 42, 44, 45); Northern Schools in **Richelieu** second floor (room 12); and Italian Schools in **Denon** first floor (rooms 9–10). Some of these rooms are closed on certain days and it is advisable to check beforehand at the information desk under the Pyramid. There are also special temporary exhibitions of pastels, cartoons and miniatures.

The department's reserves, library, archives and conservation occupy ten rooms on three levels of the Pavillon de Flore at the extreme west of Denon, accessed via the Porte des Lions. Individuals who wish to use the **Consultation Room**, which reopened in 2000, to view prints or drawings should apply in writing to the Conservateur Général, Département des Arts Graphiques, or 🖾 01 40 20 53 51. To visit the Edmond de Rothschild Collection, make an appointment on ☎ 01 40 20 50 31.

Although drawings had already existed in the Bibliothèque du Roi, it was not until 1671, when Louis XIV acquired the 5542 drawings (in addition to important paintings) collected by Everard Jabach (d. 1695) that the main nucleus of the Royal Collection was formed. To this were added drawings by Le Brun, Mignard and Coypel. By 1730 an inventory included some 8593 works, plus some 1300 drawings collected by the great connoisseur Pierre-Jean Mariette which were purchased in 1776. By 1792 some 11,000 drawings were listed, and in the following decades the figure almost doubled with the acquisition of the St Maurice au Comte d'Orsay collections, and the collections of the Dukes of Modena and of Filippo Baldinucci.

The *Codex Vallardi* (including a number of drawings by Pisanello) was acquired in 1856 and Jacopo Bellini's sketchbook in 1884. The collection was further enriched by a number of important donations in succeeding years.

Among the approximately 200 **pastel portraits** are Leonardo da Vinci, *Isabella d'Este, Duchess of Mantua*; Charles le Brun (1619–90), *Three portraits of Louis XIV*; several by Robert Nanteuil (c 1623–78); Rosalba Carriera (1657–1757), who did much to popularise the technique in France, Chardin, *His second wife* and *Self-portraits*—with spectacles, with a green eye-shade, and at his easel.

Greek, Etruscan and Roman Antiquities

This department encompasses antique art from the origins of Hellenism to the last days of the Roman Empire. Its new layout, enhanced by recent donations, runs in two directions, **Denon** lower ground floor and **Sully** first floor. From Hall Napoléon, the Denon escalator brings you to Denon lower ground floor. Beginning in rooms 1–3, the chronological circuit sets out the succession of cultures from this part of Europe. The circuit continues on Denon ground floor, in rooms A and B, across rooms 4–6, then into Sully ground floor. On Sully first floor are thematic displays of Greek pottery and Roman and Greek glass and bronzes, in elegantly decorated rooms, reminders of the Louvre's former role as a palace.

Rooms 1–3 From Denon lower ground floor you find the entrance to these rooms on your left. Objects from **Pre-Classical Greek civilisations** from the 3rd to the 1st millennium BC such as a large collection of Cycladic art (3000–2000 BC) including marble idols; pithoi from Knossos (Crete; 1700–1600 BC) and from Thera and Rhodes (14C BC); terracotta and bronze figurines and painted Minoan ceramics (Crete, 14C–12C BC) and Mycenaean art (Rhodes, 1450–1200 BC); a large Calyciform Crater (vase) depicting the *Combat of Hercules and Antaeus*; and funerary objects. *Dame d'Auxerre* (c 630 BC), of Cretan origin (part of a collection near Auxerre) a small, compact figure with her hand on her chest, and an Egyptian style wig.

Also **Archaic Greek art**, 7C–5C BC: the elegant and delicately modelled *Koré* of Samos (c 570–550 BC), one of the oldest and best authenticated works of island sculpture, inscribed 'Cheramues'; the *Rampin Head* (6C BC), a finely sculpted piece which was originally part of the statue of a horseman; bas-reliefs from the architrave of the Temple of Assos (near Troy, Turkey) representing *Hercules battling against the Triton*, a banquet, a procession of animals and centaurs; torso of Apollo (Miletus, Turkey; 5C BC); upper part of the stela, *Exaltation of the Flower*. The **Epigraphy Gallery** (room 2) has 24 Greek inscriptions, 5C BC–2C AD, is a recent innovation.

Room A Return to the Vestibule and take the escalator on the left to the **Salle du Manège**, room A (ground floor) built by Lefuel (1855–57) as the riding school of the stable complex of Napoléon III's new Louvre. It took its present name in 1879 and still has part of its original decor of 1861. This is now used to display coloured marbles such as *Old Fisherman (Seneca Dying)* and *Romulus and Remus fed by the Wolf*, and two huge Albuni basins.

Room B On Denon ground floor to the east of the Vestibule is **Galerie Daru** with antique sculptures from royal and other major historic collections including the *Borghese Crater* (or vase) (c 50 BC), the celebrated *Borghese Gladiator* (now completely restored) and the late Hellenistic *Borghese Warrior*, signed on the tree-trunk by Agasias (c 100 BC), found at Anzio, Italy, in the 17C.

The reliefs from the Temple of Zeus at Olympia (c 460 BC), after restoration, are at the top of the staircase, between the Archaic and Classical periods. On Sully ground floor, cross room 5, the **Rotunda of Mars** (created by Louis Le Vau, 1655–58) and the original entrance to the museum in 1809. Room 6, Salle de Diane, is used for information and the exhibition of recent acquisitions.

Rooms 7–17 Greek antiquities continue here, including the **Parthenon**, the **Corridor of Pan** and **Praxiteles Rooms** with originals and antique replicas: fragments of the east frieze of the Parthenon at Athens (5C BC; the greater part of the frieze, which represents the Panathenaic procession, is in the British Museum); the *Laborde Head*, from the pediment of the Parthenon. The *Venus de Milo* (Aphrodite) (room 12) found in five fragments by a peasant in 1820 on the island of Melos in the Greek archipelago is now regarded as a 2C BC copy after a 4C BC original. *Apollo Sauroktonos* (about to kill a lizard), both after Praxiteles; *Athena (Minerva) with a Necklace*, copy of the *Athena Parthenos of Phidias* (438 BC); the *Aphrodite of Cnidos*; and the *Venus of Arles*.

The elegant **Salle des Cariatides, room 17** (off room 8), Sully ground floor, the oldest surviving room in the palace, was built by Pierre Lescot for Henri II, who commissioned Jean Goujon to execute the caryatids supporting the gallery at the far end. Other decoration and the chimneypiece at the near end are by Percier and Fontaine (c 1806). This room contains antique replicas of works from the 4C BC to the Hellenistic period (3C–1C BC) by Lysippe: *Hermes Fastening his Sandal* and *Artemis, the Huntress*, known as the Diana of Versailles, acquired from Rome by François I, is after an original reputedly by Leochares. Among several Aphrodites is *Aphrodite Crouching*, from Vienne.

Rooms 18–30 Return through the Rotunda to **Etruscan and Roman Antiquities** on Denon ground floor. Among Etruscan items of great interest are five terracotta plaques from Cerveteri, Italy, (c 530 BC); the remarkable terracotta sarcophagus (also discovered at Cerveteri, by Campana, in 1850), depicting the lifelike figures of a man and his wife reclining on a funeral couch, as if conversing. The woman wears a cap (*tutulus*) and a small gorget; the man, bare-footed, is draped. Further examples of Etruscan antiquities include cinerary urns from Chiusi, bronze vessels and figurines, mirrors, jewellery and ceramics. Room 21 has terracottas, glass, jewellery and other precious objects.

Denon ground floor, **rooms 22–26**, show Roman portraits and reliefs; also frescoes, mosaics and sarcophagi; two outstanding busts in black basalt represent *Agrippa* (63–62 BC) and *Livia* (58–29 BC), wife of the Emperor Augustus. Room 27 has works from the late-Roman period, 3-5C AD.

Room 31 On the floor of the **Cour du Sphinx**, is a huge mosaic of *The Seasons* (c AD 325) from a villa near Antioch. On the walls, a frieze from the temple of Artemis at Magnesia on the Meander, depicting a battle between Greeks and Amazons (2C BC); also the god Tiber, a colossal piece found in the 16C.

Take the monumental Escalier Daru at the top of which stands the *Winged Victory of Samothrace*. This imposing statue of Parian marble, found in 1863, originally stood on a terrace overlooking the Cabeiri sanctuary on the island of Samothrace in the Aegean. The figure stands at the prow of a galley with wings spread, the draperies of her tunic clinging as if flattened by the wind. Further excavations in 1950 led to the discovery of the mutilated right hand (in a case nearby) which was probably held high to announce a naval victory, and puts the probable date of the statue as c 190 BC. The breast and left wing are of plaster.

Room 34 Sully first floor, the **Grand Cabinet du Roi Louis XIV**, built by Le Vau c 1660 is dedicated to some 100 pieces of **Greek and Roman glass**. The exhibits demonstrate various techniques used to make bottles in a variety of forms and colours, including objects for the table and other containers.

Rooms 33 and 32, Salle Henri II (ceiling decorated by Braque in 1953) and **Salle des Bronzes** contain **Greek and Roman bronzes and precious objects**. Room 33 contains the **Treasure of Boscoreale**, a collection of superbly decorated silver objects discovered in 1895 in a fine state of preservation, in a villa that was buried when Vesuvius erupted in AD 79; the silver **Treasure of Graincourt-lès-Havrincourt**; and jewellery and goldsmiths' work from all periods and regions. Room 32 contains jewellery, arms and utensils in chronological and geographical groups. Outstanding are Archaic Greek Art: *Minotaur*; statuette of *Athene*; a warrior; and *Silenus dancing* (all 6C BC); also *Pan and his Syrinx*; there are mirrors, some in their boxes decorated with scenes in relief. Classical Greek statuettes (5C BC) include *Athlete's head*, said to have been found at Benevento, Italy, probably from Herculanum 1C BC. Roman Gaul: statuettes and busts: note the eyes; and the bronze and silver plated *Fortuna*, first quarter of 3C. Also on display are a winged helmet encircled by a gold crown; gladiator's armour; the *Apollo of Piombino*, a 1C BC bronze figure, with copper encrustations—lips and nipples—which was retrieved from the sea near Piombino, Italy.

Rooms 35–38, Salles Charles X, four rooms devoted to Greek terracotta figurines, which include objects from Tanagra.

Rooms 39–47, the **Campana Gallery**, named after the Marquis Campana's collection, purchased in 1861. This is a superlative collection and the Louvre prides itself on being the world's foremost museum of **Greek vases**. Some 2000 vessels (800–400 BC) can be studied thematically according to the various decorative motifs (**room 39**), or chronologically (**rooms 40–44**). **Rooms 45–47** are study rooms. Among the vases are examples from the Geometric period; pottery from the Greek islands; vessels in the Orientalising style; pottery from Corinth; Tyrrhenian amphorae, kraters and other vessels; black-figure Attic ceramics; vases in the Attic style, including both black and red figures and vases found in the Dipylon cemetery (c 800 BC); Attic red-figure pottery (c 500 BC) including a kylix on which are Eros and Memnon, and an amphora showing Croesus on a Pyre; coloured terracottas; figurines of the Hellenistic period, especially from Myrina; and antique glassware.

Egyptian Antiquities

This impressive department is divided between Pharaonic, Roman and Christian (Coptic) Egypt. The Pharaonic section, in **Sully**, is made up of a series of thematic presentations on the ground floor and a suite of rooms arranged chronologically covering 3000 years of Egyptian art on the first floor. The sections devoted to Roman and Coptic Egypt are in **Denon**. Begin the visit by taking the Sully escalators from Hall Napoléon and crossing the Medieval Louvre to arrive opposite the large sphinx in the Crypt of the Sphinx. The first curator of the Egyptian Antiquities department was Jean-François Champollion (1790–1832), who in 1826 acquired the collection of Henry Salt (1780–1827), and further collections have been added.

Pharaonic Egypt

Room 1, in the crypt, has a *large sphinx* of great beauty carved from polished red granite. Its date remains uncertain, but the oldest inscription on it goes back to the Middle Kingdom, showing traces of the name of Amenmhat II, 1898–1866 BC. Either side are two bas-reliefs representing *Ramesses II in Worship* before the largest sphinx of all, found in front of the pyramids of Giza.

Room 2 is up the staircase on the left on the ground floor of the south wing of the Cour Carrée (also a lift). A large *statue of Nakhthorheb*, an important figure of the 26th Dynasty, marks the entrance to the department. The circuit through rooms 3–10 follows the south side of the Cour Carrée.

Rooms 3–6 The first of the series of thematic presentations introduces **Egypt through the Nile**, source of life and fertility. This is evoked by a long display cabinet which contains models of boats of the Middle Kingdom, and figurines of fish, crocodiles, hippopotami, and frogs from all periods. The limestone *Akhethetep mastaba* (tomb), room 4, found at Sakkara, is decorated with vivid scenes in bas-relief of the life of a dignitary in his rural domain, the highlight of which is the depiction of the master's meal, enlivened with music and dancing. These scenes of earthly life in the Old Kingdom (2400 BC) are echoed in paintings from the *Shrine of Wensu*, which lead on to exhibits on the theme of agriculture: tools, papyrus accounts and legal documents, and scale models. Part of room 5 is concerned with cattle breeding, hunting and fishing; also food centred around the ideal menu for the dead, sculpted on the walls of a tomb of the Old Kingdom complete with the names of the delicacies. The displays in room 6 revolve around writing and scribes. The principles and evolution of writing can be seen, together with the tools of the scribes and their patrons. There is also a display of weights and measures.

Room 7 addresses **arts and crafts** through the materials and techniques used: wood, stone, ceramics and metal. Among the exhibits are the *stela of the Chief of Craftsmen*, which recalls the pride of these men and the fine bronze statue, arms extended, of the *Horus, the falcon-god, making a libation*, was once covered in precious metals.

Room 8–10 The first room is dedicated to **dwellings and furnishings**, with domestic objects found in tombs: chairs, baskets, brooms and floor coverings, and amphorae are used to evoke a wine cellar. Room 9 contains **objects of adornment**, with beautiful examples of jewellery made in combinations of precious stones, ceramic and metal. The rarest in the collection are: gold necklace with three pendant fishes; necklace of Pinedjem I, of gold and lapis lazuli; and the ring of Horemheb. A high point in the collection are the cosmetic objects, particularly the superb spoons for cosmetic creams carved in wood, ivory and faience.

Musical instruments, including the harp, lyre, tamborine, sistrum and castanettes, are exhibited in room 10, together with games such as draughts. This brings you to the southeast angle of the Cour Carrée.

Room 11 represents the **Forecourt of the Temple and the Alley of the Sphinxes**. From the Serapeum at Sakkara come six limestone sphinxes evoking the long processional alleys called dromos. Four large cynocephali (baboons) in red granite, adoring the rising sun, formerly decorated the base of the Obelisk (see Ch. 13), at the entrance of the Temple of Luxor.

The grand staircase in the angle pavilion leads to the first floor and to **room 27** of the Egyptian Department (the middle of the chronological presentation). If you wish to see the whole of the collection do not, therefore, take this staircase. There is an escalator near room 18.

Room 12, the **Temple**, large sculptures and pieces of architecture evoke a temple and its courtyards. The first court, flanked by a portico of fine columns of pink Granite with palm-leaf capitals (5th Dynasty); statues of deities including *Sekhmet*, the lion-headed goddess; colossal statues of the kings and statues of privileged individuals. In the second court are the great deeds of the Pharaohs: the *Wall of the Annales of King Thutmosis III*; festivals. This brings you to the heart of the temple, around the *naos* or chapel sheltering the statue of Osiris are the chapels of the 'invited' gods such as elephantine gods. Also the *naos of the reign of Amasis* in pink granite; a processional boat; and the *low-relief of the King Osorkon I offering an image of the Goddess Mat*.

Room 12bis contains **objects from the Chapels**. The large circular sandstone zodiac, showing the sky, planets and constellations in 50 BC, was the ceiling of the chapel on the roof of the temple of Hathor at Dendera. Relief from a chapel from Karnak, called the **Room of the Ancestors**, with a list of kings preceding Thutmosis III, is a major document of Egyptian history.

Room 13 is found from the end of the Gallery Henry IV, via staircase descending to the **Crypt of Osiris and Royal Tomb** (elevator at end of the gallery).

Egyptians believed that Osiris had reigned in the world before becoming sovereign of the dead and deceased kings were revered as gods. The descent towards the magnificent pink granite **sarcophagus of Ramesses III** gives the impression of the descent to the hypogeum of the Valley of the Kings. The nocturnal voyage of the sun which reappears triumphant every morning, is found on the massive diorite **sarcophagus of Djedhor**. Osiris, god of the dead, is represented by a wooden statue framed by Isis and Nephthys.

Room 14 has a splendid display of **wooden mummy cases**; also stone sarcophagi like the magnificent limestone **sarcophagus of Abu-Roash** (Old Kingdom) in the palace-façade style, and the sarcophagus brought from Djedhor by Champollion. **Room 15** is behind the staircase, with a display of embalming and burial rites. This contains a **mummy of the Ptolemaic period**, with an intricately painted '*cartonnage*' (moulded linen and plaster) protection. Return via room 14.

Room 16, tombs, has displays containing objects from burial chambers of four different periods showing the evolution in funerary customs over more than 1000 years. From the end of room 15, it is possible to reach the long gallery, Galerie de Delphes.

Room 17 has **funerary equipment**. The full extent, more than 25m, of the papyrus **Book of the Dead of Hornedjitef**, is exhibited here.

Rooms 18 and 19 Gods and magic and animals, sacred and mummified, **Serapeum of Memphis**. A procession of animals associated with Egyptian gods: the *goose of Amon*, the *bull of Montou*, **Bastet**, the cat-faced goddess of Bubastis; an astonishing display of mummified animals. Also the magnificent statue of the *bull Apis*.

Take the north stairs (or lift) to the first floor. An illustrated chronology, made up of display panels each representing 1000 years, introduces the first floor circuit covering some 3000 years of Egyptian history and art.

Room 20, the **period of Nagada** (c 4000–3100 BC), the end of the Predynastic era. The highlight of this display is a dagger from Gebel-el-Arak. Its handle, carved from the canine of a hippopotamus, depicts a battle and is a very early example of relief sculpture. Also finely sculpted schist palettes.

Room 21 Thinite Period (c 3100–2700 BC). **Stela of King Zet Ouadji**, known as the Serpent King, epitomises the two great phenomena of this period: the unification of Egypt under a single crown, and the birth of writing. The name of the king is written with the hieroglyphic of the serpent. The art of low-relief was perfected, and luxury objects were made in ivory, and fine vases of coloured stone.

Room 22 Old Kingdom (c 2700–2200 BC), the period of the great pyramids: the development of the personality of the king and his funerary monument reaches its peak in the 3rd Dynasty. Finds from the pyramid of Didoufri, son of Cheops, include a small highly coloured limestone figure of a scribe seated cross-legged, the **seated scribe**, with eyes of white quartz and rock crystal; statue of the couple **Raherka and Merseankh**. The painted stone **Stela of Nefertiabet**, seated before a table with a remarkable array of offerings.

Room 23 the **Middle Kingdom** (c 2033–1710 BC), the time of the great King Sesostris was the classical period for Egyptian civilisation. The elegant *Libation Carrier*; two large wooden statues of contemporaries of Sesostris, *Chancellor Nakhti*, one of the largest wooden funerary effigies known of this period, and of the *Governor of Hapydjefai province*. Remarkable portrait statues of *Sesostris III* and of his son, *Amenemhat III*.

A small corridor contains the most beautiful stelae of this period.

Room 24 contains portraits of the dignitaries of the glorious period of the **New Kingdom** (c 1550–1353 BC) and the various objects on display show a change in style from the rigid archaism of the statue of *Prince Iahmes* to the sensual portraits of the *King Amenophis III* and *Touy*. Note the bust of *King Tuthmosis IV*, the gold dish given by Tuthmosis III to General Dejehuty and the life-size statues of *Seny Nefer* and his wife *Hatchepsut*.

Room 25 is devoted to the **New Kingdom** at the time of Akhenaton and Nefertiti (c 1353–1337 BC). The famous heretic *Akhenaton* (Amenophis IV) represented by a huge statue with elongated head, only reigned about 15 years, his memory later being held in loathing by the Egyptians. Nevertheless, he left an outstanding artistic legacy such as the Colossus. The display cases contain some of the most beautiful pieces in the Louvre: a torso, probably of *Queen Nefertiti*, in red quartzite; limestone *head of the Princess*, young yet haughty; and a statuette of the *young king with his wife Nefertiti* holding each other by the hand.

Room 26, the **New Kingdom around the time of Tutankhamun** (c 1337–1295 BC). In the first part of the room, the *'Salt' head* represents someone living during or just after the Amarnian period. Also *statue of the god Amon with Tutankhamun*, the short-lived successor of Akhenaton, became famous in the 20C when his tomb was discovered almost intact.

You now arrive at the upper landing of the south staircase, dedicated to the civilisation of Ancient Nubia. To the west is the first room of the old Egyptian Museum created at the time of Champollion, in 1827.

Room 27 New Kingdom at the time of Ramesses and other New Kingdom Pharaohs (c 1295–1069 BC). There is a magnificent fragment of painted relief depicting *Sethi I and the goddess Hathor*. The *Stela des colliers* takes up the theme from El Amarna, the *distribution of rewards from the window of the royal palace*. One display is devoted to the son of Sethi I, Ramesses II, whose long reign saw much building.

Room 28 New Kingdom (c 1295–1069 BC). The great gods are represented by a very fine statuette of *Amon and his wife Mout*; and lesser, by the small *stela of the goddess Qadech*. A wall display is devoted to the Serapeum of Memphis; and there are pectorals in gold inlaid with faience.

Room 29 King-Priests of the Saite period and Persian domination (c 1069–404 BC). The finest Egyptian bronze, the statue of *Karomama 'Divine Worshipper of Amon'*, is sumptuously decorated with inlays of gold and silver. Also the golden jewel representing the Triade Osiris-Isis-Horus; statuette of a *nude woman* in ivory is another masterpiece. The painted wood *stela of Taperet*, with two faces. There are also examples of the most beautiful statuary of the 26th Dynasty, such as the *statuette of Iahmessaneith*.

Room 30 From the **last Pharaohs of Egypt to Cleopatra** (404–30 BC). A fine *Torso of Nectanebo I*, and a limestone *statue of a falcon protecting the king*. Hellenistic influences are present in the clinging drapes on the body of the Goddess Isis. Local funerary customs maintained a strong hold, as seen in the *coffin of Tacheretpaankh* in gilded *cartonnage*, the abundant decorations recalling the mural reliefs of the large temples rebuilt at this time.

This is the last room in the main part of the Department of Egyptian Antiquities. The following room, the Salle des Colonnes, is the meeting point between the Galerie Campana (Greek vases) and the Gallery of Greek terracottas, and a rest area. For Coptic Egypt and Roman Egypt, continue through Greek Antiquities to the Winged Victory (Denon first floor), and take the staircase down to the entresol level.

Roman Egypt and Coptic Art
Rooms A, B and C This refers to the civilisations of late Antiquity in the Eastern Mediterranean. The section is situated beneath and around the Cour Visconti in **Denon** lower ground floor. From the Hall Napoléon, take the Denon escalators to the ground floor and cross the antechamber with a brief introduction to the period.

An appropriately vaulted chamber is devoted to **Funerary Objects in Egypt during the Roman period** (1C–4C AD) (room A). (Off this room to the right is *Café Denon*.) The theme is set by a painted shroud showing the deceased between Anubis and his mummy deified in Osiris. The *Mummy of Padijmenemipet*, of the Soter family, is accompanied by his coffin decorated with signs of the zodiac. Chronological displays include portraits painted on wood with wax or tempera, of Roman origin; and the plastron-masks in plaster, wood or fabric, stuccoed and painted in the ancient Egyptian tradition, all produced during the same period.

The *coffin of Chelidona* was brought to France by Champollion: the cover is decorated with symbols of air and water, necessary for the survival of the deceased in the afterworld. A large shroud (3C–4C AD) shows the deceased making a journey by boat to the underworld. Finally, the objects which accompany the deceased to the tomb: funerary statues, stelae, figurines and offerings to assure life after death.

Coptic Art
Rooms B and C eastern wing of Cour Visconti on Denon lower ground floor. Coptic Art denotes Egyptian art from the 3C AD onwards. This trend appeared in the pagan environment strongly influenced by Roman Egyptian art and among the Christian community, in particular in relation to the development of monasticism. After the Arab conquest in the mid-7C it was enriched with aspects of Muslim art. The most recent works in the Coptic collection at the Louvre date from the 14C. The 580 works showing different aspects of this art are presented both chronologically and thematically.

The emergence of Coptic art, combining Roman and Pharaonic elements, is seen in the *Horus Horseman* and the slightly more recent *shawl of Sabine*, which retains themes from pagan mythology and the decor of the Nile region. Coptic art of the 5C–8C, such as beautiful weavings and objects from daily life, is exhibited alongside thematic and iconographic displays of Christian imagery, writing and the Coptic language, and magic. Illustrations of the influence on Coptic art of the Islamic domination of Egypt include a very fine bronze *censer* surmounted by an eagle clasping a serpent, textiles woven in iridescent colours and decorative objects in bone, wood, metal and glass.

The culmination of the Coptic section is the **Baouit Room**, installed in the former amphitheatre of the Ecole du Louvre, which looks down on a display centred around a reconstruction of part of the monastery church of Baouit. This monastery, founded in the 4C and abandoned in the 12C, was excavated by French archaeologists at the beginning of the 20C. In 1903 Egypt made France the generous gift of part of the finds—paintings, sculptures, fragments of architecture, archaeological documents. A section of the monastery has been reconstructed here, its décor of wood and limestone placed on a concrete statue and there is also a model of it.

Oriental Antiquities and Islamic Art

This department, which contains objects from the Middle East apart from Egypt, was inaugurated in 1847 and has benefited from the move into larger galleries. It is divided between Oriental Antiquities: Mesopotamian and Iranian, on **Richelieu** and **Sully** ground floor; also collections from the Levant, on **Sully** ground floor. Islamic Art is on Richelieu lower ground floor. From Hall Napoléon, take the Richelieu escalator to the ground floor.

The visit starts in rooms 1a, 1b, 1c on the south of Cour Puget with objects remarkable for both their age and beauty, mainly from the ancient city states of Mesopotamia: Tello and Mari, dating from before 3000 BC.

Room 1a Archaic Mesopotamia, Sumerian Culture (3900–2900 BC), follows the development of civilisation in Mesopotamia from neolithic village origins to the Sumerians' primitive urban culture towards the end of the 4th millennium. Most finds are from Tello, formerly Girsu (Iraq). There are remarkable small objects from c 7500 BC onwards including *primitive figurines*.

Early urban culture in Sumer (c 3500–2900 BC) marked the beginnings of social hierarchy and architectural activity, towards the end of which writing was invented. The *cylinder of Uruk* (c 3100 BC) is one of the earliest examples of a seal-cylinder used to 'sign' documents. The Jemdat-Nasr period (3100–2900 BC) is represented by vessels in marble or alabaster.

During the early dynastic period (c 2900–2340 BC), writing spread and historic inscriptions appeared: see cabinet 3 concerning hieroglyphics. Among other exhibits are *foundation nails* which symbolically fixed a building to the ground and repelled evil spirits; bas-reliefs of a plumed figure, *mace of King Mesilim* (c 2750 BC) found at Tello and of Ur-Nanshe, prince of Lagash, carrying a basket of bricks on his head for the foundation ceremony; silver vase with a frieze of incised animals and the Lagash 'crest', consecrated by Entemena, Prince of Lagash; the *cone of Entemena* in terracotta, carved all round with hieroglyphics; bronze *bull's head*.

The first Lagash dynasty, founded c 2500 BC by Ur-Nanshe, is represented on a *Large Perforated Relief*. The grandson of Ur-Nanshe is commemorated in one of the oldest known historical documents, the magnificent limestone *Stela of the Vultures*, c 2450 BC (restored), from Tello. Carved on both faces, it records the victory of Eannatum, King of Lagash.

Room 1b The expansion of **Mesopotamian culture** spread in particular to Mari, on the modern Iraq-Syria border. Important excavations at the temple of the goddess Ishtar (c 2500 BC), produced an alabaster statue of the *intendant of Mari, Ebih-II*, and mother-of-pearl silhouettes of the *standard of Mari*.

Room 1c contains sculptures and precious objects of the archaic dynasties of Sumer (c 2900–2340 BC) including a *votive relief* representing musicians, the *statuette of Ginak*, and gold pendants.

Room 2 open to the east side of Cour Puget, contains larger exhibits from Mesopotamia (c 2340–2000 BC), **Empire of Akkad**, and the **last Sumerian dynasties of Gudea** and of Ur: art of the Akkadian period is represented by objects from Susa (the capital, Akkad never having been found), where they were taken in the 12C BC, and from Tello. The glory of the King and empire is idealised in royal diorite monuments: *stela of Sargon, stelae of victory; statues of King Manishtusu* (seated and standing), *obelisk of Manishtusu*. The most beautiful is the *stela of the victorious Naram-Sin*, king of Akkad, grandson of Manishtusu. In cabinet (2) judicial documents in Akkadian, which took over for a while from Sumerian as the official language. Note the quality of workmanship in the seal-cylinders carved in marble, chlorite, and porphyry, along with their 'print-outs' in clay.

The brilliant **Second Dynasty of Lagash** (2150–2100 BC) **prince Gudea**, represented by nine diorite statues in this room, one of which shows him holding a vase gushing with life-giving waters; also large clay cylinders recording, in cuneiform, Gudea's achievements as a builder; fascinating smaller objects include the goblet belonging to Gudea, decorated with serpents and winged dragons with scorpion tails; alabaster *statuette of Ur-Ningirsu*, son of Gudea; *woman with a scarf*, from Girsu; terracotta figurines (one with geese); objects concerning the construction of a temple, such as terracotta foundation nails; and furnishings from temples and tombs; late cuneiform documents.

Room 3 Mesopotamia (2000–1000 BC), Amorite Kingdom and first Babylonian Dynasty from the sites of Mari, Babylon and Eshnunna, *statue of a bull-headed man* and Larsa, *vase of Ishtar* with engraved design.

The ruins of the Amorite Palace of the King Zimri-Lim, Mari, revealed exceptional installations including two mural paintings—*Ishtar investing the king with regal powers* and a *sacrificial scene*; a *bronze lion* from the temple of Dagan; *statue of Ishtar*. Terracotta moulds from the palace kitchens. Also models of the ruins and a reconstruction of the palace. From the Temple of Dagan, a (headless) *statuette of Idi Ilum*, Prince of Mari; the *disk of Ladun-Lim*, the head of a foundation nail.

The **First Babylonian Empire** developed under the Hammurabi, (1792–1750 BC) starts a brilliant period: the freestanding *Codex of Hammurabi*, carved in black basalt, 1792–1750 BC, covered with closely written text, is one of the earliest compilations of laws. The 282 laws embrace practically every aspect of Babylonian life of c 1800 BC. Nearby are the *royal head*; bronze, *worshipper at Larsa*, on bended knee, the face and hands covered in gold leaf; bronze group of Three Rampant Ibex, with horns interlaced.

After the death of Hammurabi, Babylon declined, and the Kassites assumed power: texts of charters of donations were engraved on huge Kudurrus or boundary-stones, with symbolic images of gods.

Babylon's brilliance revived in the **neo-Babylonian Empire**, whose greatest king was Nebuchadnezzar II (605–562 BC), famous for capturing Jerusalem and deporting the Jews, as well as being a great builder: the coloured glazed-brick frieze, *lion passant*, decorated a processional route between temples; the *Esagil Tablet*, from the great temple of Marduk; *astrological calender* of Uruk; series of alabaster *statuettes of female nudes* reveal the influence of Hellenic culture (Babylon was conquered in 331 BC by Alexander the Great).

Turn right out of room 3 to room 4 for the Cour Khorsabad (see below).

Room 5 Anatolian, Cappadocian and Hittite civilisations (origins to 1000 BC): small *statuette of female nude* (mid-6th millennium BC) is considered among the first figurative symbols of a primitive fertility cult; early bronze age (3rd millennium) objects include idols and vases from the necropolis of Yortan, votive horns, a musical rattle, chariot terrets and painted ceramics. The period of Assyrian colonies in Cappadocia, c 2000 BC; Cappadocian tablets, archives in cuneiform script of business negotiations.

The Hittite Empire became one of the great powers of the Near East in the 14C and 13C BC, rivalling Egypt and the Mittani Empire: figurines in bronze; gold pendant in the form of a god; bronze casket (8C–7C).

Room 4 Cour Khorsabad, at the east end of the ground floor of Richelieu contains the celebrated reliefs from the great Assyrian palace of Khorsabad. The Assyrian Empire reached its peak between the 9C and 7 C BC, and its rulers built great palaces to exalt their achievements.

The impressive presentation against the walls of the courtyard is designed to evoke the original massive scale of the Palace of Dur-Sharrukin, Sargon II's fortress (Khorsabad). The five huge *winged bulls* with human heads, or lamassu, stood at the entrances to protect the palace from evil spirits. Three of these majestic sculptures, which have five feet so that viewed from the front they are in repose and from the side they appear in motion, are original, and one is a 19C copy. The last, a plaster cast from the original in Chicago, has its head turned towards the reliefs associated with it of *two gigantic heroes taming a lion*. Other reliefs (4m high), are forms of official propaganda which protected and decorated the base of the mud-brick walls: *bearers of the king's furnishings*, and the *frieze of the transportation of cedar wood*, from Lebanon by land and by sea. Among smaller items are tablets in copper, gold, and silver recording the foundation of the Palace of Khorsabad.

Room 6 Artefacts that have survived from the provincial palaces: Til Barsip (present Tell Ahmar, Northern Syria) rare mural paintings one featuring a blue goat; an exceptional collection of carved ivories from Arslan Tash. Kalhu (Nimrud), chosen by Assurbanipal II as his capital: reliefs from the throne room in gypseous alabaster, c 865 BC, include a *genie with a bird's head and scorpion's tail*; reliefs from the palace of Ashur at Nineveh (668–627 BC).

The **neo-Assyrian period** (9C–7C BC) is represented by bronze door plaques from Imgur-Enlil (Balawat); the annales of Tukulti-Ninurta II; figurine of the Assyrian demon Pazuzu.

Iran and the Levant

The following section is subdivided geographically into Iran (rooms 7–10 and 11–16) and the Levant—countries on the Mediterranean coast of Asia: Syria, Lebanon, Israel, Cyprus, Jordan and Turkey (rooms A, B, C, D and rooms 17–21 in Sully west and north).

Room 7 Ancient Iran (4th millennium BC). Susa, capital of the western part, was founded c 4200 BC. Three main artistic periods produced varied artefacts: Susa I (4200–3800 BC), painted ceramics; Susa II or the period of Uruk (3800–3100 BC) first attempts at metallurgy; Susa III (3100–2800 BC) birth of proto-Elamite writing.

Room 8 Susa (3rd millennium): Vase '*à la cachette*', with treasure hidden inside.

Room 9 Iran and Bactriana (3rd–beginning 2nd millennia BC): the highlands of the plateau were invaded by Iranians. Bronze arms and vessels from Luristan to the north of Susa (c 2600–1800 BC); objects from tombs at Tepe Giyan. Bactriana (Afghanistan) produced a wide range of objects, such as the remarkable statue of the *Lady of Bactriana* (c 1800 BC); bronze wheel band.

Room 10 Iran at the Middle-Elamite period (c 1500–1100 BC): royal monuments of the reign of King Untash-Napirisha; headless bronze *statue of Queen Napir Asu*, wife of King Untash-Napirisha, a considerable work weighing 1750 kg; King Shutruk Nahhunte (12C BC) and his descendants were warrior kings and great builders, responsible for the acropolis of Susa from which come several architectural elements: votive tray in bronze representing cult scenes of serpents and divinities; *moulded brick panel with goddesses and man-bull protecting a palm tree.*

Room A The countries of the Levant. Room A: Cyprus (origins to the Iron Age): its important seams of copper and its connections with the Hellenic world, gave rise to a characteristic style. Chalcolithic *statuette of a seated female* (4th millennium); other delightful models, including *boat with figures* (end 3rd millennium); *statuette of a seated god from Enkomi*; undeciphered tablet in Cypro-Mycenaean; late Bronze Age luxury and cult objects.

Room B Coastal Syria, Ugarit and Byblos (origins to Iron Age): furnishings from royal tombs and luxury items from Byblos; ceramics from Ras Shamra (ancient Ugarit); furnishings from the tombs of Minet el Beida; ivory pyxis carved with a goddess and two ibex; golden cup from the temple of Baal (c 1250–1150 BC); *stela of the god Ba'al*. Phoenician sculptures and collections of objects; embossed gold peg, known as *The Hunt*, from Ras-Shamra; *bust of the Pharaoh Osorkon* (924–895 BC) with a Phoenician dedication from the King of Byblos.

Room C Inland Syria (origins to Iron Age), subjected to influences from Mesopotamia as seen from the seal-cylinders, copper statuettes and the use of cuneiform writing: *idol with eyes*, in terracotta (c 35,000 BC); *statue menhir* in basalt from Tell Braq (2000–1600 BC); furnishings from the tomb of Til Barsip, from the temple of Ninegal, Qatna, and from other temples; *stela of Zakkus* commemorating the taking of the throne of Hamath by King Zakur; funerary stelae from Neirab or Tell Atis.

Room D Palestine (7000–1150 BC). Neolithic plaster statue from Jericho; ivories from Beersheba (Negev); Bronze Age tomb furnishings from Jericho,

Lakish, Ay and Farah; an ossuary in the form of a house; Israelite Dynasty period (1200–1150 BC), model of a sanctuary; *stela of Shihan*; the Moabite Stone, or Stela of Mesha, King of Moab (842 BC), discovered in 1868 in a remote village east of the Dead Sea. The 34-line inscription, recording victories over the Israelites in the reigns of Omri, Ahab and Ahaziah, is one of the most important, if not the earliest, examples of alphabetic writing.

The last 11 rooms are the **Sackler Wing**, on the north side of Sully. Six of these rooms complete the circuit of Iranian art, from the 14C BC to the 1st millennium BC.

Room 11–16 14C–6C BC, **Iron Age Iran and neo-Elamite dynasties**: vase in the form of a bull in red terracotta and a decorative bronze plaque originally attached to horse bits. Rooms 12–15, 6C–4C BC, the Persian Achaemenid Empire: elements from the Palace of Darius I at Susa including a huge capital in the form of heads and shoulders of bulls, one of 36 used to support the ceiling of the audience chamber (apadana); glazed brick *frieze of Persian archers—the Immortals*, and the *frieze of lions*. Room 16, 3C BC–7C AD, Parthian and Sassanian empires: Harp Player mosaic.

The last five rooms continue the theme of the Levant (following on from rooms A, B, C, D), encompassing today's Syria, Lebanon, Israel, Jordan and Turkey, during the 1st millennium BC.

Rooms 17–18 Room 17, the Phoenician kingdoms, 8C–2C BC: numerous sarcophagi and funerary monuments from the royal necropolis of Sidon; sarcophagus in basalt of Eshmunazar II, King of Sidon, in Egyptian style; the *stela of Amrit* (7C/8C BC). Room 18, the Mediterranean world, Carthage and Punic North Africa, 8C–1C BC and the Phoenician expansion to the west (8C–2C BC): marble sarcophagus of a priest; *stela Tophet of Constantine*; objects in glass.

Rooms 19 and 20 Arabia Felix and the Arabian desert (7C–3C BC) notably the Yemen, the fringes of the Arabian peninsula; the caravan cities of Palmyra and Dura Europos: stelae in alabaster from Yemen including one with a human mask; the *lintel of the Judgement of Paris* (2C BC) 3m long, from southern Syria.

Room 21 Cyprus, 9C–1C BC, a complex mixture of cultures. In the centre of the room the monumental *vase of Amathonte* carved from a single piece of limestone (3.2m in diameter) used as a water reservoir for the sanctuary of the great goddess at the summit of the acropolis of Amathonte (4C BC). Different works demonstrate the diversity of cultures of Cyprus, such as the nude *statuette of Heracles*, and the enigmatic bust of a *veiled woman*.

Islamic Art

The very beautiful display of Islamic Art, in **Richelieu** lower ground floor, to which 13 rooms have been dedicated, is shown in chronological order, from the first centuries of the Hegira (622) to modern times. Take the Richelieu escalator from Hall Napoléon to the lower ground floor and turn right. The works represented come from Muslim territories extending from Spain to India, with the exception of North Africa. Despite preconceived ideas to the contrary, there are several representations of humans and animals.

Rooms A and B Information and introduction to the Muslim world; and an explanatory survey of architecture in Islamic countries.

Room 1 First appearance of Islamic art (7C–8C): Christian, Hellenistic and Sassanid (Persian) elements synthesised into an original style. Three-legged perfume burner in bronze; blown glass vase with multiple handles; stucco panel with leaves and duck; an important series of small decorated glass flasks and recipients; and capitals influenced by Roman antiquity.

Room 2 The Abbassid world (8C–10C). An imperial art derived from Graeco-Roman Sassanian traditions. The objects in this room come mainly from Iraq, but also from western Iran and Egypt: dish *au porte-étendard* (standard-bearer), with stylised caricatures of figures typical of 10C lustreware: metallic lustre decoration was the creation of Iraqi potters in the 9C–10C. Wooden panel with stylised birds: the style of sculpted decoration with a bevelled edge was developed in Egypt under the influence of Samarran art.

Room 3 The Fatimids (909–1171) and the **Islamic West** (10C–15C). The Fatimids developed a brilliant and refined culture and a varied, often picturesque iconography: small flask in the form of a lion in rock crystal; gold bracelet decorated with musicians; quadruped (hare?) in cast bronze and engraved; fragment of applied ivory ornament with lute player; wooden plaquette with dancer (11C–12C), from Egypt; bowl decorated with a giraffe; bowl with rosace (12 C) from Syria.

    Islamic West (8C–15C). Outstanding pyxis (small box) carved in ivory in 968 for al-Mughira, son of the Calif Abd al-Rahman III (912–961) during the Umayyad Caliphate in Cordoba, Andalusia; peacock ewer; bronze lion, probably part of a small fountain.

Room 4 Eastern Iran (10C–12C). Dishes with epigraphic decor, reading: 'Science, its taste is bitter at the beginning, but at the end sweeter than honey; good health (to the owner)'; the famous Shroud of St Josse, from Khorasan, a large silk cloth (10C) decorated with elephants, camels and an inscription, brought to France after the First Crusade (1096–99) by Etienne de Blois, protector of the Abbey of St-Josse (Pas de Calais); plate with a scene of labour.

Rooms 5 and 6 Iran of the Seljuks (11C–13C). The quality, diversity and quantity of production make this period a high spot in the history of ceramics in the Muslim Orient. In room 5 an interesting series of 'provincial' ceramics decorated with champlevé and engraved slip; large basin with lion design, basin with hare, and plate with donkey. This room has a display dedicated to the sciences: celestial sphere in brass inlaid with silver (1144) is the oldest known of Arabic manufacture. Room 6 has a fine series of ceramics manufactured in urban centres using new processes; bowl with falconer on horseback; the chandelier with ducks is a technical virtuoso; ewer with a cock's head, the outer surface pierced and decorated with a turquoise slip.

Room 7 Funerary stelae and sculpted stones arranged to represent a small rural cemetery (9C–18C).

Rooms 8 and 9 Egypt, Near East, Anatolia (12C–13C), the **Ayyubids** (1071–1250) and the **Mamluks** (1250–1517). Objects from Anatolia, Jezirah and the Syro-Egyptian world, including the first examples of enamelled and gilded glass; pearlised goblet; important collection of silver encrusted metal chandeliers, bowls, vases; the Barberini Vase from the name of the Pope Urban VIII Barberini to whom this object was presented in the 17C.

One of the masterpieces of the Islamic collection (displayed separately), is the *Baptistère de Saint-Louis*, a hammered brass bowl, incised and inlaid with silver and gold (c 1300), first kept at the Sainte-Chapelle of the Château of Vincennes, and placed in the Louvre in 1852. Collection of lamps from mosques in enamelled and gilded glass; collection of albarelles and spice jars, shapes developed later in the West; basin with the name Hugues IV de Lusignan (1324–59), King of Cyprus, with an inscription in Arabic and in French.

Room 10 Mongol Iran (13C–14C). For the first time China, Iran and the West were in direct contact with each other: dish with gilded fish with a pale green base reminiscent of Chinese celadon glaze; panels with stars and crosses in lustreware (on the wall); note the astrological motif of the lion and the sun which became an national emblem in Iran in the 19C.

Room 11 Timurid, Safavid, Qajar Iran (14C–20C) and **Mughal India** (16C–19C). This vast room (beneath Cour Khorsabad) evokes, among others, the Timurid Period (14C–15C) which took its name from its founder, a Turk known in the West as Tamerlane, a pitiless conqueror. To improve the status of his homeland, Transoxiana, he systematically deported the cultural elite of towns he conquered. His greatest descendant was his son Shahruk (1407–47). The whole dynasty patronised the arts, and the early 15C in Iran is known as the Timurid Renaissance: fine jade cup carved with floral scroll and a poetic inscription.

The **Safavid period** (1501–1736). In 1501, Shah Isma'il, after taking Azerbaïdjan, conquered Iran and led a dynasty which dominated the country until 1732. In a land open to traders, western influences began to penetrate local art: the large and precious *Mantes Carpet* (because it was once at the church of Mantes) is decorated with animals and hunting scenes; carpet with animals; a rare kilim (tapestry in silk and silver thread) with storiated scenes. (The numerous rugs will be exhibited in rotation because of their fragility.)

Qajar Period (1779–1924): in 1779 power passed to Qajars who moved the political centre of the empire to Teheran (from Isfahan). Even stronger European influences penetrated and, from the mid-century, in addition to miniatures, via lithography and photography, an important school of easel painting developed. Hence the rather surprising large oil portrait of the celebrated ruler, Fath Ali Shah seated on the Peacock Throne, received as a gift by Napoléon I.

Mughal India (1526–1858). Among arms on display is Dagger with Horse's Head, and armoury known as Quatre Miroirs; hookah (narghileh) in enamelled and gilded glass with a floral decor; large velour carpet with a vegetal motif.

Room 12 The Ottoman world (14C–19C). The Louvre has many Ottoman ceramics and all the important stages of production from Iznik are represented, showing a widening palette from blue and white, through turquoise, leaf green, mauve, then greenish black, before perfecting the famous Iznik red. The motifs vary from arabesques to bunches of grapes of far-Eastern origin, indented and curved foliage, and floral decoration perfected in the design studios of Topkapı Palace: large dish, blue and white; the famous Peacock Dish; and dish with grapes; spandrels with floral decor; panel from the mausoleum of Selim II.

Room 13 Art of the book: this room exhibits (in rotation) examples of Arabic, Iranian and Mughal miniatures.

Objets d'Art

The department of Objets d'Art contains a vast and glittering array of artefacts, and in 1999 seven new rooms were opened adding 175 works from the period 1815–40 to the existing 5500 presented in the 55 rooms of Richelieu (excluding Napoléon III's apartments), plus those in the other 30 or so rooms. Objets d'Art is reached by taking the Richelieu escalators or lifts from Hall Napoléon to the first floor and heading west.

The department contains ecclesiastical and secular objects, ranging from jewellery to furnishings, from France and from other countries, which date from the end of Antiquity to the first half of the 19C. The works from the Middle Ages to Louis XIII (mid-17C) are in rooms 1 to 33, on Richelieu first floor. The circuit continues chronologically with 18C objects in rooms 34–61, Sully first floor (north). The 19C exhibits are in rooms 67–81 near the apartments of Napoléon III, Richelieu first floor. The Apartments of Napoléon III are rooms 82–92 of Richelieu. The Royal Regalia is situated quite separately in the Apollo Gallery, Denon, Room 66.

The **Middle Ages** (rooms 1–11) covers a period of about ten centuries from the end of Antiquity (476) to the Renaissance, organised chronologically and geographically.

Room 1 Two porphyry columns from the 4C basilica of St Peter in Rome flank the door. 5C. Italian metalwork and ivories, such as the ivory plaque of *Three Miraculous Cures of Christ*. Under the Merovingians (481–751), the goldsmiths' art flourished, as proven by the *jewellery and adornments of Queen Aregond*, found at St-Denis in 1959. The Carolingian Renaissance produced fine work, such as two plaques from the binding of the *psalter written by the scribe Dagulf* (783) and the bronze horseman, known as the *statuette of Charlemagne* (9C), from Metz Cathedral.

Among **Byzantine pieces** are many beautiful ivories: 6C diptych known as the *Barberini Ivory*, the *Harbaville Triptych* (10C), *triptych of the Nativity* (10C); also lapis lazuli *plaque with figures of Christ and the Virgin* (12C); the *reliquary of the stone of St-Sepulchre*, from the Sainte-Chapelle is a beautiful piece of 12C Byzantine metalwork; mosaic icons of the *Transfiguration of Christ* (11C–13C) and of *St George and the Dragon* (14C).

Room 2 Ottonian openwork ivory plaques from the Cathedral of Magdeburg (10C) and *plaque of St John* (10C) from St-Denis. From Aix-la-Chapelle, the Mozan reliquary of the *Arm of Charlemagne* (c 1170); *ewer from the Treasure of St-Denis*, in rock crystal, carved in Egypt around the end of the 10C. The *Treasure of St-Denis* includes many superb ecclesiastical ornaments commissioned or acquired by Abbot Suger, Abbot of St-Denis (1122–51): *Suger's Eagle*, an antique porphyry vase mounted in silver gilt in the form of an eagle; *vase of Eleanor of Aquitaine* in rock-crystal given by the queen to Louis VII, who gave it to Suger; antique sardonyx ewer, mounted c 1150.

Examples of **Limoges enamel** work, finely detailed and colourful: the large *casket of St Thomas Becket* (end 12C); the *ciborium of Alpais* (early 13C). Early Gothic, developing by 1200, is characterised by increasing naturalism: *cross of St Vincent of Laon*.

Room 3 Exceptional enamel work from the Limousin in the early 13C is represented by the *reliquary of St Francis of Assisi*. The Sainte-Chapelle workshop, founded by St Louis in 1239, produced the ivory *large Virgin*. Gothic ivories include the *Descent from the Cross* (mid 13C). A typical example of the refinement in art of the reign of Philippe le Bel (1285–1314) is the *ivory box with a mirror*, decorated with a couple playing chess. Second-half 13C silver-gilt *polyptych of Floreffe* (French Ardennes). A highlight of the next period is the silver-gilt *statuette of the Virgin*, presented in 1339 to St-Denis by Jeanne d'Evreux; the Italian *arm reliquary of St Louis of Toulouse* (1337) in crystal and enamelled silver gilt.

Room 4 The so-called *Ring of St Louis* (14C) from St-Denis; *gold sceptre of Charles V* with a *statue of Charlemagne*; a huge *ivory altarpiece* by the Embriachi (Italy, c 1400), presented to the abbey of Poissy by Jean, Duc de Berry; tapestry, possibly from Arras, c 1400, *L'Offrande du Coeur*.

Rooms 5–11 Room 5 has an impressive collection of Hispano-Moorish lustreware (15C–16C). Room 6, 15C metalwork: outstanding medallion with *self portrait of Jean Fouquet* (15C); this important period for the art of tapestries is demonstrated by the *Legend of St Quentin*, *Miracle of the Loaves*, and other wovenworks. Room 7, 15C–16C Italian ceramics and enamels. Faenza pioneered the development of storiated faience: *votive plaque with saints*. Room 8, Flemish tapestries, c 1500, in particular the *Life of St Anatole de Salins* (1501–06). Room 9 has tapestries and precious metalwork including the *reliquary of the hand of St Martha* (late 15C) and Room 10 is called the Salle des Millefleurs, after the delightful medieval tapestry scattered with flowers. Room 11 has samples of the technique of painted enamels developed in Limoges at the end of the 15C, and stained glass.

Rooms 12–33 The Renaissance period. The Italian Renaissance, which inspired the French Renaissance, is illustrated in **rooms 12, 13** and **14** by Italian bronzes of the 15C and first half of the 16C: Florentine and Paduan Schools.

Rooms 15 and 16 *French art at the time of François I*: painted enamels, tapestries and furniture. **Room 17** has a bronze *boy with a thorn in his foot* after the Antique, and **room 18** French and Venetian glass.

Room 19 was specially arranged to display the magnificent **tapestries**, *Maximilian's Hunts* (1531–33) which, ever since entering Louis XIV's collection, have been considered a great masterpiece and remarkably are still complete. The twelve *tapestries of the months* are after cartoons by the painter Bernard Van Orley (1488–1541) and are a unique document of court life and of rural landscapes. An outstanding collection of Italian 16C and 17C majolica ware of different types.

Room 20 the Scipio Gallery has **eight Gobelins tapestries** of the *Life of Scipio* (1688–90), from designs by Giulio Romano; **French painted enamels** (15C–16C), including superb examples from the workshops of Léonard Limosin, Jean and Suzanne de Court, Pierre Courteys, J. Pierre Reymond. On the landing, armoury (c 1556–59) which belonged to Henri II.

Rooms 21–22 French Renaissance articles: door with the initial and emblem of Henri II and Catherine de Médicis; thirteen pieces of pottery from the St-Porchaire workshop (second half 16C), the largest existing collection; painted enamel *Portrait of the Constable Anne de Montmorency* (1556), a masterpiece by Léonard Limousin; Brussels tapestry of the **Resurrection**.

Room 23 16C–17C jewellery, clocks and **watches**, in enamel, gold and precious stones, including the watch of Jacques de la Garde, gilded copper (Blois, 1510).

Room 24 Salle Charles V (1519–58) has works from Germany, Flanders and Spain, such as the *Tapestries of the Labours of Hercules* produced in Audenarde, and characterised by large cabbage leaves called aristoloches; the *Charles V Ewer and Basin* (1558–59), silver gilt and enamel, from Antwerp. Medals and plaquettes in bronze, wood or lead, from Flanders, Spain and Germany.

Room 25 Adolphe de Rothschild Room, has a painted coffered ceiling typical of Venetian Mannerism and Italian Renaissance items; one of the small bronzes is *Atlante* by Zoppo (Padua, mid-16C); Médicis porcelain and German and Italian Renaissance jewellery.

Room 26 Notable **bronzes** from the workshops of Jean Bologne and Pietro Tacca (16C–17C) and tapestries from Ferrare (1545). Jean Boulogne's (Giambologna) (1529–1608) most famous bronze is the dynamic *Nessus carrying off Deianeira*.

Rooms 27 and 28 Treasure of the Order of St-Esprit and the reconstruction of the Chapel of the Order of the Holy Spirit. Henri III founded the Order of Chivalry of St-Esprit in 1578: reliquaries, censer, mace, covered goblets, ciborium and pair of rock crystal candlesticks and embroidered vestments. Also, enamelled gold shield and helmet of Charles IX (1560–74); some of the oldest tapestries, two episodes from the *Story of Artemis* (rewoven several times since the reign of Henri IV).

Room 29 contains rare pieces of **Renaissance furniture and tapestries**: *Sacrifice of Lystra*; and a tapestry woven at Mortlake c 1630, of the *Acts of the Apostles* after Raphael. **Room 30** has a remarkable collection of the singular art of the ceramicist, Bernard Palissy, the 'inventor of rustic figurines for the king', in the form of perfectly imitated animals and rustic basins with high relief decoration; the art of enamelled pottery from the little village of Avon: figurines and decorative pieces.

Room 31 Henri IV room Tapestry woven in Paris, by Flemish weavers, of *Achilles at Scyros* (c 1630–40); Barthélemy Prieur (1536–1611), small bronzes; choir stalls from Toulouse Cathedral, 1610–12, designed by Pierre Monge; and a remarkable French armoir dated 1617.

Room 32 Pre-Gobelins tapestries, after Simon Vouet; the **beginning of the 17C** was fundamental to the history of French furniture, as the new technique of *ébénisterie* (cabinet making) appeared: a fine 17C Parisian ebony cabinet; a remarkable ensemble of bed (with hangings) and six armchairs with original embroidered velvet from the 17C Château of Effiat.

Room 33 Painting on silk outlined in embroidery of the *Story of Debora*; the exquisite piece known as the *Coffer of Anne of Austria*, second half of the 17C.

Rooms 34–65, 17C and 18C. Room 34: ceiling painting by Carolus Duran (1878) (restored) representing the *Apotheosis of Marie de Médicis*, and a pedestal table with a porphyry top. It is also the Salle Boulle, illustrating the work of the cabinet-maker, André-Charles Boulle (1642–1732) with examples of ornate Louis XIV furniture.

Room 35 Collection of **ivories** including elements of a 17C frieze by van Obstal; tortoiseshell pieces with amber, stones and metal inlay; 17C and 18C tableware and wine glasses.

Rooms 36–41 18C **French faience** and porcelain from Vincennes and Sèvres, Marseille, Moustiers and Rouen. On display in **room 42** is a large part of the Grog Carven donation of 18C furniture. In **room 43** a remarkable collection of boiseries and furniture from the Château d'Abondant, Paris c 1750.

Room 44–45 and 49 Sparkling donations of the **goldsmith's and silversmith's art**, the David-Weill and Niarchos collections: a surtout by Jacques Röettiers, made for the Prince of Condé, depicting a stag hunt; the *nécessaire* of Marie Leszczynska (1729); parts of a service ordered by the Empress Catherine II of Russia (late 18C). **Room 48**: Gobelins tapestries illustrating of the *Story of Moses*, after designs by Poussin and watches and clocks.

Room 50 Savonnerie carpet made for the Apollo Gallery (1667); French Regency furniture by Charles Cressent (1685–1768): flat-topped bureau, cupboard and chest of drawers; group of 18C chairs. **Room 51**: flat-topped bureau by Max-Emmanuel de Bavière and consoles in gilded wood (c 1715); oriental porcelain; large vases from the India Company with the arms of the Duke of Orleans.

Rooms 52–56 Outstanding examples of **Louis XV furniture** (1715–74). The Schlichting room has Gobelins tapestries and furniture by the *ébéniste* Jean-François Oeben (c 1720–63); and Salle Edmond de Rothschild has exceptional pieces inlaid with plaques of Sèvres porcelain.

Rooms 58–61 Lebaudy room contains **Louis XVI furniture** (1774–91) and is decorated with gilt and white boiseries from the Hôtel de Luynes (c 1770–75); among furniture which belonged to Louis XVI and Marie-Antoinette is a flat-topped bureau by Hauré and G. Beneman (1787); armchairs by J.-B. Senné (1748–1803). The taste for chinoiserie is seen in the Chinese wallpaper, lacquered corner-pieces and chests by Martin Carlin (c 1730–85); there is also Marie-Antoinette's writing table by Weisweiler (1784). The cabinets contain several small furnishings and precious objects which belonged to the queen.

Room 62, Salle Claude Ott: toilette in crystal and bronze made by Escalier de Crystal for the Duchess of Berry. **Room 63**: the King's bedroom at the Tuileries with the bed belonging to Louis XVIII by Jacob Desmalter. **Rooms 64 and 65**: end 18C and early 19C furniture.

Room 66 Apollo Gallery contains items originally in the **French royal collection**, including semi-precious vessels of lapis lazuli, jade, amethyst, amber, red and green jasper, agate, sardonyx, basalt, etc. Individual objects include the crown of Louis XV (1722)—after his coronation the gems were replaced by coloured stones, according to custom; the Crown Jewels retained when the rest were sold in 1887, including the Regent diamond (137 carats), discovered in India and bought by the Regent in 1717; the Côte de Bretagne ruby, which had an illustrious list of owners and was later cut into the shape of a dragon as a decoration of the Order of the Golden Fleece.

Rooms 67 and 68 Salles Valadier and Jacob Frères contain **late-18C and early-19C furniture and objets d'art**. Georges Jacob (1739–1814), who usually signed his work 'G. Jacob', had two sons, who marked their work 'Jacob Frères' until 1804, after which François-Honoré-Georges Jacob Desmalter worked on his own for another decade. The latter's son, Alphonse Jacob, who signed his work 'Jacob', flourished in the 1840s.

Room 69 A representation of the **bedroom of Madame Récamier**. In 1798 the banker, Jacques Récamier, puchased the old Hôtel Necker and the architect, Louis Berthault, was given the task of redecorating it. He designed the furniture which was made by Jacob Frères. Juliette Récamier's original taste in interior design was the prototype for the Empire Style. During the early years of the 19C, the house became one of the great sights of Paris, especially Madame Récamier's bedroom.

Rooms 70–73 Style Empire. **Room 70**: Salle Biennais is named after Biennais (1764–1843), personal goldsmith to Napoléon I. In 1810, he delivered the prestigious silver-gilt tea service of 28 pieces, ordered by Napoléon for his marriage with Marie-Louise, of which half is conserved at the Louvre; a *nécessaire* by Biennais and Lorillon, given by Napoléon to Tsar Alexander I in 1808.

Room 71 Brogniart, head of the **Sèvres porcelain** manufacture, assured the collaboration of the architects Percier, Théodore Brongniart (1733–1813) and Vivant Denon. Porcelain at this time consisted of simple forms with an elaborate, all-over, painted designs and gilding. Le Cabaret Egyptien is a Sèvres porcelain coffee-service decorated with views of Egypt, made for the wedding of Napoléon and Marie-Louise, which the Emperor took with him to St Helena.

Rooms 72–73 Severe, monumental **furniture of the Empire period** (1804–15), made by Jacob-Desmalter (1770–1841) and Thomire (1751–1843) and **room 74** contains **porcelain** produced by the Vincennes-Sèvres manufacture collected by Madame Thiers and exhibited in display cases by Jacob-Desmalter and Delafontaine.

Rooms 75–81 The seven rooms which opened in December 1999 are devoted to the **Restoration and July Monarchy period** (1814–48). **Rooms 75–77** contain objects of the period of the Restoration (1814–1830). **Room 75** is a reconstruction of the bedchamber at the Tuileries occupied by Louis XVIII then Charles; **room 76** is dedicated to porcelain produced by the Manufacture de Sevrès, including a Medicis vase and a snuff-box both decorated in cameo style; and **room 77** contains items made for the exposition of 1819 encouraged by the Directoire to stimulate national production and limit imports—especially from England. One such item is the spectacular carved crystal dressing table and chair, bought by the Duchesse de Berry.

Rooms 78–81, the **July Monarchy** (1830–48) **room 78**, the Duc d'Orleans Room, elder brother of Louis-Philppe and great patron, contains a collection of clocks and candelabra; **room 79** has furniture from the neo-Gothic salon of Marie d'Orléans, daughter of Louis-Philippe; in **room 80** (Salle Chenavard) are ceramics, silverware and neo-Renaissance objects from the Chenavard workshops produced for the expositions of 1844 and 1849. **Room 81** contains furnishings from the Audience Chamber of the Duc de Nemours.

Rooms 82–92 The **Apartments of Napoléon III** have retained their original, and somewhat ostentatious, aspect and furnishings, and constitute a unique ensemble of the period. They were created during the Second Empire to house the Ministry of State, during the project to link the Tuileries Palace to the Louvre. The work was carried out by Hector Lefuel from 1857–61 and the apartments miraculously survived the fire of 1871. The same year, they were made over to the Ministry of Finance, who remained there until the *Grand Projet du Louvre* began in 1989. Completely renovated, they opened as part of the Richelieu wing in 1993.

The reception rooms are in a sumptuous Louis XIV style. From Cour Marly, the apartments can be reached by the grand staircase (alternatively, through the early 19C rooms, or on the south, past *Café Richelieu*). The **large antechamber** has walnut panels sculpted by Nelli. Adjacent is the **introduction gallery**, with two landscapes by Daubigny, and rest areas and documentation. This opens into the **Salle Thiers** or the family salon which links both the small rooms and the large reception rooms. The first is the **Salon-théâtre**, which has a charming floral and musical decoration, and off it opens the **Petit salon de la terrasse**.

In the angle, the **Grand Salon** is the largest and most sumptuous of the rooms, glittering with gold, adorned with putti, and draped in crimson velvet. The ceiling painting by Charles-Raphaël Maréchal represents the *Linking of the Louvre and the Tuileries by Napoléon III*. The rather more sedate tones of seagreen marble and darkened wood in the **small dining room** are enlivened by gilding and *trompe l'oeil* painted wallpaper. The **large dining room** has a painted ceiling.

Sculpture

French sculpture

French Sculpture is on Richelieu lower ground floor and ground floor, organised around Cour Marly and Cour Puget, glazed and terraced courtyards that ascend to the first floor. The collections have greatly benefited from the transformation of the Richelieu Wing from government offices to magnificent galleries and courtyards, setting off to advantage larger pieces of sculpture originally designed for royal gardens or public places. From Hall Napoléon take the Richelieu escalators to the lower ground floor. Straight ahead is Crypte Girardon leading to the two courtyards. To make the visit in chronological order, take the staircase to the left just before Crypte Giradon, and go to room 1, on the south side of Cour Marly. French Early Medieval to Renaissance sculpture is on three sides of Cour Marly.

Rooms 1–6 6C–12C Romanesque sculptures, dominated by the 5C/6C columns and capitals from Notre-Dame de la Daurade, Toulouse, and the decorated early 12C doorway from the priory of St-Cecile, Estagel (Gard); also capitals from Moissac (Languedoc) and Parthenay (Poitou). In the display cabinet is a *Christ* (painted wood), early 12C; a remarkable *head of St Peter*, with eyes of inlaid lead, from the tomb of St Lazarus, Autun; and the eagle from the tympanum of Cluny. A statue column from Avignon; a relief of *St Michael and the Dragon*, from Nevers; a carved wooden seated *Virgin and Child*.

Room 3 Sculpture from mid-12C to early-13C, Romanesque to early Gothic, in the Ile de France. This intermediary period is represented by the capital of the *Annunciation and Visitation* from the Paris area, and two extraordinary historiated spiral columns, with tumbling figures, from the abbey of Coulombs; the large relief from Carrières-sur-Seine is probably one of the oldest retables left in France; notable is a group of heads from the voussoirs of the west door of the Abbey of St-Denis, erected 1135–40, during the abbacy of Suger and the turning point from Romanesque to Gothic sculpture.

Room 4 Gothic (13C) sculpture typical of the elegance of Chartres and the Paris area, including samples from Notre-Dame de Paris and St-Germain-des-Prés. *St Matthew Dictated to by the Angel* is thought to be a fragment of the jubé of Chartres Cathedral.

Room 5 Mainly devoted to **14C retables**: the retable of the Sainte-Chapelle in black and white marble; scenes from the marble retable of the abbey of Maubuisson attributed to Evrard d'Orléans; on the wall, fragments of the Choir enclosure of Notre-Dame de Paris, including the remarkable relief of *Canon Pierre de Fayel* (d. 1344).

Room 6 14C religious sculpture and funerary monuments characteristic of 14C French sculpture, including many tender examples of *Virgin and Child*, some with traces of colour. Typical of work from Basse-Normandie, mid-14C, is the *Blanchelande Virgin and Child*—the first medieval work acquired by the Louvre in 1850. Also characteristic of this period are recumbent Gothic statues. This room looks out over the Tuileries Gardens.

Room 7 Funerary statues and sculptures, of considerable importance in the 14C, such as the burial stone of Jean Casse, Canon of Noyon Cathedral; and room 8, tympanum possibly from St-Denis (13C–14C) with an exuberant green man in trefoil tracery.

Room 9 Sculptures of the time of Charles V and Charles VI from the Ile de France and Berry. These include small *statues* for the tomb of the entrails of King Charles IV (le Bel; d. 1324) and his queen, Jeanne d'Evreux (d. 1371) by Jean de Liège.

Rooms 10–11 15C sculpture from Burgundy and the Loire, two important artistic centres which developed along different lines. The celebrated *tomb of Philippe Pot*, died 1493, Grand Seneschal of Burgundy, formerly in the abbey of Cîteaux, supported by eight *pleurants* (weepers). The later Middle Ages and early Renaissance in France are represented by the superb marble high-relief of *St George and the Dragon* (1504–09), commissioned from Michel Colombe by Georges d'Amboise for the Château of Gallon. The influence of Michel Colombe is seen in the sculptures of *St Peter*, *St Suzanne* and *St Anne teaching the Virgin* (c 1500), and the *tomb of René d'Orléans-Longueville* (d. 1515); and the *Virgin of Olivet* and the *Virgin of Ecouen*, possibly from the workshop of Guillaume Regnault, nephew of Colombe; also by Regnault the *tomb of Louis de Poncher* from St-Germain-l'Auxerrois (1523).

Room 12 Partial reconstruction of the *funerary chapel of Philippe de Commynes*. **Room 13**, described as the *Passage de la Mort St Innocent*, has early 16C sculpture from the Ile de France and Champagne. The hugely ornate Flamboyant retable of the *Resurrection* has traces of polychrome. Death statue from the Auvergne, of *Jeanne de Bourbon*, Comtesse d'Auvergne, 1521, showing her being devoured by worms.

Rooms 14–17 (overlooking Rue de Rivoli). Mainly major **16C sculptors** commissioned by royalty to work both on royal residences and on funerary monuments. Their inspiration was drawn from antiquity and from the Italian Renaissance. Pierre Bontemps, *Monument of Charles de Maigny* (1556); Jean Goujon, the base of *Fountain of Innocents*, 1547–49, rue St-Denis; François Marchand. Germain Pilon: a remarkable survival from a commission by Queen Catherine de Médicis for the projected Valois chapel at St-Denis is a terracotta model for the *Virgin of Sorrows*.

Barthélemy Prieur succeeded Pilon, continuing in a more sober style, for example the recumbent marble effigies of the *Constable Anne de Montmorency and his wife*; the upper part of the *Fontaine de Diane* from the Château of Anet is the oldest surviving garden sculpture in France. Ligier Richier from Lorraine: *Child Jesus sleeping in his Crib*.

Among examples of 16C work, **room 18** is Guirand Mellot's Porte de la Salle du Grand Consistoire du Capitole de Toulouse, ordered in 1552, taken down in 1880. The first part of Louis XIII's reign (1610–43) produced little French sculpture, but from 1630 it was animated by Jacques Sarazin (1592–1660) and the Anguier brothers, notably Michel.

Room 19 Overlooking Cour Marly are **17C sculptures** including Simon Guillain's masterpiece, the *Monument of the Pont-au-Change*, which once dominated the busy crossroads opposite the Cité at the time of Louis XIII.

Cour Marly is named after the sculptures from the Parc de Marly, an estate acquired by Louis XIV in 1676 as a more private retreat than Versailles. Jules Hardouin-Mansart used water to embellish the gardens which were further adorned with Rococo style sculptures by the best artists. Sculptures in the courtyard (middle level) include *Seine*, *Marne*, *Neptune* and *Amphitrite* intended for the cascade, by Antoine **Coysevox** (1640–1720), also responsible for the equestrian groups, Mercury and Fame (1699–1702) (upper level), moved to the Tuileries in 1719. These were superseded at Marly by the magnificent *Horses of Marly* (1743–45) (opposite), of Guillaume 1er **Coustou** (1677–1746) which were subsequently placed at the end of the Champs-Elysées and brought to the Louvre in 1984. (Reproductions now stand on the Champs-Elysées and the Tuileries.)

Between the two courtyards is **room 20**. **Crypte Girardon** contains 17C–18C sculptures by Giradon, Puget, and Coysevox. In the centre is the small model for the *Equestrian statue of Louis XIV* by **François Girardon**, and at the end of the gallery, **Pierre Puget**, marble relief of the *Meeting of Alexander and Diogenes* (1671–89), made for Louis XIV. Grandiose busts of bewigged men include Coysevox's marble bust of *Jean-Baptiste Colbert* and and a bronze (posthumous) bust of *Louis II de Bourbon* 'Le grand Condé'; **J.-L. Lemoyne** marble bust of Jules Hardouin-Mansart. There is also a bust of *Marie Serre* (1706), mother of Hyacinthe Rigaud, by Coysevox.

A disparate collection of **17C–19C French sculpture** is exhibited in and around **Cour Puget**: four bronze *Captifs*, designed (1679–85) for the Place des Victoires by Desjardins (1637–94), plus four bronze reliefs and eight circular medallions, to commemorate glorious episodes during the reign of Louis XIV; Pierre Puget's Baroque *Milon of Crotona* (1671–82) and *Perseus and Andromeda* (1687–94), made for Louis XIV's Versailles, transferred to the

Louvre in 1819. Also Termes and other statues from various parks by Legros (1629–1706), Barois (1656–1726), Raon (1631–1707), Flamen (1647–1717), Marsy (1647–81), and Regnaudin (1622–1706).

Beneath the trees are 17C sculptures by Sébastien Slodtz (1655–1726) and Nicolas Coustou (1658–1733), destined for Versailles and transferred to the Tuileries in 1722. Coysevox 's lighthearted piece, *Marie-Adelaide de Savoie*, Duchesse de Bourgogne, portrays the mother of Louis XV as Diana (1710) while Jean-Baptiste Pigalle (1714–85) *Madame de Pompadour en Amitié*, marble, 1753, depicts Louis XV's favourite with flowers of all seasons. On the walls at the end are fine stucco friezes by Clodion and on the upper level, is Pigalle's *Mercury*, in lead, 1753.

Around the terrace is French sculpture for the open-air from the mid-18C to the 19C, and the first-floor galleries on the north side of the Cour Puget, rooms 21–29 and 31–33 contain small format works.

Room 21 Projects and models in plaster and terracotta for 18C tombs and funerary monuments by Bouchardon (1698–1762), Chaudet (1763–1810), Vassé (1716–72), and by Houdon (1741–1828), the marble mausoleum for the heart of Comte d'Ennery (1781). The design by Pigalle, for the *mausoleum of Marshall Saxe*, Strasbourg, St Thomas, in its architectural setting, is exceptionally elaborate.

Rooms 22–28 Small 18C works in a variety of materials by Falconet, Robert le Lorrain, Michel-Ange Slodtz and Marie-Anne Collot, pupil of Falconet; Jean-Baptiste II Lemoyne; and Guillaume Coustou (1677–1746), a terracotta of his brother Nicolas in a Turban.

Room 24 J.-B. Pigalle's, *L'Enfant à la cage*; *Voltaire Nu* in marble, 1776, a fine head on a realistic decrepit body and male portrait busts including a bronze of *Diderot* (1777), and *Self Portrait* in terracotta. **Room 25** qualifying works, high in drama but small in scale, for acceptance at the Académie royale de Peinture et de Sculpture from 1704 to 1791, by a variety of artists: Sébastien Adam, Lemoyne, Paul-Ambroise Slodtz, Thierry, Guillaume II Coustou, Monot.

Returning through the parallel galleries overlooking Rue de Rivoli, works by Jean-Jacques Caffieri (1725–92), *Corneille*, and by his rival Augustin Pajou, *Allegory of Queen Marie Leszczynska*.

Room 28 The preceding portraitists were eclipsed by **Jean-Antoine Houdon** (1741–1828). Busts of his his contemporaries include *Voltaire*, the singer *Sophie Arnould*, *Jean-Jacques Rousseau*, *Diderot*, *Benjamin Franklin* and *George Washington*.

Room 29, the **Gallery of Grands Hommes**, has statues of illustrious men commissioned in 1776 during the reign of Louis XVI from Academicians: *Molière* and *Corneille* by Caffieri; *Jean de La Fontaine* and a marble of *Nicolas Poussin* (1804), in a toga, by Pierre Julien (1731–1804). Also Houdon's bronze of *Diana the Huntress* (1790).

Room 30 is dedicated mainly to **Clodion**.

Room 31: Period of the Revolution, the Empire and the Restoration. Characteristic works are the statue of *Peace* (silver and bronze), conceived by

Vivant Denon, Director of the Louve and modelled by Chaudet (1763–1810); *Napoléon I in Coronation Robes*, marble, 1813 by Ramey (1754–1838); a mosaic by Belloni (1772–1863), *The Genius of the Emperor, Controlling Victory, brings back Peace and Abundance*, 1810, designed for the floor of Salle de la Melpomène at the Lou.

Rooms 32 and 33. From the **Romantic era**, 1820–50 virtuoso but sentimental pieces are represented by James (Jean-Jacques) Pradier: *Niobe Wounded, Psyche with a Butterfly*, the *Three Graces*; Cortot, *Immortality*, and Jacques-Edme Dumont, *Genius of Liberty*. Works by the great Romantic sculptor, François Rude (1784–1855), include *Mercury* and *Young Neapolitan playing with a Turtle*. The cases contain bronzes and plasters by the successful sculptor of animals, Antoine-Louis Barye (1795–1875), including the famous *Jaguar devouring a Hare*.

On the **upper level of Cour Puget** are monumental works of the first half of the 19C, among them: Barye's *Roger* and *Angelique riding the Hippogriffe*; large portrait heads in marble at which David d'Angers excelled; a bronze by Bosio of *Hercules fighting Achelous*; Rude's *Joan of Arc Hearing Voices*, commissioned in 1845 for a series of illustrations of women for the Luxembourg Gardens.

Italian Sculpture

The collection of Italian sculpture is in Denon, divided between 6C–15C on the lower ground floor and 16C–19C on the ground floor. Take the Denon escalator from Hall Napoléon to the lower ground floor and turn right. (On the right of the Donatello gallery, is an area for the visually handicapped with works that may be touched.)

Room 1 (a to f) Galerie Donatello was originally a stable, built 1857–59 by Lefuel, and contains Italian sculpture from the 6C–15C: *Head of the Empress Ariadne* (early 6C); Armenian stela, beginning of the 14C, in red tuff, with crosses and interlacing; marble antependium (8C–9C), with animal and vegetal decoration; two Atlantes (second half 13C) archaistic in style; a mid-13C, *Descent from the Cross* in painted wood; *Personification of the Four Cardinal Virtues: Prudence, Fortitude, Justice and Temperance*, 14C, from a funerary monument. *St Stephen* (1390–96), from the west front of Milan Cathedral demolished in 1587, the head replaced at some unknown date.

Versions of the *Madonna and Child*, in a variety of materials, mainly reliefs; life-size, seated *Madonna and Child*, in painted wood by Jacopo della Quercia. Dominating Italian sculpture in the 15C with works both elegant and sensual was the great, **Donatello**, inspired by Antiquity: *Madonna and Child*, in coloured and gilded terracotta, the half figure of the Virgin of great delicacy and pathos, probably one of the last works produced by Donatello before his departure for Padua (1443); Donatello and his studio: *Madonna Worshipping the Child* (the Piot Tondo), a roundel of terracotta with wax medallions (under glass, partly restored); after a lost original by the master, *Madonna of Verona*, in *cartapesta* (*papier mâché*). The *Virgin surrounded by four angels*, by Agostino di Duccio, made for Piero de Medici, is a virtuoso example of marble low relief; the three reliefs of the *Madonna and Child*, by Mino da Fiesole, give a masterly effect of transparent fabrics.

Notable is the marble roundel of the *Young Christ and St John the Baptist*, by

Desiderio da Settignano, carved to give an astonishing impression of depth.

Among portrait busts: by Benedetto da Maiano (1442–97) vigorous bust of *Filippo Strozzi*; and from a Florentine workshop (late 15C), *La Belle Florentine*. Two decorative panels in marble by Fiesole and Giovanni Dalmata came from the lower part of the Mausoleum of Paul II in the old basilica of St Peter's, Rome.

Room 2 Bottega della Robbia (15C–16C) is a small gallery devoted to a collection of enamelled earthenware, in characteristic blue and white, and yellow and green, of the Florentine workshop of the della Robbia (Andrea, 1435–1525), Giovanni (1469–c 1530), Luca (1475–c 1548) and Benedetto Buglioni (1459–1521), including *St Sebastian, Madonna and Child with Three Cherubims*, and *Christ on the Mount of Olives*.

Room 3 to the left contains the Spanish collection.

For the continuation of Italian sculptures take the Mollien Staircase up to Denon ground floor. On the landing is the large *Nymph of Fontainebleau*, a bronze bas-relief by Benvenuto Cellini, made for the Porte d'Orée at Fontainebleau but placed, until the Revolution, above the gateway of the Château d'Anet.

Room 4 Michelangelo Gallery: with low vaults and polychrome marble floor, is a suitably grand setting for Michelangelo's *Slaves*, with works from 16C–19C. Pass first through the monumental portal of the Palazzo Stanga at Cremona, attributed to Pietro da Rho.

This leads to the most celebrated works in the department, the two *Slaves*, 1513–15, by Michelangelo Buonarotti (1475–1564): *The Captive*, struggling for his freedom, and the sensuous *Dying Slave*. Both were both intended for the tomb of Pope Julius II, but given to Henri II in 1550 by Robert Strozzi, were placed for some time at the Château of Ecouen (see Ch. 40) and then transferred to Cardinal Richelieu's collection.

Among several works by (or attributed to) Gian-Francesco Rustici is *Apollo's Victory over the Python*, marble; *The Young River*, by Pierino da Vinci (1531–54), related to Leonardo; examples of work in bronze by Northern sculptors who spent most of their working life in Italy: Jean Bologne (Giambologna) (French), *Mercury Flying* (1580), and Adrien de Vries (Dutch), *Mercury Carrying off Psyche*, made (1593) for the castle of Prague, but ending up in French royal parks.

Of the **high Baroque period**, works by **Bernini** (1598–1680) include *Angel carrying the Crown of Thorns* (terracotta, Rome, c 1667); and the bust of *Cardinal Richelieu*, modelled on the triple portrait of Richelieu by Philippe de Champaigne in London.

At the end of the gallery are works by Antonio Canova, *Psyche revived by the Kiss of Cupid*, and *Cupid and Psyche standing*; and Bartolini (1777–1850), *Nymph with a Scorpion* (marble, 1837).

Spanish Sculpture

The small collection of Spanish Sculpture, 12C–18C, is squeezed between the Italian and the Northern Sculpture collections in **room 3** on Denon lower ground floor and contains examples of capitals from the Visigothic and Mozarab periods. Also works in alabaster from royal tombs of the Catalan Monastery of Poblet; monumental Gothic doorway, richly decorated with vegetal motifs and an *Annunciation*; an extraordinary work illustrating a Franciscan legend, of the *Dead St Francis*, in polychrome wood with eyes of glass, teeth of bone, and cord of hemp, probably mid-17C.

Northern Sculpture
Continue through the Spanish section to Northern Sculpture, 12C–16C, in the west of Denon lower ground floor.

Room A English 15C, alabasters from Nottingham. **Room B**: *Virgins* (12C–15C) in **International Gothic style**, from the Rhenish lands, Netherlands, Baveria, Germany, Salzburg and Lorraine. Notable is the 12C Bavarian *Crucifixion* carved in lime wood, the emaciated and touching figure of Christ wearing a long pleated perizonium. There is also a celebrated *Virgin and Child* from Isenheim, near Colmar, originally the central part of retable carved in lime wood which lends itself well to complicated drapery.

Room C German and Dutch works from the later Gothic period, 15C–16C, among the reliefs and sculptures is a **Virgin of the Annunciation**, kneeling, in painted alabaster, by Riemenschneider; a naked *Magdalen* (La Belle Allemande), in painted lime wood, Augsburg (c 1515) by Gregor Erhart (d. c 1540); a *Crucifixion* in oak from the Brabant, end 15C; *Retable of the Passion*, in polychromed oak, Antwerp, c 1510.

Renaissance sculpture is represented by the *Tombstone of Jean de Coronmeuse*, Abbot of St Jacques de Liège (c 1525–30); and, attributed to Schro (active 1545–68), bust of the *Elector Ottheinrich von der Pfalz*, in alabaster.

Art from Africa, Asia, Oceania and the Americas at the Louvre
This collection is exhibited at the western extremity of Denon. The recommended entry is the Portes des Lions on the south (Seine) side of the Louvre and the visit is included in the general ticket to the Louvre.

This collection opened in the here in April 2000 and is made up of a sample of some 120 key works belonging to a new museum planned for 2004 on Quai Branly. The works for the future museum have been gathered together from the Musée de l'Homme, Musée National des Arts d'Afrique et d'Océanie, and certain provincial museums, as well as from overseas.

The visit is organised around the four main cultural regions, Africa, Asian, Oceania (Pacific and Australia) and the Americas. The visitor is greeted by an ancient African statue of a man of the Nagada II period, from pre-dynastic Egypt (5000–4000 BC). Among other African works is a remarkable Ife head in terra-cotta from Nigeria. A stone sculpture, which once belonged to André Breton, from the Island of Nias opens the Asiatic sector, while a c2000-year old sculpture from Chupicuaro, Mexico, is at the centre of the room devoted to the Americas.

16 • The Museums of the Union Centrale des Arts Décoratifs

■ Arrondissement: 75001
◉ Tuileries, Palais Royal-Musée du Louvre, Pyramides
◭ Châtelet-Les-Halles

Union Centrale des Arts Décoratifs (UCAD)

Usually known as the Musée des Arts Décoratifs, the main entrance is at 107 Rue de Rivoli. UCAD is quite autonomous from the Louvre Museum, although housed in the north-west part of the Palais du Louvre and extends into a section of the Rohan wing (**Map 8; 1**). This once overcrowded and somewhat stuffy museum is emerging as a modern masterpiece of museology following a major programme of restoration and expansion. Some sections of the museum are still being renewed and it is due to be open in its entirety by the end of 2002.

The museum consists of the Museum of Decorative Arts, the Museum of Fashion and Textile, and the Museum of Advertising and there is also a Library. It is open Tues–Fri 11.00–18.00, Sat, Sun 10.00–18.00, Wed to 21.00, closed Mon and public holidays (☎ 01 45 55 57 50). One ticket gives admission to all three museums and temporary exhibitions. There is a bookshop and boutique selling replicas and good quality objects of contemporary design on the ground floor, and a very pleasant café (ticket holders only) at the heart of the Museum of Advertising.

History of the collection

The history of the collection is bound up with the Union Centrale des Beaux-Arts appliqués à l'Industrie and the Société du Musée des Arts Décoratifs (founded in 1864 and 1877 respectively), which in 1882 merged to become the Union Centrale des Arts Décoratifs. In 1901 work began on the rehabilitation of the interior of the Pavillon de Marsan, and the Musée des Arts Décoratifs was inaugurated in May 1905. Today, its inventory lists over 140,000 items. In 1935 the Musée Nissim de Camondo, 63 Rue de Monceau, was affilliated to the Union (see Ch. 28).

The new space for the **Musée de la Publicité** (advertising), designed by Jean Nouvel, opened in 1999. This pioneering concept demands a particular approach, and Nouvel describes the space or 'Square' (3rd floor) which it inhabits as a metaphor for the urban environment where advertising is part of everyday life. Brought together here are all the techniques used in advertising: showcases for objects, posters and original drawings as well as screens, projectors, video monitors, computers, luminous news-boards and so on. This concept is epitomised by the convivial café in this Square, which is situated adjacent to the multimedia library where researchers or the public may freely browse the advertising database. This museum mounts some four temporary exhibitions a year on specific themes drawn from material in the collection.

Musée de la Mode et du Textile

The Musée de la Mode et du Textile is on two floors of the Rohan wing of the Louvre. The collection of costumes, from the 17C to the 20C, accessories and textiles is presented thematically and changed every year.

History of the collection

The collection had its origins in the Union Française des Arts du Costume (UFAC), established in 1901, since when its collections of costumes and accessories have been very considerably increased, partly due to donations. A proportion has been acquired with the participation of several famous fashion houses—among the more notable names being Balenciaga, Chanel, Dior, Fath, Givenchy, Lanvin, Patou, Ricci, Rochas, Saint-Laurent, Schiaparelli, Ungaro and Worth. The growth of the industry was spectacular during the latter half of the 19C when some 158 couturiers existed in Paris. By 1872 this had risen to 684 and in 1895 to 1636 (six of whom employed 400–600 workers each), not including small independent dressmakers.

The holdings, which are being increased continually, include 20,000 costumes and 35,000 accessories of all types (including a rare collection of umbrellas, Second Empire hats, costume jewellery, fans, shoes, handbags and gloves); some 21,000 samples of textiles (prints, tapestries, laces, embroideries, braids); and patterns and pattern-books. To complete the museum, one further floor is made over to a Fashion and Textile Documentation Centre. This holds a photographic library of 215,000 images, a slide library with 300,000 images, 15,000 commercial catalogues of the second half of the 20C to the present day, 6500 books, 250 periodical titles (about 100 complete series), and a collection of 50,000 drawings and engravings. The museum also contains a textile laboratory.

Musée des Arts Décoratifs

The Musée des Arts Décoratifs contains an outstanding collection of French decorative and ornamental art from medieval times to the present, most of which will be exhibited on a permanent basis. Objects range from Italian primitives, tapestries, porcelain, paintings and furniture from the Middle Ages to the present. It is especially rich in 17C, 18C and 19C objets d'art. There are also diverse pieces such as Islamic artefacts, notably carpets, and Art Nouveau and Art Deco interiors. The new layout will include both period rooms and series of objects, such as ceramics, silverware and jewellery. The richly endowed 20C collection (from 1900 to contemporary) will extend from the ground to the 9th floor in the Pavillon de Marsan. At the time of writing, the nine **Gothic and Renaissance rooms** have already opened, therefore until the transformation is complete is it possible only to give an idea of what will be on display in future in the rest of the museum.

Gothic and Renaissance works are presented in a group of nine rooms on the 3rd floor. **Room 1** exhibits thematically, and in rotation, 13C–16C tapestries. **Room 2**, Salle du Maître de la Madeleine. Various periods of the Middle Ages are represented in this room which is named after the Tuscan creator of the panel *Virgin and Chld between St Andew and St James*, last quarter of the 13C. This work is one of the oldest Italian works in a French collection and blends the Byzantine tradition with an increasing naturalism evolving in Italy at this period. Slightly later is Bernardo Daddi's **Miracle of St Peter the Martyr** (1338) and **San Elpidio a Mare** by Giacomo di Nicola da Recanati typifies International Gothic style.

Spanish works include several painted wooden altar fronts, a retable panel by the Catalan, Pedro Garcia de Benabarre (14C), and the elegant **Coronation of the Virgin** by Juan de la Abadia the Elder (end 15C). Also painted panels from Germany and France and two panels, c 1515–20, attributed to the Master of the triptych of the Crucifixion of Antwerp. A wooden statue of an **Angel** (Parisian region) is typical in stance and expression of the late 13C.

Room 3, Salle Raoul Duseigneur, is arranged as a French bed-chamber of the late Middle Ages furnished mainly by objects from the Château de Villeneuve Lembron in the Auvergne, and a tapestry from Arras entitled **Romance of the Rose** (c 1400).

Room 4, Salle Maciet, contains portraits of **Marie de Clèves** and **Charles d'Orléans**, parents of Louis XII. The tapestries, with scenes of rustic and courtly life, and the furniture illustrate the transitional phase of the late Middle Ages. Evoking the interior of a church, **room 5**, **Gallery of Retables**, has stalls with misericords, as well as Belgian, Italian, German and French carved and painted retables, including a rare example on a large scale from Barcelona, the Retable of St John the Baptist by Luis Borrassá (active 1380–1424). Also 15C–16C religious statuary.

Room 6, Salle des arts du feu, brings together objects (13C–16C) made or decorated by techniques involving firing, such as enamels, French and German stoneware, Hispano-Mauresque earthernware, Italian majolicas, small Renaissance bronzes and a collection of Venetian glass as well as an enamelled terracotta piece from the workshop of the Buglioni in Florence (c 1520).

Room 7 is named after Emile Peyre, who bequeathed all the Italian paintings in the museum. The 55 painted panels (restored), unique in France, once decorated the beams of the Santa Colomba monastery at Cremona. There are also *cassoni* (painted marriage chests), paintings and sculpture. The Cabinet de Travail, **room 8**, depicts a private study of the mid-16C. The small portraits and the Renaissance motifs of the intarsia (marquetry) panels are typical of France at this period. The Salle des vitraux, **room 9**, brings together 16C stained-glass panels from Leiden, and French and Italian furnishings set off by false marble walls (dating from the 1960s), representing the increasing desire during the Renaissance for comfort and luxury. Also **Venus and Cupid**, **The Honey Thief** by Cranach the Elder (1472–1553)

Other items in the decorative arts collection include, from the time of **Louis XIII to the Second Empire period** (17C–early 19C), examples of panelling of c 1707 from 7 Pl. Vendôme, and oak-panelling of c 1735; a ceiling of c 1710 by Claude Audran (1658–1734) from the Hôtel Bertier de Flesselles, Rue de Sévigné, and another of c 1715 from the Hôtel de la Comtesse de Verrie in the Rue du Cherche-Midi; also decorative panels by N. Coypel and by Hubert Robert;

painted panels in the Etruscan style (c 1780); and a number of carved wood brackets, panels, picture-frames and mirrors.

In the **furniture collection** are 17C–18C chairs exemplifying the evolution of styles; a fine marquetry cabinet of c 1670; a marquetry armoire attributed to Boulle of c 1680 and another by Charles Cressent (c 1725); various pieces in the Chinese taste and Chinoiserie objects. Also chairs by members of the Jacob family; a boat-shaped bed by F. Baudry (1827).

Among the **paintings** are a *Portrait of the Chancellor d'Anguesseau* by Robert Tournières; a pastel of Molière; *Venetian Scenes* by Michele Marieschi (1710–43); and monastic scenes by Alessandro Magnasco; garden scenes by Pillement; flower studies (1614–15) by G. Pini; watercolours by Lavreince, J.-B. Huet, Debucourt and Mallet; an early work (c 1806) by Ingres, *The Casino of Raphael at Rome*; and *Houdon's Studio*, and the *Gohin Family*, both by Louis Boilly. Also a series of wax-portrait moulds, some by G.-B. Nini (c 1717–80), and a collection of portrait-miniatures.

Among the extensive **ceramic collections** are examples from St-Cloud, Moustiers, Strasbourg, Rouen (some exhibiting surprisingly strong Chinese influence), Sceaux, Sinceny, Marseille; *faïences en trompe-l'oeil* and *faïences* fine china; ware from Vincennes, Sèvres, Mennecy and Chantilly; biscuit figures, and a curious terracotta of a girl playing with her pet dog, by Clodion (1738–1814); an important collection of Chinese cloisonné; and Delft and Meissen porcelain.

There are also such diverse fine quality objects as door furniture; bronze appliqués, ornaments and also a coiffeuse used by Joséphine at the Tuileries; silverware; mathematical instruments; pewter; clocks and watches; ivory boxes; snuff grinders; rings; cutlery; *nécessaires*; embroidered purses; shuttles; walking-sticks; paperweights; pipes; plaster plaques; statuettes; glass ornaments; decorative embossed leather cases; and book-bindings. There are also toys.

Also in the collection are Charles le Brun's projects for tapestries of *The Months* and furniture and furnishings in the Louis-Philippe and Second Empire (Napoléon III) styles.

From the **late-19C, 20C and Contemporary collections** are complete interiors, including three rooms (boudoir, bedroom and bathroom) designed for Jeanne Lanvin by Armand Rateau, in 1920–22. There are also examples of the applied arts: metal, ceramic and glass including glass by R. Lalique, and paintings by Marie Laurencin, Maurice Denis and Matisse, among others. There is also jewellery of the period. The Art Nouveau exhibits contain a room with woodwork by Georges Hoentschell, furniture by Hector Guimard, Emile Gallé, Louis Majorelle and A. Charpentier. Among smaller objects are a lamp by L.C. Tiffany, glass by Lalique, Dammouse, and Gallé, ceramics by Carriès, Chaplet, Delaherche, and others and metalwork by Hirtz, Dunan and Gaillard. Leading artists and designers from 1945 onwards are represented by such objects as a table by Giacometti and chair by Niki de Saint-Phalle.

The important **Bibliothèque des Arts Décoratifs** (Library), with some 120,000 volumes and periodicals, is being modernised and will reopen during 2000/2001.

17 • North of the Rue de Rivoli

■ Arrondissements: 75001, 75002

🔒 Concorde, Tuileries, Pyramides, Palais-Royal

🚇 Auber

Angélina, 226 Rue de Rivoli, ☎ 01 42 60 82 00. Famous café and tea and coffee shop for indulgent snacks, £

L'Ardoise, 28 Rue du Mont-Thabor, ☎ 01 42 96 28 18. Small, contemporary bistrot, good value and crowded, £

Le Dauphin, 167 Rue St-Honoré, ☎ 01 42 60 40 11. Convenient, inexpensive, but choose carefully, £

Café Drouant, 18 Rue Gaillon, ☎ 01 42 65 15 16. The less expensive café version of a historic restaurant, ££

Gérard Besson, 5 Rue du Coq-Héron, ☎ 01 42 33 14 74. Rather grand, with a new dining room, and classic, expensive delicacies—especially good desserts, £££

A la Grille St-Honoré, 15, Place du Marché St. Honoré, ☎ 01 42 61 00 93. Good traditional cooking, £

Juvenile's, 47 Rue de Richelieu, ☎ 01 42 97 46 49. A Scots-owned tapas bar, for Spanish sherry and wines from all over. Great snacks, £

Kinugawa, 9 Rue du Mont-Thabor, ☎ 01 42 60 65 07 (also on Rue St-Philippe-du-Roule, 8e). Excellent Japanese fare, impeccable service, but costly, ££

Le Meurice, Hôtel Meurice, 228 Rue de Rivoli, ☎ 01 44 58 10 50. Somewhat OTT decor but superb down-to-earth cooking. Lunch menu, £££

Pile ou Face, 52bis Rue Notre-Dame des Victoires, ☎ 01 42 33 64 33. Cosy old-fashioned ambience with Normandy produce, ££

Restaurant Costes, Hôtel Costes, 239 Rue St. Honoré, ☎ 01 42 44 50 25. Very fashionable, very chic, Italianate setting, trendy food, and pricey, ££

Restaurant Lescure, 7 Rue de Mondovi, ☎ 01 42 60 18 91. Rustic bistrot serving good reliable food at very good prices, £

Le Soufflé, 36 Rue du Mont-Thabor, ☎ 01 42 60 27 19. Not difficult to guess their speciality—which has been served here since time immemorial; go for the traditional one au Grand-Marnier, £–££

Vaudeville, 29 Rue Vivienne, ☎ 01 40 20 04 62. Art Deco brasserie in the Flo chain, ££

Café de Vendôme, 1 Pl. Vendôme, ☎ 01 55 04 55 55. Classic French cooking in a classy *quartier*, ££

Around the Palais Royal is a wide choice, some with tables on the terraces of the Palais-Royal Gardens:

Le Grand Véfour, 17, Rue de Beaujolais, ☎ 01 42 96 56 27. Lunch menu slightly less expensive, but worth it for the 18C decor, £££

There are several small eateries in the quartier:

Willi's Wine Bar, 13 rue des Petits-Champs, ☎ 01 42 61 05 09, English run with interesting food, £

L'Incroyable, Rue Montpensier /Rue de Richelieu ☎ 01 42 96 24 64. Famously inexpensive, £

Rue Montpensier/gardens of Palais-Royal:

La Gaudriole, ☎ 01 42 97 51 36, £

Pierre au Palais Royal, 10, Rue de Richelieu, ☎ 01 42 96 09 17. A traditional restaurant updated, used by locals, ££

This district, centrally placed between the Louvre, Place de la Concorde and the Opéra, is a strange mixture of Parisian elegance and tourist trash. Prestigious boutiques selling jewellery, fashion and antiques jostle with souvenir stalls selling models of the Eiffel Tower and T-shirts emblazoned with Parisian motifs. In and around famous streets such as Rue de Rivoli, Rue St-Honoré and Rue de la Paix and the ultra elegant Place Vendôme, are some of the finest and most luxurious hotels, but also more modest establishments. Likewise, there is an abundance of grand and not-so-grand, restaurants, cafés and teashops. In the district there are two well-established English bookshops. Less obvious places to visit are the Comédie-Française, the gardens of the Palais Royal and the church of St-Roch.

Rue de Rivoli

Constructed in 1811–56 and named in honour of Napoléon's victory over the Austrians in 1797, Rue de Rivoli runs east from Pl. de la Concorde (**Map 2; 7–8**; see Ch. 13) following the Tuileries Gardens and the Louvre. The street begins at the west, at the corner of Rue St-Florentin, with the 18C **Hôtel de la Vrillière** (or de Talleyrand), designed by Chalgrin, and the inspiration for the later American Embassy building (see Ch. 27). The statesman, Charles Maurice de Talleyrand-Périgord (1754–1838) died in this building. A uniform range of arcaded buildings runs from here to Pl. du Palais-Royal—handy on a rainy day.

As you wander down Rue de Rivoli you come across the British booksellers, W.H. Smith at no. 248. Further on, the Hôtel Meurice, 228 Rue de Rivoli, saw the capture (25 August 1944) of General von Choltitz, commander of the German forces in Paris after he refused orders to destroy the capital's principal buildings. The *salon de thé Angélina* at no. 226 is the smart place for tea or, even better, hot chocolate, and *Galignani's Bookshop*, no. 224, established here since 1855, stocks English and French books and magazines. It was established by M. Galignani and his English wife, Anne Parsons, who in 1815 started out by publishing an English newspaper, guides to Paris and reprints of English books. A bronze-gilt statue of *Joan of Arc* by Frémiet stands in Place des Pyramides. Diagonally opposite (no. 107) is the Musée des Arts Décoratifs (see Ch. 16) and at no. 99 is the entrance to the underground shopping precinct, the Carrousel du Louvre (see Ch. 14).

Rue St-Honoré

Rue St-Honoré runs parallel to Rue de Rivoli but has a totally different atmosphere and in many respects is more interesting. Linking the two towards the west is Rue Cambon where, at no. 5 (previously no. 3) Stendhal lived between 1810 and 1814. This street crosses Rue du Mont-Thabor and at the corner with Rue St-Honoré stands the Church of the Assumption, built in 1670 as the chapel of the convent of the Haudriettes and now used by the Polish community. Turn east on Rue St-Honoré and you soon come to Rue de Castiglione. The Hôtel Lotti at no. 7 was described in George Orwell's *Down and Out in Paris and London* (1933).

Place Vendôme

Rue de Castiglione opens out to the north into Place Vendôme (**Map 2; 8**), of refined and distinguished 18C elegance; like so much of Paris, it is resplendent at night.

History of the Place Vendôme

The Place was conceived in 1686 and construction proceeded under the direction of Jules Hardouin-Mansart at the end of the 17C. It owes its name to a 17C *hôtel particulier* built by César, Duc de Vendôme, son of Henri IV and Gabrielle d'Estrées, which stood on this site. The hôtels with their grand and unified façades were completed in the 18C. Homes for bankers gradually became high-class commercial properties and apartments. Nos 11–13 is the Ministère de la Justice (since 1815). Frédéric Chopin died at no. 12 in 1849. The *Ritz* was established at no. 15 in 1898, keeping much of its 18C decoration, and the *Bristol* at no. 3, and there are a number of expensive jewellers and boutiques.

Dominating the Place is the **Colonne de la Grande Armée** (or the Vendôme Column), constructed by Gondouin and Lepère in 1806–10 in the style of Trajan's Column in Rome to replace an equestrian statue of Louis XIV by Girardon (the left foot of which is in the Musée Carnavalet).

History of the Colonne de la Grande Armée

Spiraling up the 43.50m high column is a band of bronze bas-reliefs, designed by Bergeret and made from the metal of 1250 Russian and Austrian cannon captured at the Battle of Austerlitz in 1805. The statue of Napoléon at the summit is a copy by Dumont (1863) of the original by Chaudet torn down by the royalists in 1814. The present statue narrowly escaped destruction in 1871 when a group of Communards, encouraged by the artist Gustave Courbet, demolished the column. Courbet went into exile in Switzerland after being condemned to finance the re-erection of the column in 1875 and died in Switzerland in 1877.

The once fashionable **Rue de la Paix** (now lined with travel agencies and airline offices) leads north to the Pl. de l'Opéra (see Ch. 24). Turn right down Rue Casanova towards the Place du Marché-St-Honoré for an alternative route back to Rue St-Honoré and yet another aspect of the *quartier*. The old market place has been transformed with a building by Ricardo Bofill featuring columns and glass but Rue du Marché-St-Honoré has retained some of the neighbourhood atmosphere. On the corner of the Place and Rue is the site of a Dominican convent where the Jacobin Club met in 1789–94 (now a restaurant).

St-Roch

Further east on Rue St-Honoré, steps ascend to St-Roch (**Map 2; 8**). Hemmed in by buildings and on a narrow street, the impact of this fine Baroque church is lost yet it is one of the largest churches in Paris and rich in paintings and monuments. From the 17C–19C, this was a wealthy and elegant *quartier*.

History of St-Roch

The body of the church, with a classical layout, was begun between 1653–90 to plans by Jacques Lemercier, and was finally completed in 1719 thanks to a generous donation from the banker John Law. In the meantime (1706–10), Jules Hardouin-Mansart added the circular Chapel of the Virgin to the north. The elegant façade was the work of Robert de Cotte, 1736–38. The church was consecrated in 1740, then extended further with the Chapel of the Calvary (c 1750) to produce a dramatic sequence of Baroque spaces. Between 1750 and 1770, at the initiative of Curé Jean-Baptiste Marduel, St-Roch was endowed with a grandiose ensemble of painted and sculpted decoration of which only a sample remains as many were lost at the Revolution. New works were commissioned in the 19C and there are numerous interesting furnishings and monuments, some acquired from defunct churches. The organ case dates from 1752 although the instrument has been modified several times. The stalls and the upper part of the pulpit are 18C. The total length of the interior is an impressive 126m.

To the left of the entrance is a medallion of the dramatist *Corneille* (1606–84), who is buried in the church. In the first chapel in the right aisle (east) are a bust of *François de Créquy* (d. 1687) by Coysevox and the *tomb of the Comte d'Harcourt* (d. 1666) by Renard. The second chapel contains a statue of *Cardinal Dubois* (d. 1723) by G. Coustou and a monument, by Huez, to the astronomer *Maupertuis* (1698–1759). In the dome of the Chapel of the Virgin is a restored painting of the *Assumption* by Jean-Baptiste Pierre, 1756, and *Glory*, by Falconet (1756), in stucco against the arcade, was part of a group replaced by the marble *Nativity* by Michel Anguier, from Val-de-Grâce. There are also 17C paintings by E. Le Sueur and Claude Vignon, and 18C works by Germain Drouais and Jean Restout. The **Communion Chapel** has a curious tabernacle inspired by the temple in Jerusalem (c 1840), and some fine stained glass depicting St Denis the Areopagite (1849) by Régnier.

Continuing around the church, on the west side, on the last pillar of the ambulatory, is a bust of *Le Nôtre* (d. 1707) by Coysevox. In the transept is a plaster of *St Andrew* by Pradier (1823), and a statue of *St Augustin* by Huez (1766); also a canvas of *St Denis Preaching* by Joseph-Marie Vien, 1767 and 19C murals. The next chapel contains a monument to the *Abbé de l'Epée* (see Ch. 7). The 3rd chapel (beyond the transept) contains the remains of a monument to *Pierre Mignard* (1610–95) by Jean-Baptiste II Lemoyne, 1744. And in the last chapel is a painting by Théodore Chassériau.

The eastern section of Rue St-Honoré is where Napoléon suppressed the Royalist rising of 5 October 1795 and, at no. 163, a plaque reminds us that Joan of Arc was wounded near this spot. At the junction with Av. de l' Opéra is Pl. André-Malraux, with a view northwest towards the Opéra and two fountains by Davioud. Rue de Rohan runs a short distance south to Rue de Rivoli, to the arch leading to Pl. du Carrousel. Opposite is the **Théâtre Français** (Map 8; 1), usually known as the **Comédie-Française**.

History of the Comédie-Française

As an institution the Comédie-Française dates from the amalgamation in 1680 of the Hôtel de Bourgogne actors with Molière's old company, which had already absorbed the Théâtre du Marais. In 1812 Napoléon signed a decree (in

Moscow) reorganising the Comédie-Française, which is still a private company although controlled by a director nominated by the government and enjoying a state subsidy. The present theatre was built in 1786–90 by Victor Louis, but largely remodelled and restored several times, the last in 1974.

In the foyer is the seated statue of *Voltaire* by Houdon and the chair in which Molière was sitting when acting in *Le Malade Imaginaire* and taken fatally ill. The theatre also owns various statues of actors and dramatists, including *Talma* by David d'Angers, *Dumas fils* by Carpeaux, *Mirabeau* by Rodin, and a statue of *George Sand* by Clésinger; also the portrait of *Talma* by Delacroix and other paintings by Lemoyne, Caffieri, Van Loo, Mignard and Coypel. The auditorium ceiling was painted by Albert Besnard (1913). (Occasional visits organised by the Monuments Historiques.)

An inscription high up on the corner of Rue de Valois (on the eastern side of Palais-Royal) marks the site of the Salle de Spectacle du Palais-Cardinal, occupied by Molière's company from 1661 to 1673, and by the Académie Royale de Musique from 1673 until a fire in 1763.

The Palais-Royal

Adjoining the Théâtre Français is the Palais-Royal. This name applies not only to the original palace but also to the extensive range of buildings and galleries surrounding the gardens to the north. This area has a fascinating history and the delightful enclosed pedestrian oasis is entered from neighbouring streets by several passages.

History of the Palais-Royal

The Palais-Royal proper, originally known as the Palais-Cardinal, was designed by Jacques Lemercier in 1634–39 for Richelieu, Louis XIII's chief minister, to be near the Louvre. The Cardinal (d. 1642) bequeathed it to the king, who died soon afterwards (1643). Anne of Austria (d. 1666) then regent, took up residence there with her sons Louis XIV and Philippe d'Orléans, and called it Palais-Royal. They had to beat a hasty retreat during the Fronde in 1648 and when Louis XIV returned he installed himself at the Louvre. Queen Henrietta Maria, widow of Charles I of England, and her daughter lived in the palace, which was altered by Mansart.

In 1763 fire destroyed the east wing and the theatre. The houses and galleries around the gardens were the work of the architect Victor Louis. They were built as a speculative venture in 1781–86 by Philippe-Egalité, descendent of the Orléans side of the royal family, who was heavily in debt, and let out as shops and cafés. He was also responsible for the Théâtre-Français, and the Théâtre du Palais-Royal, in the northwest corner dates from the same period.

Over the years the cafés became at different times a rendezvous for political activists, literati and various insalubrious activities, since the police were excluded from entry. On 13 July 1789 Camille Desmoulins delivered in the gardens the fiery harangue which precipitated the fall of the Bastille the following day, and Charlotte Corday purchased the knife to kill Marat in one of the boutiques here.

The name then changed to the Palais-Egalité and it became government offices only to return, in 1814, to the Orléans family and its earlier name. It was the residence of Louis-Philippe until 1832 but in 1848 it was plundered by revolutionaries. The palace was rebuilt by Chabrol in 1872–76 after damage during the Commune. It is now occupied by the Conseil d'Etat and the Ministère de la Culture et de la Communication.

The buildings in the **Cour de l'Horloge**, facing Pl. du Palais-Royal, were erected by Constant d'Ivry, with sculptures by Pajou and Franceschi. The façade on the north side, overlooking the Cour d'Honneur, was completed by Fontaine, who also restored the east and west wings. The so-called **Galerie des Proues** (prows) on the east, is the only relic of Lemercier's 17C building. To the north, the Cour d'Honneur is separated from the gardens by the Galerie d'Orléans, a double Doric colonnade by Fontaine (1829–31), which was restored and cleared of its shops in 1935. In 1985–86, Daniel Buren's 250 puzzling truncated black-and-white fluted columns of differing heights, above and below ground, were installed in the Cour d'Honneur; and Pol Bury's mobile steel spheres animate the pools of the Galerie d'Orléans.

The large rectangular enclosed **gardens**, less frequented than others in the centre of Paris, were renovated in 1992. South is the Cour d'Honneur, north the Galerie Beaujolais, on the west the Galerie de Montpensier, and opposite the Galerie de Valois. Enfilades of limes planted in 1970 flank a formal parterre, often planted with tulips, and a fountain. Under the arcades on three sides are specialist and antique shops, and restaurants, creating an altogether harmonious ensemble. The *Grand Véfour*, at nos 79–82 Galerie de Beaujolais, was the fashionable rendezvous of writers in the Second Empire and is now a restaurant of high repute. In 1785, there was museum of waxworks at 17 Galerie de Montpensier, founded by Curtius, Mme Tussaud's uncle. The *Café du Caveau* (nos 89–92) was the meeting place of the partisans and past residents include the writers Colette and Jean Cocteau.

Immediately east of the Palais-Royal is the Rue de Valois, with (nos 1–3) the Pavillon du Palais-Royal (1766); at nos 6–8, once the Hôtel Melusine, the first meetings of the French Academy took place in 1638–43. The ox sculptured above the door recalls its period as the restaurant Boeuf à la Mode from 1792 to 1936.

In the parallel street to the east, Rue Croix-des-Petits-Champs, is the entrance to the **Banque de France** (**Map 8; 1**), founded in 1800 and moved here in 1811. The buildings incorporate the former Hôtel de la Vrillière, built by Mansart in 1635–38 and restored by Robert de Cotte in 1713–19, later known as the Hôtel de Toulouse from its occupancy by the Comte de Toulouse, son of Louis XIV and Mme de Montespan. Within the bank is the profusely decorated Galerie Dorée, one of the first of its kind in the 17C (occasional visits organised by the Monuments Historiques).

To the northeast of the Bank lies the circular **Pl. des Victoires**, laid out by Jules Hardouin-Mansart in 1685; the surrounding houses were designed by Pradot. The equestrian statue of *Louis XIV* by Bosio (1822) replaces the original, destroyed in 1792; the bas-reliefs on the pedestal depict the *Passage of the Rhine*, and *Louis XIV Distributing Decorations*.

Immediately northwest in the surprisingly provincial-looking Pl. des Petits-Pères, is **Notre-Dame-des-Victoires**, or the church of the Petits-Pères, dedicated in 1629 by Louis XIII to commemorate the capture of La Rochelle from the Huguenots in the previous year. On the site of a former chapel, it was begun by Pierre Le Muet in 1629–32; Libéral Bruant designed the transept and last bay of the nave 1642–66, and it was completed only in 1740 by Sylvain Cartault. The plan of the interior derives from the Gesù in Rome, with communicating chapels around the nave. Every interior wall is plastered with ex-voto tablets and the organ case and carved stalls date from 1740. The second chapel on the left contains the tomb of the composer Jean-Baptiste Lully (1633–87) by Pierre Cotton, with a bust by Gaspard Collignon; in the choir are seven paintings (1746–55) by Carle van Loo.

The adjoining street leads north to the **Palais de la Bourse** or Stock Exchange (group visits only, ☎ 01 49 27 10 00). Built by Brongniart and Labarre in 1808–27, it is a typical Neo-classical building of the period with a grandiose Corinthian peristyle to which the north and south wings were added in 1903.

Rue du Quatre-Septembre to the north was driven in 1864 through an old district which has kept some interesting houses around Rue Feydeau, built on Louis-XIII fortifications, and the Rue des Colonnes. Rue Vivienne leads south from the Bourse along the east side (right) of the Bibliothèque Nationale (see Ch. 18), where there are several 17C–18C houses.

On the left, at the corner of Rue Colbert, stands part of the **Hôtel de Nevers**, built by Mazarin in 1649 to house his library. Further on is a fountain of 1708, and beyond (right) in the Sq. Louvois, the Fontaine Louvois, by the younger Visconti (1844). The Square was laid out in 1839 on the site of a theatre (the Salle Louvois) built in 1794, which housed the Opéra until 1820. No. 12 Rue Chabanais, immediately to the west was the setting of Toulouse-Lautrec's painting *Au Salon* (1894).

Continue south on Rue de Richelieu passing at the corner of Rue Molière the Fontaine Molière by Visconti (1844): the dramatist is by Seurre and the figures of Comedy by Pradier. The street ends at the Pl. André-Malraux.

18 • The Bibliothèque Nationale de France-Cardinal de Richelieu

■ Arrondissement: 75002

Bourse; Pyramides, 4 Septembre

Auber

This is a banking/stockbroking area, and local restaurants are well-patronised at midday.

Le Grand Colbert, 2, Rue Vivienne ☎ 01 42 86 87 88. A pretty place in the restored Galérie Colbert, ££

Le Vaudeville, 29 Rue Vivienne, ☎ 01 40 20 04 62. Part of the Flo group, Art Deco interior, speedy and popular, £

A Priori Thé, In Galerie Vivienneé ☎ 01 42 97 48 75. Another pretty café/teashop which closes at 18.00, £

Rôtisserie Monsigny, 1 Rue Monsigny, ☎ 01 42 96 16 61. Near the Banque de France, popular with locals for lunch and but also good after-theatre meals; traditional cooking by Jacques Cagna, ££

Canard d'Avril, 5 Rue Paul

Lelong, ☎ 01 42 36 26 08.
South-western French cooking
inevitably includes hearty duck
specialities, £
Au Pays de Cocagne, 1 rue Réamur,

☎ 01 40 13 81 81. A young, modern restaurant in the Espace Tarn
(Tarn Tourist Office), therefore also
south-western cuisine, £

Bibliothèque Nationale de France-Cardinal de Richelieu

The Bibliothèque Nationale de France-Cardinal de Richelieu (National Library of France; **Map 3; 7**) has been here since the 17C and, with the British Library, is one of the two largest in Europe. But in 1998 there was a huge upheaval when a major part of the collection was transferred to the new Bibliothèque National de France-François Mitterand, east of Gare d'Austerlitz (see Ch. 6), changing the emphasis of the attractive Richelieu-Louvois site and prompting the reorganisation of its space. An Institut National d'Histoire d'Art created in this location brings together various national collections. Special collections remain at the old building, among them manuscripts, prints, photographs, maps and plans, music, coins, medals, antiquities, and the collection from the performing arts. There are several areas open to the public, including the Musée du Cabinet des Médailles et Antiques and the temporary exhibition rooms, Galerie Mansart and Galerie Mazarine.

The main entrance is in the west façade at 58 Rue de Richelieu and 2 Rue Louvois (☎ 01 47 03 81 26). Look out also for the renovated covered passages behind the Bibliothèque. In the recently renovated Galerie Colbert (1826), off Rue des Petits Champs, is the commecial showcase of the Library. The adjacent Galerie Vivienne (1823) (between Rues Vivenne and des Petits Champs) is a smart shopping arcade.

History of the Bibliothèque Nationale de France

The buildings of the Bibliothèque Nationale de France consist of a group of 17C *hôtels particuliers* added to and amended until the end of the 19C. In 1666 Colbert installed the Bibliothèque du Roi in one of his houses on Rue Vivienne, next to the Hôtel Mazarin which had been added to by Mansart in 1654. It was first opened to the public for two days a week in 1692. In 1724 the buildings were extended by Robert de Cotte and in 1826 the library spread into Galerie Mazarin, the former Hôtel Chevry and Hôtel Tubeuf, built by Le Muet in 1635, up to Rue des Petits-Champs. Between 1857 and 1873, Henri Labrouste carried out a number of modifications to the building, including the delicate cast- and wrought-iron frame supporting a cluster of domes suspended over the Main Reading Room.

Formerly known as the Bibliothèque Royale and the Bibliothèque Impériale, it originated in the private collections of the French kings. Largely dispersed at the end of the Hundred Years War, the Library was refounded by Louis XII and moved to Blois. During the next two centuries it was at Fontainebleau, and then Paris, before finding its present home in Rue de Richelieu. Guillaume Budé (c 1468–1540) had earlier been appointed the first Royal Librarian. It was enriched by the purchase or gift of many famous private libraries and smaller collections (including that of Colbert), and at the Revolution its range was extended with the confiscation of books from numerous convents and châteaux. In 1793 an act was passed that a copy of every book, newspaper, etc printed in France should be deposited by the publishers in the Bibliothèque Nationale.

The main entrance vestibule is on the right of the Cour d'Honneur. The **Reading Room**, opposite the main entrance, covered by Labrouste's nine faience cupolas (which seats 259 readers as against the 2000 in the new Bibliothèque Nationale-F. Mitterand) can now be glimpsed through the doors (guided visits in French, 14.30 first Tuesday of every month). **Galerie Mansart**, to the right at the foot of the stairs, was formerly Mazarin's sculpture gallery—note his arms above the door and the carved foliage and paintings by Grimaldi. The **Cabinet des Estampes** beyond contains about 11 million items varying from master prints to postcards, posters and wallpaper samples.

The **Department of Music** contains two million works including collections of musical scores, books on music, and MSS (among them Mozart's *Don Giovanni*) previously in the Library of the Conservatoire de Musique. The Manuscripts department has an awesome collection, with more than 530,000 MSS, of which some 10,000 are illuminated, ranging from the oldest book, an Egyptian manuscript c 2000 BC, to manuscripts, by authors such as Marcel Proust and Jean-Paul Sartre. The Department of Maps and Plans has 90000 items, including 104 globes.

Temporary exhibitions are held frequently, and the permanent collection, the Cabinet des Medailles et Antiques, is in Galeries Mansart and Mazarine.

Musée du Cabinet des Medailles et Antiques

The Musée du Cabinet des Medailles et Antiques, open Mon–Fri 13.00–17.45, Sat 13.00–16.45, Sun 12.00–18.00 (☎ 01 47 03 83 30), has four exhibition rooms on two floors. Take the stairs on the left of the entrance. The collection brings together the collections of the kings of France. Founded in the 16C, it contains objects known to have been in royal hands some time before that date, and has over 500,000 coins and medals, from Antiquity to the present day and some 30,000 antiquities and other objects, many of outstanding quality.

Near the entrance is a Parian marble torso of Aphrodite (Hellenistic period), while in showcases on this and on the mezzanine floor are examples of French and foreign coins and medals, engraved cameos and jewels. Notable is the *Grand Camée*, from the Sainte-Chapelle, representing the Apotheosis of Germanicus, with Tiberius and Livia—the largest antique cameo known; the aquamarine intaglio of *Julia, daughter of Titus*, a particularly fine carved portrait; an engraved Chaldaean stone (1100 BC), found near Baghdad; the agate nef (incense boat) from St-Denis; Sassanide Dish (c 5–7 AD); the sardonyx Cup of Ptolemy; the Patère de Rennes (a Roman gold dish found in 1774); a Merovingian chalice and oblong paten (6C), from Gourdon, in the Charollais; a bust of Constantine the Great, once the head of the cantor's wand at the Sainte-Chapelle; and a series of ivory chessmen (11C–12C), once reputed to have belonged to Charlemagne (d. 814).

Other cases contain Renaissance medals and bronzes; Egyptian terracottas and painted limestone statuettes; Roman bronze statuettes; ancient arms and armour, and domestic utensils; Greek and Etruscan vases, including a red-figured amphora, signed Amasis; cyclix of Arcesilaus, king of Cyrene; vase of Berenice (239–227 BC), from Benghazi, and other ceramics; gold objects from the tomb of Childeric I, at Tournai; ivory consular diptychs, and Byzantine diptychs; gold bullae of Charles II of Anjou, king of Naples (1285–1309), of Baldwin I, Emperor of Constantinople in 1204–06, and of Edmund, Earl of Lancaster, titular king of Sicily, 1255–63; gold coins found at Chécy (Loiret); a Celtic bracelet (Aurillac; 5C–6C); a silver hoard from the temple of Mercurius Canetonensis

(Berthouville, Eure), including silver figurines and vessels of the 2C BC and others of the best Greek period.

Also displayed is the so-called Throne of Dagobert, on which the kings of France were crowned: a Roman curule (seat of office) chair of bronze, with arms and back added in the 12C by Suger. The restored Salon Louis XV, decorated by Van Loo and Natoire, with *dessus de portes* by Boucher, has its original coin cabinets.

19 • Place du Palais-Royal to Les Halles

■   Arrondissements: 75001, 75002, 75004

🚇   Palais Royal-Musée du Louvre, Louvre-Rivoli, Les Halles,
     Etienne-Marcel, Châtelet

🚊   Châtelet-les-Halles

 Au Chien qui Fume, 33 Rue du Pont-Neuf, ☎ 01 42 36 07 42. A good old-timer going back to 1740, serving traditional dishes and sea food, £

Au Pied de Cochon, 6 Rue Coquillière, ☎ 01 42 36 11 75. The 24-hour brasserie established when the produce market still functioned; popular but a bit overpriced, ££

L'Alsace aux Halles, 16 Rue Coquillière, ☎ 01 42 36 74 24. Filling food from Alsace, ££

Benoit, 20 Rue St-Martin, ☎ 01 42 72 25 76. Pricey classic bistrot cooking, £££

Bistro Caveau François Villon, 64 Rue de l'Arbre Sec, ☎ 01 42 36 10 92. Authentic setting and not too expensive, ££

Bistrot de la Place, 2 Pl. du Marché Ste-Catherine, ☎ 01 42 78 21 32. The charming square and terrace are the main attributes, £–££.

Bistrot du Louvre, 48 Rue d'Argout, ☎ 01 45 08 47 46. Modern, courteous and unpretentious, ££

Less expensive are:

Fish and Fun, 55 Blvd de Sébastopol, ☎ 01 42 21 10 10. Friendly, quick fish joint, £

La Grille Montorgeuil, 50 Rue Montorgeuil, ☎ 01 42 33 21 21. Brash, but good value, £

Le P'tit Gavroche, 15 Rye Ste-Croix-de-la-Bretonnerie, ☎ 01 48 87 74 26. Basic and hearty, £

Ostréa, 4, Rue Sauval, ☎ 01 40 26 08 07. Seafood brasserie tucked away near Les Halles, reasonably priced, £

Pharamond, Rue la Grande Truanderie, ☎ 01 42 33 06 72. A classic bistrot, wonderful Art Nouveau décor, with reliable cooking, ££

Louis Philippe Café, 66 Quai de l'Hôtel de Ville, ☎ 01 42 72 29 42. Attractive setting, terrace, £

Le Temps de Cerises, 31 Rue de Cerisaie, ☎ 01 42 72 08 63. Small and friendly café, weekday lunch good value, £

Relais du Sud-Ouest, 154 Rue St-Honoré, ☎ 01 42 60 62 01. Reliable, a real local lunchtime place, £

This chapter covers the modern quarter of Les Halles and the important old churches of St-Germain-l'Auxerrois and St-Eustache. As always in Paris, the picturesque and historic abut the crass and commercial, a case in point being Rue St-Denis.

Walking east from Pl. du Palais-Royal, with the façade of the Palais-Royal on your left (see Ch. 17), follow Rue St-Honoré along the north side of the **Louvre des Antiquaires** (☎ 01 42 97 27 00). This building of 1852, formerly the department store of the Grands Magasins du Louvre, was acquired in 1975 by the British Post Office Staff Superannuation Fund as an investment, then gutted. Since 1978 it has accommodated, on three floors, some 250 professional antique-dealers' stalls, open to the public daily from 11.00–19.00, except Monday (also closed on Sunday from mid July–mid September). They can organise transport, settle customs formalities and provide certificates of authenticity, etc. Frequent lectures and exhibitions.

To the east is the classical-Mannerist **Temple de l'Oratoire** (1621–30, 18C façade), designed by Clément Métezeau the younger, and in which Jacques Lemercier and François Mansart had a hand. Originally the French mother church for the Congregation of the Oratory, it was assigned by Napoléon in 1811 to the Calvinists. In Rue de Rivoli is a monument of 1889 by Crauk to Admiral Coligny (1519–72), the chief victim of the massacre of St. Bartholomew, wounded nearby.

Returning to Rue-St-Honoré, turn right (east) to find the **Fontaine du Trahoir**, its stalactites and shells surrounding a nymph, sculpted by Boziot. It was rebuilt by Soufflot in 1778, replacing one by Goujon. Rue du Louvre leads north to the small Pl. des Deux-Ecus. Off Rue Jean-Jacques-Rousseau to the southwest is the once elegant **Véro-Dodat arcade** (1822), named after Messieurs Véro and Dodat. To the east of Pl. des Deux-Ecus is the refurbished circular mid-18C building, the **Bourse du Commerce** (Map 8; 1). Formerly the Corn Exchange, it received its metal-framed dome in 1811 and was remodelled in 1888. It can be visited on weekdays. The fresco representing international commerce around the upper part of the interior hall has been entirely renovated as has the glass dome. (Guided visits, ☎ 01 55 65 55 65.)

A fluted Doric column adjoining its southeast side was once part of the **Hôtel de la Reine** (later Hôtel de Soissons, in the garden of which stock-jobbing or brokering took place from 1720), built for Catherine de Médicis in 1572 on the site of the earlier Hôtel d'Orléans which had belonged to Blanche of Castile (d. 1252). The column may have been used as an astrologer's tower.

Les Halles

The Bourse de Commerce is now the only remaining evidence in Paris of the Halles Centrales, which by mid-1969 had been moved to extensive modern markets at Rungis (c 11km south of Paris and north of Orly airport). Markets had stood here since the early 12C, but the ten huge pavilions constructed by Victor Baltard (1805–74) in the 1850s immediately to the east, together with two additional market halls completed in 1936, were demolished by 1974 (with the exception of no. 8, which was re-erected at Nogent-sur-Marne). What Zola described as *Le ventre de Paris* is no more, although it is still referred to as the *trou* or hole.

The radical redevelopment of the whole area of Les Halles was much criticised on aesthetic grounds, but there were prodigious technical problems to be resolved such as the underground railway-station, a major intersection of the RER system, at the bottom of the *trou*; road tunnels, underground parking, air-conditioning plants, skillfully disguised behind the façades of houses; and the erection of buildings, which to some extent harmonise with the old. A number of architects took part in the project, including for a time Ricardo Bofill.

The **Forum des Halles** (Map 8; 2), its ribbed and glazed courtyard forming the sunken lid to the *trou*, and embellished by curious pink marble statuary entitled *Pyègemalion* (sic), by the Argentinian sculptor Julio Silva, has had a very mixed reception since it was inaugurated in September 1979 and is now somewhat run down.

To the north and east of the Forum are terraces on which mirrored mushroom-shaped pavilions have sprung up. Gardens covering nearly 5 hectares have been laid out to the west, planted with 600 trees while plants trail over metal structures and 11 fountains play along. There is a sundial and a 'listening' head, *l'Ecoute*, by Henri de Miller, a large greenhouse, alleys named after poets, and a children's play garden of six fantasy worlds designed by the sculptor, Claude Lalanne.

Seen across the flattened area and gardens, St-Eustache comes into its own, as do the Bourse du Commerce and the astrological tower. Nearby, the restored Fontaine des Innocents (see below) is also set off to advantage. There are large areas of pedestrian precincts east and west of the transverse Blvd de Sébastopol, and the reopening of the Pompidou centre has revived this district, which is a hub of activity of every kind.

From the western side of the Bourse du Commerce, Rue du Louvre continues north. On the right is the **Hôtel des Postes** (1880–84), the main Post Office of Paris: opposite, in the elegant Hôtel d'Ollone (built in 1639 and altered in 1730), is the Caisse d'Epargne (or Savings Bank).

History of the Hôtel des Postes

From the 13C to the 18C the University of Paris was responsible for the postal service for private citizens, while from 1461 the royal mail was carried by relays of post riders. In 1719 the University lost its privilege and all mail was controlled by the royal service. In 1757 the postal headquarters was in the Hôtel d'Hervart.

From just north of the Bourse du Commerce, heading east, in Rue Coquillière are numerous restaurants, including *Au Pied de Cochon* where all-night revellers used to eat oysters for breakfast when the old market was in full swing.

St-Eustache

Dominating the area is the splendid silhouette of St-Eustache (**Map 8; 2**). Begun in 1532, perhaps by Pierre Lemercier, it was consecrated in 1637. It appears to be a Gothic structure with supporting flying buttresses but, typical of this transitional period, on closer inspection it is seen to have Renaissance details and decorations.

History of St-Eustache

The Neo-classical main west doorway, completed only in 1754–88, is totally out of keeping with the rest of the church, but both transepts have round-headed doorways (c 1638–40), the decoration restored. A passage from Rue Montmartre leads to the north transept. The open-work bell-tower, known as the Plomb de St-Eustache, above the crossing, has lost its spire, and above the Lady Chapel in the east is a small tower built in 1640 and rebuilt in 1875.

The church was the scene of the riotous Festival of Reason in 1793, and in 1795 became the Temple of Agriculture. St-Eustache has always been noted for its music. Here Berlioz conducted the first performance of his *Te Deum* (1855) and Liszt his *Messe Solenelle* (1866) and it is now the venue of an organ festival in June and July.

The **interior** is a striking combination of Gothic plan and Renaissance decorative motifs. The nave is short and the double aisles and chapels continue round the choir, while the wide transepts do not extend beyond the chapel walls. Square piers are flanked by three storeys of superimposed orders, the vaulting is Flamboyant with heavy pendant bosses, and above the high arcades is a small gallery. In the chapels are restored paintings from the time of Louis XIII and the 11 lofty windows of the apse were executed by Soulignac (1631), possibly from cartoons by Philippe de Champaigne. The churchwardens' pew was designed by Pierre le Pautre and carved by Carteaux, c 1720 and the unadorned stalls were acquired from the convent of Picpus (see Ch. 33). The **organ**, with an ornate case by Victor Baltard (1854), is one of the most important in Paris.

The second chapel on the south, the musicians' chapel, commemorates Rameau, Franz Liszt and Mozart's mother. On the trumeau of the transept door-way is a 16C statue of St John and the second choir chapel has a *Pietà* attributed to Luca Giordano. The glass of the fifth chapel, which features St Anthony, was given by the Société de la Charcuterie de France. On the altar of the Lady Chapel is a *Virgin* by Pigalle (1748) accompanied by murals by Thomas Couture (1856).

As you return by the north aisle, in the first choir chapel is the very fine but incomplete *tomb of Colbert* (d. 1683), designed by Le Brun, with statues of *Colbert* and *Fidelity* by Coysevox, and of *Abundance* by Tuby. In the next chapel is a painting of the *Supper at Emmaus*, school of Rubens, a 17C French painting of the burial of a martyr. *The Ecstasy of the Virgin* (c 1627) in the third chapel is by Rutilio Manetti. Above the north-west door is the *Martyrdom of St Eustace* by Simon Vouet.

Rue de Turbigo leads northeast from St-Eustache towards Pl. de la République, soon reaching Rue Etienne-Marcel, in which, to the left (at no. 20), rises the **Tour de Jean-sans-Peur**, a graceful defensive tower of c 1400 once incorporated in the Hôtel de Bourgogne. Part of this mansion (see no. 29) was used from 1548 until the turn of the 18C as a theatre, where plays by Corneille and Racine were performed.

The next street to the east, **Rue St-Denis**, is one of the oldest routes in Paris. Parallel to the old Roman road, now Rue St-Martin, it leads to the Royal necropolis of St-Denis (see Ch. 39). Partly pedestrianised, this narrow, bustling, street is lined with sandwich bars and seedy shops. At no. 135, in its northern section, an inscription indicates the former position of the Porte St-Denis or Porte aux Peintres, a gateway in the walls of Philippe Auguste. No. 142 is the Fontaine de la Reine (1730). On no. 133 are statues from the medieval Hôpital de St-Jacques, once on this site.

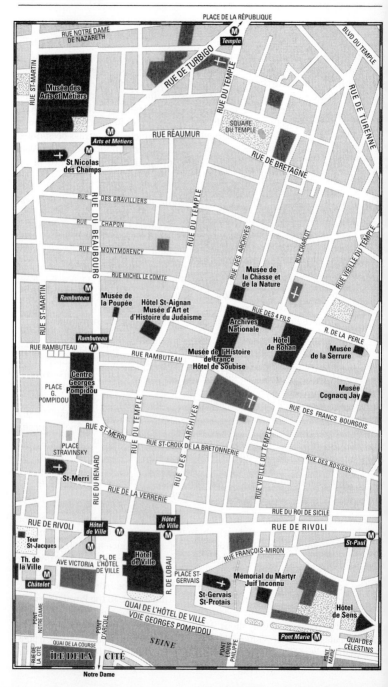

PLACE DE LA RÉPUBLIQUE

RUE NOTRE DAME DE NAZARETH

Temple Ⓜ

RUE DE TURBIGO

BLVD DU TEMPLE

RUE ST-MARTIN

Musée des Arts et Métiers

RUE DU TEMPLE

SQUARE DU TEMPLE

RUE DE TURENNE

RUE RÉAUMUR

Ⓜ Arts et Métiers

RUE DE BRETAGNE

St Nicolas des Champs

RUE DES GRAVILLIERS

RUE DU BEAUBOURG

RUE CHAPON

RUE DU TEMPLE

RUE DES ARCHIVES

RUE CHARLOT

RUE VIEILLE DU TEMPLE

MONTMORENCY

RUE MICHEL LE COMTE

Musée de la Chasse et de la Nature

RUE ST-MARTIN

Ⓜ Rambuteau

Musée de la Poupée

Hôtel St-Aignan Musée d'Art et d'Histoire du Judaïsme

RUE DES 4 FILS

Archives Nationale

Hôtel de Rohan

R. DE LA PERLE

Musée de la Serrure

Ⓜ Rambuteau

RUE RAMBUTEAU

RUE RAMBUTEAU

Musée de l'Histoire de l France Hôtel de Soubise

Musée Cognacq Jay

Centre Georges Pompidou

PLACE G. POMPIDOU

RUE DES FRANCS BOURGEOIS

RUE ST-MERRI

RUE DU TEMPLE

RUE ST-CROIX DE LA BRETONNERIE

RUE DES ARCHIVES

RUE VIEILLE DU TEMPLE

RUE DES ROSIERS

PLACE STRAVINSKY

RUE DU RENARD

St-Merri

RUE DE LA VERRERIE

RUE DU ROI DE SICILE

RUE DE RIVOLI

Hôtel de Ville Ⓜ

Hôtel de Ville Ⓜ

RUE DE RIVOLI

Tour St-Jacques

St-Paul Ⓜ

Th. de la Ville

Ⓜ Châtelet

AVE VICTORIA

PL. DE L'HÔTEL DE VILLE

Hôtel de Ville

R. DE LOBAU

PLACE ST-GERVAIS

RUE FRANÇOIS-MIRON

Mémorial du Martyr Juif Inconnu

St-Gervais St-Protais

Hôtel de Sens

QUAI DE L'HÔTEL DE VILLE

VOIE GEORGES POMPIDOU

Pont Marie Ⓜ

QUAI DES CÉLESTINS

PONT NOTRE DAME

PONT D'ARCOLE

SEINE

PONT LOUIS PHILIPPE

PONT MARIE

QUAI DE LA COURSE

RUE DE LA CITÉ

ÎLE DE LA CITÉ

Notre Dame

THE MARAIS

Oberkampf

BLVD J. FERRY

BLVD VOLTAIRE

BLVD DU TEMPLE

Filles du Calvaire

RUE OBERKAMPF

RUE AMELOT

BLVD VOLTAIRE

St-Ambroise

St-Ambroise

0 — 200 yards
0 — 200 metres

St Sébastien Froissart

RUE SAINT-SÉBASTIEN

Richard Lenoir

N

BOULEVARD BEAUMARCHAIS

RUE ST-CLAUDE

St Denis du St Sacrement

RUE DE TURENNE

RUE AMELOT

RUE DU CHEMIN VERT

BOULEVARD RICHARD LENOIR

RUE SEDAINE

RUE ST-GILLES

Chemin Vert

Bréguet Sabin

Musée Carnavalet

R. DES FRANCS BOURGEOIS

R. DE TURENNE

PLACE DES VOSGES

RUE DE LA ROQUETTE

Bastille

Hôtel de Sully Caisse Nat. des Monuments Historiques et des Sites

RUE DE BIRAGUE

Musée Victor Hugo

Bastille

RUE SAINT-ANTOINE

PLACE DE LA BASTILLE

RUE DE CHARENTON

St-Paul St-Louis

Bastille

Opéra de Paris Bastille

VILLAGE ST-PAUL

RUE BEAUTREILLIS

Bastille

BOULEVARD HENRI IV

BOULEVARD BOURDON

BLVD DE LYON

RUE DE LYON

BLVD DE LA BASTILLE

QUAI DES CÉLESTINS

Bibl. de l'Arsenal

You then reach on the left **St-Leu-St-Gilles**, built in 1235, the nave reconstructed after 1319. The aisles were added in the 16C; the choir, still partly Gothic, in 1611 (and reconstructed in 1858–61 to make way for the adjacent boulevard). The façade and windows were remodelled in 1727 and a crypt excavated in 1780. The church contains three alabaster reliefs (in the sacristy entrance) and a sculptured group of St Anne and the Virgin, by Jean Bullant (second south chapel). The organ gallery is by Nicolas Raimbert (1659).

Going south on Rue St-Denis you reach the small Sq. Joachim du Bellay, on part of the site of the medieval Cimetière des Innocents, the main burial ground of Paris until 1785, when the remains, probably including those of La Fontaine, were transferred to the catacombs (see Ch. 7). Traces of the arches of the cemetery galleries are still to be seen on nos 11 and 13 in the Rue des Innocents.

The restored Renaissance **Fontaine des Innocents** was originally erected in 1548 in the neighbouring Rue St-Denis by Pierre Lescot, with bas-reliefs by Jean Goujon (now in the Louvre). It was remodelled and set up here by Payet c 1788 and the south side was decorated by Pajou.

South of the Fontaine des Innocents are several small streets, including Rue des Lombards, intersected by Blvd de Sébastopol which leads south to Place du Chatelet (see Ch. 21).

20 • The Beaubourg and the Centre Pompidou

■   Arrondissement: 75004
🔒   Rambuteau, Hôtel de Ville, Châtelet
🚇   Châtelet-Les Halles

Grizzli, 7 Rue St-Martin, ☎ 01 48 87 77 56. Good sturdy regional food, in 1900-style bistrot, £–££

In the Pompidou Centre:
Forum Café on Level 1
Coffee Shop on Level 2; and on

Level 6
Restaurant Georges, ☎ 01 44 78 47 99. A Frères Costes enterprise, as in all the best museums, with zany colour décor, panoramic terrace, open at night (priority entrance for the restaurant), £–££

The reopening of the **Centre Pompidou** (Map 8; 2) has injected a new lease of life into the whole district known as the Beaubourg.

History of the area

Literally translated as beautiful market town, the Beaubourg was once a small rural community, surrounded by vineyards, but it was gathered within the boundaries of the city of Paris when Philippe-Auguste's walls were built in the 13C. The main artery was Rue Beaubourg, and the focus the church of St-Merri. This ancient quarter, still boasting some fine 17C and 18C houses, was carved up in the 19C with the building of Rue Rambuteau and Blvd Sébastopol and by the 1930s had fallen into neglect and was partly demolished. Its character radically altered when the Centre Georges Pompidou opened in 1977.

Bounded to the west by the frankly unsexy Blvd de Sébastopol and Rue du Renard, relics of the old Beaubourg can be found in the narrow streets such as Rue Quincampoix (parallel to the east), although most houses date from the 17C–18C. Pl. Edmond-Michelet opens at the junction with Rue Aubry le Boucher and from here is a diagonal view across Rue St-Martin to the Centre Pompidou (see below) on the Plateau de Beaubourg, a two-hectare site divided between the building and the large sloping piazza. Just north at the junction of Rue Bernard-de-Clairvaux, leading east into the redeveloped Quartier de l'Horloge, and Rue Brantôme, is an imaginative modern clock, with automata, by Jacques Monestier (1979).

Immediately south of the Centre is Pl. Igor-Stravinsky, flanked by relics of the Rue Brisemiche. A novel installation is the **fantasy fountain** with amusing coloured mobile sculptures by Nikki de St Phalle and Jean Tinguely, in keeping with the Pompidou centre but setting up a cruel visual contrast with its neighbour, the church of St-Merri (or St-Merry).

St-Merri

St-Merri (1515–52; **Map 8; 2**), stands at the intersection of the two major Roman axes, the present Rue St-Martin and Rue de la Verrerie. The dingy exterior of the church belies a noble interior which has retained many original furnishings. It replaced at least two older churches that covered the grave of St Médéric of Autun (d. c 700), and was built in Flamboyant Gothic at a time when Renaissance styles were taking over. The porch, although damaged, is carved with pinnacles and friezes. In the 18C the interior was given a Baroque décor. From 1796–1801 it became the Temple of Commerce. The west front is notable for its rich decoration, but the statues are mostly poor replacements of 1842. The northwest turret claims the oldest bell in Paris (1331); the southwest tower lost its top storey in a fire.

The **nave and choir**, like Notre-Dame, are of equal length and have simple quadripartite vaults except over the crossing which has lierne vaults and a pendant boss. A frieze of animals, leaves and figures runs around the nave above the arcades. The window tracery has flame-like curves. There is a double aisle on the right (south)—one for the canons and one for the public, and a single on the left. The church lost its 16C wooden jubé early in the 18C. The Slodtz brothers undertook the sculptured embellishments in the 18C: Michel-Ange Slodtz designed the **pulpit** (1753) and the gilded Glory above the main altar, and added marble veneer and stucco to the choir chapels. The dark oak organ case dates from 1647, modified in the 18C and in 1857. Saint-Saëns was organist here.

Immediately to the right of the entrance is a Renaissance screen, and in the first outer chapel of the south aisle are the remains of the 13C church. Further on is a large **chapel** by Boffrand (1743–44), with three oval cupolas, beautiful bas-reliefs by Paul-Ambroise Slodtz (1758), and a *Supper at Emmaus* by A. Coypel. The 17C painting above the choir's south entrance of the *Virgin and Child* was one of a pair by C. Van Loo, but its opposite number was stolen.

In the **left aisle**, the first chapel contains a 15C tabernacle; the third a *Pietà* attributed to Nicolas Legendre (c 1670); the 4th, a painting by Coypel (1661). From the fifth, a staircase descends to the crypt (1515), which has grotesque corbels and the tombstone of Guillaume le Sueur (d. 1530). The church was decorated with murals in the 19C, some by Chassériau, in the third chapel north of the choir. The painting of *St Merri Liberating Prisoners* in the north transept is by Simon Vouet.

There is some good **stained-glass** contemporary with the church in the upper windows, although much was taken out in the 18C, and the lower windows are mainly 19C. The nave windows belong to the early 16C; outstanding are the two west windows, depicting the life of *St Nicholas of Myre* and of *St Agnes*. The stained glass of the choir and transept is attributed to Pinaigrier and dated c 1540.

The quarter around St-Merri, with its narrow and picturesque alleys, retains several characteristic old houses that survived the rage for demolition during the Halles-Beaubourg redevelopment scheme. Rue des Lombards, named after the Italian bankers and money changers who frequented it in the Middle Ages, continues to the east by the Rue de la Verrerie. It is said that the writer Boccaccio (1313–75), whose mother was French, was born near the junction of Rue des Lombards and Rue St-Martin.

Centre Pompidou

The Centre Georges Pompidou (**Map 8; 2**), was reborn with a great fanfare on 1 January 2000, following a huge campaign of renovation and reorganisation lasting 27 months. Home to the national collection of modern art, one of the most important in the world, its official title is the **Centre National d'Art et de Culture Georges-Pompidou**. It was named after the former president who, in 1969, conceived the idea of a centre to encompass all aspects of modern culture. The hype surrounding its building, the first great project of its kind, tended to overshadow the importance of the collections that it was built to house. The space made available was divided so that only part was built on, and the other part became the lively **Piazza Beaubourg** which slopes down from Rue St-Martin to the main entrance. This has become the theatre of all kinds of street entertainment, bridging the gap between the neighbourhood and the more formal events inside the Centre.

The Centre is proud of its interdisciplinary status which aims to offer the public the widest possible range of 20C culture. It comprises four departments: Le Département du Développement Culturel (DDC) which oversees the whole thing; Le Musée National d'Art Moderne/Centre de Création Industrielle (MNAM/CCI); La Bibliothèque Publique d'Information (BPI), a multi-media free-access public library; and L'Institut de Recherche et Coordination Acoustique-Musique (IRCAM), bringing together musical creation and technological research, housed in a separate building. The Centre also hosts activities such as dance, music, cinema and new technology and a new departure is the *Carrefour de la création*, exploring technological innovation.

• The museum and exhibition centre is open Wed–Sun, 11.00–21.00. Closed Tues and 1 May; (☎ 01 44 78 12 33). There are three types of tickets: National Museum of Modern Art/Centre for Industrial Creation, certain exhibitions, the Brancusi studios and the Panorama; major exhibitions only; or a one-day pass combining both. There is a designer boutique on Level 1, and bookshops on Levels 0 and 4. There are cafés on Levels 1 and 2 and a restaurant on Level 6 (see above). The rearrangement of the Centre has liberated more space on Levels 4 and 5 for the permanent collection of the **Museum of**

Modern Art and Industrial Creation (MNAM/CCI) allowing 1400 works owned by the museum to be on view at any time.

History of the building

The building, arguably the most controversial since the Eiffel Tower, is a 15,000-ton metal box, 166m long, 60m wide, and 42m high and has a glazed surface of 11,000m². Its functional elements—air conditioning, elevators, etc.—are mainly on the exterior, picked out in primary colours. This frees up maximum space inside on seven floors (5 above ground) totaling 70,000m². The Anglo-Italian team that designed the Pompidou Centre included the architects Richard Rogers and Renzo Piano, in association with G. Franchini and the Ove Arup group. Renzo Piano has been in charge of the restructuring.

Following its inauguration on 31 January 1977, the building suffered excessive wear and tear inflicted by a far greater number of visitors than it was designed to accommodate. The complete facelift began in 1995, and involved the piazza and all the areas adjacent to the Centre. One of the most daring features of the building is the external escalator encased in a glazed tube which writhes up the façade, providing access to each of the upper five floors. Previously this drew a huge volume of visitors simply for the ride, but it is now accessible only to ticket-holders (the cost of entry is not excessive).

The **main entrance** to the Centre on Level 0 is from the piazza and escalators take you to the upper floors. There is another entrance on Rue du Renard-Beaubourg to the east. Level 4 houses the **Contemporary Collections** (1960 onwards), and Level 5 the **Historical or Modern Collections** (1905–60). Visitors are channeled to the Historical Collections (Level 5) via the Contemporary Collections (Level 4) in a deliberate attempt to make sure the later works are not overlooked. There is additional space on Levels 1 and 5 for temporary exhibitions. The **Library** (BPI) occupies most of Levels 1, 2 and 3 (over 350,000 volumes, 250,000 transparencies, 12,000 records, reference material, films and video-cassettes plus periodicals, CDs, documentary films, etc.) and Level 1 is reserved for conferences, cinema, theatre, dance and other events.

Musée National d'Art Moderne/ Centre de Création Industrielle

The Musée National d'Art Moderne (MNAM/CCI) is made up of nine sections: Historical, Contemporary, Graphic Arts, Photography, New Media, Art Films, Architecture, Design and a Documentary section. One objective of the much improved layout is to show the parallel developments in these different fields. The examples are selected from some 45,000 works by 4245 artists, architects and designers covering most of 20C artistic creation.

The Historic or Modern Collections

Rooms dedicated to one artist are juxtaposed with other rooms arranged thematically. The main sections relate to Cubism and Modernism, Dadaism, Abstraction, De Stijl and the Bauhaus, and eight rooms are devoted to Surrealism. There are also sections concentrating on Classical Forms and Mature Works (in the 1940s) of artists such as Matisse, Bonnard, Braque, Picasso, and Dubuffet. The last rooms, entitled *Un ultime face-à-face*, feature works from the closing of this period (1950–60) with one room dedicated to Matisse's cutouts. On the exterior terraces are sculptures by Henri Laurens, Joan Miró, and

Alexander Calder. (Works may occasionally be shown in rotation.) The Brancusi workshop is separate building entered from the Piazza (see below).

The Historic or Modern Collections, 1905–60, on Level 5, are introduced by Douanier Rousseau, *La Guerre* (1894) and Picasso, *Petite fille sautant a la corde*, (1950) (**room 1**). Along the wide central area are key works starting with Matisse, *Le Luxe* (1907) contrasting with Picasso, *Etude d'une des Demoiselles d'Avignon* (1907); these are followed by Raymond Duchamp-Villon, *Le Cheval Majeur* (1914–76) a three-dimensional interpretation of Cubism; Delaunay, *Poet, Philippe Soupault* (1922), Antoine Pevsner, *Masque* (1923), Giacometti, bronze sculpture entitled, *Table* (1933-69), Chagall, *A la Russie, aux ânes et aux autres* (1911), Matisse, Polynesian cutouts (1946), Picasso, *Atelier de modiste* (1925/26), Henri Laurens, *L'Automne*, Georges Braque, *Still Life* (1932).

The first great 20C movement in art, **Fauvism** (**room 2**), with its violent, impasto colour and contorted forms, is represented by André Derain, *Le Faubourg de Collioure* (1905), *Les deux Péniches*; Georges Braque, *L'Estaque* (c 1906); Raoul Dufy, *Les Affiches à Trouville*. Other artists briefly involved with Fauvism were Camoin; Albert Marquet, *Matisse in his Studio* (1905). And from the Fauve pallette of Henri Matisse, *Algerienne* (1909), *Intérieur, Bocal de Posissons Rouges* (1914) as well as a brush with Abstraction, *Porte-fenêtre à Collioure* (1914) and the bronze sculpture *Deux Negresses* (1908). Other Fauve artists include Maurice de Vlaminck, *Les Arbres Rouges* (1906); Othon Friesz (1879–1949), *Portrait de Fernand Fleuret* (1907); Albert Marquet, *La Plage de Fécamp*, *Portrait d'André Rouveyre*, and *Bassin du Havre*.

Further works by **Matisse** in the collections include *L'Odalesque à la Culotte Rouge*, and the highly decorative *Figure Décorative sur Fond Ornemental* (1925–26). The museum also owns several of his bronzes including *Nu Couché* (1907), *Jeanette I* and *IV* (1910–13) and *Nu de Dos I, II, III, IV* (1930); by **Picasso**, *Portrait d'une Jeune Fille*, *Femme en Collier* (1917); and *Portraits of Mme Paul Eluard*, and of *Dora Maar*.

Rooms 3 and 5 The development of **Cubism**, between 1907 and 1914, is followed through the works of its creators, Braque and Picasso, from the Analytical (until c 1911) to the Synthetic phase, alongside masks and carvings from Gabon and the Ivory Coast which deeply influenced the Cubist vision. **Braque**, *Route à l'Estaque* (1908), *Le Guéridon, Nature Morte au Violin, L'Homme à la Guitar* (1914), etc; **Picasso**, *Le Joueur de Guitare* (1910), *Femme Assise* (1910), *Buste de Femme* (1909–10). You can see Cubist collages, c 1911–14 (**room 6**) along with Picasso's curtain for Erik Satie's ballet *Mercure* (1924). Other major artists who experimented with Cubism were Juan Gris, *Le Petit Déjeuner* (1915), Francis Picabia, *Udnie* (1913), Marc Chagall, *La Mort* (1908), *Le Cimetière* (1917). Three-dimenstional 'Cubist' objects were produced by Henri Laurens (montage), *La Bouteille de Beaune* (1918); Lipchitz, and Raymond Duchamp (1876-1918).

Room 4 has work by Georges Rouault (1871–1958): *Polichinelle* (1910), and religious paintings such as *La Sainte Face* (1933). Fernand Léger moved from a lyrical interpretation of Cubism, *La Noce* (1911–12) to a rigorous personal style, *Contraste de Formes* (1913), and with Amédée Ozenfant and Jeanneret (Le Corbusier) (1887–1965), developed an ordered form of Cubism known as **Purism**. The work of the sculptor Alexander Archipenko shows the influence of the Cubist movement.

Room 7 From the period immediately preceding the First World War are works by the brilliant young Henri Gaudier-Brzeska. **Dada** was born in 1916 in Zurich out of the horrors of that War. Anti-art, provocative and funny if sometimes obscene, it was taken up by Marcel Duchamp, *Le Verre des Célibataires (Les Neuf Moules Mâlic)* (1914–15), George Grosz, *Remember Uncle August, the Unhappy Inventor* (1919); Kurt Schwitters, *Merz* (1926), Man Ray, *Cadeau* (1921–63); Francis Picabia, *L'Oeil Cacodylate* (1921) and *Dresseur d'animaux* (1923); Otto Dix, *Souvenir de la Galerie des glaces à Bruxelles*, 1920, and Hans Arp.

Room 8 European pioneers in **Expressionism** were Frantisek Kupka, *Autour d'un Point* (1911), Ernst-Ludwig Kirchner, *La Toilette* (1913–20), and Marc Chagall. The Russians Michel Larionov, a member of the German Die Brücke group, and Natalia Goncharova, *Les Porteuses* (1911) contributed to the avant garde movements.

Rooms 10–15 show the overlapping themes of **Abstraction, de Stijl** and the **Bauhaus**. Many of the developments, in fine and applied arts, were born of the fertile breeding ground of the Bauhaus and cross-pollinated with movements throughout Europe. The museum is very rich in works by the Russian-born **Wassily Kandinsky** which demonstrate one artist's progression from early Fauve-type landscapes to the floating, detached shapes of *Avec l'Arc Noir* (1912) and *Tableau sur Fond Clair* (1916). A member, with Kandinsky, of the Blaue Reiter group in Munich and then of the Bauhaus (1922–33), was **Paul Klee** among whose works are *Villas at Florence* (1926) and *Arrow in the Garden* (1929). **Constructivism**, described as somewhere between utopia and integration, is represented by artists such as Oskar Schlemmer (also a member of the Bauhaus), Antoine Pevsner (1884–1962) *Construction in Space* (1923–25), Baumeister, Pougny, Malevich, and the Italian Futurists, Luigi Russolo (1885–1947), *Dynamisme d'une automobile* (1911) and Balla.

The **de Stijl** group of Dutch artists, associated with the magazine of the same name (1917–32), produced the pure abstraction of Van Doesburg, *Composition* (1920), and Piet Mondrian, *Composition* (1937) and *New York City I* (1942) and Georges Vantongerloo *S x R3* (1933-34). Forms of abstraction are found in the sculpture of Constantin Brancusi, *La Muse Endormie* (1910) and *Le Coq* (1935).

Rooms 14–15 The development between 1920 and 1940 in **architecture and furniture**, using drawings, models, furniture and other objects, ranges from designs for Russian villages to the work of Le Corbusier, Jean Prouvé and Robert Mallet-Stevens and theoretical projects from De Stijl. The influence of the Bauhaus and de Stijl is seen in furniture designs, notably Marcel Breuer's armchair *Club 33* (1925), and the resolutely progressive ideas of the Union of Modern Artists, Pierre Jeanneret and Alvar Aalto (Finland).

Room 16 Robert Delaunay combined Cubism with light and colour to produce vibrant works celebrating modern life in such compositions as *Joie de Vivre* (1930) and *Rythme* (1934), and *Manège de Cochons* (1922). By Sonia Delaunay are *Rythme* (1938) and *Electriques* (1914) and Hans ArpArp, Hans (1888–1966), *Concrétion Humain* (1934). The large works by **Fernand Léger** (**room 17**) who returned to a figurative style after the First World War, range from *La Lecture* (1924) and *Composition aux Trois Figures* (1932) where equal importance is given to objects and figures, to the Purist composition of 1927,

244 • THE BEAUBOURG AND THE CENTRE POMPIDOU

Composition with Four Hats. Léger who, like Delaunay, sought to reconcile art and science, produced strictly unsentimental works combining dynamic flat decorative forms with free colour: *Composition aux Deux Perroquets* (1935–39), and *Les Loisirs—Hommage à Louis David* (1948–49). In the same rooms are Henri Laurens, *Cariatide assise* (1929–30) and *L'adieu* (1941); also works by Alberto Magnelli (1888–1971), *Jean Hélion, Au cycliste* (1939) and *A rebours* (1947).

Other **sculpted works** in the collections include: Lipchitz, *Head of Gertrude Stein* (1920), *Figure* (1926–30); Gargallo, *Statue of the Prophet*; the highly personal three-dimensional work of Alexander Calder (1898–1976) in wire: *Josephine Baker* (1926); mobiles—*Disque Blanc, Disque Noir* (1940–41); in wood *Requin et Baleine* (c 1933); Alberto Giacometti, *Portrait de Jean Genet* (1955).

Rooms 19–26 Surrealism had its roots in Dada, literature, Freud's theories and the hallucinatory paintings of Giorgio di Chirico, such as *Premonitory Portrait of Guillaume Apollinaire* and *Melancholy of an Afternoon* (1914). Its poet-painters, led by André Breton, had a far-reaching effect on all aspects of art. **Max Ernst** *Ubu Imperateur, l'Intérieur de Vue* (1929), *Loplop Présente une Jeune Fille* (1930) and his collage *La Femme 100 Têtes* (1929) and the bronze *Le Capricorne* (1948); **Salvador Dali**, *Hallucination Partielle* and *l'Ane pourri* (1928), and the chilling works of **Alberto Giacometti** including *La Pointe à l'Oeil* (1931), *Femme égorgée* (1932–33), *Objet désagréable à jeter* (1931) as well as *La Boule suspendu* (1930). **René Magritte**, *Le Double Secret* (1927), *Le Modèle Rouge*, *A Quatre Heures d'Eté, l'Espoir* (1929), and *Six Images de Lénin sur un Piano* (1931).

The individual, poetic style of **Joan Miró** came under the spell of Surrealism as in *La Sieste* (1925), *Le Catalan* and *L'Addition,* as did Picasso briefly in *Figure* (c 1927) and *Minotaure* (1943). Among the Surrealist rooms is an evocation of Breton's studio (**room 23**) with a variety of objects found or collected, and works by Yves Tanguy, Man Ray, Picabia, etc. Surrealism in Europe and the United States, **room 24**, has work by Matta, Arshile Gorky, Masson, Jackson Pollock, Wilfredo Lam, *L'ange (l'Insecte/La danseuse)* (c 1935), Roberto Matta, *Xpace and the ego* (1945). Surrealist sculpture and engravings include Julio Gonzalez (1876–1942), *Femme se coiffant* (1931) and *Femme à la Corbeille* (1953), Hans Bellmer, *La Poupée* (1934–37) and Hans Arp, *Danseuse* (1925). Reference to Luis Buñuel's *L'Age d'Or* (1930) is a tribute to Surrealist cinema.

Room 27–28, Return to Order in European Painting, 1920–30, addresses the post First World War period when artists sought inspiration from the timeless reassurance of neoclassical art. Works from this period include Picasso, *La Liseuse* (1920), *Arlequin, Nature Morte à la Tête Antique* (1925); Otto Dix, *Portrait of Sylvia von Harden* (1926) an uncompromising portrait of a journalist, a woman and an era and *Comte St-Genois d'Anneaucourt* (1927); Balthus, *La toilette de Cathy* (1933) and *Alice* (1933); Max Beckmann, *Fastnacht Paris* (1930). Also work by Miró, *l'Intérieur (La Fermière)* (1922–23); Jean Fautrier (1898–1964) *Le sanglier écorché* (1927); Max Beckman, *Mardi Gras Paris* (1930); Bonnard, *Portrait des Frères Bernheim de Villers* (1920); Vuillard, *Portrait de Jeanne Lanvin* (1933); and portraits by Derain and di Chirico.

Room 29, School of Paris, was a loose grouping of artists who worked in Paris in the first part of the 20C Amedeo Modigliani, *Tete de femme* (1912–13) (sculpture) and *Portrait of Dedie* (c 1918), Chaïm Soutine, *Le Groom* (1928), and

Portrait of Miestchanioff; Foujita, My Interior (Still Life with Clock), (1921), and Francis Gruber. Later members of the School of Paris included abstract painters such as Maria Elena Vieira da Silva, *La Bibliothèque* (1949); Jean Fautrier, *Femme Douce* (1946); and Antoni Tàpies (b. 1923).

Room 30 Later works of **Bonnard** and **Matisse** 1930–40 bear witness to the influence on the chromatic range of their work of the light of the south of France. In the large *Grand Intérieur Rouge* (1948) Matisse experiments with the expressive qualities of colour and in *La Blouse Roumaine* (1940), *Liseuse sur Fond Rouge* with simplification of form. Pierre Bonnard, moved to the Côte d'Azur c 1925 to concentrate on interpreting light, forms and character exclusively with colour: *Nu à la Baignoire* (1931), *Coin de Table* (1935), *L'Atelier au Mimosa* (1939–46). **Rooms 31–34** show mature works of **Braque** and **Picasso**, 1920–1940. Braque's interiors and sombre still lifes include *Le Duo* (1937), and *Le Billard* (1944), prizewinner at the Venice Biennale in 1948. These contrast with Picasso's grating figures, *Femmes aux pigeons* (1930), the brightly coloured *La Muse* (1935); *L'Aubade* (1942) is an experiment with a variety of materials. A late work by Magritte, *Stropiat* (1947), was recently acquired by the museum. **Art Informel**, non-geometric abstraction of 1950s, was practised by Jean Fautrier, *Tête d'otage No. 21* (1945), Wols, Hans Hartung and Nicolas de Staël, La *Vie Dure* (1946).

Jean Dubuffet was the main exponent of **Art brut** (raw art) as in *Dhô tel Nuancé d'Abricot* (1947) and Pierre Alechinsky, Karel Appel and Bram Van Velde (Dutch) were members of a group of Northern painters known as 'Cobra'. Also Giacometti's bronze head, *Diego* (1954).

Rooms 36–39, the last rooms, bring together **American Abstract Expressionists**: typical of **Jackson Pollock**'s, drip technique is '*Number 26 A*', *Black and White*, which are echoed in the lyrical abstraction of Hantaï; Pierre Soulages's (b. 1919) huge canvases trace a form in space in black and white. The colour fields of Mark Rothko and Barnett Newman have a mystical rapport with Joan Miró, *Bleus I, II and III* (1961), and Lucio Fontana, *Black Sculpture, Spatial Concept* (1947). Also works by Yves Klein, *Ci-gît l'espace* (1960), Jean Degottex and Arshile Gorky and Etienne Martin's accumulation of found material is entitled *The Coat* (1962). Among figurative painters of the post-war period are Alberto Giacometti, *Portrait de Jean Genet* (1955), and Francis Bacon *Van Gogh in a Landscape* (1957), *Three People in a Room* (1964). A space is devoted to Matisse's cutouts: *Deux Danseuses* (1937–38), *Le Ciel* (1946), *Nu Bleu II and III* (1952), *La Tristesse du Roi* (1952) and projects for the chapel at Vence.

Room 40, **Architecture** 1940–60, concentrates on industrial and urban planning. On the exterior terraces are monumental sculptures by Henri Laurens, *La Grande Baigneuse* (1947), Joan Miró, and Alexander Calder.

There is a rich **photographic collection** of some 12,000 prints, considered a vital document in the history of photography, including images by Man-Ray, Dora Maar, Brassaï and Lászlo Moholy-Nagy.

The Contemporary Collections

The Contemporary Collections, Level 4, cover the period from 1960 onwards and are exhibited thematically, by style or by artist. Only part of the museum's large collection can be exhibited at one time and the selection and emphasis will change approximately every year to 18 months. Considerable space is dedicated to architecture and design for the period.

Individual rooms are dedicated to Jean Dubuffet; Edward Kienholz (1927–94); Jacques Monory, Joseph Beuys (b. 1921), Jean-Pierre Raynaud, Dan Graham, Gerhard Richter, Annette Messager, Douglas Gordon, Ben and Christian Boltanski, and to the main movements of the last 40 years of the 20C. The works shown are representative of the many and varied mediums used in the second half of the 20C: painting, sculpture, casting, photomontage, photography, video, drawing, recycling, performance art, cinetics.

Large, playful fantasies open the collections and focus your mind and set the tone for what is to follow: a mechanised sculpture by Jean Tinguely, *Requiem pour une Feille Morte* (1970) and Claes Oldenburg's (b. 1929) slightly scary *Giant Ice Bag* (1969–70); Ben's *Magasin* (1958–73), a montage on a monumental scale, of disparate objects making a Dadaistic anti-art statement; two figurative sculptures, Thomas Schütte, *Sans Titre* (1996), Alain Séchas, *Le Mannequin* (1985); and Jean Dubuffet's *Jardin d'hiver* (1968–70), a monochromatic 'environment'.

The museum is well endowed in **Pop Art**, which developed in England and the USA. in the 1960s. Artists include Andy Warhol, *Ten Lizes* (1963); Claes Oldenburg, *Ghost Drum Set* (1972); Robert Rauschenberg, *Oracle* (1962), Christo (b 1935) *Package and Wrapped Floor* (1968); and James Rosenquist, *President Elect* (1960–61). **Nouveau Réalisme**, a new perception of reality, was a parallel development, re-interpreting the ready-mades of Marcel Duchamp, founded in Paris in 1960 by Yves Klein (1928–62). Among the Nouveaux Realistes were Martial Raysse, *America, America* (1964) a huge neon-lighted metal hand; Arman (b. 1928); *Home Sweet Home* and *Chopin's Waterloo*; Niki de Saint-Phalle and Tinguely, sculptures in the Stravinsky fountain; César, *Compression des voiture*; Oyvind Fahlström, *The Planetarium* (1962–63); Raymond Hains, *Ach Alma Manetro* (1949); also Jacques de la Villeglé, François Dufrêne, Daniel Spoerri, Mimmo Rotella and Gérard Deschamps.

Although the founder of Nouveau Réalisme, **Klein** himself is known above all for his monochromatic works in blue, a deep ultramarine that he patented as IKB, because he believed blue has no tangible reality. He produced 194 IKBs from 1955–1962: *Monochrome bleu (IBK 3)* (1960), *L'arbre, grande éponge bleu* (1962).

Abstract Expressionism or **Conceptual Art** is represented by Joseph Kosuth (b. 1945); Willem de Kooning, *Woman* (c 1952); Barnett Newman, *Shining Forth (to George)* (1961); Mark Rothko's modern icons; colour field painting of Frank Stella, *Parzeczew II* (1971).

Other artists whose work may be on view are Jasper Johns, (b. 1930) *Figure 5* (1960); Alain Jacquet (b. 1939) *Le Déjeuner sur l'Herbe*; Pierre Soulages (b. 1919), *Peinture* (1979) all black; Ellsworth Kelly (b. 1923); Andy Warhol, *Electric Chair* (1966); Frank Stella (b. 1936) *La Vecchia del'orto* (1986); Richard Lidner (1901–78), David Hockney and Jim Dine.

Movements and artists of the 1970s include **Kinetic art** with Agam's restored *Du Salon* (1972); and **Fluxus**, with work by Joseph Beuys, Ben, Robert Filliou and Erik Dietman; among the museum's vast reserves of **Arte Povera** is the work of Giuseppe Penone, *Albero* and *Soffio 6*; Annis Kounellis (b. 1936) *Sans titre*; Pino Pascali (1935–68) *Le Penne di Esopo*; Mario Merz, *Che fare* (c 1968–69); Boetti (1940–94); and Luciano Fabro (b. 1936). There are representative works of

Antiforme: Eva Hesse, *Seven Poles* (1970); Robert Morris, curious yet eloquent felt *Wall Hanging* (1969–70); Richard Serra, *Plinths* (1967); and Tony Cragg (1949). **Minimalism and Conceptual Art**: Pierre Soulages all black *Peinture* (1979), Joseph Kosuth, *One Colour, Five Adjectifs* (1966), Stanley Brouwn, *Trois pas = 2587 mm* (1972–73) and Bertrand Lavier, *D'après Caton l'Ancien* (1975).

Among **Paintings 1970–90**, during a period of crisis, questioning and reaffirmation, are the striped installations of Daniel Buren (b. 1938), *Jamais Deux Fois la Même* (1967–2000) on the north and south extremities of the museum. Also Claude Rutault, *Toiles à l'unité* (1973) and *Légendes* (1985); Markus Lüpertz (b 1941), *Exekution* (1992); Jörg Immendorff, *Die Table* (1999); and works by Niele Toroni, François Rouan, Jean-Michel Alberola, Gérard Gasiorowski, as well as Malcolm Morley, *Cradle of Civilisation with American Woman* (1982) and Georg Baselitz (b. 1938), *Ralf III* (1965) and *Die Mädchen von Olmo* (1981).

Examples of **Op Art, Kinetic Art and Geometric Abstraction**, hard-edged works, optical or otherwise, began with Joseph Albers, *Hommage to the Square* (1956), and were developed by the great master of op art, Victor Vasarély, *Hô II* (1948–52), *Procion, neg* (1957). Other artists in this group are Jesus Rafael Soto (b 1923) and Yaacov Agam (b 1928), *Amenagement de l'antichambre des apparts proviens du Palace de l'Elysées* (1972–74).

Considerable space is needed for **Installations and Special Works** (1960–80), some disturbing, some funny, some puzzling, focusing on 'representation': Jacques Monory, *Narrative Figuration*, a series using photos and film; Dorothea Tanning (b. 1910), *Chambre 202/Hôtel du Pavot* (1970); Edward Kienholz, *While Visions of Sugar Plumbs Danced in their Heads* (1964); Jean-Pierre Raynaud, *Container Zéro* (1988); Joseph Beuys, a mysterious work made for a *Happening Infiltration for Grand Piano* (1964–66), and *Skin* (1984) and by the same artist, *Plight* (1958–85), a padded room; Dan Graham, *Present Continuous Past(s)*, (1974); Annette Messager (b. 1943), *Les Pensionnaires* (1971–72) a series of vitrines, and Boltanski, *Saynètes comiques* and *A Fictive Autobiography*, a new type of storytelling.

Four Questions is the selection of 30 objects of the 1980–90s (paintings, photographs and graphic arts) by one artist, Fabrice Hybert, crammed into a small space, but its seemingly humdrum arrangement is almost reassuring in contrast with the more worrying or outrageous installations and montages in the museum.

Works from **1990 to the Present** include those produced by the Centre Pompidou such as Douglas Gordon, *Feature Film* (1999), and recent acquisitions: Claude Closky, the large series *De 1 à 1000* (1993), Xavier Veilhan, *Le Supermarché* (1997–98), Jean-Marc Bustamante, *Lum. 6.91*, Thomas Struth, *Church of Frari* (1995), Marc Quinn, *The Great Escape* (1996). Installations of this period are: *United Enemies* (1993–1994) by Thomas Schutte, Patrick Tosani, *CDD IX* (1996), Jana Sterback, *Vanitas* and *Robe de Chair pour Albinos Anorexique* (1987). A new look at the human figure involving casting, sculpture, photography, video, etc. includes Mona Hatoum's, *Corps étranger*, Valérie Jouve, *Sans titre no. 54* (1998), Marie-Ange Guilleminot (b. 1960), *La Rotateuse* (1995), and Gilles Barbier, *Polyfocus* (1999).

Space is set aside for the history of **Architecture and Design** from the 1960s to the 90s, presented through maquettes, models, drawings and objects. Megastructures and utopias are characteristic of the work of architects during the

1960s such as Robert Le Ricolais, Richard Buckminster, Louis Kahn, Kenzo Tange, the Archigram group, and Hans Hollein. Designers included Joe Colombo, Gaetano Pesce, Eero Saarinen, Pierre Paulin, Olivier Mourgue, Roger Tallong, and so on. Pop Art exercised a considerable influence on the 60s designs, for example the sofa *Safari* (1968) by Archizoom Associati. Representative of the period 1970–80 is the work of architects such as Tadao Ando, Christian de Portzamparc, Jean Nouvel, Norman Foster, Richard Rogers, Bernard Tschumi, and Frank Gehry, and designers Ettore Sottsass, Michele de Lucchi, Gaetano Pesce and Martin Sezakely. Architecture in the 1990s features the work of Dominique Perrault, Jean Nouvel, Kazuyo Sejima, Anne Lacaton and Jean-Philippe Vassal and the designs of Alberto Meda, Ron Arad, Jonathan Ive and Philippe Starck.

The **Museum Gallery** and the **Graphic Arts Gallery** are reserved for temporary exhibitions, and the **Salon du Musée** is a documentary centre with catalogues, videos, CD roms, and database open to visitors.

On the north of the Piazza Beaubourg is a small extension which opened in January 1997, designed by Piano, enclosing a garden and the **Atelier Brancusi** moved from 11 Impasse Ronsin. Here, exactly reconstructed, are the four studios of Constantin Brancusi's workshop, complete with sculptures, models, plinths, etc, plus photographs and other memorabilia. The layout allows visitors to circulate around the exterior of the studios and view them from different angles. This small but dignified haven of monumental tranquility should not be missed.

North-east of the Pompidou Centre, at 22 Rue Beaubourg, in Impasse Berthaud, is the **Musée de la Poupée**, with French dolls and others from around the world (☎ 01 42 72 73 11).

21 • South of Rue de Rivoli, from the Louvre to Place de l'Arsenal

■ Arrondissements: 75001, 75004

🚇 Louvre-Rivole, Châtelet, Hôtel-de-Ville, St-Paul, Sully-Morland, Pont Marie, Bastille

At two ends of the scale on Quai de l'Hôtel de Ville:
Galerie 88, at no. 88, ☎ 01 42 72 17 58. Fun and inexpensive international cuisine, £
Miravile, no. 72, ☎ 01 42 74 72 22. Reasonable set menu, otherwise expensive with some excellent dishes, ££

Restaurants on Rue François-Miron:
Le Relais St-Paul, no. 33, ☎ 01 48 87 34 20. Traditional fare, £–££
Les Vapeurs du Marais, no. 50, ☎ 01 42 71 99 00. Fish with specialities such as bouillabaisse, £–££
Marchand de Vins, no. 52, ☎ 01 48 87 15 40. Wine bar with food, £

The Auld Alliance, no. 80, ☎ 01 48 04 30 40. Hard to believe, a Scottish pub, serving Saturday brunch, £
Café de la Poste, 13 Rue Castex, ☎ 01 42 72 95 35. Little gem, tucked away, excellent value, £
Les Vins des Pyrénées, 25 Rue Beautreillis, ☎ 01 42 72 64 94.

Agreeable, lively and reasonable, £
Thanksgiving, 20 rue St-Paul, ☎ 01 42 77 68 28. Old setting, American regional cooking of the best, £
Le P'tit Comic, 6 Rue Castex, ☎ 01 42 71 32 62. Serves mainly crèpes, surrounded by *bandes dessinés*, £

Here we pick up Rue de Rivoli again, at the eastern extremity of the Palais du Louvre. This section was laid out at the time of Napoléon III to allow rapid access for troops to the Hôtel de Ville in case of emergency. Rue de Rivoli (and its extension Rue St-Antoine), slices the Marais in two. In the wedge-shaped area south of these street and bordered by the Seine are two major squares, Place du Châtelet and Place de l'Hotel de Ville, as well as the church of St-Germain-de-l'Auxerrois and some quiet and picturesque streets. Rue St-Antoine ends at the popular and trendy Bastille district (See Ch. 22).

Where Rue du Louvre crosses Rue de Rivoli to Pl. du Louvre there is a view of the east façade of the Palais du Louvre (See Ch. 14). This supposedly is the area where Caesar's legions encamped in 52 BC. The Mairie of the 1st Arrondissement (1859) opposite, according to Viollet-le-Duc, was intended as a caricature of the adjoining church. The conspicuous Neo-Gothic north tower was added the following year.

St-Germain-l'Auxerrois

St-Germain-l'Auxerrois (**Map 8; 1**), a Gothic church of the 13C–16C, was drastically altered in the 18C and restored (1838–55), under the direction of Lassus and Baltard. The most striking exterior feature is the **porch**, by Jean Gaussel (1435–39), with a rose window, and above it, a balustrade, which encircles the building. The transeptal doorways (15C) and Renaissance doorway (1570) (seen from the neighbouring schoolyard), north of the choir, are noteworthy.

History of St-Germain-l'Auxerrois

The church, dedicated to the 5C St Germanus, Bishop of Auxerre, stands on the site of a Merovingian sanctuary. A second church replaced it in the 11C, which was replaced by the present building in the 13C. The ringing of its bells for matins on 24 August 1572 was the signal to commence the slaughter of Huguenots, known as the Massacre of St Bartholomew. The building was desecrated during the Revolution and sacked by a mob in 1831.

Royal artists and architects of the Valois Court were buried in St-Germain: the poets Jodelle and Malherbe; the architects Lemercier, De Cotte,Gabriel and Le Vau; the artists Coypel, Boucher and Chardin; the sculptors Coysevox, N. and G. Coustou; and the engraver Israël Silvestre.

The **interior** (78m by 39m) is double-aisled. The alterations of 1745, mingled the classicism of the 18C with 14C–15C architecture and converted the piers into fluted columns and heightened their capitals. The organ case, from Sainte-

Chapelle, was designed by Pierre-Noël Roussel and made by Lavergne in 1756. Opposite the entrance are two 17C white marble holy water stoups. The brass pendant chandeliers are 18C.

The **royal pew** (1682–84), in the north aisle, a *tour-de-force* of wood carving, was designed by Le Brun and executed by François Mercier. The wood is worked to represent a baldaquin with draperies above fretworked panels and supported by Ionic columns and pilasters. Behind it is a 16C Flemish sculpted triptych with painted wings and, in the aisle-chapel opposite, is another altarpiece (1519) in carved wood, from Antwerp. The pulpit is 17C. The outer south aisle is occupied by the Chapel of the Virgin, late 13C, with a Tree of Jesse designed by Viollet-le-Duc and above it a 14C Virgin of the Champagne School. The 15C St Mary of Egypt and the 13C St Germanus (Germain), were originally in the porch.

Fragments of the destroyed **rood-screen**, sculpted by Jean Goujon, are preserved in the Louvre, and the wrought-iron choir-railings date from 1767. On the left at the choir entrance is a wooden statue of *St Germanus*, seated; on the right a stone figure of St Vincent (both 15C). Only the transepts have their original 15C–16C stained-glass. The font was designed by Mme de Lamartine.

Above a small door in the ambulatory (south side) is a late-15C polychrome Virgin. The first inner bay, the oldest part of the church, is the base of the 12C belfry. In the 4th chapel are marble statues of *Etienne d'Aligre and his Son*, both Chancellors of France (d. 1635; 1677); 6th chapel, a relic of a *Pietà* by Jean Soulas (1505); and in the 7th chapel, effigies from the tomb of the Rostaing family (1582 and 1645). There are several 19C frescoes by Guichard, and windows by Lusson.

Further east on Rue de Rivoli is Sq. St-Jacques, a public garden since 1856 and the first of a series of green areas created by Haussman who was busy transforming the district at the time. In the centre rises the Flamboyant Gothic **Tour St-Jacques**, dating from 1508–22. Since 1797 this is the only relic of a series of churches standing on this site from the 9C dedicated to St Jacques-la-Boucherie and was a rallying point for pilgrims on the road to Santiago de Compostella in Spain. In the 17C Blaise Pascal carried out experiments here, and from 1836 it was used as a shot-tower until creatively restored in 1858 by Ballu. At the end of the 19C it became a meteorological station.

Adjoining to the southwest is the hectic **Pl. du Châtelet** (Map 8; 4), bounded by the Seine, here crossed by the Pont au Change (see Ch. 1). The Place is named after the vanished Grand Châtelet, a fortress gateway leading to the Cité, once the headquarters of the Provost of Paris and the Guild of Notaries. It was begun in 1130, and demolished between 1802 and 1810. There is a plan of the fort on the front of the Chambres des Notaires on the north side of the square.

On the east side is the Théâtre de la Ville, restored after a fashion and reopened in 1980, only to be severely damaged by fire in 1982. To the west is the Théâtre du Châtelet (1862), where Communards were court-martialled in 1871. In the centre is the Fontaine du Châtelet (or de la Victoire or du Palmier) dating from 1808 and 1858. An inscription indicates the position of the Parloir aux Bourgeois, the seat of the municipality of Paris from the 13C until 1357 (see below).

From the north side of the Place, Av. Victoria, named in honour of Queen Victoria's visit to Paris in 1855, leads east to the **Pl. de l'Hôtel-de-Ville** (Map 8; 4), another large pedestrianised square with fountains which is frequently used for public gatherings. The **Hôtel de Ville**, on the eastern side of the square is the

Hôtel de Ville

administrative centre of the City authorities and its elaborate 19C façade is grandly floodlit at night. The Place was known until 1830 as Pl. de Grève, as ships had moored on the strand or *grève* in this area since the 11C. It was the location for public executions, many incredibly barbarous, of Protestants, assassins, sorceresses, highwaymen, murderers, revolutionaries, and the like. It was often a rendezvous for unemployed or dissatisfied workers, who were said to *faire grève*, which came to mean to go on strike.

The Hôtel de Ville stands on the site of its historic predecessor, begun c 1532 and burnt down by the Communards in 1871. This caricature replica, in the style of the French Renaissance, was built (on a larger scale) in 1874–84 from the plans of Ballu and Deperthes. Its façades are embellished with statues of eminent Frenchmen; its interior is also lavishly adorned in the official taste in architecture of the period, with sculpture, elaborate carvings and murals, including Puvis de Chavannes' *The Seasons*. The platforms of the Métro station, Hôtel de Ville, are decorated with illustrations of the old building and its splendid interior. Limited visits the first Monday of each month at 10.30. Book in advance ☎ 01 42 76 50 49. At 29 Rue de Rivoli, on the north side of the building, is the Municipal Tourist Office (☎ 01 42 76 43 43).

History of the Hôtel de Ville

In 1264 Louis IX created the first municipal authority in Paris by allowing the merchants to elect magistrates (*échevins*), led by the *prévôt des marchands*, who was also head of the *Hanse des marchands de l'eau*. This merchant guild, which had the monopoly of the traffic on the Seine, Marne, Oise and Yonne, took as their emblem a ship, a device which still graces the arms of the city. Their first meeting-place was known simply as the Parloir aux Bourgeois; later they met at the Grand-Châtelet itself; and finally, in 1357, the Provost Etienne Marcel bought the Maison aux Piliers or Maison du Dauphin, a mansion in Pl. de Grève, for their assemblies. In 1532 plans for an imposing new building were adopted but work was stopped at the second floor, and the new designs were not completed until 1628.

This was where in 1789 the 300 electors nominated by the districts of Paris met. On 17 July, Louis XVI received the newly-devised *tricolore* cockade from the hands of Jean Sylvain Bailly, the Mayor. On 10 August 1792, the 172 commissaries elected by Paris gave the signal for a general insurrection. In 1794

Robespierre took refuge here but was arrested on 27 July and dragged, injured, to the Conciergerie. In 1805 it became the seat of the Préfet de la Seine and his council, and was the scene of numerous official celebrations.

The Swiss Guards put up a stout defence of the building during the July Revolution of 1830. In 1848 it became the seat of Louis Blanc's provisional government and witnessed the arrest of the revolutionary agitators Armand Barbès and Louis-Auguste Blanqui. The Third Republic was proclaimed here in 1870 (4 September) and, in the following March, the Commune. On 24 May 1871 the building was evacuated before being set ablaze by its defenders.

In 1944 the Hôtel de Ville was a focus of opposition to the occupying forces by the Resistance movement who, by 19 August, had established themselves in the building repelling German counter-attacks until relieved by the arrival of Général Leclerc's division five days later.

Just across Rue de Rivoli from the north-east corner of the Hôtel de Ville at 22 Rue des Archives, is the **Temple des Billettes**, built in 1756 for the Carmelites, but since 1812 used by the Lutherans. On the north side is the only medieval cloister extant in Paris, a relic of an older convent. Completed in 1427, there are sometimes exhibitions under its Flamboyant vaults.

To the east of the Hôtel de Ville, between two of its annexes, lies **Pl. St-Gervais,** with its elm tree, a reminder of the famous elm of St-Gervais, beneath which justice used to be administered; the proverbial expression for waiting for Doomsday is, ironically, *Attendre sous l'orme* (the elm). This was one of the first inhabited areas on the Right Bank, and Rue François-Miron follows the course of a Roman road which led from Lutetia to Senlis.

St-Gervais-St-Protais

Dominating the eastern side of Pl. St-Gervais is St-Gervais-St-Protais (**Map 8; 4**) The cult of Gervase and Protase was popular in the early Middle Ages and this was one of the oldest parishes on the Right Bank, going back to the 6C. It is thought that the sanctuary was rebuilt in the 13C. Despite the Classical façade, the body of the present church is a late Gothic structure begun at the end of the 15C.

History of St-Gervais-St-Protais

The original plans are attributed to Martin Chambiges, whose work was continued by his son Pierre. The lower stages of the tower are an early 15C survival. The façade (1616–21), by Clément II Métezeau, is posited as an early example in Paris of the correct sequence of the three Classic orders: Doric, Ionic and Corinthian. The choir and transepts date from rebuildings of 1494–1578 and the nave was continued in Flamboyant Gothic between 1600–20, with lierne and tierceron vaults, despite the strength of Italian Renaissance influence at this time. Work on some of the chapels and tower went on until 1657.

The painter Philippe de Champaigne (1602–74), the writer Paul Scarron, Paul (1610–60) and the dramatist Crébillon the Elder (1674–1762) are buried here. François Couperin (1668–1733) and seven members of his family served as organists from 1653 to 1830. The organ (16C–17C), known as the **Couperin organ**, survives albeit restored and enlarged several times and the case rebuilt in the 18C.

The **interior**, impressively lofty and stylistically unified, has several works of art. The high windows of both nave and choir contain painted glass of c 1610–20 by Robert Pinaigrier and Nicolas Chaumet.

In the south aisle, the third chapel has an altar commemorating some 50 victims of the bombardment on Good Friday 1918, when a German shell struck the church. In the fourth are seven low 17C painted panels of the *Life of Christ*. Painted glass of 1531 by Pinaigrier, restored in the 19C represents, in the fifth chapel, the *Martyrdom of St Gervais and St Protais*, and in the sixth the *Judgement of Solomon*. The eighth chapel contains the *tomb of Michel le Tellier* (d. 1685), by Mazeline and Hurtrelle; the bearded heads supporting the Chancellor's sarcophagus are from the tomb of Jacques de Souvré (d. 1670), by François Anguier, the rest of which are in the Louvre. The Lady Chapel, a heady example of

West façade, St-Gervais-St-Protais and the elm tree

Flamboyant Gothic (1517) with complicated vaults and a bravura pendant boss, also retains fine original glass (restored in the 19C) of the *Life of the Virgin*.

In the **north aisle** is a plaque commemorating the consecration of an earlier church, 1420. All that remains are the first two levels of the belfry above the sacristy, which retains a good iron grille of 1741. The next chapel is the Chapelle Dorée (1628) with its original decoration; in the adjacent chapel are a 13C high relief of the *Dormition of the Virgin* (below the altar), and a portrait by Pajou (1782) of *Mme Palerme de Savy*.

In the **choir**, the first seven stalls in the upper row were remade in the 17C; the rest are mid-16C with interesting misericords. The 18C bronze-gilt candelabra and cross were designed by Soufflot. Against the north entry-pillar is a 14C Virgin, known as N.-D. de Bonne-Délivrance; and on either side of the altar, wooden statues of the patron saints, by Michel Bourdin (1625).

The south façade of the church can now be seen since the area has been the subject of clearance and restoration. The façades of some houses in Rue des Barres, behind the building, are worth looking at, and the surrounding streets, in the pleasing *quartier* of St-Paul have some fine 17C and 18C elevations and details.

The stepped **Rue François-Miron**, leading east from St-Gervais, is an imposing and interesting street. Nos 2–14, built c 1735, are adorned with wrought-iron work with an elm motif (see above); nos 30, 36 and 42 all have good features. Nos 11 and 13 are late medieval timber-framed houses.

In Rue Geoffroy-l'Asnier (to the right) at no. 26 is the **Hôtel de Chalons-**

Luxembourg (1608), with a magnificent doorway (1659). No. 22 is a handsome 17C elevation, and at no. 17, is a Jewish Study Centre with, on the angle with Rue Grenier-sur-l'eau, a memorial to an Unknown Jewish Martyr.

Further east in Rue François-Miron, at no. 44 is **La Maison d'Ourscamps** (1585), an outstanding building occupied by the l'Association de Paris historique, built around a timbered and jettied courtyard and over a vaulted 13C cellar. The former townhouse of the Abbey of Ourscamps (near Noyon), it provided accommodation for students of Notre-Dame school as well as serving as a warehouse for produce from the country property. (Open Mon–Sat 14.00–18.00, occasionally Sun.)

No. 68 is the **Hôtel de Beauvais** (1655–60) by Le Pautre (under restoration). The 18C Hôtel Hénault de Cantobre at no. 82 (note the wrought iron) is home to the **Maison Européenne de la Photographie** (☎ 01 44 78 75 00), entrance on 5–7 Rue de Fourcy. This centre for contemporary photography has a library, auditorium, and exhibition spaces, open Wed–Sun 11.00–20.00.

To the right in Rue de Jouy, no. 7, the **Hôtel d'Aumont**, by Le Vau (1648) and François Mansart (1656), has some of its original decoration, including work by Le Brun.

Beyond, Rue du Figuier leads right to the **Hôtel de Sens** (**Map 9; 3**), built 1475–1519 for the archbishops of Sens, when the bishopric of Paris was suffragan to the metropolitan see of Sens (before 1623); it is older than the Hôtel de Cluny (see Ch. 5), the only other important example of 15C domestic architecture in Paris. Unfortunately, after long neglect, the Hôtel de Sens was poorly restored; since 1911 it has housed the Bibliothèque Forney, a reference library for the fine arts.

To the east, Quai des Célestins commands attractive views of the Ile St-Louis. On the left, at no. 32, is the site of the **Tour Barbeau** which completed, on the river bank, the northern perimeter of Philippe Auguste's defensive wall. One of the best sections of this can be seen from the adjacent Rue des Jardins-St-Paul across the school playground.

The neighbouring Rue St-Paul had acquired its name before 1350; at no. 32 a fragment of the belfry of the vanished church of St-Paul-des-Champs survives. See below for the eastern end of the Quai des Célestins.

Between Rue des Jardins-St-Paul and parallel Rue St-Paul, the former gardens of King Charles V were restored and rearranged in 1970–81 in a series of courtyards perfect for browsing, called the **Village St-Paul**, with antique craft boutiques (open Thur–Mon 11.00–19.00).

The north end of Rue des Jardins-St-Paul brings you to Rue St-Antoine, an ancient thoroughfare retaining several elegant façades.

A few paces to the west is **St-Paul-St-Louis** (**Map 9; 3**), or the Grands-Jésuites, built for that Society by Louis XIII in 1627–41 to replace a chapel of 1582. The Jesuits were suppressed in 1762, and St-Paul was added to the original name in 1796 to commemorate the demolished St-Paul-des-Champs.

History of St-Paul-St-Louis

Building work, including the handsome Baroque portal, was supervised by Martellange until 1629, and François Derrand saw it through to its completion in 1641, while Turmel was responsible for the interior decorations. Its florid style, inspired by 16C Italian churches, is a good example of French

Jesuit architecture. The clock on the façade came from the church of St-Paul. The church was restored by Baltard in the 19C and the statues on the façade are 19C (by Lequesne, Etex and Préault). Richelieu said the first mass here.

The ornate **interior** is imposing but light, retaining the original clear glass with floral friezes. The 55m high dome over the crossing, was the third to be built in Paris (after the Petits Augustins and the Carmes). In the pendentives are medallions of the four Evangelists and, in the drum, *trompe l'oeil* paintings of Clovis, Charlemagne, Robert le Pieux and St-Louis (19C). Most furnishings have been dispersed, some to the Louvre, and the tomb of Henri II to Chantilly. The suspended silver angels carrying the embalmed hearts of Louis XIII and XIV have, of course, long gone.

However, the church still contains some fine works. In the north transept, is the beautiful painting *Christ in the Garden* by Delacroix, and opposite *St Louis Receiving the Crown of Thorns*, school of Vouet (1639); and in the south, *Louis XIII offering a Model of the Church to St Louis* by Vouet. There is also good wood carving and 17C ironwork. Buried here are Bishop Huet of Avranches (d. 1721), and Louis Bourdaloue, confessor to Louis XIV.

Turning east along Rue St-Antoine, you shortly reach (left; no. 62) the most elegant and prestigious *hôtel particulier* in the Marais, the **Hôtel de Sully** (or de Béthune-Sully; **Map 9: 3**). It is occupied by the Caisse Nationale des Monuments Historiques et des sites, who can give information about guided tours to the sites and monuments of Paris (booklet *Visites Conférences* available in most museums, ☎ 01 44 61 21 69/01 44 61 21 70) and has an excellent bookshop, open Tues–Sun.

The mansion (1624–30), thought to be by Jean du Cerceau, was acquired by Sully, the minister of Henri IV, in 1634. The courtyard, a fine example of Louis-XIII style, abounds in carved decorations, notably around the dormers and six bas-reliefs in niches, the females representing the Elements and the males Autumn and Winter. Spring and Summer are on the garden façade, a subdued echo of the courtyard. The entrance pavilions and the interior, extensively restored, still have their 17C ceilings and panelling. Extended by an orangery, the Petit Sully, in 1634–41, it is possible to walk through the garden out into Place des Vosges.

The photographic archives of the Caisse Nationale, which sells photographs and is invaluable to the student of French art and architecture, are at 4 Rue de Turenne, adjacent to the west.

From just east of the Hôtel de Sully, the short Rue de Birague approaches the southern entrance of the Pl. des Vosges (see Ch. 22); nos 12 and 14 have elegant features.

On the south side of Rue St-Antoine is Rue Beautreillis. Beneath the carriage-entrance of no. 22, the Grand Hôtel de Charny, are some woodcarvings in purest Louis XIII style. No. 10 was the Hôtel des Princes de Monaco, built c 1650, but altered in the 18C–19C. To the right in Rue Charles V is the imposing Hôtel d'Aubray (no. 12) of 1620. No. 10, the Hôtel de Maillé, retains its Louis XIII façade and no. 15, opposite, dates from 1642. Nos 7 and 9 Rue Beautreillis, late 16C, are fine bourgeois houses.

On reaching Rue des Lions, with a number of 17C–18C mansions, including no. 10 and no. 11, in which Mme de Sévigné, famous for her *Lettres* lived in 1645–50, turn left and then right to return to the Quai des Célestins.

No. 4 Quai des Célestins, the stately **Hôtel de Fieubet**, formerly Hôtel de St-Pol, with an interesting courtyard, was renovated and decorated by Le Sueur and Vicotte after plans by Jules Hardouin-Mansart for Gaspard de Fieubet, Chancellor to Anne of Austria. Unfortunately in 1857 it was transformed into a pastiche of Italo-Spanish Baroque.

At no. 1 Rue de Sully, on the far side of Blvd Henri-IV, in the quiet Quartier de l'Arsenal (named after the arsenal established here by Henri IV), is the **Bibliothèque de l'Arsenal** (Map 9; 5) which is open to visitors during temporary exhibitions.

History of the Bibliothèque de l'Arsenal

The library was founded in 1757 by Antoine-René, Marquis de Paulmy d'Argenson (1722–87), and sold by him to the Comte d'Artois (Louis XVI's brother) in 1785. Supplemented by other collections, it became State property in 1792, opened to the public in 1797 and has been a department of the Bibliothèque Nationale since 1977. Nodier, Hérédia, Mérimée and Anatole France were librarians here. It is installed in the former residence of the Grand Master of Artillery, built for the Duc de Sully in 1594 and embellished (1718–45) by Boffrand. The Salon de Musique has superb Louis-XV woodwork, and the Apartment of the Duchesse de La Meilleraie has a ceiling by Vouet.

This prestigious library has an encyclopaedic collection of early printed volumes and is known particularly for its incomparable series of illuminated MSS including the *Psalm Book of St-Louis*. Added to these are engravings, musical works and maps and an almost complete collection of French dramatic works. The Gordon Craig collection was acquired in 1957 and the library continues to acquire illustrated works by contemporary artists and engravers and original contemporary bindings.

At 21 Blvd de Morland in the **Pavillon de l'Arsenal** is an information centre on the architecture and urban planning of Paris with permanent and temporary exhibitions (Mon–Sat 10.30–18.30, Sun 11.00–19.00; ☎ 01 42 76 33 97).

Return to Blvd Henri-IV, and turn right past the Caserne des Célestins (barracks of the Gendarmerie Mobile, built on the site of the Celestine monastery founded in 1362, and suppressed in 1779). Take the Rue Castex (left) back to Rue St-Antoine. On the corner is the circular **Temple de Ste-Marie**, originally the chapel of the Convent of the Visitation, and now a Protestant church. It was built by François Mansart in 1632–34. The unscrupulous Surintendant des Finances, Nicolas Fouquet (1615–80) and Henri de Sévigné (Mme de Sévigné's husband, killed in a duel in 1651) were buried here. Vincent de Paul was almoner of the convent for 28 years.

A few paces to the west, at no. 21, is the Hôtel de Mayenne (or d'Ormesson), with a turret and charming staircase. Now the Ecole des Francs-Bourgeois, it was built by Jean or Jacques II du Cerceau in 1613–17, and modified by Boffrand in 1709.

To the east, a tablet on 5 Rue St-Antoine marks the position of the court of the Bastille (see Ch. 22), by which the Revolutionary mob gained access to the fortress. Near the junction of this street and the Pl. de la Bastille was the site of the great barricade of 1848, and also the last stronghold of the Communards in 1871.

22 • The Marais, Place de la Bastille, Place des Vosges

■ Arrondissements: 75003, 75004, 75012

🚇 Bastille, St-Paul, Hôtel-de-Ville, Rambuteau, Temple, Arts-et-Métiers, Réamur-Sébastopol

L'Ambroisie, 9 Pl. des Vosges, ☎ 01 42 78 51 45. The haute cuisine does not always live up to the awesome ambience, £££

Auberge Nicolas Flamel, 51 Rue Montmorency, ☎ 01 42 71 77 78. Reputedly the oldest house in Paris, and very beautiful, with good old recipés, £–££

Baracane, Bistrot de l'Oulette, 38 Rue des Tournelles, ☎ 01 42 71 43 33. Plain, dependable, low-key bistrot that one expects to find in Paris but rarely does. £

Au Bascou, 38 Rue Réamur, ☎ 01 42 72 69 25. Excellent Basque bistrot which attracts locals and visitors, £

Bofinger, 5 Rue de la Bastille, ☎ 01 42 54 13 67. Brasserie Flo group with Art Nouveau décor and dependable food, ££

Les Enfants Gâtés, 43 Rue des Francs-Bourgeois, ☎ 01 42 77 07 63. Lively bar, a favourite in the *quartier*, offering some vegetarian dishes, £

Les Fous d'en Face, 3 Rue du Bourg-Tibourg, ☎ 01 48 87 03 75. Real bistrot, good wines, good prices, £

Chez Jenny, 39 Blvd du Temple, ☎ 01 42 74 78 78. Serves game and seafood, £

Mariage Frères, 30 Rue du Bourg-Tibourg, ☎ 01 42 72 28 11. Tea with everything—original cooking, £

Chez Marianne, 2 Rue des Hospitalières-St-Gervais, ☎ 01 42 72 18 86. Jewish/Eastern European dishes in lively atmosphere. Book, £

Chez Omar, 47 Rue de Bretagne, ☎ 01 42 72 36 26. The place to experience a really good coucous, simple setting but sought after, £

Le Reconfort, 37 Rue de Poitou, ☎ 01 42 76 06 36. North African influence on the cooking, and delicately used spices, £

Under the arcades of Place des Vosges:
Ma Bourgogne, no. 19, ☎ 01 42 78 44 64. Go for the atmosphere and setting, £–££

In Rue des Rosiers, at the heart of the Marais:
Jo Goldenberg, no. 7, ☎ 01 48 87 70 39. Famous Jewish deli/restaurant, £

Hammam Café, no. 4. Kosher food in Art Nouveau Turkish baths, trendy, £

Le Loir dans la Théière, no. 3, ☎ 01 42 72 90 61. *Salon de thé* and light lunches, £

The northern part of the Marais (see map pp 236–237), one of the most interesting districts of old Paris, is bounded by the Grands Boulevards on the north and east, by Blvd de Sébastopol to the west, and by the Rue de Rivoli to the south. In spite of past neglect, demolition and some rebuilding, it remains substantially as developed in the 17C. Numerous buildings of outstanding architectural interest, many of them restored in recent years, offer a fascinating reminder of the elegance of this period. There are a number of museums in the Marais. The smaller ones are covered in this chapter, while the four major ones, Musée Carnavalet, Musée Picasso, Musée Cognacq-Jay and a new addition, the Museum of Jewish Art and History in Rue du Temple, are covered in Chapter 23. The southern sector of the Marais and the Beaubourg are described in Chapters 20 and 21.

History of the area

So called from the marshy land (*marais*, marsh or morass), the district only became habitable with the arrival of the Knights Templar and other religious houses who settled here in the 13C and converted the marshes into arable land. Royal patronage began with Charles V who, anxious to forget the associations of the Palais de la Cité with the rebellion of Etienne Marcel in 1358, built the Hôtel St-Paul here. In the 16C, the Hôtel de Lamoignon and Hôtel Carnavalet were built, but the seal of royal approval came with the construction of the Pl. Royale (1605; later known as the Pl. des Vosges, see below).

Courtiers built themselves houses as near to the Pl. Royale as possible, and the Marais remained the most fashionable residential area of Paris until the creation of the Faubourg St-Germain in the early 18C. The Revolution ended its long reign of fashionability, the nobles fled, the State confiscated their property and sold it to craftsmen, mechanics and merchants who flooded into the area, bringing a totally different aspect to the *quartier* while the grand buildings fell into neglect. Much of the Marais is still animated by trade and commerce and it is again a fashionable place to live, while its museums and picturesque streets attract many visitors.

Place de la Bastille

Immediately east of the Marais lies Pl. de la Bastille (**Map 9; 4**), laid out in 1803. The ground plan of the famous fortress prison is marked by a line of paving-stones in the Place beneath which some of its cellars are said to survive. Its keep (a model of which is in the Musée Carnavalet) stood on the west side, across the end of Rue St-Antoine, and the main drawbridge was slightly north of the junction with Blvd Henri-IV. The July Column (see below) stands approximately in the centre of what was the east bastion. The Canal St-Martin now runs beneath the Place, appearing to the south in the Port de Plaisance de l'Arsenal (1806), which flows into the Seine. The canal boat trips start from here (see p 27). The area between the port and Blvd de la Bastille was turned into a garden in 1982–83.

History of the Place de la Bastille

The Bastille (or Bastille St-Antoine), originally a bastion-tower defending the eastern entrance to Paris, developed under Charles V into a fortress with eight massive towers, immensely thick walls, and a wide moat. Nevertheless, prisoners managed to escape. By the reign of Louis XIII, the Bastille had become almost exclusively a state prison for political offenders, among whom were the mysterious Man in the Iron Mask (1698–1703) and Voltaire (twice). The arbitrary arrest by *lettre de cachet*, imprisonment without trial, made the Bastille a popular synonym for oppression. Many illustrious names are among those held here, often for obscure reasons: the Duchesse du Maine and Mme de Tencin; John Vanbrugh the playwright/architect for most of 1692; another inmate was the notorious Marquis de Sade, who wrote *Justine* and other racy works here.

On 14 July 1789, the Revolutionary mob, aided by a few troops, attacked and overwhelmed its defenders, murdered the governor, the Marquis de Launay, and freed a handful of prisoners. Work on its demolition was immediately put in hand.

The **July Column** (Colonne de Juillet) is not connected with the storming of the Bastille, but was erected by Louis-Philippe in 1840–41 to commemorate the 504 victims of the *Trois Glorieuses* (three days' street-fighting) of July 1830, who are buried in vaults beneath the circular base of the column. The victims of the Revolution of February 1848 were subsequently interred here, and their names added to the inscription. The bronze-faced column, 51.5m high, is surmounted by a bronze-gilt figure of Liberty.

To the south east of the Place, on the site of the former Gare de la Bastille, is the **Opéra National de Paris Bastille** (Map 9; 6), a sophisticated and costly structure with a slightly clinical look and convex façade, built to celebrate the bicentenary of the Revolution. Its design, by Carlos Ott, a Uraguayan-born Canadian, was chosen from 744 projects and is a far cry from Garnier's Opera House.

Incorporating the latest technical equipment, the Opéra Bastille is noted for its excellent acoustics. The building covers a vast area and comprises a main auditorium with seating for 2700, a so-called *Salle modulable* for 600 to 1000, and a studio seating 280. Granite, wood and glass are used in the uncluttered décor of the main auditorium, which has excellent sightlines. There are several rehearsal rooms for the orchestra, chorus and ballet, numerous studios, extensive workshops, scenery stores and costumes as well as two restaurants. The scene changes are made by bringing into position any of six separate platforms, including the stage, without needing to shift scenery behind the scenes. There are guided visits lasting just over an hour at certain times (☎ 01 40 01 19 70). Both ballet and opera are performed here. Box office: ☎ 08 36 69 78 68, fax 01 44 73 13 74, www.opera-de-paris.fr.

Opéra Bastille

For the Faubourg St-Antoine, to the east, see Ch. 31.

Nos 2–20 in Blvd Beaumarchais, leading north from Pl. de la Bastille, are built on the site of a luxurious mansion and garden belonging to the dramatist Caron de Beaumarchais (1732–99).

Rue de la Bastille leads northwest from Pl. de la Bastille, north of and parallel to Rue St-Antoine, to Rue des Tournelles, where no. 28 is the **Hôtel de Mansart-Sagonne**, built for himself in 1674–85 by Jules Hardouin-Mansart and decorated by Le Brun and Mignard. Rue du Pas-de-la-Mule leads left to Pl. des Vosges; beyond, no. 50 has a splendid façade.

Place des Vosges

Pl. des Vosges (**Map 9; 3**), built 1606–11, has a specific charm unlike any other square of Paris. At the heart of the Marais, this large quadrangle is surrounded by 39 houses built on a uniform plan with brick, stone and stucco façades, arcaded ground floors and simple dormers. Trees were not planted in the central gardens until 1783, damaging the overall symmetry, so the ideal time to visit is in winter when the leaves have fallen.

The main approach to Pl. des Vosges, from Rue St-Antoine, is by Rue de Birague, passing through the Pavillon du Roi (see below).

History of the Place des Vosges

The Place occupies the site of the royal Palais des Tournelles, the residence of the Duke of Bedford, English regent of France in 1422 after the death of Henry V. In 1559, during the marriage celebrations of Elisabeth de France to Philippe II of Spain, Henri II was accidentally killed by Montgomery at a tournament. His widow, Catherine de Médicis consequently abandoned the palace. The square in its present form was laid out for Henri IV, possibly by Louis Métezeau or Baptiste du Cerceau, as the Place Royale and was inaugurated by Louis XIII in 1612. The slightly taller king's pavilion was built above the gateway in the centre of the south side, and the queen's was the corresponding building on the north (no. 28). In the earlier part of the reign of Louis XIV this was one of the most fashionable addresses in Paris, and the centre of the *Nouvelles Précieuses* satirised by Molière. It acquired its present name in 1799, after the department of the Vosges was first to discharge its liabilities for the Revolutionary Wars.

At the corners of the square are fountains (1816), and in the centre an indifferent equestrian statue of Louis XIII (1825) set up to replace one destroyed in 1792.

No. 6 is the **Maison Victor Hugo**, open 10.00–17.40, closed Mon and public holidays (☎ 01 42 72 10 16), in which Victor Hugo lived in 1832–48 (second floor), perhaps of more interest for his numerous pen and wash drawings (c 350) than for the memorabilia. The upper rooms provide an opportunity to enjoy the view over the Place.

Things to see include the bust of *Hugo* by Rodin; *Portrait of Juliette Drouet* by Bastien-Lepage; *The Première of Hernani* by Besnard; *Portrait of Adèle Foucher*, the poet's wife, by Louis Boulanger; *Hugo on his Death-bed* by Bonnat; and works by Célestin Nanteuil and Delacroix. There is also furniture and woodwork, designed or carved by Hugo.

No. 7, the Petit-Hôtel de Sully, was built by Jean Androuet du Cerceau. The writers Théophile Gautier (in 1831–34) and Alphonse Daudet lived at no. 8, the Hôtel de Fourcy (1605) and no. 21 was the mansion of Cardinal de Richelieu.

From the northwest corner of Pl. des Vosges you cross Rue de Turenne (where to the left, in the court of No. 23, is the Hôtel de Villacerf, of c 1660, with a fountain), and enter Rue des Francs-Bourgeois. (For the north part of the Rue de Turenne, see below.)

At the corner of Rue des Francs-Bourgeois and Rue de Sévigné is the imposing **Hôtel Carnavalet**. Begun in 1548 for Jacques de Ligneris, President of the Parlement, it is built around a courtyard with sculptures by Jean Goujon. It was altered in 1660 by François Mansart, who built the present façade but retained the 16C gateway with statues by Goujon. Further alterations were made in 19C and 20C. It now contains the Musée Carnavalet (see Ch. 23). In 1989 the museum was extended into the Hôtel le Peletier de St-Fargeau, built by Pierre Bullet for Michel de Peletier in 1687–90. Mme de Sévigné lived here from 1677 until her death in 1696; her apartments were on the west side, opposite the entrance. The building was acquired by the municipality in 1866 and the museum was inaugurated in 1880.

Immediately west of the Hôtel Carnavalet, at 11 Rue Payenne, the Hôtel de Polastron-Polignac, houses the Swedish Cultural Centre and **Musée Tessin**, with paintings by Alexander Roslin (1718–93) and others. No. 13, the Hôtel de Lude, is a good example of an early 18C mansion. There is a small lapidary collection in the Sq. Georges-Caën opposite.

South of the Hôtel Carnavalet, on the corner of the Rue Pavée, no. 24 is the fine **Hôtel Lamoignon**, named after a 17C occupant, which was built in 1584 for Diane de France, legitimised daughter of Henri II. Possibly the work of J.-B. Androuet du Cerceau, it has colossal Corinthian pilasters and curved pediments. It now houses the **Bibliothèque Historique de la Ville de Paris**, containing over 400,000 volumes and 100,000 manuscripts relating to the history of the city, and to the Revolution.

Rue Pavée brings you to Rue des Rosiers, the old Jewish quarter (parallel with Rue des Francs-Bourgeois), an atmospheric street with some interesting restaurants.

On the south side of Rue des Francs-Bourgeois, no. 31 is the Hôtel d'Albret, built c 1640 by François Mansart, with an 18C street façade. At the end of the courtyard of no. 33 is a fragment of Philippe Auguste's walls. At 8 Rue Elzévir, leading north, is the **Hôtel de Donon**, since 1990 the home of the Musée Cognacq-Jay (See Ch. 23). The restored mansion, dating from 1575, was built for Médéric de Donon, but several alterations were made in the mid 17C.

On the corner of the transverse Rue Vieille-du-Temple (right; no. 54) is one remaining turret (c 1510), of the heavily restored Hôtel Héroult.

A short distance south is the **Hôtel des Ambassadeurs de Hollande** (no. 47), built by Cottard in 1657–60. On this site stood the house of the Maréchal de Rieux, in front of which on his return from Isabeau de Bavière's residence (see below), the Duc d'Orléans was assassinated in 1407 by Jean sans Peur's (Duke of Burgundy) thugs.

For the north half of Rue Vieille-du-Temple, see below.

On the left you pass **N.-D. des Blancs-Manteaux**, a reference to the white habits of an order of mendicant monks established here in 1285 by Louis IX. The

18C door came from St-Barthélemy in the Ile de la Cité, demolished in 1863 and inside is a Flemish style rococo pulpit (1749).

At 55 Rue des Francs-Bourgeois are the offices of the Crédit Municipal, formerly the Mont-de-Piété (a government pawnbroking establishment), founded by Louis XVI in 1777.

Beyond at no. 60 is the imposing portal of the **Hôtel de Soubise** (Map 9; 1), the home of the **Museum of the History of France of the National Archives**. Open 12.00–17.45 Mon–Fri, 13.45–17.45 Sat–Sun, closed Tues (☎ 01 40 27 60 96), frequent temporary exhibitions.

History of the Hôtel de Soubise

The first mansion here was the Hôtel de Clisson, built in the 14C by Constable Olivier de Clisson, supporter of Charles V against the English. The turreted Gothic gateway of 1380 (58 Rue des Archives), is a vestige of this building and a rare example of 14C architecture in Paris. Bolingbroke (later Henry IV) gave a farewell banquet here in 1399 before setting out for England. Purchased in 1553 by François de Lorraine, the Duc de Guise and his wife Anna d'Este, there is a suggestion that this was where the St-Bartholomew's Massacre was planned, and the Day of the Barricades began in 1588. In 1700 the mansion was sold to François de Rohan-Soubise and Anne de Rohan-Chabot. Between 1705 and 1712 the architect Delamair transformed the building, re-orientating the main entrance onto Rue des Francs Bourgeois.

The Archives Nationales have been housed here since 1808, ensuring the survival of the interior decoration (1712–45) and the splendid Cour d'Honneur, with its colonnade, has copies of *The Four Seasons* by Robert le Lorrain on the façade.

From 1736 Germain Boffrand, commissioned by the Prince of Soubise, produced a masterly design for an oval pavilion connecting rooms in the north wing, and then revamped the interior in curviliniar French Rococo or Rocaille décor. On the ground floor are the Prince's Apartments with decoration by Boucher, Carle Van Loo, L.-S. Adam, J.-B. Lemoine II, Restout, and others. A 19C staircase leads to the Princess's Apartments and the Grand Antichambre (the Guises' Guard Room). The chapel bears traces of the Chapelle de Clisson of 1375 transformed in 1533 and the Chambre d'Apparat (Ceremonial Bedroom), heavy with stucco, contains a reproduction of the princess's bed from Boffrand's engravings. The oval Princess's Salon is a stunning piece by Boffrand and Natoire in white and gold.

The **Hôtel de Rohan** (open to the public during special exhibitions) known also as the Hôtel de Strasbourg, was begun in 1704 by Delamair and successively inhabited by four cardinals of the Rohan family, all of whom were bishops of Strasbourg. From 1808 to 1925 the mansion was occupied by the Imprimerie Nationale. In the second courtyard is a fine relief of the *Horses of Apollo* by Robert le Lorrain. Only the rooms of the first floor have conserved their original decoration (mid-18C) and are hung with Gobelins and Beauvais tapestries. The Cabinet des Singes contains Chinese style paintings by Christophe Huet (1745–50), and the Cabinet des Fables comes from the Hôtel de Soubise and dates from the time of Boffrand.

From Rue des Archives leads Rue de Braque with some fine houses: nos 4–6, the

17C Hôtel Le Lièvre de la Grange; no. 7 belonged to the Comte de Vergennes (1717–87), Louis XVI's foreign minister to and supporter of American Independence. At the corner of Rue des Archives and Rue des Haudriettes is a fountain, with a naiad sculpted by Mignot (1765).

Diagonally opposite at 60 Rue des Archives is the grand **Hôtel de Guénégaud** by François Mansart (c 1650), containing the **Musée de la Chasse et de la Nature** and an exclusive Hunting Club. Open 10.00–12.30, 13.30–17.30, closed Tues, ☎ 01 42 72 86 43. The museum contains a variety of hunting weapons, from the 16C–19C, from France and other parts of Europe; powder flasks, daggers, cross-bows, etc. and stuffed big game, swords, porcelain decorated with hunting scenes and Mexican terracotta animals. Among the paintings are *Philip the Fair* (Philip I of Spain; father of the Emperor Charles V) in falconer's costume, and *La Chasse de Diane* by 'Velvet' Brueghel and van Balen. There are also a number of works by François Desportes (1661–1743); and by Chardin, Oudry, Carle Vernet and Monet.

In Rue Charlot, leading northeast from Rue des Quatre-Fils, is St-Jean-St-François, built as a Capuchin chapel on the site of a *jeu de paume* and completed in 1715.

Further along Rue des Quatre-Fils you meet Rue Vieille-du-Temple; at no. 87 is the Hôtel de Rohan (see above).

From the intersection of Rues Vieille-du-Temple (no. 90 was the site of the Jeu de Paume des Marais, used as a theatre from 1634–73) and des Quatre-Fils, a short detour takes you towards the northeastern section of the Marais via the Hôtel Salé. Take Rue de la Perle to Pl. de Thorigny where on the right (no. 1) is the **Hôtel Libéral-Bruant**, named after one of the architects of Les Invalides and built in 1685 for his personal use. It has a perfectly harmonious pedimented elevation, decorated with four busts in niches. It now houses the **Musée de la Serrure** (or Musée Bricard). Eugène Bricard, was the 19C collector of this splendid decorative door-furniture, including locks, keys, handles and plaques of all periods. Open Mon 14.00–17.00, closed Sat, Sun, ☎ 01 42 77 79 62.

A few paces to the southeast bring you to Rue du Parc Royal. No. 4, was built c 1620. No. 10, the restored Hôtel de Vigny, of the same date, is now the offices of the Centre National de Documentation du Patrimoine–Inventaire Général. Rue Payenne leads back towards the Hôtel Carnavalet.

Northeast on Rue de Thorigny, to the left, is the **Hôtel Salé (Map 9; 1)** an elegant mansion also called the Hôtel Aubert de Fontenay and the Hôtel de Juigné, but it became known as the Hôtel Salé on account of the huge profits its owner made from salt tax. The largest house in the Marais, it is a prime example of a *hôtel particulier* of the 17C between court and garden. It now contains the Musée Picasso (See Ch. 23).

Rue Ste-Anastase leads, right, off Rue de Thorigny into Rue de Turenne, where no. 60 is the Hôtel du Grand-Veneur, with a fine boar's head on the façade, while no. 66 retains traces of the Hôtel de Turenne, built for the great marshal's father. On the site of the chapel of the convent later installed here, the church of **St-Denis-du-St-Sacrement** was built in 1835 in neo-Greek style, by Godde, and contains a painting of the *Descent from the Cross* by Delacroix. At the junction of Rue Debelleyme, leading northwest, and Rue Vieille-du-Temple is the Hôtel d'Espinay, no. 110, with a remarkable staircase. This *quartier* has a number of art galleries.

No. 78 Rue des Archives (the next main street to the southwest), was built by Bullet (c 1660), with a beautiful staircase by Le Muet.

Further north is **Sq. du Temple (Map 4; 7)**, at the centre of the densely populated Quartier du Temple, one of the 24 squares created during the Second Empire. Until the late-12C this was the site of the stronghold of the Knights Templar. The headquarters of their order in Europe until 1313, it was then occupied by the Order of St John. Today this garden boasts many different trees and a lake with a cascade made with rocks from the Forest of Fontainebleau.

History of the Sq. du Temple

The area owned by the Templars lay for the most part between this point and Pl. de la République to the northeast (see Ch. 24). Before the Revolution it was occupied by wealthy families, artisans who did not belong to the corporations and therefore were free from many restrictions, and debtors who were protected here from legal action.

The palace of the Grand Prior of the Knights of St John was renowned for its luxuriousness but, with the Revolution, the Tour du Temple (1265) was transformed into a prison, and in August 1792 Louis XVI and the royal family were taken from the Tuileries and incarcerated here. (Objects from the prison are now in the Musée Carnavalet.)

A short distance to the north (195 Rue du Temple) is **Ste-Elisabeth**, founded in 1628 by Marie de Médicis. The main feature is the boiseries including, in the ambulatory, 17C carvings of scriptural scenes from the abbey of St-Vaast at Arras.

Rue Réaumur leads west from Sq. du Temple, passing (left) Rue Volta, in which no. 3, of c 1300, is possibly the oldest surviving house in Paris. Rue Réaumur crosses Rue de Turbigo to meet Rue St-Martin (the original Roman road to the north from Lutetia) between the former Abbey of St-Martin-des-Champs (right) now occupied by the Musée National des Arts et Métiers (see Ch. 23), and (left) the 15C **St-Nicolas-des-Champs** (Map 3; 8). This large church, the third on this site, dates mainly from the 15C and the Flamboyant north façade and west portal date from that time. Extensions to the nave in the 16C account for the Renaissance south door, inspired by a design by Philibert Delorme. The interior was classicised c 1745 and the organ case, some parts going back to 1610, is richly decorated. The church is well endowed with paintings (16C–19C) by such as Simon Vouet, Lallement, Coypel, Bonnat and J.-P. Laurens.

Return to Rue du Temple by turning east along Rue des Gravilliers (just south of St-Nicolas-des-Champs). 13 Rue Chapon (the first turning right, going south), has an interesting court. Nos 101–103, the Hôtel de Montmorency, the residence of Fouquet in 1652, has its entrance at 5 Rue de Montmorency. No. 51 in this street, the Maison du Grand-Pignon, restored in 1900, was built in 1407 by Nicolas Flamel.

Rue Michel-le-Comte, parallel to the south, retains a number of early 17C houses. Nos 67–87, on the west side of Rue du Temple, provide a charming ensemble of 17C houses. One of the best, the **Hôtel de St-Aignan** at no. 71, became the home of a new museum for Jewish art and history (see Ch. 23) in 1999.

History of the Hôtel de St-Aignan

The Hôtel de St-Aignan, designed by Pierre le Muet, was completed in 1650 for Cardinal Mazarin's Superintendent of Finances. An unprecedented example of civil architecture in Paris, the giant Corinthian order is deployed in the magnificent courtyard. On the south side, masking a section of Philippe

Courtyard of the Hôtel St-Aignan, Musée d'Art et d'Histoire

Auguste's boundary wall, is a *trompe l'oeil* façade creating an illusion of space and symmetry. The mansion was acquired by the Duc de St-Aignan in 1688, at which time the main staircase was installed and the garden façade enlarged. Le Nôtre was involved in the design of the garden. The 20C restoration, begun in 1978, is based on the late 17C design and the recreation of the 18C garden is underway.

No. 79, c 1620, altered after 1751, the Hôtel de Montmor, has a fine gateway and attractive pediment in the courtyard. No. 41, the Auberge de l'Aigle d'Or (17C), is the last remaining example in Paris of a coaching inn of the period. The square turret on no. 24 dates from 1610; and an inscription on no. 17 indicates the site of the house of du Guesclin (1372–80). Rejoin the Rue de Rivoli at the Hôtel de Ville (see Ch. 19).

23 • Museums in the Marais: Carnavalet, Cognacq-Jay, Picasso, Arts et Métiers, Jewish Art

> ■ Arrondissements: 75003
>
> 🚇 Bastille, St-Paul, Rambuteau, Temple, Arts-et-Métiers, Réamur-Sébastopol
>
> Restaurants and cafés: see Chapters 21 and 22.

Musée Carnavalet, Musée de l'Histoire de Paris

The Musée Carnavalet (**Map 9; 3**) is housed in the grand Hôtel Carnavalet (See Ch. 22) 23 Rue de Sévigné and, since 1989, Hôtel le Peletier de St-Fargeau, linked to the main building by a gallery on the first floor. This is an important collection which traces the history of Paris from prehistory to the early 20C

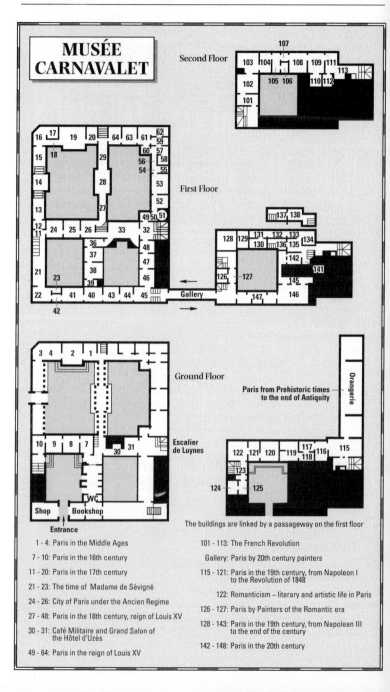

MUSÉE CARNAVALET

Second Floor

First Floor

Ground Floor

Paris from Prehistoric times to the end of Antiquity

Orangerie

Escalier de Luynes

Gallery

Shop **Bookshop**

WC

Entrance

The buildings are linked by a passageway on the first floor

1 - 4: Paris in the Middle Ages

7 - 10: Paris in the 16th century

11 - 20: Paris in the 17th century

21 - 23: The time of Madame de Sévigné

24 - 26: City of Paris under the Ancien Regime

27 - 48: Paris in the 18th century, reign of Louis XV

30 - 31: Café Militaire and Grand Salon of the Hôtel d'Uzès

49 - 64: Paris in the reign of Louis XV

101 - 113: The French Revolution

Gallery: Paris by 20th century painters

115 - 121: Paris in the 19th century, from Napoleon I to the Revolution of 1848

122: Romanticism – literary and artistic life in Paris

126 - 127: Paris by Painters of the Romantic era

128 - 143: Paris in the 19th century, from Napolean III to the end of the century

142 - 148: Paris in the 20th century

through paintings, sculpture, furniture and decors. Especially charming are the reconstructed interiors saved from mainly 18C Parisian mansions when Haussmann was demolishing many buildings in the 19C. Open 10.00–17.40, closed Mon and public holidays (☎ 01 42 72 21 13).

The bronze statue of Louis XIV in the centre of the **courtyard** is by Coysevox. Of the sculptures in the courtyard, the best are those by Jean Goujon on the entrance arch and above the door on the left. The reliefs of *The Seasons,* on the side opposite the entrance, were probably done under his direction. On the right, the relief above the door is a 19C copy of the one opposite; those on the first storey are by Van Obstal (1660). In autumn 2000 the 17C Orangerie, a unique example in Paris, opened after renovations. It now contains a new exhibition of neolithic finds from Bercy, including pirogues (canoes) of c 2000–4000 BC, and a presentation concerning the research that has been carried out on the origins of Paris up to the end of the Roman period.

The **entrance** to the museum is to the right of the courtyard. After passing through a vestibule, off which is a bookshop, you turn left into the **Salles des Enseignes**, with shop and tavern signs of the 15C–19C and maquettes of Paris during the last century. Beyond these rooms is the foot of the Escalier de Luynes. On the ground floor are Archaeological, Renaissance and 18C sections. The period rooms (restored 1996) are on the first floor. The Hôtel le Peletier de St-Fargeau has displays relating to Paris from the Revolution to the 20C.

Ground floor

The colonnaded Pavillon de Choiseul, between the Cour de la Victoire (right) and Cour des Drapiers, brings you to the section (**rooms 1–4**) given over to the early history of Paris, with maquettes of Gallo-Roman Lutetia, and its layout during the Merovingian period; fragments of masonry and collections of glass, terracottas, and coins. Also displayed are bronze objects, jewellery, buckles and arms, together with parts of a sarcophagus.

Return through the colonnade, to (right) the Renaissance rooms (**5–10**). As well as a maquette of the medieval Cité there are several interesting paintings with views of Paris by French, Flemish and Dutch artists; and *Portraits of Mary Stuart in 1561*, wearing a white mourning veil, and of *Catherine de Médicis* (both School of Clouet); the *Duc de Guise* (known as Le Balafré from his scar) attributed to François Quesnel, and an anon. *Portrait of Henri III*. In the Salle Bleu are early views of Paris and 16C prints.

In the panelled **Salon Ledoux** (1762), designed by Claude-Nicolas Ledoux (1736–1809), saved from the Café Militaire (formerly in Rue St-Honoré) are Martin Drolling's *Portrait of Ledoux*, attributed to Callet, and *Portraits of Ledoux's Daughter*, and his *Wife*. **Room 31** contains some magnificent gilt panelling of 1767 from the Hôtel d'Uzès, Rue Montmartre, also from designs by Ledoux.

First floor

To follow a more or less chronological sequence, begin with **rooms 24–26**, the former apartment of the prolific letter writer Mme de Sévigné, now known as the Salles des Echevins, devoted to Paris during the Ancien Régime. Note the monumental chimneypiece of the Louis-XIII period and several portraits of aldermen by de Troy and Duplessis; by Largillière portrait of *Françoise Boucher d'Orsay* in 1702.

The **Salles Sévigné, rooms 21–23**, with late 17C panelling, were lived in by Mme de Sévigné's son. Room 21 was used as a portrait gallery, and contains a pastel portrait of her by Nanteuil, and a portrait by Mignard of her daughter, *Mme de Grignan*. Among souvenirs is the japanned desk that Mme de Sévigné brought from the Château des Rochers near Vitré and a collection of faience.

Rooms 12–20 describe the transformation of Paris during the reigns of Louis XIII and Louis XIV, recorded in views of the city and evoked by the interiors of grand town houses. In the first room, *Pont Neuf*, c 1633; **room 13**, *Views of the Place Royale* (now Pl. des Vosges), and of the *Cité from the Quai de la Tournelle*, c 1646, and several views by Abraham de Verwer. **Room 14** has engravings of buildings, and **room 15** further views, including the *Observatoire* by Pierre-Denis Martin and also his *View from the Quai de Bercy*. **Room 16** contains early 18C panelling from the Hôpital de la Pitié, and views of popular scenes. **Room 17** displays richly painted and gilded boiseries of c 1656 from the Hôtel Colbert de Villacerf at 23 Rue de Turenne; in **room 19** is panelling from the grand cabinet doré by Le Brun from the Hôtel de la Rivière, 14 Pl. des Vosges, with ceiling painting by Le Brun. **Room 20** contains another ceiling painting (1651), also by Le Brun, from the same mansion and recently restored.

The remainder of the rooms are in Louis XV and Louis XVI styles. These rooms contain interiors from *hôtels particuliers* originally situated in smart *quartiers* such as the Faubourg St-Germain and Faubourg St-Honoré. Two have been meticulously redecorated using the 18C technique *peinture à la colle*. The colour schemes, all of which are different, vary according to the period, and were scrupulously researched. The panelling has relief decoration in both wood and stucco. Fabrics were specially woven to match the decor, carefully differentiating between what is authentic and what is remade. The antique furniture is from various sources and includes an important furniture collection donated in 1965 by Henriette Bouvier.

Rooms 27–29 contain views of Paris between 1720 and 1760, notably those by Charles-Léopold de Grevenbroeck and Nicolas Raguenet (1715–93) including *The regatta near the Pont Notre-Dame*, showing houses flanking the bridge.

Room 32 is a reconstruction of a stairwell from the Hôtel de Luynes, decorated with *trompe-l'oeil* paintings of peopled balconies, by P.A. Brunetti (1748). In **room 39** is a collection of wax portraits and a beautiful study by Boucher, *Le Pied de Mlle O'Murphy*; **room 41** Chardin's *Game of Billiards*, and Etienne Jeaurat (1699–1789), the *Transport of 'filles de joie' to La Salpêtrière*. **Room 46** contains a portrait of the *Abbé Tournus Praying* by Restout. **Room 47** is devoted to the theatre during the reign of Louis XV. **Room 48** has a portrait of *D'Alembert* by Catherine Lusurier and a *Portrait of Voltaire* after Nicolas de Largillière and Voltaire's armchair.

Aspects of Paris during the later years of the reign of Louis XV and that of Louis XVI are depicted in **rooms 49–64**. **Room 53** has two genre paintings by Michel Garnier (1753–1819), of interest for their depiction of costume; **rooms 56–57** topographical and architectural paintings, while **room 57**, decorated by Boucher and Fragonard c 1765, comes from the house of the engraver Gilles Demarteau in the Rue de la Pelleterie. **Rooms 59–64** contain paintings by de Machy, Hubert Robert (including his *Demolition of the Houses on the Pont Notre-Dame in 1786* and on the *Pont au Change in 1788*), J.-B. Lallemand, Debucourt, Alexandre Noël and others.

From room 45, take the passage (which may contain exhibitions) to the **Hôtel le Peletier de St-Fargeau**, and then up a staircase. This brings you to the first of a dozen rooms devoted to the French Revolution.

In **rooms 101–104** are *La Fête de la Fédération*, a large painting by Thévenin, and *La Déclaration des Droits de l'Homme*. Also an anon. *Portrait of Mirabeau*, and a view of the *Revolutionaries in the Jeu de Paume, Versailles, 20 June 1789*, school of David; the keys of the Bastille; *The Storming and Destruction of the Bastille* by Hubert Robert; and a model of the prison cut from one of its stones under the direction of Palloy, the demolition contractor, and other souvenirs of the event; historical scenes of events preceding the fall of the Bastille by J.-B. Lallemand; a *Self-portrait Bust*, attributed to Curtius, a relation of Mme Tussaud; and an anon. *Portrait of Dr Guillotin*.

Life in the Prison du Temple from 10 August 1792, is evoked in **rooms 105–106** and painted there in 1793 is a *Portrait of young Louis XVII* by J.-M. Vien fils. Two paintings by Jean-Jacques Hauer: *Louis XVI's Fairwell to his Family*, and *Louis XVI taken away from His Family*; paintings of the *Execution of the King* and of *Marie-Antoinette*. **Rooms 107–108** concern the Convention and the Terror, with prison scenes by Hubert Robert and anonymous portraits of main political figures of the period; scenes by de Machy and Hubert Robert (*The Prison of St-Lazare*). **Rooms 109–114**: the Directoire and the period of the Revolutionary wars. Room 13: colourful gouaches by Pierre-Etienne le Sueur, and room 14: Sèvres porcelain depicting revolutionary emblems.

Stairs and a lift descend to the ground floor and **room 115**, devoted to the Consulate and First Empire, with Gérard, portraits of *Mme Récamier seated* and of the actress *Mlle Duchesnois*; Pierre-Paul Prud'hon, *Portrait of Talleyrand in 1807*; Robert Lefèvre, *Portrait of Napoléon in 1809*; the Death-mask of Napoléon and his *Nécessaire de Campagne*, among other souvenirs.

Room 116 covers the Restoration period. Gérard, *Portrait of Charles X*. **Rooms 117–118** have paintings of Paris, notably by E. Bouhot, *View of the Palais des Tuileries seen from the Quai d'Orsay*; Corot, *The Pont St-Michel and Quai des Orfèvres*.

Events surrounding the Revolution of July and the July Monarchy, in **rooms 119–120**, include a maquette depicting the arrival of the Duc d'Orléans at the Hôtel de Ville, 31 July 1830; a plaster model by F. Rude of the *Departure of the Volunteers*, for his relief on the Arc de Triomphe; François Dubois, *The Erection of the Obelisk of Luxor in the Pl. de la Concorde*, together with a painting of the scene by Geslin.

Room 121 covers the Second Republic: Horace Vernet, *Portrait of Arago*; anon., *Portrait of Pierre-Joseph Proudhon* and several paintings by H.-V. Sebron and J.J. Champin. **Rooms 122, 124–25**: the Romantic period, with portraits by Henri Lehmann of *Liszt*, and of *Marie d'Agoult*; of the divas *Marietta Alboni* and *Malibran* by A.-J. Péignon and Henri Decaisne respectively. A collection of miniature caricature sculptured busts in bronze or plaster of famous artists and musicians by Jean-Pierre Dantan, notably those of *Berlioz*, *Verdi*, and also the *Duke of Wellington*.

At the top of the adjacent stairs, designed by Pierre Bullet, **rooms 126–127**, are more views of Paris. From the landing is a view of two huge bird's-eye *Panoramas of Paris* c 1852 by Victor Navlet.

Second Empire souvenirs in **rooms 128–129** include the Prince Imperial's cradle (1856); a *Portrait of Baron Haussmann* attributed to Henri Lehmann; a pastel *Portrait of Mérimée* by Simon Rochard; anon. *Arrival of Queen Victoria at the Gare de l'Est to attend the Universal Exhibition of 1855*; *View of the levelling of the Colline de Chaillot in 1867 for the Exhibition*, and a panoramic view of that exhibition.

Room 130, events during the Siege of Paris in 1871: artillery in the Jardin des Tuileries in late September 1870; Gambetta leaving Paris by balloon; sketches by Puvis de Chavannes for his *The Pigeon*, and *The Balloon*; and Corot, *Paris Burning*. **Room 131**: *The Commune*, illustrated by G. Boulanger.

Cross room 132 to **room 133**: *Portrait of Blanqui* by Eugène Carrière; views by Victor Dargaud and E.-M. Lansyer. **Room 135**: several Parisian views, among them Lépine, *The Seine at Passy*; Jongkind, *The Rue St-Séverin at night*; Guillaumin, *The Seine at Bercy*; and Lebourg, *Notre-Dame under Snow*.

Room 136 is devoted to portraits of literary figures, among them, P.L. Mita, *Nadar*; Eugène Carriere (1849–1906), *Edmond de Goncourt*; L. Montegut, *Daudet Writing*; Boldini, a pastel of *'Gyp'*; Gustave Doré, *Charles Philipon*. **Room 137–138** depict the Belle Epoque, with several works by Jean Béraud (1849–1935).

The reconstruction in **room 141** of the Art Nouveau decor (1899; by Henri Sauvage) is of a private room from the Café de Paris, which stood at 39 Av. de l'Opéra until demolished in 1954. In adjoining **rooms 142–143** is the reassembled decoration of 1900 for the jewellery shop of Fouquet, in Rue Royale, designed by Alphonse Mucha (1860–1939).

Room 146 contains the Baroque-style decoration of the ballroom of the Hôtel de Wendel, designed in 1924 by the Catalan artist Josep Maria Sert, the theme of which is the Procession of the Queen of Sheba.

In **room 147** are furniture and mementos from the homes of Paul Léataud, Marcel Proust, and Anna de Noailles, all of whom used to write in bed. Among portraits here are Countess Greffulhe, the *Abbé Mugnier*; J.-E. Blanche, *Princesse Jean de Broglie*, *Cocteau in 1913*, and *René Crevel*; Foujita, *Jean Rostand* (the biologist son of Edmond); and Romaine Brooks, *Natalie Barney*.

On leaving this room, turn to look at the caryatids from the Café de Paris (see room 141 above) and the *Portrait of André Wormser* by Albert Besnard. Keep straight ahead along the passage (**room 148**) before descending the stairs to the exit.

Musée Cognacq-Jay

Since 1990 Musée Cognacq-Jay (**Map 9; 3**) has been at 8 Rue Elzévir, the Hôtel de Donon (see Ch. 22). The museum was started by Ernest Cognacq (1835–1928), founder of the Magasins de la Samaritaine, and was inaugurated in 1929. Open 10.00–17.40, closed Mon and public holidays (☎ 01 40 27 07 21).

This is an intimate and perfectly maintained museum, entirely devoted to the 18C, with a profusion of objects in 20 small rooms on four floors and in the impressively beamed attic. Many of the rooms contain beautiful panelling with rocaille decoration, some removed from the Château d'Eu (Normandy), and some original 17C panelling.

Among outstanding pieces of **furniture** are a Beauvais tapestry covered set of chairs by J.-B. Lelarge; marquetry work by Denizot, Weisweiler, A.; a bureau by Boulle in ebony inlaid with a variety of materials; a small desk in holly by Oeben;

a Louis XVI bed *à la polonaise*. The collection of ceramics and porcelain includes a colourful pair of Kien-Lung cranes (porcelain); also terracotta busts by J.-B. Lemoyne of the Maréchal de Saxe and the Maréchal de Lowendal; Meissen porcelain and French terracotta figures, including Clodion, Project for the tomb of Mme Dubarry's dog; a rare collection of enamelled and jewelled boxes and other small objects. It has an unusually large collection—for Paris—of English paintings of the period.

A pick of the outstanding portraits includes Boucher, *Mme Baudouin*, his *Daughter*; Gérard, *Mme Bauquin du Boulay and her Niece*; Marguerite Gérard, *Claude-Nicolas Ledoux*, the architect; Hugh Douglas Hamilton, *Lady Carhampton (?)*; Adélaïde Labille Guiard, *Comtesse de Maussion*; Largillière, *The Duchess of Beaufort (?)*; Maurice Quentin Delatour, *Mme la Présidente de Rieux*, *Self-portrait*, *Man in a Blue Waistcoat*, and *The Marquis de Bérenger*; Thomas Lawrence, *Princess Clémentine de Metternich*; Nattier, *Madame Henriette*, *Marie Leszczynska*; Perronneau, *Charles Lenormant du Coudray*; Reynolds, *Lord Northington*; attributed to Romney, *Female portrait*; John Russell, *Miss Power*; Elisabeth Vigée-Lebrun, *The Vicomtesse de Mirabeau Playing a Guitar* and *A Dancer*.

Other works include Boucher, *La belle Cuisinière*, Canaletto, two *Venetian scenes*; Chardin, *Still Life with a Copper Cauldron*; Morland, *The First Steps*; Wright of Derby, *The Young Bird-Catchers*; Rembrandt, *Balaam's Ass* (1626; an early work); Ruisdael, *The Old Oak*; G.-B. Tiepolo, *Cleopatra's Banquet*; Watteau, *Gilles Ó l'Orée du Bois*, and *Return from the Hunt*, one of a set of four, two of which are in the Wallace Collection, London; also works by Fragonard, Greuze, Guardi and Hubert Robert.

Among the *galante* scenes are a number by Boilly, Pierre-Antoine Baudouin (1733–69), Nicolas-Ren, Jollain (1732–1804), Nicolas Lavreince (1737–1807) and J.-B. Mallet (1759–1835).

Musée Picasso

The whole building **Hôtel Salé** (**Map 9; 1**), 5 Rue de Thorigny (see Ch. 22), was thoroughly restored before receiving the collection of works by Picasso (1881–1973), acquired by the State in lieu of death duties. From the entrance hall across the courtyard, a majestic staircase sweeps you up to the collections.

• Open summer: 1 Apr–30 Sept, 09.30–18.00, 1 Oct–31 March 09.30–17.30, closed Tues 1/1, 25/12, (☎ 01 42 71 25 21). Free guided visits for individuals and groups in English (not summer) Fri 14.30. Facilities for the disabled include the loan of wheelchairs.

This is a favourite visit for anyone who loves both modern art and fine houses. It has an extensive collection of works by Picasso and a number of canvases by other artists owned by the artist. The large collection of drawings and prints is displayed in rotation. The galleries are arranged in approximately chronological order to show Picasso's development from 1894–1972.

The collection includes from Picasso's early period, just after his first visit to Paris, his haunting **Blue Period** *Self-portrait* (1901) painted when he was 20; and *Celestina* (1904). Between the **Rose Period** *The Two Brothers* (summer 1906) and *Self-Portrait* (autumn 1906), after his discovery of Iberian art, there is a change of direction. The culmination of this was his seminal work of 1906–07 now in New York (*Les Demoiselles d'Avignon*) for which the Museum has some preparatory works. Representative of his **Cubist** era (1907–15) are the well-known *Still-life with Chair Caning* (1912), his first collage, made with rope and oil-cloth printed with a design of chair caning; a three-dimensional interpretation of Cubism is *Sculpted Female Head* of his companion Fernande Olivier; the synthesis of collage and sculpture produced the witty construction of 1915, *Violin*; in total contrast he began to make Ingresque portraits such as *Portrait of Olga Khoklova seated* (1917), the Russian dancer who became his wife in 1918.

Bathers (Biarritz, 1918) recalls summer by the sea; from his **Classical Period** come *Jug and apples*; *Women Running along a Beach* (1922); *The Pipes of Pan* (1923). *Paul as a Harlequin* and *Paul as a Pierrot* show his small son in fancy dress. Although Picasso was never part of the Surrealist group, its influence plus the impact of his personal problems at the time emerge in the aggression of *The Kiss* (1925), *Large Nude in a Red Armchair* (1929) and *Figures by the Sea* (1931).

In early 1930, Picasso painted a *Crucifixion* and worked on a series of sculpted female heads. Paintings of the period include the voluptuous *Sleeping Nude* (1932) and a portrait of his model and then lover, *Marie-Thérèse Walter*. The themes of the bull fight and the Minotaur recur throughout Picasso's art: *Corrida* (1933) and the drawing *Minotaur* (1936). Towards the end of the 1930s there was a new focus in the artist's life, represented in *Portrait of Dora Maar* (1937); and in 1938, he painted his small daugher, *Maya and her Doll* (1938). His political anguish later in the decade is reflected in *Cat with a Bird* (1938).

During the war, Picasso assembled and sculpted the cryptic *Bull's Head*, from bicycle parts, and large *Man with a Sheep* (1943). His stays in Antibes with Françoise Gilot from the summer of 1946 inspired *Skull*, *Sea Urchins* and *Lamp on a Table* (1946). He became passionately interested in ceramics while in the south of France: *Vase: Woman with a Mantilla* (1949). Animals and birds always played an important role in his work, as in *Nanny-Goat* (1951). Later works include *Massacre in Korea* (1951); *Dejeuner sur L'Herbe* (both burlesque and tribute to Manet; 1960); *Woman with Open Arms* (1961) and *The Young Artist* (1972).

Among works collected by Picasso now belonging to the State, are Balthus, *The Children*; Cézanne, *Château Noir*; Corot, *Little Jeannette*; Miró, *Self-portrait*; Modigliani, *Seated Girl*; Henri Rousseau, *Self-Portrait with Lamp*, *The Artist's Wife*, and *The Sovereigns*; Renoir, *Seated Bather*; and works by Braque, Matisse and René-Hilaire de Gas (1770–1858; grandfather of Edgar Degas).

The Musée National des Arts et Métiers and the Abbey Church of St-Martin-des-Champs

The Musée National des Arts et Métiers (**Map 3; 8**) described as the museum of technical innovation, has its entrance at the corner of Rue Réamur and Rue Vaucanson. The museum reopened in March 2000 following considerable renovations and its large collection is now set off to advantage in a refreshing new display. Incorporated in the museum is the **Abbey Church of St-Martin-des-Champs**, restored in 1854–80. The choir has perhaps the earliest Gothic vault in Paris (1130–40), while the aisleless nave dates from the 13C. Open 10.00–18.00, Thur to 21.30, closed Mon and public holidays, ☎ 01 53 01 82 00. Bookshop. There are two temporary exhibitions a year in the Illustration Room.

St-Martin-des-Champs, Musée des Arts et Métiers

History of the Abbey Church of St-Martin-des-Champs

The priory of St-Martin-des-Champs, founded in 1060 by Henri I and presented to the Abbey of Cluny by Philippe I in 1079, stood outside the city walls until the early 14C. During the Revolution it was taken over by an educational institution. Its dependencies were later used as a small-arms factory and in 1798 were assigned to the Conservatoire des Arts et Métiers, founded in 1794. The collections of Vaucanson and other scientists were assembled here and in 1802 it opened as the Musée des Techniques. The library (42.80m by 11.70m) is now installed in the former refectory, a 13C masterpiece, probably built by Pierre de Montreuil (architect of the Sainte-Chapelle), its vaulting supported by a central row of columns (recalling those of the Eglise des Jacobins at Toulouse), and with a reader's pulpit at the east end. The external side of the southern doorway is a good example of decorated Gothic, and the sole relic of the original cloisters. Further south is the restored 13C portal of the church (not entered from here; see below). The turret is a comparatively recent addition.

From the spacious entrance hall take the lifts to the 2nd floor and then work downwards. The museum is arranged over three floors and divided thematically into Scientific Instruments, Materials, Construction, Communication, Energy, Mechanics, and Transport. The chapel is also used for exhibits. Each of these subjects is sub-divided chronologically into pre-1750, 1750–1850, and 1850–1950, and 1950 onwards. From the 80,000 objects in the collection (it also has some 20,000 works on paper), the items exhibited demonstrate the evolution of all the major technical inventions since the 16C. These objects are not only technically and scientifically brilliant but they are also beautiful, skilful or curious.

In the extensive collection of **Scientific Instruments** are astronomical and surveying instruments for calculating time, distance, weight, temperature etc. including Arsenius's great astrolabe of 1569, **Pascal**'s calculating machine, 1642, and timepieces and clocks by Berthoud, Lepaute, Bréguet, Janvier and other famous 18C horologists. There are also Abbe Nollet's instruments of natural philosophy, the laboratory of Jaques-César and Alexandre Charles, Buffon's circular mirror with variable focus, an anemometer (1734) for measuring the speed of wind—the oldest known instrument integrating a system of recording data, and the contents of **Lavoisier**'s (1743–94) laboratory. Exhibits range from Foucault's experiments with the measurement of speed of light (1862) which took place in the Observatory to the cyclotron from the Collège de France (1937) and a Cray-2 Super computer (1985). **Materials** includes natural products (paper, ceramics, iron, linen, glass, wool, etc.) a vitrine with glass produced by Emile Gallé at the turn of the 20C, and the development of plastics.

On the **first floor** you go through the *cabinèt de dessins* before coming to **Construction** which addresses the development from traditional methods using wood and stone through to the greatest revolution in the 19C with the introduction first of metal frames and then concrete, and finally their combination as reinforced concrete as in the Théatre du Champs-Elysées (1911–13) by Perret. The large area devoted to **Communication** covers a multitude of techniques: writing, and printing, from **Gutenberg** (1438) to the mechanised printing press (1750–1850); the development of photographic equipment and apparatus used by **Daguerre**, Niepce, Lumière and others, and the pioneering days of photography and cinematography; historical equipment such as the optical telegraph invented by Chappe (see Ch. 31), **Edison**'s phonograph (1877); objects illustrating the development of recording, radio and television; discoveries by Bell, global satellites in the 20C, and the various means of communication open to us today.

Energy is based on three main stages, from water and wind-mills, including the Machine de Marly (see end of Ch. 35), to the invention of the steam engines, with a model of Watt's steam engine, to electricity. And there is also an example of energy saving with a model of the bioclimactic house (1999). **Mechanics** includes automation, machine tools, levers and mills, and has an example of the sliding lathe by Vaucanson (18C). Also, for the less mechanically minded and children, the utterly charming **Theatre of Automata**, including Marie-Antoinette's Joueuse de Tympanon, which goes into action on the first Wed and third Sun of every month at 14.00, 15.00 and 16.00 and the second Thur of every month at 18.00. 19.00 and 20.00.

On the ground floor level are various modes of **Transport** demonstrating the development from wind and animal power, to steam then motorised vehicles. Among the museum's excellent collection are two prototypes of the motor car, Cugnot's steam-carriage of 1770 and one by Serpollet (1888) and early petrol-driven vehicles such as a Panhard (1896), Peugeots of 1893 and 1909, a Berliet phaeton (1898), a De Dion-Bouton (1899) and a Renault of 1900. Pioneering aeroplanes include those of Ader (1897), Esnault-Pelterie (1906), the plane in which Blériot made the first flight across the Channel (1909) and a Bréguet of 1911.

The **Chapel** has become a shrine to technology and science. Foucault's pendulum has been returned to its original place in the chancel; there is Scott's steam engine, the first steam powered bus, called L'Obéissante made by Amédée Boillée, the model for the *Statue of Liberty* by Bartholdi, and Ader and Blériot aircraft and a model of the Vulcan engine from the Ariane rocket.

At the north-west corner of the building is the Fontaine du Vertbois (1712) which, with the adjoining tower, has been restored.

Musée d'art et d'histoire du Judaïsme

The museum in a splendid 17C mansion, the Hôtel St-Aignan (**Map 8; 2**; see Ch. 22) at the heart of the quarter known in Yiddish as the *Pletzl*, was made available at the initiative of Jacques Chirac in 1986, then Mayor of Paris, and opened in 1999. It brings together collections which were dispersed between the Musée d'Art Juif in Montmartre (now closed), and a collection that had been languishing in the reserves at the Hôtel de Cluny including the Strauss-Rothschild collection. The building has been imaginatively adapted to fulfill the functions of a modern museum and is deceptively extensive. It incorporates an important media library (book, video and photo), an auditorium, children's workshop and temporary exhibition space. The galleries contain explanatory texts and audio guides in English are available. Open Mon–Fri 11.00–18.00, Sun 10.00–18.00, ☎ 01 53 01 86 60. There is a gift shop, bookshop and café.

A main theme of the museum is Jewish communities that have congregated on French soil over the centuries, such as European Jews who migrated to France in the 19C and those from North Africa in the 20C. Three sections are, however, reserved for specifically French Jewish history and art: the Middle Ages, the process of emancipation from the French Revolution to the Dreyfus Affair; and the 20C. The identification of Jewish applied art generally adheres to different criteria at certain historic periods (although there are exceptions): from the Middle Ages to the 18C, it depends on the artist or craftsman, the type of decoration, motif or iconography, and the function, while the recent period is covered by the title the Jewish Presence in 20C Art.

Enter at the far side of the courtyard, beneath the St-Aignan family coat of arms. Off the reception hall is the main staircase to the permanent collections starting on the first floor with the **Introductory Room**. Here the antiquity of the Jewish people is evoked through its relationship to a text, a language, a homeland, and its particular destiny of exile, using handwritten Hebrew texts and translations. **Rooms 2–6**: medieval France, contains gravestones, manuscripts and four rare objects, a Hanukkah lamp, a wedding ring, an alms box and a seal; a display devoted to Jews in Italy, from the Renaissance to the 18C, includes synagogue furniture such as a Holy Ark from Modena, and among marriage objects are a marriage ring and illuminated marriage contracts; a fascinating ensemble of Hannukkah lamps of all types, origins and periods, representing the diversity of Jewish customs worldwide; the meeting of two diaspora in Amsterdam in the 16C and 17C, is narrated through engravings; a *sukkah* decorated with a view of the Holy City serves as the focal point for a display concerning the central role of Jerusalem. The following **rooms 7 and 8** (divided between the first and second floors, taking you past the **Library** on the second mezzanine) are devoted to the traditional Ashkenazi and Sefardi worlds, with

Hannukkah lamp

models of synagogue architecture and silverware including a highly ornate 17C Torah case from Vienna, as well as fine textiles.

The next section (**room 9**) enters the **Era of Emancipation**, which began with the French Revolution. Vital events in 19C French Judaism are illustrated with documents, paintings and other objects, and includes more than 3000 items from archives donated by the grandchildren of Captain Dreyfus (1859–1935). A transitional sequence (**room 10**) illustrates the important intellectual role of Jews in Europe at the turn of the century, including the emergence and spread of **Zionism** and Yiddish culture. Graphics are used to highlight the Jewish cultural renaissance in Germany and Russia at the beginning of the 20C focusing on folklore, ornament, biblical subjects and calligraphy, all versions of artistic expression linking Jewish themes and identity. **Room 11**, arranged on several levels, brings you to the **Jewish Presence in 20C Art**, with the work of artists of the School of Paris, such as Lipchitz, Soutine, Marcoussis, Orloff, Modgliani, El Lissitsky, Zadkine and Chagall who absorbed contemporary artistic developments in a very personal manner often breaking away from the exclusively religious iconography which had dominated Jewish art until then.

Room 12 builds up a documentary picture of European Judaism around the theme of the Jewish community which inhabited the Hotel de St-Aignan in 1939 in the *Pletzl*. The only reference to the Holocaust is very personal to this community. In a tiny courtyard is a low-key but moving installation by Christian Boltanski which consists of plaques naming the former residents. During the roundup of Parisian Jews in 1942, seven residents were arrested and in all, 13 former members of the community were deported and died. The last gallery (**room 13**) is entitled the **Contemporary Jewish World**.

24 • The Grands Boulevards

■ Arrondissements: 75002, 75004, 75008, 75009, 75010
🚇 Concorde, Madeleine, Opéra, Richelieu-Drouot, Rue Montmartre, Bonne-Nouvelle, Strasbourg-St-Denis, République
🚈 Auber

Top of the range, £££ *Lucas-Carton*, 9 Pl. de la Madeleine, ☎ 01 42 65 22 90. Temple of gastronomy by Alain Senderens and decor by Majorelle, the Art Nouveau cabinet maker; pricewise, the sky's the limit
Chez Maxim, 3 Rue Royale, ☎ 01 42 65 27 94. Posh place since the 1890s now owned by Pierre Cardin

Café de la Paix, 12 Blvd des Capucines, ☎ 01 40 07 30 20, Décor by Garnier, architect of the Opéra; you could limit your visit to one drink

££ range
Le Trente, 30 Pl de la Madeleine, ☎ 01 47 42 56 58. The restaurant of the food-store Fauchon, overlooking the Place, and with a garden, serving pretty delicious dishes

Au Petit Riche, 25 Rue Le Peletier, ☎ 01 47 70 68 68. Tidy old-time bistrot with honest cooking
Le Grand Café, 4 Blvd des Capucines, ☎ 01 43 12 19 00. 20s-style brasserie with 24-hour service
Café Runtz, 16 Rue Favart, ☎ 01 42 96 69 86. Near Opéra Comique, a veritable *weinstube* with an Alsace flavour, open late.

More economical, £
L'Amanguier, 20 Blvd de Montmartre ☎ 01 47 70 91 35 and 110 Rue de Richelieu, ☎ 01 42 96 37 79. Small group of reliable restaurants

Léon de Bruxelles, 8 Pl. de la République, ☎ 01 43 38 28 69. Chain specialising in *moules et frites*
Le Grand Café, 4 Blvd Des Capucines, 75009, ☎ 01 43 12 19 00 (near Opéra), modern 'Belle Epooque' style brassierie, seafood, traditional and modern lighter cooking

Teashops
L'Arbre à Cannell, 57 Passages des Panoramas, under the arches in a 19C *chocolatier*
Ladurée Royale, 16 Rue Royale, ☎ 01 42 60 21 79. The classy stop for tea and macaroons

The once fashionable Grands Boulevards are a succession of wide thoroughfares extending in a curve from Pl. de la Madeleine to the Bastille. They were laid out in 1670–85 on the site of the inner ramparts built by Charles V in the 14C and fortifications built by Louis XIII in 1633–37 already demolished some decades earlier. Although not quite the debonair district of the dashing boulevardiers that it was in the 19C, it combines commerce with entertainment—opera, theatre, cabaret and cinema and still draws the crowds. There are also historic links with developments in art and cinema in the 19C and at the beginning of the 20C. But the further east you *flânez*, the less glamorous it becomes. The Métro line Météor (Line 14), which opened in 1999, runs east between Madeleine and and Bibliothèque.

A good place to start this expedition is from **Rue Royale** which, as far as Rue St-Honoré, is lined with uniform 18C facades, shops of quality and restaurants (see above)—at no. 3 is the famous *Maxim's*. The **Musée Bouilhet-Christofle**, at no. 9, is devoted to the art of the silversmith; and no. 11 is **Lalique**. René Lalique (1860–1945), goldsmith and jeweller, caused a sensation when he displayed his designs in glass at the International Exhibition of 1900.

The street is closed by **Ste-Marie-Madeleine**, or simply La Madeleine (**Map 2**; 6–8), built in the style of a Greco-Roman temple and surrounded by a majestic Corinthian colonnade, which is visually counterbalanced by the Assemblé National building across the river.

History of Ste-Marie-Madeleine

Two earlier churches had been demolished unfinished, in 1777 and 1789, before Pierre-Alexandre Vignon (1763–1828) started work in 1806 on the orders of Napoléon, who, before he had thought of the Arc de Triomphe, intended it as a Temple of Glory for the Grande Armée. It was finished by Huvé in 1842. In the pediment is a relief of the Last Judgement by Lemaire;

the bronze doors are adorned with bas-reliefs of the Decalogue by Triqueti (1838). The memorial service for those who died when Concorde crashed in ths summer of 2000 was held here.

The **interior** abounds in gold leaf and coloured marble, paintings, mosaics and sculptures, and has a fine Cavaillé-Coll **organ**. The nave is covered by three cof-fered domes and the east end by a half dome, with an enfilade of columns around the sanctuary. In chapels on either side of the entrance are the *Marriage of the Virgin*, by Pradier, and the *Baptism of Christ* by Rude; and the group of the *Ascension of the Magdalen* (1837), on the high-altar, by Marochetti adds a touch of high drama.

On the eastern side of the Pl. de la Madeleine is a small flower market. At no. 2 stood the Café Durand, where Zola wrote *J'Accuse*, an open letter denouncing the army and defending Dreyfus, published in *L'Aurore*, on 13 January 1898. On Rue de Sèze is *Fauchon*, the most famous of all Parisian grocery stores, whose win-dow displays are a mouth-watering work of art.

The southern section of Blvd Malesherbes, leading northwest from the Madeleine, is dominated by **St-Augustin**, an early example of the use of iron in church construction (1860–71), by Baltard, architect of the former Halles. Marcel Proust spent much of his youth at no. 9 Blvd Malesherbes.

Blvd de la Madeleine, the westernmost of the Grands Boulevards, leads northeast and becomes Blvd des Capucines, which crosses Pl. de l'Opéra (see below). Running southeast from the Boulevard towards Pl. Vendôme is Rue des Capucines. Off its north side Rue Edouard-VII leads to a small place containing an equestrian statue of *Edward VII* (by Landowski), a frequent visitor to Paris as Prince of Wales and king, and a promoter of the Entente Cordiale which was established between Britain and France in 1904.

At 14 Blvd des Capucines a tablet records the first exhibition of a cinema film given by the brothers Lumière (28 December 1895), and a few days later the first demonstration of X-rays, a discovery of Dr Roentgen, took place in the same room. No. 35 was once the studio of Nadar (Félix Tournachon; 1820–1910), the portrait-photographer and aeronaut. The first Impressionist Exhibition was held here in 1874, with paintings by Renoir, Manet, Pissarro, Monet, etc. Included in this exhibition of 1874 was Monet's *Impression Soleil levant* (1872) (depicting the port of Le Havre in mist) which gave the group its name (see Ch. 29).

Opéra Garnier

The focal point of the busy Pl. de l'Opéra (**Map 2; 6**) is Garnier's opera (of the phantom) house to the north. If you feel the need for a little bit of Belle Epoque extravagance, enjoy the view of the recently cleaned façade from the elegant ter-race of *Café de la Paix*.

• Open 10.00–17.00 every day (☎ 01 40 01 25 14); there are also guided tours at 13.00 (closed 1/1, 1/5 and during matinées). Gift and bookshop in the Hall d'Acceuil. Bookings (for both ballet and opera performances): ☎ 08 36 69 78 68/www.opera-de-paris.fr.

History of the Opéra Garnier

Opéra Garnier, an appropriately lavish monument to the grandiose period of the Second Empire, was built in 1861–75 from the designs of Charles Garnier (1825–98). It was recently renovated, and the public areas can be visited (auditorium when not in use). There is a bookshop and library in the entrance. The first opera-house in Paris was established in 1669 by Perrin, Cambert and the Marquis de Sourdéac on the Left Bank, between the Rue de Seine and the Rue Mazarine and the first director was Lully (from 1674), under whom it acquired its secondary title of Académie Royale de Musique.

The façade, flanked by a flight of steps, is grandly adorned with coloured marbles and sculpture. On either side of the arcade opening into the vestibule are allegorical groups, including (right) *The Dance* by Carpeaux (a copy by Paul Belmondo, original is in the Musée d'Orsay). Above are medallions of composers; and bronze-gilt statues of other composers and librettists are seen between the monolithic columns of the loggia. Behind the low dome of the auditorium is a triangular pediment crowned by a statue of *Apollo of the Golden Lyre*.

The second vestibule contains the box-office, beyond which is the **Grand Staircase**, with its white marble stairs 10m wide and a balustrade of onyx and rosso and verde antico lit by elaborate chandeliers. On the first floor, where the staircase divides, is the entrance to the stalls and the amphitheatre, flanked by caryatids, and on each floor are arcades of monolithic marble columns. The Avant-Foyer leads to the Grand Foyer; glass doors communicate with the Loggia overlooking the Pl. de l'Opéra, and by the middle door is a bust of *Garnier* by Carpeaux.

The **auditorium** is resplendent in red plush and gilt, and has five tiers of boxes. The dome, resting on eight pillars of scagliola, was painted, in disturbing contrast to the rest of the décor, in 1964 by Chagall with murals inspired by nine operas. The huge stage is 60m high, 52m wide and 37m deep, behind which is the Foyer de la Dance (the scene of many paintings of ballet dancers by Degas; see Musée d'Orsay), with a mirror measuring 7m by 10m.

The small **Museum of the Opera** (a department of the Bibliothèque Nationale de France) is in the Rotonde de l'Empereur to the left of the Grand Staircase. This charming museum mounts permanent and temporary exhibitions from its complete collection of the scores of all operas and ballets performed here since its foundation, over 100,000 drawings of costumes, scenery and photographs and paintings of artistes as well as memorabilia including objects belonging to Diaghelev. Open 10.00–17.00, closed 01/01, 01/05, 08/05 (☎ 01 40 01 17 89).

At 9 Rue Scribe is the **Musée Fragonard**, of the history of perfume, open 09.00–17.30.

Av. de l'Opéra leads southeast towards Pl. André-Malraux (see Ch. 17) and is crossed by Rue Louis-le-Grand. Napoléon and Joséphine Beauharnais were married in 1796 at 3 Rue d'Antin (the next cross-street), which was then the Mairie of the 2nd arrondissement. The Fontaine Gaillon (1828), just to the east in the Rue St-Augustin, is by Visconti and Jacquot.

Immediately behind the Opéra, facing Pl. Diaghilev, are the department stores of *Galeries Lafayette* (1898), to the west, *Au Printemps* (1889; remodelled since), with huge and remarkable central halls, and a *Marks & Spencer*.

Just east of the former is Rue de la Chaussée-d'Antin, leading north to La Trinité (see Ch. 25) where Mozart stayed at no. 5 in 1778 and Chopin in 1833–36.

Blvd des Italiens (the continuation northeast of Blvd des Capucines), whose many famous cafés have often been replaced by cinemas and commercial buildings, derived its name from the Théâtre des Italiens (1783), where Donizetti's *Don Pasquale* was first performed in 1843. Sir Richard Wallace (1819–90), who collected many of the works of art now in the Wallace Collection, London (see Ch. 30), had a home in Rue Taitbout (north of the boulevard).

The next street, **Rue Lafitte**, was named after Jacques Laffitte, 1767–1844, the financier (see Ch. 38). At the far end of the street you can see N.-D.-de-Lorette with Sacré-Coeur in the background (Chs 25 and 26). At nos 39 and 41 stood Ambroise Vollard's art gallery, the dealer who strongly supported avant-garde artists. He introduced the work of Gauguin and Cézanne to the public and organised the first exhibitions in Paris of works by Picasso and Matisse (1901 and 1904 respectively).

It was in the parallel **Rue Le Peletier** (to the east) that Orsini tried unsuccessfully to assassinate Napoléon III in 1858, but managed to kill or injure 156 other people. No. 3 was the Café du Divan, frequented by Balzac, Gautier, Nerval and Baudelaire.

In Rue de Marivaux (opposite) stands the **Opéra-Comique-Salle Favart** (entrance, 2 Rue Boïeldieu) with a bijou auditorium built 1894–96. The Opéra-Comique originated in a company that produced pieces during local fairs, and in 1715 purchased from the Opéra the right of playing vaudevilles interspersed with ariettas. Discord between the two theatres continued until in 1757 Charles Favart (1710–92) finally established the rights of the Opéra-Comique, which moved to this somewhat confined site in 1783.

At the junction of the boulevard with that of Blvd Montmartre and Blvd Haussmann (only extended to this point in 1927), Rue Drouot leads north past (no. 6) the Mairie of the 9th arrondissement in a mansion of 1746–48, and no. 9 (left), the **Hôtel des Ventes de Paris**, or Nouveau Drouot (named after Napoléon's aide-de-camp) rebuilt in the 1980s, the main auction-rooms of Paris, the French equivalent of *Christie's* or *Sotheby's*, where important sales are held from February to June. Pissarro painted 13 views of Blvd Montmartre from a window of the Grand Hôtel de Russie, which stood at 1 Rue Drouot.

Rue de Richelieu leads south to the Bibliothèque Nationale Richelieu (see Ch. 18). At no. 10, in the short Blvd Montmartre (some way from Montmartre) is the **Musée Grévin** (☎ 01 47 70 85 05), a waxwork collection on the same lines as Mme Tussaud's in London. Opposite is the pretty Théâtre des Variétés, the scene of several of Offenbach's successes. In the block on the right between Blvd. Montmartre and Rue St-Marc is a *dédale* of 19C arcades, leading off Passage des Panoramas (gaslit in 1817), and on the right is Passage Jouffroy.

The Rue Montmartre, so named since 1200, leads southeast towards St-Eustache (see Ch. 19).

Rue du Faubourg-Montmartre, heading north west towards the former suburb of Montmartre, recalls the time when the boulevard formed the city boundary. Rue Geoffroy-Marie, a turning off to the right, leads through a mainly Jewish quarter, towards the Rue Richer. Here at no. 32 is the cabaret known as the *Folies-Bergère*, originally the Café Sommier Elastique (springy mattress!), founded in 1869 to produce vaudevilles. Manet's *The Bar at the Folies-Bergère* was painted in 1881.

Continuing east from Blvd Montmartre is **Blvd Poissonnière**. To the north, at 2 Rue du Conservatoire (beyond the Rue Rougemont), is the Conservatoire National d'Art Dramatique, a small theatre of 1802, Paris's first music academy.

The boulevard is now crossed by Rue Poissonnière (right) and its northern extension, the Rue du Faubourg-Poissonnière, the route taken by fishmongers of old on their way to Les Halles. Beyond this junction, the line of boulevards is continued by Blvd de Bonne-Nouvelle, on the northern side of which is the façade (1887) of the Théâtre du Gymnase. To the south, steps lead up to N.-D. de Bonne-Nouvelle, rebuilt in 1824.

The short and seedy Blvd St-Denis (**Map 3; 8**), lies between two triumphal arches, Porte St-Denis and the Porte St-Martin. **Porte St-Denis**, a triumphal arch 23m high, designed by Blondel, was erected in 1674 to commemorate the victories of Louis XIV in Germany and Holland. The bas-reliefs, designed by Girardon, were executed by the brothers Anguier. It faces Rue St-Denis, or Voie Royale, once the processional route of entry into Paris, and last so used on the occasion of Queen Victoria's visit in 1855.

On the far side of Blvd de Sebastopol, which with its northern extension, Blvd de Strasbourg, stretches from Pl. du Châtelet to Gare de l'Est, you pass the **Porte St-Martin**, another triumphal arch in honour of Louis XIV, c 18m high, built in 1674 by Bullet, and decorated with bas-reliefs of contemporary campaigns, by Desjardins and Marsy (south side) and Le Hongre and the elder Legros (north).

Rue St-Martin (the original Roman road leading north from Lutetia) leads south to the Musée National des Arts et Métiers (see Ch. 23), off which the Rue N.-D. de Nazareth runs left.

Two famous theatres in Blvd St-Martin, the **Théâtre de la Renaissance**, managed by Sarah Bernhardt in 1893–99, and the **Théâtre de la Porte-St-Martin**, burnt down during the Commune and rebuilt, are a reminder of the numerous theatres that sprang up in this area after 1791, with the emancipation of French theatre. In fact so frequent were performances of passionate and bloody melodramas that this became known as the Boulevard du Crime.

Pl. de la République (Map 4; 7), on the site of the Porte du Temple and the junction of seven important thoroughfares, was laid out on the edge of this proletarian district in 1856–65 by Haussmann for strategic reasons, but is still the rallying point for demonstrations. The pedestal of the *Monument de la République* (1883; 25m high), with an allegorical female proffering an olive branch and bronze bas-reliefs by Dalou.

At the corner of Rue Léon-Jouhaux (previously Rue de la Douane) leading northeast from the Place, was Daguerre's workshop in 1822–35. The Théâtre Lyrique was one of many (including Des Funambules, 1816–62) that stood on a section of Blvd du Temple demolished by Haussmann. Beyond Pl. de la République to the east is the Canal St-Martin (see Ch. 31).

25 • Gare de l'Est to Gare St-Lazare

Arrondissements: 75003, 75009, 75010

République, Gare de l'Est, Gare du Nord, Poissonnière, N.-D.-de-Lorette, Trinité St-Lazare, St-Augustin, Madeleine

Auber

Two brasseries with superb décor in the same chain (Flo), where you can count on traditional fare, are:

Brasserie Flo, 7 Cour des Petites Ecuries, ☎ 01 47 70 13 59, the original Flo, authentic 1886 setting for Alsatian food and wine, ££

Julien, 16 Rue du Fb. St-Denis, ☎ 01 47 70 12 06. Sinuous Art Nouveau surroundings and imaginative dishes, ££

Terminus Nord, 23 Rue de Dunkerque, ☎ 01 42 85 05 15. Yet another Flo brasserie, but 1920s this time, opposite Gare du Nord therefore handy for Eurostar travellers, £–££

Le Châteaubriant, 23 Rue Chabrol, ☎ 01 48 24 58 94. An Italian restaurant near Gare de l'Est, impeccable cooking, ££

Chez Catherine, 65 Rue de Province, ☎ 01 45 26 72 88. A classic bistrot to refuel after a shopping spree, ££

Chartier, 7 Rue du Fb.-Montmartre, ☎ 01 47 70 86 29. Known the world over, big, busy and basic, £

The Cricketer Pub, 41 Rue des Mathurins, ☎ 01 40 07 01 45. Typical English pub patronised by the French, £

Chez Michel, 10 Rue Belzunce, ☎ 01 44 53 06 20. Also close to Gare du Nord, Breton specialities, one-price menu, £

In the Nouvelle Athènes district:
La Table de la Fontaine, 5 Rue Henri-Monnier, ☎ 01 45 26 26 30. Charming bistrot with a modern twist, £

Le Convivial, 47 Rue St-Georges, ☎ 01 42 85 22 35. Classic/Provençal cooking in a subdued atmosphere, £–££

This district may not be rated as a main tourist attraction, but it is crossed by visitors who have travelled to Paris by train from the north (including Eurostar) or the east, or those on their way to Montmartre. In the once fashionable residential parts are two intimate and atmospheric museums in the former homes of Gustav Moreau and Ary Scheffer.

Blvd de Magenta runs northwest from Pl. de la République to the outer boulevards, linking Gare de l'Est and Gare du Nord. At its intersection with Blvd de Strasbourg is the church of **St-Laurent**. On the site of a 6C basilica near the old Roman road, this church has undergone endless alterations. The present building was begun before 1429 but retained an older north tower. The nave was vaulted (some splendid pendant bosses) and the choir remodelled in 1655–59, with a high-altar by Antoine le Pautre. Further work was carried out in the 16C–17C, and the

Lady Chapel dates from 1712. The 17C façade was demolished in 1862–65 in favour of a Flamboyant one, Haussman's choice, and the spire erected.

Just to the north is **Gare de l'Est** (**Map 4; 3–5**), its courtyard on the site of the medieval St Lawrence fair. On the other side of the boulevard was the Prison de St-Lazare, rebuilt as a hospital, from 1632 the headquarters of the Lazarists or Priests of the Mission, founded in 1625 by Vincent de Paul (1576–1660).

Blvd Magenta crosses Rue La Fayette before passing (right) the **Gare du Nord** (**Map 3; 4**) with its iron and glass interior and Neo-classical façade by Hittorff (1863). It is the terminus for TGV Eurostar, of the line from Calais, Boulogne, etc., and for TGV Nord and TGV Thalys. There is also a rapid shuttle service to Charles de Gaulle airport. The new RER EOLE line opened in 1999 and is sited in the underground station Magenta between the two mainline stations.

In the thickly populated cosmopolitan Quartier de la Chapelle, between the main-line stations to the north, is **St-Denis-de-la-Chapelle** (13C, but much restored), where Joan of Arc received communion in November 1429 before besieging Paris. Adjacent is a modern basilica, **Ste-Jeanne-d'Arc**, begun in 1932, the main part of reinforced concrete completed later by Pierre Isnard, and consecrated in 1964. Adjacent is one of the last covered markets in metal, the Marché de la Chapelle, 1885.

Turning southwest along the Rue la Fayette, you pass another work by Jacques Hittorff, **St-Vincent-de-Paul** (1824–44), of Roman inspiration. Two square towers dominate a pedimented portico of 12 Ionic columns approached by a cascade of steps. The interior frieze was painted by Hippolyte Flandrin (1809–64) and the dome by Picot. On the altar is a *Crucifixion* by Rude and the main **organ** is the work of Cavaillé-Coll.

South, via Rue d'Hauteville, is Rue de Paradis, where at no. 30bis is the showroom of the glass-maker *Baccarat*, replacing one existing since 1764, and the **Musée de Cristal** (☎ 01 47 70 64 30).

Return to Rue la Fayette crossed further west by Rue Cadet where, at no. 16, is the **Musée du Grand Orient de France**, with material relating to European Freemasonry (☎ 01 45 23 20 92). At this intersection, the Rue de Châteaudun leads west to pass **N.-D.-de-Lorette**, another basilican church, built in 1823–36 by Hippolyte Lebas, with a portico of four Corinthian columns. The interior has coffered vaults and colonnade.

Rue des Martyrs, from behind the church, is the old route up to Montmartre, a lively *quartier*, full of eating places, already well known for its cabarets in the 18C. North west from the church, Rue N.-D.-de-Lorette ascends to the small and charming Pl. St-Georges. The *lorettes*, or *demi-mondaines*, who inhabited the area in the 19C, were a favourite subject of the caricaturist Gavarni (1801–66), and are represented on his monument here by Denys Puech. During the 19C this was at the centre of an area developed by Lapeyrière and dubbed *la Nouvelle Athènes*—so named by Dureau de la Malle in the *Journal des débats* in 1823. The luxury Greek-Revival style buildings, designed by Auguste Constantin among others, attracted businessmen, bankers, writers such as the writer brothers Goncourt and artists.

No. 27 Pl. St-Georges is the **Fondation Dosne-Thiers**. The residence of President Thiers (1797–1877) from 1822 to 1871, it contains the **Bibliothèque Thiers**—80,000 volumes on the history of France since the Revolution and the Napoleonic collection of Frédéric Masson. Temporary exhibitions are held here; apply for permission to visit the Masson collection. Opposite, at no. 28, is an over-ornate 19C neo-Renaissance mansion, briefly home to the Marquise de Païva before her house on the Champs-Elysées was completed (see Ch. 27).

At the top of Rue St-Georges is a small theatre of the same name, the façade decorated in *trompe l'oeil*. Off Rue d'Aumale is Square d'Orléans, where Chopin lived at no. 9 and Georges Sand at no. 5. Rue St-Georges continues downhill, and in the parallel Rue de la Rochefoucauld, to the west is the **Musée Gustave Moreau**, containing a collection of some 18,000 paintings and drawings left by Moreau (1826–98) to the State. Open Mon, Wed 11.00–17.15, other days, 10.00–12.45, 14.00–17.15, closed Tues, 1/1, 1/5, 25/12 (☎ 01 48 74 38 50).

The walls of this creaking, evocative studio on two floors are covered with paintings by the leading Symbolist whose use of colour and surprisingly liberal teaching methods profoundly influenced the next generation of artists. A former pupil, George Rouault, was the first curator of this museum. Among the works on display are *The Apparition* and *Salome*, of 1874–76, *Mystic Flower* (1890), *Hésiode et la Muse*, *Jupiter and Semele* (1895). A picturesque spiral staircase leads to the upper floor where watercolours are exhibited by rotation and drawings can be viewed in cases with movable panels. Degas' *Portrait of the Artist*, dated 1867, also hangs here. On the first floor it is possible to see the tiny apartment in which Moreau and his parents lived, full of family souvenirs.

To the west, off Sq. de la Trinité, stands **La Trinité**, built in 1863–67 by Ballu in a hybrid, unappealing style characteristic of the Second Empire, with a tower 63m high. Messiaën was organist here for some years in the 1930s. It was erected on the site of the disreputable Cabaret de la Grande Pinte, later Les Porcherons. In front of the church is a welcome patch of greenery, with fountains also by Ballu and sculptures by Duret.

From a point northeast of the church, Rue Pigalle and Rue Blanche climb northeast and north towards Montmartre. Between the two is Rue Chaptal. Tucked away at the end of a cobbled courtyard at no. 16 is the **Musée de la Vie Romantique**, in the Maison Renan-Scheffer, with collections devoted to George Sand and Ary Scheffer; it is also used for temporary exhibitions. Scheffer brought together here the artistic glitterati of the era and his great-niece, daughter of the philosopher Ernest Renan, carried on the tradition. The house remained in the family for about 150 years. As well as the house, the studios built by Scheffer for teaching and receiving guests, contain paintings and memorabilia. Open 10.00–17.40, closed Mon and public holidays (☎ 01 48 74 95 38).

To the west of La Trinité, Rue Clichy climbs gently north to Pl. de Clichy. No. 16 is the **Casino de Paris**, where Josephine Baker starred, and to the south, Rue de Mogador leads to the Opéra.

Rue St-Lazare leads west from Sq. de la Trinité to **Gare St-Lazare** (Map 2; 4–6), a terminus of the western region of the SNCF. Its interior was the subject of paintings by Monet in 1877 (see Ch. 9). To the west of the station, the Rue de Rome leads northwest through the Pl. de l'Europe, painted by Caillebotte in 1877.

Rue du Havre leads south from Gare St-Lazare, where no. 8, the **Lycée Condorcet**, founded in 1804, occupies the former buildings (with a Doric cloister court) of a Capuchin convent; on the site of its chapel (in the parallel street to the east) is St-Louis d'Antin by Brongniart (1782). The street continues south as Rue Tronchet to the Madeleine (see Ch. 24).

Blvd Haussmann, one of the main streets in the area, commemorates Eugène-Georges, Baron Haussmann who, as Préfet de la Seine, initiated extensive urban development in central Paris. Work began here in 1857 as part of a scheme to construct an unbroken thoroughfare from Blvd Montmartre to the Arc de Triomphe, and was only completed in 1926.

A short distance to the west, on the south side of Blvd Haussmann, is Sq. Louis XVI (**Map 2; 6**), formerly the Cimetière de la Madeleine. Here lie the bodies of the victims of the panic of 1770 in the Pl. de la Concorde (see Ch. 13), together with the Swiss guards massacred on 10 August 1792 and all those guillotined between 26 August 1792 and 24 March 1794. In the square is the **Chapelle Expiatoire** erected in 1815–26 from the plans of Fontaine in the style of a classical funeral temenos. Built by order of Louis XVIII, it was dedicated to the memory of Louis XVI and Marie-Antoinette, whose remains, first interred in the graveyard on this site, were removed to St-Denis in 1815 (see Ch. 39). The Chapel is open Thur, Fri, Sat. 13.00–17.00 (closed 1/1, 1/5, 25/12).

Inside are two marble groups: ***Louis XVI and his confessor Abbé Henry Essex Edgeworth*** (1745–1807) by Bosio (below which is inscribed the king's will, dated 25 December 1792) and ***Marie-Antoinette supported by Religion***, by Cortot, the latter figure bearing the features of Mme Elisabeth. (Below is inscribed a letter said to have been written by the queen to her sister-in-law from the Conciergerie on 16 October 1793.) The bas-relief by Gérard above the doorway represents the removal of their remains.

26 • Montmartre

■ Arrondissement: 75018

▣ Pl. de Clichy, Blanche, Pigalle, Anvers, Abbesses, Lamarck-Caulaincourt

In this very touristy area, there are some eating places worth seeing out:

A Beauvilliers, 52 Rue Lamarck, ☎ 01 42 54 54 42. Elegant restaurant and classic cooking, ££

Le Bouclard, 1 Rue Cavallotti, ☎ 01 45 22 60 01. Lively atmosphere and hearty dishes, £–££

Le Cottage Marcadet, 151bis Rue Marcadet, ☎ 01 42 57 71 22. Bold and unusual recipés, ££

Le Moulin à Vins, 6 Rue Burg, ☎ 01 42 52 81 27. Rustic bar, quality wines, and food, £

Au Négociants, 27 Rue Lambert, ☎ 01 46 06 15 11. On the edge of the tourist circuit, informal ambiance, simple traditional food, £

Le Perroquet Vert, 7 Rue Cavallotti, ☎ 01 45 22 49 16. Traditional cooking and cosy atmosphere, £

Rendez-vous des Chauffeurs, 11 Rue des Portes-Blanches, ☎ 01 42 64 04 17. Unpretentious, even unglamorous, but popular, especially the prices, £

Le Restaurant, 32 Rue Véron, ☎ 01 42 23 06 22. Bohemian atmosphere and varied cooking, £

Le Sancerre, 35 Rue des Abbesses, ☎ 01 42 58 08 20. Café/bar open 07.00 to 02.00, £

Au Virage Lepic, 61 Rue Lepic, ☎ 01 42 52 46 79. Good value, low key, budget bistro, £

Montmartre is a must for almost every visitor to Paris, drawn by numerous associations: the old village atmosphere, the Moulin Rouge, chansonniers, cabarets, bohemians, its reputation as a centre of artistic and political fement in the 19C, and the Sacré-Coeur basilica which seems so mystical from the distance high above Paris. Surprisingly, despite its popularity, the *quartier* around the 'Butte' has retained a distinct atmosphere, best discovered on foot, and an hour or two may be pleasantly spent wandering around here or sitting in a café in Place du Tertre, familiar from the paintings of Utrillo, among others. But first of all, there is Clichy to negotiate.

Pl. de Clichy (**Map 2; 4**) was the site of the Barrière de Clichy, which on 30 March 1814 was defended against the approaching Prussian troops by pupils from the Ecole Polytechnique and the Garde Nationale under Marshal Moncey. The action is commemorated by a bronze group by Doublemard (1869).

To the east of Pl. de Clichy with all its restaurants and cinemas, is the wide Blvd de Clichy and its continuation, Blvd de Rochechouart. These form the southern boundary of Montmartre proper and are the focus of the sleazy night life where colourful crowds congregate around Pl. Pigalle and Pl. Blanche. Yet close to these seedy centres there are residential districts and more salubrious nightlife.

The Place and Blvd de Clichy were frequently painted by Renoir, Van Gogh (in 1887), Signac and many other artists working in the vicinity. The first turning, right, off Blvd de Clichy is Rue de Douai: which shortly crosses Pl. Adolphe-Max (formerly Pl. Vintimille), a district formerly much frequented by artists and writers: Dickens, George Sand, Bonnard, Vuillard, Zola among others.

History of Montmartre

Over a century ago Montmartre was made more accessible by the construction of new streets ascending through the northern slums and poor artists migrated there because it was both picturesque and cheap, making it an artistic centre for about 30 years. Around 1881 the famous *Le Chat Noir* (84 Blvd de Rochechouart; closed in 1897) opened, advertising the attractions of the district. Then the serious artists gradually retreated and have now all but vanished. The atmosphere of that bohemian era was vividly brought to life by Henri de Toulouse-Lautrec, whose studio was at 5 Av. Frochot, near the Pl. Pigalle. Seurat had a studio at 128 bis Blvd de Clichy from 1886, and died nearby; Signac's studio in 1886–88 was at no. 130 in the Boulevard, where Picasso lived in 1909. Degas died at no. 6 in 1917, where his protegée, Mary Cassatt, had painted.

Cimetière de Montmartre

Av. Rachel, the first turning on the left off Blvd de Clichy going east, leads to the main entrance of the Cimetière de Montmartre, on the western slope of the Butte (**Map 2; 2**), partly spanned by a viaduct.

Although not quite as famous as that of Père-Lachaise, it is nevertheless fascinating both for its tombstone art (by Bartholdi, David d'Angers, Falguière, Rodin and Rude) and the celebrities buried here. It extends over 11 hectares under the shade of some 750 trees and opened in 1825. Plans of the graveyard indicating where the illustrious are buried are available at the main entrance. Among the avenues of tombs are memorials to 18C–20C writers, such as Gautier, De Vigny, the Goncourt brothers, Alexandre Dumas fils, Stendhal, Heine, Murger, Zola (a huge red marble monstrosity), Feydeau, Maxime du Camp, Renan and Giraudoux; or composers: Berlioz, Delibes, Offenbach, Halévy, Adam and Ambroise Thomas; also Adolphe Sax; the artists remembered here include Fragonard, Greuze, Delaroche, Carle Vernet, Horace Vernet, Diaz de la Peña and Degas; the actors Frédéric Lemaître and Louis Jouvet; the dancers Vestris, Taglioni and Nijinsky; Mme Récamier, Pauline Viardot and Marie Duplessis ('La Dame aux Camélias'); as well as Waldeck-Rousseau, Marshal Lannes (heart only), Hittorff, Fourier, Ampère, Dr Charcot and Miles Byrne, the United Irishman.

From Pl. de Clichy, **Rue Caulaincourt** is carried over the cemetery by a viaduct, which is the most convenient approach to Montmartre by car. Toulouse-Lautrec kept a studio for a decade prior to 1897 at no. 21 and Renoir at no. 73 c 1910, where the Swiss artist Steinlen (1859–1923), died.

Continuing along Blvd de Clichy, you pass (left) the once-famous *Moulin Rouge*, founded by Joseph Oller, which was inaugurated on 1 May 1889, now a cabaret-restaurant. Just after Pl. Blanche at no. 72 is the recently opened **Museum of Erotic Art** (open 10.00–02.00 every day). Pl. Pigalle was the site of the Café de la Nouvelle Athènes, long an artistic rendezvous, notably of Manet and Degas.

To climb to the Butte, at Pl. Blanche turn left up the steep Rue Lepic towards the rebuilt **Moulin de la Galette**. Vincent van Gogh and his brother, Théo, lived at no. 54 in 1886; the dancer La Goulue began her career here, and it was painted by Renoir in 1876 and Bonnard in c 1905, among others. In Av. Junot, off Rue Lepic, is the Modern Movement house built in 1926 by Adolphe Loos, the Viennese purist, for the Dadaist writer, Tristan Tzara. An alternative route to the Butte de Montmartre is via Rue Houdon to Pl. des Abbesses to find one of only two surviving complete Art-Nouveau Métro entrances (Abbessess) by Guimard in cast iron and still glazed. Also **St-Jean de Montmartre** (1894–1904), one of the first churches in reinforced concrete by Baudot, pupil of Labrouste. Follow Rues Le Tac and Tardieu for the alternative means of ascending to Montmartre, by funicular, every 5 minutes all day; there is also the Montmartrobus, from Pigalle and the Marie du 18e, every 12 minutes.

Rue Norvins brings you to the legendary **Pl. du Tertre** (Map 3; 1) with its rapid-portrait artists always touting for business, much commercialism, and crowded cafés, maintaining a holiday atmosphere summer and winter.

To the east of Pl. du Tertre stands **St-Pierre-de-Montmartre**, the successor of an earlier church built to commemorate the martyrdom of St Denis, a relic of a Benedictine nunnery founded in 1134 by Adélaïde de Savoie (d. 1154). It was consecrated in the presence of her son Louis VII by Pope Eugenius III in 1147 and is one of the oldest churches in Paris.

The severe façade dates from the late 17C and the bronze doors (1980) were made by T. Gismondi. Inside, against the west wall, are two ancient columns with 7C capitals; two other capitals, one at the apse entrance and another in the north aisle, are of the same date. The Romanesque nave has 15C vaulting; the north aisle dates from 1765 and the south c 1838, both vaulted 1900–05. The transept and the choir retain Romanesque elements with, over the choir, one of the earliest examples in Paris of a ribbed vault (1147). The apse was rebuilt in the late 12C. The tomb of the foundress lies behind the altar. The altar itself is the work of J.-P. Froidevaux, consecrated in 1977, and the glass installed in 1954, is by Max Ingrand.

In the adjacent Jardin du Calvaire (closed) are Stations of the Cross executed for Richelieu. Foundations of a Roman temple have been discovered to the north of the church, while in the derelict graveyard (open only on All Saints Day) is the tomb of the navigator Bougainville (1729–1811); also buried here is the sculptor Pigalle (1714–85).

The Butte Montmartre

The Rue Azais, to the south, leads to the terrace below the Basilique du Sacré-Coeur, which affords a rare opportunity for a panoramic view of Paris—with a rash of skscrapers erupting on the skyline—without suffering vertigo.

History of the Butte Montmartre

An obvious vantage point, the history of the Butte Montmartre is one long series of sieges and battles. The Butte was occupied by Henri of Navarre in 1589 when besieging Paris and the final struggle between the French and the Allies took place here in 1814. On 18 March 1871, at 6 Rue des Roses to the north east of the Butte, Generals Thomas and Lecomte were murdered by insurgents and their deaths precipitated more drastic government action against the Communards.

The Butte Montmartre rises 130m above sea-level and 104m above the level of the Seine, and is thought of as the highest point in Paris (although Belleville in the 20th arrondissement is, in fact, slightly higher; see Ch. 29). Various derivations of the name include Mons Mercurii, Mons Martis or Mons Martyrum; the two first presuppose the existence of a Roman temple on the hill; the last the probability that St Denis and his companions, SS. Rusticus and Eleutherius, were beheaded at the foot of the hill, and according to tradition, St Denis then walked to the site of the Basilica of St-Denis (see Ch. 39), carrying his severed head. The site of the martyrdom is said to be where the Chapelle du Martyre stands, in the convent at 9 Rue Yvonne-le-Tac, just east of the Métro Abbesses. It was in the crypt of the chapel built here that Ignatius de Loyola and his six companions, including Francisco Xavier, taking the first Jesuit vows, founded the Society of Jesus (1534).

Sacré-Coeur

In 1873 the National Assembly decreed the building of a basilica here as an expiatory offering after the Franco-Prussian War of 1870–71. The result, the Sacré-Coeur (**Map 3; 1**), visible from almost every part of Paris, is a conspicuous white stone edifice in a Romanesque-Byzantine style derived from St-Front at Périgueux.

History of Sacrè-Coeur

The cult of the Sacred-Heart became popular after the first pilgrimage in 1873 to Paray-le-Monial in Burgundy, the site of a 17C revelation. Work on the church began in 1876 from the plans of Abadie (who had recently restored St-Front in Périgueux), and although used for services in 1891, it was not consecrated as a basilica until 1919. It is built of Château-Landon stone, which whitens with age.

The two statues at the front of the basilica depicting *Joan of Arc* and *St Louis* are by Hippolyte Lefebvre. Bronze doors with a delicate vegetal design invite you in, but it is hard to reconcile the radiant white exterior with the unremitting gloom of the interior. 100m long and 75m across the ambulatory, it is surmounted by a dome 83m high, and abutted by a square campanile in which hangs the *Savoyarde*, one of the world's heaviest bells: 19 tons.

The surfaces of this church of pilgrimage are extensively decorated with **mosaics**, executed by Luc-Olivier Merson, the huge (largest in the world) one above the high altar depicting *Christ and the Sacred Heart worshipped by the Virgin, Joan of Arc and St Michael*. The glass is 20C.

Both the crypt and the dome can be visited for a fee. The dome, not surprisingly, provides more views—inside and out; from the external gallery you can see the 80 columns (each with a different capital).

Flights of steps descend the steep slope of the Butte through the gardens of Sq. Willette (the funicular runs on the west side). Rue de Steinkerque continues downhill to Blvd de Rochechouart and Pl. d'Anvers.

The former village atmosphere of **Old Montmartre**, with its cottages and little gardens, can be glimpsed in places. In Rue des Saules, leading north from Rue Norvins, the Clos Montmartre was created in 1933 and planted with vines which are harvested each October and vinified in the Marie du 18e Arrondissement. No. 4 in this street is *Au Lapin Agile* (named after the rabbit of M. André Gill who commissioned the sign), made famous by its artistic clientele. Maurice Utrillo is buried in the nearby Cimetière St-Vincent.

Some idea of the way it was can be experienced at the charming **Musée de Vieux-Montmartre** (12 Rue Cortot), installed in a 17C house with a garden, which originally belonged to Rosimond, an actor in Molière's troupe. Occupants over the years included Renoir in 1875, Emile Bernard, Léon Blum, Suzanne Valadon, and her son Maurice Utrillo. The museum records the history of the district, including the legend of the martyrdom of St Denis and the history of the Abbey; it also contains ephemera and material of local interest ranging from 18C porcelain made locally at the Manufacture of Clignancourt to a reconstruction of a Montmartrois Bistrot; and exhibits evoking local Cabarets notably the Chat Noir, theatre of shadows.

Just off Place to Tertre in Rue Poulbot is the **Espace Montmartre Salvador Dali** (☎ 01 42 64 40 10) with over 300 works by the Surrealist artist. Close by is Pl. Emile-Goudeau, a favourite artistic area c 1910. No. 13 was the famous **Bateau-Lavoir** (rebuilt since a fire in 1970), the ramshackle residence at different times of Picasso, Modigliani, Van Dongen, Derain, Gris, and Max Jacob, where Picasso conceived his ground-breaking *Demoiselles d'Avignon* and where a banquet was held in honour of Douanier Rousseau.

At the foot of the Butte Montmartre, in a Pavilion built by Baltard, is the **Musée d'Art Naïf-Max Fourny**, open 10.00–18.00 every day (☎ 01 42 58 72 89) (with a restaurant). A variety of temporary exhibitions and performances are held here.

27 • Avenue des Champs-Elysées

Arrondissement: 75008

Concorde, Champs-Elysées-Clemenceau, Franklin D. Roosevelt, George-V, Charles de Gaulle-Etoile

Charles de Gaulle-Etoile

This area has some of the classiest and most costly restaurants, but if you want a special treat without totally breaking the bank, look at the set-price lunch menus:

Chiberta, 3 Rue Arsène Houssaye, ☎ 01 53 53 42 00. Refined and straightforward cuisine in a beautiful setting

Les Elysées du Vernet, Hôtel Vernet, 25 Rue Vernet, ☎ 01 44 31 98 98. Southern cuisine, glass ceiling by Eiffel. One of the best.

Lasserre, 17 Av. Franklin-Roosevelt, ☎ 01 43 59 53 43. Neo-classical décor with a retractable ceiling, favoured by politicians

Laurent, 41 Av. Gabriel, ☎ 01 42 25 00 39. Wonderful food at astronomic prices—but an excellent value lunch and dinner set-price menu

Ledoyen, First floor, Carré Champs-Elysées, ☎ 01 53 05 10 01. Flemish cuisine of high quality

Taillevent, 15 Rue Lamennais, ☎ 01 44 95 15 01. Perfection all around

Restaurants with specialities and character around the ££ range, include

Androuèt, 6 Rue Arsène-Houssaye, ☎ 01 42 89 95 00. This world-famous where cheese is king has moved to this new address

L'Alsace, 39 Av. des Champs-Elysées, ☎01 43 59 44 24, as the name would suggest, Alsatian cooking (*choucroute*) and a busy brasserie

Bar des Théâtres, 6 Av. Montaigne, ☎ 01 47 23 34 63, inexpensive late-night bar-brasserie where you might catch a glimpse of glamour

Cercel Ledoyen, Carré des Champs-Elysées, ☎ 01 47 42 76 02. The Ground Floor version of Ledoyen (above) but easier on the pocket

Fouquet's, 99 Av. des Champs-Elysées, ☎ 01 47 23 70 60. The most famous café on the Champs with the names of stars in brass

Ladurée, 75 Av. des Champs-Elysées, ☎ 01 42 82 40 10, an attractive salon de thé and restaurant which is also a *patissier* and *chocolatier*

La Salle à Manger, 17 Av. Kléber, t 01 44 28 00 17. Intimate, luxurious and stylish, ££–£££

For snacks or less-expensive meals (£):

Drugstore Publicis Champs-Elysées ☎ 01 44 43 79 00, the 60s hangout still produces a reasonable meal

Le Petit Yvan, 1bis Rue Jean Mermoz, ☎ 01 42 89 49 65. The sort of bistrot you are always hoping to find

Restaurant du Rond-Point, Théâtre Renaud-Barrault, av. Franklin-Roosevelt, ☎ 01 42 56 22 01, patronised by theatre people

The Champs-Elysées

To the west of Pl. de la Concorde extend the Champs-Elysées, through which the **Av. des Champs-Elysées** (Map 1; 6/2; 7), probably the most famous avenue in the world, gently ascends for nearly 2km to the striking silhouette of the Arc de Triomphe. Although the impressive perspectives remain and Parisians and visitors alike still flock there, time has taken its toll on the Champs-Elysées and its former elegance is a little faded. To bring it back to life, some 300 additional trees were planted a few years ago which helps to redress the balance and, when lit up at night (especially at Christmas) the old magic returns. The Champs-Elysées is the focus for numerous state occasions and commemorations, as wide ranging as the celebration of liberation in 1944 and France's soccer victory in the World Cup of 1998.

History of the Champs-Elysées

At the beginning of the 17C, this low-lying area was still marshland, but after a decree issued 1667 to create a promenade in the same perspective as the Tuileries gardens, it was drained and in 1670 laid out to designs by Le Nôtre's. Its name was changed from Grand-Cours to Champs-Elysées early in the 18C. The Marquis de Marigny (brother of Mme de Pompadour) had it replanted in 1765 and the avenue was extended to the Pont de Neuilly in 1774. It was used from 1814 to 1816 as a military encampment for allied troops and the gardens consequently suffered severely. The area became fashionable during the Second Empire, and in 1858, the gardens were re-landscaped in the less-formal English style and have remained virtually unchanged since then.

The Champs-Elysées consists of two parts. The first and smaller section, at the Concorde end, is made up of the gardens created in 1838 extending as far as the Rond-Point des Champs-Elysées. The other section is the commercialised avenue, flanked by offices and showrooms, cinemas and banks, expensive restaurants and fast-food outlets, which continues northwest to Place Charles de Gaulle.

From the Pl. Clemenceau (**Map 2; 7**), Av. de Marigny leads north, passing (left) the Théâtre Marigny by Garnier (1883) and an open-air stamp market (Thur, Sat and Sun) to the walled gardens of the Palais de l'Elysée, but mere mortals are forbidden to tread the flanking *trottoir*. Av. Gabriel runs parallel to the north side of the Champs-Elysées past the gardens of the Palais de l'Elysée, of the British Embassy and of the American Embassy (1931–33) at the corner of Rue Boissy-d'Anglas (see Ch. 28).

On the south side, between the Petit (left) and Grand Palais, both built for the Exhibition of 1900, Av. Winston Churchill leads to the most eye-catching bridge on the Seine, **Pont Alexandre-III** (1896–1900) named after the Tsar of Russia who laid the first stone at a moment of entente cordiale between the two countries. A single elegant steel arch, 107.50m long, abundantly decorated with lamps and sculptures, it was given a thorough revamp a few years ago. The avenue and bridge create a typically grand Parisian vista across the Seine to the gleaming dome of Les Invalides (see Ch. 11).

Among the specimen trees, memorials and statues of the **Jardins des Champs-Elysées** enveloping, on the south side, the The Musée du Petit Palais and the Grand Palais, are secreted various restaurants (*Ledoyen*, *Laurent* and *Pavillons de l'Elysées* and *Gabriel*), two theatres and a Punch and Judy created in 1818.

Six radiating avenues and six fountains create the **Rond-Point des Champs-Elysées**, and to the southwest extends the wide Av. Montaigne.

The Musée du Petit Palais

The Musée du Petit Palais is found in the Petit Palais (**Map 2; 7**), a fine building with pediment and dome echoing Les Invalides across the Seine. It was built by Charles Girault, and opened its doors in 1902 as the Musée des Beaux-Arts de la Ville de Paris. In 2001, after a hundred years of service, the museum is closing to undergo a thorough overhaul to bring it into line with the finest museums of Paris. The renovations are likely to continue until 2003 and during that time the building itself will be enhanced, the space for permanent, temporary and rotating exhibitions will be extended and the garden and fountains put in order. This will enable the extremely prestigious collection of fine and applied arts to be set off to greater advantage. The museum, whose entrance is on Av. Winston Churchill, mounts frequent temporary exhibitions.

The museum owns works stretching from Antiquity to 1925, covering different types of artistic expression in particular periods. It divides roughly into two sections. The first is Ancient Art, encompassing everything from Egyptian and Classical Antiquities to 18C European, made up mainly of four bequests: Dutuit, Tuck, Ocampo and Marie. The other is French 19C–20C comprising purchases and commissions by the Ville de Paris in the 19C and a considerable number of bequests.

The **Dutuit Collection** is made up of Gallo-Roman bronzes; Egyptian statuettes; and an extensive collection of Greek ceramics, a collection of Grolier bindings also majolicas, Bernard Palissy and Saint-Porchaire ceramics, Limoges enamels, ivories, German and Burgundian wood carvings and paintings by Cranach the Elder, Velvet Brueghel, and Cima de Conegliano, and other works of the Italian Renaissance. The second major group of works is from the **Edward Tuck Collection**, comprising Chinese porcelain of the K'ang-Hsi period (1662–1722) and an extensive collection of 18C works including Sèvres and Meissen porcelain, Battersea enamels, Beauvais tapestries, paintings by Greuze, Poussin, Largillière, Hubert Robert, and sculptures by Houdon and Puget, and a Louis XV furniture.

There are paintings of the **Dutch school** by Willem van de Velde (1611–93), Hobbema (1638–1709), Ter Borch, Metsu, Rembrandt, Teniers the Younger, Jan Steen, Jordaens, Adriaen van de Velde. **19C–early 20C French painting** is represented by a fine cross section from Rococo to Impressionism and beyond, with works by Fragonard, Géricault, Doré, James Tissot, Courbet. Among many fine portraits are those by Leon Bonnat (1833–1922), Baudry, Sargent and Courbet. Other compositions include works by Ingres and academic artists such as Chassériau, Boulanger, Granet, and Alphonse Legros Le Lutrin.

Masterpieces of the 19C owned by the museum include Courbet's Realist masterpiece *Girls on the Banks of the Seine* (1856); and by Daumier and Jules Breton. Landscape painting can be followed through the work of Corot, Boudin, Rousseau, and Jongkind, to Sisley, Pissarro; Monet, *Sunset at Lavacourt*; two women artists of the 19C, Mary Cassatt, Berthe Morisot, are represented in the collections. Portraits include: Manet, *Portrait of M. Duret*; Renoir, *Portrait of A. Vollard*, *Woman with a Rose*; Cézanne, *Portrait of Ambroise Vollard*; and by Vuillard and Bonnard. Other works by Cézanne include the *Three Bathers* (c 1879–82) which once belonged to Matisse; also works by Gauguin, *Old Man with a Stick*; Toulouse-Lautrec.

19C sculpture includes Denis Puech, Dalou, Carpeaux, Renoir and Rodin. There are ceramics by Gauguin, and jewellery and glass by Lalique, Tiffany, Gallé and Georges Fouquet.

The **Grand Palais** (Map 2; 2. ☎ 01 44 13 17 17, recorded information), like the Petit opposite, was built in 1897 for the Exposition Universelle, with a classical façade, surmounted by a lofty portico and has space for block-busting temporary art exhibitions. The western half is made over to the **Palais de la Découverte**, devoted since 1937 to spreading scientific knowledge imaginatively. It contains a planetarium and has displays relating to astronomy, physics, earth and life sciences and dinosaurs as well as plenty of interactive facilities. Open 09.30–18.00, Sun and public holidays 10.00–19.00, closed Mon, 1/1, 1/5, 14/7, 15/08, 25/12 (☎ 01 56 43 20 20). Bookshop and café.

On Av. Franklin Roosevelt is the Théâtre du Rond-Point (Renaud-Barrault Company) by Davioud (1860), with a restaurant. At no. 25 Av. des Champs-Elysées is the former **Hôtel de la Païva** (1866), in florid neo-Renaissance style, built for a beautiful courtesan, the Marquise de Païva, where artists and writers were entertained. It is now home to the Travellers' Club and at no. 127 (left) beyond the upper end of the Av. George-V, is the **Office de Tourisme de Paris**, open every 09.00–20.00 all year except Sundays in winter and public holidays 11.00–18.00; closed 01/05, ☎ 01 49 52 53 54.

Two streets beyond, at 107 Rue La Boétie, are showrooms of the **Institut Géographique Nationale**, where a large range of French maps is on sale.

Twelve avenues radiate starwise from Pl. Charles-de-Gaulle (formerly Pl. de l'Etoile, and still commonly known as such: **Map 1; 5**), around which traffic roars alarmingly.

The Arc de Triomphe

In the centre of this traffic chaos stands serenely the grandiose Arc de Triomphe the largest triumphal arch in the world (almost 50m high, and 45m wide), erected to the glory of the French army and Napoléon's megalomania.

History of the Arc de Triomphe

Napoléon's desire to raise a triumphal arch began to take shape in 1806. Designed by Chalgrin, the arch was completed only in 1836, so that at the time of the Emperor's marriage to Marie-Louise of Austria (1810) it was necessary to build a mock arch for the wedding procession. Still unfinished by the time of the fall of the Empire in 1814, it was not until 1823, when Louis XVIII dedicated it to his armies returning victorious from Spain, that work began again under Huyot. The project was finally brought to a close at the time of Louis-Philippe when Blouet took over in 1832, remaining faithful to Chalgrin's ideas, and Blouet also supervised the decoration, carried out by several of the best sculptors of the day. On an intensely cold day in 1840 the funeral cortège bearing Napoléon's ashes passed under the Arch. The Pl. de l'Etoile, designed after the Arch was built by Haussmann, and the uniform façades of the hôtels between each avenue were by Hittorff in 1854–57. These have no access from the place but are reached from the Rues Tilset and Pressbourg.

La Marseillaise *by François Rude*

To reach the Arch safely, take the tunnel from the Champs-Elysées. Open 1 Apr–30 Sept, 09.30–23.00; 1 Oct–31 March 10.00–22.30. Closed mornings 8/5 and 11/11; all day 1/1, 1/5, 14/7, 25/12, ☎ 01 55 37 73 77. It contains a museum of the history of the monument, but the greatest attraction is the **observation platform** at the top. From here, until late into the evening, there are spectacular views down to the star pattern of the street below, along the great vista of the Champs Elysées or towards the huge Grande Arche de la La Défense. Take time, however, to see the **sculptures at ground level**, especially the colossal groups in high relief on the main façades. Facing the Champs-Elysées are (right) the *Departure of the Army in 1792* or *La Marseillaise* by Rude, undoubtedly the most dynamic composition of the four, and (left) the *Triumph of Napoléon in 1810*, by Cortot. Facing the Av. de la Grande-Armée are (right) the *Resistance of the French in 1814*, and (left) the *Peace of 1815*, both by Etex. The four spandrels of the main archway contain figures of *Fame* by Pradier, and those of the smaller archways have sculptures by Vallois (south side) and Bra. Above the groups are relief panels of the campaigns of 1792–1805 including (north) the *Battle of Austerlitz*.

On the **row of shields** in the attic storey are inscribed the names of battles of the Republic and the Empire, although some were not in fact French victories! Below the side arches are the names of some hundreds of generals who took part in these campaigns with the names of those who fell in action underlined.

Beneath the arch is the **Tomb of the Unknown Soldier**, victim of the 1914–18 War. The flame has burnt constantly since 11 November 1923. At its foot is a bronze plaque representing the Shaef shoulder-flash, dated 25 August 1944, the day of the liberation of Paris from the German occupation.

To the west, the Av. de la Grande Armée leads gradually downhill to Porte Maillot, with the towers of La Défense rising some distance beyond: see latter part of Ch. 30.

28 • Rue du Faubourg-St-Honoré to Parc Monceau

Arrondissements: 75008, 75017

Concorde, Madeleine, St-Philippe-du-Roule, Pl.-des-Ternes, Villiers, Monceau, Charles de Gaulle-Etoile

Charles de Gaulle-Etoile

L'Ampère, 1 Rue Ampère, ☎ 01 47 63 72 05. Traditional, friendly bistrot, £

Baumann Ternes, 64 Av. des Ternes, ☎ 01 45 74 16 66. Alsatian specialities in a lively atmosphere, £

Billy Gourmand, 20 Rue de Toqueville, ☎ 01 42 27 03 71. Polished and pretty cooking and setting, ££

Le Boeuf sur le Toit, 34 Rue du Colisée, ☎ 01 43 59 83 80. Venerable 20s brasserie, once patronised by Cocteau, varied dishes, ££

Les Bouchons de François Clerc, 22 Rue de la Terrasse, ☎ 01 42 67 25 95. Standard prices and food, excellent affordable wines, £–££

Les Cigales, 127 Rue Cardinet, ☎ 01 42 27 83 93. Provençal to the hilt, £

Goldenberg Wagram, 69 Av. de Wagram, ☎ 01 42 27 34 79. Classic Jewish cooking—ranging from sandwiches to a full meal, £

Le Grenadin, 44 Rue de Naples, ☎ 01 45 63 28 92. Contemporary setting and modern cuisine, ££

La Grande Batelière, 9 Av. de Wagram, ☎ 01 47 70 85 15. Speciality caviar; Yiddish, Russian, and eastern European cuisine, £–££

Les Gourmets des Ternes, 87 Blvd. de Courcelles, ☎ 01 42 27 43 04. Archetypal bistrot with check tablecloths, and good simple food, £

La Marée, 1 Rue Daru, ☎ 01 43 80 20 00. Modernised fresh seafood cooking in a revamped setting, ££

Niel 4 Saisons, 73 av Niel, 17, ☎ 01 44 40 28 15. Traditional, early 1900 décor, floral terrace, £
La Soupière, 154 Av. de Wagram, ☎ 01 42 27 00 73. Seasonable menus, with rare mushrooms a speciality. Good value lunch menu, £–££

Leading chefs-restauranteurs, Jacques Cagna, Michel Rostang and Guy Savoy, opened 'bistrots' in this area where you can sample their craft somewhat less expensively than at their main establishments.
Owned by Rostang:
Bistrot d'à Côté Flaubert, 10 Rue G. Flaubert, ☎ 01 42 67 05 81 Hustly-bustly atmosphere, ££
Bistrot d'à Côté Villiers, 16 Av. de Villiers, ☎ 01 47 63 25 61, ££
Michel Rostang, 20 Rue Rennequin, ☎ 01 47 63 40 77. His main restaurant, lucious, £££
Owned by Guy Savoy:
Guy Savoy, 18 Rue Troyon, ☎ 01 43 80 40 61. Noble rusticity, of the very best. £££

Le Bistrot de l'Etoile-Troyon, 13 Rue Troyon, ☎ 01 42 67 25 95. One of Savoy's bistrots, opposite his main restaurant, £–££ *Le Bistrot de l'Etoile-Niel*, 75 Av. Niel, ☎ 01 42 27 88 44, £–££	Owned by top chef Jacques Cagna: *La Rotisserie d'Armaillé*, 6 Rue d'Armaillé, ☎ 01 42 27 19 20. Bistrot with innovative goodies, £

The Faubourg-St-Honoré *quartier*, in the vicinity of the Elysées Palace, is one of the most luxurious in Paris, liberally sprinkled with embassies, expensive hotels and restaurants, up-market boutiques, jewellers and fashion houses. Further northwest are two important collections of fine and decorative arts, the Musée Jacquemart-André and the Musée Nissim de Camondo, in impressive private mansions donated by the owner/collectors. Parc Monceau is one of the older and favourite gardens of Paris.

Rue du Faubourg-St-Honoré is the northwest continuation of Rue St-Honoré starting from Rue Royale (see Ch. 24), and ending at Pl. des Ternes. It follows the course of the medieval road from Paris to the village of Roule and became fashionable at the end of Louis XIV's reign. In the 18C the grandeur of its mansions made it a rival to the Faubourg St-Germain as an aristocratic quarter. Now this street, up to and around Avenue Montaigne, is adorned with all the designer names, Dior, Chanel and Nina Ricci, et al. and the long-established instituion *Hermes* at no. 24.

On the left at no. 33 Rue du Faubourg-St-Honoré is the exclusive Cercle Interallié (1714), the Russian Embassy during the Second Empire. No. 35, the Hôtel de Charost, since 1825, is home to the **British Embassy** (Map 2; 7).

History of the British Embassy

The 4th Duc de Charost commissioned Antoine Mazin to build the mansion in 1722. In 1785 it was let to the Comte de la Marck, during whose tenancy much of its interior decoration was completed and the English style garden laid out. It was bought in 1803 by Pauline Bonaparte (later Princess Borghese), much of whose furniture remains. She sold the house to the Duke of Wellington in 1814 for £32,000, complete with numerous clocks, chandeliers, candelabras and chimneypieces. Berlioz and Harriet Smithson were married in the chapel in 1833, with Liszt as best man and Thackery to Isabella Shawe in 1836.

The British Embassy church of St Michael is in Rue d'Aguessau opposite. No. 41 is the Hôtel Pontalba, built by Visconti and restored by E. de Rothschild.

The **Palais de l'Elysée**, the official residence of the President of the Republic since 1873 (no admission), stands at the corner of Av. de Marigny. This heavily guarded mansion was built by Molet as the Hôtel d'Evreux in 1718 but has been greatly altered and enlarged since.

History of the Palais de l'Elysée

Mme de Pompadour once occupied it, as did Murat, Napoléon I, who signed his second abdication here in 1815, and Wellington. Napoléon III lived here as Président from 1848 until he moved, as Emperor, to the Tuileries in 1852. It then reverted to its use as a residence for visiting heads of state (including Queen Victoria in 1855 and Elizabeth II in 1957).

No. 11 Rue des Saussaies was the Gestapo headquarters in Paris during 1940–44 with a plaque in memory of victims of the Gestapo. Continuing along Rue du Faubourg-St-Honoré you pass (right) the Ministère de l'Intérieur (Home Office), built in 1769–84 behind a gilded wrought-iron gate flanking Pl. Beauvau. Further on, beyond Av. Matignon, stands **St-Philippe-du-Roule**, built 1774–84 by Chalgrin and added to in the 19C, on the site of the parish church of Roule and later enlarged. The sculpture of *Religion* on the pediment is by Duret, and the basilical style interior contains Chassériau's ceiling painting, *Descent from the Cross*.

At 45 Rue La Boétie (to the north) is **Salle Gaveau**, one of the more important concert-halls in Paris.

Rue du Faubourg-St-Honoré now crosses Av. de Friedland which leads west to the Arc de Triomphe (see Ch. 27). At 208 Rue du Faubourg-St-Honoré, beyond Av. Friedland, are the buildings of the old Hôpital Beaujon (1784); opposite, at 11 Rue Berryer, is the former Hôtel Salomon de Rothschild. Honoré Balzac died in 1850 where 12 Rue Balzac now stands and a statue (1902) of him by Falguière stands at the intersection with Av. de Friedland (see also Rodin's version, Ch. 7).

Just beyond the intersection with Av. Hoche is **Salle Pleyel** (1927), the largest concert-hall in Paris, radically revamped in 1981. In Rue Daru, parallel to the north, is the exotic neo-Byzantine **Russian Orthodox church** of St-Alexander-Nevsky (1859–61).

From behind St-Philippe-du-Roule (see above) Rue de Courcelles crosses Blvd Haussmann. At 38 in Rue de Courcelles (then 48) Dickens lodged in 1846; from 1901–05 Proust lived at no. 45 in a cork-lined sound-proof room, before moving to 102 Blvd Haussmann where he remained until 1919. The Galerie Ching Tsai Loo at no. 48 is a unique red building in Chinese style commissioned in 1926 for an Oriental art dealer.

The Musée Jacquemart-André

The Musée Jacquemart-André (**Map 2; 5**) at 158 Blvd Haussmann, is one of the lesser-known but very rewarding museums of Paris, with a remarkable collection of French 18C art and Italian Renaissance art, in the setting designed and lived in by the collectors. Following extensive renovations completed in 1996 the Italian Museum and the private apartments can be visited, and there is an elegant *Salon de thé* on the ground floor in the former dining room complete with a G.B. Tiepolo fresco and tapestries, *The Legend of Achilles*. Open 10.00–18.00 daily (☎ 01 42 89 04 91) each visitor is issued with an autoguide. There is a boutique.

The house was built c 1870 by Edouard André (d. 1894), who in 1881 married the painter Nélie Jacquemart, and in 1912 she bequeathed the collection to the Institut de France.

Ground floor

In the entrance hall is a Winterhalter, *Portrait of Edouard André*, who came from a rich Protestant banking family. In the first room are two oval paintings by Boucher, *Toilette of Venus* and the *Sleep of Venus*, Nattier, *Portrait of the Marquis d'Antin*, Canaletto, *St Mark's Square* and *The Rialto, Venice*; Chardin, *Still life*; and a bust of *Pigalle*. This leads to the spacious **Grand Salon**, with magnificent 18C woodwork and mirrors, four Gobelins tapestries, and busts by Coysevox, Houdon, and *Henri IV* by Barthélémy Tremblay.

The first in a suite of small rooms off the Grand Salon contains a Beauvais tapestry called *Russian Games*, after Le Prince, a Savonnerie carpet (1663), a Louis XIV fireplace and a Guardi painting. The **Cabinet de Travail**, with a painted ceiling attributed to Tiepolo, has works by Greuze, Fragonard and Lancret and, on the desk, a portrait of *Nélie Jacquemart* who painted Edouard André's portrait in 1872. The Boudoir contains Vigée-Lebrun's, *Countess Skravonska* and paintings by David, Reynolds and Hubert Robert.

In the **Library** are Egyptian antiquities as well as gems of Flemish and Dutch paintings such as Rembrandt, *Amalia von Solms*, *Pilgrims at Emmaus*, *Dr Arnold Tholinx*; Van Dyck, *Count Henry of Peña*, *Time Cuts the Wings of Love*; Franz Hals, *Portrait of a Man*; Ruysdael, *Landscape*: also Philippe de Champaigne's *Portrait of A Man* and the *Boucicaut Book of Hours*, which belonged to Diane de Poitiers.

The other large reception room the opposite side of the Grand Salon, used as a **Music Room**, in sumptuous Second Empire style has a different atmosphere, with red damask walls and ebony furniture. It contains a small Fragonard *Head of an Old Man*; works by Vigée-Lebrun and Largillière and a Beauvais tapestry from a cartoon by Boucher, called *Autumn*.

The **Winter Garden** is an unusual oval space at the end of the building with a beautiful swirling double staircase designed by Henri Parent with antique sculptures. The **Smoking Room** has objects brought back from the Orient by Mme André, including a 14C mosque lamp. There are also paintings from England by Joshua Reynolds, Gainsborough and John Hoppner (1758–1810). On the staircase is a marvellous fresco by Tiepolo, *Henri III welcomed by Federigo Contarini to the Villa de Mira*.

First floor

On the first floor are three rooms of the museum dedicated to the Italian Renaissance. This prodigious collection includes 82 14C and 15C paintings and a handful from the 16C. Major works include four 15C versions of the *Virgin and Child* by Botticelli, Perugino, Francesco Botticini (1446–97) and Baldovinetti (1422–99); Uccello, *St George and the Dragon*; Vittore Carpaccio, *The Embassy from Hippolytos* (1493–95) and *Six Saints from a Coronation of the Virgin* (1493), by Carlo Crivelli; large retable by Botticini, *Pietà with Saints*, in its original frame. There is a fine a coffered ceiling decorated with *Four Couples in a Garden*; a miniature *Annunication* (1430–40) by Mariano d'Antonio; a banner (1444) by Pietro di Giovanni di Ambrogio; Giorgia Schiavone, *Profile of a Man*, on parchment. Also Bernadino Luini, *Virgin with SS. Margaret and Augustine*; a brilliant little *Virgin and Child* by Cima da Conegliano (end 15C); oval painting by Signorelli (1441–1523) of the *Holy Famliy with St John the Baptist*; also Giovanni [?] Bellini, *Virgin and Child*, Mantegna, *Mocking of Christ*.

Italian sculpture includes works by Laurana, Jacopo Sansovino and a small bronze relief by Donatello. A number of 15C marble doorways have been re-erected and among terracottas from the della Robbia workshops, is an *Angel of the Annunciation* by Andrea della Robbia. There is a Florentine wood and marquetry bench with the Strozzi arms (end 15C) and marquetry choir-stalls, c 1505 (Northern Italian).

At the end of the visit are three intimate rooms of the private apartments.

The Rue de Téhéran, a few paces to the east, climbs north across Av. de Messine to meet Rue de Monceau.

The Musée Nissim de Camondo

The Musée Nissim de Camondo, 63 Rue de Monceau (**Map 2**; **3**), an annexe to the Musée des Arts Décoratifs, was bequeathed by Count Moïse de Camondo (died 1935) as a memorial to his son Nissim, killed in 1917 (his daughter and grandchildren died at Auschwitz). The mansion itself dates from 1911–14, but the interior décor uses 18C panelling or reproductions, such as the wrought-iron balustrade of the staircase, to create the setting for the outstanding collection of antique furniture, carpets, tapestries and tableware. The house has been almost completely restored and fabrics remade to replicate the original.

Open 10.00–17.00, closed Mon and Tues, ☎ 01 53 89 06 40. From the entrance hall, with a red marble fountain (1765) from the Château de St-Prix, Montmorency, and a flat-topped desk by J-H. Riesener, stairs lead up past a pair of corner cupboards decorated with Japanese lacquer attributed to B.V.R.B., and a pair of armchairs upholstered in Savonnerie tapestry.

First floor

The **Grand Bureau** has a pair of low cabinets by Leleu; a roll-top desk and secretaire by Saunier, the latter from the Château de Tanly; desk-armchair of 1778; a white marble-topped table by M. Carlin from the Château de Bellevue; two low chairs known as *voyeuses*, designed for watching the gaming tables, by Séné; chairs by N.Q. Foliot covered in Aubusson tapestry (scenes from La Fontaine); Aubusson tapestries with six fables from La Fontaine after Oudry; a Beauvais screen with the fable of the *Cock on the Dunghill*; bronze bust of *Mme Le Comte* by Coustou; Vigée-Lebrun, *Bacchante*.

The **Grand Salon**, overlooking the garden, has white and gold panelling from a private town house at 11 Rue Royale; a pair of covered vases carved from petrified wood, from the collection of Marie-Antoinette; marquetry cabinet and tables by Riesener; round table and *bureau de dame* (with Sèvres porcelain plaques) by Carlin; tables by A. Weisweiler, D. Roentgen and R.V.L.C. (R. Vandercruse, called Lacroix); suite of furniture (which belonged to Sir Richard Wallace), including two sofas and an armchair by G. Jacob; a six-leaved Savonnerie screen; Vigée-Lebrun, *Mme Le Coulteux du Molay*; *La Pêcheuse*, a Beauvais tapestry, after Boucher; and among Savonnerie carpets, one (*L'Air*) woven for the Grande Galerie of the Louvre (1678) and one made in 1660.

Salon Huet, seven panels and three *dessus de portes* of *Scènes pastorales* painted by J.B. Huet, dated 1776; marquetry roll-top desk by Oeben; pair of cabinets by Garnier and Carlin; sofa, *bergères* and chairs by Séné; a folding screen by J.B. Boulard, delivered in 1785 for Louis XVI's Salon des Jeux at Versailles.

Salle à Manger, with a view of the Parc Monceau, console and a pair of serving tables by Weisweiler; pair of small cabinets by Leleu; silver by Auguste and Roettiers (the latter's work was ordered by Catherine II of Russia for Orloff). Sèvres porcelain, known as the Buffon set, decorated with birds. **Galerie**, sofa and chairs by P. Gillier; Aubusson tapestries, after Boucher, *La Danse Chinoise*.

Petit Bureau, furniture by Topino, Riesener and R.V.L.C., among others; snuffboxes, clocks, Chinese porcelain (Kien-Loung); four *Views of Venice* by Guardi; Oudry, sketches for Gobelins tapestries of *Les Chasses de Louis XV*; three paintings by H. Robert. On the stairs leading to the second floor, two Aubusson tapestries in the Chinese style, after Boucher.

Second floor

Galerie, sofa and chairs by Nogaret; a series of engravings after Chardin; 18C Chinese porcelain. Turning right into the **Salon Bleu**: pair of tables attributed to Riesener; low bookcase by Weisweiler; red morocco casket embossed with the arms of Marie-Antoinette; 18C and 19C views of Paris; a family portrait by Gautier-Dagoty (c 1770); watercolour of the *Quai Malaquais* by T. Boys; Chinese porcelain of the 17C–18C.

Bibliothèque, an oak-panelled oval room, contains a drop-front desk by Leleu; two bronze and Sèvres biscuit candelabras by Blondeau after Boucher; Aubusson tapestry screen (1775). **Chambre à Coucher**: furniture by Cramer, Topino and G. Jacob. Among paintings: Danloux, *Rosalie Duthé*; Lavreince, *The Singing Lesson*; Lancret, *Les Rémois*; Drouais, *Alexandre de Beauharnais as a Child*; Savonnerie carpet (1760) for the chapel at Versailles. **Deuxième Chambre**: secretaire attributed to Riesener and various *Scènes de Chasse*. The **bathroom** and **dressing room** of the early 20C are also open to the public and the **kitchens** have recently opened.

At 7 Av. Vélasquez, a parallel street to the north, is the **Musée Cernuschi**, bequeathed to the city in 1895 by the collector (of Maltese origin). In many ways it complements the more comprehensive collections of Oriental art in the Musée Guimet and Musée d'Ennery (see pp 305 and 314 respectively). Open 10.00–17.40, closed Mon and public holidays, ☎ 01 45 63 50 75.

Of particular interest are the funerary figurines of the T'ang and Wei dynasties, neolithic terracottas, and bronze vases of the Chang dynasty (14C–11C BC). There are outstanding paintings on silk of horses and grooms of the T'ang period (8C). Note also the collections of clasps, mirrors, and jade amulets. On the first floor is an extensive collection of bronze objects from Louristan and Iran (8C–7C BC), a bronze basin of 5C–3C BC and porcelain of various periods.

Parc Monceau

The neighbouring Parc Monceau (**Map 2; 3**. 88 hectares) is an appropriately elegant garden for this smart district. It derives its name from a vanished village, and is a remnant of a private park laid out by Carmontel in 1778 for Philippe-Egalité d'Orléans, Duc de Chartres, and father of Louis-Philippe. Its gardener was Thomas Blaikie (1750–1838), a Scotsman. It was then known as the 'Folie de Chartres', and certain picturesque details remain.

Near the northeast corner is the **Naumachie**, an oval lake with a graceful Corinthian colonnade, which may have come from either the Château du Raincy or from the projected Valois chapel at St-Denis. To the east of the lake is a Renaissance arcade from the old Hôtel de Ville; to the west is the **Rotonde de Chartres**, a toll-house, by Ledoux, in the 18C city wall erected by the Farmers-General. Used as a keeper's lodge, the building was disfigured in 1861 when the columns were fluted and a dome added. The four monumental gates are by Davioud, and scattered among the ornamental trees and shrubs and colourful flowerbeds are several statues, including *Ambroise Thomas* by Falguière (1902), *Guy de Maupassant* by Verlet (1897).

There are various imposing mansions in the streets to the north, including those in Rue de Prony, leading northwest. Off this street, Rue Fortuny turns northeast to the re-named Pl. du Gén. Catroux (formerly Pl. Malesherbes but still

Métro Malesherbes). Slightly to the north is the **Salle Cortot**, a concert-hall (78 Rue Cardinet).

Batignolles

Further northeast, in the Batignolles, some picturesque areas still survive the pressures of modernisation, and deserve exploration. In 1989 the **Promenade Pereire**, a *promenade plantée*, was created on top of the RER line between Rue Bayen (Porte Maillot) and Pl. Maréchal-Juin. This clever camouflage consists of open gardens alternating with enclosed squares in a continuous walkway. The *quartier* gave its name to a school of Impressionist painters under the leadership of Manet (see the painting by Fantin-Latour in the Musée d'Orsay).

In the **Cimetière des Batignolles** (best approached by the Av. de Clichy, and some distance northwest of the Cimetière de Montmartre) lie Verlaine, André Breton and Léon Bakst.

The Av. de Villiers leads northwest from the Pl. du Gén. Catroux, in which no. 43 is the **Musée Henner** (open 10.00–12.00, 14.00–17.00, closed Mon), devoted to the work of Jean-Jacques Henner. Some distance further west, near the Porte de Champerret, stands **Ste-Odile** (1938–46), with a flattened dome and rocket-like tower. Nearby, at 41 Blvd Berthier, John Singer Sargent had his studio c 1883–86, which was taken over by Giovanni Boldini.

29 • Chaillot, Passy and Auteuil

■ Arrondissement: 75016

Concorde, Alma-Marceau, Iéna, Trocadéro, Passy, La Muette, Porte-d'Auteuil

L'Adresse, 4 Rue Beethoven, ☎ 01 40 50 84 40. Interesting dishes and bargain prices, £

Bar des Théâtres, 6 Av. Montaigne, ☎ 01 47 23 34 63. Relatively inexpensive, lively, open late, some glamorous clientele, £

Le Bistrot de l'Etoile Lauriston, 19 Rue Lauriston, ☎ 01 40 67 11 16. Arguably Guy Savoy's best bistrot, £

La Butte Chaillot, 110bis Av. Kléber, ☎ 01 47 27 88 88. Another Savoy bistrot, good value menus, £–££

Driver's, 6 Rue Georges-Bizet, ☎ 01 47 23 61 15. Young clientele, freshly prepared food, automobile décor, £

Faugeron, 52 Rue de Longchamp, t 01 47 04 24 53. Classy elegance, every detail taken care of, £££

La Gare, 19 Chaussée de la Muette, ☎ 01 42 15 15 31. In an old train station, with a terrace, £–££

Le Noura, 27 Av. Marceau, ☎ 01 47 23 02 20. Lebanese cooking, delightful terrace, inexpensive, £

Port Alma, 10 Av. de New York, ☎ 01 47 23 75 11. Excellent seafood at a wide range of prices, ££

Le Petit Rétro, 5 Rue Mesnil, ☎ 01 44 05 06 05. Charming surroundings and classic menu, £–££
Le Relais du Parc, 55-57 Av. Raymond-Poincaré, ☎ 01 44 05 66 10. North African cooking in neo-colonial English setting, ££
Le Scheffer, 22 Rue Scheffer, ☎ 01 47 27 81 11. A step back in time to traditional bistrot-style food and prices, £
Le Totem, Palais de Chaillot, Pl. du Trocadero, ☎ 01 47 27 28 29, with splendid views of the Eiffel Tower, £
Le Vivarois, 192 Av. Victor Hugo, ☎ 01 45 04 04 31. 60s décor for delicious classic modern cuisine, £££

This chapter covers a section of the 8e and the whole of the 16e arrondissement bordered by the Champs-Elysées, the Seine and the Bois de Boulogne, a smart residential area characterised by large 19C and 20C apartment blocks, with prime examples of architecture by Perret, Jeanneret and le Courbusier. Several pleasant gardens and wide avenues contribute to the grand atmosphere of this area, while around Rue de Passy, which has a more intimate feel, there is a good shopping.

The *quartier* also boasts the most stunning view of the Eiffel Tower. There are several museums in the 16e which, although important, may be less familiar to visitors to Paris: Musée Marmottan, Musée d'Art Moderne de la Ville de Paris, Musée Guimet and, in the Palais de Chaillot, the Musée de l'Homme and the Musée de la Marine.

From Pl. de la Concorde (see Ch. 27) follow the Seine along Cours la Reine and its extension, Cours Albert-1er westwards to Pl. de l'Alma. This was the route laid out in 1616 along the old road to the villages of Chaillot, St-Cloud and Versailles, and the Roman canal bringing water from Chaillot. The parallel Port de la Conférence, flanking the river, takes its name from the Conference Gate (demolished in 1730), the entry point of the Spanish ambassadors in 1660 who discussed with Mazarin the proposed marriage between Louis XIV and María Teresa. In the gardens near Pont Alexandre III is a statue of *Simon Bolivar on horseback* by Frémiet.

Pont des Invalides (Map 7; 1, west of the Pont Alexandre-III) dates from 1827–29, but was rebuilt in 1879–80 and enlarged in 1956. The statue of a *zouave* (an Algerian solider belonging to the French light infantry corps) on **Pont de l'Alma** (1974) comes from the original bridge and was once used as a gauge in estimating the height of the Seine in flood.

Lalique, the glassmaker, designed the glass and metal doors of his house at no. 40 Cours Albert-1er. Near Place de l'Alma are several monuments including Belgium's *Gratitude to France* by Rudder (1923) and to the Polish patriot *Adam Mickiewicz* by Bourdelle. The **Flame of Liberty**, on the west side of Place de l'Alma, presented to Paris by the International Herald Tribune, has acquired a new significance since the death of Princess Diana in 1997 in the nearby underpass.

Just across the Seine at the south end of Pont de l'Alma is the public entrance to the **sewers** (*égouts*) of Paris. This formidable system was laid out by the engineer Eugène Belgrand (1810–78) at the time of Haussmann, and is a far cry from the *grand égout* described by Victor Hugo in *Les Miserables*. Part of the total 2100km of the working city sewers may be visited by guided tour or independently between 11.00–17.00 (winter to 16.00); restricted entry after heavy rain. There is an audiovisual, a room showing future technology and even a gift shop.

Several handsome streets radiate north from Pl. de l'Alma (**Map 1; 8/7; 2**), many of the mansions being the showrooms of haut-couturiers. At 13 Av. Montaigne, leading northeast, is the **Théâtre des Champs-Elysées**, a pioneering structure by Auguste Perret (1911–13). This excellent concert hall was decorated by several others artists as well as Bourdelle who designed the reliefs, and its early days scintillated with performances by Ballets Russes and the first rendition of Stravinsky's *Rite of Spring*. On the west side of Av. George-V, leading northwards, is the American Church of the Holy Trinity (1885–88), built in a Gothic style.

Av. de New York, with its continuations, follows the north bank of the Seine for some distance before bearing west to the Porte de St-Cloud. Parallel to the long narrow Allée des Cygnes (Isle of Swans) lying mid-stream south of Pont de Bir-Hakeim, is the cylindrical **Maison de la Radio** (or de l'ORTF; **Map 5; 4**), designed in 1960 by Henri Bernard, impressive in size even if its tower is out of proportion to the rest of the building. The **Musée Radio-France**, devoted to radio, is at 116 Av. du Président-Kennedy, but it may only be visited with a guided tour starting hourly from 10.30–16.30 (but not 12.30) closed Sun, ☎ 01 42 30 33 83.

At the southern end of the Allée des Cygnes, crossed here by the Pont de Grenelle (rebuilt 1875), is a reduced size bronze replica of Bartholdi's *Statue of Liberty* facing downstream, presented to France by the United States. The original stands at the entrance to New York harbour and another smaller replica is in the Jardin du Luxembourg (see Ch. 8).

Av. du Président-Wilson leads west from the Pl. de l'Alma, from which Av. Marceau immediately branches off right towards the Arc de Triomphe. On the left is **St-Pierre-de-Chaillot** (1937), a neo-Romanesque church mainly of concrete, by Emile Bois, the façade covered with reliefs of the life of St Peter. It replaced an 18C parish church.

To the right in Av. du Président-Wilson is the **Hôtel Galliéra** (1888–92), built in Italian Renaissance style to house the Duchesse de Galliéra's (d. 1889) collection of 17C Italian art. In the end she bequeathed it to the city of Genoa. Since 1977 the building has housed the **Musée Galliéra de la Mode et du Costume** (of the Ville de Paris). Set in gardens, its entrance is at 10 Av. Pierre-1er de Serbie. Parts of the extensive collection, enriched by donations, are shown in rotation in a series of temporary exhibitions covering specific themes or periods. Open 10.00–17.40 during exhibitions, closed Mon and public holidays, ☎ 01 56 52 86 00, www.paris-france.org.

Normally there is a display of dresses, designs, costume and fashion-plates, photographs and an astonishing variety of accessories, lingerie and other forms of clothing, from costume jewellery to shoes, as well as dolls and wigs.

Musée d'Art Moderne de la Ville de Paris

On the south side of the avenue stands the **Palais de Tokyo** (**Map 6; 1–2**) constructed for the Universal Exhibition of 1937 (by Aubert, Dondel, Viard and Dastugue) on the site of a military bakery, itself replacing the old Savonnerie or soap manufacture (see also Gobelins, Ch. 6). The wall of the terrace is decorated with bas-reliefs by Janniot; and here, with other statues by Bourdelle, is a bronze of *La France*, installed in 1948, with the inscription 'Mother, here are your sons who fought so long and hard' (Charles Péguy).

The building consists of two wings, the eastern one housing the **Musée d'Art Moderne de la Ville de Paris**. Frequent temporary exhibitions are held here, in which case the permanent collection may in part be on view. Open 10.00–17.30, closed Mon and public holidays, ☎ 01 53 67 40 00. There is small café and a bookshop/boutique.

The museum was inaugurated in 1961 to house the municipal collection of 20C works built up from donations since 1930, plus acquisitions. It owns important works from the School of Paris and other European artists and a growing contemporary collection.

Leading to the permanent exhibition is the *Chambre de Méditation* (1969) by Tania Mouraud and *La Mer*, a projection by Ange Leccia. **Rooms 1–6** are arranged chronologically up to the 1960s, starting with sculptures from Africa and Oceania (Pacific) and paintings by Georges Rouault, followed by Fauve works from 1905 by Matisse, *Pastoral* (1905), Derain, *Three Figures seated on the Grass* (1906), Dufy, *The Aperitif*, as well as Vlaminck. Next is Cubism with works by Picasso such as *L'Evocation*, a tribute to his friend Casagemas, donated by Vollard, *Still Life with Pipe* (1914) and *Pigeon with Peas* (1911); Braque, *Tête de Femme* (1909); also Gris, Derain, Henri Laurens and Jacques Lipchitz. The **Section d'Or** or Orphic Cubists' are represented by Albert Gleizes, Jean Metzinger and André Lhote and other later variations of Cubism by Léopold Survage and Louis Marcoussis.

Works by artists who participated in the **Dada** movement include Kurt Schwitters, Jean Crotti, Francis Picabia and a Surrealist section brings together work by De Chirico, Andre Masson, Max Ernst and Victor Brauner.

Robert Delaunay and Fernand Leger have an important part in the collections. murals by the Delaunays, **Rythmes** Léger, Robert Delaunay, *The Cardiff Team: Disks* (1918).

Different aspects of **Abstraction**, from between the Wars, is illustrated by the works by Franz Kupka, Auguste Herbin, Jean Arp and Jean Fautrier. A room devoted to the diverse movements of the 1920-30s bring together the School of Paris artists, such as Chaim Soutine, Modigliani, *Woman with a Fan*, Chagall, *Le Rêve*, and particularly Bonnard, *Nude in the Bath*.

Rooms 7–14 contain post-1960s works, starting with styles of abstraction by Pierre Soulages, Jean Degottex, Martin Barré's *bombes* and Lucio Fontana's lacerations, along with work by Hantaï. Work of the **Nouveau Réalisme** group includes *décollages d'affiches* by Jacques Villeglé and Raymond Hains, an *accumulation* by Arman, a *compression* by César, and a *néon* by Martial Raysse. Then there are figurative works, based on urban societies, by Adami, Arroyo, Cueco, Monory, Rancilla and Télémaque. From the 70s are works by Viallat, Dezeuze, Buraglio. And representing **Arte Povera** are Giovanni Anselmo, Giulio Paolini, Luciano Fabro, Mario Merz and Giuseppe Penone. One room is devoted to the **Narrative Art of the 1970s** with Parisian artists such as Boltanski, Messager and Sarkis.

Work of the 1980s includes paintings, sculptures, installations and objects by Jean-Pierre Bertrand, Thomas Schütte and Ettore Spaletti among others. And for the 1990s, new technologies include videos and large photographs by Jean-Marc Bustamante, Rosemarie Trockel, Patrick Tosani.

Aside from these rooms, there are Niele Toroni's *Cabinet de Peinture* (1989) and Daniel Buren's *Murs de peinture*, as well as two versions of Matisse's *Dance*

(1931–32) created for the Barnes Foundation in the USA and the vast wall decoration of 250 panels, *Fée Eléctricité*, painted by Raoul Dufy for the Pavilion of Light at the 1937 Exhibition.

To the west is the Pl. d'Iéna (**Map 1; 1**), from which seven streets diverge. 2 Av. d'Iéna is the residence of the US ambassador. To the north of the Place stands the Musée Guimet.

The Musée Guimet

The Musée Guimet at 6 Pl. d'Iéna (**Map 1; 7**), with its annex at 19 Av. d'Iéna, was founded in Lyons in 1879 by Emile Guimet (1836–1918), presented by him to the State, transferred to Paris and inaugurated in 1889. In 1945 it officially became the Département des Arts Asiatiques des Musées Nationaux, Guimet's original collection having been considerably augmented, and now includes those of the Asiatic department of the Louvre, illustrating the arts of India and the Far East. The museum has been closed for restoration and reopened in January 2001, ☎ 01 56 52 53 00, open 10.00–18.00, closed Tues.

The only rooms currently open, the **Galeries du Panthéon Bouddhique**, are housed on two floors in the former Hôtel Heidelbach, at 19 Av. d'Iéna. Open 09.45–18.00, closed Tues, ☎ 01 40 73 88 11. These galleries largely concentrate on sculptures related to the Buddhist cult in Japan (some 250) and—to a lesser extent—in China. Its garden is laid out in the Japanese style.

Major works in the museum are listed below by country.

Cambodia: Khmer sculpture, including a statue of Hari-Hara (pre-Angkorian style; late 6C), uniting in one person the two gods Siva and Vishnu; lintel of 7C–12C; sculpture of 9C–10C; female divinity (early 9C); Vishnu in the Kulen style; Brahma in the Koh Ker style; pediment from the temple of Banteai Srei (967); carvings of a lion, an elephant and of the magic serpent, Naga (12C). Also sculptures in the Bayon style (12C–13C); each meditative statue wears the enigmatic 'Angkorian smile'; portrait of King Jayavarman VII; frieze of dancing *apsaras*.

Champa Art of Assam (central Vietnam): a head of Buddha (9C) and a dancer with two young elephants (10C).

Java: heads of Buddha (8C–9C); lintel decorated in the Prambanan style (9C); bronzes (7C–9C), and statuettes of Avalokitesvara and Kubera, gods of riches—note the seven treasure-pots at his feet; leather marionettes for a shadow-theatre; a painted fabric calendar from Bali.

Siam (Thailand): stuccoes from P'ra Pathom (c 8C); Buddhas of the Schools of Sukhodava and U-Thong (14C–15C); head of Buddha (16C); painted and worked leather hangings.

Laos: Buddha with a begging-bowl.

Burma: lacquered wooden Buddha and illuminated MSS.

Tibet: statue in gilded bronze of Dakini; and statuettes decorated with coloured stones; religious objects, jewellery and silverwork. Paintings illustrating the life of Buddha, gods and saints.

Nepal: Buddhist paintings and statues of wood and gilded bronze.

India: funerary furniture and stone sculpture from near Pondicherry; clay sarcophagus, pottery and jewellery. Mathurâ and Amarâvatî sculpture (2C–4C); serpent-king (sandstone); marble bas-reliefs; Buddhas. Among objects of the 'classical' period (4C–8C), a Buddha in the Gupta style; Torso of a finely sculpted sandstone Buddha (mid 5C); steles of Pâla Art (8C–12C); South Indian stone sculpture; bronzes of Siva; beautiful gouaches and watercolours of the Mogul, Rajput and Pahâri period (16C–18C), including one of Louis XIV when young.

Pakistan and Afghanistan: examples of Græco-Buddhist Gandara sculpture (1C–5C); decorative bas-relief (schist); figurines from the Buddhist monastery of Hadda, including a Genie carrying a floral offering and a demon in a fur; fragments of frescos from the monastery of Kakrak (c 5C); the Treasure of Begram (1C–2C): Græco-Roman and Syrian objects, Indian ivories and Chinese lacquerwork discovered together by the French archaeological mission to Afghanistan in 1937 and 1939–40.

China: carved bone objects of the Chang Dynasty (16C–11C BC) and important collections of archaic bronze implements, ritual vases and arms, from Ngan-Tang, capital of the dynasty; ritual vase in the shape of an elephant; a 'p'an' bowl of the Chou Dynasty (11C–5C BC); the Treasure of Li-Yu, a remarkable find from the Warring Kingdoms Dynasty (5C–3C BC), notably a jade, turquoise and gold-ornamented sword. Jades: the earlier ones in the form of symbols (Pi, the sky; Tsong, the earth; Kwei, the mountain, etc.) and bronzes. Tombstone (Han Dynasty; 206 BC–AD 220); Buddha from Yun-Kang (5C); heads of Bodhisattva and Kasyapa, from Long-men (early 6C); Ananda and Kasyapa, disciples of Buddha (Suei Dynasty; 561–618), marble with traces of polychrome; Dvarapàla, guardian of the temple and funerary statuettes of the T'ang Dynasty (618–906); gilded bronzes of the Wei, Suei and T'ang dynasties (5C–10C), including a small stele representing Sakyamuni and Pradhutaratna, dated 518; lacquer-work; polychrome bowls of the Han Dynasty and Sung Dynasty (960–1279); black lacquer cabinet decorated in gold (17C).

Japan: Jômon and Yayoi pottery (2000–1000 BC and 1C BC–3C AD respectively); figurines (Haniwa) of the era of the Great Tombs (5C–6C); wooden Buddhas (8C–9C); carved masks of the Nara Dynasty (8C); portraits of bonzes (14C–15C); pottery for the tea ceremony ('Cha-no-yu'); Imari Kakiemon and Satsuma porcelain; sword-furniture (kozukas); screens, one illustrating the arrival of the Portuguese in Japan (16C).

Korea: gilded bronze crown and silverware from the kingdom of Silla (5C–6C); and ceramics.

The museum also has an important collection of **Chinese porcelain**, formed principally from the Calmann Collection—'three colour' ware (T'ang Dynasty), celadon, black and white wares (Sung Dynasty)—and from the Grandidier Collection: Ming (1368–1643) and Ch'ing (1644–1912) dynasties.

Central Asia: Buddhist paintings from Touen-houang; votive banners, one representing Kasyapa in old age, dated 729.

This area has a plethora of buildings of the 1930s, such as the Palais du Conseil

Economique et Social, between Pl. d'Iéna and the Palais de Chaillot, a late work by Auguste Perret (1937–38), originally designed for a Musée des Travaux Publics. The north wing, for the Western European Union, was added in 1960–62.

Av. du Président-Wilson leads to **Pl. du Trocadéro (Map 6; 1)** (named after a fort near Cádiz occupied by the French in 1823), on the former Colline de Chaillot. Six avenues fan out from this semi-circle and in the centre stands an equestrian statue of Maréchal Foch (1851–1929). On the southeast is the Palais de Chaillot (see below) and its gardens and fountains.

History of the Place du Trocadéro

This prestigious site overlooking the Seine, la Colline de Chaillot was chosen in the 16C by Catherine de Médicis as the site of a royal palace, later embellished by Anne of Austria. In 1651 Henrietta Maria established the Convent of the Visitation here but this was destroyed during the Revolution and Napoléon planned to use the site for a palace for his son, to eclipse the Kremlin. However the disasters of 1812 intervened and his dream was never realised.

To the west, steps lead to the small Cimetière de Passy, containing the graves of Debussy, Gabriel Fauré, Manet and Berthe Morisot.

From the terrace of the Palais de Chaillot the **Trocadero Gardens** descend to the Seine, creating the setting for a number of statues as well as fountains which include a battery of 20 jets shooting almost horizontally—stunning when illuminated at night. Beyond Pont d'Iéna (1806–13), on the opposite bank, the Eiffel Tower pierces the horizon and orchestrates a dramatic vista across the Champ-de-Mars to the Ecole Militaire and the Unesco buildings, see Ch. 12.

The double bridge downstream Pont de Bir-Hakeim (formerly Pont de Passy, 1903–06), both Métro and road bridge, was named after a French victory in North Africa in 1942.

The Palais de Chaillot

The Neo-classical Palais de Chaillot (**Map 6; 1**), on the southeast side of the Pl. du Trocadéro, was erected for the Paris Exhibition of 1937, replacing the earlier Palais du Trocadéro by Davioud for the 1878 Exhibition. The form of the present building, by Carlu, Boileau and Azéma was determined by the old one. The former central pavilion was removed to create a terrace and the wings were encased within the two curved extensions.

On the entrance level is *Le Totem* restaurant, benefitting from the fine view of the Eiffel Tower, and a bookshop.

Beneath the terrace of the Palais de Chaillot, flanked by gilded bronze statues, is the **Théâtre de Chaillot**, seating over 2000, home of the Théâtre National de Chaillot, decorated by Bonnard, Dufy and Vuillard, among others. The third General Assembly of the United Nations took place here in 1948.

The Palais de Chaillot is undergoing a number of alterations: in the Paris wing (east), the **Musée des Monuments Français** is under restoration; in the Passy wing (west), are the **Musée de la Marine** and the **Musée de l'Homme**. The **Aquarium du Trocadéro** is being rebuilt and due to re-open in 2001. The **Musée du Cinéma** is being relocated to Bercy (See Ch. 33).

The **Musée des Monuments Français** is disappearing until 2003 for a total overhaul. The museum, founded by Viollet-le-Duc in 1879 as the Musée de Sculpture Comparée, contains faithful replicas of masterpieces of French sculpture, architecture, murals and stained-glass. To those familiar with the great French monuments *sur place*, it is a strange experience to find them grouped together here. The renovations will allow an increase in the number of exhibits on display and extend the chronology from the 12C through to the period between the Wars.

On the ground floor of the west wing of the Palais de Chaillot is the **Musée de la Marine**, worth a visit even for the most confirmed land-lubber, open 10.00–17.50, closed Tues and 25/12, 1/01, 1/05 (☎ 01 53 65 69 69). It has a remarkable collection of material illustrating French naval history through to the 21C, including and series of models of ships and a number of fine paintings of maritime subjects include Vernet's *Ports of France*. A team of restorers can be observed at work, and consulted if desired.

The main gallery, right of the entrance, is dominated by the richly carved poop of the *Reale* (1690–1715), some of the sculpture of which is attributed to Puget. Note the paintings (nos 61 and 62) of the *Embarkation of Henry VIII for the Field of Cloth of Gold* by Bouterwerke (a copy of the original by Vincent Volpi) and a *View of Amsterdam* by Bakhuysen (1664). Four anonymous views of Malta (nos 138–9) and two views of Port Mahon (nos 147 and 416, the latter by Joseph Chiesa) are also of interest, and a number of marine paintings by Jean-François Hue.

In the centre of the gallery are displayed 13 (15 completed of the original 24 commissioned) views of the *Ports of France* painted between 1754–65 by Claude-Joseph Vernet, depicting Dieppe, Antibes, tuna-fishing near Bandol, Rochefort, La Rochelle, Cette, two views of Toulon, two of Bordeaux, two of Bayonne, and Marseille.

You pass the richly ornamented **Emperor's Barge** (1811) before entering a section devoted to lighthouses and leading to the area used for temporary exhibitions. Along a parallel gallery are further sections displaying thematic topics, such as navigation and voyages of discovery, 18C shipbuilding, the merchant navy, and early steamships. The history of the French Navy includes the first armoured frigate *La Gloire*, launched in 1859, and continues through to the present with the nuclear aircraft carrier *Charles de Gaulle* due to join the French Fleet in the early 21C.

Musée de l'Homme

The Musée de l'Homme (Museum of Mankind), on the first and second floors of the west wing, brings together three laboratories of the Muséum National d'Histoire Naturelle (see Ch. 6): Biological Anthropology, Prehistory and Ethnology, its primary objective being educational and research. It has a comprehensive library, photographic library, cinema and various technical services. The collections are fascinating but some of the galleries are slightly outdated. Open 09.45–17.15, closed Tues and public holidays; ☎ 01 44 05 72 72, recorded message ☎ 01 44 05 72 00.

The sequence begins on the first floor with an anthropologcal presentation of **human evolution** entitled *Tous parents, tous différents* (All related, all different); next is an exhibit called *6 milliards d'hommes* (6 billion people) addressing the question of mankind in his environment with a number of information screens (in English and French); *La nuit des temps* shows man's development from Primate to Neolithic with the reconstruction of a prehistoric dig evoking prehistoric man and his world.

You then embark on a worldwide ethnological journey where different societies are encapsulated through their arts, crafts and customs. The continent of **Africa** is divided into two sections, south of the Sahara with Madagascar, and North Africa and Middle East. The section devoted to Black Africa is especially rich with reliefs and other artifacts from the Royal Palace of the ancient kingdom of Dahomey (present Republic of Benin); masks from Gabon, Guinea and Mali; bronzes, terracottas and funerary urns from Tchad, and frescoes from Ethiopia. The diversity of the Arab world, including the three main religions and nomadic life, is described through colourful items including costumes, jewellery and domestic artefacts.

At the far east end of the next floor are the **Arctic communities**, mainly Lapp and Eskimo. An important display is dedicated to the Ammassalik Eskimos from the east coast of Greenland, which shows these people at a specific moment in their evolution with items collected in 1934–35. The **Asian Gallery** is introduced by the reconstruction of a traditional wooden Turkish house containing some beautiful items associated with marriage rites, the bazaar and the traditional life of women, especially skills involved in preparing a *trousseau* such as embroidery and lace making. A section devoted to an expedition at the end of the 19C to remote areas of China, Tibet and Burma, contains outstanding objects and photographs of life there. A striking reference to Laos and Cambodia in the South-East Asian Gallery includes the interior of a house and a Buddhist altar; Thailand and Malaysia are evoked through masks and shadow figures used in theatrical and dance performances; and Japan is conjured up through its traditional costumes. The **Galerie d'Océanie** retraces migrations between 40,000 BC and 600 AD from southwest Asia to the South Pacific and evokes the diverse cultures of the south seas with examples of rites, festivals, and social life as well as different types of architecture. (The exhibit of the Marquesas Islanders' art and way of life from prehistory to French colonisation is being renovated.)

The **Americas** section, revamped in 1992, is set out as a voyage of discovery from Alaska to Tierra del Fuego, illustrating the various and varied peoples of the Americas. It contains an excellent section devoted to the American Indian; the reconstruction of part of the Palace of Teotihuacan in Mexico decorated with frescoes; a suspended bridge of the type made by the Incas leading to civilisations of the Andes to discover the kind of treasures that attracted the Conquistadors; and there is even an evocation of the Amazonian forest. The **Arts and Techniques** gallery illustrates the diversity of solutions given to mankind within the planetary ecosystems as well as the stages of technical evolution of *Homo sapiens*. Lastly there is a fascinating collection of some 400 **musical instruments** underlining the universal importance of music in all its diversity. Concerts are held here. At the time of writing the European gallery is being rearranged (for France, see Musée national des Arts et Traditions populaires, Ch. 30).

Rue Franklin (no. 8 was Clemenceau's residence from 1883–1929) leads southwest from Pl. du Trocadéro and is continued by Rue Raynouard. From their junction at Pl. de Costa Rica, Rue de Passy, high street of the old village of **Passy**, runs west to the Jardin du Ranelagh (see below).

Steps descend to the left in Rue Raynouard to Sq. Charles Dickens, where the old vaulted cellars of Passy Abbey shelter the **Musée du Vin en France** (10.00–18.00, closed Mon); ☎ 01 45 25 63 26, restaurant in the 14C cellars (lunch only).

Tucked away at no. 47 Rue Raynouard is **Maison de Honoré de Balzac** (10.00–17.40, closed Mon and public holidays, ☎ 01 55 74 41 80. **Map 5; 4**), not only a memorial to the writer but also to rural Passy. His home in 1841–47, this is where he hid from creditors and wrote *La Cousine Bette* among other novels. The museum contains memorabilia including the famous coffee pot (he was heavily dependent on caffeine), and a reference library. One room is devoted to Madame Hanska, whom Balzac knew for 18 years but married only five months before he died. The ivy-covered Rue Berton, behind the house, is a charming lane characteristic of the old *quartier*.

Rue des Vignes leads to the Chaussée de la Muette and the east end of the **Jardin du Ranelagh** (**Map 5; 1–3**), part of the ancient royal park of La Muette. Le Petit Ranelagh was named after its fashionable namesake in London in 1774 and was a favourite place to go dancing for over a century. It is graced with a statue of *La Fontaine* (1984) by Corréla. Nearby in 1783 the first balloon ascent in France was made by Pilâtre de Rozier and the Marquis d'Arlandes in a balloon created by the Montgolfier brothers.

The royal Château de la Muette, originally a hunting-lodge, restored by Louis XV for Mme de Pompadour, disappeared in 1920. The modern mansion, just north of the Jardin du Ranelagh and east of the Porte de la Muette, was built by Baron Henri de Rothschild, and is now the property of the OECD (Organisation for Economic Cooperation and Development).

Musée Marmottan

Tucked away on the west side of the Ranelagh gardens, at 2 Rue Louis-Boilly, is the Musée Marmottan (**Map 5; 1**), an increasingly popular but still intimate museum in a 19C *hôtel particulier*. Best known for its celebrated works by Monet and other Impressionists, the basis of the museum was in fact the collection of Empire paintings, furniture and bronzes bequeathed to the Institut de France by Paul Marmottan in 1932, supplemented by further donations, among them medieval miniatures and 19C paintings. This eclectic but already brilliant collection was enhanced in 1997 with a bequest of 155 works from descendants of Berthe Morisot, Denis and Annie Rouart. In recent years the Monet room has been renovated, there are porcelain displays on the first floor, and the clocks have been put in working order. Temporary exhibitions are frequently held in the museum. Open 10.00–17.30, closed Mon, ☎ 01 44 96 50 33; gift and bookshop.

From the original collection are Flemish, German and Italian paintings, including *Resurrection of Lazarus*, School of Lucas Cranach, and *Descent from the Cross*, Hans Muelich. To this were added the outstanding **Wildenstein Collection** of 228 medieval illuminated miniatures assembled in a gallery on the left of the entrance (due for restoration). Among the French works are a page from the *Hours of Etienne Chevalier* by Jean Fouquet, *Alchemy* by Jean Perreal, the depiction of a boar-hunt (late 15C); and some by Jean Bourdichon, *The Kiss of Judas*. Italian illuminations include several by Lucchino Giovanni Belbello da Pavia (fl. 1430–62); and the remarkable Renaissance page of parchment *The Baptism of Constantine* by Giovanni dei Corradi with the intial 'P' made up of elements of Classical architecture. There are also some Flemish works of the period. An outstanding 15C French tapestry illustrates the *Story of Ste Susanne*.

The collection of **First Empire** works is made up of decorative and fine arts: furniture by Jacob Frères and Pierre-Antoine Bellangé; an extraordinary geographical clock, designed in 1813 but altered after the fall of the Empire, inlaid with painted Sèvres porcelain medallions representing time zones (it revolves at 16.00 each day); and a *surtout de table* by Thomire, in gilded bronze; there is also porcelain of the period. Paintings include a portrait of *Désirée Clary* by Gérard; *A Young Woman* by Lawrence; a *View of Fontainebleau* by Bidault and Boilly, and by the latter, *Portrait of a Captain of the First Company of Musketeers*. There are drawings by Fragonard and Hubert Robert.

The **Impressionist collections** come from four donations, Donop de Monchy, Michel Monet, Duhem and, as mentioned, Rouart. The most notorious of all Impressionist works, *Impression Sunrise* by Claude Monet, was part of the de Monchy donation. First shown in 1874, this painting gave its name, albeit derisive at the time, to the most important artistic movement of the 19C. In 1985 this priceless canvas and others were stolen from the Marmottan, but happily all were recovered five years later in Corsica.

Grouped together, these works provide a fine overview of the development of 19C painting from Corot, *The Lake at Ville-d'Avray seen Through Trees*, to late Monets. Carolus Duran, *Portrait of Monet*; of *Monet and his Wife* by Renoir and, by **Monet** himself, *The Beach at Trouville*, *Walking near Argenteuil*, *A Train in the Snow*, *Argenteuil in the Snow*, *The Pont de l'Europe Gare St-Lazare*, *Vertheuil in the Mist*, one of the series of Rouen Cathedral, *Effects of Sunlight–Sunset*, the two atmospheric renditions of *The Seine at Port-Villez*, and *London, the Houses of Parliament* reflecting on a glinting Thames; also sketches for his later canvases and several caricatures. Most haunting are variations on the theme of the gardens at Giverny: waterlilies, willows, wisteria and the Japanese Bridge and their reflections in the ponds. The Giverny works form a complementary collection to those in the Orangerie (see Ch. 13).

The wealth of this small museum does not end here: there is the glowing *Bowl of Tahitian flowers* by Gauguin; Degas, *Portrait de Madame Ducros*; Berthe Morisot's sensitive *Small Girl with a Basket*, *At the Ball*, *Self Portrait*, *Le Cerisier* and others; Sisley, *The Canal du Loing in Spring*; Renoir, *Girl in a White Hat* (pastel); and paintings by Caillebotte, Guillaumin, Jongkind, Pissarro and Le Sidaner, *Daybreak at Quimperlé*. There are also paintings by Ernest Rouart, Morisot's son, and the collector Henri Duhem (1860–1941) himself. Drawings by Constantin Guys, Boudin, Morisot and Signac, among others.

To the south is the residential district of Auteuil, bordering the Bois de Boulogne. Henri Bergson lived at 47 Blvd de Beaséjour, skirting the Jardin du Ranelagh, and the Goncourt brothers (Edmond 1822–96 and Jules 1830–70) lived and died at 67 Blvd de Montmorency.

From Blvd de Montmorency, turn left into Rue de l'Assomption and right into Rue Docteur-Blanche. At 8–10 Sq. Dr-Blanche are two villas designed in 1923 by by Le Corbusier (1887–1965) (Charles-Edouard Jeanneret), **Villa Jeanneret** and **Villa La Roche**. The former contains the library of the Le Corbusier Foundation which holds a large part of the Le Corbusier archives.

Villa La Roche is open to the public and can be visited Mon–Thur 10.00–12.30, 13.30–18.00, Fri to 17.00, closed Sat, Sun, public holidays and August (☎ 01 42 88 41 53). Villa La Roche is a prime example of the spirit of Le Courbusier and an essential visit for anyone interested in the Modern Movement. The house, built for a Swiss banker, Raoul La Roche, is designed around a main hall leading to two different sections of the house—private and public. The overall impression is of light and carefully articulated space.

At the southern end of Blvd de Montmorency is the Porte d'Auteuil, the south east entrance to the Bois de Boulogne (see below), and an approach to the A13 autoroute and the Blvd Périphérique. From Pl. de la Porte d'Auteuil, Blvd Exelmans swings south east to reach the Seine at Pont du Garigliano. Southwest of the Porte d'Auteuil is the **Jardin des Serres d'Auteuil** (Municipal Nursery Gardens), part of Louis XV's botanic gardens, with remarkable glasshouses. Nearby is the Roland-Garros tennis stadium, where the French Open takes place every June.

In the small **Cimetière d'Auteuil**, in the Rue Claude-Lorrain (south of and parallel to the Blvd Exelmans), lie Hubert Robert, Mme Helvétius, Carpeaux, Gavarni and Gounod.

30 • Bois de Boulogne, Neuilly and La Défense

■ Arrondissements: 75016, 92200, 92060
🚇 Porte-d'Auteuil, Muette, Porte-Dauphine, Porte-Maillot, Les Sablons, Esplanade de la Défense Grande-Arche de la Défense
🚏 Grande-Arche de la Défense

In and around the Bois de Boulogne are several restaurants in pleasant setting. Several on the Allée de Longchamp:
L'Auberge du Bonheur, ☎ 01 42 24 10 17, £
L'Orée du Bois, at no. 1, ☎ 01 40 67 92 50, £
La Grande Cascade, Allée de Longchamp, ☎ 01 45 27 33 51. The most expensive, £££

On Route de Suresnes, two fairly expensive restaurants:
Le Pavillon Royal, ☎ 01 40 67 11 56, ££
Pré-Catelan, ☎ 01 45 24 55, £££

In the 19C stables in Bagatelle Park:

Les Jardins de Bagatelle with tables outside in the summer, ☎ 01 40 67 98 29
Le Chalet des Îles, at the Lake, ☎ 01 42 88 04 69, ££
Le Pavillon des Princes, 69 Av. de la Porte d'Auteuil, ☎ 01 47 43 15 15. A seafood restaurant, ££

A totally different, but novel modern setting, is La Défense. Cafés and bars: *Le Café de la Place*, in the CNIT
Café-internet in the Extrapole building
Les Tours (bar), 49 passage Coupole.

Restaurants in Sector 4:
Le Bistrot à Vin, 86 esplanade Charles de Gaulle, ☎ 01 47 76 11 94 £

Le Malongo Café, 16 place de la Défense, La Défense 4, light meals and snacks in a pleasant setting (terrace) ☎ 01 55 91 96 96, £

L'espace Brasserie du Toit, ☎ 01 49 07 27 27. A new eating place at the top of the Grande Arche, £

Le Brantôme en Périgord, 8 bis, place Charras, Courbevoie, ☎ 01 43 34 50 93. Opposite Défense 5, for impeccable Perigordian cooking, ££

In the Neuilly district:

Le Bistrot d'à Côté Neuilly, 4 Rue Boutard, Neuilly, ☎ 01 47 45 34 55. Michel Rostang, £–££

Toit de Passy, 94 Av. Paul Doumer, ☎ 01 45 24 55 37, ££

Two contrasting sites on the periphery of Paris come together in this chapter: the Bois de Boulogne, lung of Paris, with its green spaces, water features and famous rose garden, the Parc de Bagatelle; and to the north across the Seine, the ultra-modern urban *quartier* of La Défense known best for the Grande Arche. Between is the residential suburb, Neuilly-sur-Seine, leading to the Musée National des Arts et des Traditions Populaires.

The Bois de Boulogne

The Bois de Boulogne (Map 5; 1), at 845 hectares, is slightly smaller but better known than its counterpart at the other end of the city, the Bois de Vincennes. The Bois de Boulogne is a tiny remnant of the Forest of Rouvray, part of the band of forest once surrounding ancient Lutetia. Tamed, landscaped, subdivided, it encompasses gardens, lakes and the Longchamp racecourse. It lies immediately to the west of the 16e arrondissement of Paris (Chaillot, Passy and Auteuil: see Ch. 29), and was originally restricted on the east by part of the peripheral fortifications of the city. Now the Blvd Périphérique tunnels below the eastern and southern edges of the Bois, which is bounded on the north by Neuilly. The suburb of Boulogne-Billancourt lies to the south, and the Seine to the west, on the far side of which rise the hills of Mont Valérien, St-Cloud, Bellevue and Meudon. (Warning: Do not stray into the Bois at dusk or after dark.) There are some museums in the vicinity.

History of the Bois de Boulogne

Although the châteaux of La Muette, Madrid and Bagatelle, and the abbey of Longchamp were erected on its borders, the Bois was neglected until the middle of the last century. Quantities of timber went for firewood during the Revolution and a large part of the Allied army of occupation bivouacked here after Waterloo. It was the haunt of footpads and often the scene of suicides and duels. In 1852 it was handed over by the State to the City, transformed into an extensive park, and became a favourite promenade of the Parisians. The model was Hyde Park in London, which had so impressed Napoléon III. More trees were felled in 1870 to reduce protective cover for the Prussians. The equestrian scenes which were such a favourite subject of Constantin Guys often had the Bois in the background. Thousands of trees were lost during the storms in December 1999.

There are four main entrances to the Bois from central Paris, namely **Porte Maillot** (at its northeast corner); **Porte Dauphine** (at the western end of the Av. Foch);

Porte de la Muette (at the south end of the Av. Victor-Hugo); and **Porte d'Auteuil** (at its southeast corner). Between the last two is the subsidiary **Porte de Passy**.

The Bois is divided diagonally by the long Allée de Longchamp, leading south-west from the Porte Maillot towards the Carrefour de Longchamp and a popular equestrian rendezvous. It is intersected by the Route de la Reine Marguerite (from the Carrefour de la Porte de Madrid to the Porte de Boulogne, on the south side of the Bois).

From the Etoile (Place Charles de Gaulle) two avenues lead directly to the Bois: Av. Victor-Hugo to Porte de la Muette (Victor Hugo, 1802–85, died in a house on the site of no. 124); and the majestic Av. Foch (the creation of Napoléon III and Haussmann), to Porte Dauphine. The latter, with gardens along each side, is the widest in Paris. From its inception in 1855 it had a succession of names before the death of the illustrious general in 1929. At Porte Dauphine there is one of the two surviving complete Art Nouveau Métro station entrances of 1900 by Hector Guimard. Nearby is a monument (between nos 17 and 22) to Adolphe Alphand (1817–91) by Dalou and Formigéz, who laid out Av. Foch, the Bois and many other parks in Paris.

At 59 Av. Foch, is the **Musée d'Ennery**, with a small but important collection of Oriental art formed by the dramatist Adolphe d'Ennery (Eugène Philippe; 1811–99); the building also houses a collection of Armenian art. Open Thur, Sun 14.00–18.00, ☎ 01 47 23 61 65. No. 80 Avenue Foch was the home of Claude Debussy (1862–1918). Southwest of the park entrance is a huge build-ing (1955–59) constructed for NATO but now housing university faculties.

Parc de Bagatelle

Further west, skirted by the Route de Sèvres à Neuilly, are the walls of the Parc de Bagatelle (24 hectares). It is open to the public until dusk (fee), and there is a restaurant (expensive).

This delightful and well-tended oasis, made up of several gardens in different styles, is most famous for its rose-garden, at its best in mid-June, when the annual International New Rose competition takes place in the Orangerie. However, ear-lier in the year it is carpeted with spring flowers. Concerts are also held here. Landscaped with a wide selection of trees, and with follies, streams, waterfalls and lakes, the planting shows the influence of the Impressionists' preference for massed blooms—the Garden Conservator in 1905, J.-C.-N. Forestier, was a friend of Monet. As well as the roses, there are irises, wisteria, clematis and water lilies.

The elegant little **Château de Bagatelle**, replacing an earlier residence, was built for a wager within 64 days by Bélanger for the Comte d'Artois, later Charles X, in 1779. The dome was added in 1852. It was acquired by the Ville de Paris in 1904.

History of the Château de Bagatelle

During the Revolution it was turned into a tavern and later became the resi-dence of Sir Richard Wallace (1818–90), supposed natural son of the Marquess of Hertford. Wallace had a town house at 25 Rue Taitbout where he collected art treasures (now in the Wallace Collection, London) in addition to those he had inherited from his half-brother the eccentric Richard Seymour Conway, 4th Marquis of Hertford (1800–70), who had bought the mansion in 1835 and died here. Hertford's own brother, Lord Henry Seymour (1805–59) was founder of the exclusive Jockey Club. Wallace was also a great benefactor of Paris, which he provided with drinking fountains in 1873, after the 1870–71 war, when he also helped to equip ambulances. He founded the Hertford British Hospital in Paris (opened 1879) and built the Anglican church of St-George (1887–88; Rue Auguste-Vacquerie, off Av. d'Iéna).

To the west are various sports grounds (including polo and *tiercé*); to the south-west is the Hippodrome de Longchamp, opened in 1857. On the north side is a windmill (restored), almost the only relic of the Abbey of Longchamp, founded in 1256 by St Isabel of France, sister of Louis IX.

From the Carrefour de Longchamp (just east of the windmill), a road leads due east past the Grande Cascade (an artificial waterfall) to skirt the enclosure of the Pré-Catelan (according to legend, named after the troubadour Arnaud Catelan, murdered here c 1300). The **Jardin Shakespeare** has specimens of plants and trees mentioned in Shakespeare's plays.

Further east are buildings of the Racing Club de France, flanking the west bank of the Lac Inférieur, with two linked islands. Boats may be hired on the east bank. To the south is the Lac Supérieur, beyond the Carrefour des Cascades; in the south-east corner of the Bois, is the **Hippodrome d'Auteuil** (steeplechasing).

N.-D.-des-Menus, in Av. J.-B. Clément, leading southwest from the Porte de Boulogne, although frequently restored, still has its 14C nave. Beyond (right) are the **Jardins Albert Kahn**, including one laid out in Japanese style. Open daily April–November.

In the Rue Denfert-Rochereau is a series of buildings in the Modern Movement style of 1926–27, by L.-R. Fischer, Le Corbusier and Robert Mallet-Stevens; also at the angle of Rue des Arts and Allée des Pins are two *résidences-ateliers* of 1924, by Le Corbusier. There are more examples of experimental architecture of the 1920s by Auguste Perret, and André Lurçat in Rue du Belvédère and in Rue Nungesser-et-Coli (near Parc des Princes), an apartment block (1932) by Le Corbusier.

On the northern edge of the Bois, near the Jardin d'Acclimation, is the **Musée National des Arts et des Traditions Populaires (Museum of Folk Arts and Traditions)**. The museum is housed in a building by Jean Dubuisson, completed in 1966, just west of the Carrefour des Sablons. Open 09.45–17.15, closed Tues, ☎ 01 44 17 60 00.

The museum is not on the beaten track but well worth exploring. Dedicated to the ethnological heritage of France, it is a fascinating tribute to **French craftsmanship and provincial life** with a huge range of objects, beautiful and quaint, attractively displayed. Originally focusing on the pre-industrial era, it is gradually extending to encompass the modern period. It is an important research centre with all the resources which that implies, and has a bookshop and gift shop. Several rooms are devoted to temporary exhibitions.

The visit runs through a series of interconnecting galleries subtly lit to show off the thousands of exhibits, which are arranged thematically mainly covering aspects of rural life. Themes include the techniques of gathering, hunting and fishing as distinct from livestock farming, including bees, horses and cattle. There are displays that explain the processes, from raw material to finished product, used in bread-making, viticulture, tailoring, wood-turning and furniture making, ceramics, and stonemasonry. The rhythm of country or village life from the cradle to the grave is evoked by groups of objects associated with christenings, customs and beliefs, festivals, popular mythology and the Christian tradition. Time for relaxing is provided by fairs, games, dance and music and folk art. The reconstruction of a shepherd's hut from the Aubrac (Massif Central), a craftman's house from Finistère (Brittany) or an Alpine chalet give an insight into daily life in remote regions.

Northwest of the museum is the **Jardin d'Acclimatation** (linked to Porte Maillot by a little train, Wed, Sat and Sun 13.30–18.00; every day during school holidays), with activities for children including a mini-farm (its former inmates were eaten in 1870), a playground, radio-controlled boats, and the **Musée en Herbe** with workshops for children.

Neuilly-sur-Seine

From the Arc de Triomphe (see Ch. 27), Av. de la Grande Armée descends north west to **Porte Maillot**, a great meeting of principal routes and the site of extensive blocks of buildings in recent years, commanded on the north side by the International Centre and the Palais des Congrès and one of the Aérogares (or air terminals) of Paris.

A short distance to the northwest, near Pl. du Gén. Koenig (Pl. de la Porte des Ternes), stands N.-D. de la Compassion, a mausoleum in the Byzantine style (1843).

Beyond Porte Maillot, the wide Av. Charles-de-Gaulle bisects Neuilly-sur-Seine, once the most fashionable suburb of Paris. It was partially laid out in what was formerly the park of Louis-Philippe's château (built in 1740, burned down in 1848), and later developed as a colony of elegant villas but more recent apartment blocks temper the distinctive character of the neighbourhood.

Its southern half retains the attraction of being adjacent to the Bois de Boulogne. In the old cemetery lie Anatole France and André Maurois and in the **Cimetière de Lavallois-Perret**, the suburb north of Neuilly, lie the revolutionary Louise Michel (1830–1905) and Maurice Ravel (1875–1937).

Av. Charles-de-Gaulle leads to **Pont de Neuilly**, a stone bridge by Perronet (1768–72, almost entirely rebuilt in 1935–39), which replaced an earlier bridge erected in 1606 after Henri IV and Marie de Médicis were almost drowned in the Seine here. The central section of the bridge stands on the northern extremity of the Ile de Puteaux; to the north is the Ile de la Grande Jatte, painted by Seurat in 1884.

La Défense

This erect statement of 20C commerce and architecture is a far cry from Chantecoq Hill where Geneviève, *pucelle* of Nanterre and future patron saint of Paris, shepherded her sheep (see Ch. 4). La Défense, the culmination of Parisian bravado in the last century, is a distinctive and familiar silhouette to the west of Paris beyond the Arc de Triomphe and the Seine. Dominating the *grattes-ciel* is **La Grande Arche**, an arch which dwarfs all others. This is an unusual visit, but fascinating for anyone interested in modern architecture and works of art. It has marvellous views, and on a sunny day or a warm evening the esplanades of this young and dynamic *quartier* are a hive of activity. There is also a good a choice of eating places.

History of La Défense

La Défense takes its name from a monument by Barrias (1883) commemorating the defence of Paris against the Prussians in 1871. In 1958 a government project to set up a business centre on this area took shape and 750 hectares,

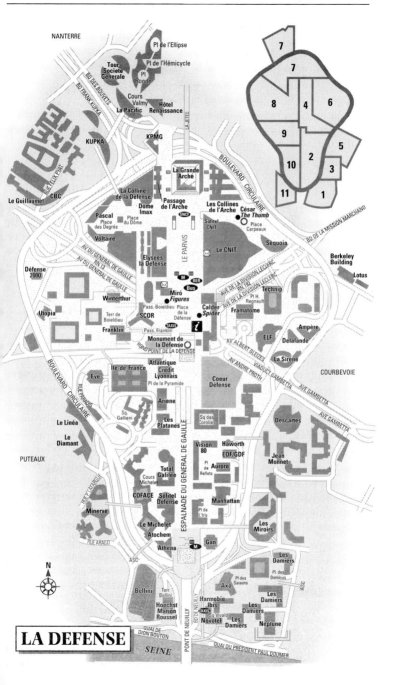

LA DEFENSE

belonging to the three adjacent communes of Courbevoie, Nanterre and Puteaux, on the edge of Paris, were earmarked. EPAD, a public organisation, was set up to take overall responsibility for the development and the project will be completed by 2007. The construction of the RER line in 1970 brought La Défense within rapid reach of central Paris, and its commercial success is undisputed with 99% of the office space occupied by some 3600 national and multinational organisations. The first building of consequence was the triangular-shaped flat-domed exhibition hall, the CNIT Centre (1958), which has the largest concrete vaulted roof in the world. Another pioneering building was the 34 storey Tour Hoechst-Roussel, adjacent to Pont de Neuilly.

This is a revolutionary two-tier city, the upper level being car-free with all rail and road traffic networks hidden below ground including the RER, Métro and bus stations and car parks (26,000 spaces). Since 1998 much-needed improvements have been carried out to the main hall of the station of Grande Arche de la Défense. Consequently, the district is an unpolluted pedestrian paradise. It is also totally self-contained with hotels and apartments, cafés and restaurants, shops and cinemas (Dôme Imax), exhibitions and an **Automobile Museum** (1 pl. du Dôme, La Défense 7); there is a university in neighbouring Nanterre.

The whole area is divided into 11 sectors and it is wise, if you are heading somewhere in particular, to know in advance the relevant sector number. Emerging directly from the RER station or Métro (line 1), you arrive on the Parvis (the main esplanade) close to **La Grande Arche** (see below) (sectors 4/7). The CNIT, with cafés and shops, is on the north side of Le Parvis (sector 4). To the east is Place de la Défense with Calder's red **Spider** stabile, and close to this is Espace Info-Défense (☎ 01 47 74 84 24) for current information. From here you can look down on the 19C monument of La Défense on the Rond-Point below.

Nearby is **Expo EPAD**, a permanent exhibition that explains the history and development of the district, and the most recent major building project, the Coeur

Défense, designed by J.-P. Viguier, covering 190,000 m^2, on the site of the old Esso building. It is, in fact, a group of buildings standing perpendicular to the esplanade comprising two slender 38-storey towers and three low buildings separated by covered streets and with a glass Atrium.

The vast expanse of main esplanade is the prolongation of the greatest of all Parisian perspectives, planned in the 17C as a royal highway between Paris and St-Germain-en-Laye. But the project was never completed, but by 1863 Napoléon III had extended the Avenue de la Grande-Armée as far as Chantecoq Hill and placed a statue of Napoléon I there. This was later replaced by Barrias' *La Défense de Paris*. The kilometre-long esplanade is bordered by green

La Défense

spaces and enlivened with a variety of sculptures, fountains and murals. There are some 50 works, witty and monumental, among them: Agam, *The Esplanade Fountain*, with mosaics made in Venice; César, *The Thumb*; Miró's fantasy figures; Takis, *Pool* and *17 Light Signals*; Moretti, *Le Moretti*, a 32m high ventilation shaft transformed by 672 fibre glass tubes in different colours; Venet, *Indefinite Double Lines*; and installations by Calder and Caro.

The **Grande Arche** can be visited, Mon–Fri 11.00–17.00, Sat, Sun 10.00–17.00; closed Tues. A Danish architect, Johann Otto von Spreckelsen, chosen by M. Mitterrand from 424 projects, came up with this unusual design, which was completed in mid 1989. Although called an arch it might better be described as a colossal hollow cube. It is 110m square, open on two sides, and sits on 12 huge piles sustaining a weight of 300,000 tonnes. The whole is pivoted slightly from the main axis of La Défense and suspended below the arch is a cloud-like awning. A series of exterior elevators rise to the summit from where there is an awesome view over the surrounding buildings and down the straight vista to the Arc de Triomphe, the Tuileries and finally the Louvre. On the top floor is space for temporary exhibitions of contemporary art and a brasserie/restaurant.

Some of the most eye-catching buildings to the south of the arch are the angular Pascal Towers (1983) and to the east, the dark monolithic Framatome Tower (46 storeys) (1974), so far the tallest—reflecting the prismatic ELF Tower (1985) adjacent. Further east rises the Descartes Tower (1988) and beyond, the GAN Tower (1974) and the triangular-shaped AXA Tower (1974). Facing the arch, on the other side of the main axis, is the sharp-angled Athena Tower (1984). The Coeur Défense site is east of the CNIT.

An extensive development further west incorporates **Parc André Malraux**, the largest park created in Paris since the beginning of the century, covering 25 hectares and using soil extracted from the commercial district. This is part of an ambitious scheme to improve Nanterre, the préfecture of the département of Hauts-de-Seine further northwest, under which the A14 motorway runs to meet the A13 and the new A86 running north–south.

31 • Place de la République to La Villette

Arrondissements: 75010, 75019
République, Colonel Fabien, Jaurès, Porte de la Villette, Porte de Pantin, Buttes-Chaumont, Jourdain, Télégraphe, Belleville, Pyrénées

Near the Canal St-Martin are:
Au Gigot Fin, 56 Rue de Lancry, ☎ 01 42 08 38 81. Modest and unpretentious, £
Astier, 44 Rue Jean-Pierre Timbaud, ☎ 01 43 57 16 35.

Quality-price ratio make this restaurant reliable and popular, £ *Café de la Musique*, Cité de la Musique, ☎ 01 48 03 15 91. Modern and trendy, a Frères Costes establishment, £

In the Cité des Sciences et de l'Industrie, ☎ 01 40 05 82 00. Restaurants and bars include: *Cafeteria* and *Croq'cité*, Level 2; *Bars* in Explora and in the Géode.

Upholding the tradition of the quartier around La Villette for meaty cuisine:
Au Cochon d'Or, 192 av. Jean-Jaurès, ☎ 01 42 45 46 46, ££
Le Bistrot du Cochon d'Or, 192 av. Jean-Jaurès, ☎ 01 42 45 46 46, £
Au Boeuf Couronné, 188 av. Jean-Jaurès, ☎ 01 42 39 54 54, a huge 1930s brasserie, £
Dagorno, 190 av. Jean-Jaurès, ☎ 01 40 40 09 39, ££.

In and around the Parc des Buttes Chaumont:
Le Pavillon du Lac, ☎ 01 42 02 08 97/40 40 00 95
Le Pavillon Puebla, corner S. Bolivar and Rue Botzaris, ☎ 01 42 08 92 62. Attractive, rather grand, with terrace and views, ££
La Mandragor, 74 rue Botzaris, ☎ 01 42 39 86 18, £

In the Belleville district:
Le Baratin, 3 Rue Jouye-Rouve, ☎ 01 43 49 39 70. Popular wine bar with excellent vintages, and food, £
Le Zéphyr, 1 Rue Jourdain, ☎ 01 46 36 65 81. 50s bistrot with a great-value lunchtime menu, £

This chapter covers an area on the eastern side of Paris. It is often assumed that La Villette is a long way from the city centre but in fact it takes only about 20 minutes by Métro from Opéra and it is an easy journey for anyone arriving at or staying near Gare du Nord. It is worth devoting a full day to the area as there is plenty to see and do. La Villette is synonymous with the Cité des Sciences et de l'Industrie, the huge centre devoted to modern technology set in a large park crossed by the Canal de l'Ourcq. An alternative means of travelling to the district is by canal (see p 27). On the opposite side of the park is the more recent (1996) Cité de la Musique with concert halls and the magical Museum of Music. To the south are two charming small parks, Parc des Buttes Chaumont and Parc de Belleville.

To the east of Pl. de la République is Sq. F. Lemaître at the point where the underground canal, camouflaged by Blvd. Jules Ferry gardens, becomes the overground **Canal St-Martin** (1806–25; **Map 4**) (cruises from Bassin de l'Arsenal (see p 27), flanked by the Quai de Valmy and Quai de Jemmapes.

North of here is the charming Passerelle de Dieu (1884–85), level with Rue L.-Jouhaux, a metal pedestrian revolving bridge over the Canal. The third bridge after this is another turning footbridge, Pont Grange-aux-Belles, at the tree-lined double lock, Ecluses des Récollets.

Hôtel du Nord, alongside Ecluses des Récollets (101 Quai des Jemmapes) became famous when it featured in the 30s' film, and now has a bar and occasional music. At this point, Quai de Jemmapes has some eye-catching architecture: no. 112 an Art Deco relic of 1908, with striking bay windows in an iron and concrete; no. 116 uses red brick and white tiles in a Post-Modernist miscellany (1986) and no. 132 is an elegant steel, glass and brick (1896) industrial building.

Opposite is Rue de la Grange-aux-Belles, near which stood the **Gibet de Montfaucon**, the Tyburn of Paris, set up in the 13C and finally removed in

1790. The gallows proved fatal to three Surintendants des Finances: Enguerrand de Marigny, who erected it; Jean de Montaigu, who repaired it; and Semblançay, who tried to avoid it. Rue Bichat (off Rue de la Grange-aux-Belles) leads to the entrance of the **Hôpital St-Louis** (Map 4; 2–4), founded by Henri IV and built by Claude Vellefaux in 1607–12. It is an excellent and now rare example of the early Louis XIII style, and its courtyards and chapel may be visited on application at the porter's lodge; the chapel is open most afternoons (except Saturday).

The last bridge is level with Rue Louis-Blanc, where at no. 26 is another elegant steel building of 1906, and the new Paris Industrial Tribunal. The canal runs under Pl. du Stalingrad from where there are views of the Bassin de la Villette. Here, in the shadow of the overhead Métro line, on a small island site, stands the **Rotunde de la Villette**, built as a toll-house by Ledoux in 1789 (see Chps 7, 28 and 33), illuminated at night.

At 44 Rue de Flandre, leading north east from the northern side of the Place, is a relic of the old Portuguese Jewish Cemetery, in use between 1780 and 1810.

La Villette

The 19C cattle-market and abattoirs of La Villette were modernised in the 1960s but were abandoned in the early 1970s. The ambitious project of converting the extensive site of some 55 hectares into a multicultural public park extending to both sides of the Canal de l'Ourcq, and of building a city of science in its northern half and a city of music in the south, was realised between 1980 and 1996.

The south entrance to the park and the Cité de la Musique is best approached from the Métro, Porte de Pantin, while the Cité des Sciences (see below) is more conveniently reached from the Métro Porte de la Villette.

The Cité de la Musique

A complex of dynamic and varied buildings designed by Christian de Portzamparc is laid out on either side of the south entrance to the park. On the west side, at 211 Av. Jean-Jaurès, stands the new **Conservatoire de Paris**, ☎ 01 40 40 45 45, whose history goes back to 1765, containing practice and recording studios, three concert halls, a database library and many other facilities.

The larger building on the east side, the **Cité de la Musique** at 221 Av. Jean-Jaurès, ☎ 01 44 84 44 84, is designed for a variety of events in connection with music including a wide range of concerts. It encompasses a museum with an amphitheatre and a flexible concert hall (with the possibility of a variety of seating configurations); also workshops for the young, information and documentation centres for various services.

• The Cité and the museum are open Tues–Sat 12.00–18.00, Sun 10.00–18.00, Fri to 19.30, closed Mon. Guided visits for groups Tues–Sat 09.00– 12.00 by prior reservation only, ☎ 01 44 84 46 46. The main entrance to the Cité de la Musique is opposite the Fontaine aux Lions next to which there is a café-restaurant (open 08.30–02.00) where musical interludes include jazz on Wednesday evenings. There is an extensive boutique-bookshop in the centre.

The **Musée de la Musique** exhibits some 900 instruments, paintings, sculptures and works inspired by music, and holds temporary exhibitions. As well as collecting and conserving, the museum aims to give visitors the opportunity

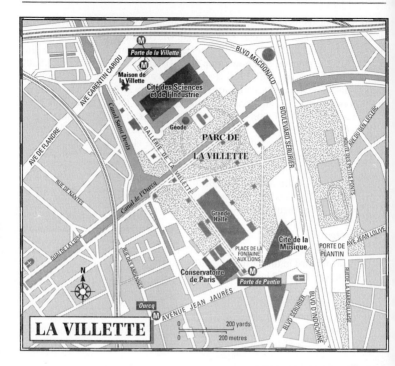

both to see and to hear musical instruments. Various types of guided tours are available and the 230-seat amphitheatre within the museum is the focus for concerts of historic instruments. The collection, on several floors, is imaginatively presented to illustrate the evolution of music and instruments, and the role of composers, musicians and patrons and allows the instruments to be admired for both their physical and musical beauty. To fully appreciate the collection, infrared headsets provide both a spoken and a musical commentary; and there are interactive terminals for visual information.

The museum boasts some exceptional and even unique sets of instruments, notably: 17C Venetian archlutes; guitars by Voboam; an outstanding collection of French stringed instruments from the 18C and 19C; Cremona violins by Amati, Stradivarius and Guarnerius del Gesù; recorders by Hotteterre; Flemish harpischords by the celebrated Rucker dynasty; 18C French harpsichords; pianofortes by Erard and Pleyel; an exceptional collection of brass instruments by Adolphe Sax; 20C instruments, including an electronic violin by Max Mathews, a MIDI saxophone and Frank Zappa's E-Mu synthesizer; also unique instruments from around the world, such as a 17C Sàrangi from northern India and a 19C chest drum from Zaire.

The **Parc de la Villette**, designed by Bernard Tschumi, is an innovative exercise in urban renewal with areas particularly appealing to children. Between the Place de la Fontaine aux Lions (Cité de la Musique) and the Cité des Sciences et de l'Industrie, a passageway covered by an undulating awning parallel to the western side of the Grande Halle leads across the park and crosses the Canal de l'Ourcq (the south bank of which is skirted by another transverse passageway) to enter the northern sector. Alternatively, there is a path that takes you on a winding route across most of the 35 hectares through prairies and picnic areas, mischievous modern sculptures, gardens with themes such as *Miroirs, Vents et Dunes, Brouillards, Bamboo*, and past 24 follies of bright red enamelled metal, laid out on a grid pattern. General information ☎ 01 40 03 75 75. There are canal trips between la Villette and Pl. Stalingrad, Métro Jaurès.

From the Cité de la Musique, the gleaming sperical Géode draws you across to the northern half of the park and the Cité des Sciences et de l'Industrie (see below). Near this is the **Maison de la Villette**, the restored rotunda of the veterinary surgeon, the only 19C building left, now housing a small museum devoted to the history of the district.

Cité des Sciences et de l'Industrie

The main entrance (north) to the Cité des Sciences et de l'Industrie is from Porte de la Villette at 30 Av. Corentin-Cariou. (There is a second entrance on the west.) Most of the facilities and amenities, including a science bookshop, boutique and bank, are on the main entrance level. There are various cafés.

• Open (including the Géode) Tues–Sat 10.00–18.00, Sun 10.00–19.00, closed Mon and 1/5, 25/12. The admission charges vary depending on the combination of visits. Information, ☎ 01 40 05 80 00. Headphones are available (several languages, including English).

The massive rectangular block forming the Cité des Sciences et de l'Industrie, covering over 3 hectares, was inaugurated in March 1986. The auction-hall of a slaughter-house, begun on this site but abandoned incomplete in 1973, was incorporated into the new structure. The imaginative adaptation by Adrien Fainsilber reflects the scale of the site and incorporates the natural environment by introducing the themes of water, light and vegetation. On the south side of the building are three 32 x 8m glasshouses with plants establishing a point of transition between the building and the park; natural light floods in through two huge glazed cupolas; and the whole structure is surrounded by a moat. The main hall or nave is 100m long and 40m high and there are five levels to explore. Transparent lifts ascend within a stainless steel framework (there are also escalators).

The aim of the Cité is to demystify and popularise science, making it serious yet entertaining in order to attract all types and ages of visitors. The objective is to help to explain how scientific discoveries, innovative technology and revolutionary changes evolve hand-in-hand with industry and business. To this end there are many and varied activities using all kinds of models, multimedia displays and hands-on experiences to encourage discovery and exploration. At the core of the Cité, on **levels 1 and 2**, covering 30,000m² is **Explora**, a series of imaginative exhibitions covering science, technology and industry. The **South Gallery** offers journeys through six exhibitions: Automobile, Aeronautics, Space, Ocean, Environment and Energy. Among the several scale models are the submarine *Nautilus*, a model of the Ariane 5 rocket, 1:5 scale, 13m high; and a Mirage IV jet. The **North Gallery** is the fun area, with interactive and entertaining presentations involving the sensory, conceptual and technical capabilities of human mechanics in five exhibitions: Images, Computer Science, Expression and Behaviour, Sound, and Mathematics. The mezzanines have exhibitions illustrating fundamental questions about ourselves and the universe. The **Greenhouse**, garden of the future, is the most recent permanent exhibition. There are also temporary exhibitions.

An especially delightful area is the **Cité des Enfants**, designed specifically for children and divided into a wide variety of activities, for 3 to 5 year-olds and 5 to 12 year-olds, following itineraries through the science village. (A leaflet in English on the displays and exhibitions is available in English.) The **Techno cité**, designed for children from 11 years old, is an initiation into technology and includes several different types of robots, and a section devoted to computers and communications technology. There is also an **aquarium** and a **cinema** and a **Médiathèque** (multi-media library) open to the public on the ground floor.

Immediately to the south, reached from the main hall but outside the main building, are further entertainments. The **Géode** is an omnimax cinema of 36m diameter. The exterior of the spherical dome is clad in 6433 triangular plates of polished steel and inside are some 395 tiered seats facing a huge hemispheric cinema screen of $1000m^2$ and 26m in diameter. Specially adapted films are projected at a vertiginous optical angle of 180°. Cinaxe is a total film experience using advanced technology to create a realistic simulation. The **Argonaute** is a full-scale submarine, launched in 1957.

Pl. du Colonel-Fabien, Av. Mathurin-Moreau leads to the west entrance of the **Parc des Buttes Chaumont** (southwest of La Villette), one of the most picturesque and least known of Parisian parks (23 hectares), in the midst of the district of Belleville. The park was created during Haussmann's régime in 1866–67 by Alphand and Barillet from a decidedly unpromising terrain. The bare hills (*monts chauves*) of extensive gypsum (plaster of Paris) quarries, where rubbish was dumped, were transformed into craggy scenery. Lawns slope down to a lake spanned by a suspension bridge leading to a rocky promontory topped off with a tiny Classical temple. Among the well-tended flowerbeds are two restaurants and various entertainments for children. Near the southeast side of the park, Rue Fessart leads east, crossing Rue de la Villette (where at no. 51 the artist Georges Rouault was born in 1871) to the Gothic-revival **St-Jean-Baptiste** (by Lassus, 1854–59).

South of the church, Rue de Belleville continues east, passing a developing area to the north, to the **Cimetière de Belleville**. An inscription to the right of the entrance in the Rue du Télégraphe records that Claude Chappe experimented here with the aerial telegraph that was to announce the victories of the French Revolutionary Wars. Originally called Tachygraphe, it was set up in 1792 on this site and was the basis of lines to Lille and Strasbourg.

Belleville

Belleville in the 20th arrondissement, bordered by Rue de Belleville, has become quite the in-place, to live in and to visit. This cosmopolitan *quartier* has a seething bazaar (Tues and Fri) on Blvd de Belleville, and there are ethnic stores and cafés of every description and music of all types (Edith Piaf was born in 1915 at 72

Rue de Belleville). Although Belleville has not escaped some fairly cruel modernisation, there are still narrow streets with small residences, and abandoned warehouses around courtyards that harbour a number of artists who have contributed to the conservation of this area, and who open their workshops in May during several days of *Portes Ouvertes*.

Above it is the highest point in Paris (128m) around which a garden, the **Parc de Belleville**, was created in 1988, with an impressive rocky terrace providing a truly panoramic view of Paris.

32 • Père-Lachaise Cemetery

■ Arrondissement: 75020

☺ Père-Lachaise, Alexandre-Dumas, Philippe-Auguste

Les Allobroges, 71 Rue des Grands-Champs ☎ 01 43 73 40 00. Pleasant décor, considerate service and refined cooking, £–££

The Cimetière de l'Est, better known as Père-Lachaise (**Map 10; 1–2**), is the largest (47 hectares) and long the most fashionable cemetery in Paris. On a hill overlooking Paris, it is visited for its green spaces, in order to pay tribute to the late and great who lie there, or to view its monuments. Some of the tombs and monuments are fine works of art by leading 19C and 20C French sculptors, others are simply outrageous kitsch. The main entrance is in Blvd de Ménilmontant. It is open 08.00–17.30 every day. Visits in English, Saturday 15.00.

History of Père-Lachaise Cemetery

Père François de La Chaise (1624–1709) was the confessor of Louis XIV and lived in the Jesuit house rebuilt in 1682 on the site of a chapel. The property, situated on the side of a hill from which the king, during the Fronde, watched skirmishing between Condé and Turenne, was bought by the city in 1804 and laid out by Brongniart, and later extended several times. But this cemetery is not reserved for Roman Catholics, and buried side-by-side are Jews, Buddists, Muslims and non-believers.

The first interments were those of La Fontaine and Molière, whose remains were transferred here in 1804. The monument to Abélard and Héloïse, set up in 1779 at the abbey of the Paraclete (near Nogent-sur-Seine), was moved here in 1817, its canopy composed of fragments collected by Lenoir from the abbey of Nogent-sur-Seine.

The plan on pp 326–327 will help you to track down some of the tombs of the illustrious dead interred here and, when you are exhausted, there are pleasant areas for sitting or admiring the view of Paris. Either side of the main alley, the **central sector** (24 hectares) is classed as historic site, and the eastern part of this (9.5 hectares), where Chopin and Géricault are buried, designated **Secteur Romantique**. The tomb of Oscar Wilde (his body was moved here nine years after his death in 1900),

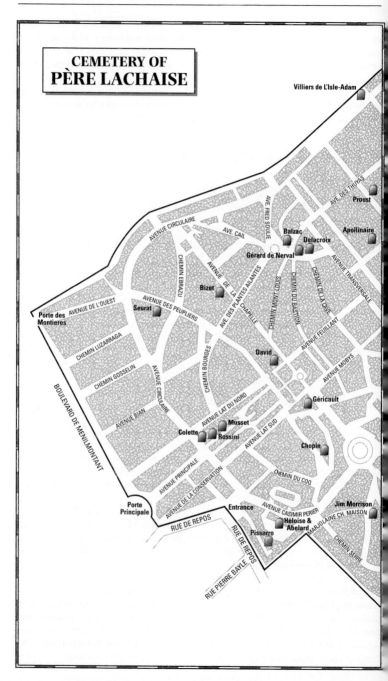

CEMETERY OF
PÈRE LACHAISE

Villiers de L'Isle-Adam

Proust

AVE. DES THUYAS

Apollinaire

AVENUE CIRCULAIRE

AVE. CAIL

Balzac

Delacroix

AVE. FRED SOULIÉ

Gérard de Nerval

AVENUE TRANSVERSALE

CHEMIN DU BASTION

CHEMIN DE LA CAVE

CHEMIN EBRAZU

AVENUE DE LA

Bizet

AVENUE DES PLANTES AILANTES

AVENUE DE LA CHAPELLE

CHEMIN MONT-LOUIS

Seurat

AVENUE DES PEUPLIERS

Porte des Montieres

AVENUE DE L'OUEST

AVENUE FEUILLANT

CHEMIN LUZARRAGA

David

CHEMIN BOURGES

AVENUE MOBYS

CHEMIN GOSSELIN

BOULEVARD DE MENILMONTANT

AVENUE CIRCULAIRE

AVENUE BIAN

Géricault

AVENUE LAT DU NORD

Musset

Colette

Rossini

AVENUE LAT SUD

Chopin

AVENUE PRINCIPALE

AVENUE DE LA CONSERVATION

CHEMIN DU COQ

Porte Principale

Entrance

AVENUE CASIMIR PERIER

Jim Morrison

RUE DE REPOS

Héloise & Abelard

MARJOLAINE CH. MAISON

Pissarro

RUE DE REPOS

CHEMIN SERRE

RUE PIERRE BAYLE

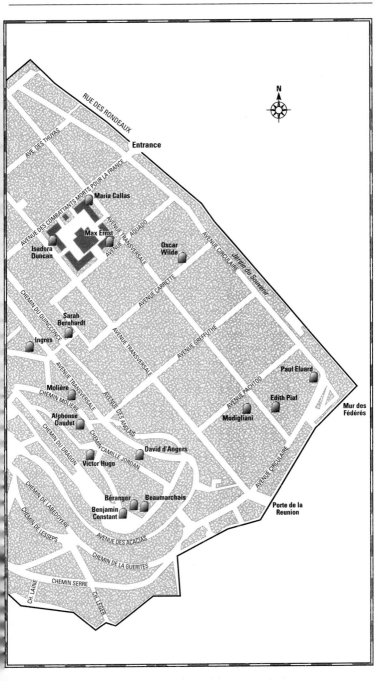

RUE DES RONDEAUX

AVE DES THUYAS

Entrance

N

AVENUE DES COMBATTANTS MORTS POUR LA FRANCE

Maria Callas

AVENUE ARAGO

AVENUE TRANSVERSALE

Max Ernst

Isadora Duncan

Oscar Wilde

AVENUE CIRCULAIRE

Jardin du Souvenir

AVENUE CARRETTE

CHEMIN DU QUINCONCE

Sarah Bernhardt

AVENUE TRANSVERSALE

Ingres

AVENUE GREFFULHE

AVENUE TRANSVERSALE

Molière
CHEMIN MOLIÈRE

Paul Eluard

AVENUE PACTHOD

Edith Piaf

Alphonse Daudet

AVENUE DES ANGLAIS

Modigliani

CHEMIN DU DRAGON

CHEMIN CAMILLE JORDAN

David d'Angers

Mur des Fédérés

Victor Hugo

CHEMIN DE LABEDOYERE

Béranger

Beaumarchais

Benjamin Constant

AVENUE CIRCULAIRE

CHEMIN DE LESSEPS

AVENUE DES ACACIAS

Porte de la Reunion

CHEMIN DE LA GUERITES

CH. LAINE

CHEMIN SERRE

CH. LEGER

designed by Jacob Epstein, vies in popularity with the simpler grave of the rock star Jim Morrison, who died accidentally in Paris in 1971. Huge mausoleums such as that of the Princess Elisabeth Deminoff contrast with the realistic bronze by Dalou of the young journalist Victor Noir shot in cold blood by Pierre Bonaparte in 1870.

In the eastern corner of the cemetery is the **Mur des Fédérés**, against which 147 Communards were shot on 28 May 1871; and here also is a monument to the many thousand Frenchmen who died either in German concentration camps or during the Resistance of 1941–44 and other deeply moving tributes to victims of Nazism. Thousands of Parisians still visit the cemetery on 1 November, All Saints' Day (*Toussaint*).

The list of the famous is endless. Among **writers** are Beaumarchais, Victor Hugo, Béranger, Proust, Balzac, Benjamin Constant, Gérard de Nerval, Alfred de Musset, Daudet, Apollinaire, Henri de Régnier, Barbusse, Bernardin de Saint-Pierre, Villiers de l'Isle-Adam, Colette and Eluard.

Composers and musicians buried here include Grétry, Boieldieu, Hérold, Pleyel, Cherubini, Bizet, Reynaldo Hahn, Chausson, Kreutzer, Chopin, Lalo, Gustave Charpentier, Auber, Poulenc, as well as the singer Adelina Patti.

Artists and sculptors are also numerous: David, David d'Angers, Pradier, Pissarro, Corot, Doré, Ingres, Gros, Daumier, Daubigny, Clésinger, Guillaume Coustou, Alfred Steven, Barye, Prud'hon, Delacroix, Géricault, Seurat and Modigliani.

There is a representative selection of **Napoléon's marshals**: Davout, Kellermann, Lefèbvre, Masséna, Ney, Murat, Victor, Macdonald, Suchet, and generals Foy, Junot, Reille, Savary, Marbot and Baron Larrey.

Other celebrities include Talma, Isadora Duncan, Sarah Bernhardt and Yvette Guilbert, Marie Walewska, Champollion, Parmentier, Blanqui, Baron Haussmann, Percier, Fontaine, René Lalique, Saint-Simon, Lammennais, Michelet, Arago, Monge, and Branly.

Among the **British names** are Sir William Keppel (1702–54), second Earl of Albemarle; Gen. Lord John Murray (1711–87); Adm. Sir Sidney Smith (1764–1840); Gen. Sir Charles Doyle (1770–1842); and Sir Richard Hertford-Wallace (1818–90), the connoisseur and benefactor of Paris (see Ch. 30) and Mary Clarke (Mme Mohl, 1793–1883).

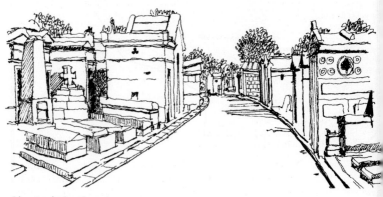

Père-Lachaise Cemetery

North of the Rue de la Roquette, opposite the main entrance of the cemetery, stood the Prison de la Grande-Roquette. From 1853 to 1899 condemned prisoners were held at La Roquette while awaiting execution. Here in 1871 50-odd Commune hostages were shot, although c 130 were also released. Thiers' victorious government forces of 'law and order' then proceeded to round up thousands of Communards—both repentant and defiant—and in two days shot out-of-hand 1900 of them in retaliation or 'in expiation'.

To the southeast of the cemetery, approached by Blvd de Charonne (forking off Blvd de Ménilmontant) and Rue de Bagnolet, stands **St-Germain-de-Charonne**, a rustic church of the 13C–14C, restored in the 19C, retaining its village cemetery (the only other in Paris being St-Pierre-de-Montmartre). **St-Jean-Bosco** (1937), of concrete and with a lofty tower, stands a short distance southeast of the junction of Blvd de Charonne and Rue de Bagnolet.

33 • Faubourg St-Antoine

■ Arrondissements: 75011, 75012

Ⓔ Bastille, Nation, Gare de Lyon, Ledru Rollin, Bercy, Cour St-Emillion

🚆 Gare de Lyon, Nation

Les Allobroges, 71 Rue des Grand Champs, ☎ 01 43 73 40 00. Traditional bistrot fare plus more ambitious cooking, £–££

L'Auberge Aveyronnaise, 40 Rue Fabriel-Lamé, ☎ 01 43 40 12 24. A home-from-home for the Aveyronnais in Paris, £

A La Biche au Bois, 45 Av. Ledru Rollin, ☎ 01 43 43 34 38. Friendly, old fashioned good quality, £

La Gourmandise, 271 Av. Daumesnil, ☎ 01 43 43 94 41. Carefully presented classics, £

Le Grand Bleu, opposite 46 Blvd de la Bastille, ☎ 01 43 45 19 99. A fish restaurant alongside the port de l'Arsenal, £

Chez Paul, 13 Rue Charonne, ☎ 01 47 00 34 57. Vintage bistrot, generous portions, lively atmosphere, £

La Sologne, 164 Av. Daumesnil, ☎ 01 43 07 68 97. Refined cooking and restful setting, ££

Au Trou Gascon, 40 Rue Taine, ☎ 01 43 44 34 26. Reliable and robust Gascony cooking, ££

Le Train Bleu, Pl. Louis Armand, Gare de Lyon, ☎ 01 43 43 09 06. Magnificent turn of the century décor, pity about the food, ££

Le Viaduc Café, 43 Av. Daumesnil, ☎ 01 44 74 70 70. Simple snacks.

Les Zygomates, 7 Rue Capri, ☎ 01 40 19 93 04. Atmospheric bistrot in an old butcher's shop, pretty good cooking, £

This off-the-beaten-track *quartier* around Place de la Nation and Gare de Lyon has, in the last decade, become a very popular area for restaurants, night-life and as a residential quarter. Contributing to this are Opera Bastille (Ch. 22), the improvements to the Port de Plaisance at Bastille and the redevelopment of the Bercy area. The district around Ave. Daumesnil has sprung to life because of the innovative use of the obsolete railway tracks. Under the arches are trendy shops, the Viaduc des Arts, and the tracks above have metamorphised into a walk through a series of gardens, the Promenade Plantée. There is also the benefit of the new Métro line Météor.

Rue du Faubourg-St-Antoine (Map 9; 3)leads east-southeast from Pl. de la Bastille to Pl. de la Nation through an area memorable in the history of the Revolutions of 1789 and 1848. It was also the scene of skirmishing during the Fronde (1652), when Turenne defeated Condé. Since the late 13C it has been a centre of cabinet-making, and there are still busy workshops in the courtyards and passages hidden behind 18C façades. This vibrant, varied area has a number of flourishing antique shops and galleries.

At no. 1 Rue du Faubourg-St-Antoine, leading away from Pl. de la Bastille (see Ch. 22) and the new opera-house, Joseph Fieschi in 1835 hatched his plot to assassinate King Louis-Philippe (see Blvd du Temple)—it failed, but 18 others were killed. At no. 61 (left), at the corner of Rue de Charonne, is the Fontaine Trogneux (1710).

To the left (north), Rue St-Bernard leads to **Ste-Marguerite**, built in 1634 but many times altered since. Behind the high altar is a *Pietà* by Girardon. It is believed that the 10-year-old Louis XVII, who in all probability died at the Temple (see Ch. 22), was buried in the graveyard here in 1795, together with other victims of the Revolution.

South of Rue du Faubourg-St-Antoine at this point is the **Hôpital St-Antoine**, rebuilt in 1905 but retaining part of Lenoir's 18C building for the former Abbaye de St-Antoine-des-Champs.

Several thoroughfares converge on the spacious **Pl. de la Nation**, at the centre of which is a colossal bronze group representing the *Triumph of the Republic*, by Dalou (1899). It was known formerly as the Pl. du Trône (named after the throne erected for Louis XIV's triumphal entry in 1660 with Marie-Thérèse); in 1794 no fewer than 1306 victims of the Terror were guillotined here. Between 1793 and 1880 it was known as the Pl. du Trône-Renversé.

To the east of the *cirque* are two **pavilions**, built as toll-houses by Ledoux in 1788, each surmounted by a Doric column 30.50m high; one with a statue of Philippe Auguste (by Dumont), the other, of Louis IX, by Etex.

Cours de Vincennes—once the scene in Easter Week of the Foire aux Pains d'Épice, a festival dating back to the 10C, when bread made with honey and aniseed was distributed by the monks of the Abbey of St-Antoine—leads directly east from Pl. de la Nation to Porte de Vincennes, and beyond to the Château de Vincennes (see Ch. 34).

Rue Fabre-d'Églantine leads south to Rue de Picpus, where, at the end of the garden at no. 35, a convent of Augustinian nuns, is the little **Cimetière de Picpus** (open 14.00–16.00 or 18.00, except Mon), a private burial ground for émigrés and descendants of victims of the Revolution, including La Fayette and the families of Chateaubriand, Crillon, Gontaut-Biron, Choiseul, La Rochefoucauld, Montmorency, Talleyrand-Périgord, Rohan-Rochefort, Noailles Salignac-Fénelon and many others.

Starting again from Pl. de la Bastille, a short distance southeast in Rue de Charenton, is the rebuilt Hospice des Quinze-Vingts, founded as an asylum for 300 blind people by Louis IX in 1260.

In the parallel Av. Daumesnil are two imaginative new installations making use of the old elevated railway line. The 60 arches of the **Viaduc des Arts** are home to arty boutiques where 46 different craftsmen and artists work on or create traditional and contemporary objects, as varied as musical instruments, textiles, furniture and sculpture. Above the viaduct is a walkway called the **Promenade Plantée**, a series of planted areas and gardens leading from near Opéra Bastille (close to Rue Ledru-Rollin) to Vincennes (Rue Edouard-Lartet), created out of the old rail track giving views of a little-known district of Paris including the unnerving repetition of a replica of Michelangelo's *Dying Slave* (see Louvre) on the police-station façade. There are a number of access points and four new gardens along the way: Jardin Hector-Malot, the Jardins de Reuilly, the Jardin de la Gare de Reuilly, and the Jardin Charles-Péguy.

Rue de Lyon leads south from Pl. de la Bastille to the **Gare de Lyon (Map 9; 8)**, terminus of lines to Dijon, Grenoble, Lyon, the south of France and Italy, including TGV. It preserves a *fin-de-siècle* buffet called *Le Train Bleu* behind the Beaux-Arts facade. Opposite the station once stood the Mazas Prison, where 400 Communards were rounded up and massacred by Thiers' troops in 1871. On its south side the station is now overlooked by tower blocks, including the Tour Gamma A, 195 Rue de Bercy, containing offices of the Observatoire économique de Paris (Institut National de la Statistique et des Etudes Economiques), a mine of information.

Rue Van Gogh leads southwest from the station across the new Pont Charles-de-Gaulle, spanning the Seine linking Gare de Lyon to the Gare d'Austerlitz (see Ch. 6). Further west is Pont d'Austerlitz (originally 1802–07), rebuilt in stone in 1855 and widened in 1886, it spans the Seine to Pl. Valhubert and Gare d'Austerlitz. Not far southeast of Gare de Lyon are the new Ministère de Finances offices along Blvd de Bercy, leading to the widened Pont de Bercy (1864).

On the far side of the boulevard stands the hexagonal **Palais Omnisports** (1984), a turf-clad stunted pyramid topped by a tubular platform supported by four cylindrical towers, which holds 17,000 spectators.

Alongside the stadium is one of the newest Paris gardens, **Parc de Bercy**, completed in 1997, covering 14 hectares parallel with the Seine, where the bonded wine warehouses once stood, and opposite the preposterous towers of the new Bibliothèque Nationale, Mitterand (see Ch. 6). The novel fountain, *Canyoneaustrate*, by Gérard Singer, lies between the Palais Omnisports and the *grande prairie*, an open grassy area of the Parc de Bercy. Further on is a combination of intimate thematic gardens (Kitchen, Rose, Scented, etc.) a maze, and a token vineyard serving as a reminder of the previous activity of the *quartier*. A canal leads to a small lake in the southeastern section accessed by a footbridge over Rue Joseph-Kessel (Métro Cour St-Emilion) and another series of gardens. Many mature trees are integrated into the landscape and three existing buildings, namely the Pavillon de Bercy, the Maison du Jardinage and the Maison du Lac, as well as an 18C folly. Transformation work began in autumn 2000 on the former American Centre building (by Frank Gehry) in Bercy Park, which will become the **Maison du Cinéma**, incorporating the Musée Henri Langlois, previously at the Palais de Chaillot.

The **Musée des Arts Forains**, at 53 Av. des Terroirs de France, is a fairground museum. (Groups only by appointment, ☎ 01 43 40 16 22). Rue Joseph-Kessel leads to Pont de Tolbiac, and further east is the Pont National carrying the Périphérique, and the Porte de Bercy, gateway to the A4 motorway to the east.

34 • Vincennes

■ Arrondissement: 94300
🔒 Château de Vincennes
📍 Line A: Vincennes

There is a variety of restaurants in the Bois de Vincennes:
Le Restaurant du Plateau de Gravelle, ☎ 01 43 96 99 55, £
Le Chalet de la Porte Jaune, Lac des Minimes, ☎ 01 43 28 80 11, £

Le Chalet des Iles, Ile de Reuilly, ☎ 01 43 07 77 07, £
Le Chalet du Lac de Saint-Mande, ☎ 01 43 28 09 89, £
La Chesnaie du Roy, Route de la Pyramide, ☎ 01 43 74 67 50, £

Vincennes is at the eastern extremity of Paris (at the end of Line 1 on the Métro) and the château, which has been undergoing a lengthy restoration, was one of the glories of the French monarchy in the 14C and 15C. A little outside the usual tourist route, on a fine day the château visit might be combined with a walk along the Promenade Plantée (see Ch. 31), and there is the added attraction of the Bois de Vincennes with its Parc Floral.

Château de Vincennes
Approximately 2km east of the Porte de Vincennes, easily reached by Métro, RER or, with a bit more effort, on foot (see above), stands the impressive bulk of the former royal residence, the Château de Vincennes, part of which is now occupied by the armed forces. By the 16C this huge rectangular construction comprised nine square towers linked by fortified walls surrounded by a moat. Enclosed within were a keep, chapel and buildings of different periods. All the towers, except the Tour du Village (entrance), which lost only its statues, were reduced to the level of the walls in the 19C. The French historian Michelet called it 'the Windsor of the Valois'.

• The château is open 10.00–12.00 and 13.15–18.00 (1 Oct–31 Mar to 17.00), closed 1/1, 1/5, 01/11, 11/11, 25/12. ☎ 01 48 08 31 20. Guided visits only inside the buildings (usually in French unless pre-booked for groups) although the exterior has free access. Gift/bookshop.

History of the Château de Vincennes
A royal property since 1178 under Louis VII (1137–80), it became Louis IX's (1226–70) second residence after Paris and remained a royal stronghold until the 14C. The keep or donjon, begun by Philippe VI, the first of the Valois, in 1337 at the beginning of the 100 Years War, was completed by his grand-

son Charles V (1364–73) around 1370, who also built the ramparts in about seven years and started work on the Chapel in 1379, replacing that built by Louis IX. This great fortress was then the political capital of the kingdom and the illustration of 'December' in the *Très Riches Heures du Duc de Berri*, or Fouquet's panel for the *Hours of Etienne Chevalier* (at Chantilly) give an idea of its splendour and importance in the 15C. The foundations of the Pavillons du Roi and de la Reine (the Queen Mother, Anne of Austria) (to the southeast) were laid in the 16C and completed nearly a century later when the château, then in Mazarin's possession, was altered and decorated by Le Vau. It was used as refuge for the court during the problems of the Wars of Religion and by Mazarin to protect his collection during the problems of the Fronde.

Deserted by the court in favour of the palace at Versailles (c 1680), Vincennes was gradually stripped of its furnishings, and its glory, to become first, a porcelain factory (1745; transferred to Sèvres in 1756), then a cadet school and finally, in 1757, a small-arms factory. By 1788 it was put up for sale but found no purchaser, and was rescued from destruction by the Revolutionary mob by La Fayette in 1791. When, in 1808, Napoléon converted it into an arsenal, the surviving 13C buildings were demolished. By 1840 it was used as a fortress, to the detriment of much of Le Vau's decoration. Degradation continued during the Second World War when German occupying forces installed a supply depot, and the Pavillon de la Reine was partially destroyed by an explosion in 1944 when they evacuated.

There are many historical associations, some sombre, with Vincennes: Louis X died in the castle in 1316, Charles IV in 1328, and Charles V was born here in 1337. Both Charles IX (in 1574) and Mazarin (in 1661) died here as well as Henry V of England in 1422, seven weeks before the death of Charles VI whom he should have succeeded as king of France. During the reign of Louis XIII, the keep was used as a state prison. In March 1804 the Duc d'Enghien (son of the Prince de Condé), after arrest on Napoléon's orders, was tried by court-martial and shot the same night in the château. Général Daumesnil, governor at different periods between 1809 and his death in 1832, famously retorted, when summoned to surrender to the Allies in 1814, 'First give me back my leg' (lost at the Battle of Wagram). It is not generally known that Mata Hari was shot here in 1917; and in 1944, three days before evacuating it, a plaque records that the Germans shot some 30 hostages against the interior of the ramparts.

Cross the moat to enter the fortress beneath the 48m high **Tour du Village**. The campanile on the tower was rebuilt in 2000 and reproduces the 14C clock installed by Charles V in the keep, an innovatory but costly undertaking at that time. The bell of 1369, which is struck from outside, still survives, and would originally have been used for liturgical purposes although, being semi-public, it also came to signify the hours of the working day. The route passes between a range of buildings in military occupation. On the right is the **Acceuil Charles V** and the entrance, ticket office and shop.

Past this building on the right the huge **donjon** or keep, a 52m tall square tower flanked with round turrets, rises above its free-standing turreted enceinte. (It is undergoing lengthy and complicated renovations and therefore closed). Charles V's quarters were on the second floor and a plaque records the death of

Henry V of England whose body was taken to Westminster for burial. The finest of its type still standing in France, the donjon is a sophisticated construction consisting of a series of superimposed vaulted chambers using iron girders to stabilise the upper floors.

The areas dating from the time of Charles V which can be seen on the guided visit include the ramparts and the **Sainte Chapelle**, founded 14C and completed in 1552. This, like other chapels with the same dedication, was modelled on the royal chapel on the Ile de la Cité but here there is no lower level. The Flamboyant façade has a magnificent rose-window surmounted by an ornamental gable filled with tracery. The bare interior contains graceful vaulting, tracery and sculptures and, at the east end, seven stained-glass windows by Beaurain (16C) restored after an explosion in 1870. In the oratory is a monument to the Duc d'Enghien (see above; by Deseine, 1816).

To the south, through a portico, the immense **Cour d'Honneur** opens out and, beyond, the monumental main entrance at the time of Mazarin, the **Tour du Bois**. On the right is the **Pavillon du Roi** (now containing military archives), and opposite, the **Pavillon de la Reine** where Mazarin died in 1661. Both were completed by Le Vau in 1654–60. The Pavillon de la Reine, where two rooms with their painted decor have survived, contains the **Navy Insignia Museum** and is open to the public on Wednesdays, 14.00–17.00. The **Musée des Chasseurs** in the Tour du Roi, containing tombs of the heroes of the Algerian war in the 19C, is being restored.

The **Bois de Vincennes** which at 995 hectares is slightly larger than the Bois de Boulogne, has many attractions, both botanical and sporting. The forest was first enclosed in the 12C and replanted in 1731 by Louis XV who converted into a park for the citizens of Paris. In the 19C there were many transformations and embellishments including three lakes and, after further land was ceded to the Bois in 1860, more lakes and avenues were created. Although unfamiliar to the majority of visitors it is worth leaving time for a stroll here even if only as far as the beautiful **Parc Floral** created in 1969, to the southeast of the château. The naturally flat terrain was given a contoured relief and two irregular-shaped lakes

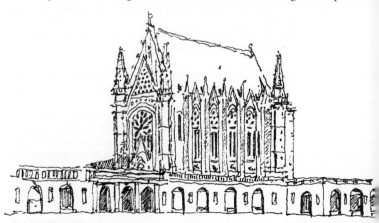

Sainte-Chapelle

provide a focus. Within the 31 hectares are thematic gardens, rhododendrons and water plants plus a wealth of modern sculptures and two restaurants. Beyond are stadiums, sports grounds, a cycle track and a racecourse for trotting races. Further east is **Lac des Minimes**, a tropical garden and an Indo-Chinese pagoda.

Near the racetrack to the south of the Bois is a farm and an arboretum and towards the southwest end, approached from the château by Av. Daumesnil, is the **Parc Zoologique de Vincennes**, the main zoo of Paris. Beyond that is Lac Daumesnil, south of which is a Buddhist temple. There is a project to recreate the large 17C Le Nôtre gardens.

Av. Daumesnil leaves the Bois at the Porte Dorée (or Porte Picpus), just north of which is the building of the former Musée National des Arts Africains et Oceaniens (75012), with an ornately sculpted façade. The museum has closed and its collections are transferring to the Musée Branly in the 15e, opening in 2004 (see Ch. 12 and Louvre).

Some 3.5km northeast—as the crow flies—in the **Parc de Montreau**, at 31 Blvd Théophile Sueur, Montreuil (91300), open Wed–Fri 14.00–17.00, Sat 14.00–18.00, Sun 10.00–18.00, is the **Musée de l'Histoire Vivante**, open Wed–Fri 14.00–17.00, Sat 14.00–18.00, Sun 10.00–18.00, ☎ 01 48 70 61 62, largely devoted to the Socialist ethic and the history of the revolutions of 1830 and 1848, the Paris Commune and other proletarian movements.

Around Paris

35 • From Paris to Versailles, via Sèvres and Saint-Cloud

Getting there

By rail

To Versailles The most convenient way to travel is by RER line C5 to the terminus nearest the palace, Versailles-Rive Gauche. There are also trains from the Gare St-Lazare to Versailles-Rive Droit, and from the Gare Montparnasse to Versailles-Chantiers. Alternatively, take the Métro to the Pont de Sèvres, then bus 171.

To Sévres, St-Cloud Tramway (line T2) between Issy-Val-de-Seine and La Défense stops at Parc de St-Cloud and Sèvres. Mainline trains from St-Lazare or La Défense to St-Cloud. Métro Lines 9 and 10. Buses 52, 72, 160, 169, 171, 175, and 179.

By road

Take the A13 motorway and the first exit after passing through the tunnel at St-Cloud. A road leads southwest towards the Château of Versailles (parking in the Pl. d'Armes). An alternative is the N10, bearing south west from the Porte de St-Cloud over the Pont de Sèvres.

On the way to Versailles, there are places of interest and museums, reached by the N10 or by public transport.

In the suburb of Boulogne-Billancourt are the **Musee des Années 30**, 28 Av. André-Morizet, ☎ 01 48 04 52 80 (Métro, Marcel-Sembat); **Musée et Jardin Paul Landowski**, 14 Rue Max-Blondat, ☎ 01 55 18 46 41 and the **Musée-Bibliothèque Marmottan**, 7 Pl. Denfert-Rochereau, ☎ 01 41 10 24 70 (both Métro Boulogne-J.-Jaurès) and **Musée Albert Kahn**, Jardins et collection, 14 Rue du Port, ☎ 01 46 04 52 80.

The main reason to visit **St-Cloud** is for its park, the Domaine National de Saint-Cloud (460 hectares), ☎ 01 41 12 02 90, with its sophisticated cascades and fountains, grand perspectives and views over Paris. Philippe d'Orléans (Monsieur), younger brother of Louis XIV employed Le Pautre and Hardouin-Mansart to design a palace and cascades, and Le Nôtre for the gardens. St-Cloud's porcelain factory (1695–1773) and palace both burned down, the latter during German occupation, 1870–71, and the ruins were cleared away in 1891.

From the main entrance you pass former outbuildings of the château, one of which contains a very modest **museum**, open Wed, Sat and Sun 14.00–18.00. On the terrace, the site of château is marked out with flowerbeds and yews. North of this is the English-style **Jardin de Trocadéro** with a small lake, created at the time of Louis XVIII and in the opposite direction is the Horseshoe Pond extended by an alley to a green amphitheatre created in the 18C. Below the château terrace is a large pond that serves as reservoir for the **Grande Cascade**. This magnificent example of hydraulic magic, using only gravity, is brought to life on Sundays in June. The upper part of the cascade, all of which is decorated with sculptures of figures, sea monsters, masks and *rocailles*, was designed by Le

Pautre in 1660–65 and the lower part designed by Hardouin-Mansart in 1698–99. Not far from here is the **Grand Jet**, which goes back to the 16C, and a fountain with six nymphs. To the west, beyond the terrace, is the fountain with 24 water jets, long perspectives, alleys, more basins, fountains and woodland. During the gales of Christmas 1999, 17,500 trees were lost but are being replaced. There are several cafés in the park.

In **Sèvres** at the southeast corner of the park is **Musée National de Céramique de Sèvres** (Métro: Pont de Sèvres), created at the beginning of the 19C, open 10.00–17.00, closed Tues (☎ 01 41 14 04 20). Porcelain is still produced here and there is a boutique selling replicas and modern pieces.

The porcelain factory founded in 1738 was moved here from Vincennes in 1756 at the request of Mme de Pompadour, and since 1760 has been State-controlled. Among designers of Sèvres porcelain were E.-M. Falconet and J.-B. Pigalle. There are on display some 5000 pieces of ceramics from France and other countries, from the Middle Ages to the present. On the ground floor, are Islamic ceramics, Hispano-Moresque ware, Delft ware, Italian majolica and European historical collections from the 16C to 18C. On the first floor are 17C and 18C European porcelain and faience from Nevers, Moustiers, Rouen, Strasbourg, Marseille and Sceaux; and copies of Oriental pieces manufactured at St-Cloud, Mennecy, Meissen, Chantilly, Vincennes and Saxe (Meissen). And of course there is Sèvres porcelain, from 1740 to the present day. Temporary exhibitions are held on the second floor.

On a height some 3km north is the fort of Mont Valérien (1830). Off Blvd Washington is an American Military Cemetery.

In Sèvres off the N10 towards Ville d'Avray, the Maison des Jardies', 14 Av. Gambetta, was the country retreat of Balzac in 1837–41. It was later the home of Léon Gambetta (1838–82), one of the proclaimers of the Republic in 1870, and from 1879 to 1882 president of the Chamber (open Mon and Fri 1.30–15.15). The 18C church in Ville d'Avray (mainline station), contains frescoes by Corot, who often painted the lakes in the Bois de Fausses Reposes, further southwest.

Immediately southeast of Sèvres is **Meudon** (Celtic Mellodunum), whose benefice Rabelais enjoyed in 1551–52 and where Wagner wrote *The Flying Dutchman* in 1841. The Villa des Brillants, the **Rodin Museum** at Meudon, was the sculptor's home from 1895 until his death in 1917. The property can be visited between 1 May and 30 September (Fri, Sat, Sun 13.30–18.00, ☎ 01 41 14 35 00). On display are casts of Rodin's major works and the sculptor's collection of antiquities in the garden.

Further south is the **Observatoire d'Astronomie Physique**. The building, formerly the Château Neuf, was built for the Grand Dauphin (Monseigneur, the son of Louis XIV), by Hardouin-Mansart, but a fire in 1870 reduced it to a single storey. The terrace commands a wide view and the Forêt de Meudon extends to the south and west.

From Sèvres, the N10 continues southwest (through the suburbs of Chaville and Viroflay) to (c 8km) Versailles.

Versailles

Brasserie Maitre Kanter, part of a chain but reliable food, quick and efficient.
Brasserie La Fontaine, ☎ 01 39 51 57 79. In the annexe of the Trianon Palace, less pricey (therefore less amazing food) but with a great ambience, ££
Brasserie du Théâtre, 15 Rue des Réservoirs, ☎ 01 39 50 03 21. Mirrored setting serving genuine brasserie food, ££
La Flotille, ☎ 01 39 51 41 58. In the Park of the Château, wins hands down for the setting, and the food matches up to it, ££
La Marée de Versailles, 22 Rue au Pain, ☎ 01 30 21 73 73. Mouthwatering seafood, ££
Le Potager du Roy, 1 Rue du Maréchal-Joffre, ☎ 01 39 50 35 34. Fresh ingredients; good lunch menu, ££

Le Quai No. 1, 1 Av. de St-Cloud, ☎ 01 39 50 42 26. Seafood, ££
Restaurant de la Reine, 8 Rue de la Chancellerie, ☎ 01 39 50 07 82. Intimate atmosphere and refined cuisine, ££
Les Trois Marches, 1 Blvd de la Reine, ☎ 01 39 50 13 21. In the Trianon Palace Hotel, elegant restaurant overlooking the park of the chateau and exquisite cuisine to match, £££

There is a good choice of restaurants of all categories in Rue Satory and around the Place du Marché, both areas are about 10 minutes walk from the château and a good alternative to the crowded eating places around Place des Armes.

- Tourist Information Office: 2bis Avenue de Paris, 78000-Yvelines. ☎ 01 39 24 88 88, fax 01 39 24 88 89 (guided visits of the town).

The *préfecture* of the *département* of Yvelines, with a population of some 90,000, Versailles lies in a low sandy plain between two lines of wooded hills. The town is dignified and affluent, reflecting its regal history, and the regularly laid out streets and imposing avenues converge on the château and its park, drawing the visitors who flock there with good reason. The château dominates Versailles, yet the town itself is worth spending a little time on and it makes an extremely pleasant base outside Paris, especially if you prefer a more rural setting or to take advantage of the musical entertainment and see the fountains play on summer evenings. It falls into distinct *quartiers* around its two main churches, the cathedral of St-Louis and the church of Notre-Dame, it has many elegant 17C and 18C buildings, a lively market area, and hotels and restaurants of all categories. There are also numerous sites of interest in the *département*.

The Quartier Notre-Dame, known as the New Town, of Versailles, is to the northeast of Place des Arms (in front of the château). At the heart of this busy district is the **Church of Notre-Dame** (1684–86), by Jules Hardouin-Mansart, the covered market and the antiques area around the old Court House of 1724 and dungeons.

West of this *quartier*, the Hôtel des Réservoirs, originally built by Lassurance for Mme de Pompadour, still bears the marquise's arms. Proust isolated himself

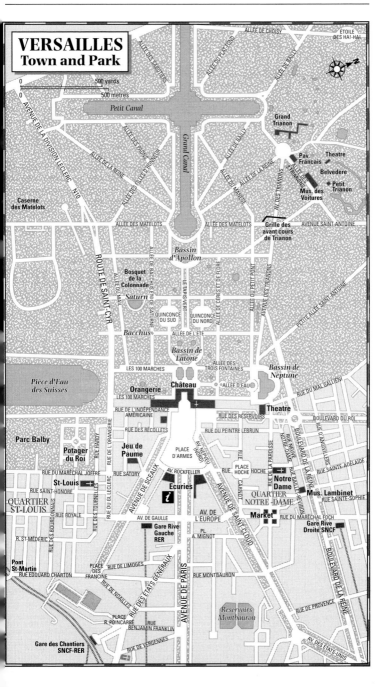

VERSAILLES
Town and Park

0 ____ 500 yards

0 ____ 500 metres

ALLÉE DE CHOISY

ÉTOILE
DES HAI-HAI

ALLÉE DU PLAFOND

ALLÉES SABOTIÈRES

AVENUE DE LA DIVISION LECLERC — N10

ALLÉE DE BAILLY

AV. DE BAILLY

Petit Canal

ALLÉE DE LA REINE

ALLÉES PAONS

ALLÉE DES AILES D'HONNEUR

ALLÉE DE LA REINE

ALLÉE DE BAILLY

ALLÉE DU MANÈGE

AV. DES TRIANONS

ALLÉE DES TRIANONS

Grand Canal

**Grand
Trianon**

Pav.
Francais

Theatre

Belvedere

Petit
Trianon

Mus. des
Voitures

**Caserne
des Matelots**

ALLÉE DES MATELOTS

ALLÉE DES MATELOTS

Grille des
avant cours
de Trianon

AVENUE SAINT-ANTOINE

*Bassin
d'Apollon*

ALLÉE DE BACCHUS ET DE SATURNE

LE RAPIN VERT

ALLÉE DE CÉRÈS ET DE FLORE

ALLÉE DU PETIT PONT

AVENUE DES TRIANONS

PETITE ALLÉE SAINT-ANTOINE

**Bosquet
de la
Colonnade**

Saturn

QUINCONCE
DU SUD

QUINCONCE
DU NORD

ROUTE DE SAINT-CYR

ALLÉE DU MAIL

Bacchus

ALLÉE DE L'ÉTÉ

*Bassin de
Latone*

ALLÉE DES
TROIS FONTAINES

*Bassin de
Neptune*

RUE DU MAL GALLIENI

LES 100 MARCHES

ALLÉE D'EAU

*Pièce d'Eau
des Suisses*

Orangerie

Château

LES 100 MARCHES

RUE DE L'INDÉPENDANCE
AMÉRICAINE

RUE DES RÉSERVOIRS

Theatre

BOULEVARD DU ROI

RUE DES RÉCOLLETS

RUE DU PEINTRE LEBRUN

RUE NEUVE
NOTRE-DAME

RUE DE LA PAROISSE

BOULEVARD DE LA REINE

RUE SAINTE-ADÉLAÏDE

Parc Balby

RUE HARDY

RUE DE L'ORANGERIE

PLACE
D'ARMES

AV. DE ST INGRID

RUE HOCHE

PLACE
HOCHE

RUE DE LA PAROISSE

RUE DE BAILLE-REUNION

**Potager
du Roi**

**Jeu de
Paume**

AV. ROCKFELLER

RUE HOCHE

**Notre
Dame**

RUE SAINTE-SOPHIE

RUE DU MARÉCHAL JOFFRE

RUE SATORY

Ecuries

AVENUE DE SAINT-CLOUD

**QUARTIER
NOTRE-DAME**

Mus. Lambinet

St-Louis

AVENUE DE SCEAUX

CARNOT

Market

RUE DU MARÉCHAL FOCH

RUE SAINT-HONORE

RUE DE GLI LECLERC

**QUARTIER
ST-LOUIS**

RUE DES TOURNELLES

AV. DE
L'EUROPE

**Gare Rive
Droite SNCF**

RUE ROYALE

AV. DE GAULLE

**Gare Rive
Gauche
RER**

PL.
A. MIGNOT

R. ST-MÉDÉRIC

RUE DU BOURDONNAIS

BOULEVARD DE LA REINE

**Pont
St-Martin**

PLACE
DES
FRANCINE

RUE DE LIMOGES

AVENUE DE PARIS

RUE MONTBAURON

RUE DE PROVENCE

RUE EDOUARD CHARTON

RUE DE NOAILLES

RUE DES ÉTATS GÉNÉRAUX

*Reservoirs
Montbauron*

AV. DES ÉTATS-UNIS

PLACE
R. POINCARRÉ

RUE
BENJAMIN FRANKLIN

**Gare des Chantiers
SNCF-RER**

RUE DE VERGENNES

here for almost five months in the latter half of 1906. The elegant Théâtre Montansier (no. 13), founded by the actress Mlle Montansier, was built by Heurtier and Boulet in 1777.

A short walk to the northeast at 54 Blvd de la Reine is the **Musée Lambinet**, housed in a mid-18C mansion. In the collection are sculptures by Houdon and early prints with interesting views of Versailles.

At no. 1 Blvd de la Reine (further west) is the **Trianon Palace**, a luxury hotel built by René Sergent, the architect of the Plaza Athénée in Paris, in 1910.

History of the Trianon Palace Hotel

During the First World War the Trianon Palace was a hospital for British troops and in April 1917 the Allied Military Committee installed its permanent War Council here. It was chosen by Allied politicians for meetings preceding the signing of the Treaty of Versailles in the château. In the conference room is a plaque recording the handing of conditions for peace by Georges Clemenceau to the German High Command on 7 May 1919. The building was requisitioned by the Royal Air Force in 1939, by the Luftwaffe in 1940 and by the Americans in 1944 when it was again the meeting place for decisions that settled the peace. Since then the Trianon Palace Hotel's original architectural splendours have been lavishly restored.

Av. de Paris, leads directly east from the château and divides the Quartier Notre-Dame from the Quartier St-Louis. No. 21 occupies the Hôtel de Mme du Barry (1751, private) its monumental portal by Claude-Nicolas Ledoux. Comte Robert de Montesquiou (1855–1921), on whom Proust based his Baron Charlus and Huysmans his Jean des Esseintes in *A Rebours*, lived at no. 53. At the western extremity of Av. de Paris, north and south, facing the entrance to the Chateau across Place des Armes, are the **Grande** and the **Petite Ecurie** (Stables).

On the south side of Av. de Paris is the quieter **Quartier St-Louis**, or Old Versailles, begun at the time of Louis XIV. No. 4 Av. de Paris is the Hôtel de Ville, 1899, and at no. 22 is the **Hôtel des Menus Plaisirs**, the warehouse built for Louis XV where theatrical scenery and props, and other playthings were stored. Immediately south of the château is the **Grand-Commun**, built by J. Hardouin-Mansart in 1684 to accommodate court functionaries. Adjacent is the former Hôtel de la Guerre (1759) and Hôtel des Affaires Etrangères et de la Marine (1761), now the municipal library, with Louis XV decoration.

From here Rue du Vieux-Versailles (left) leads to the historic **Jeu de Paume**, the royal tennis-court (1686) (open May–Sept, Sun 14.00–17.00). On 20 June 1789, the deputies of the Third Estate, finding themselves locked out of the States-General, adjourned here and, with the astronomer Bailly as their president, swore not to separate until they had given France a proper constitution. This is known as the Oath of the Tennis Court.

Cross Rue de l'Orangerie and turn down Rue du Maréchal Joffre. To the east is the church of **St-Louis** (1742–54) by Jacques Hardouin-Mansart de Sagonne, a rare example of a church of the period of Louis XV. A restrained version of Baroque, it was designated a cathedral in 1802. To the west is the **Potager du Roi**, formerly Louis XIV's kitchen-garden and now a horticultural college (open April–Oct, Sat and Sun, 10.00–18.00). And to the east is the pretty little St-Louis Square, with 18C houses.

36 • The Château and Gardens of Versailles: the Trianons

Versailles must be the best known château in the world. When it was new royalty all over Europe desired to emulate it. Now it is one of the main attractions for anyone visiting France, and with good reason. The combination of palace, museum and gardens is stunning, let alone the summer displays when the fountains play. However, when planning your visit, bear in mind that it is almost impossible to see more than a part of the immense ensemble of château, Trianons and Park in one day, especially at the height of the season. To appreciate everything fully would take at least two days. The State Apartments tend to get saturated throughout the morning, so an alternative is to visit the Grand and Petit Trianons first before returning to the main building.

 There is a *café* (Cour de la Chapelle, near Entrance A) and a restaurant, *La Flotille*, in the gardens opposite the Grand Canal.

- **Opening times**: the **château** is open 2 May–30 Sept 09.00–18.30; 1 Oct–30 Apr 09.00–17.30, closed Mon, certain public holidays and during official ceremonies. **Gardens and park** (open every day, 07.00–dusk summer, 08.00–dusk winter); and p 355 for the **Grand and Petit Trianons** (open 1 Apr–30 Sept 12.00–18.30; 1 Nov–31 March 12.00–17.30). **Les Grandes Heures du Parlement** is an independent museum presented by the National Assembly, open 09.00–18.30 2 May–30 Sept 09.00–17.30 1 Oct–30 Apr, closed Mon (☎ 01 39 67 07 73; audioguide).

Guided and non-guided visits

There is a variety of visits, some independent, some guided, and some only available at certain times. The ticket to all guided and audioguided visits includes admission to the State Apartments. Tickets are valid all day. There is a reduced rate after 15.30 every day, and all day Sunday.

Non-guided visits, Entrance A (audioguide available): the State Apartments, Hall of Mirrors, and Apartments of the Queen; Museum of the History of France: Crusades Rooms, the 17C Historical Galleries, Hall of Battles and 1830 Room (not continuously open, ☎ 01 30 83 77 88/01 30 83 76 20).

Visits with audioguide commentary, Entrance C: Louis XIV's Chamber, Hall of Mirrors and Apartments of the Dauphin and Dauphine.

Guided visits, Entrance D: Private Apartments of Louis XV and Louis XVI; of Marie-Antoinette; the Opera and Chapel; a Day in the Life of Louis XIV. To check availability and openings, it is advisable to enquire in advance from the Bureau d'Action Culturelle, ☎ 01 30 83 77 88. Individual reservations can be made on the spot for the same day. (Group reservations for visits without guide for State Apartments, ☎ 01 30 83 77 43; guided visits ☎ 01 30 83 77 88.) There are also themed visits (in French only) from Sept–June (☎ 01 30 83 77 89). In summer, a guided visit to the woodland groves (☎ 01 30 83 77 80).

Entrance A in Cour de la Chapelle: visitors' entrance for individuals for the non-guided visit, general information, currency exchange and hire of audioguide.

Entrance C: visit to the King's Chamber with audioguide or with a guide.
Entrance D: ticket sales for guided visits.
Entrance B for groups, on the north side of the Cour Royale.
Entrance H facilities for the handicapped.
There are various information and ticket offices, cloakrooms (obligatory for umbrellas, parcels) and bookstalls.

Calèches Horse-drawn carriages are a recent innovation for getting around the park. They run regularly between the château and the Trianons, they run a regular tour of the park and, during the Grandes Eaux Musicales, there is also a tour of the Trianon Gardens. Tues–Sun, 11.30–16.30 Oct–Apr, 10.30–18.00 May–Sept (☎ 01 30 97 04 40).

Music Performances in the château and gardens: Centre de Musique Baroque, concerts ☎ 01 39 20 78 10; Nouveaux Plaisirs, concerts and dance, ☎ 0803 808 803; Fêtes de Nuit and Grandes Eaux Musicales (Productions du Roi Soleil) summer performances in the gardens, ☎ 01 30 83 78 88.

History of the Château de Versailles

Versailles emerged from obscurity in 1624, when Louis XIII built a hunting lodge here, which was subsequently developed into a small château, with a garden laid out in 1639. The royal estate originally covered an area of 6614 hectares, surrounded by a 43km-long wall and entered by 22 gates. The domain was reduced to 815 hectares after the Revolution. The real creator of Versailles was **Louis XIV**, who in 1661 conceived the idea of building a lasting monument to his reign. **Louis le Vau** was entrusted with the renovation and embellishment of the old building around the Cour de Marbre, while **Le Nôtre** laid out the park. After Le Vau's death in 1670 the work was continued by his pupil **François d'Orbay**, and the interior decoration was supervised by **Charles le Brun**. In 1682 Louis XIV transferred the court and seat of government here from St-Germain. Jules Hardouin-Mansart, appointed chief architect in 1676, radically remodelled the main body of the château and built the two huge north and south wings, giving the immense façade (with its 375 windows) a total length of 580m, and began work on the chapel.

The workforce employed on the building and in laying out and draining the grounds was impressive. In 1684 each day there were 22,000 men and 6000 horses at work and the exhorbitant expenditure impoverished France. In 1687 Mansart started work on the **Grand Trianon**. The life at Court, where its members would orbit, moth-like, around the imperious figure of the *Roi soleil*, was a superficially scintillating scene disguising monotonous routine, rigid protocol and ceremonious etiquette which, coupled with intrigue and hypocrisy, governed the daily drama of Versailles. The Duc de Saint-Simon's *Memoires* describe it all inimitably.

The main wings were divided up into numerous diminutive suites to house individual courtiers and their families. Under **Louis XV** a series of royal apartments, decorated in the current style, were incorporated; and one of the colonnaded pavilions in the entrance court, the interior of the opera-house and the **Petit Trianon** were built by Jacques-Ange Gabriel. Louis XVI redecorated a suite of apartments for Marie-Antoinette and built the rustic village or Hameau.

The château was the birthplace of Louis XV (1710–74), Louis XVI (1754–93), Louis XVIII (1755–1824) and Charles X (1757–1836).

The independence of the United States was formally recognised by Britain, France and Spain in the Treaty of Versailles, signed in 1783. The meeting of the Assembly of the States-General was held in Versailles in 1789, where on 20 June the deputies of the Third Estate formed themselves into the National Assembly. On 6 October an angry mob, some 7000 strong, led by the women of Les Halles, marched to Versailles and forced the royal family to return with them to Paris, where they were confined to the Tuileries. The place was then pillaged.

By 1792, having been uninhabited for over two years, Versailles was denuded of its finery, and the Grand Canal quite dry. In 1814 the palace was occupied by Tsar Alexander I and Friedrich Wilhelm III of Prussia. Under the **Restoration**, the second colonnaded pavilion was completed by Dufour, but the building later deteriorated from neglect. Louis-Philippe did irreparable damage to the château by housing a museum here.

In the **Franco-Prussian War** Versailles became the HQ of the German armies operating against Paris. The château was used as a hospital and Moltke occupied no. 38 Blvd de la Reine. On 18 January 1871, King Wilhelm I of Prussia was crowned German Emperor in the Galerie des Glaces; on 26 January the peace preliminaries were signed at Bismarck's quarters at 20 Rue de Provence. In 1871–75 the National Assembly sat in the opera-house, and here the Third Republic was confirmed on 25 February 1875. The general restoration of the complex began after the appointment of Pierre de Nolhac as curator in 1887.

During the **First World War** Versailles was the seat of the Allied War Council, and the Peace Treaty with Germany was signed in the Galerie des Glaces on 28 June 1919. Further extensive restorations were made in 1928–32, thanks largely to the donations of the Rockefeller Foundation, and were continued after the Second World War under the curatorship of Gerald van der Kemp. During that war, the Allied GHQ was at Versailles from September 1944 until the following May, and many buildings were requisitioned by the military.

The wide Avenues de St-Cloud, de Paris and de Sceaux converge on Pl. d'Armes, east of the château, bounded to the east by the **Grandes Ecuries** (south) and the **Petites Ecuries** (north), the royal stables, built by Mansart in 1679–85 to accommodate 200 carriages and 2400 horses. Communards were incarcerated here in 1871. Their façades have been restored, and converted into a **Carriage Museum**, containing Louis XVIII's hearse. It is advisable to check opening hours (☎ 01 30 83 77 88).

The Château de Versailles

The gateway to Château de Versailles, with Mansart's original grille, is flanked by groups of sculptures: (right) *France Victorious over the Empire* by Marsy, and *Victorious over Spain* by Girardon; and left, *Peace* by Tuby and *Abundance* by Coysevox. The Avant-Cour or Cour des Ministres is bounded by detached wings once assigned to secretaries of state. In the centre is the *Equestrian Statue of Louis XIV* (erected 1836) and beyond, the Cour Royale, between two colonnaded pavilions dating from 1772 (right) and 1829.

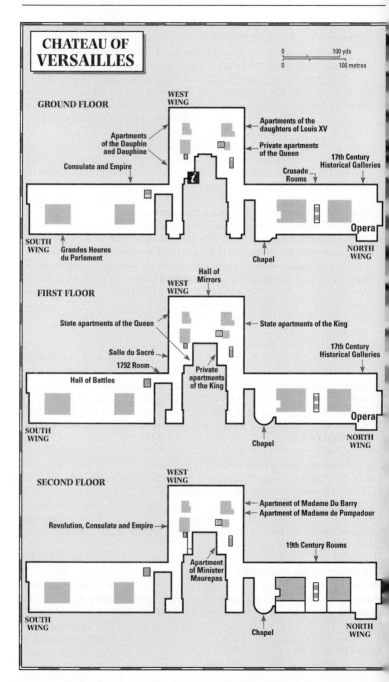

CHATEAU OF VERSAILLES

0   100 yds
0   100 metres

GROUND FLOOR

WEST WING

Apartments of the daughters of Louis XV

Apartments of the Dauphin and Dauphine

Private apartments of the Queen

Consulate and Empire

17th Century Historical Galleries

Crusade Rooms

SOUTH WING

Grandes Heures du Parlement

Chapel

Opera

NORTH WING

FIRST FLOOR

Hall of Mirrors

WEST WING

State apartments of the Queen

State apartments of the King

Salle du Sacré

1792 Room

Hall of Battles

Private apartments of the King

17th Century Historical Galleries

SOUTH WING

Chapel

Opera

NORTH WING

SECOND FLOOR

WEST WING

Apartment of Madame Du Barry

Apartment of Madame de Pompadour

Revolution, Consulate and Empire

19th Century Rooms

Apartment of Minister Maurepas

SOUTH WING

Chapel

NORTH WING

In the time of Louis XIV, only those who possessed the 'honours of the Louvres'—called 'cousin' by the king, and who had the right to bring their coach or chair or liveried servants into the great Courtyard of the Louvre—had the right to enter by this route.

Note the **Cour de Marbre**, a deep, marble-paved recess at the end of the Cour Royale; this was the courtyard of Louis XIII's château and the nucleus of the whole, before being transformed by Le Vau and Mansart.

Independent non-guided (audioguides available) ~ Entrance A

Ground floor Adjacent to the Entrance Hall is the Vestibule de la Chapelle, with handsome carved and gilded doors and containing a marble relief by Nicolas and Guillaume Coustou of Louis XIV crossing the Rhine.

The visit begins on the first floor in the upper **Vestibule de la Chapelle**, decorated with *Virtues* by various sculptors, and a striking view of the Chapel and Royal Gallery, the door of which has a chased lock by Desjardins.

Grands Appartements du Roi (King's State Apartments). These have kept their original decorations of marble inlay, sculptured and gilded bronzes, carved doors and painted ceilings, executed under the supervision of Charles le Brun. The original furniture, however, was sold after the Revolution. The **Salon d'Hercule**, one of the most impressive in the château, was fitted up by Louis XV in the Louis XIV style and inaugurated in 1739. The decoration revolves around the great work by Paolo Veronese, *Dinner in the House of Simon* given to Louis XIV in 1664, and placed in a grand moulded frame (Jacques Verberckt), as was the other Veronese, *Eliezer and Rebecca*. On the ceiling is the *Apotheosis of Hercules* by François Lemoyne (1733–36) (restoration due January 2001) and Antoine Vassé (1729–34) was responsible for the elaborate bronzes.

The **Salon de l'Abondance** was used as a refreshment room at royal receptions. The ceiling-painting here is by Houasse (restored). The portraits are those of Louis XIV's eldest son, *The Dauphin*, and of his grandsons, *Duc de Bourgogne* and *Philip of Anjou* (later V of Spain), all by Rigaud; and those of Louis XV by J.-B. van Loo.

The **Salon de Vénus**, the main entrance to the State Apartments, and named after its painted ceiling (also by Houasse), is noteworthy for its marble decorations in early Louis XIV style. The carved doors are by Caffieri; above are bronze bas-reliefs. The mural decorations of this salon (and the succeeding one) are original. In the central alcove is a statue of *Louis XIV in Antique Costume* by Jean Warin; on either side of the room are *trompe-l'oeil* paintings by Jacques Rousseau.

The **Salon de Diane**, the former billiard room, is named after the ceiling painting by Gabriel Blanchard and contains a bust of Louis XIV (then aged 27) by Bernini (1665).

The **Salon de Mars**, once the guardroom, later a gaming-room and subsequently a ballroom and concert-room, has a ceiling by Audran, Jouvenet and Houasse. The paintings above the doors are by Simon Vouet and the portraits of Louis XV and Marie Leszczynska are by Carle van Loo.

The **Salon de Mercure**, a card-room at the time of Louis XIV and where after his death that monarch lay in state for eight days, has a ceiling by J.-B. Champaigne. The tapestry, by Le Brun, was woven at the Gobelins (1668–72); the clock, with automata, of 1706, is by Antoine Morand.

The **Salon d'Apollon**, the former throne-room (in which the thone was silver), is the last room of the King's State Apartments. In the centre of the ceiling is Charles de la Fosse's masterpiece, depicting *Louis XIV (the Roi Soleil) as Apollo in a Chariot Escorted by the Seasons*. The portrait of the king in royal regalia is Rigaud's copy of that in the Louvre.

Galerie des Glaces This, together with its antechambers, the Salons de la Guerre and de la Paix, form a grandiose decorative ensemble. The **Salon de la Guerre**, completed in 1678, keeps its original decoration of coloured marble and bronze and still has three of the six busts of Roman emperors, bequeathed by Mazarin. Over the mantlepiece is a superb stucco medallion of Louis XIV on horseback by Antoine Coysevox. The ceiling painting, the first of a series designed by Charles le Brun, represents *France Victorious, Bearing on her Shield the Portrait of Louis XIV*.

The **Galerie des Glaces** (Hall of Mirrors), 73m long, 10.5m wide and 12.3m high, is a scintillating masterpiece of the Louis XIV style. It was begun by Jules Hardouin-Mansart in 1678 and its decoration, by Le Brun, was completed in 1686. Among the artists employed were Caffieri, Coysevox, Le Comte and Tuby, for the sculptures; Cucci for the mirror frames; and Ladoireau for the trophies on the walls.

The gallery is lit by 17 windows looking on to the park, and facing these are an equivalent number of bevelled mirrors of equal size, altogether an installation of excessive luxury in the 17C. The red marble pilasters have bronze capitals decorated with cocks' heads, fleurs-de-lys and suns. The cornice of gilded stucco is adorned with crowns and the collars of the Orders of the Saint-Esprit and St Michael. The marble statues of Venus, Paris, Mercury and Minerva in the niches are copies from the Antique; some other statues are also copies of originals. Twenty silvered bronze and Bohemian glass chandeliers illuminate the gallery. It is easy to imagine the the the scene, at the time of Louis XIV, with candlelight falling on the lavish furnishings and fabrics.

The central ceiling-painting, by Charles Le Brun, represents *Louis XIV Omnipotent*, while the numerous other paintings depict the subjection of Holland, the Empire and Spain, the Peace imposed by Louis on his enemies, his embassies abroad, the Protection of the Arts and of the People, and the great Foundations established during his reign.

Appartements de la Reine You now enter the **Salon de la Paix**, the queen's card-room. The ceiling completes Le Brun's scheme, depicting *France Bringing the Benefits of Peace to Europe*. Over the chimneypiece (left unfinished by Le Brun) is a painting by Lemoyne (1729), showing *Louis XV Offering Peace*, following his great-grandfather's example.

The **Salle des Gardes de la Reine**, with marble decoration of the period of Louis XIV, retains its ceiling by Noël Coypel. It was here that the revolutionary mob, having mounted the adjacent staircase, burst in, and where three of the Swiss Guards died in the queen's defence.

The **Antichambre**, where the king and queen had supper in public, was formerly the queen's guardroom. The portrait of *Marie-Antoinette in 1779* is by Mme Vigée-Lebrun, who also painted that of the queen with her children (1787). Three other portraits, by Adélaïde Labille-Guiard, depict the *Duchess of Parma*, and *Mesdames Elizabeth, Adélaïde and Victoire* (Louis XIV's aunts). It was in this room on 1 January 1764 that Mozart, not quite eight years old, was invited with his father to attend the Grand Couvert.

The **Salon des Nobles**, or Peers' Salon, was the queen's presence-chamber. The ceiling is by Michel Corneille (d. 1708); the tapestry portrait of *Louis XIV* is by Cozette (after L.-M. van Loo).

The **Chambre de la Reine**, the first of the Grands Appartements de la Reine (Queen's State Apartments), has been lavishly restored to its appearance when Marie-Antoinette fled from it on the morning of 6 October 1789. The chimney-piece has been brought back from the Trianon; the silk hangings were copied at Lyon from pieces of the original material supplied by Lyon in 1787. The balustrade is a reconstruction. Both Marie-Thérèse and Marie Leszczynska died in this room (1683 and 1768, respectively), and the confinements took place here of the queens of France. The jewel cabinet of Marie-Antoinette is by Schwerdfeger (1787); her bust was executed by Félix Lecomte. Above the doors are allegorical paintings of the *Children of Louis XV* by Natoire and de Troy; the grisaille panels of the ceiling are by Boucher.

Following on from the Salles des Gardes is **Salle du Sacré** (Coronation Room), previously referred to as the Grande Salle des Gardes. This room has been restored since its alterations by Louis-Philippe. The ceiling-painting is by Callet and the *dessus de portes* (panel above the door) are by Gérard; on the walls are huge paintings by David depicting *Napoléon Presenting Eagles in the Champ-de-Mars* (1804), and his *Crowning of the Empress Josephine at Notre-Dame* (a copy of that in the Louvre); and *Murat at the Battle of Aboukir* (1799) by Gros.

A small room leads to the **Salle de 1792**, containing military portraits, and originally the Salle des Marchands, to which vendors of goods were admitted for the convenience of the inmates of the palace. The **Escalier des Princes**, by Mansart, gave access to the south wing, once reserved for the princes of the blood.

Musée de l'Histoire de France

The following rooms may be visited independently but are not permanently open. The **Salles des Croisades**, on the ground floor of the North Wing, are five rooms installed by Louis-Philippe. The route to them takes you through a gallery with plaster casts of royal effigies from St-Denis. Decorated in the Troubadour style of the Romantic era, they contain paintings of the important events in the Crusades.

Galerie des Batailles (not permanently open), nearly 120m long, constructed at the time of Louis-Philippe by combining most of the Royal Family's appartements on the first floor, which displays a dull selection of huge canvases representing French military achievement—perhaps the only one of note being *The Battle of Taillebourg*, by Delacroix.

Galeries historiques du Dix-septième Siècle (17C Gallery), North Wing, ground and first floors, is open intermittently as a non-guided visit and consists of 21 rooms. There is an impressive collection of portraits and historical paintings from the accession of the Bourbons to the throne of France to the death of Louis XIV: Anon., *Henri IV in Armour*; Rubens, *Mary de Médicis*; Philippe de Champaigne, *Cardinal Richelieu, Mère Agnès Arnauld*; and there are portraits of the sculptors, artists and writers of the period. These rooms also include *Views of Versailles* by Pierre-Denis Martin; portraits of *La Grande Mademoiselle,*

Henriette d'Angleterre and several court beauties painted by the Beaubrun brothers; Nocret, *Anne of Austria*; and Le Brun, *Turenne*.

The mid-19C **Questel Staircase** ascends to the first floor, with battle scenes by Van der Meulen and an *Equestrian portrait of Louis XIV in 1672*, by Houasse. Views of royal châteaux: *St-Germain and Vincennes* by J.-B. Martin, *Marly* and *Trianon* by P.-D. Martin, *St-Cloud* by Allegrain; also a fine bust by Nicolas Coustou of *Colbert*. Portraits and self-portraits by Antoine Coypel, Largillière, Rigaud, Mignard, and Ferdinand Elle; Antoine Benoist, wax portrait of *Louis XIV aged 68*.

Les grandes heures du Parlement (☎ 01 39 67 07 73) is an independent exhibition in the South Wing on the ground floor presented by the French National Assembly. The museum is laid out around the Chamber, built in 1875, for meetings of Congress, i.e. both houses of parliament, Senate and National Assembly, where amendments to the Constitution are debated and ratified. The exhibition follows the birth of the National Assembly from the Revolutionary period to the present day and explains the history of the French parliamentary system. There are sections devoted to the work of deputies, the role of the Senate, the creation of the European Union and international relations as well as parliaments throughout the world.

Visits with Audioguide commentary ~ Entrance C

Appartements de Louis XIV, du Dauphin et de la Dauphine takes you up the Queen's Staircase to the first floor and through the guard room. To the right is a suite of four rooms known as those of Mme de Maintenon (1635–1719), who later became Louis XIV's confidante. As his morganatic wife, she occupied the suite from 1684 to 1715. Most of the business of state was transacted in her bedchamber. No trace remains of the former decoration of Mme de Maintenon's apartments, which are now occasionally used for temporary exhibitions.

The first room of the Appartements du Roi is the **Salle du Gardes du Roi**, and from there you enter the **Première Antichambre** in which Louis XIV dined in public at 10 o'clock, with his back to the fireplace. The **Seconde Antichambre**, adjacent, is known as the **Salon de l'Oeil-de-Boeuf** since 1701 because of its oval bull's-eye window. It was in this room that the courtiers would wait for admission to the king's *lever*. The decorations are original, including the stucco frieze showing children's games on a gold background by Van Cleve, Hurtrelle and Flamen, among others. A curious picture by Nocret represents the Olympian gods and goddesses with the features of the royal family.

Three doors open onto the Galerie des Glaces and another on the left leads into the Queen's Apartments. (Stairs behind a mirrored door descend to the Apartments of the Dauphin(e), see below.)

The lavishly restored **Chambre du Roi**, Louis XIV's bedchamber (in which he died on 1 September 1715), overlooks the Cour de Marbre. Here the ceremonious *lever* (rising) and *coucher* (retiring) of the king, who used to lunch daily at a little table placed before the middle window, took place. It was from the balcony of this room that Marie-Antoinette and Louis XVI, at La Fayette's suggestion, showed themselves to the mob on 6 October 1789. The decorations of carved wood and the balustrade separating the (reconstructed) bed from the rest of the room have been regilded, but are in part original: most of the rich brocades and other fabrics are modern, woven at Lyon, scrupulously copying the original materials. The sculpture of gilded stucco above is by Nicolas Coustou. The chimneypieces date from 1761, with bronzes by Caffieri; the bust of *Louis XIV* is by Coysevox. There is a self-portrait by Van Dyck.

The adjacent **Cabinet du Conseil**, dates in its present form from 1755, with boiseries by Antoine Rousseau. Note the two Sèvres vases and the table on which the Treaty of Versailles was signed in 1783.

From the Cabinet du Conseil you return through the **Galerie des Glaces** (see above) back to the Oeil-de-Boeuf room, with paintings by Lancret, and descend to the ground floor, to the **Apartments of the Dauphin and Dauphine**. The rooms look out onto the gardens and were, in their time, occupied by eight dauphins and their wives. They have been repeatedly altered and much of the original decoration was spoiled or even destroyed by Louis-Philippe.

The Antichambre gives access to the Dauphin's **Seconde Antichambre** which contains some of Nattier's masterpieces: *Marie Leszczynska in a Houserobe*; *Madame Adélaïde*, and a sketch for *Madame Adélaïde Disguised as Air*, part of a decoration for the Large Drawing Room.

The **Chambre** with green decoration, later the bedroom of the Dauphin Louis (1729–65), son of Louis XV, with portraits by Tocqué of *Marie-Thérèse-Antoinette-Raphaelle d'Espagne*; Louis-Michel van Loo, *Felipe V of Spain* and *Elisabeth Farnese*; Nattier, *Louise-Elisabeth de France* (Duchess of Parma); also the copy, made by Marie Leszczynska, of a painting of a farm by Oudry, signed Marie, Reine de France. The splendid furnishings include *boiseries* by Verberckt, a red lacquer cabinet by Bernard van Rysenburgh, and the marble chimneypiece with figures by Caffieri; the **Grand Cabinet** (Dauphin's Study), at the corner of the building, has a splendid view of the gardens. Regilt, and with chairs by Georges Jacob and a flat-topped desk by van Rysenburgh, it also contains portraits of the *Daughters of Louis XV* by Nattier and a terrestrial and celestial globe by Mancelle, 1781. The **Small Library** has four seascapes by Joseph Vernet.

The **Cabinet de la Dauphine** (Inner Room) retains part of its charming woodwork decoration and over the doors are Oudry, *The Four Seasons*, and Nattier, *Marie-Josèphe de Saxe*. The chambre also has a *lit à la polonaise* (with four columns and an ornate canopy). Louis XVI, Louis XVIII and Charles X were born in this room, which was also the bedroom of Marie-Antoinette on her arrival in France from Vienna in May 1770.

In the **Grand Cabinet** are paintings by, Jean-Baptiste van Loo, *Stanislas Leszczynski and Catherine Opalinska, Queen of Poland*; Belle, *Marie Leszczynska and the Dauphin*; Rigaud, *Samuel Bernard the banker*; Stiemart (after Rigaud), *Cardinal Fleury*; School of Rigaud, *Philibert Orry*; Tocqué, *Marquis de Matignon*.

The **Seconde Antichambre** has several portraits by Alexis Simon Belle, among them *Marie-Anne-Victoire* (Maria-Anna-Victoria; Infanta of Spain, betrothed to Louis XV when she was three, who in 1729 married the future José of Portugal); attributed to Pierre Gobert (after Nattier), *Peter the Great of Russia* (who visited Versailles in May 1717); François Stiemart, *Marie Leszczynska*; J.-B. van Loo and Parrocel, *Louis XV on Horseback*; J.-L. Lemoyne, *Bust of Philippe, Duc d'Orléans*. The **Première Antichambre** or Guard Room contains Rigaud; *Louis XV as a child*; Santerre, *The Regent Orléans*; Largillière, two unknown members of the Parlement; Pierre-Denis Martin (le Jeune), *Departure of Louis XV from the Lit de Justice* and *The Consecration of Louis XV at Reims*.

Guided visits

Chapel, Opéra and Private Apartments of Louis XV and Louis XVI can only be visited on a guided tour—the chapel is open once a month for services (enquire at the information desk).

The **Chapel**, with its colonnade of Corinthian columns, was begun by Jules Hardouin-Mansart in 1699 and completed in 1710 by Robert de Cotte. The high altar is of marble and bronze with sculptures by Van Clève, above which is the organ. François Couperin was one of the great organists who played here. The central ceiling-painting is by Antoine Coypel, and above the royal pew is a *Descent of the Holy Ghost* by Jouvenet.

The **Opéra**, or **Salle de Spectacles**, at the far end of the North Wing, is reached through two galleries. The Foyer de l'Opéra, retains its 18C decoration by Pajou. The Opéra, although planned in the 1680s, was built for Louis XV by Gabriel in 1770. It was first used on the occasion of the marriage of the Dauphin (Louis XVI) and Marie-Antoinette, when Lully's *Perseus* was performed. It was repainted under Louis-Philippe, and in 1855 was the scene of a banquet given in honour of the King of Sardinia's theatre in Turin, it is a perfect example of Louis XV decoration, having been skilfully restored (1955–57) by Japy, even the upholstery being copied from the original specifications. Seating 700 spectators and with a stage second in size only to the Paris Opéra Garnier, it is now reserved for rare gala performances.

On the first floor of the north side of the Cour de Marbre, you visit the **Cabinets du Roi** or **Petits Appartements du Roi** (private apartments of the king), known as the Inner Apartments in Louis XIV's day, where the king kept his most precious art treasures. This series of rooms was transformed by Louis XV in 1735 to provide a retreat from the tedious etiquette of his court.

The **Petits Appartements de Louis XV et de Louis XVI** include the **Chambre de Louis XV**, the bedroom in which the king died of smallpox on 10 May 1774; with boiseries by Jacques Verberckt and a bust of his mother, the *Duchesse de Bourgogne*, by Coysevox. The **Cabinet de la Pendule** derives its name from Passemant's clock, placed here in 1754, executed by Dauthiau, with chased designs by Caffieri, surmounted by a crystal globe marking the phases of the sun, moon and planets: note also the barometer by J.-B. Lemaire.

The **Cabinet des Chiens**, with a frieze of hunting scenes and decorated with flower-paintings, was occupied by lackeys and the king's favourite hounds. Adjacent is the **Salle à Manger des Retours de Chasse** overlooking the much-altered Cour des Cerfs.

The **Cabinet Intérieur du Roi**, in the angle, is the grandest room in the apartment, with panelling and mirror frames considered the finest made by Verberckt. The original furniture of the time of Louis XV is still in place, with the famous rolltop desk by Oeben and Riesener (1760–68). The **Arrière Cabinet** or Private Study, where Louis XV met his secret agents, led into the apartments of Madame Adélaïde.

The **Cabinet de Musique de Mme Adélaïde**, also with fine gilded *boiseries* by Verberckt, is where, in December 1763, Mozart played the harpsichord before Mme Adélaïde (1732–1800, 4th daughter of Louis XV) and other members of the family. The **Bibliothèque de Louis XVI** (with Louis-XV furniture) was decorated by Antoine Rousseau. The chimneypiece is by Boizot and Gouthière, and the candelabrum is attributed to Thomire.

The **Salle à Manger** took its present shape in 1769. Sometimes known as the Porcelain Room, as an exhibition of Sèvres was held here each Christmas in Louis XVI's time, it is elegant with blue drapes and Sèvres porcelain plaques of hunting scenes. The chairs, 1786, are by Séné and Boulard. The Salle de Billiard and Salon des Jeux, where Louis XIV's collections of paintings and gems were displayed, became part of Mme Adélaïde's suite.

Petits Appartements de la Reine Marie-Antoinette The guided tour of these apartments starts on the first floor of the south side of the Cour de Marbre, after ascending the Queen's Staircase and crossing the guard room via an access made especially for today's visitors.

The small and cramped private suite of Marie-Antoinette, situated between the state rooms and courtyards, give a fascinating insight into the private life of the court. The apartment retains its superb decoration of the time of Marie-Antoinette. Among the rooms visited are the **Salle de Bains** and the **Nouvelle Bibliothèque** used by the ladies-in-waiting. In the **Salon de la Reine**, with elaborate decoration by the brothers Rousseau, she received her intimate friends, and her musicians, Gluck and Grétry, and sat to Mme Vigée-Lebrun for her portraits. Next is the **Bibliothèque**, with imitation bookshelves over the doors and adjustable shelving. The **Méridienne** or Sofa Room, is an octagonal room redesigned by Mique in 1781, with the Queen's day bed, the original pedestal table and two armchairs by Georges Jacob with replica upholstery. Then there are two very small rooms, the second the former boudoir of the Duchesse de Bourgogne with its wood panelling of 1701.

The visit continues with exquisite rooms used by the Queen for informal entertaining. These include the **Salle à Manger**. Next to this is a bijou **salon** (Billiard Room, it can only hold a maximum of 10 people) for withdrawing after the meal, the modern fabrics copied from the original. There was a direct and discreet route between the King's and Queen's bedroom along back corridors, looking over the Dauphin's rooms.

The tour then descends to the ground floor to the part of a three-room apartment adapted in 1784 for Marie-Antoinette, comprising a charming pale blue and white **Salle de Bains** with a Louis XVI bed, and a Bibliothèque, its décor lost in the 19C.

Cross the **Galerie Basse**, two parallel galleries below the Galerie des Glaces, between courtyard and garden. Completely altered since Le Vau designed it in 1669, the steps between the two compensate for the difference in level between the Old and New Châteaux. This was where Molière gave several of his plays, including the first performance of *Tartuffe* (1664); it has been remodelled and contains several false arches. This brings you to a chambre, in pale green, with Georges Jacob bed and chairs and a dressing table by Riesener. It contains the last state portrait of Marie-Antoinette (1788) by Vigée-Lebrun.

The four rooms—the Grand Cabinet, Inner Cabinet, Antichambre and Chambre—which make up the **Appartements du Capitaine des Gardes**, also part of this visit, contain some important paintings by Duplessis and Hubert Robert; also a painting of Marie-Antoinette, aged ten, dancing at Schönbrunn. On a chest-of-drawers is a copy of the famous diamond necklace which was the subject of a scandal in 1785. A scheming woman, calling herself Countess de la Motte-Valois, perusaded Cardinal de Rohan to buy the necklace to give to Queen Marie-Antoinette. When the necklace subsequently disappeared the Cardinal was arrested at Versailles. The scandal which ensued brought discredit on the Queen despite the fact that she was not at all implicated in the affair.

Appartements de Mme de Pompadour et de Mme du Barry (temporarily closed since the storms of 1999). These adjacent rooms are on the attic floor of the North Wing (guided visit). Mme de Pompadour (1721–64) occupied her diminutive suite from 1745 to 1750 when, no longer the king's mistress but still his confidante, she moved to the ground floor. Mme du Barry (1743–93), lived in these apartments from 1769–74 only. The beautiful *boiseries* have been restored and repainted in their original colours.

18C rooms and Appartments des filles de Louis XV, Mesdames Victoire and Adélaïde may only be visited by appointment (for groups or individuals at group rates). These rooms are on the ground floor adjacent to the Royal Apartments, and include the Hall of the States General.

The **Première Salle**, once part of the former Bathing Apartment (a suite of bathrooms), was later occupied by Mme Victoire, an accomplished musician to whom Mozart dedicated his first six harpsichord sonatas in 1784. The paintings are: Barthémy Olivier, *The English Tea-Party*, with Mozart at the harpsichord, and J.-B. Charpentier, *The Cup of Chocolate*; there also works by L.-M. van Loo and Tocqué. In the following rooms are paintings over the door of the *Fables of La Fontaine* by Oudry, and a commode by Riesener. There are also a harpsichord by Blanchet, some good *boiseries* and furniture, and portraits such as Nattier, *Mme Adélaïde*.

The first room of **Mme Adélaïde's Apartments**, has *dessus des portes* by J.-B. Restout of the *The Seasons*. The **Chambre** in which Mme de Pompadour died has fine chairs by Foliot and the bust of the Dauphin by Pajou. The **Grand Cabinet** is endowed with a Gagliano violin belonging to Mme Adélaïde.

Adjoining the landing of the Escalier de la Reine is the Escalier de Stuc, which ascends to the second floor where, in the Attique de Chimay and Attique du Midi, are displayed an outstanding **Collection of Historical Paintings** illustrating the early Napoleonic period. Visits by appointment only.

Several rooms contain views of the many battles fought in the Revolutionary and Napoleonic wars, among them works by Louis-François Lejeune, Giuseppe-Pietro Bagetti, Nicolas-Antoine Taunay, Gén. Bacler d'Albe and Carle Vernet. Among the men and moments recorded on canvas are Gros, *Napoléon at Arcole*; one of five copies made by David of his *Napoléon crossing the Alps*; J.-F. Hue, *Napoléon visiting camp at Boulogne*. War at sea is also illustrated, including George Healy's copies of Hoppner's portraits of *Lord Nelson* and *Lord St Vincent*, and of Lawrence's *William Pitt*.

Portraits of the imperial family are dominated by Gérard's *Napoléon as Emperor of the French*, also his *Madame Mère*; Robert Lefèvre, *Portrait of Napoléon*; F.-A. Lethière, *Josephine*; Vigée-Lebrun, *Portrait of Marie-Annunciade-Caroline Bonaparte*. Also an unfinished pastel of *Marie-Antoinette* by Alexandre Kucharsky; Girodet , *Chateaubriand* and *J.-B. Bellay, Deputy for St. Dominique*; David, *Pope Pius VII*; Gérard, *Comte Regnaud de St. Jean d'Angely* and *Murat*.

Other rooms, devoted to the Restoration of the Bourbons, the July Monarchy, Second Empire and Third Republic are on the second floor of the North Wing.

The Gardens of Versailles

The magnificent gardens are reached by passages leading north and south of the Cour Royale. Laid out with geometrical precision, they have carefully planned vistas, straight tree-lined walks, artificial lakes and ponds. Interspersed among the groves and clumps of trees, lawns and terraces, are statues and vases of marble and bronze. The ultimate embellishment is the famous fountains. Some of the more fragile or damaged original statues have been replaced by casts.

History of the gardens

André le Nôtre (1613–1708), the celebrated landscape-gardener, designed the gardens for Louis XIV. The fountains and hydraulic machinery were the work of Jules Hardouin-Mansart and the engineer François Francini, while the sculptural decoration was carried out under the supervision of Le Brun and Mignard.

The gardens were first laid out in 1661–68. The preliminary work of levelling and draining the site was prodigious and thousands of trees were brought here from all parts. Inspired by Italian originals, but interpreted on a scale hitherto unknown, Versailles represents the masterpiece of French gardening. In their general lines and their Classical sculptural decoration, the gardens remain as planned, but it was not until the 18C that trees were planted to the present extent, so that what we now see are really the gardens of Louis XV and Louis XVI.

A 20-year programme of replanting provoked by the gales of 1990 was violently interrupted by the devastating storm of 25–26 December 1999, when some 10,000 trees were blown down. Among the 80 per cent of rare species and historic trees lost were two junipers planted by Marie Antoinette, the Virginian Tulip tree, and the Cedar planted in 1772 near the Hameau. The huge task of replanting began in March 2000 and has engendered enormous support from the public and from French, American and Canadian enterprises as well as Franco-American associations.

• The **gardens and park** are normally open from 07.00 until dusk in the summer (from 08.00 in winter) to pedestrians (no picnics); cars are admitted to the park on payment, and to the Trianons (via Blvd de la Reine, north of the château). A *petit train* (☎ 01 39 54 22 00) and *calèches* (☎ 01 30 97 04 04) provide transport around part of the gardens and to the Trianons most days. The **fountains** play on certain Sundays in May–Oct only (for information, ☎ 01 30 83 77 88). As well as the Grandes Eaux Musicales and the Grandes Fêtes de Nuit, there is a variety of performances in the gardens (information ☎ 01 30 83 78 88).

The central axis of the main terrace commands wonderful views, and the terrace itself is adorned with bronze statues after the Antique, cast by the Keller brothers, amongst them, *Apollo, Bacchus* and *Silenus*; also marble vases of *War* by Antoine Coysevox, and Peace by Tuby. The **Parterre d'Eau** (Water Garden), has two large ornamental pools decorated with bronzes (1690).

On the right (north) of the terrace extends the **Parterre du Nord**, where the original design of Le Nôtre has been largely respected. Just beyond is the **Fontaine de la Pyramide** by François Girardon, and among the sculptures in the cross-walk (left) is *Winter*, also by Girardon. The **Allée d'Eau**, designed by Perrault and Le Brun (1676–88), leads directly to the **Bassin de Neptune** (1740), the largest fountain-basin in the gardens.

The **Bosquet des Trois Fontaines** (parallel to the Allée d'Eau), runs parallel to the main axis, passing (right) the **Bains d'Apollon**, within a grove laid out by Hubert Robert under Louis XVI, in a romantic spirit very different from Le Nôtre's formal symmetry.

To the left of the Parterre d'Eau is the **South Garden**, whose steps are surrounded by 17C sculptures of *Children mounted on Sphinxes* (Sarrazin and Lerambert). You then come to the **Orangerie** by Mansart, into which Communards were herded in 1871 prior to their imprisonment. Two flights of steps, known as the Cent Marches, descend alongside it.

Further south, beyond the St-Cyr road, you see **Pièce d'Eau des Suisses** (682m long by 134m wide), excavated in 1678–82 by the Swiss Guards, many of whom are said to have died of malaria during the operation.

Return to the Parterre d'Eau and continue west to the **Marches de Latone**, monumental flights of steps. From here before you is the magnificent perspective of the gardens, whose symbolic layout is based on the myth of Apollo. And in the opposite direction the full impact of the façade of the château comes into focus. Flanking the steps are the Fountains of Diana and of Dawn, with statues of *Air* by Etienne le Hongre, and *Diana the Huntress* by Martin Desjardins.

The steps descend to the oval **Bassin de Latone** (Latona, or Leto, mother of Artemis and Apollo, insulted by Lycian peasants, had them turned into frogs by Zeus.) At the foot of the steps is Latona with her Children Apollo and Diana.

Further west extends the so-called **Tapis Vert** (or Allée Royale), a lawn 330m long and 36m wide, lined with marble vases and statues, many of them copies from the Antique. On the left is *Venus* by Pierre le Gros and *Achilles at Scyros* by Vigier. Towards its far end (right) is the entrance to the **Bosquet des Dômes**, with several statues, including *Acis and Galatea* by Tuby.

Almost opposite, beyond the far side (south) of the Tapis Vert, in the **Bosquet de la Colonnade**, is a circle of marble arches by Mansart (1685–88), in the centre of which once stood the *Rape of Proserpine* by Girardon.

At the far end of the Tapis Vert is the **Bassin d'Apollon**, with the impressive group of *Apollo's Chariot* by Tuby in the centre. To the right is the Petite Venise, where Louis XIV's Venetian gondoliers were housed.

Beyond the Bassin d'Apollon, and separated from the gardens by railings, is the **Petit Parc**, divided by the **Grand Canal**, 1650m long and 62m wide, the scene of Louis XIV's boating parties. Almost at its central point it is crossed by a transverse arm (c 1070m), extending from the Grand Trianon, to the north, to the few remaining buildings of the former royal menagerie.

To return to the château, cross the **Salle des Marronniers**, a chestnut grove behind the Colonnade, to pass the Bassin de Saturne or de l'Hiver. South of this is the Bassin du Miroir, followed by the Bassin de Bacchus or de l'Automne, with sculptures by Girardon and Marsy and then, right, the glade known as the Bosquet de la Reine.

The most direct pedestrian approach to the Trianons and the Hameau is to follow the Allée d'Eau leading north from the terrace behind the central block of the palace to the Grille de Neptune, then turn left and veer slightly northwest along the Av. de Trianon, approximately 20 minutes' brisk walk. But a more interesting route is to bear half right (northwest) from the Grand Canal (see above and on plan).

The Grand Trianon

The Grand Trianon, a miniature palace designed by Jules Hardouin-Mansart and Robert de Cotte, was built for Louis XIV in 1687 as a retreat from the formality of court life, although with sumptuous marble decorations comparable with those of Versailles itself. It replaced a flimsy summer-house for picnics, tiled inside with blue and white Delftware, and known as the 'Porcelain Trianon', erected on the site of the village of Trianon, which had been razed in 1663.

The buildings, sacked at the Revolution, were redecorated for Napoléon, who frequently stayed here with Marie-Louise, his second wife, and the Empire furniture which he installed still remains. In the 1960s, accurate work of reproduction of fabrics of the period was undertaken and the Grand Trianon was renovated to receive heads of state on official visits.

On the left of the courtyard, with the open colonnade or peristyle ahead, is the visitors' entrance. Off the entrance, the **vestibule** contains views of Versailles and Chambord by Allegrain and Pierre-Denis Martin respectively, and a console table by Jacob-Desmalter.

In the **left wing** a corridor leads to **Empress Josephine's Boudoir**, containing a gondola-shaped sofa, to the right of which is the splendidly mirrored Salon des Glaces, furnished with a handsome set of white and gilt chairs covered with Beauvais tapestry. The **Salon des Colonnes** is one of the most beautiful rooms in the Trianon, with Napoléon's bed (1809) from the Tuileries. The **Antichambre de la Chapelle** was transformed in 1691, but still contains a small sanctuary. Beyond is the open peristyle of Languedoc marble pillars.

Cross the peristyle (originally an open loggia) to the **right wing**, first entering the Salon Rond, with paintings entitled *Flowers and Fruit of America* by Desportes. At the time of Louis XIV, this served as a vestibule opening onto a theatre which stood here until 1703, then the apartment was further transformed in the 18C and 19C. The **Salon de Musique** has a bronze table with Vosges granite top, two consoles by Jacob-Desmalter, and the Beauvais tapestry-covered set of chairs. Next comes the Grand Salon and Salon des Malachite, the latter with a malachite bowl given by Alexander I of Russia after the Treaty of Tilsit in 1807.

From the adjoining Salon Frais, built to protect fragile blooms in the upper garden, with four *Views of Versailles* by J.-B. Martin, you turn left into the gallery, decorated by Mansart, with good views south over the terrace. It contains views of the *Gardens of Versailles and Trianon*, at the time of Louis XIV, 21 by Jean Cotelle (1645–1708), two by Allegrain and one by J.-B. Martin. The Salon des Jardins looks out onto the Grand Canal. The suite of rooms beyond is not open to the public. Adjacent to the Salon Frais is the **Salon des Sources**, with *Views of Versailles* by P.-D. Martin (1663–1742) and Charles Chastelain (1672–1740).

The next five rooms which make up the **Appartement de l'Empereur** are visited only with a guide. They once formed the Apartments of Mme de Maintenon, and were later occupied by Stanislas Leszczynski, former king of Poland (1741), Mme de Pompadour, and Napoléon with Marie-Louise.

The **gardens** were laid out by Mansart and Le Nôtre. To the west is the Water Buffet (the main fountain), also designed by Mansart, with bas-reliefs and figures of *Neptune* and *Amphitrite*. A bridge leads from the Jardin du Roi, behind the palace, to the gardens of the Petit Trianon.

The Petit Trianon

To the east is the Petit Trianon (1762–68), with two floors and an attic storey. This charming pavilion was built by Ange-Jacques Gabriel for Louis XV as a country retreat for himself and Mme de Pompadour, who did not live to see it completed. Mme du Barry then occupied it. It was a favourite residence of Marie-Antoinette, and was subsequently occupied by Pauline Borghese, Napoléon's sister. To the left of the courtyard is a chapel.

Many of the rooms in the Petit Trianon retain their original decoration, including chimneypieces by Guibert in the dining room and grand salon. In the dining room, traces of a trap-door, through which it was intended that tables would appear ready-laid, are still visible in the floor. The entrance is in the former billiard room and the first floor is open to the public for a non-guided visit of ten rooms all containing paintings and furnishings of quality. The attic storey may be visited on a guided tour (☎ 01 30 84 76 18).

The **gardens** of the Petit Trianon were originally a *ménagerie* and botanical garden laid out by Bernard de Jussieu for Louis XV, a passionate botanist, but were altered for Marie-Antoinette in the English style (1774–86). Louis XVI had a little garden here where he liked to pick his own herbs.

To the west of the main building is the **French Garden Pavilion**, built in 1750 by Gabriel, with a good view of the façade of the palace. To the north is the **theatre** (1780; by Richard Mique), where Marie-Antoinette made her début in court theatricals, beyond which is the octagonal **Belvedere** (also by Mique), with charming interior decoration by Le Riche, overlooking a small lake. The queen was resting in a grotto here when, on 6 October 1789, she was told the news that a revolting mob had broken into Versailles.

Some few minutes' walk to the northeast, on the far side of a larger lake, are remains of the **Hameau**, a theatrical hamlet built in 1783 for Marie-Antoinette to indulge her taste for nature, as popularised by Jean-Jacques Rousseau. The ensemble was, in fact, a working farm whose produce was used at the château. It comprises a mill, the Maison de la Reine (with a dining-room, drawing room, and Chinese cabinet room, plus a billiard room), the boudoir on the right; a pigeon-cote and the Tour de Marlborough.

You can return past the Temple d'Amour (1778; by Mique), with its Corinthian colonnade and Mouchy's copy (1780) of Bouchardon's statue of *Cupid cutting his bow from the club of Hercules*, to return to the courtyard of the Petit Trianon, and the exit.

Petit Trianon

37 • Malmaison

Rueil-Malmaison

Getting there
Rueil-Malmaison is reached either by road (N13; 7.5km) from the Pont de Neuilly, or by RER, Line A (direction St-Germain-en-Laye), to Rueil-Malmaison, and the 144, 241, 244 or 467 bus to the town centre and walk across the park of Bois-Préau. Alternatively, from La Défense take the bus no. 258 to the château.

Tourist information
Tourist Information Office, 160 Avenue Paul-Doumer, 92500-Rueil-Malmaison, ☎ 01 47 32 35 75, www.rueil-tourisme.com.

In Rueil Malmaison:
Auberge du Théâtre, 4 Rue du Bel Air, ☎ 01 47 77 04 36. Intimate setting, quality cooking reasonably priced, £

Chanteric, 1 Place Richelieu, ☎ 01 47 08 46 91. Hearty dishes of southwestern France, £

El Chiquito, 126 Avenue Paul-Doumer, ☎ 01 47 51 00 53. Elegant and refined seafood restaurant, ££

Le Jardin Clos, 17 Rue Eugène-Labiche, ☎ 01 47 08 03 11. Traditional cuisine and setting, with garden, £

La Terrasse, 28 Rue de la Libération, ☎ 01 47 16 02 80. Rustic setting for gastronomic delights, ££

In Rueil 2000:
Côté Italie, 5 Place des Impressionnistes, ☎ 01 47 08 47 62. Italian cooking with terrace on the banks of the Seine, £

La Maison Fournaise, Ile des Impressionistes, ☎ 01 30 71 41 91. The *guinguette* once patronised by the Impressionist painters, £

Rueil-Malmaison, which is on the banks of the Seine to the west of Paris, has close associations with the early Empire period through the Châteaux of Malmaison and of Bois-Préau. And Malmaison has a particular connection with the Empress Joséphine, as the grounds provided the opportunity for her to indulge her passion for plants. The suffix Malmaison was added in 1928.

This is an attractive town with walks along the Seine as well as a Japanese and a rose garden near the tourist office. In the church of Rueil (1584, west façade of 1635 by Lemercier), is the tomb of the Empress Joséphine (1825), and that of Hortense de Beauharnais is in the chapel erected in 1858 by her son, Napoléon III. He also donated the 15C Florentine organ-case by Baccio d'Agnolo. In the former Mairie is a fascinating **Museum of Local History** (open 14.30–18.00 Mon-Sat) ranging from the neolithic period to the time when the Impressionists patronised the *guinguettes* on the banks and the islands of the Seine near Rueil.

The Château de Malmaison

• Open Mon, Wed, Thur, Fri 10.00–12.00, 13.30–16.30; Sat, Sun 10.00–17.00; closed Tues, 1/1, 25/12. ☎ 01 41 29 05 55; combined ticket with Bois-Préau.

History of the Château de Malmaison

The château was built c 1620 and became, from 1799, the country residence of Napoléon and Joséphine, who chose it because of the park then covering 800 hectares, with the intention of rebuilding the house. The work of transforming the interior was entrusted to Fontaine and Percier. Malmaison's interesting collections concentrate on the earlier Napoleonic period, the Consulate and on Joséphine and her children Eugène (1781–1824) and Hortense (1783–1837). Its annexe (see below) is devoted to Napoléon in exile and the Napoleonic legend. The Empire period (1804–15) is covered by the Musée Napoléon I at Fontainebleau.

Joséphine (Marie-Josèphe Rose) Tascher de la Pagerie (1763–1814), born in Martinique, the daughter of a nobleman, had married Alexandre, Vicomte de Beauharnais, in December 1779; he was guillotined in 1794. In 1796 she married Bonaparte, who crowned her Empress in 1804. Josephine retired here, with her children after her divorce in December 1809, and continued to develop her interest in botany and gardening. She died at Malmaison five years later of a chill caught while entertaining visiting allied sovereigns.

Malmaison was later bought by María Cristina of Spain, and in 1861 was acquired by Napoléon III. Despoiled of most of its contents, it was sold in 1896 to the philanthropist Daniel Osiris (1828–1907), who refurnished it and presented the château to the State as a Napoleonic museum.

The house contains superb collections of furniture and fittings, carpets, porcelain, silver, clocks (all in working order), and a variety of objets d'art of the early Napoleonic period: among the furniture are several pieces made specifically for the Consul and his wife by Jacob Frères and other *ébenistes*, and such personal pieces as Joséphine's bed (designed by Jacob-Desmalter), dressing-table, dressing case and embroidery frame. Show-cases display a large number of smaller souvenirs. All the rooms on the ground floor have been returned to their former state according to Fontaine and Percier's original drawings for the interior. Restoration work began in 1985 to recreate the original Neo-classical decor by the painstaking removal of layers (up to eight) of subsequent paint, followed by retouching where necessary.

Ground floor

The enclosed porch or vestibule in the form of a tent was added in 1800. The **Main Hall**, in Antique style, contains marble busts of members of the Bonaparte family; a number of others are displayed throughout the building. The

Château de Malmaison

paintwork in the **Billiard Room** has been stripped back to the original of 1812, and contains some furniture by Jacob-Desmalter from the great gallery and an Empire-style billiard table. In the **Drawing Room** (Salon Doré) are severe Egyptian-style furnishings by Jacob Frères and paintings by Gérard and by Girodet of the *Apotheosis of the French who died in the Revolutionary Wars*, both inspired by Ossian's poems. The restoration of the delightful **Music Room** was completed in April 1999. It contains Joséphine's harp and the pianoforte belonging to Hortense, and at the time of Joséphine was used as a gallery as depicted in the painting by Garnerey.

To the left of the Main Hall, the **Dining Room** has frescoes of dancers by Louis Lafitte inspired by Pompeii, and the **Council Chamber**, the setting for the creation of the Legion of Honour, has been returned to its original design by Percier of a military tent. The adjoining **Library**, also by Percier and Fontaine, has books retrieved from Napoléon's personal collection, a travelling chest for books used by him during his campaigns and a the desk from the Tuileries Palace.

Among the many fine portraits in Malmaison are Gérard, *Napoléon in Grenadier Uniform* (1804/5), *Joséphine Seated*, and *Madame Mère*; Isabey's drawing of *Napoléon as First Consul at Malmaison*; Bacler d'Albe, *Gén. Bonaparte* (1796/7); Girodet, *Queen Hortense*; David's original of *Bonaparte crossing the St-Bernard Pass* (five replicas elsewhere); Gros, *The First Consul after Marengo*; Pierre-Paul Prud'hon, the *Empress Joséphine* c 1809; also paintings collected by Joséphine who had a penchant for Troubadour-style works inspired by the Middle Ages.

At the foot of the stairs to the first floor is a *Head of Napoléon* by Canova. On this floor were the apartments of Napoléon, of Hortense and Eugène, and of Joséphine. The Emperor's rooms, in part reconstructed, display various memorabilia, and his former **Bedroom** replicates the original as closely as possible. The painting of *Joséphine* (1809) by Gros shows the park of Malmaison. The small rooms of Joséphine's accommodation have altered less. Her **State Bedroom**, restored as it was after 1812 to an unusual but elegant red and gold tent-like oval, is where she died. The Empress's **Ordinary Bedroom,** which she preferred, is brighter and lighter and due to be restored. Other rooms contain the Austerlitz Table, in Sèvres porcelain and bronze, commemorating Napoléon's victory; porcelain including the beautiful Egyptian tea set (Sèvres), Napoléon's last present to Joséphine before the divorce; mementos of friends of the Empress (including a bust of *Charles James Fox* by Ann Seymour Damer); a book by Redouté; and exhibits linked with the history of Malmaison.

On the **second floor** are Joséphine's original wardrobes and various court apparel, including two dresses that belonged to her. There is also space for temporary exhibitions.

In the **gardens**, of which only six hectares remain of 200, are beds planted with those varieties of rose grown by Joséphine with the help, until 1805, of her English gardener, Mr Howatson. The gardens were celebrated in their time and her blooms were later reproduced in coloured drawing by Pierre-Joseph Redouté. The famous cedar planted by Joséphine to celebrate the victory of Marengo in June 1800 can be seen from the music room.

To the left of the entrance lodge, on your way out, is the **Coach House**, with Napoléon's *landau en berline* used at Waterloo and taken by Blücher, also the St-Helena hearse, presented by Queen Victoria. Behind is the **Pavillon Osiris**, with collections of caricatures, medallions and snuffboxes propagating the Napoleonic legend, and a portrait of *Tsar Alexander I* by Gérard. Beyond the other side of the entrance drive is a summer-house used as a study by Napoléon when First Consul.

From opposite the entrance, a few minutes' walk through the park will take you to the **Château de Bois-Préau**, dating from 1700, and acquired by Joséphine in January 1810 as an annexe in which to accommodate her entourage and visitors, and to house part of her collections. It was later sold and in 1926 bequeathed to the State by its then American owner, the millionaire Edward Tuck (see also Petit-Palais, Ch. 27). Open Thur–Sun summer 12.30–18.30, winter 12.30–18.00, closed Tues and public holidays. At the time of writing the Château de Bois-Préau is closed for renovation and no date has been announced for the reopening.

Rooms on the first floor are devoted exclusively to the period of Napoléon's years of exile. On 17 October 1815 he disembarked from the *Northumberland* and settled in his enforced residence at Longwood on the remote south Atlantic island of St-Helena, where—under the eye of Sir Hudson Lowe, the governor—he was to remain until his death on 5 May 1821.

Here, in addition to the camp-bed in which he died, are numerous souvenirs of his years of captivity, among them his *nécessaire* no. 3 (by Biennais), silver flasks and other plate, his grey coat and hat, boots and slippers, apart from furniture; a book given to Napoléon by Lord Holland; Marchand's sketch of the dead emperor; and his death-mask, moulded by Antommarchi, his Corsican doctor. His remains were brought back to France and placed in Les Invalides in December 1840; see p 153.

The **Petite Malmaison**, now privately owned, was constructed in 1805 for Joséphine as a place to receive and entertain visitors when they visited the greenhouses, which were originally attached to it but no longer exist. The house can be visited by appointment (☎ 01 47 49 48 15) and is open on Sundays from 1 June–30 Sept.

Rueil 2000 is a surprisingly attractive modern area on the banks of the Seine looking out towards the Ile de Chatou, also known as the Ile des Impressionnistes (off the N190). On the island is the last remaining *guinguette* (an out-of-town café which also offers music and dancing), the *Maison Fournaise*, now a restaurant (☎ 01 30 71 41 91) with a museum (Thur–Sun 11.00–17.00, ☎ 01 34 80 63 22). As the setting of Renoir's *Le Déjeuner des Canotiers* (1881), this location has been revived as a tribute to the Impressionists who came to paint and eat here. An Impressionist Festival is held one Sunday in June.

The N13 follows the south bank of the Seine, passing at **Bougival**, with a Romanesque church tower, the house where Bizet died (1875) and the *datcha* built by Turgenev, open Sun 10.00–18.00 (groups by appointment only, ☎ 01 45 77 87 12).

38 • St-Germain-en-Laye

Getting there

St-Germain-en-Laye is easily reached from central Paris by the RER Line A1 (about 25 minutes from Charles de Gaule-Etoile station). This line replaces the first railway constructed in France, in 1837, which made the Seine Valley accessible in the 19C to many Parisians, but resulted in the destruction of part of the garden of the château. Bus no. 258 runs from La Défense. **By road**, near the Autoroute A14/N13 interchange, or via the N13 and N184.

Tourist information

Maison Claude Debussy, 38 Rue au Pain, 78100-Saint-Germain-en-Laye, ☎ 01 34 51 05 12, fax 01 34 52 36 01; www.ville-st-germain-en-laye.fr.

Brasserie du Théatre, Pl. du Château, ☎ 01 30 61 28 00. Good traditional brasserie with 1930s' décor, £

Cazaudehore, 1 Av. Prés. Kennedy, ☎ 01 30 61 64 64. Classy classical cuisine, with terrace for al fresco summer eating. Expensive, £££

Ermitage des Loges, 11 Av. des Loges, ☎ 01 39 21 50 90. Mediterranean flavour in summer, £–££

La Feuillantine, 10 Rue des Louviers, ☎ 01 34 51 04 24. Cosy and popular, with reliable food, so book ahead, £

Pavillon Henri IV, 21 Rue Thiers, ☎ 01 39 10 15 15. Fine cooking in an historic setting, £££

La Petite Province, 16 Rue du Vieil Abreuvoir, ☎ 01 39 73 88 88. Wine bar with up-market vintages, serving regional food, £

Tarte Julie, 3 Rue Vieil Abreuvoir, ☎ 01 39 73 95 11. A tea shop specialising, as its name suggests, in tarts, £

Le Vieux Fourneau, 31 Rue Wauthier (near Pl. du Marché), ☎ 01 39 73 10 84. Home cooking, and paella a speciality, £

St-Germain-en-Laye, on the edge of the Forest of St-Germain, is an attractive small town with royal connections. Its splendid site, well-kept 17C–18C mansions and elegant shops make is a worthwhile short expedition from the centre of Paris by RER. The RER station brings you out opposite the huge, recently restored château which dominates the town. The château is home to the important **Musée des Antiquités**, the national museum of prehistory, and stands in a park abutting the forest. From its vast terrace designed by Le Nôtre there are splendid views of Paris. The district has links with several musicians and painters, giving rise to two museums, the **Claude Debussy Musée** and the **Maurice Denis Museum** (Musée du Prieuré). Near St-Germain-en-Laye are the site of the former **Château Marly** at Marly-le-Roi, the Château de Maisons at Maison-Lafitte and, the 20C **Villa Savoye** designed by Le Courbusier.

Château de St-Germain-en-Laye

The strategically sited royal château, dominating a bend of the Seine, was one of the principal seats of the French Court until abandoned by Louis XIV in 1682 in favour of Versailles. It also afforded refuge to Henrietta Maria of England (1644–48). After 1688 this was the residence—and Court—of James II (1633–

1701) who died here, as did his wife, Mary of Modena (1658–1710) who helped the impoverished English who filled St-Germain. In 1862 Eugène Millet restored the old castle to its 16C form and adapted it to house a museum of Gallo-Roman archaeology. The château has been undergoing a long project of restoration to return the exterior to its former grandeur, and improvements have been made to the museum.

History of the Château de St-Germain-en-Laye

The first château, erected in the 12C by Louis VI, was enlarged by St-Louis (Louis IX), who built the free-standing chapel in 1230–38. During the 100 Years War, the Black Prince in 1346 destroyed the castle, sparing the chapel. Later in the 14C, Charles V demolished the ruins and rebuilt the château within the 13C walls incorporating the chapel. Building started again in 1539 during the reign of François I and the work was continued by Philibert de l'Orme for Henri II in 1557, who began the Château-Neuf, below the original castle (or Château-Vieux), a vast structure completed by Henri IV. The infant Mary Stuart lived here from October 1548 until her marriage to François II in April 1558

In 1638 Louis XIV was born in the Château-Neuf, and large sums were spent on improving it during the years 1664–80 while Le Nôtre designed the terrace c 1660. The Château-Neuf was demolished in 1776, except for the Pavillon Henri IV (now a hotel) and the Pavillon Sully, at the foot of the steep slope east of the town, in the suburb of Le Pecq. After the Revolution the castle was used as a military prison for three decades until in 1862 Napoléon III restored the building and installed the Museum of Celtic and Gallo-Roman Antiquities.

In 1962, a century after the first museum, the **Musée des Antiquités Nationales** was opened here. The impressive collections trace the existence of man from his origins to the Middle Ages. The displays, which are in chronological order, have in part been revamped and rearranged. Open 09.00–17.15, closed Tues, certain public holidays, ☎ 01 39 10 13 21. There is a boutique and bookshop. The château is interesting both from the point of view of the building and its history, and the museum.

The **Chapel** (1230–38, ground floor), attributed to Pierre de Montreuil, slightly predates the Sainte-Chapelle in Paris (see Ch. 1). François I and his first wife, Claude de France (1499–1524; daughter of Louis I), Louis XIV and his son, the Grand Dauphin, were baptised here. It has lost most of its furnishings over the years and contains copies only of tombs from the Alyscamps at Arles.

Museum of National Antiquities

Rooms 1 to 9 on the mezzanine floor range from the **Palaeolithic and Neolithic** periods through to the Bronze and Iron Age and Celtic Gaul. Here you can see engraved and sculpted bone and stone, such as the Lady with the Hood, from Brassempouy (Landes), carved from mammoth tusk, c 21,000 BC; objects made of reindeer antler c 11,000 BC, from the Dordogne; an enigmatic engraved menhir from the Aveyron of the 3C BC. Items from the **Bronze Age** include bracelets, torques and other gold objects as well as 8C BC armour from the Haute-Marne. Of the Hallstatt period (1st Iron Age; 800–450) and the La Tène culture (450–52 BC), is a good collection of bronze vessels and jewellery and a container for mead or wine. Of the **Celtic period** is a reconstructed chariot burial from La Gorge-Meillet (Marne) and a maquette of the fortified site of Alèsia.

The first floor, **rooms 10–16**, concentrates on the **Gallo-Roman period**, with sections displaying Celtic divinities and those from the Graeco-Roman world, including figures of Venus and Mercury; ex-votos and their mould; an exemplary display of silver utensils, glassware, bronze lamps, scales, handles, keys and sigillate pottery. Other rooms contain small sculptured objects—birds, boars, horses and human figures including a reclining couple with a dog at their feet, from Bordeaux; a collection of jewellery, buckles, fibulae, games, and a collection of arms. A large mosaic pavement of the 3C from St-Romain-en-Gal (on the Rhône opposite Vienne) depicts a rustic calendar of the seasons. Adjacent are various agricultural implements. There are also collections of jewellery, plaques, glassware, and buckles from the Merovingian period, and the arms of the Chef de Lavoye, possibly a close companion of Clovis, with an exceptional collection of arms with cloisonné decoration. One room is devoted to comparative archaeology with objects from Egypt and other countries.

To the north of the château is the **Grand Parterre**, originally part of a scheme by Le Nôtre between 1662 and 1674, which once included the Jardin de la Dauphine to the east, now planted with rows of elms, and the Grande Terrasse. The Jardin Anglais was created in the 19C. At its south-east corner, at 21 Rue Thiers, is the **Pavillon Henri-IV**, a hotel since 1836, where Dumas wrote *The Three Musketeers* and *The Count of Monte Cristo*.

The 1.95km of the **Grande Terrasse of St-Germain** extends northeas across the park of St-Germmain-en-Laye, commanding a splendid view of Paris—particularly of La Défense: Notre-Dame is approximately 21km to the east. At the far end is the Grille Royale, the entrance to the Forêt de St-Germain, the former royal hunting preserve, of some 3500 hectares with pleasant drives and walks.

Town of St-Germain-en-Laye

The church of St-Louis (opposite the château), designed c 1765 by N.-M. Potain, but not completed until early 19C, contains the tomb of James II of England, erected at the request of George IV, and in which his partial remains were re-interred in 1824.

Behind the church, at 38 Rue au Pain, leading southwest is the tourist information office and, in the same building, the **Musée Claude Debussy** (open Tues–Sat 14.00–18.00).

The composer Claude Debussy (1862–1918) was born here on 22 August 1862 at 38 Rue au Pain, and spent his childhood in this fine 17C–18C house built around a courtyard where his parents owned a small shop. The museum contains a collection of memorabilia presented by Madame de Tinan, the composer's daughter-in-law, arranged to follow the development of the composer. On the second floor is a **Salon de Musique** equipped with a Bechstein c 1915 to reproduce faithfully Debussy's music.

The continuations of Rue au Pain (Rues A. Bonnefant and de Mareil) lead you, after a few minutes' walk to the **Musée du Prieuré**, 2bis Rue Maurice-Denis (Wed–Fri 10.00–12.30 and 14.00–17.30; Sat, Sun, to 18.30; ☎ 01 39 73 77 87).

A former royal hospital founded by Mme de Montespan in 1678, in 1905 Maurice Denis (1870–1943) rented a studio here and from 1914 until his death the property became his home. Denis was co-founder and principal theorist of the Nabis ('prophets' in Hebrew), and the museum, inaugurated in 1980, throws an interesting light on the development of Modern art. The bequest by his family and the group of artists known as the Nabis has been increased by acquisition over 15 years.

Among important works by Maurice Denis are *Self Portrait* (1921), with the Prieuré in the background; *Portrait of Paul Sérusier*; *Portrait of his Mother*; *Marthe, his First Wife, in the garden at dusk*; *Ladder in the Foliage*; *Pilgrims at Emmaus*; *Jacques Portelette aged four*; *Mme Ranson and her Cat*. Other artists represented in the collection include Louis Anquetin (1861–1932), *Self-Portrait*, *Woman in Black*; Emile Bernard (1868–1941), *Portrait of Dom Verkade*; Pierre Bonnard (1867–1947), *Screen with Rabbits, My Grandmother*; Thérèse Debains (1907–74), *Woman in a Straw Hat*; Charles Filiger (1863–1928), *Christ in the Tomb* (c 1890); Paul Gauguin (1848–1903), *The Patron's Daughter* (1886); Georges Lacombe (1868–1916), carved wood *Bust of Maurice Denis*; Paul-Elie Ranson (1864–1909), *The Witches*; Paul Sérusier (1864–1927), *Portrait of his Wife, Breton Girl*; Félix Vallotton (1865–1900), *Bookshelves*; Edouard Vuillard (1868–1940), *Garden at l'Etang-la-Ville, The Reservoir*.

There are also several designs for wallpapers and stained glass by Maurice Denis together with furniture and examples of the decorative arts of the period, including ceramics by the Daum brothers of Nancy.

The **Chapel** was decorated entirely by Maurice Denis (who was a devout Catholic) with blue frescos and Stations of the Cross, and he also designed the glass, with the exception of the round Visitation by Marcel Poncet. The adjacent Studio was built by Auguste Perret in 1912 for Maurice Denis when he was working on the frieze for the Théâtre des Champs-Elysées and is now the venue of temporary exhibitions.

Chambourcy

At Chambourcy, 4km west of St-Germain, is the 18C **La Roseraie**, 64 Grande Rue, which was the home of André Derain (1880–1954) from 1935, with his studio still intact. It is open to the public on the 4th Saturday and Sunday of each month and some Bank Holidays (☎ 01 30 74 70 04).

Poissy

Northwest of St-Germain-en-Laye at Poissy is Le Corbusier's **Villa Savoye** (1929), at 82 Rue Villiers (RER Line A and bus 50 to Les Œillets). Open 1 Apr–31 Oct, 09.30–12.30, 13.30–18.00; 2 Nov–31 Mar, to 16.30; closed Tues and public holidays, ☎ 01 39 65 01 06.

One of Le Corbusier's virtuoso designs, the house was built in 1919–31 for Pierre and Eugenie Savoye who lived here until 1940. The Villa was damaged when expropriated during the War but a long and careful restoration (ending in 1997) has brought it to as near as possible to its original state. This house known as 'les Heures Claires' was carefully designed to take advantage of the site which then commanded splendid views towards Paris (now somewhat obscured). A seemingly simple design, it incorporates the architect's basic tenets of modernism. The exterior view presents a white box on pilotis or stilts, with a flat roof and horizontal rhythm. The interior is a more complex articulation of space and light, combining large windows and a roof terrace with practical living spaces.

Two writers, Emile Zola and Maurice Maeterlinck, lived in the village of Médan (train from St-Lazare to Villennes-sur-Seine) to the northwest of Saint-Germain-en-Laye. The former's house, **Maison d'Emile Zola**, is open Sat–Sun and public holidays 14.00–18.30, and the **Château of Médan** acquired by Maeterlinck, is open all year to groups by appointment (☎ 01 39 85 86 59).

Marly-le-Roi

Some 4km south of St-Germain, to the west of the N386, stood the royal **Château of Marly**, its name preserved in the town of Marly-le-Roi, built in 1679–86 by Jules Hardouin-Mansart for Louis XIV, and a favourite retreat from the formality of Versailles. Unlike other royal residences, Marly was planned as a group of 12 guest-houses around the central royal pavilion, and dedicated to carefree conviviality. The buildings and the parkland setting were fully integrated and much use was made of *trompe l'oeil* and water.

The famous *Marly horses*, by Coysevox and Coustou, which adorned the pools, were gradually transferred to the Tuileries between 1719 and 1794 (see Louvre). Sold at the Revolution, the château was used as a factory until 1809. Then plundered for its stone, it was finally demolished in 1816. Vestiges remain of the park, where the famous hydraulic **Machine de Marly** stood. It was originally constructed in 1681 to raise water from the Seine to the Marly aqueduct, which in turn carried it to Versailles. New machinery had been installed in 1855–59, taking its water from an underground source, but the whole thing was dismantled in 1967.

In the Park of Marly-Louveciennes, as part of a visit to the park, is the **Musée-Promenade de Marly-le-Roi et Louveciennes**, which evokes the great days of Marly through paintings, etc, and has a room dedicated to the Machine de Marly, open Mon–Fri 10.00–12.00, Wed to Sun, 14.00–17.30, closed public holidays, ☎ 01 30 61 61 35.

The **church** of Marly-le-Roi was also built by Mansart (1689) and contains some works originally in Versailles. At Port-Marly in the Seine Valley (bus no. 10 from Saint-Germain-en-Laye) is the Renaissance-style **Château de Monte-Cristo** where Alexandre Dumas lived and worked. Open 1 Apr–1 Nov, Tues–Fri 10.00–12.30, 14.00–18.00, Sat–Sun 10.00–18.00; winter, Sundays only, 14.00–17.00 (☎ 01 30 61 61 35).

Maisons-Laffitte

Maisons-Laffitte, birthplace of Jean Cocteau (1889–1963) is about 4km north of St-Germain-en-Laye. A racehorse centre, there are training-stables, a **Musée du Cheval de Course** and a racecourse. Although the railway station was known as Maisons-Laffitte as early as 1843 (see below) the town adopted the name officially only in 1882.

The celebrated **Château de Maisons** was built 1634–46 for René de Longueil (1596–1677), first Marquis de Maisons, a Surintendant des Finances before Fouquet. Recognised as the masterpiece in classical style of François Mansart (1642–51), it has remarkable interior decoration. Open 1 Apr–15 Oct, 10.00–12.00, 13.30–18.00; 16 Oct–3 March to 17.00, closed Tues and 1/1, 1/5, 1/11, 11/11, 25/12, ☎ 01 39 62 01 49. The visit includes the Racehorse Museum.

History of Maisons-Laffitte

The property was bought in 1777 by the Comte d'Artois (later Charles X) and partly redecorated by Bellanger. It was deserted at the Revolution and its contents dispersed. In 1804 it was acquired by Marshal Lannes, Duc de Montebello, and was sold in 1818 to Jacques Laffitte (1767–1844), a banker and speculator who had profited from the Napoleonic Wars. In 1833 he demolished the stables and sold off the estate. Further fragmented by a subsequent owner, Tilman Grommé, a Russian artist, the shell of the château was saved from demolition in 1905 when it was acquired by the State and restored.

From the entrance hall, decorated in the Doric order, ascends the great staircase, one of Mansart's masterpieces, embellished with putti executed by Philippe de Buyster. Rooms that may be visited include the Salles des Graveurs, with a *trompe l'oeil* ceiling, and collections of prints and plans; and the Salon des Captifs, with a coffered ceiling, and a fireplace carved by Gilles Guérin; the Vestibule d'honneur, with reliefs by Jacques Sarrazin. Also the Ball Room hung with early 18C Gobelins tapestries of the **Hunts of Maximilian**; the King's Bedroom with a replica 17C bed; the Salon à l'Italienne, containing a portrait by Van Dyck of the **Countess of Bedford**; and the domed Cabinet aux miroirs, with a marquetry floor. The south wing, redecorated by the Comte d'Artois, contains the former Queen's suite, transformed by Lannes. Voltaire wrote *Marianne* when a guest here in 1720.

The N308 leads southeast across a meander of the Seine towards La Défense (see latter part of Ch. 28) and central Paris. The road passes, after crossing the Pont de Bezons (south of Colombes), the site of a château in which Henrietta Maria (1606–69) died. The widow of Charles I of England, she was buried at St-Denis.

39 • St-Denis

Getting there
By car

St-Denis is reached from Paris by turning off the A1 autoroute about 3km north of the Porte de la Chapelle; from elsewhere, autoroute A86, or the N1, N14, N186 and N214. By train, Métro Line 13 to St-Denis-Basilique, or RER Line D to St-Denis (RER Line B to La Plaine/Stade de France).

Tourist information
1 Rue de la République, 93200 St-Denis (☎ 01 55 87 08 70).

Arts et Rencontres, Jardin Pierre de Montreuil, 11 Allée des 6 Chapelles, ☎ 01 48 20 40 62. Café with a cultural theme, £
Les Arts, 6 Rue de la Boulangerie, ☎ 01 42 43 22 40. Traditional and franco-oriental cuisine, £
Le Boeuf est au 20, 20 Rue Gabriel-Péri, ☎ 01 48 20 64 74. Standard dishes and wide range of menus, £
Les Cours de l'Abbaye, 8 Rue des Boucheries, ☎ 01 48 09 84 13. Rustic dishes from the south-west of France, £
Le Mélody, 15 Rue Gabriel Péri, ☎ 01 48 20 87 73. Provençal specialities and well as tried and trusted favourites, £

Le Panoramique, Stade de France, Porte T, ☎ 01 55 93 04 40. Excellent cooking and pleasant atmosphere overlooking the stadium, ££

Au Roi du Couscous, 63 Rue du Landy, ☎ 01 42 43 20 25. The place to enjoy Algerian dishes, £

La Table Ronde, 12 Rue de la Boulangerie, ☎ 01 48 20 15 75. Filling food such as choucroute, cassoulet and couscous, £

St-Denis draws visitors mainly because of the Basilica (Cathedral since 1966) with its royal tombs, but it is also a lively and cosmopolitan suburb with an injection of new projects, not the least of which is the vast sports stadium, the Stade de France. The town centre has been transformed since the 1980s by imaginative redevelopment of commercial, domestic and educational buildings, involving architects such as Roland Simounet and Oscar Niemeyer. A small garden, **Place Pierre de Montreuil**, was created in 1998 on north side of the basilica, setting off the north door with its 12C–13C sculptures, and indicating on the ground the extent of the unfinished Valois rotunda with the monogram of Henri II and Catherine de Médicis in the centre (see below).

Starting from this garden and linking the basilica and the stadium is a new **historic trail** of 20 engraved steel markers indicating events and monuments associated with the past and present of St-Denis along the way. In St-Denis there are also two museums—a museum of Art and History and a museum of silverware—which make the very easy journey from the centre of Paris even more worthwhile. A music festival is held here in the summer.

History of St-Denis

An important commercial centre since the Middle Ages, the **Foire** (fair) **de St-Denis** began in the 8C, and the celebrated **Foire du Lendit** (held in the spring) was established here in 1050 and received royal recognition from Louis VI until 1552. The present **market** is the largest in the Ile-de-France (Tues, Fri and Sun). The 19C Grande Halle of the market and the 18C Maison des Arbalétriers (drying house), now a café, have been restored. When Paris got rid of its dirty industries in the mid-19C, many came to St-Denis, and the canals were built at that time. Then the industries gradually disappeared, the canals have little traffic and the district is crossed by the busy A1 and A86.

Basilica (Cathedral) of St-Denis

The Gothic Cathedral of St-Denis was supposedly built over the burial place, c 250, of the missionary apostle of Lutetia, Denis (Dionysius), and his companions Rusticus and Eleutherius. This was known as Catolacus, 11km north of Paris, on the Paris–Beauvais route. St Denis was considered the first Bishop of Paris and by the 12C he was ousting St Martin of Tours as national saint. The new basilica begun in the 12C is celebrated for pioneering what became known as Gothic architecture.

• Open 1 Apr–30 Sept, 10.00–19.00, Sun 12.00–19.00; 1 Oct–31 March to 17.00, Sun to 17.00, closed 1/1, 1/5, 1/11, 11/11, 25/12, ☎ 01 48 09 83 54.

History of the Basilica of St-Denis

The abbey of St-Denis was founded c 475, traditionally at the instance of St Geneviève, and enlarged in 630–38 by Dagobert, who also founded a Benedictine monastery. The first substantial church on the site was built by Abbot Fulrad in 750–75, and here in 754 Pope Stephen III consecrated Pepin the Short, his wife and sons, thus establishing them securely on the throne that Pepin had recently usurped. This church was itself replaced by another built by the powerful and influential **Abbot Suger** (abbot 1122–51)—a momentous occasion in the history of architecture, for the new style adopted was the prototype of what became known as Gothic. The narthex (west porch, c 1135–40), crypt and apse (1140–44) survive from this period of construction. The rebuilding of the nave had barely begun before Abbot Suger's death, and the rest of the building, notably the nave and transepts, dates from 1231–81, following the designs of Pierre de Montreuil (d. 1267). The chapels on the north side of the nave were added c 1375. Already strong links between the Crown and the Abbey were reinforced at the time of Abbot Suger who, from 1127, was adviser to Louis VI and Louis VII, and Regent during the Second Crusade (1147–49).

Dagobert had chosen to be buried close to the saintly relics of Denis and the Abbey Church finally became the sole royal mausoleum. With the exception of Philippe I, Louis XI, Louis-Philippe and Charles X, all the French kings since Hugh Capet were buried here. As well as its role as protector of royal bodies and souls, in 1120 Louis VI accorded it the privilege of keeper of the **royal insignia**, including the oriflamme (the military standard), and the coronation regalia. Its association with royalty and the fact that 13 bishops attended the dedication of the choir in 1144, assured the spread of its style of architecture throughout northern France.

In 1422 the body of Henry V lay in state at St-Denis on its way from Vincennes to Westminster, and here **Joan of Arc** came seven years later to dedicate her armour. Henriette d'Angleterre, daughter of Charles I, was buried here in 1670 where her mother, Henrietta Maria, had been buried the previous year.

After injudicious alterations in the 18C, the abbey was suppressed at the Revolution and its roof stripped of lead. During the Terror, the tombs were rifled, their contents dispersed and the corpses of the kings tossed into a common pit.

The best of the monuments were saved from destruction by Alexandre Lenoir, who preserved them in his Musée des Petits-Augustins (Ecole des Beaux-Arts), from where they were later returned and drastically restored. Renovation of the fabric of the basilica was taken in hand in 1805, but in 1837 the north tower was struck by lightning. Debret undertook the rebuilding of the tower, but it collapsed in 1845 and was reconstructed by **Viollet-le-Duc** who, with Darcy, carried out subsequent restoration to the basilica. The explosion of a nearby bomb-dump in 1915 caused further damage and additional restoration work was started in 1952. It was designated a cathedral in 1966.

Exterior

The **west front**, a development from the great Norman churches, notably St-Etienne in Caen, inspired generations of Gothic façades. Mighty buttresses divide the elevation vertically into three sections, corresponding to the internal stucture of the church. An original element is the crenellated caesura between the façade and the set-back tower (originally twin towers). Three west portals, deep and finely profiled, animate the lower part of the façade. The central one is larger than the others and sets up a different rhythm in the central bay. The sculpture in the tympana and voussoirs of all three portals has been terribly abused and was heavily reworked in the 19C.

The *Last Judgement* of the **central tympanum** has a few original elements—the images of God and Christ, and the Dove and the Lamb. The **north door** was possibly decorated with a mosaic in the first instance, representing for the first time on a tympanum a *Virgin in Majesty*. The present 19C carvings show the story of St Denis. The signs of the zodiac on the jambs are 12C.

The **south door tympanum** has scenes from the *Life of St Denis*, mainly 12C but with 19C heads. The *Labours of the Month* on the jambs are 12C. The high relief statues of Old Testament kings in the jambs, which was a turning point in the integration of sculpture with architecture (coming before those at Chartres), were destroyed in 1771. Another innovative feature of the west façade is the large **oculus** (it is not known how it was originally subdivided) high in the central bay, the precursor of the rose window of Gothic architecture.

Suger undertook the enlargement of the **east end** in honour of a new shrine and to allow for the increasing number of pilgrims. The exterior of Suger's **apse** appears less innovatory than the west end, with Romanesque round-headed windows and relieving arches around the crypt, although the windows of the chapels are Gothic. The upper storeys with flying buttresses date from the 1230s. By Suger's death in 1151, the two ends of the church were still linked by the 8C construction. When the rebuilding of the nave and transept was undertaken during the mid-13C, the upper level of Suger's choir was destroyed and whether flying buttresses had originally been used can only be hypothesised. The transeptal portals, each with a pioneering Rayonnant rose window, are mid-13C work.

Interior

Suger added to the west of the existing 8C church the large **narthex** supporting three chapels, an early medieval concept. But characteristic of Early Gothic are the rib vaults which spring from strong piers enlivened by clusters of elongated shafts, and the tall openings between them. Supposedly the oculus in the west was a practical solution to lighting the low central chapel above the narthex. Work to rebuild the 8C **nave** began in earnest in 1231. The junction between the narthex and nave is awkward. In contrast, the overall effect of the wide nave, slender shafts and exceedingly fine tracery, glazed triforium and vast expanses of glass in the clerestory, is elegant and lives up to its comparison with a lantern of light. The **transepts** are generous to allow for the royal tombs. They are pierced north and south with magnificent **rose windows** squared up to fill the whole of the bay and continuing behind the open triforium below, the first of their kind and emulated at Notre-Dame in 1258. The glass is 19C.

Suger began the reconstruction of the **east end** immediately after the completion of the west, in 1140. The work consisted of enlarging both the crypt and, above it, the choir, and creating the double ambulatory. In 1144, 20 new altars were consecrated. This construction clinches St-Denis's reputation as the birthplace of Gothic: the shallow undulating chapels opening wide into the double ambulatory and linked to it by ribbed vaulting (an ingenious combination of round and pointed ribs), and the enormous ratio of glazed to solid wall. The use of slender columnar supports, rather than compound piers, looks back to

Romanesque east ends. This is probably explained by a desire to harmonise the ambulatory with the 8C building still in place. The elegant arrangement of columns allows an uninterrupted view through to the large windows of the radiating chapels, two in each, fulfilling Suger's aim of filling the church with 'wonderful and uninterrupted light'. The axial chapels of the crypt and ambulatory were both dedicated to the Virgin.

From Suger's records, it is known that the central vessel was rib-vaulted. The carved and inlaid high stalls of the ritual choir (1501–07) are from the chapel of Georges d'Amboise at the Château de Gaillon; the low stalls are 15C work from St-Lucien, near Beauvais. In the choir is a charming 12C Virgin, originally at the abbey of Longchamp.

The **crypt**, entered on either side of the choir, was constructed by Suger around the original Carolingian martyrium built by Abbot Fulrad, the site of the grave of St Denis and his companions. There are some 12C capitals and traces of wall paintings, and excavations have revealed Gallo-Roman Christian tombs and the tomb of Queen Aregonde, Clovis's daughter-in-law, and fragments of earlier churches.

The **central chapel** was the Bourbon burial vault until the Revolution, and contains the sarcophagi of Louis XVI and Marie-Antoinette (see Chapelle Expiatoire; Ch. 25), and those of Louis XVIII among other 18C–19C sovereigns. The **ossuary** on the north side contains the bones that were thrown into a pit when many tombs were rifled in 1793. On the south side is a 19C cenotaph in memory of the Bourbon kings, including Henri IV and Louis XIV. The **stained glass** in the Lady Chapel dates from the 12C, placing it among the oldest in France, albeit restored in the 19C. Among the 15 panels that have survived, mounted in modern glass in the east end, is a *Tree of Jesse*, in which Abbot Suger himself is represented. The baptistry window, designed by J. J. Gruber in 1932, is vividly different.

On the south side of the ambulatory are a copy of the Oriflamme and statues of Louis XVI and Marie-Antoinette at prayer, commissioned by Louis XVIII.

The tombs

The tombs—described below—are a remarkable collection of funerary sculpture from the mid-12C to the mid-16C. Among tombs in the **south aisle**, are those of Louis d'Orléans (d. 1407) and of Valentine de Milan (d. 1408), an Italian work of 1502–15, commissioned by Louis XII. This combines a figure in repose, in the French tradition, on an Italian-style sarcophagus where the twelve apostles replace the more usual *pleurants*. Opposite, against the southwest pillar of the crossing, is the heart-tomb of François II (d. 1560), by Germain Pilon and Ponce Jacquiau. Also in the south aisle, the urn (1549–55) by Pierre Bontemps, containing the heart of François I.

In the **south transept**, the tomb of **François I** (d. 1547) and Claude de France (d. 1524), a masterpiece by Philibert Delorme, begun in 1547, is a classicised version of the tomb of Louis XII (see below), in the form of a triumphal arch. Much use is made of coloured marbles skilfully worked by Bontemps. The royal pair appear kneeling, with their children, on the upper level, and again, recumbent, below. On the east side of the south transept are the tombs of **Charles V** (d. 1380), a remarkable likeness sculpted by André Beauneveu, commissioned before the king's death; the statue of his queen, Jeanne de Bourbon comes from the Célestins church in Paris. Bertrand du Guesclin (d. 1380), High Constable of France, is one of the few commoners buried here. The tomb of Charles VI (d. 1422) also resides in this transept.

At the west end of the **choir** is the tomb of **Philippe III**, le Hardi (d. 1285) by Jean d'Arras, using black and white marble, one of the first portrait statues. There is also a masterly effigy of his queen, Isabella of Aragón (d. 1271), and the tomb of **Philippe IV**, le Bel (d. 1314). At the left of the steps to the sanctuary is the 13C tomb of **Dagobert** (d. 638), with relief sculptures on three levels in a pinnacled niche, showing the torment and redemption of the king's soul, and a beautiful statue of Queen Nanthilde (13C). The figures of Dagobert and his son are 19C restorations. Nearby is the tomb of Léon de Lusignan (d. 1393).

Tomb of Louis XII and Anne de Bretagne

On the north side of the **ambulatory**, you pass the tombs of (left) Blanche and Jean (both d. 1243), children of Louis IX, a rare example of a tomb in metalwork and enamel. Transferred from St-Germain-des-Prés is a remarkable slab in cloisonné mosaic (11C), of Frédégonde (d. 597), queen of Chilperic I; and **Childebert I** (d. 558), of the mid-12C, the oldest funerary effigy in France. In the chapel at the top of the steps, are draped statues of *Henri II* (d. 1559) and *Catherine de Médicis* (d. 1589) by Germain Pilon (1583). In the sanctuary is the Altar of the Relics (by Viollet-le-Duc), on which are placed the reliquaries, given by Louis XVIII, of St Denis and his fellow-martyrs.

In the **north transept** is the temple-like tomb of **Henri II**, part of a grandiose scheme on the part of his queen, Catherine de Médicis, which included a huge rotunda in the Italian style on the north transept—never completed and demolished in the 18C (see above, Place Pierre de Montreuil). Famous artists linked with its construction were Primaticcio, Lescot, Bullant, and A. du Cerceau and the tomb, designed by Primaticcio in 1560–73, was placed there by Henri IV. The monument, with recumbent and kneeling effigies of the king and queen, was sculpted by Germain Pilon and others. Here also are the tombs of **Philippe V** (d. 1322), **Charles IV** (d. 1328), **Philippe VI** (d. 1350) and **Jean II** (d. 1364), the last two by André Beauneveu. In the choir are tombs of **Louis X** (d. 1316) and his son **Jean I** (d. 1316).

The **north aisle** contains the tomb of **Louis XII** (d. 1515) and Anne de Bretagne (d. 1514), covered by a baldaquin, commissioned by François I and made by Giovanni di Giusto, a Florentine, c 1515–31. On the upper part, the royal pair are represented in life. Below, they are depicted after death in a remarkably sensitive manner (in contrast with the heavy allegorigal figures surrounding them), and the chapel-like tomb enclosing the *transi* and the *transie* (the effigies of the dead pair) introduces a new element in funerary monuments. Bas-reliefs illustrate episodes in the king's career.

Among other 13C–14C tombs, are that of Louis de France (d. 1260), the eldest son of Louis IX, with Henry III of England as one of the *pleurants* in the cortege around the base—an early example of this imagery.

To the south of the basilica are restored **monastic dependencies**. Rebuilt in the 18C by Robert de Cotte and Jacques V Gabriel, they were occupied after 1809 as a Maison d'Education de la Légion d'Honneur, for the daughters of members of the Legion. (To visit, check with the Tourist Office.)

Musée d'Art et d'Histoire

Some five minutes' walk further south, at 22 bis Rue Gabriel Péri, the museum of the town's history Musée d'Art et d'Histoire (open 10.00–17.30, Sun 14.00–18.30, closed Tues and public holidays, ☎ 01 42 43 05 10) is installed in a Carmelite convent founded in 1625. The chapel (closed for restoration) by Mique, with an Ionic portico, has a fine compartmented cupola (1780), built while Louise de France was in residence (1770–87). St-Denis is one of the most researched towns in France since revealing important finds during excavations for the Métro in 1972, and the museum was installed in the former convent in 1981. Three wings of the original cloister survived and the fourth has been replaced. Pious 18C mottos on the convent walls have been restored.

In the former chapter house is the reconstituted **Pharmacy of the Hôtel-Dieu** (demolished 1907) with other souvenirs of the former hospital. The refectory and kitchen of the Carmelite convent have been converted into an excellent archaeological and historical section explaining the role of the town since the time of ancient Catolacus—on the tin route across northern Europe, at the time of medieval St-Denis with its pilgrimage and fairs, in the evolution from monarchic to communist associations, and in modern industries as varied as Pleyel pianos (until 1962), chemicals, Christofle glass, and gas—evoked in André Lhote's painting of the *Usine à Gaz, St-Denis et Gennevilliers*, 1937.

The **history of the Carmelites** is recorded in the restored cells on the upper floor, one with memorabilia specific to Madame Louise, daughter of Louis XV. Works from the Besson donation, notably by Albert André, are shown in adjacent rooms. On the second floor is a huge and fascinating collection devoted to the Commune de Paris (1870–71). The museum owns some 4000 engravings and lithographs by Daumier (not necessarily on view).

The recent modern wing of the cloister leads to the section devoted to the poet **Paul Eluard** (1895–1952), born in St-Denis. The exhibits include some of Eluard's manuscripts and works by Zadkine, Picasso, Max Ernst, Cocteau, Giacometti and Françoise Gilot, a *Portrait of Paul Eluard* (1952) by André Fougeron, as well as rare editions illustrated by his painter friends.

The **Musée Christofle**, containing decorative silverware and tableware, is best approached from the Métro Porte de Paris, then follow Blvd Anatole France to the southwest across the Canal St-Denis, and turn right. The museum, which until now has been exclusively for pre-booked tour groups, will be opening its doors to the public at the beginning of 2001. (Check opening times with the Tourist Office.) Here are replicas of historical interest and original pieces of the art of the gold- and silversmith produced by the Société Christofle since its establishment in 1830. The company became the most important producer of silverware in France in the 20C.

The **Stade de France**, at Plaine-St-Denis, is the stadium for football, rugby and athletics as well as large concerts, which was built in two years and opened in 1998 for the World Cup. It can be visited except on event days. A spectacularly well-organised complex, it seats up to 80,000, and the elliptical roof over the seating suspended from steel beams appears to hover like a flying saucer. The stadium has brought a new impetus and vast improvements to the area, particularly the efficient public transport services (Métro line 13, RER Lines B and D). There is an gourmet restaurant, the *Panoramique*, in the stadium (see above).

40 • Ecouen

Getting there
By train

Ecouen (95440, Val d'Oise) can be reached by **train** from Gare du Nord (suburban lines direction Luzarches or Persan-Beaumont par Montsoult), to Ecouen-Ezanville station, then the 269 bus (direction Garges Sarcelles) to the Mairie d'Ecouen. The Château is reached on foot by a path to the left of the Mairie. An alternative route from the station is to take the footpath through the woods (about 20 minutes' walk).

By car

Take Autoroute A1 from Porte de la Chapelle, exit 3 and N401, N1 (to Sarcelles) then N16.

A small town, it is dominated by the magnificent Renaissance Château d'Ecouen which houses the Musée National de la Renaissance, inaugurated in 1977. The collection follows on chronologically from the Musée du Moyen Age in Paris. The town itself is of little interest except for the church of St-Acceul which has some notable stained-glass in its choir (1544).

The Musée National de la Renaissance

● Open 09.45–12.30, 14.00–17.15, closed Tues and 1/1, 1/5, 25/12. ☎ 01 34 38 38 50. The Park is open in the summer 08.00–19.00 and in winter to 18.00.

The intention of this elegant and well-organised museum, which is less visited than others on the outskirts of Paris, is to give an overview of the decorative arts of the Renaissance. The Château d'Ecouen was an obvious choice of setting for the museum as it is a prime example of Renaissance architecture, but there was also an urgent need for space to house the series of large tapestries of David and Bathsheba, stored for a long time at the Hôtel de Cluny.

History of the Musée de la Renaissance

The construction of the château began c 1538 for the Constable Anne de Montmorency. Among major artists employed were the sculptor Jean Goujon and the architect Jean Bullant. The building was put to a variety of uses during the Revolutionary period, and in 1805 became a school for the daughters of members of the Légion d'Honneur. Many of its embellishments, including an altar by Goujon from the chapel, were removed during the Revolution, and reverted to the Duc d'Aumale, who chose to include them in his château at Chantilly.

Built in two stages, beginning 1538 and 1547, the château is arranged around a courtyard, with square pavilions on the angles and moats on three sides. The elevations are simply articulated with pilasters and string courses, and ornamentation confined to the dormer windows, which show a progression in styles from the west to the north wings. After 1547, work began on the interior to provide luxurious apartments for the owners and the King, Henri II, and porticos were added. Those on both sides of the north wing have Henri II's insignia. The south portico, which uses the Colossal Order for the first time in France, is ascribed to Jean Bullant. It was intended as the setting for Michelangelo's *Slaves* (see Louvre, Ch. 15) given to Montmorency by Henri II.

Ground floor

The **entrance**, through the east wing, is a replacement, in 1807, of the superimposed galleries with an equestrian statue of the Constable, designed by Goujon or Bullant, destroyed in 1787 (a fragment of its decorative sculpture is in the museum).

From here, turn left into the **chapel**, which has delicately carved Renaissance-style woodwork and painted Gothic ribbed vaulting and contains an unusual retable depicting the Passion (1534–78). Incorporated in the decoration are the coats of arms of Anne de Montmorency and Madeleine de Savoie.

The following series of rooms on the ground floor begins with the **armoury** which has a profusely decorated chimneypiece in the School of Fontainebleau style, the first of 12 depicting biblical themes which are a feature of Ecouen. The arms and armour include stirrups with the emblem of François I, and armour from the workshops of Maximilian I of Germany c 1510–20. The former **kitchens** contain a collection of fragments of stonework from Ecouen and carved wooden screens and other Renaissance carvings from the Château of Gaillon. The **room of Roman heroes** has rare painted leather hangings from Normandy with Roman heroes and the chimneypiece shows *The Tribute to Caesar*.

A group of small rooms is devoted to collections of magnificent **alabaster, carved wooden plaques** and **panels and small sculptures**. There are also pear-wood and box-wood statuettes, mainly German or Flemish. The outstanding bronze figurines include *Jupiter* by Alessandro Vittoria, *Virgin and Child* by Niccolò Roccatagliata, and fornicating satyrs by Riccio. Next there are some superb examples of metalwork, including damascened, cutlery and a collection of Renaissance door-furniture.

Among the mathematical instruments and watches in the **Clock Room** are a celestial sphere in gilded copper and an exquisite automated timepiece masquerading as a miniature ship, by Hans Schlotlheim of Augsburg. An unusual piece is the splendid inlaid silversmith's workbench from Germany (1565), a full-scale working model made for a nobleman's pleasure rather than as a craftsman's tool.

The angle room, known as the **Catherine de Médicis Chamber**, has three tapestries showing the *Battle of St-Denis* (10 November 1567) and a portable triptych with painted enamels. The Queen's room has a monumental fireplace from a house in Rouen, and in the next room are sculpted and enamelled terracottas by Luca della Robbia as well as French sculptures including *The Three Fates*, in marble, by Germain Pilon, and *The Compassion of the Father* in terracotta. The museum owns a precious collection of portraits in wax in the form of medallions; it also has ten carved *mascarons* (heads) originally on corbels (c 1600) of the Pont-Neuf in Paris, and two from the Palais du Louvre.

First floor

The first floor has been arranged to evoke the owners' and king's residence as it was after 1547. In the South Wing were the apartments of Anne de Montmorency and his wife, Madeleine. In the décor are reminders of his role as commander of the army—his emblem, a sword and blue eaglets, features in his arms. The decorated chimneypiece in the **Constable's Chamber** has a scene of *Esau Hunting* and there are two School of Fontainebleau paintings. The reconstructed **Constable's Library**, above the chapel, is reached by a spiral staircase from these apartments. It has its original and unique décor of wooden panels inlaid with gilt arabesques and the monogram of Anne de Montmorency. The **Apartments of Madeleine de Savoie**, mainly a reconstruction, follow those of the Constable. In the antechamber is an Italian spinet (1570) and the chambers contain a 16C Venetian bureau inlaid with painted mother-of-pearl and notable carved doors (from elsewhere). Abilgail's Pavilion takes its name the painted decoration of the fireplace.

The long **Psyche Gallery** was originally grandly decorated with stained glass and paving (remnants of which are exhibited elsewhere), and murals. The finely carved stone fireplaces are from Châlons-en-Champagne (1562), with reliefs of *Christ and the Samarian Woman*, and *Actaeon surprising Diana in her Bath*.

This room houses the raison d'être of the museum, the celebrated series of tapestries entitled *The Story of David and Bathsheba* (Brussels c 1510). It is possible that Jan van Roome was involved in their creation. Individualistic portrayal of the figures and architectural settings, typically Renaissance, is combined with a foreground reminiscent of medieval millefleurs. Stylised flowers form the border and the colours are still strong. The story, reading from left to right, begins with a scribe before an open book recording the episodes and each of the ten tapestries contains several scenes. David, despised by his wife, brings the ark to Jerusalem, then departs for battle against the Ammonites at Rabbah, with Uriah, husband of Bathsheba. After seducing Bathsheba, David sends Uriah to his death and Bathsheba is received at David's court. The prophet Nathan predicts the death of their child, while allegorical figures put Lust to flight. David and Bathsheba's child dies and David appeases God's anger by fasting and praying. He then resumes the battle and takes Rabbah. As the story ends the scribe closes the book.

A small room in the west wing and the series of rooms that follow are the apartments of the king. **Henri II's Chamber** has a painted ceiling with the king's monogram and crescent, and a chimneypiece featuring *Saul in Anger Slaughtering Two of his Cattle*.

Beyond a carved wooden staircase, from the Chambre des Comptes of the Palais de la Cité, is the **Salle d'honneur**, which has the only sculpted marble chimneypiece at Ecouen. Attributed to Jean Bullant, c 1558, the coloured marble was a gift of Cardinal Farnese. The paved floor, originally in the Psyche Gallery, was made by Masséot Abaquesne (mid 16C), who made his name through his work at Ecouen. Displayed in this room are two tapestries of the *Fructus Belli* series (the other six dispersed elsewhere), woven in Brussels, 1546–48, by Jean Baudouyn from cartoons by Giulio Romano, which show the soldiers' payday and the general's dinner. In the next rooms are painted leather panels with scenes from Scipio and a chimneypiece with the Judgement of Solomon and some fine secular stained glass from Ecouen, with the emblems of Anne de Montmorency, Catherine de Médicis, François I and Henri II. The last room on this floor has **embroideries** made for Sully when he was Grand Master of the Artillery and occupied the Arsenal in Paris.

Second floor

The first room is devoted to a remarkable group of **ceramics** from Iznik (ancient Nicaea, in northwest Turkey), dating largely from 1555–1700. There is also **stained glass** mainly from churches around Paris. French ceramics are represented by 16C tile panels, and ceramics by Masséot Abaquesne including a magnificent tiled floor of 1550 and pharmacy pots; also two rare pieces from the Saint-Porchaire workshops, c 1560, and faience attributed to Bernard Palissy. There is a room dedicated to **cassoni**, painted panels from 15C Florentine marriage-chests, depicting the Trojan Horse and other Classical scenes; Limoges enamel plaques and portraits (by Léonard Limousin, Nardon Pénicaud, Pierre Reymond, Pierre Courtois and others); also collections of majolica, glass and among the jewellery, a swan pendant from Germany. Among fine examples of the **gold- and silversmith's craft** are notably a statuette of *Daphne* by Wenzel Jamnitzer, a goblet in the shape of a snail (Netherlands; c 1700) and several magnificent examples from Nuremberg and Augsburg.

41 • Sceaux

 Getting there
By train

RER Line B, stopping at Bourg-la-Reine, Sceaux or Parc de Sceaux.
By car

The N20 leads south from the Porte d'Orléans to (10km) Sceaux.

Tourist information
Sceaux, ☎ 01 46 61 19 03. 92330, Sceaux (Hauts-de-Seine).

The double **Aqueduct de Arceuil** crosses the valley of the Bièvre 2km south of the Blvd Périphérique. The lower part was built in 1613–23 by Marie de Médicis to supply the Luxembourg fountains; it was preceded by a Roman aqueduct, built in the 4C to bring water to the Palais des Thermes. Both Erik Satie and artist Victor Vasarely lived in the suburb of Arceuil.

After 4.5km the broad Allée d'Honneur climbs west from the N20 to the entrance of the **Château de Sceaux**. A 19C building replaced the sumptuous 17C château built for Colbert, which, during the first half of the 18C, was the scene of the literary and artistic court of the ambitious Duchesse du Maine (1676–1753). Voltaire wrote *Zadig* here; and works by Racine, Molière and Lully were performed in the adjacent Orangerie (left), constructed by Jules Hardouin-Mansart (1684; restored). To the right is the Pavillon de l'Aurore, by Perrault.

Since 1937 the **Musée de L'Ile de France** has been installed in the château, which was restored between 1992 and 1994. This illustrates the history and topography of the area around Paris. It is well worth visiting, not only for its site, but for the wealth of interesting material depicting the appearance of, and life in, the environs of the capital in past centuries. It also contains a documentation centre (by prior appointment). Open 10.00–18.00 Apr–Sept, otherwise

10.00–17.00, closed Tues 1/1, Easter, 1/5, 1/11, 11/11, 25/12, ☎ 01 46 61 06 71 or 01 41 13 70 41.

The museum is arranged around four main themes. The ground floor is devoted to the History of the Property and its main owners, from the time of Colbert's original château to the one built by Lesoufaché in 1857 for the Duke of Trevise. The **Grand Salon** (room 3) contains portraits of *Colbert* attributed to Lefebvre, and of the *Duchess of Maine* by De Troy. The **Small Green Room** (room 5), with a charming view, shows a large collection of Sceaux ceramics. The **Library** (room 7) contains Sevres, St-Cloud and Vincennes ware.

Room 9 on the first floor, the **Royal Residences Room**, displays paintings, engravings and furniture evoking the châteaux of Marly, St-Germain-en-Laye or Choisy, as they were. The **Landscape Rooms** (rooms 11, 12, 13 and 17) show the area as it was between the 17C and 20C, with a room dedicated to a number of views by Paul Huet (room 13). Lastly, there are rooms containing works given by artists, such as the watercolours and engravings by Dunoyer de Segonzac and the famous series *Hostages* by Jean Fautrier.

The majestic park, laid out by Le Nôtre, forms one of the more attractive open spaces near Paris and contains, south of the château, a series of cascades leading to the Octagon, to the west of which is the Grand Canal. From here you have a view of the Pavillon de Hanovre, moved here in 1934 from the Blvd des Capucines.

A short distance northwest of the château, across the park, is the **old church-yard** of Sceaux, where the fabulist Florian (1755–94) is buried. The simple tombs of Pierre (1859–1906) and Marie Curie (née Sklodowska; 1867–1934), the discoverers of radium, are in the local cemetery.

Some 2.5km west, in the Parc de la Vallé aux Loups, is the restored residence of Chateaubriand (in 1807–18).

Further afield

42 • Fontainebleau

Getting there
By train

Distance from Paris, 60km (40 miles). From the Gare de Lyon, there are **trains** to Fontainebleau-Avon (45 min) and from there Cars Verts (every 15 minutes) to the château.

By car

Take the A6 motorway (Porte d'Orléans/Lyon exit from the périphérique), then the N37. After the junction where the N37 joins the N7, the road crosses part of the Forêt de Fontainebleau (see below). At 7km after leaving the motorway, a crossroad leads right 1km to the village of Barbizon (see below).

Tourist information

Opposite the Château at 4 Rue Royale, 77300 Fontainebleau (Seine et Marne), ☎ 01 60 74 99 99, www.tourisme77.net. From the Tourist Office, during the main season, are guided walks of the town (in French), rides in horse-drawn *calèche* or by petit train. Autoguides (also in English) are available for the town, Château and gardens.

In Fontainebleau, 77300 (Seine-et-Marne):

Le Beauharnais, 27 Pl. Napoléon, ☎ 01 60 74 60 00. Very good value, set-price meals, and relaxed setting, ££

La Carpe d'Or, 7 Rue d'Avon, ☎ 01 64 22 28 64. Handy for the Château, reasonably priced, £

Le Caveau des Ducs, 24 Rue de Ferrare, ☎ 01 64 22 05 05. Superb 17C cellar and Burgundian cooking, £–££

Auberge du Mont-Chauvet, Route des hauteurs de la solle, ☎ 01 64 22 92 30, £

Table des Maréchaux, 9 Rue Grande, ☎ 01 60 39 50 50. Traditional quality cooking, ££

In Barbizon, 77630:

Auberge du Manoir Saint Hérem, 29 Grande Rue, ☎ 01 60 66 42 42. ú

Les Allouettes, 4 Rue Antoine Barye, ☎ 01 60 66 41 98. Outdoor eating and pretty inside, with good traditional cuisine, £–££

Hostellerie Les Pléiades, 21 Rue Grande, ☎ 01 60 66 40 25. The painter Daubigny lived here; good fresh classic fare, £–££

Fontainebleau is one of the most pleasant resorts within easy reach of Paris and popular with Parisians who want to live outside the capital. It has the dual attractions of the Château and the forest, both magnificent. The Château really came into its own at the time of François I in the 16C and was much appreciated by Napoléon as a comfortable home. Indeed, the château, despite its grand connections, has a surprisingly intimate atmosphere. More recently, the area was the HQ of NATO and is now internationally known for its professional and academic institutions such as the international business school, INSEAD, the Office National des Forêts, and the Ecole des Mines.

History of Fontainebleau

For centuries Fontainebleau was an important royal residence, used as a royal hunting-lodge in 1137 and later fortified. Thomas Becket, when in exile, consecrated the chapel of St-Saturnin in 1169. In 1259 Louis IX founded monastery of Trinitarians here and this is where Philippe IV (le Bel) (1268–1314) was born and died. James V of Scotland spent December 1536 at Fontainebleau, before his marriage with Madeleine, daughter of François I.

As Charles VII and his successors deserted Fontainebleau for the Loire, the château's present form is largely due to François I (1494–1547), who found the place almost derelict. After 1527 he assembled a group of mainly Italian architects and artists to rebuild and decorate it, among them Sebastiano Serlio (1475–1554), G.B. Rosso, Francesco Primaticcio) and Nicolò dell'Abbate, with Gilles le Breton as the chief French architect. The Italian Mannerist style that became naturalised here became known as the School of Fontainebleau, marked by its often extreme, etiolated elegance. More alterations were made during the reigns of Henri II and Henri IV whose son, Louis XIII, was born and baptised here in 1601. Both François II and Henri III were also born at Fontainebleau.

In 1657 it was the scene of the the assassination of Monaldeschi, the favourite of ex-Queen Christina of Sweden (see below); and Louis XIV signed the Revocation of the Edict of Nantes here in 1685.

Napoléon I spent 12 million francs on renovating the Château. At the time of his coronation in 1804 he received Pius VII at Fontainebleau; the second visit by the Pope, from June 1812, was less auspicious, as the Emperor forced Pius to spend 19 months as his prisoner until he renounced temporal power. This is where on 6 April 1814 Napoléon signed the act of abdication and bade farewell to his Old Guard, departing for Elba on the 20th, only to return on 20 March 1815 via Grenoble to review his grenadiers and lead them to the Tuileries.

The château was again restored, at enormous cost, by Louis-Philippe in neo-Renaissance style. It suffered during six-months occupation in 1870–71 by the Prussians; while from 1941 it was the headquarters of General von Brauchitsch, until liberated by General Patton in August 1944. From 1949–66 it was the military HQ of the Allied powers in Europe. The last important political event at the Château was the European Summit in June 1984.

The Rue Royale and Blvd Magenta (in which there are several old mansions) converge on the Pl. du Gén. de Gaulle, in which the doorway of the Hôtel du Cardinal de Ferrara, built 1544–46, is arguably the most authentic surviving work of architect, painter and theorist Sebastiano Serlio (restored in 1995). At 88 Rue St-Honoré is the **Musée Napoléonien d'Art et d'Histoire Militaire** (14.00–17.00, closed Sun and Mon).

The Musée National du Château de Fontainebleau

- Open summer 09.30–17.00; July and Aug 09.30–18.00; Nov–May 09.30–12.30, 14.00–17.00; closed Tues, 1/1, 1/5. Last entry 45 minutes before closing (☎ 01 60 71 50 70). Information panels throughout the Château are printed in five languages. Photos permitted without flash. Access for the handicapped to the State Apartments. The visitors' entrance and Salle d'Acceuil with information on the château (hire of audioguide) and region is in the Louis XV wing, to the right of the courtyard. There is a well-stocked shop for books and souvenirs of the Château. For the Musée Napoléon I, see below.

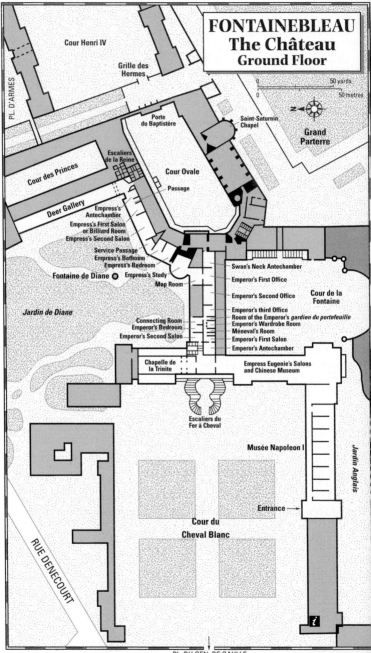

FONTAINEBLEAU
The Château
Ground Floor

Cour Henri IV

Grille des Hermes

PL. D'ARMES

Porte du Baptistère

Saint-Saturnin Chapel

Grand Parterre

Escaliers de la Reine

Cour Ovale

Cour des Princes

Passage

Deer Gallery

Empress's Antechamber

Empress's First Salon or Billiard Room

Empress's Second Salon

Service Passage

Empress's Bathroom

Empress's Bedroom

Fontaine de Diane

Empress's Study

Map Room

Swan's Neck Antechamber

Emperor's First Office

Emperor's Second Office

Cour de la Fontaine

Jardin de Diane

Connecting Room

Emperor's Bedroom

Emperor's Second Salon

Emperor's third Office

Room of the Emperor's *gardien du portefeuille*

Emperor's Wardrobe Room

Méneval's Room

Emperor's First Salon

Emperor's Antechamber

Chapelle de la Trinité

Empress Eugenie's Salons and Chinese Museum

Escaliers du Fer à Cheval

Musée Napoléon I

Jardin Anglais

Entrance →

Cour du Cheval Blanc

RUE DENECOURT

i

PL. DU GEN. DE GAULLE

The Château is composed of many distinct buildings erected over the centuries, mostly of two storeys. As much of the stone (local sandstone) is unsuitable for sculpture, its exterior is plain when compared to its richly decorated interior. The interior also reflects the fashions and tastes of different periods and occupants, providing fascinating examples from the Renaissance to the Second Empire, and in several places different styles are juxtaposed. There is a superb collection of furnishings—some original to the rooms, some acquired—and fabrics, many reproduced in the 20C from original designs.

The Pl. du Gén. de Gaulle provides a good view of the west front of the château; the massive wrought-iron grille marks the site of a former wing which closed the courtyard. This vast space (152m by 112m), **Cour du Cheval-Blanc**, also called the Cour des Adieux, is where Napoléon made his farewell. It has a horse-shoe-shaped staircase of 1634 by Jean Androuet du Cerceau (which replaced one by Le Breton begun in 1531) in the main façade which dates from the 16C and is monogrammed with the F of François I. This wing, articulated by pavilions with high slate roofs, is in sandstone and rendered stone. Despite the different building phases and complex alterations, there is, at first glance, a certain conformity in the elevations from the sympathetic use of similar materials. The low wing on the left, also from the time of François I but heavily modified during the intervening time, introduces brick. The south wing, known as the Louis XV wing, which replaced the Galeries d'Ulysse demolished in 1739, is built in brick and stone to harmonise with its neighbours.

First floor, State Apartments

Follow the corridor to the **Escalier de Stuc** with its false marbling and, on ascending to the first floor, turn right through the antechamber with a 19C stained-glass panel by L-C. Maréchal, to enter the **Galerie des Fastes**. Built by Napoléon III, it displays a collection of paintings recording special events or celebrations in the château.

The **Galerie des Assiettes**, is decorated with 128 Sèvres porcelain plates (1839–44) painted with views of Fontainebleau and other royal residences and, curiously, one with a scene of Niagara Falls and another of Twickenham; the ceiling is decorated with murals on wood by Ambroise Dubois (1543–1614).

From the **Vestibule du Fer à Cheval** (named after the courtyard), which has three original massive oak doors of the Louis XIII period (17C), you enter the first of the **Salles Renaissance**, the 64m long **Galerie François I**, with magnificent doors, built in 1528–44, to link the Trinitarian chapel and the donjon. A private gallery, for which the King kept the keys, his initial and salamander device are conspicuous. The decoration is *à la française*, with wood panelling on the lower walls, and stucco, paintings and fresco above. The stucco reliefs by Rosso were completed after his death by Primaticcio, the strongest example of Italian influence in the decoration of the château, and at the origin of the First School of Fontainebleau. The frescoes represent allegorical and mythological scenes, with reference to the life of the king. This gallery was restored under Napoléon III, but one painting was left to show how it originally looked. Seen from the windows is the carp lake, a novelty created by Henri IV and subsequently a trend setter.

Turn right to the **Salle des Gardes** (part of the State Apartments), completed c 1570 at the time of Henri IV, which retains its original frieze. The ceiling (the design of which is reproduced on the marquetry floor) was redesigned by Louis

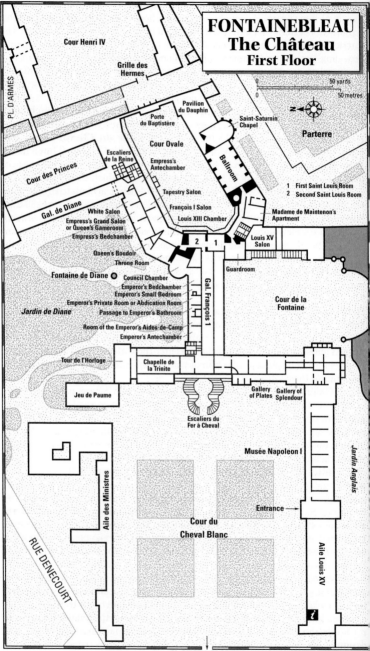

**FONTAINEBLEAU
The Château
First Floor**

Cour Henri IV

Grille des Hermes

PL. D'ARMES

Pavilion du Dauphin

Porte du Baptistère

Saint-Saturnin Chapel

Parterre

Cour Ovale

Escaliers de la Reine

Empress's Antechamber

Ballroom

Cour des Princes

Tapestry Salon

1 First Saint Louis Room
2 Second Saint Louis Room

Gal. de Diane

White Salon

François I Salon

Louis XIII Chamber

Madame de Maintenon's Apartment

Empress's Grand Salon or Queen's Gameroom

Empress's Bedchamber

2 1

Louis XV Salon

Queen's Boudoir

Throne Room

Fontaine de Diane

Council Chamber

Guardroom

Emperor's Bedchamber

Emperor's Small Bedroom

Emperor's Private Room or Abdication Room

Passage to Emperor's Bathroom

Room of the Emperor's Aides-de-Camp

Emperor's Antechamber

Gal. François 1

Cour de la Fontaine

Jardin de Diane

Tour de l'Horloge

Chapelle de la Trinité

Jeu de Paume

Gallery of Plates

Gallery of Splendour

Escaliers du Fer à Cheval

Musée Napoleon I

Jardin Anglais

Aile des Ministres

Entrance →

RUE DENECOURT

Cour du Cheval Blanc

Aile Louis XV

i

PL. DU GEN. DE GAULLE

XIII, and the room was redecorated in 1834–36, ending up as a combination of Louis XIII and Empire styles. The woodwork is of the 17C. The chimneypiece, with a bust of Henri IV attributed to Matthieu Jacquet, was made from several pieces recovered from elsewhere. The original furniture in this and the following suite of rooms was sold and replaced in the first decades of the 19C. It includes a number of pieces by Alphonse Jacob-Desmalter (c 1840), placed as they were during the Second Empire.

The royal suite of François I was converted by Louis XIV into the **Appartements de Mme de Maintenon**. Much of the furniture, including the Boulle commode, were installed during the 19C. It is said that Louis signed the disastrous Revocation of the Edict of Nantes in the Grand Salon in 1685, and the *boiseries* are, in part, of that date. Adjacent is the antechamber of the former **Salle de Spectacle**. Fabrics were rewoven in 1982. This wing contained the Belle Cheminée (beautiful fireplace) dismantled in 1725.

The splendid 30m-long **Salle de Bal**, was begun by Gilles le Breton, but transformed by Delorme. It was originally an open loggia in the Italian style but glazed later, and commands the best view of the Cour Ovale and of the donjon of Louis IX. The design of the elaborate coffered walnut ceiling is reproduced on the parquet floor, a conceit of Louis-Philippe. The décor is generously endowed with the interlaced monograms of Henri II and of the Queen, Catherine de Médicis, C, which somewhat ambiguously, can also be interpreted as the D of Diane de Poitiers, the Royal mistress. Primaticcio designed, and Nicolò dell'Abbate executed in 1552 the now much-restored mythological scenes. The satyrs flanking the fireplace are copies of the originals melted down at the Revolution.

The adjacent **Chapelle de St-Saturnin** (1541), replaced the one consecrated by Becket.

The **Escalier du Roi** was the last part of the Château to be built during the Renaissance. The heavily ornate upper part of the well was formerly the **Bedchamber of Anne de Pisseleu, Duchesse d'Etampes**, the mistress of François. But this was transformed into a staircase after a design by Gabriel in 1749. The sculptures are ascribed to Primaticcio and the frescoes, in which the king is depicted as Alexander the Great in eight episodes from the life of the Macedonian hero, were painted by Nicolò dell'Abbate from Primaticcio's designs. The stucco figures are of the period of Jean Goujon. From the windows your look across the Cour Ovale to the doors of the **Porte du Baptistère**.

The **Sovereign's State Apartments** included what are known as the **First and Second St-Louis Rooms**. The second room, the bedchamber, is in the old castle keep. These later became the king's public dining room. The archway adjoining was opened in 1757 and the rooms were redecorated in 1836 and embellished by paintings of the 1780s depicting episodes in the life of Henri IV, but still retain some 17C works by Ambrose Dubois. The fine marble bas-relief of *Henri IV à cheval* (1599; by Jacquet) comes from the Belle Cheminée mentioned above.

The **Salon Louis XIII**, formerly the Cabinet du Roi or Chambre Ovale, retains some early 17C decoration, restored in 1837, and most of its original paintings by Dubois of *The Loves of Theagenes and Chariclea*, although three were removed in 1757 to open wider doors to make room for the voluminous dresses of the ladies. In this room Marie de Médicis gave birth to Louis XIII in 1601. The furniture is a mixture of 17C and 19C.

Salon François I, originally the bedroom of Eleanor of Austria, second wife of François I, has a medallion of Venus and Adonis by Primaticcio over the chimneypiece, and on the walls are several Gobelins tapestries of hunting scenes. Those in the adjacent **Tapestry Salon** illustrate the *Story of Psyche*, while the adjoining **Empress's Antechamber** contains three of *The Seasons* (spring is missing).

The long (over 80m) **Galerie de Diane**, was built c 1600, for Marie de Médicis to take walks during bad weather. Barrel-vaulted, it was decorated with paintings illustrating the *Myth of Diana* and the *Victories of Henri IV*. By the 19C it had fallen into disrepair and was renovated by Napoléon I. Since 1858 has served as a library.

You return through the **Appartements de la Reine**, whose 18C decor was refurbished by Napoléon for Joséphine. All the rooms were entirely restored in the 1990s, the fabrics and carpets rewoven and they are, indeed, splendid. The **White Salon**, arranged in 1835 by Louis Philippe for Queen Marie-Amélie has mid- and late 18C fireplace and wainscoting. The charmingly named **Queen's Gamesroom** (Salon des Jeux) or Salon de l'Impératrice reproduces the original Neo-classical designs of the time of Marie-Antoinette (1786) with stucco by P.-L. Roland. The room is displayed alternately with Louis XVI or First Empire furnishings.

The glitzy **Chambre de l'Impératrice** (or the Room of 19 Queens), has an ornate Louis XIV ceiling and its walls covered by silk rewoven in Lyon in the 20C. Marie-Antoinette's bed, with her initial M, made for this room in 1787 by Sené and Laurent, was in fact never used by her. It also has replicas of the the former hangings. The 19 queens who used the room included Marie de Médicis, Marie-Thérèse, Marie Leszczynska, Marie-Antoinette, Joséphine, Marie-Louise, Marie-Amélie and the Empress Eugènie. Napoléon's armchair was made specially for him and adapted to his needs. The **Queen's Boudoir**, an unrestored delight with delicate painted panels, contains furniture by Riesener and Georges Jacob of 1786, was made for Marie Antoinette.

The former bedroom of Henri IV, became the ostentatious **Throne Room of Napoléon** in 1808, and is the only Throne Room in France, with an interesting juxtaposition of styles. It has conserved some of its original trappings from the mid 17C, but most of the panels were carved in the 1750s. Among outstanding pieces of furnishing from the Napoleonic era are the Savonnerie carpet, the rock crystal candelabra by Chaumont, the standards flanking the throne surmounted by the initial N and an eagle, designed by Percier and Fontaine for St-Cloud and moved here in 1808, and the Napoleonic bees on the baldaquin. The portrait of Louis XIII is after Philippe de Champaigne.

A passage where papers were burned during the time of Louis XV, leads to the richly decorated **Salle du Conseil** (Council Chamber), an exceptional room with a lighthearted Rococo décor mainly 1751–53. The five ceiling paintings by Boucher represent the *Sun Beginning its Race and Chasing the Night*, and the *Four Seasons*. On the walls are are paintings *en camaïeu* (monochrome) in alternate blue and pink, framed by gilded panels, by Carle van Loo and J.-B. Pierre. In rather harsh contrast is the First Empire furniture.

The private **Napoléon I's Imperial Apartments** were restored to their original splendour in the last decade of the 20C after years of renovations entailing the revival of almost forgotten crafts. These six rooms, used by Napoléon as campaign headquarters, back onto the Grande Galerie of François I and overlook the Jardin de Diane. Originally built for Louis XVI, Napoléon took them over and had them entirely refitted from 1804. The **Emperor's Bedroom**, dripping with gilt and chandeliers, contains the sumptuously draped ceremonial bed for which the new fabrics are faithful copies of the originals. The **Small Bedroom of the Emperor**, showily bright green and red, contains his mechanical desk ordered from Jacob Desmalter, and his camp bed, the only one he could sleep in, with camouflage. The **Salon Particulier** (Private Room) contains all the original furniture of 1808, and is also known as the Abdication Room as it contains the table where he signed the Abdication on 6 April 1814. The bathroom is trimmed in deep gold fabric and the chairs (Louis-Philippe) in the **Aides-de-Camp's Room** are upholstered with Beauvais tapestry and the carpet rewoven in 1995. The **Antechambre** contains two large paintings and Empire furniture.

Stairs descend to the ground floor and to the **Chapelle de la Trinité** built for Henri II by Philibert Delorme on the site of Louis IX's foundation. Martin Fréminet, inspired by Michelangelo, was largely responsible for its sumptuous decoration (1608–14), with the vault-paintings set in ornately moulded and heavily gilded stucco frames. The elaborate altarpiece by Francesco Bordoni (1633) surrounds a painting of the *Deposition* by Jean Dubois, Ambroise Dubois' son. It was restored in the late 20C. It was the scene of the marriage of Louis XV and Marie Leszczynska in 1725; in 1810 of the baptism of the future Napoléon III; and in 1837 of the marriage of Ferdinand, Duc of Orléans (1810–42; eldest son of Louis-Philippe) to Helen of Mecklenburg-Schwerin.

Musée Napoléon I

The Musée Napoléon I is installed on two floors of the Louis XV wing (1738–74), on the south side of the Cour des Adieux. This is devoted to the period of the First Empire (1804–15) and complements the collections at Malmaison and Bois-Préau which concentrate on the Consulate and his years on St-Helena (see Ch. 37). Almost every room contains remarkable examples of the furniture of the period by eminent cabinet makers.

Evoking the period are busts and portraits of members of the Imperial family, including Gérard's portraits of *Napoléon I* and *Joséphine*, in their coronation robes, surviving regalia, robes and decorations. The Grand Vermeil, the silver-gilt surtout of table decoration by Henry Auguste presented by the city of Paris, and porcelain and cutlery, is on display. There are souvenirs of Marie-Louise (1791–1847), whom Napoléon married in 1810. One room concentrates on the Roi de Rome (1811–32) with, among other reminders of his childhood, his cradle, by Thomire-Duterme. Other members of the extensive Bonaparte family to whom the Emperor dispensed favours are not forgotten, and a room is devoted to his mother, Mme Mère, née Maria Letizia Ramolino (1750–1836), widowed with eight children when aged 35.

At the west of this wing, is the Théâtre Napoléon III (1857; by Hector Lefuel) incorporated here after the former theatre burnt out. Visits can be arranged through the Tourist Office.

Empress Eugénie's Salons and the Chinese Museum

The Musée Chinois is part of Empress Eugénie's suite in the Louis XV pavilion overlooking the Carp Pond. It contains Oriental artefacts collected by Napoléon III's Empress at a time when these were fashionable. Many of the objects displayed were spoils of the Franco-British expedition to China in 1860 including some from the Summer Palace, such as 18C golden vases, while other items were ambassadorial gifts.

Petits Appartements de l'Empereur et de l'Impératrice

Visit by guided tour only (in French); ☎ 01 60 71 50 60 from 09.30 for the daily times of visits. Most of these rooms still have their late 18C decoration and Empire furniture and were occupied by Napoléon and his staff, members of the royal family or royal mistresses from 1808. Among the furnishings are the Emperor's richly canopied bed (1804) by Jacob-Desmalter. There are other pieces by Jacob-Desmalter, Jacob-Frères, Boulle, and some attributed to Riesener. The apartments also include the Map Room, the Empress's Study and Second Salon, and and the Galerie des Cerfs decorated by Alexandre Denuelle, commissioned by Napoléon III, with stags' heads and paintings of the 1860s. This was the scene of the Marquis de Monaldeschi's assassination in 1657; the chain mail he was wearing and the sword that pierced it, are on view.

The exterior of the Château

After visiting the interior, it becomes evident that the château is arranged around several main courtyards. Each is a testament to different phases of building, and the complexity of the structure is compounded by the different names given to each courtyard according to successive episodes in its history. Starting off from the northeast corner of the Cour des Adieux, and passing the **Jeu de Paume** (real tennis court) on your right, the path brings you to the **Jardin de Diane** which was formerly entirely closed by an orangery built by Henri IV in brick and stone, similar to the existing building on the east, the Galeries de Diane and des Cerfs, with busts in niches, c 1600.

In the centre of the garden is a bronze **fountain** with the huntress Diana surrounded by hounds and stags' heads. The original was placed here in 1603, but suffered at the Revolution, and was partially replaced in 1813. The present 17C Diana is after an antique and was installed in place of the original in 1813. The dogs' and stags' heads, recovered from the Louvre, are by Pierre Biard (1603). At the base of the Tour de l'Escalier of the building on the west side of the garden, is a doorway with Egyptian caryatids and children bearing the arms of François I.

Go around this wing, following the line of the moat, to the **Porte Baptistère** (Dauphine), a domed monumental entrance designed by Primaticcio for Henri IV, the entrance to the Cour Ovale. Around the original oval courtyard was the 12C castle whose donjon remains practically unaltered. In 1601, after the Court had fled Paris because of the plague, this was the scene of the baptism of Louis XIII.

Opposite a gateway of 1640, decorated with heads of Mercury by Gilles Guérin, opens onto the **Cour Henri-IV**, 1606–09. Enclosed on three sides by buildings in a combination of brick and render, these were originally the kitchens and staff quarters, distanced from the main building to minimise fire risk. The main entrance to Cour Henri IV is to the north, facing the Pl. d'Armes.

To the south of Cour Henri IV, through the central pavilion with the curved façade, is the **Grand Parterre** (Parterre du Tibre), a formal garden with ornamental ponds designed by Le Vau and Le Nôtre, but divested of its pattern of box hedges. Beyond the round pool of Tiber to the south, and beyond the waterfall and canal to the east, is the forest. On the right, past the apse of the Chapelle St-Saturnin, is the **Porte Dorée** by Le Breton, an important relic of the building campaign of François I. This, the least altered structure of the time (c 1528–40), gives an idea of the original impact of Italian Renaissance art on French architects and builders. An Italianised fortified gate is flanked by two towers, in the manner of Gaillon (Eure); most innovative are the three superimposed open bays.

A passage leads into the **Cour de la Fontaine** framed by buildings of different eras: the François I gallery, the Henri IV terrace, apartments of Henri II, the elegant building by Primaticcio with double staircase and, opposite, the large pavilion of Gabriel, built in 1750. The large dogs of Fô guard the old entrance to the Chinese rooms of Empress Eugénie. To the south and southwest extends the **Etang des Carpes**, with its island pavilion from the time of Henri IV, rebuilt by Louis XIV and restored by Napoléon. The **Jardin Anglais**, laid out for Napoléon, reflects 19C fashion.

The 84-hectare park extends to the east of the parterre with straight alleys radiating star-shaped from a junction, alongside the canal, dug by order of Henri IV, which is about 1200m long.

A little way to the east, beyond the walls, is the town of **Avon**, once more important than its neighbour. The 13C–16C church contains a number of interesting tombstones, as well as the tomb of the assassinated Monaldeschi. In the cemetery lies the writer Katherine Mansfield (1888–1923) who died near here.

The Forest of Fontainebleau

The approximately 17,000 hectares Forest of Fontainebleau, known in the past as the Forest of Bière, surrounds the château and is the objective of as many visitors. It attracted royalty in the past because of its good hunting, and today it draws the crowds for the sheer beauty of its landscape, for walking and rock climbing, and for its flora and fauna. Made accessible by several good roads, there is also still space to get away. It is densely wooded in parts, predominantly with oak, but also with pines, beech and birch, while other parts are rocky wildernesses interspersed with sandy clearings. Some of the more picturesque sites are the **Gorges de Franchard**, for the 12C **Ermitage** and the view; and the **Désert d'Apremont**, for the rock formations, some 4km west and northwest respectively of the Carrefour de la Libération. Also the **Heights of the Solle** for the view of the racecourse and the beeches of the **Gros Fouteau**. The IGN Map 401 includes this area.

Barbizon

Now a sophisticated resort of artists and celebrities, Barbizon lies 8km northwest of Fontainebleau, via the N7 (or take unmarked Routes Forestières through the forest and past the sites mentioned above). This well-manicured village liberally sprinkled with boutiques and bistrots becomes very crowded at weekends. In the mid-19C, it was the headquarters of the Barbizon group, which counted among them Millet, Théodore Rousseau, Corot, Diaz de la Peña and Daubigny. The first two were buried at Chailly-en-Bière, just north of the main road, where Bazille, Monet, Renoir, Sisley and Seurat also painted.

The **Musée de l'Auberge Ganne** opened in 1995 in the *auberge* frequented and decorated by many of these artists during the years 1848–70. The museum is open 1 Apr–12 Nov 10.00–12.30, 14.00–18.00; 13 Nov–30 March to 17.00, open all day Sat, Sun and most public holidays, closed Tues; ☎ 01 60 66 22 38. A modest building, it has been imaginatively transformed into a bright exhibition area around a little garden-courtyard. On the entrance level is an audio-visual room and three rooms evoking the *auberge* when it was run by the Ganne family. On the first floor the former bedrooms have displays recalling Barbizon at the time of the painters, with photographs, drawings, engravings and paintings. The *Painters in the Forest of Fontainebleau* by Coignet (1798–1860) sums up the importance of the surroundings to the group who pioneered painting *en plein air*. The walls and furniture in an upper room, decorated by the artists have been restored to make a touching souvenir of the former painter-clients. The **Maison Atelier de Théodore Rousseau**, further along the street, is used for temporary exhibitions.

Index

A

Abaquesne, Masséot (mid 16C) 375
Abbate, Nicolò dell' (c 1512–71) 379, 383
Abbey Church of St-Martin-des-Champs 272
Adam, Sébastien Adam (1705–78) 215
Allée de Longchamp 314
Allée des Cygnes 158
American Church of the Holy Trinity 303
American Embassy 291
André, Albert (1869–1954) 372
Andrea del Sarto (1486–1530) 189
Angelico, Fra (c 1387–1455) 186, 187
Anguier, Michel (1614–86) 214
Antoine, J.-D. (1771–75) 124, 145
Antonello da Messina (1430–79) 188
Apollinaire, Guillaume (1880–1918) 149
Arc de Triomphe 293
Arc de Triomphe du Carrousel 165
Arceuil 376
Archipenko, Alexander (1887–1964) 242
Arènes de Lutèce 107
Arp, Hans (1888–1966) 156, 244
Arras, Jean d' 371
Artigas, Llorens (1892–1988) 156
Assemblée National 144
Au Pied de Cochon 234
Auteuil 311
Automobile Club 162
Av. des Champs-Elysées 291
Av. Daumesnil 331
Av. de Friedland 297
Av. des Gobelins 113
Av. de la Motte-Picquet 151
Av. de l'Observatoire 127
Av. du Président-Wilson 303
Avon 387

B

Baccarat 283
Backhuysen, Ludolf (1631–1708) 186
Bacon, Francis (1909–92) 245
Baltard, Victor (1805–74) 233, 235, 278
Balthus (b. 1903) 244
Balzac, Honoré 310
Banque de France 228
Barbizon 387
Barois (1656–1726) 215
Barrias, Ernest (1841–1905) 141
Bartholdi, Auguste (1834–1904) 127
Bartolommeo di Giovanni (active end 15C) 188
Barye, Antoine-Louis (1796–1875) 135,

(1795–1875) 216
Baselitz, Georg (b. 1938) 247
Bastille 258
Bateau-Lavoir 289
Batignolles 301
Baudelaire, Charles 143
Baudry, F. (c 1725–36) 222
Baumgarten, Lothar (b. 1944) 117
Bazille, Frédéric (1841–70) 137
Beaubourg 238
Beauharnais, Joséphine de 357, 358
Beauneveu, André (1335–1401/3) 370
Beham, H. S. (1500–50) 183
Behrens, Peter (1860–1940) 141
Bellangé, P.-A. (1758–1827) 311
Bellechose, Henri (c 1380–c 1440) 175
Belleville 324
Bellini, Giovanni (c 1430–1516) 188, 298
Bellini, Jacopo (c 1400–71) 187
Bellmer, Hans (b. 1902) 244
Belloni (1772–1863) 216
Benedetto da Maiano (1442–97) 217
Benoist, Marie-Guillemine (1768–1826) 180
Bénouville, Léon (1821–59) 181
Berchem, Nicolas (1620–83) 186
Bergson, Henri (1851–1941) 311
Bernard, Emile (1868–1941) 140
Bernini, Gianlorenzo (1598–1680) 167, 217, 345
Beuys, Joseph (1921–85) 246, 247
Bibliothèque de l'Arsenal 256
Bibliothèque de France 111
Bibliothèque Historique de la Ville de Paris 261
Bibliothèque Mazarine 124
Bibliothèque Nationale de France-Cardinal de Richelieu 230
Bibliothèque Ste-Geneviève 100
Bibliothèque Thiers 283
Blaikie, Thomas 300
Blanchard, Jacques (1600–38) 178
Blondel, Nicolas François (1618–86) 281
Blvd de Clichy 286
Blvd Edgar-Quinet 119
Blvd Haussmann 285, 297
Blvd de l'Hôpital 111
Blvd des Invalides 146
Blvd des Italiens 280
Blvd de la Madeleine 278
Blvd de Magenta 282
Blvd du Montparnasse 119
Blvd du Palais 83
Blvd Périphérique 159
Blvd Raspail 122

C

Atlas section

INDEX TO ATLAS MAPS

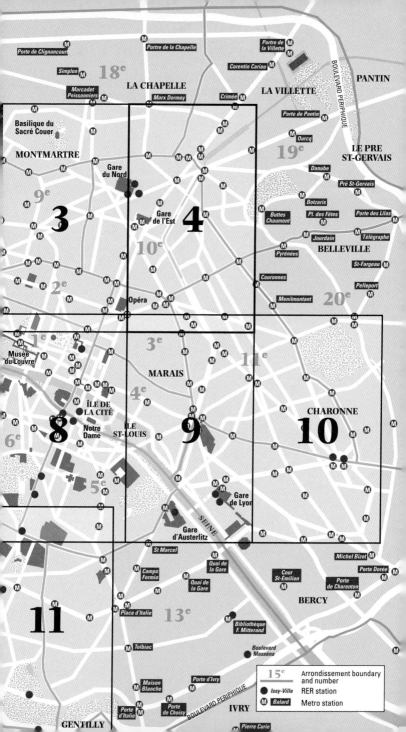

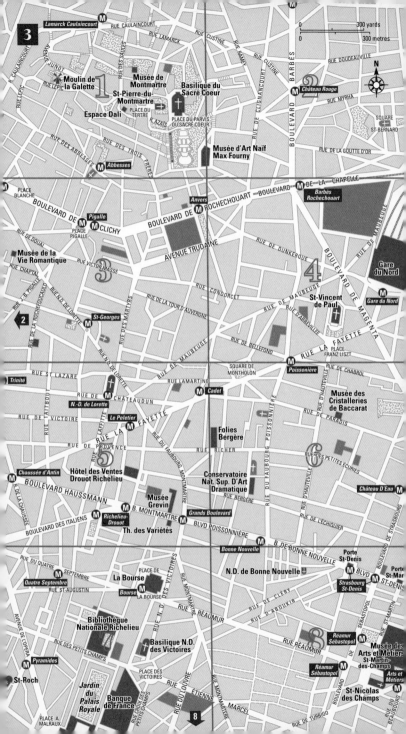

3

Lamarck Caulaincourt Ⓜ RUE CAULAINCOURT

RUE LAMARCK

RUE CUSTINE

RUE RAMEY

RUE DOUDEAUVILLE

0 — 300 yards
0 — 300 metres

N

R. CAULAINCOURT

AVENUE JUNOT

RUE LEPIC

RUE DES SAULES

Moulin de la Galette

Musée de Montmartre

St-Pierre-du-Montmartre

Basilique du Sacré Coeur

1

Espace Dali

PLACE DU TERTRE

RUE AZAIS

PLACE DU PARVIS DU SACRÉ-COEUR

BOULEVARD BARBÈS

Château Rouge Ⓜ

2

RUE MYRHA

SQUARE ST-BERNARD

RUE DE CLIGNANCOURT

RUE DES ABBESSES

RUE DES TROIS FRÈRES

Abbesses Ⓜ

Musée d'Art Naïf Max Fourny

RUE DE LA GOUTTE D'OR

PLACE BLANCHE

BOULEVARD DE CLICHY

Anvers Ⓜ BOULEVARD DE ROCHECHOUART

DE LA CHAPELLE Ⓜ

Barbès Rochechouart

Pigalle Ⓜ

PLACE PIGALLE

Ⓜ CLICHY

RUE DE DOUAI

AVENUE TRUDAINE

RUE DE DUNKERQUE

BOULEVARD DE MAGENTA

RUE DE MAUBEUGE

Gare du Nord

Musée de la Vie Romantique

RUE VICTOR MASSÉ

3

RUE CHAPTAL

RUE DE LA ROCHEFOUCAULD

RUE DE B. PIGALLE

RUE N.D. DE LORETTE

RUE DE CONDORCET

RUE DE LA TOUR D'AUVERGNE

4

St-Vincent de Paul

RUE D'ABBEVILLE

Gare du Nord Ⓜ

2 ◀

St-Georges Ⓜ

RUE DES MARTYRS

RUE DE MAUBEUGE

RUE DE BELLEFOND

RUE LA FAYETTE

PLACE FRANZ LISZT

Trinité Ⓜ

RUE ST LAZARE

RUE N.D. DE LORETTE

RUE LAMARTINE

SQUARE DE MONTHOLON

Poissonière Ⓜ

RUE DE CHABROL

RUE D'HAUTEVILLE

Musée des Cristalleries de Baccarat

RUE DE CHÂTEAUDUN

Cadet Ⓜ

N.-D. de Lorette

RUE DE TAITBOUT

RUE DE LA VICTOIRE

Le Peletier Ⓜ

RUE LA FAYETTE

RUE DE PROVENCE

RUE DU FAUBOURG POISSONNIÈRE

RUE DE PARADIS

Folies Bergère

RUE RICHER

Chaussée d'Antin Ⓜ

Hôtel des Ventes Drouot Richelieu

5

BOULEVARD HAUSSMANN

R. DE LA CHAUSSÉE

BOULEVARD DES ITALIENS

RUE DE LA FAYETTE

RUE DU FAUBOURG MONTMARTRE

Conservatoire Nat. Sup. D'Art Dramatique

RUE BERGÈRE

RUE D'HAUTEVILLE

RUE DES PETITES ÉCURIES

6

Château D'Eau Ⓜ

RUE DE L'ÉCHIQUIER

Richelieu-Drouot Ⓜ

Musée Grevin

B. MONTMARTRE

Grands Boulevard Ⓜ

BLVD POISSONNIÈRE

Th. des Variétés

Bonne Nouvelle Ⓜ

B. DE BONNE NOUVELLE

Porte St-Denis

Porte St-Mar

RUE DU QUATRE SEPTEMBRE

PLACE DE LA BOURSE

N.D. de Bonne Nouvelle

BOULEVARD DE STRASBOURG

Quatre Septembre Ⓜ

La Bourse

RUE ST-AUGUSTIN

Bourse Ⓜ

LA BOURSE

RUE N.D. DES VICTOIRES

RUE MONTMARTRE

RUE RÉAUMUR

RUE DE CLÉRY

RUE D'ABOUKIR

Strasbourg St-Denis Ⓜ

ST-DENIS

AVENUE DE L'OPERA

Bibliothèque Nationale Richelieu

RUE DES PETITS CHAMPS

Basilique N.D. des Victoires

PLACE DES VICTOIRES

RUE RÉAUMUR

SÉBASTOPOL

Réamur Sébastopol Ⓜ

Musée des Arts et Métiers

Pyramides Ⓜ

RUE ÉTIENNE

RUE DU LOUVRE

Réamur Sébastopol Ⓜ

St-Martin-des-Champs

St-Roch

Jardin du Palais Royale

Banque de France

RUE CROIX DES PETITS CHAMPS

RUE MONTMARTRE

RUE MARCEL

RUE DE TURBIGO

Arts et Métiers Ⓜ

St-Nicolas des Champs

PLACE A. MALRAUX

8 ▼

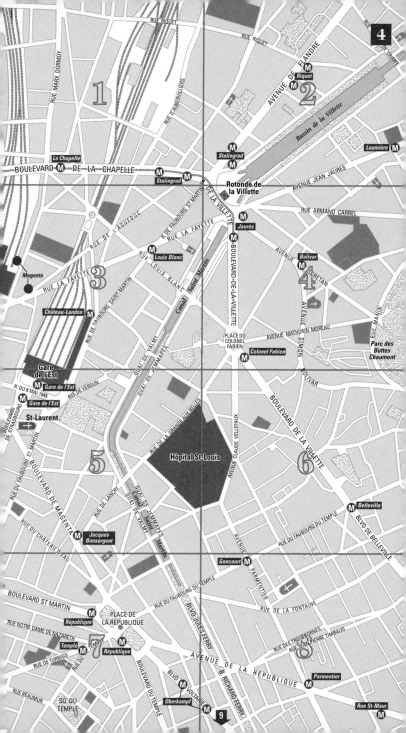

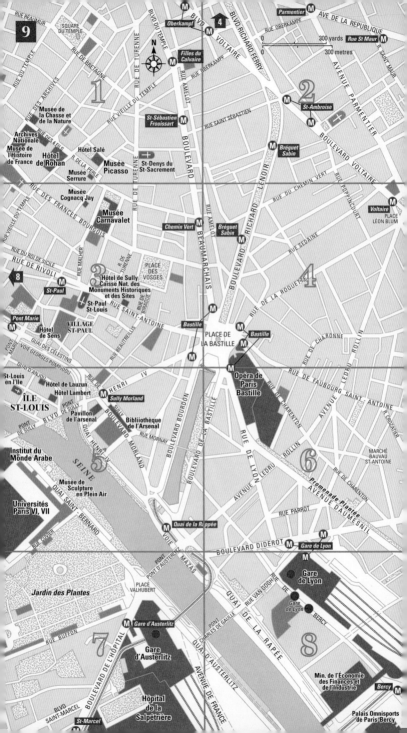

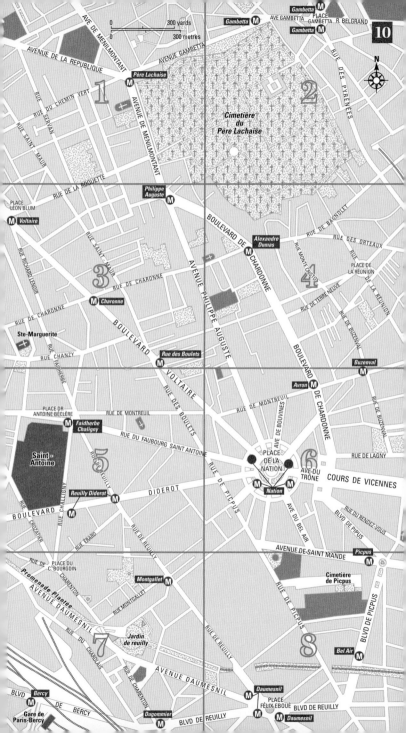

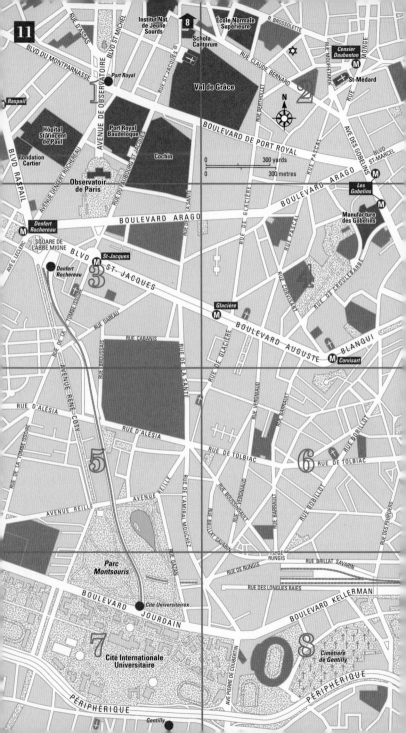

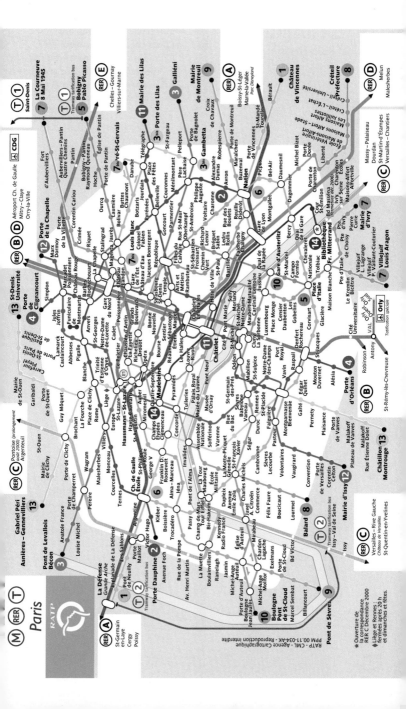

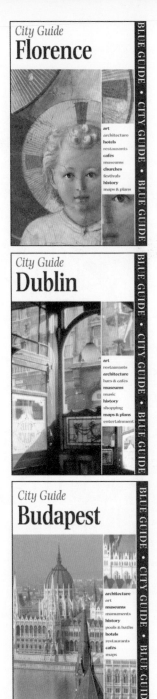

BLUE GUIDE • CITY GUIDES • BLUE GUIDES • BLUE GUIDE

City Guide
Florence

art
architecture
hotels
restaurants
cafés
museums
churches
festivals
history
maps & plans

- **22 walks provide a personalised tour of Florence's outstanding galleries, museums and churches, accompanied by excellent city maps and a variety of well-chosen restaurants in all price ranges where you can savour Tuscan specialities**

- Alta Macadam
  8th edition, 2001
  384pp
  ISBN 0–7136–5454–6
  £13.99

City Guide
Dublin

art
restaurants
architecture
bars & cafés
museums
music
history
shopping
maps & plans
entertainment

- **from Celtic gold body ornaments at the National Museum to Francis Bacon's extraordinary studio at the Hugh Lane Gallery and mouth-watering delicacies in Temple Bar's Meeting House Square Market, Blue Guide *Dublin* is packed with information about this lively and historic city**

- Brian Lalor
  2nd edition, 2001
  192pp
  ISBN 0–1736–5354–X
  £10.99

City Guide
Budapest

architecture
art
museums
monuments
history
pools & baths
hotels
restaurants
cafés
maps

- **stunning architecture, wonderful museums, thermal pools and bath-houses, café society, Jewish Budapest ~ these are just some of the topics covered by our locally based author in this Blue Guide**

- Bob Dent
  2nd edition, 2001
  224pp
  0–7136–5776–6
  £11.99